Sailor Moon

4

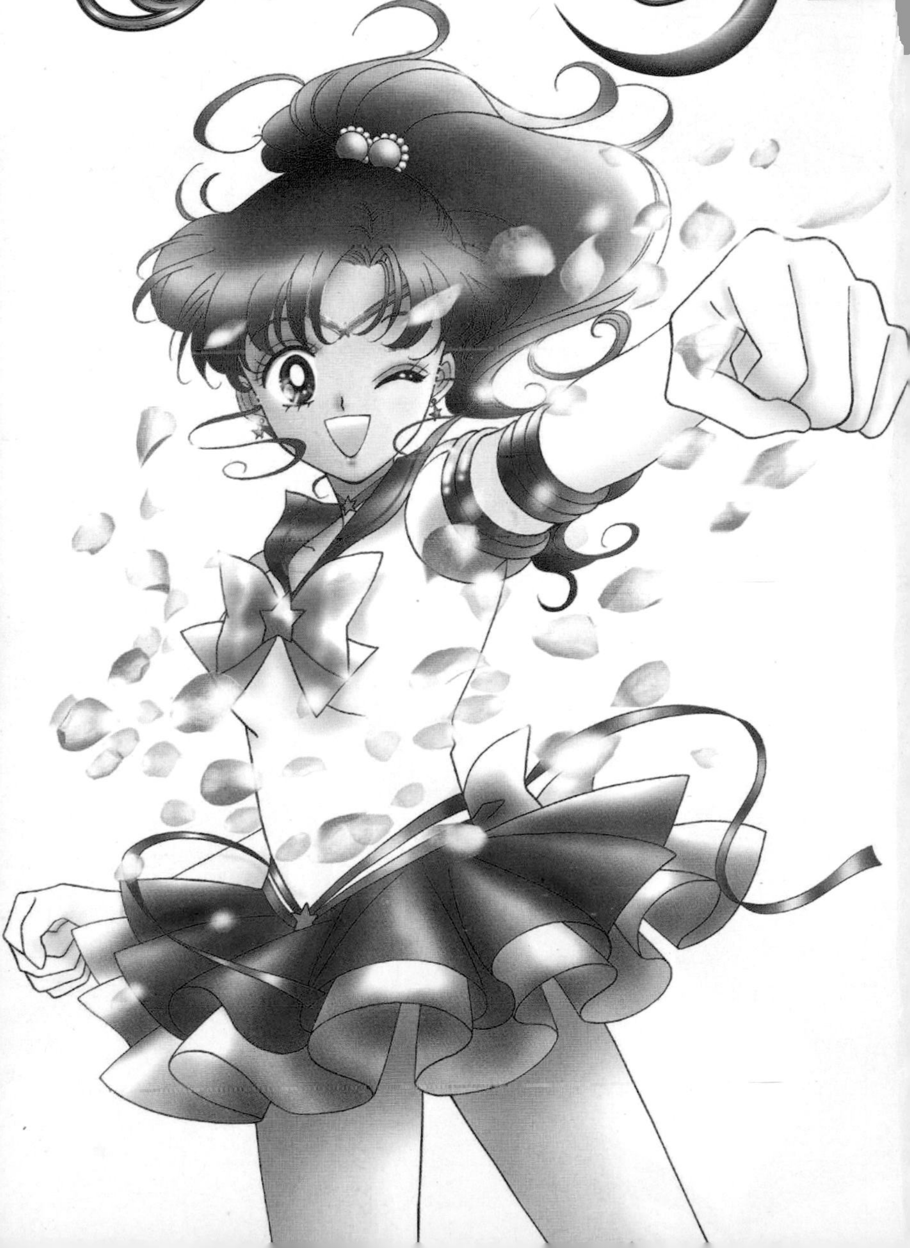

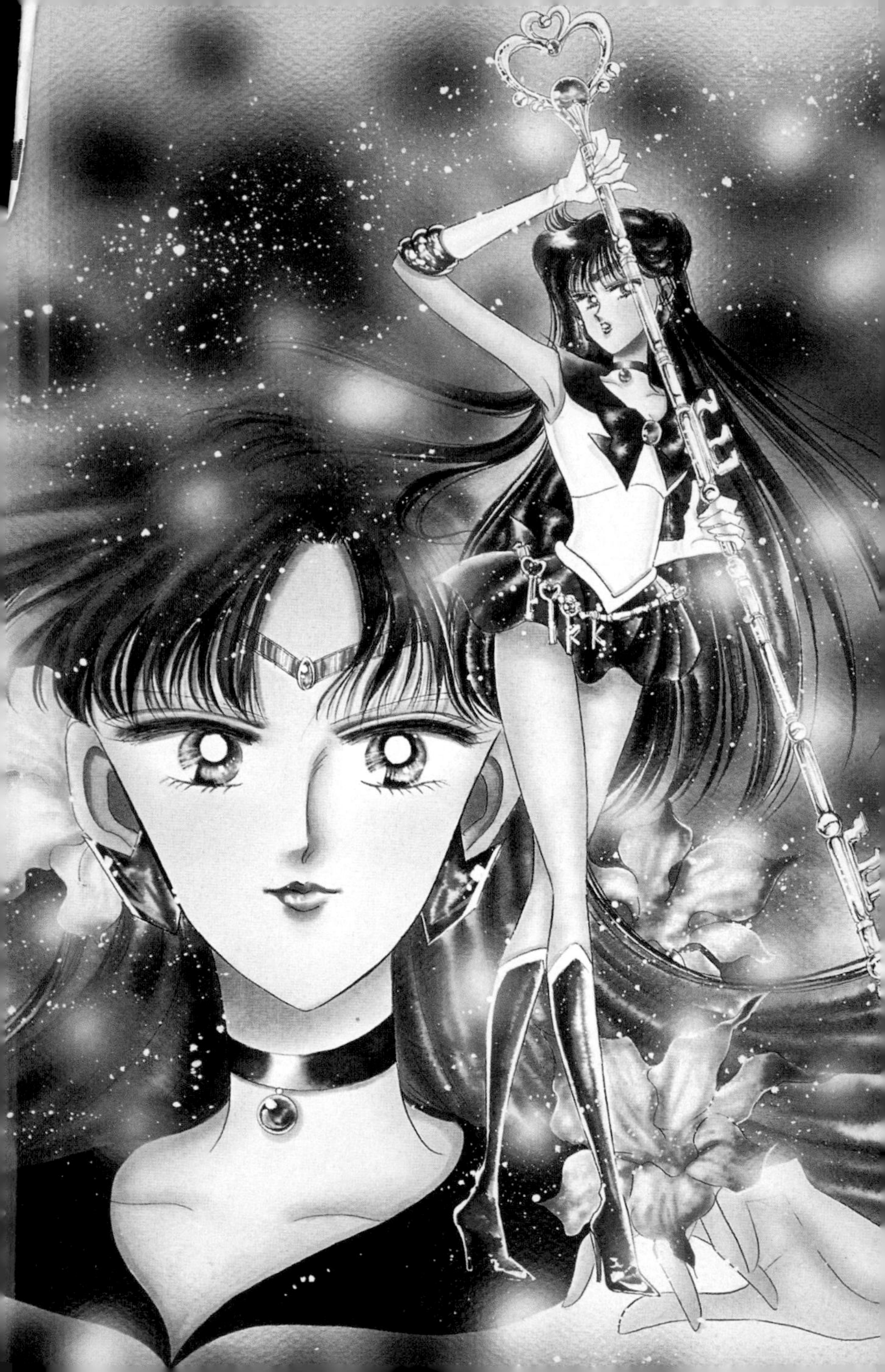

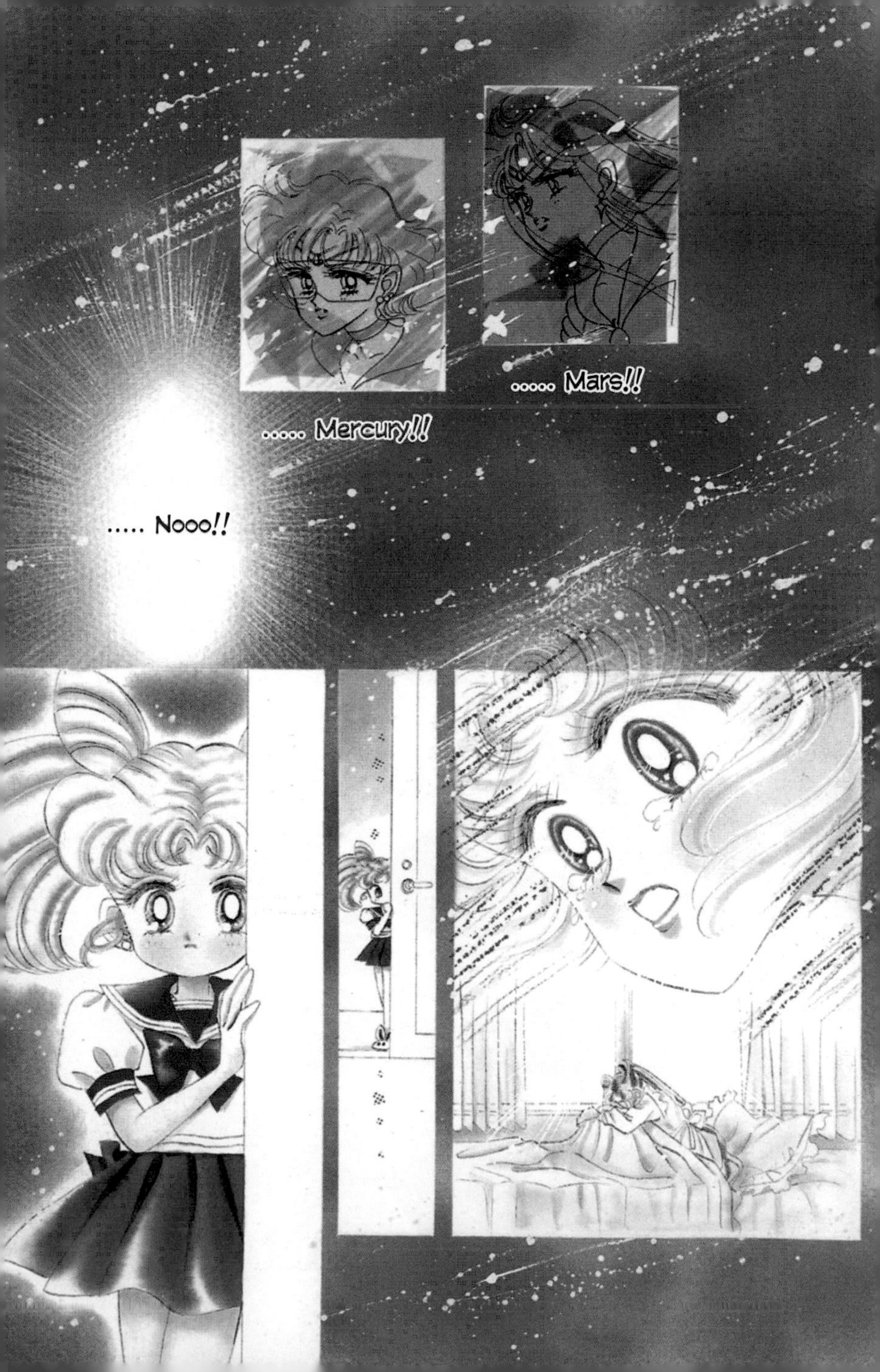
...... Mars!!
...... Mercury!!
..... Nooo!!

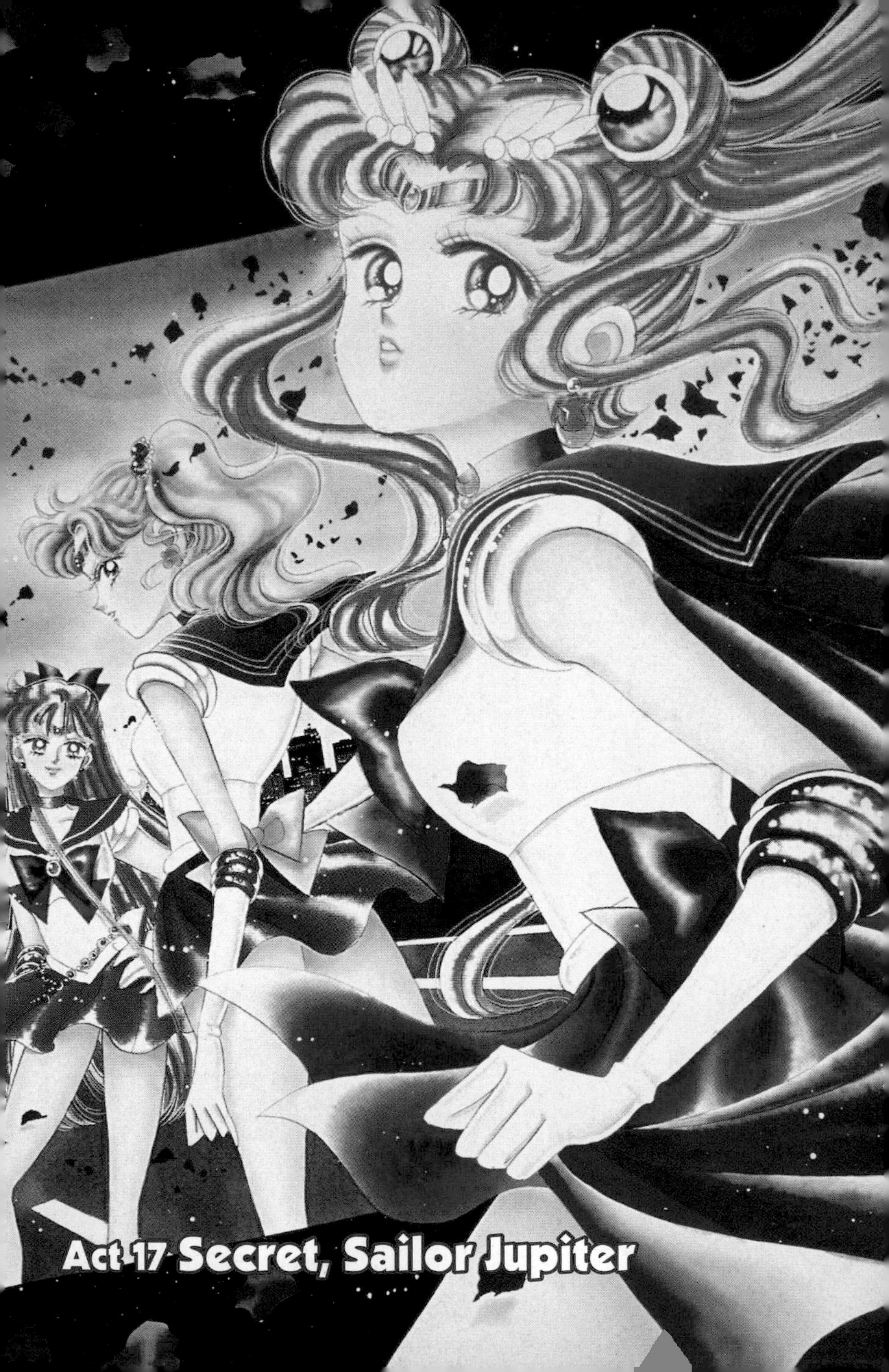

Act 17 Secret, Sailor Jupiter

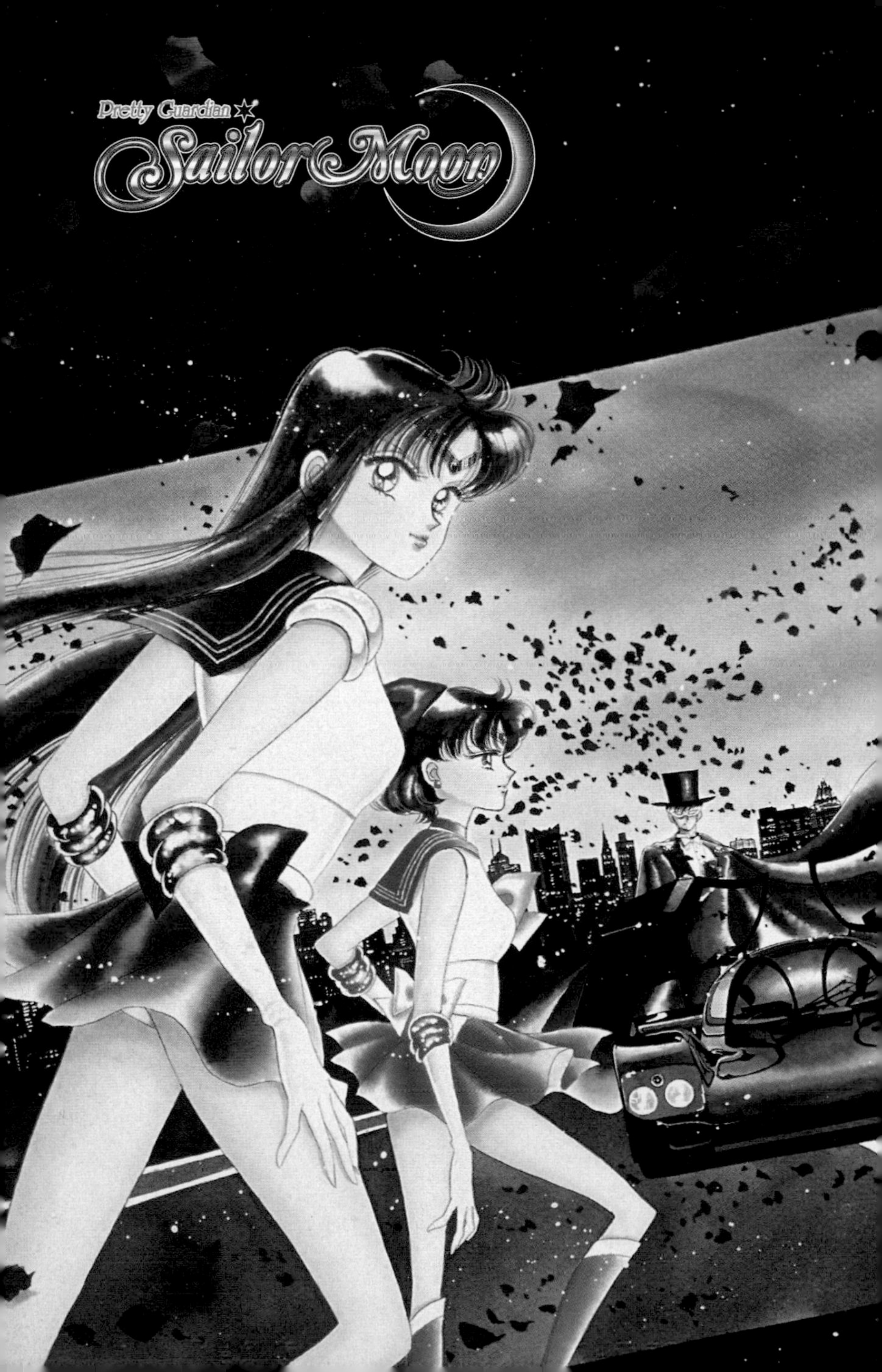
Pretty Guardian
Sailor Moon

CONTENTS

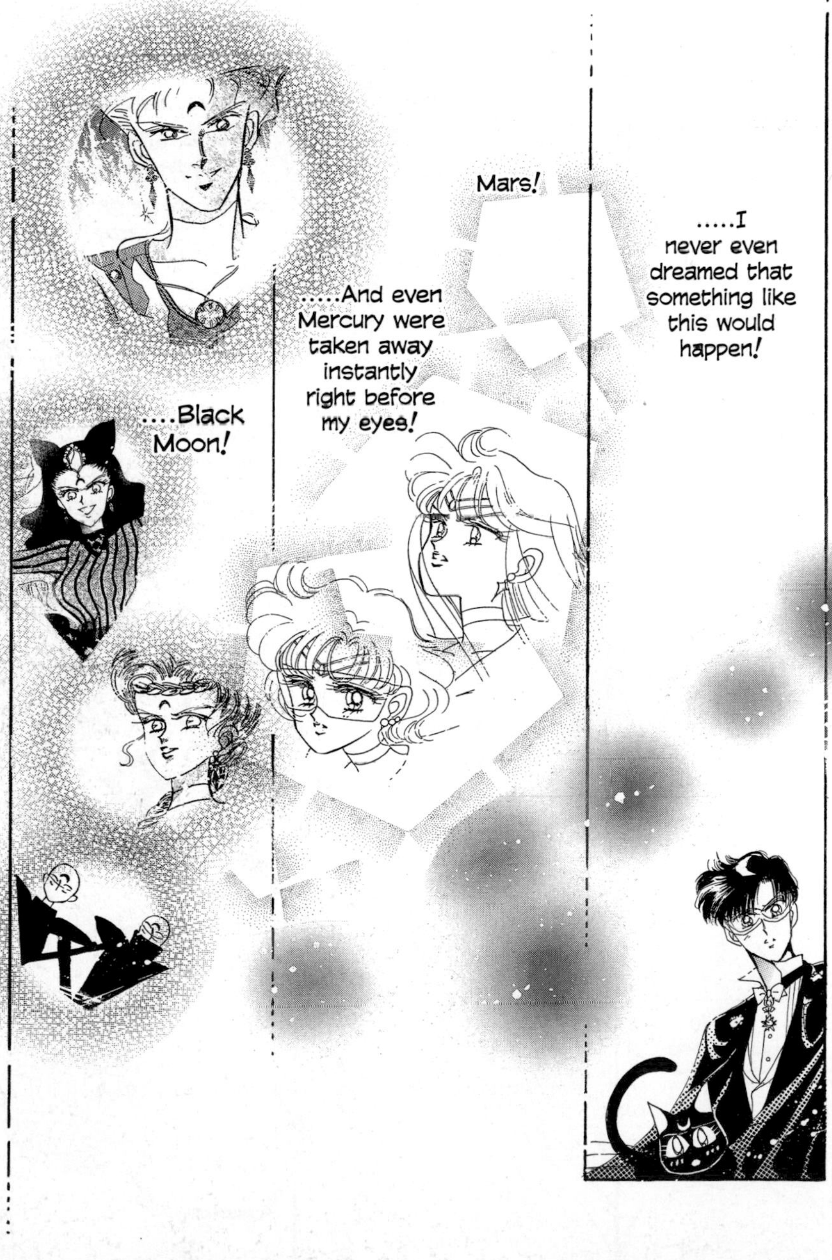
.....I never even dreamed that something like this would happen!
Mars!
.....And even Mercury were taken away instantly right before my eyes!
.....Black Moon!

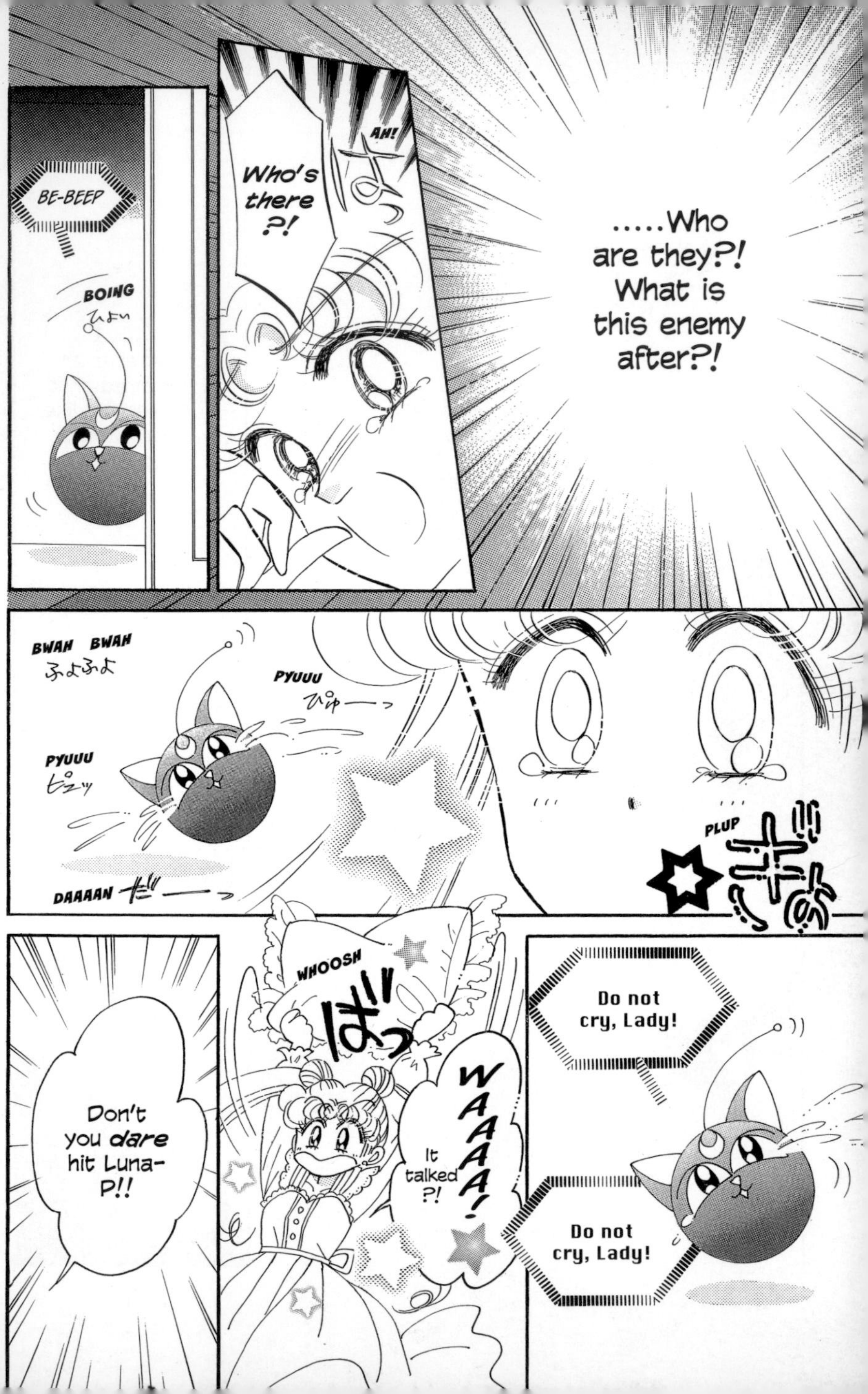
.....Who are they?! What is this enemy after?!
AH!
Who's there?!
BE-BEEP
BOING
ひょい
PLUP
PYUUU
ぴゅーっ
BWAH BWAH
ふよふよ
PYUUU
ピュッ
DAAAAN
だーっ
Do not cry, Lady!
Do not cry, Lady!
WHOOSH
ばっ
WAAAAA!
It talked?!
Don't you *dare* hit Luna-P!!

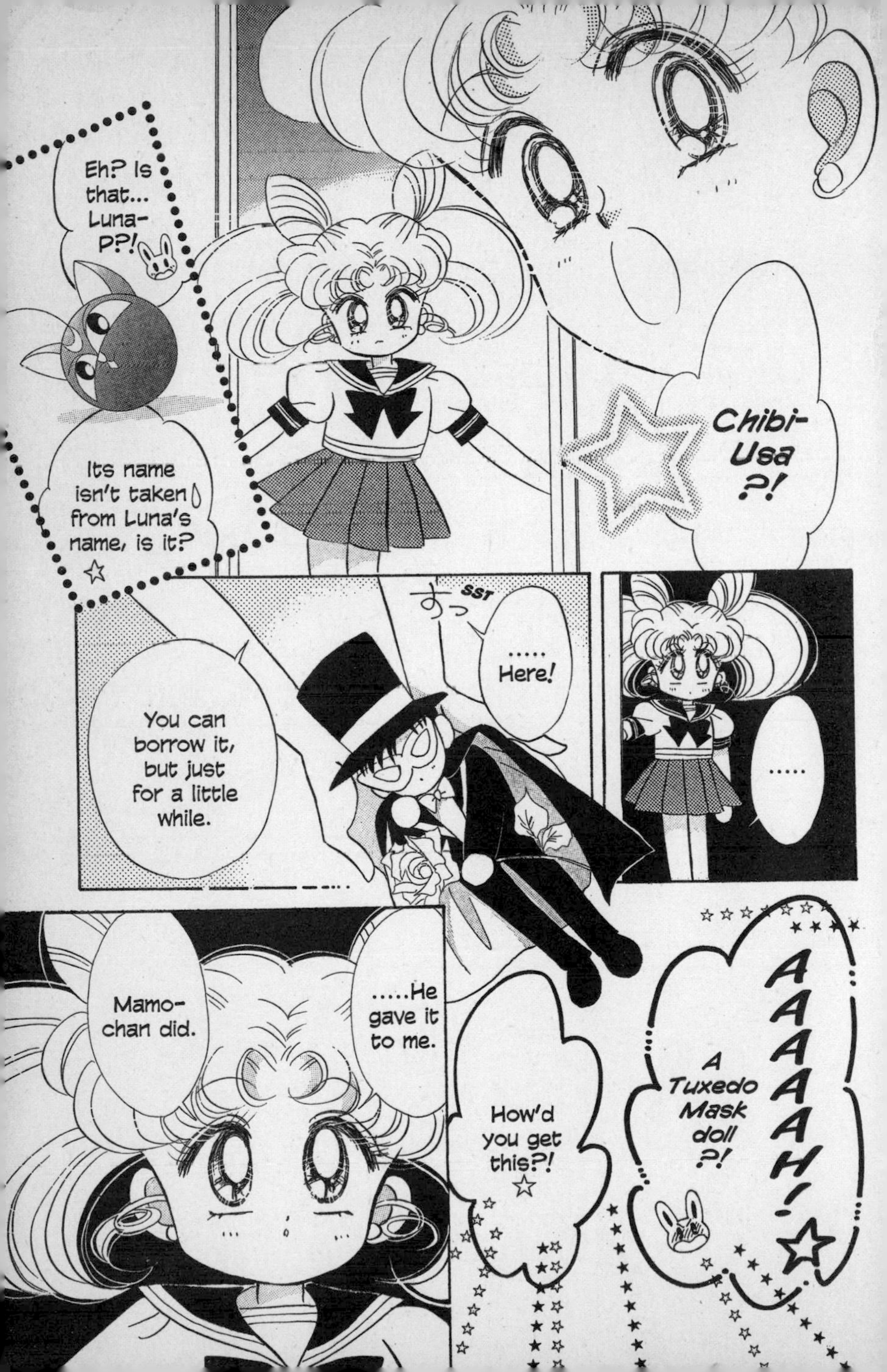
Chibi-Usa ?!
Eh? Is that... Luna-P?!
Its name isn't taken from Luna's name, is it? ☆
.....
すっ SST
..... Here!
You can borrow it, but just for a little while.
AAAAAH! ☆
A Tuxedo Mask doll ?!
How'd you get this?! ☆
.....He gave it to me.
Mamo-chan did.

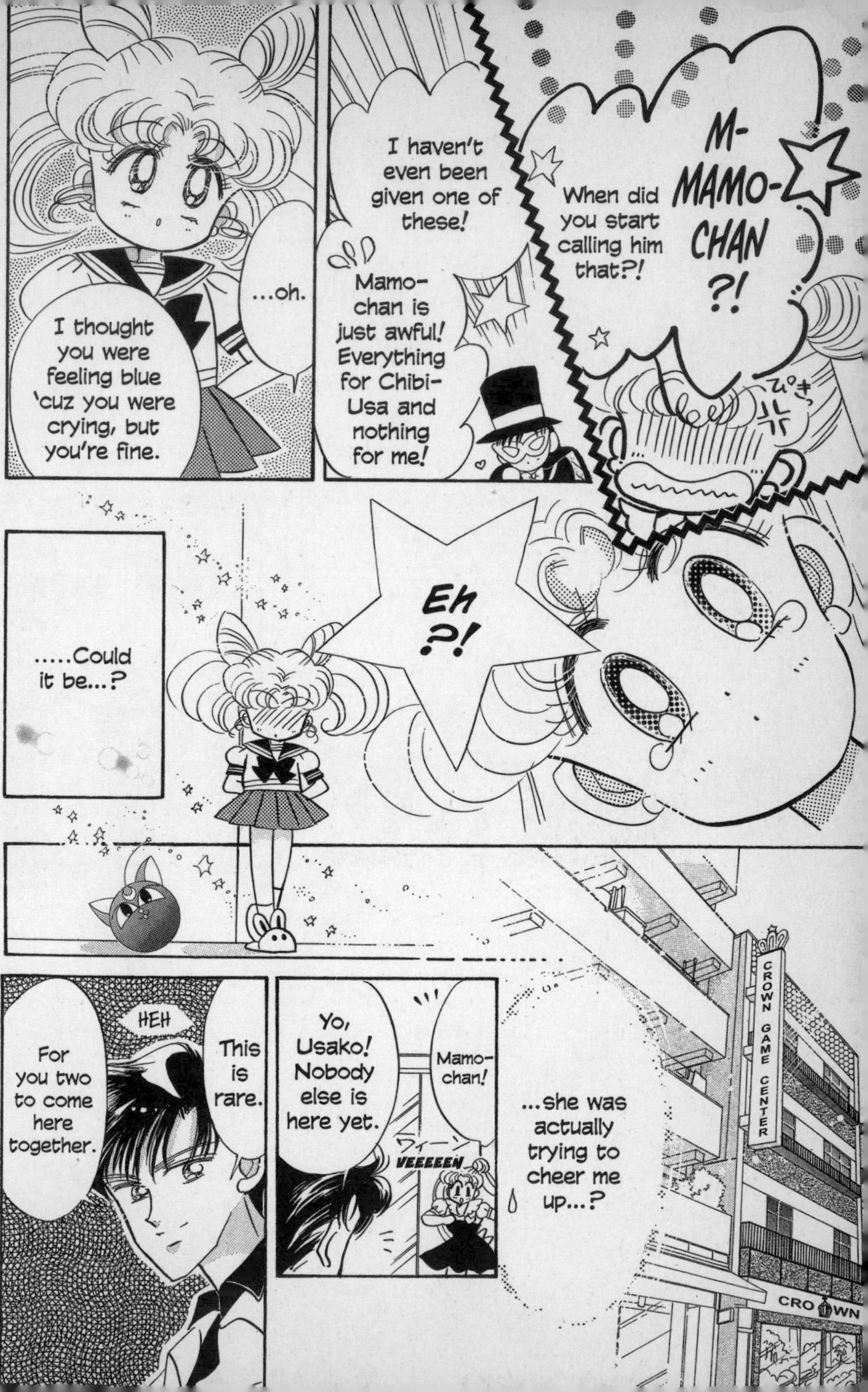
M-MAMO-CHAN?!
When did you start calling him that?!
ぴきっ
I haven't even been given one of these!
Mamo-chan is just awful! Everything for Chibi-Usa and nothing for me!
...oh.
I thought you were feeling blue 'cuz you were crying, but you're fine.
Eh?!
.....Could it be...?
...she was actually trying to cheer me up...?
CROWN GAME CENTER
CROWN
Mamo-chan!
Yo, Usako! Nobody else is here yet.
ヴィーン
VEEEEEN
HEH
This is rare.
For you two to come here together.

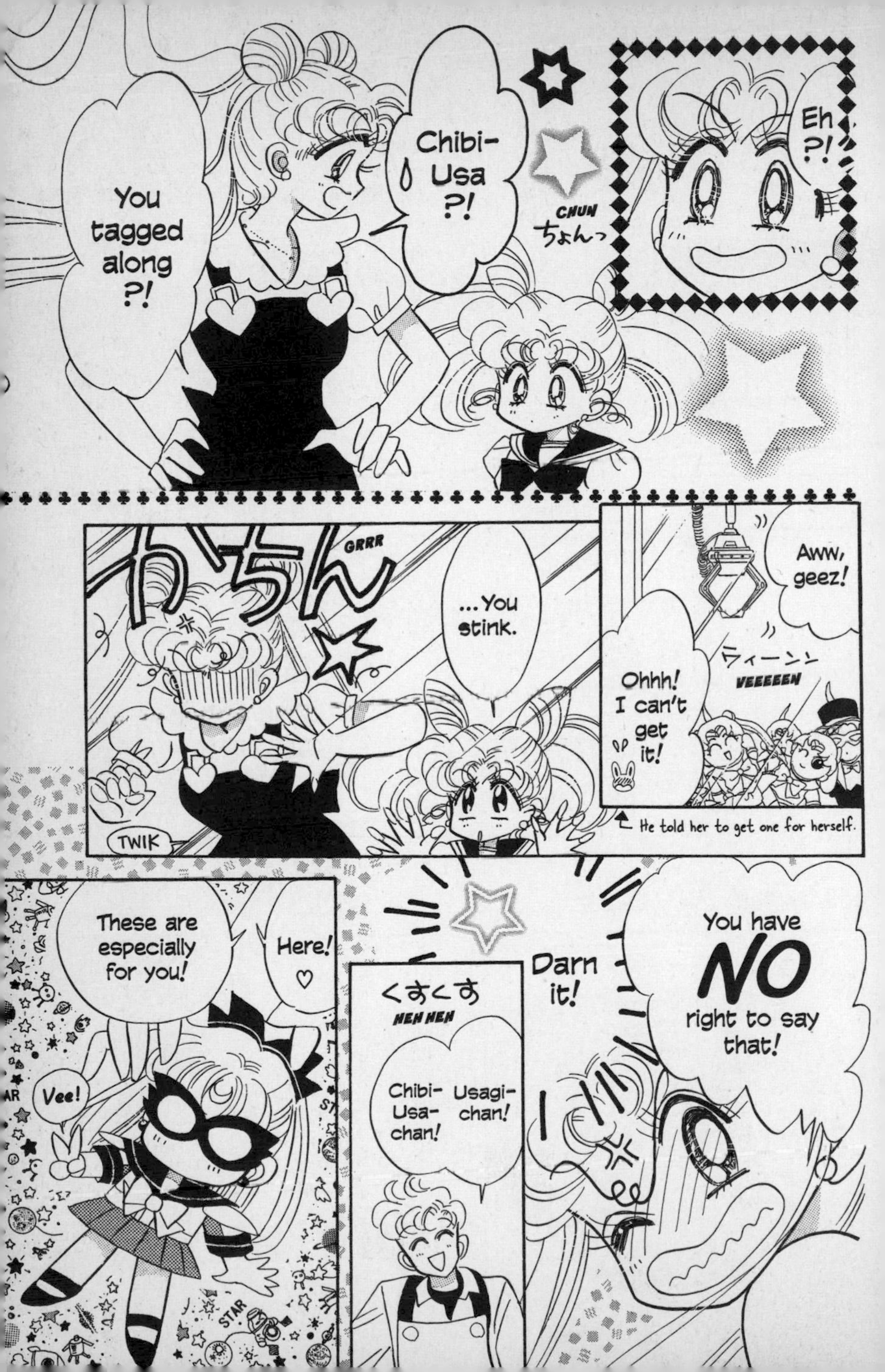
Eh?!
Chibi-Usa?!
CHUN
ちょんっ
You tagged along?!
Aww, geez!
ウィーンン
VEEEEEN
Ohhh! I can't get it!
He told her to get one for herself.
GRRR
...You stink.
TWIK
You have NO right to say that!
Darn it!
くすくす
HEH HEH
Usagi-chan!
Chibi-Usa-chan!
Here! ♡
These are especially for you!
Vee!

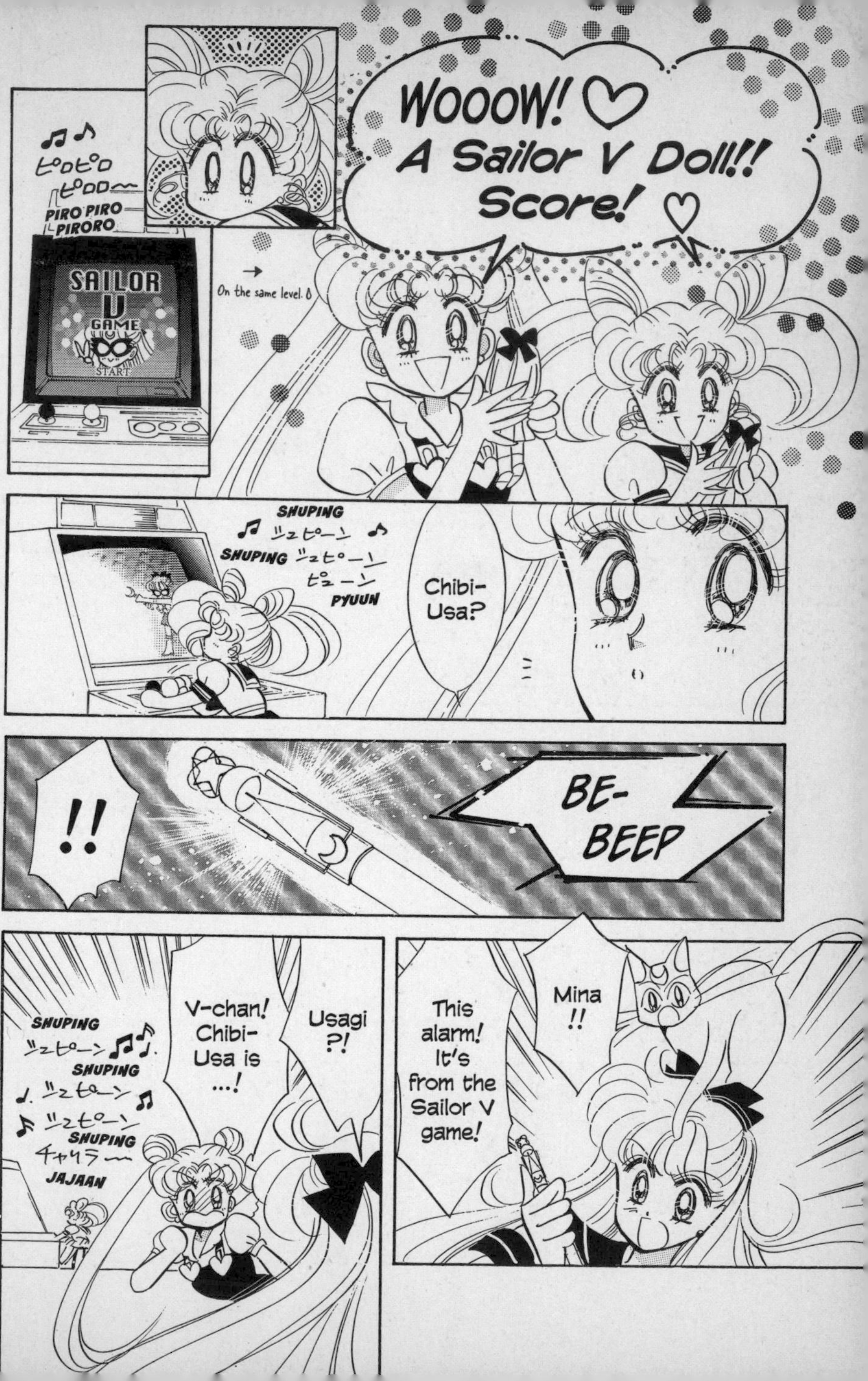
WOOOW! ♡ A Sailor V Doll!! Score! ♡
♫♪ ピロピロ ピロロ〜
PIRO PIRO PIRORO
SAILOR V GAME
START
→ On the same level. 0
Chibi-Usa?
SHUPING ♫ ジュピーン ♪
SHUPING ジュピーン
ピューン PYUUN
BE-BEEP
!!
Mina !!
This alarm! It's from the Sailor V game!
Usagi ?!
V-chan! Chibi-Usa is ...!
SHUPING ジュピーン ♫♪
SHUPING ♩ ジュピーン ♫
♪ ジュピーン SHUPING
チャリラ〜 JAJAAN

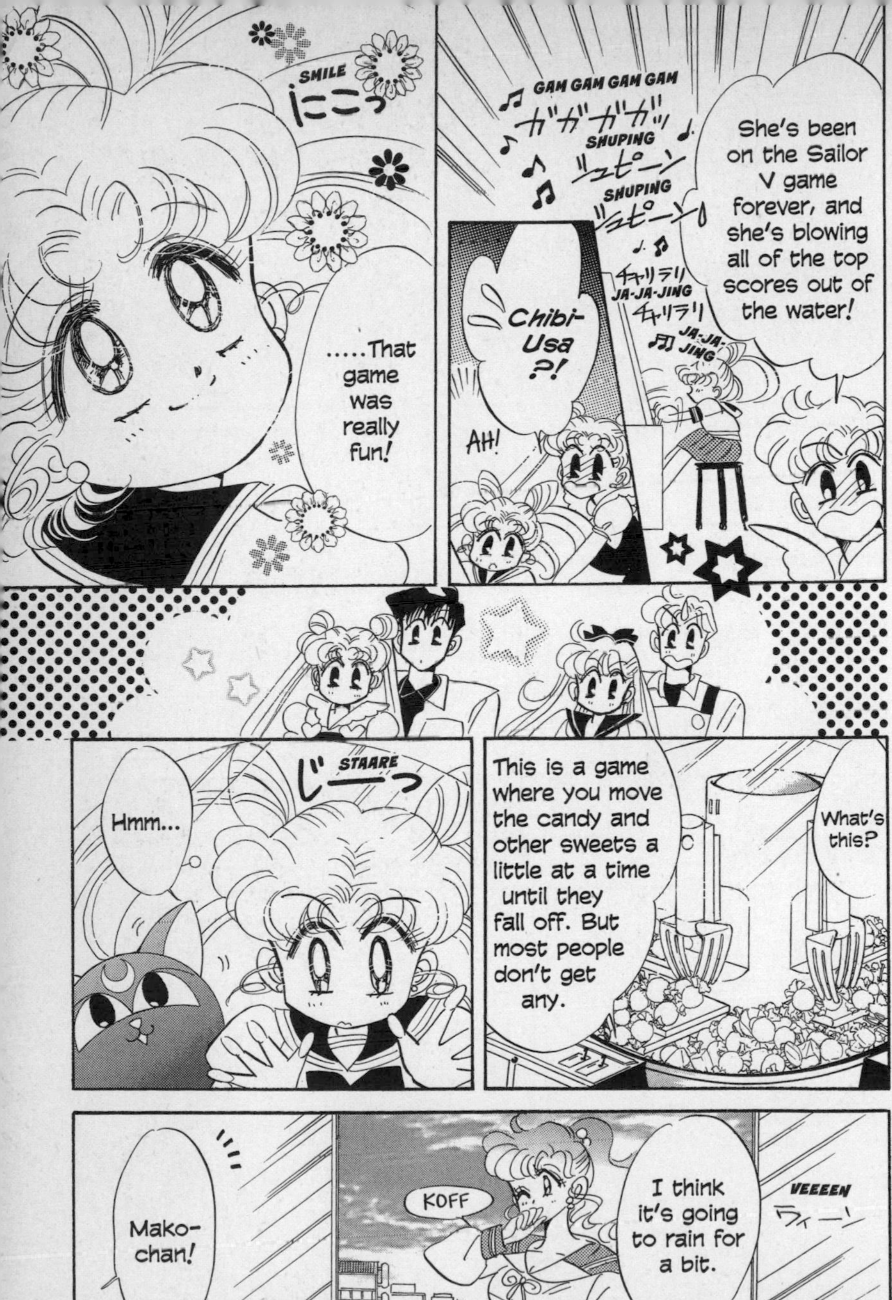
She's been on the Sailor V game forever, and she's blowing all of the top scores out of the water!
GAM GAM GAM GAM
ガガガガッ
SHUPING
ジュピーン
SHUPING
ジュピーン
JA-JA-JING
チャリラリ
チャリラリ
JA-JA-JING
Chibi-Usa ?!
AH!
SMILE
にこっ
.....That game was really fun!
What's this?
This is a game where you move the candy and other sweets a little at a time until they fall off. But most people don't get any.
STAARE
じーっ
Hmm...
VEEEEN
ウィーン
I think it's going to rain for a bit.
KOFF
Mako-chan!

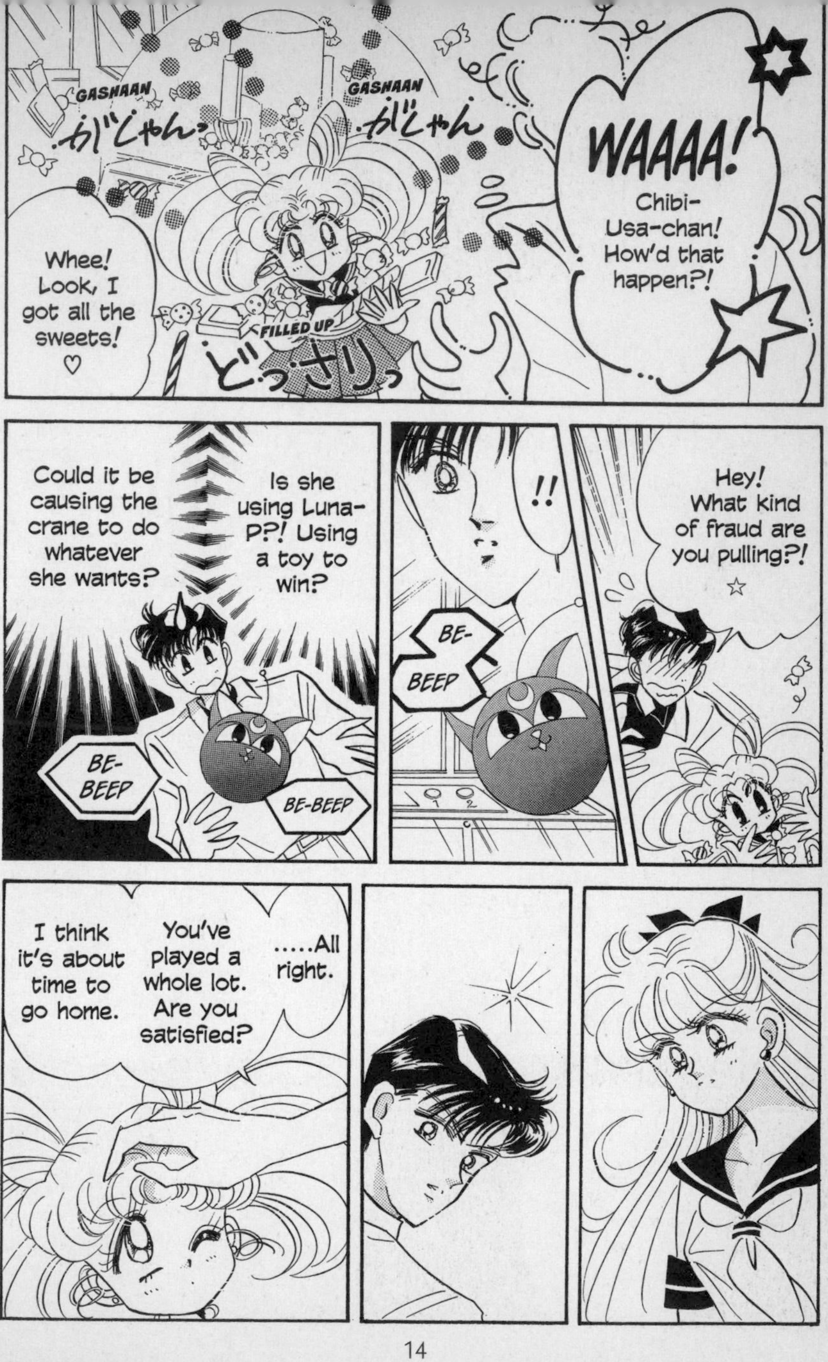
WAAAA!
Chibi-Usa-chan! How'd that happen?!
GASHAAN
がじゃん
GASHAAN
がじゃん
Whee! Look, I got all the sweets! ♡
FILLED UP
どっさり
Hey! What kind of fraud are you pulling?!
!!
BE-BEEP
Is she using Luna-P?! Using a toy to win?
Could it be causing the crane to do whatever she wants?
BE-BEEP
BE-BEEP
.....All right.
You've played a whole lot. Are you satisfied?
I think it's about time to go home.

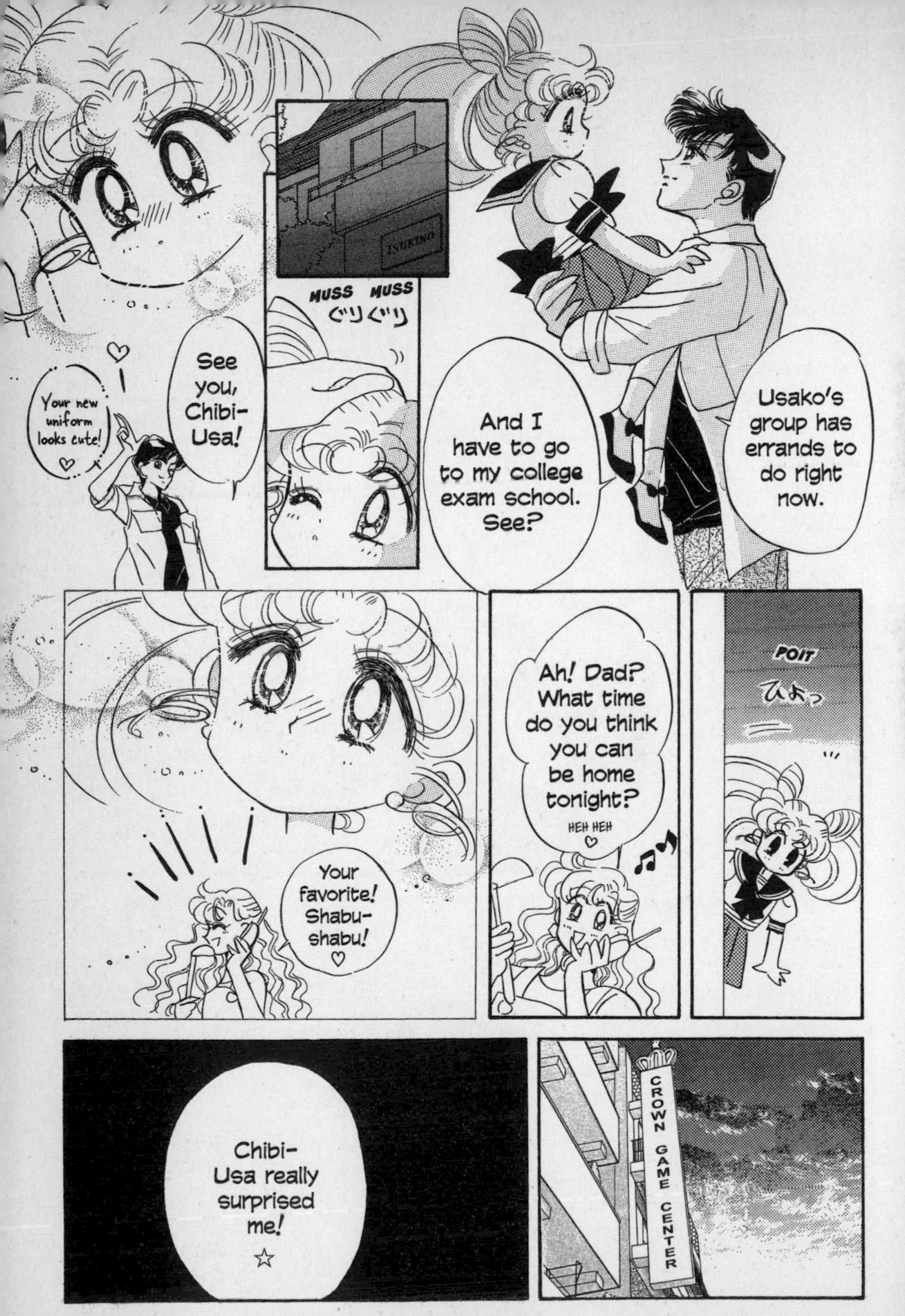

Usako's group has errands to do right now.
And I have to go to my college exam school. See?
TSUKINO
MUSS MUSS
ぐりぐり
See you, Chibi-Usa!
Your new uniform looks cute! ♡
POIT
ひよっ
Ah! Dad? What time do you think you can be home tonight?
HEH HEH ♡
Your favorite! Shabu-shabu! ♡
CROWN GAME CENTER
Chibi-Usa really surprised me! ☆

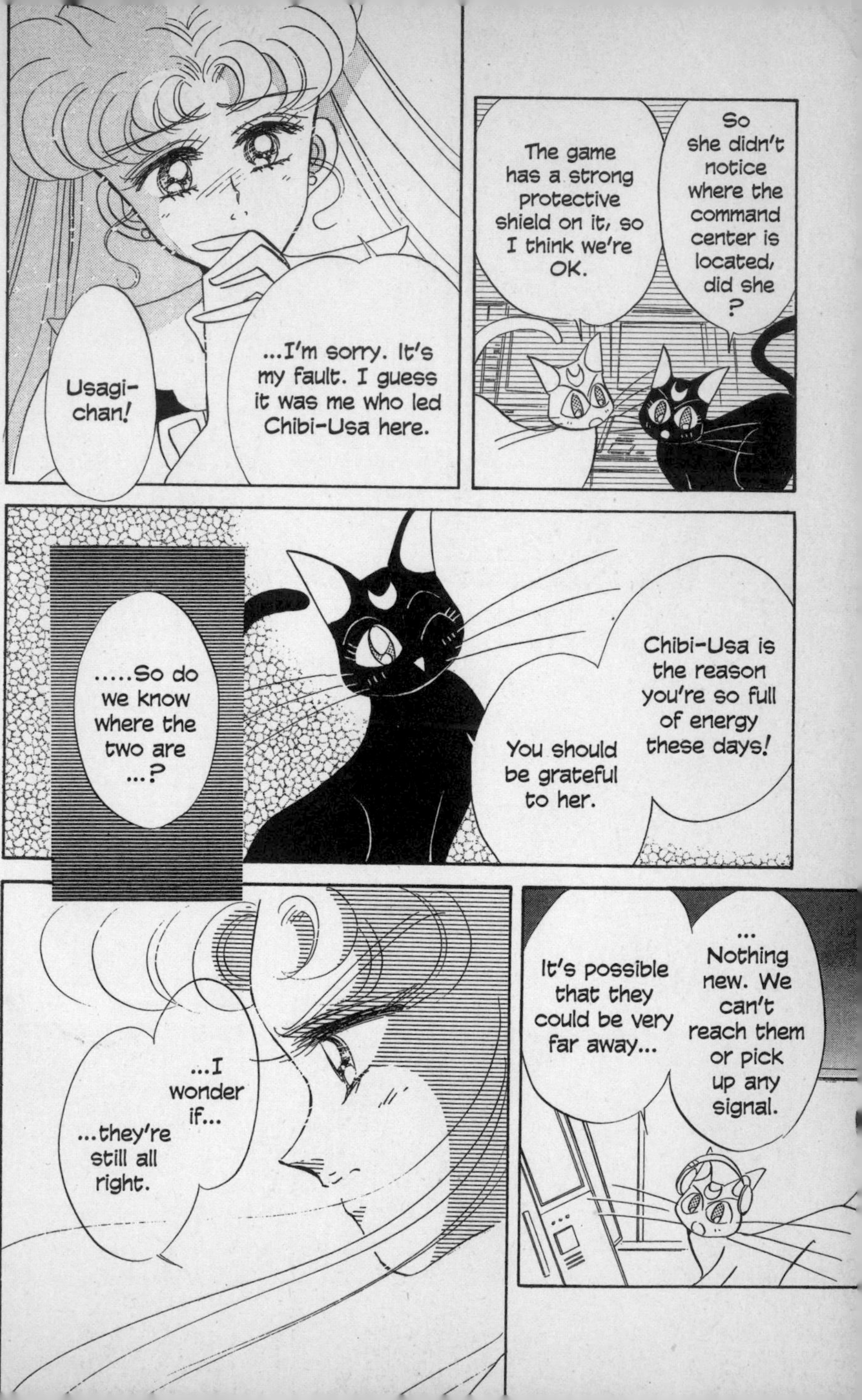
So she didn't notice where the command center is located, did she?
The game has a strong protective shield on it, so I think we're OK.
...I'm sorry. It's my fault. I guess it was me who led Chibi-Usa here.
Usagi-chan!
Chibi-Usa is the reason you're so full of energy these days!
You should be grateful to her.
.....So do we know where the two are ...?
... Nothing new. We can't reach them or pick up any signal.
It's possible that they could be very far away...
...I wonder if...
...they're still all right.

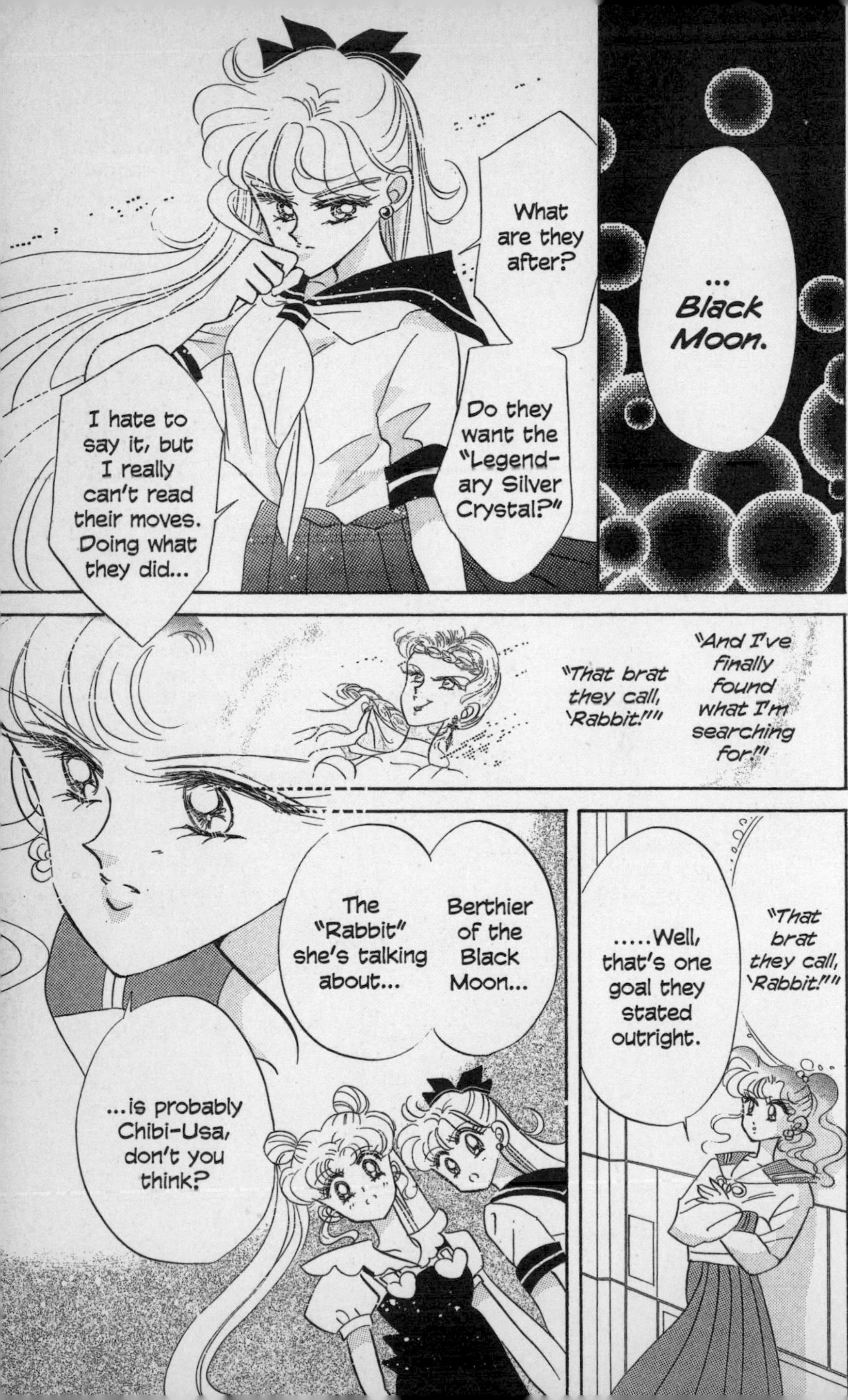
... Black Moon.
What are they after?
Do they want the "Legendary Silver Crystal?"
I hate to say it, but I really can't read their moves. Doing what they did...
"And I've finally found what I'm searching for!!"
"That brat they call, 'Rabbit!'"
"That brat they call, 'Rabbit!'"
.....Well, that's one goal they stated outright.
Berthier of the Black Moon...
The "Rabbit" she's talking about...
...is probably Chibi-Usa, don't you think?

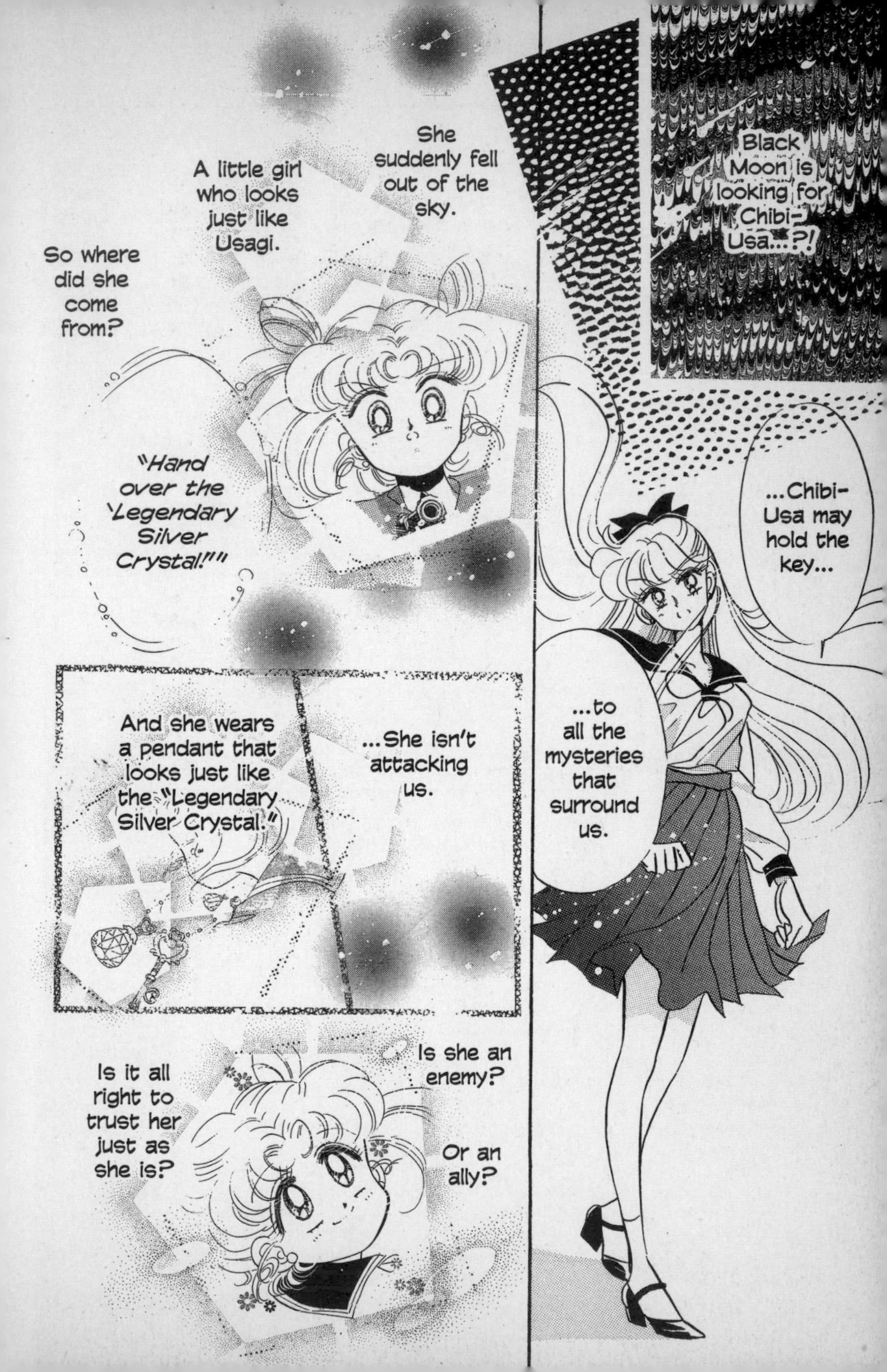
Black Moon is looking for Chibi-Usa...?!
...Chibi-Usa may hold the key...
...to all the mysteries that surround us.
She suddenly fell out of the sky.
A little girl who looks just like Usagi.
So where did she come from?
"Hand over the 'Legendary Silver Crystal!'"
...She isn't attacking us.
And she wears a pendant that looks just like the "Legendary Silver Crystal."
Is she an enemy?
Or an ally?
Is it all right to trust her just as she is?

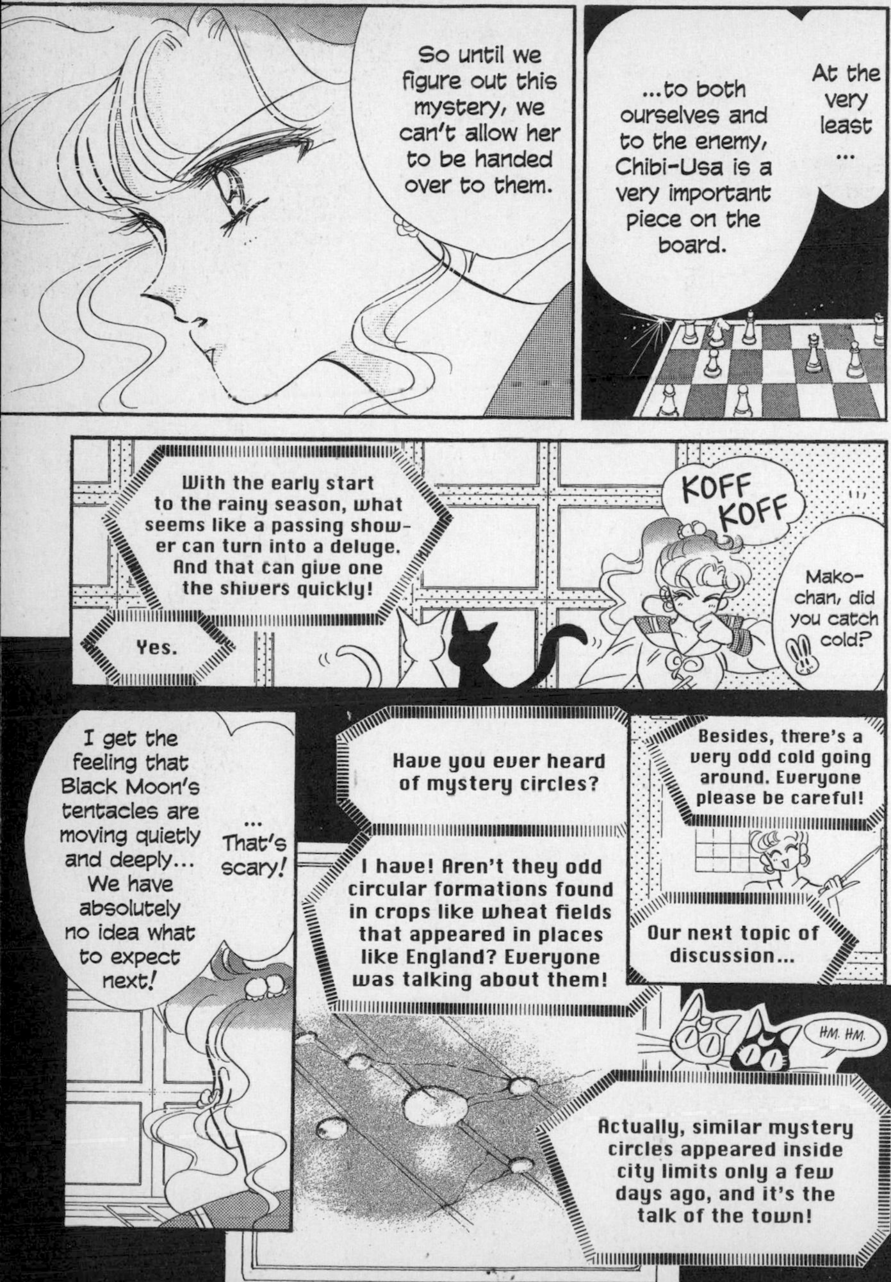

At the very least ...
...to both ourselves and to the enemy, Chibi-Usa is a very important piece on the board.
So until we figure out this mystery, we can't allow her to be handed over to them.
KOFF KOFF
Mako-chan, did you catch cold?
With the early start to the rainy season, what seems like a passing shower can turn into a deluge. And that can give one the shivers quickly!
Yes.
Besides, there's a very odd cold going around. Everyone please be careful!
Our next topic of discussion...
Have you ever heard of mystery circles?
I have! Aren't they odd circular formations found in crops like wheat fields that appeared in places like England? Everyone was talking about them!
HM. HM.
Actually, similar mystery circles appeared inside city limits only a few days ago, and it's the talk of the town!
I get the feeling that Black Moon's tentacles are moving quietly and deeply... We have absolutely no idea what to expect next!
... That's scary!

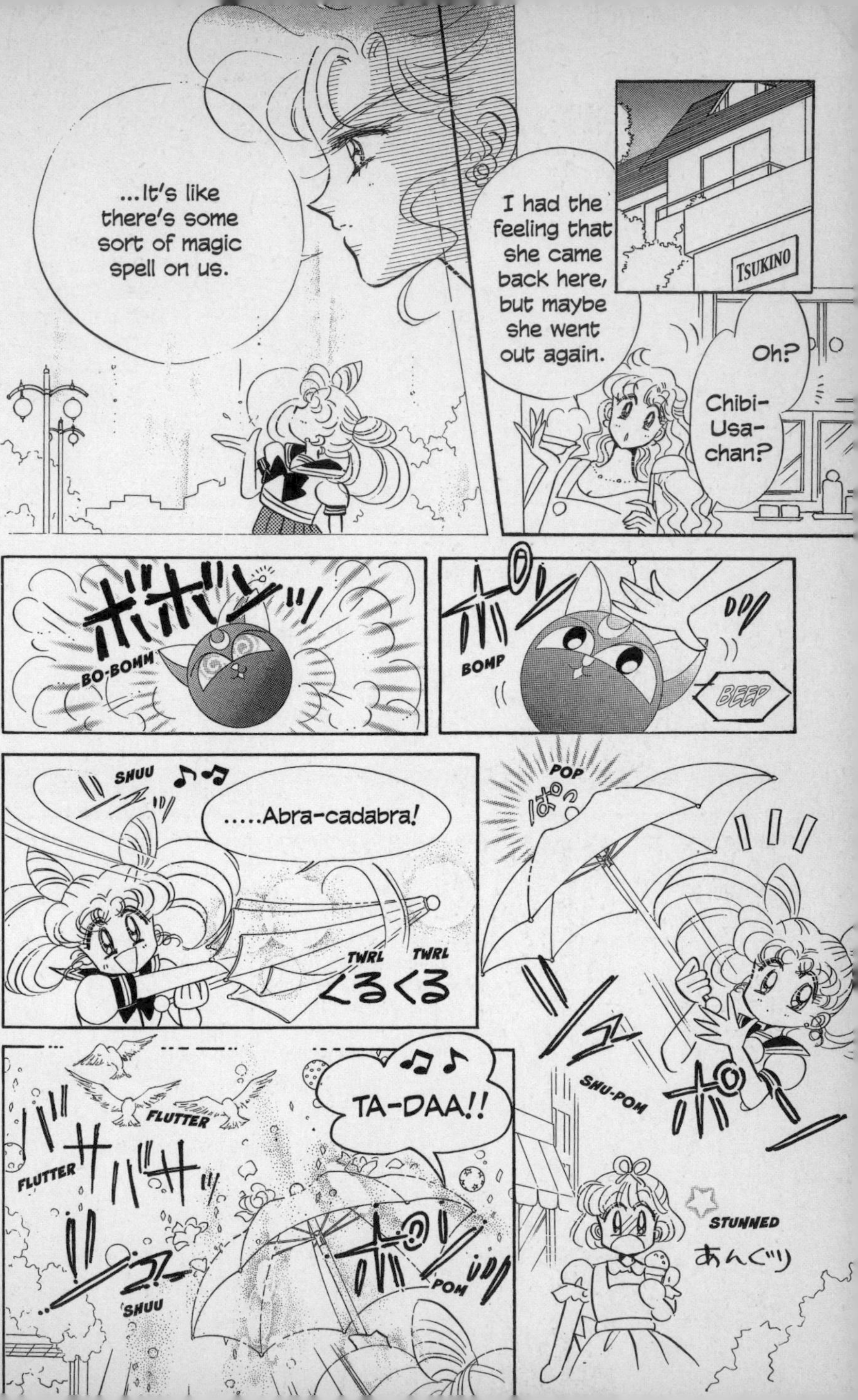
TSUKINO
I had the feeling that she came back here, but maybe she went out again.
Oh? Chibi-Usa-chan?
...It's like there's some sort of magic spell on us.
BOMP
BEEP
BO-BOMM
POP
ぱっ
SHU-POM
SHUU
.....Abra-cadabra!
TWRL TWRL
くるくる
STUNNED
あんぐり
TA-DAA!!
FLUTTER
FLUTTER
SHUU
POM

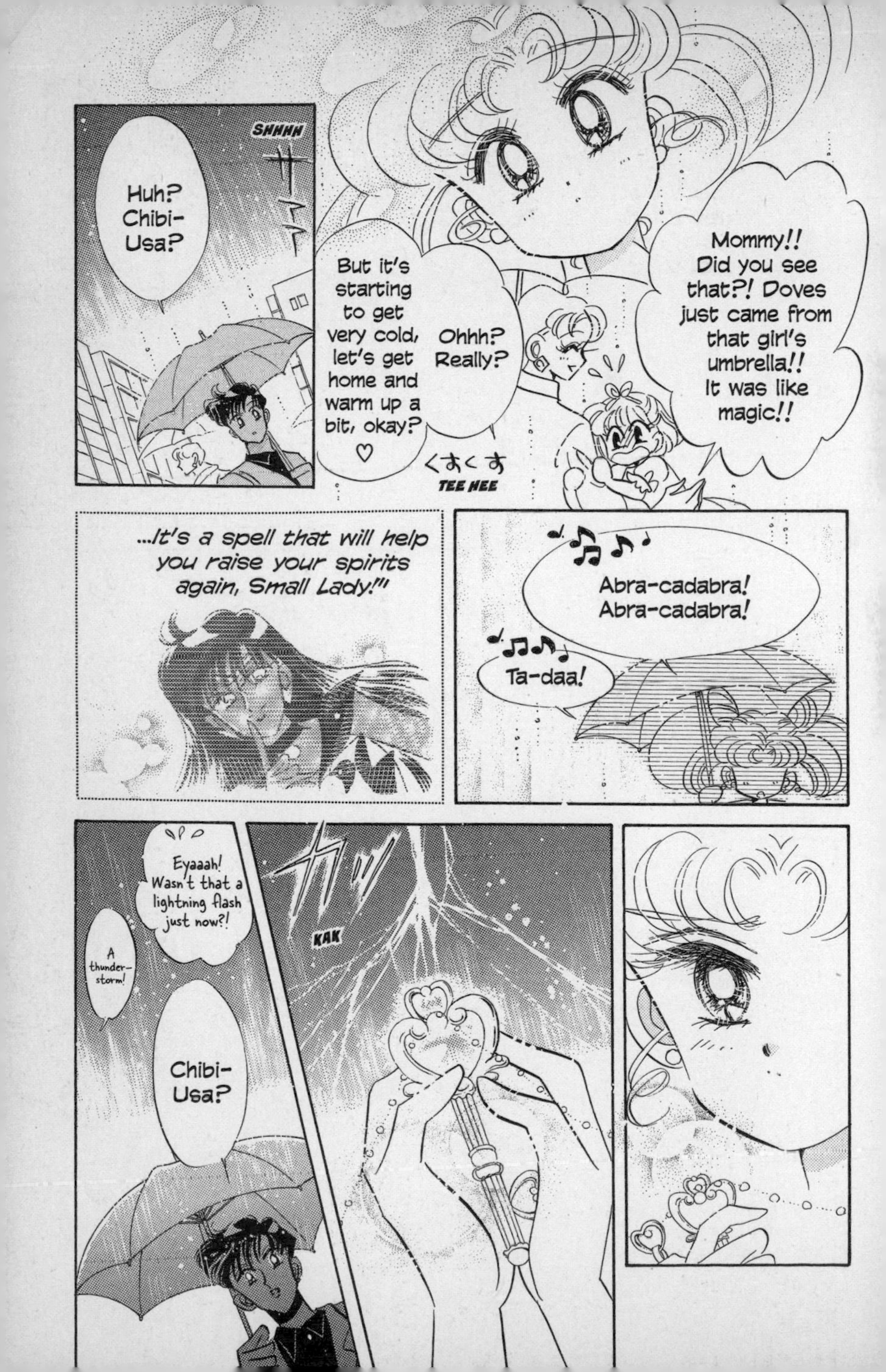
Mommy!! Did you see that?! Doves just came from that girl's umbrella!! It was like magic!!
Ohhh? Really?
But it's starting to get very cold, let's get home and warm up a bit, okay? ♡
くすくす
TEE HEE
SHHHH
Huh? Chibi-Usa?
Abra-cadabra! Abra-cadabra!
Ta-daa!
...It's a spell that will help you raise your spirits again, Small Lady!'"
KAK
Eyaaah! Wasn't that a lightning flash just now?!
A thunder-storm!
Chibi-Usa?

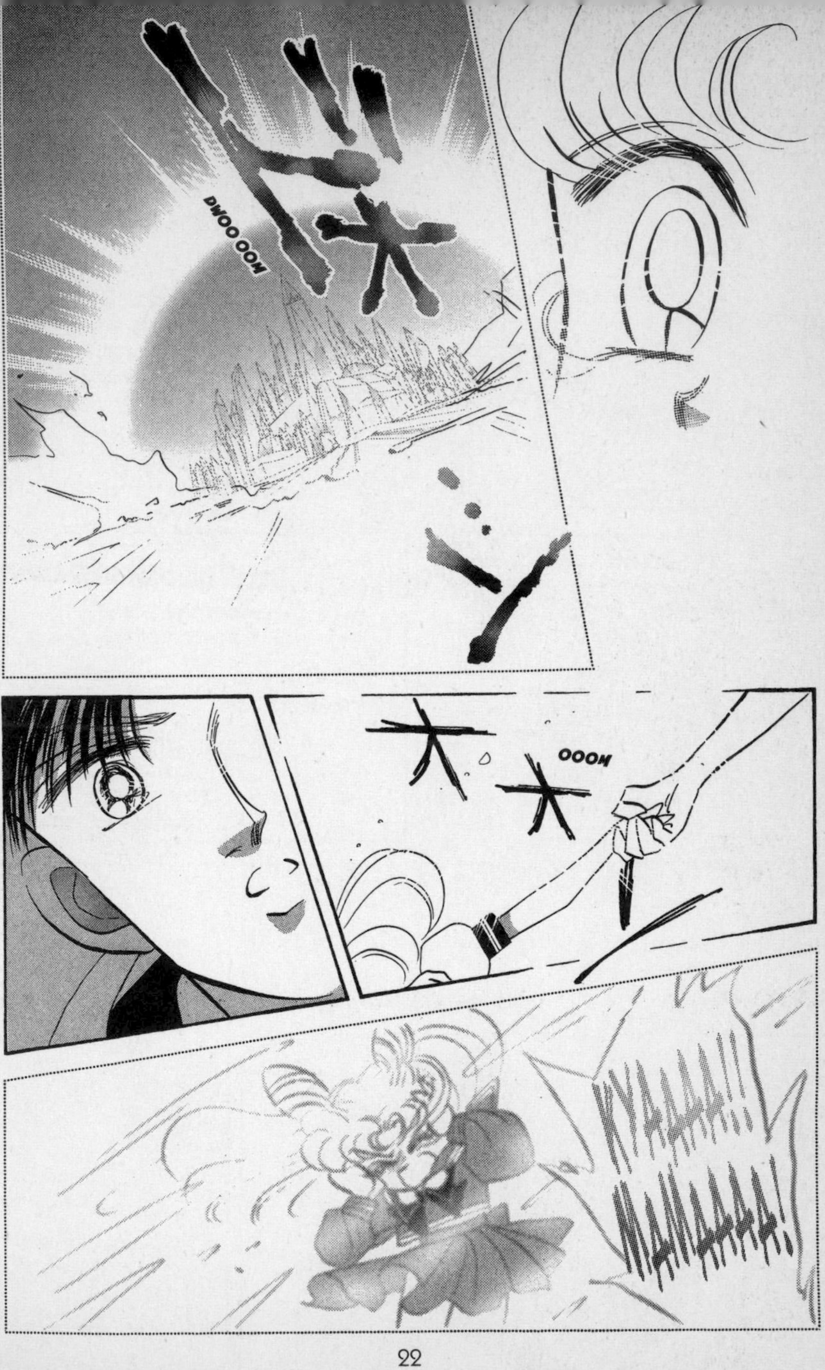
DWOO OOM
OOOM
KYAAAA!!
MAMAAAA!

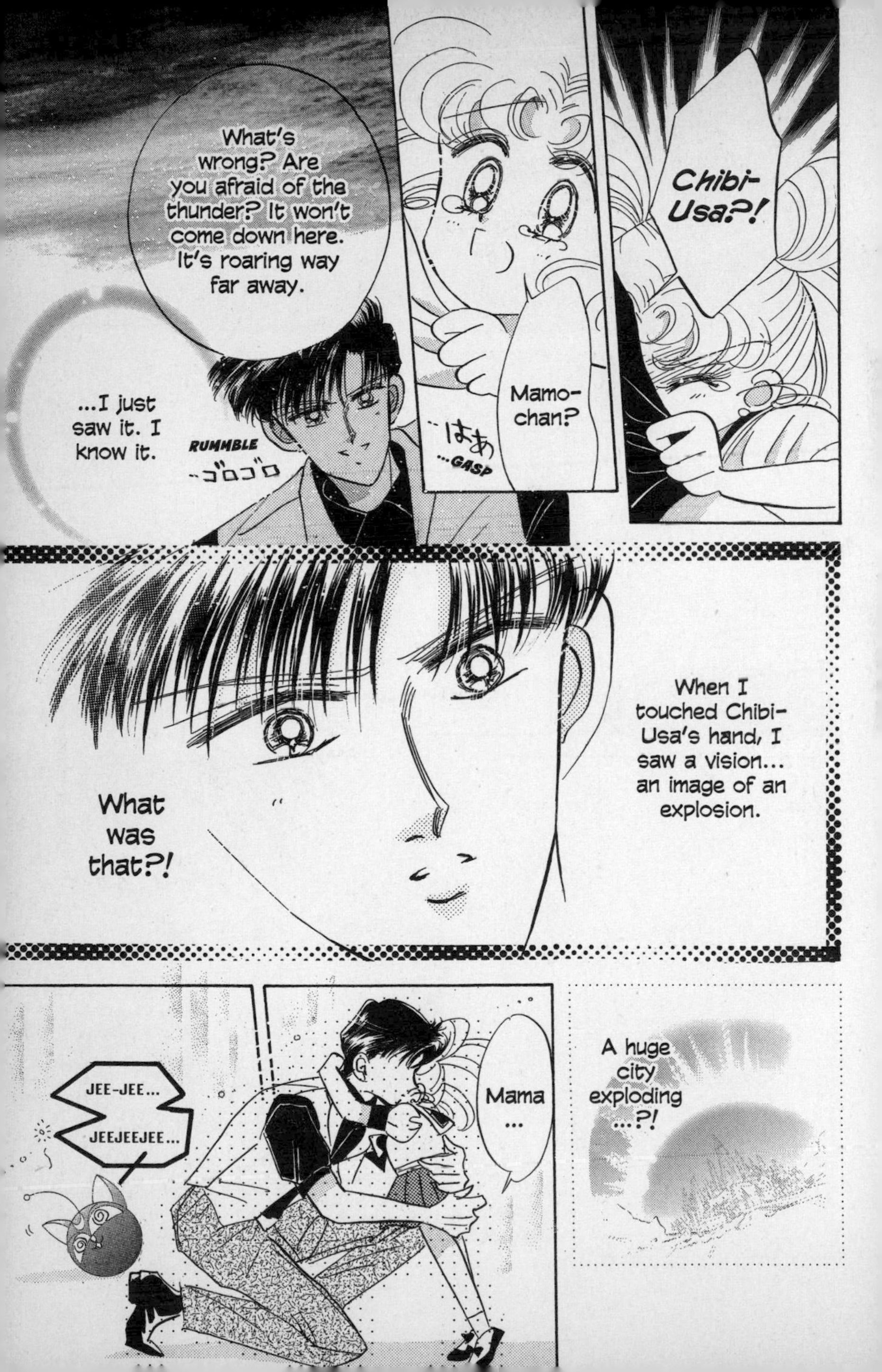
Chibi-Usa?!
Mamo-chan?
はあ
...GASP
What's wrong? Are you afraid of the thunder? It won't come down here. It's roaring way far away.
RUMMBLE
ゴロゴロ
...I just saw it. I know it.
When I touched Chibi-Usa's hand, I saw a vision... an image of an explosion.
What was that?!
A huge city exploding ...?!
Mama ...
JEE-JEE...
JEEJEEJEE...

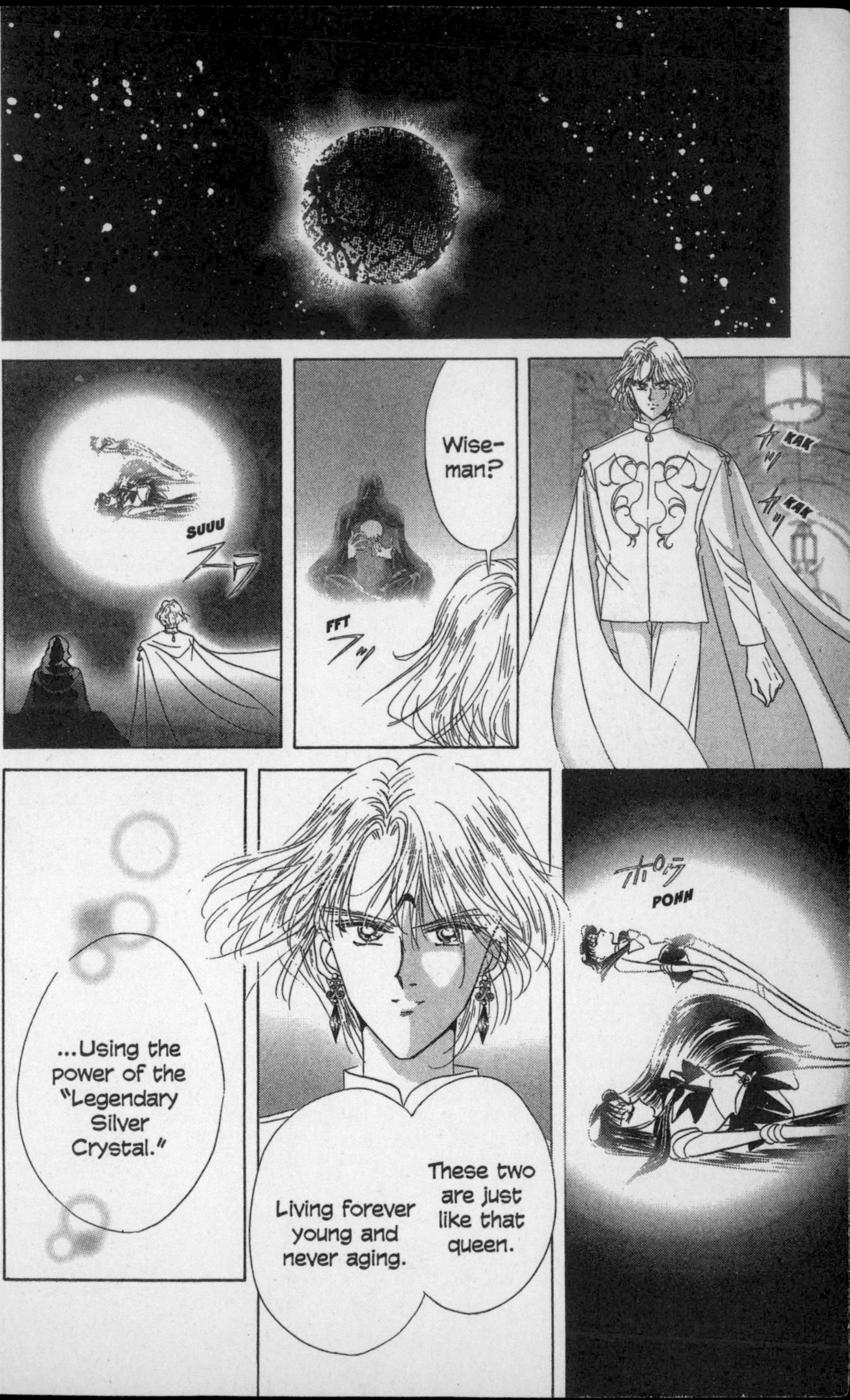
KAK
KAK
Wise-
man?
FFT
SUUU
PONH
These two are just like that queen.
Living forever young and never aging.
...Using the power of the "Legendary Silver Crystal."

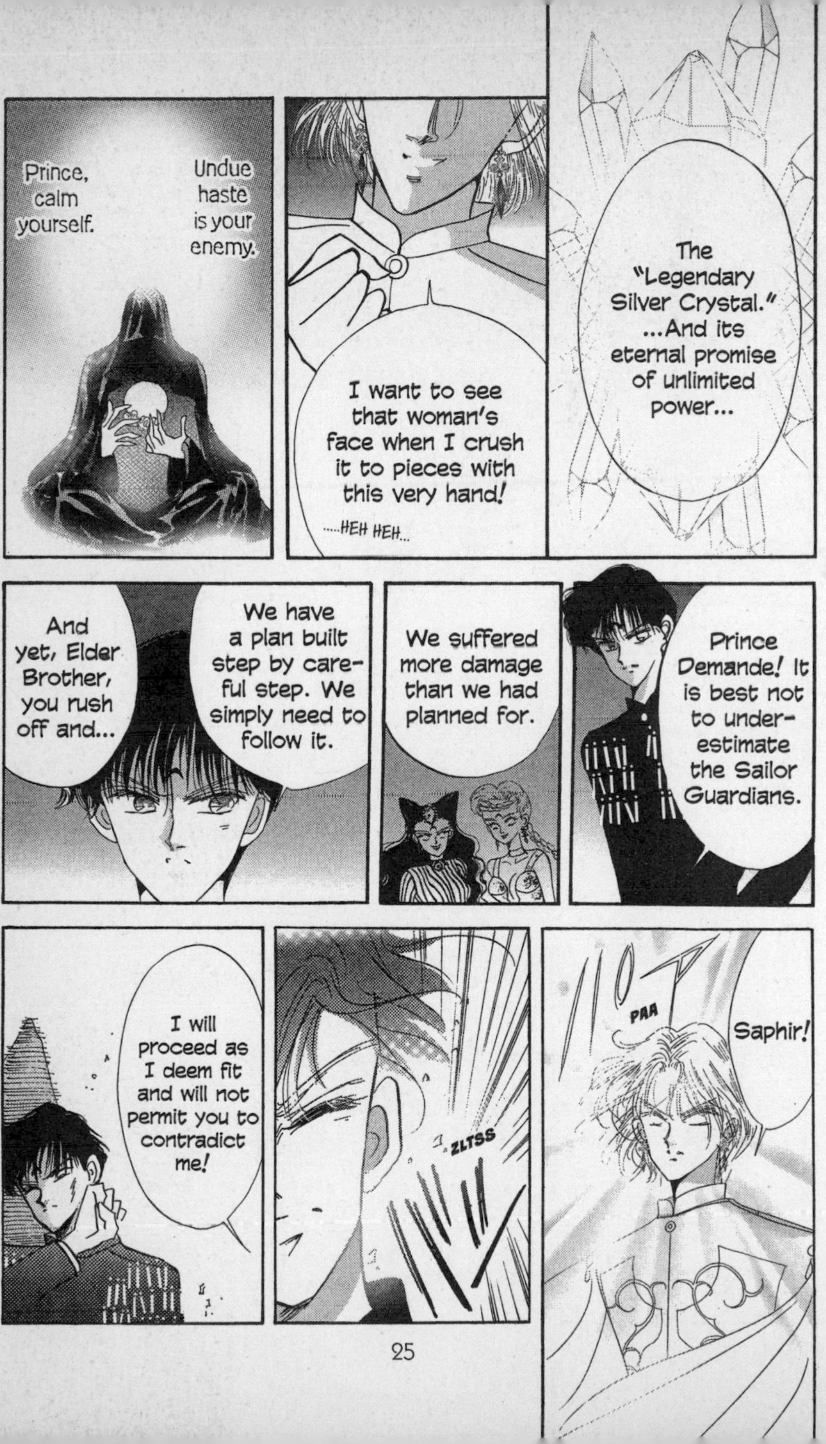
The "Legendary Silver Crystal." ...And its eternal promise of unlimited power...
I want to see that woman's face when I crush it to pieces with this very hand!
...HEH HEH...
Undue haste is your enemy.
Prince, calm yourself.
Prince Demande! It is best not to underestimate the Sailor Guardians.
We suffered more damage than we had planned for.
We have a plan built step by careful step. We simply need to follow it.
And yet, Elder Brother, you rush off and...
PAA
Saphir!
ZLTSS
I will proceed as I deem fit and will not permit you to contradict me!

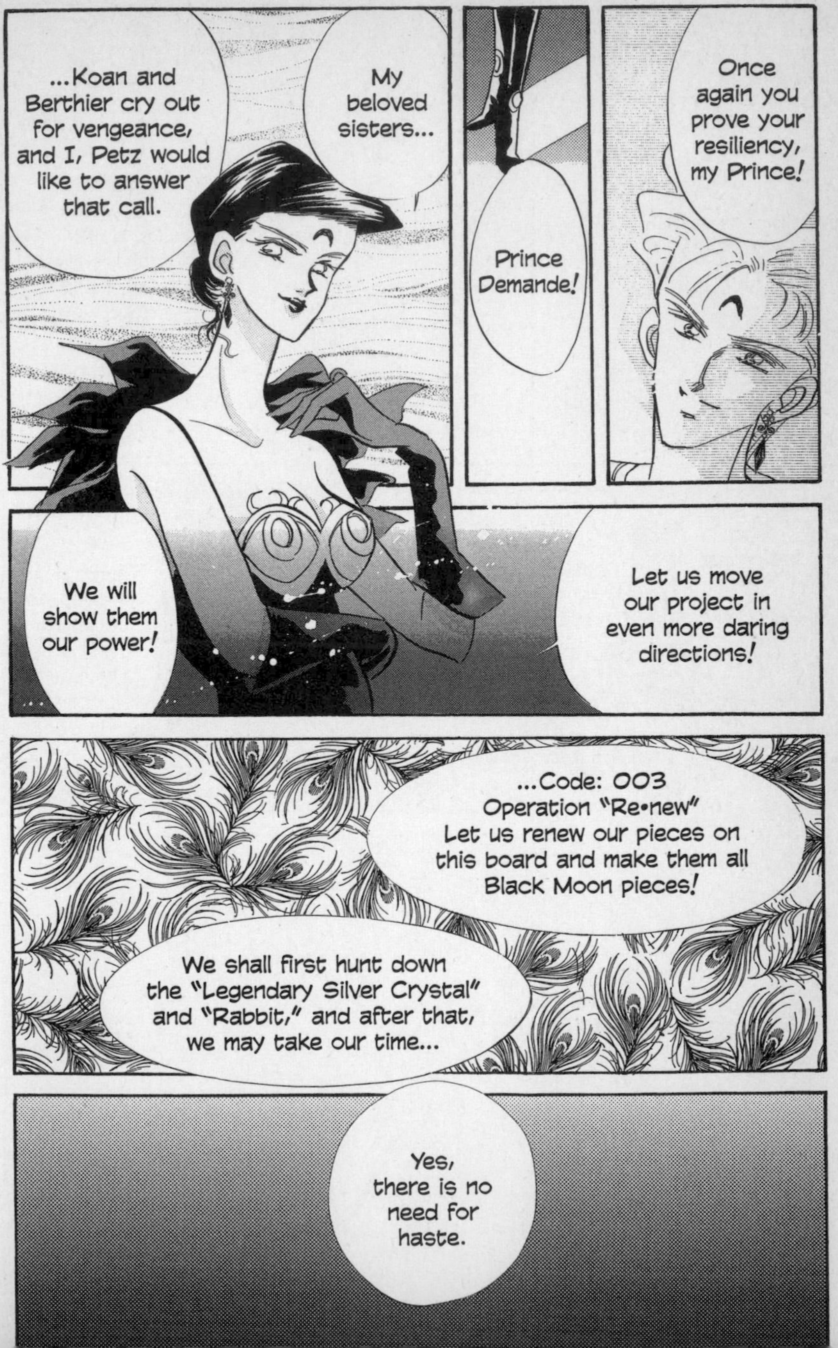
Once again you prove your resiliency, my Prince!
Prince Demande!
My beloved sisters...
...Koan and Berthier cry out for vengeance, and I, Petz would like to answer that call.
Let us move our project in even more daring directions!
We will show them our power!
...Code: 003 Operation "Re•new" Let us renew our pieces on this board and make them all Black Moon pieces!
We shall first hunt down the "Legendary Silver Crystal" and "Rabbit," and after that, we may take our time...
Yes, there is no need for haste.

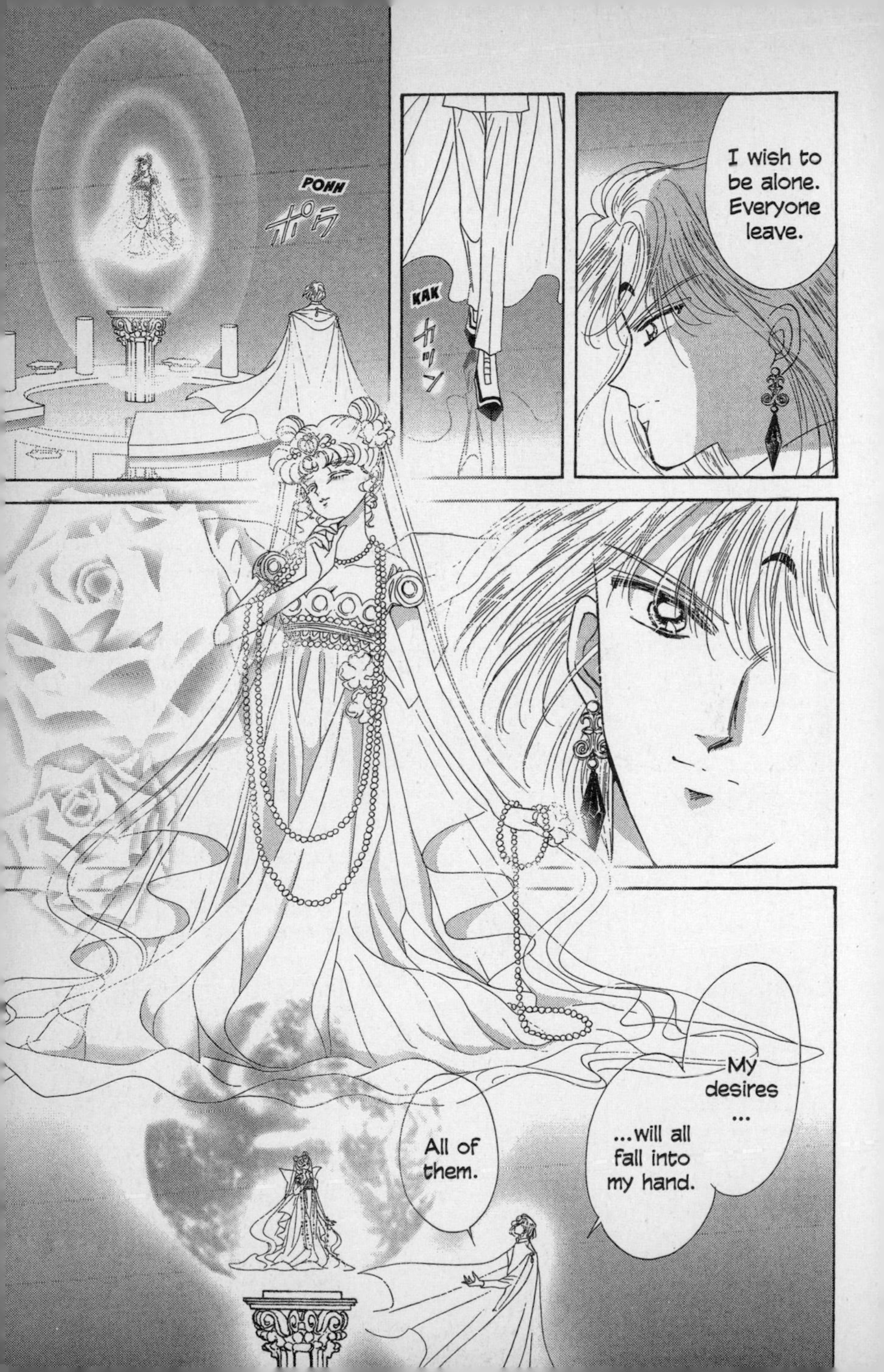
I wish to be alone. Everyone leave.
KAK
PONN
My desires ...
...will all fall into my hand.
All of them.

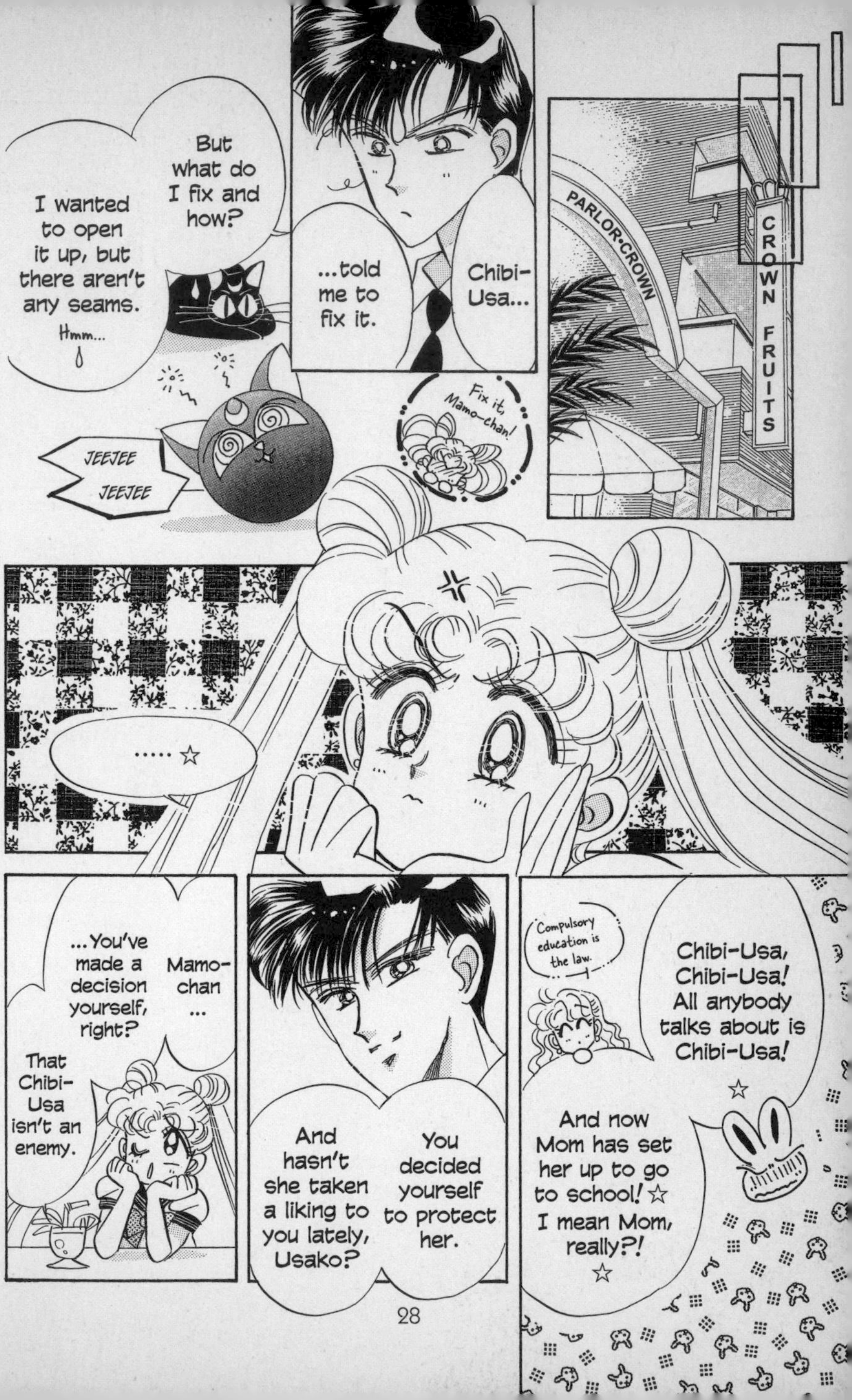
CROWN FRUITS
PARLOR·CROWN
Chibi-Usa...
...told me to fix it.
But what do I fix and how?
I wanted to open it up, but there aren't any seams.
Hmm...
Fix it, Mamo-chan!
JEEJEE
JEEJEE
..... ☆
Chibi-Usa, Chibi-Usa! All anybody talks about is Chibi-Usa! ☆
Compulsory education is the law.
And now Mom has set her up to go to school! ☆ I mean Mom, really?! ☆
You decided yourself to protect her.
And hasn't she taken a liking to you lately, Usako?
Mamo-chan...
...You've made a decision yourself, right?
That Chibi-Usa isn't an enemy.

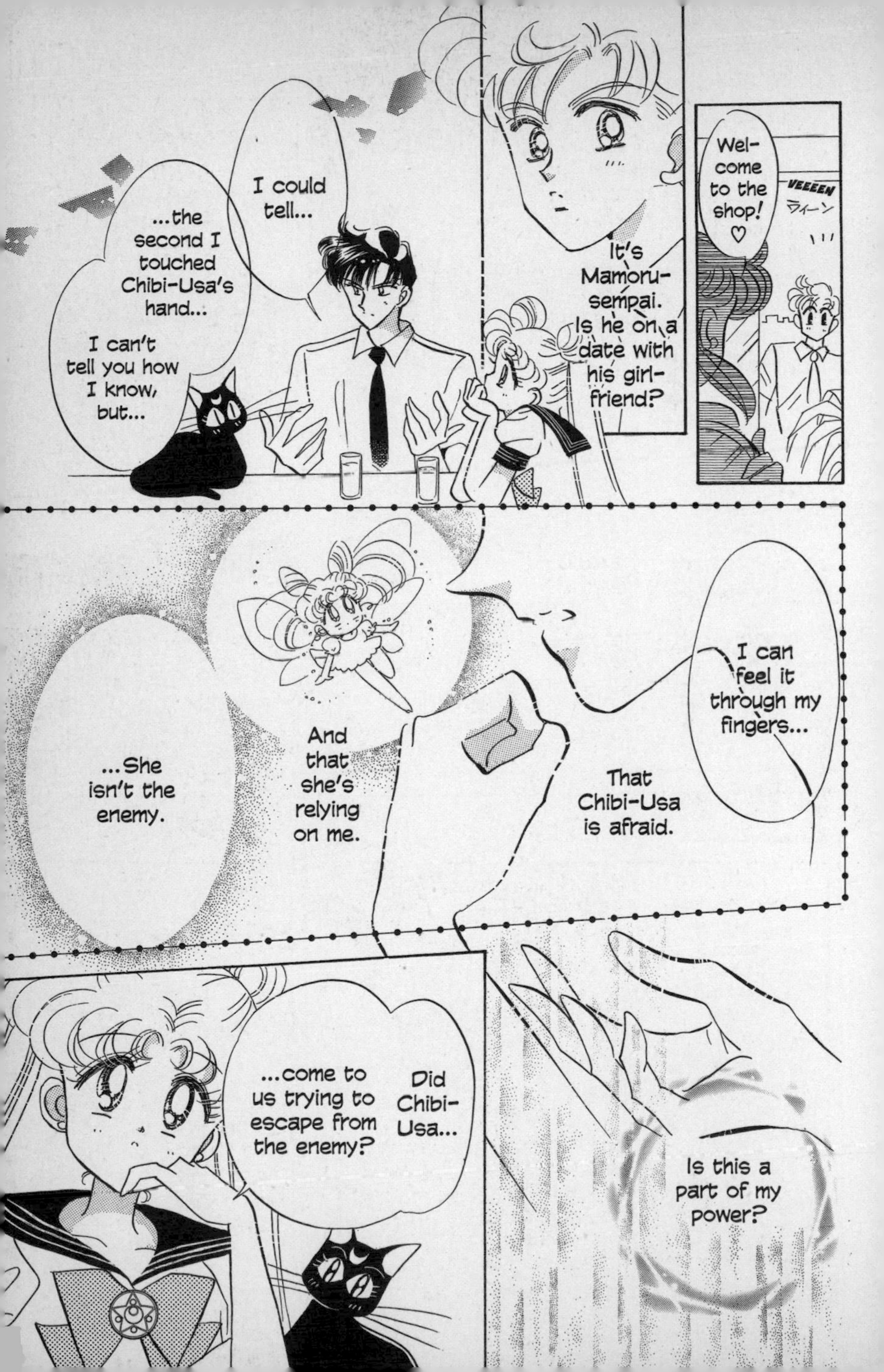
Wel-come to the shop! ♡
VEEEEN
ラィーン
It's Mamoru-sempai. Is he on a date with his girl-friend?
I could tell...
...the second I touched Chibi-Usa's hand...
I can't tell you how I know, but...
I can feel it through my fingers...
That Chibi-Usa is afraid.
And that she's relying on me.
...She isn't the enemy.
Is this a part of my power?
Did Chibi-Usa...
...come to us trying to escape from the enemy?

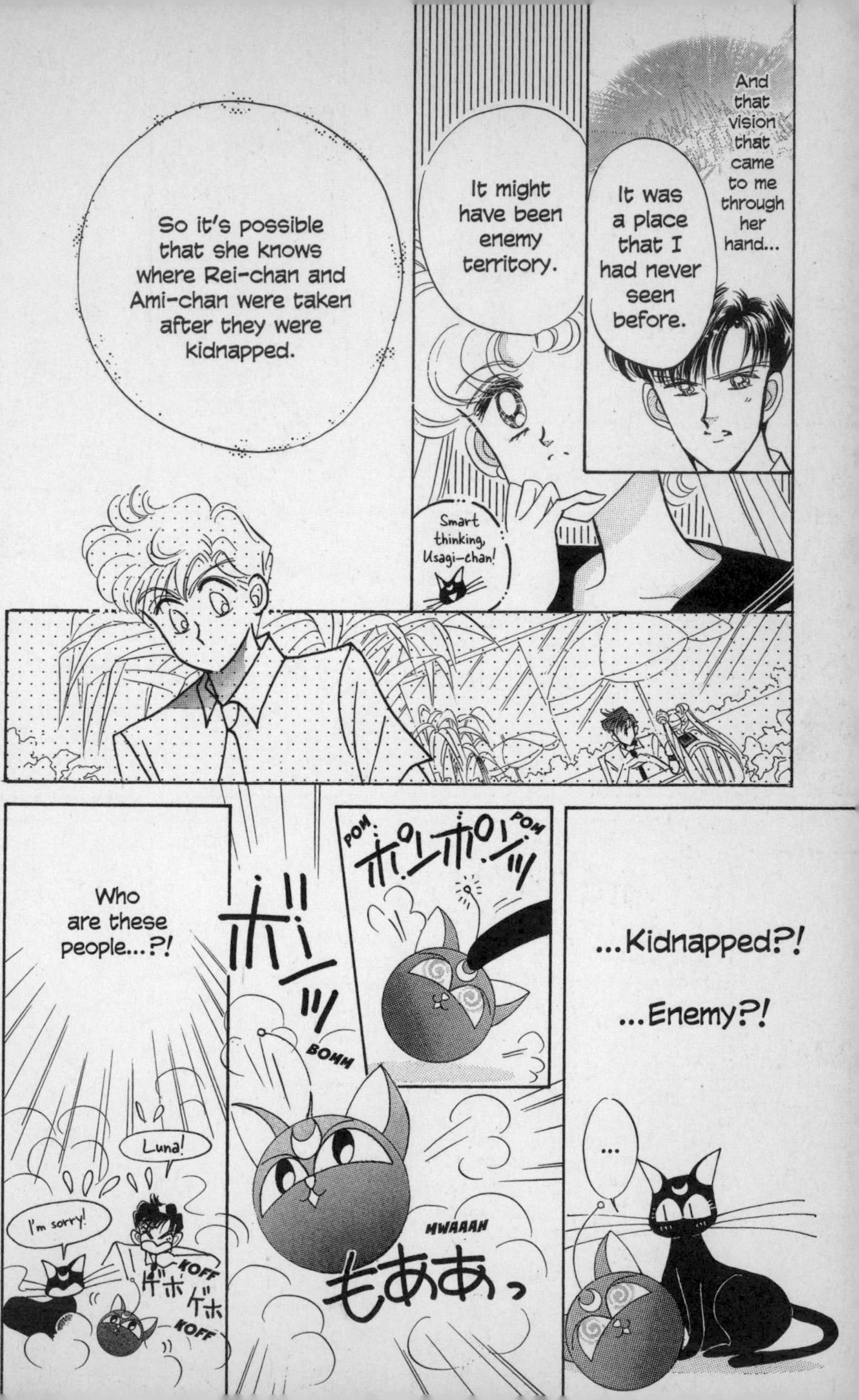

And that vision that came to me through her hand...
It was a place that I had never seen before.
It might have been enemy territory.
Smart thinking, Usagi-chan!
So it's possible that she knows where Rei-chan and Ami-chan were taken after they were kidnapped.
...Kidnapped?!
...Enemy?!
...
POM POM
ポンポンッ
ボンッ
BOMM
MWAAAH
もあぁっ
Who are these people...?!
Luna!
I'm sorry!
KOFF
ゲボゲホ
KOFF

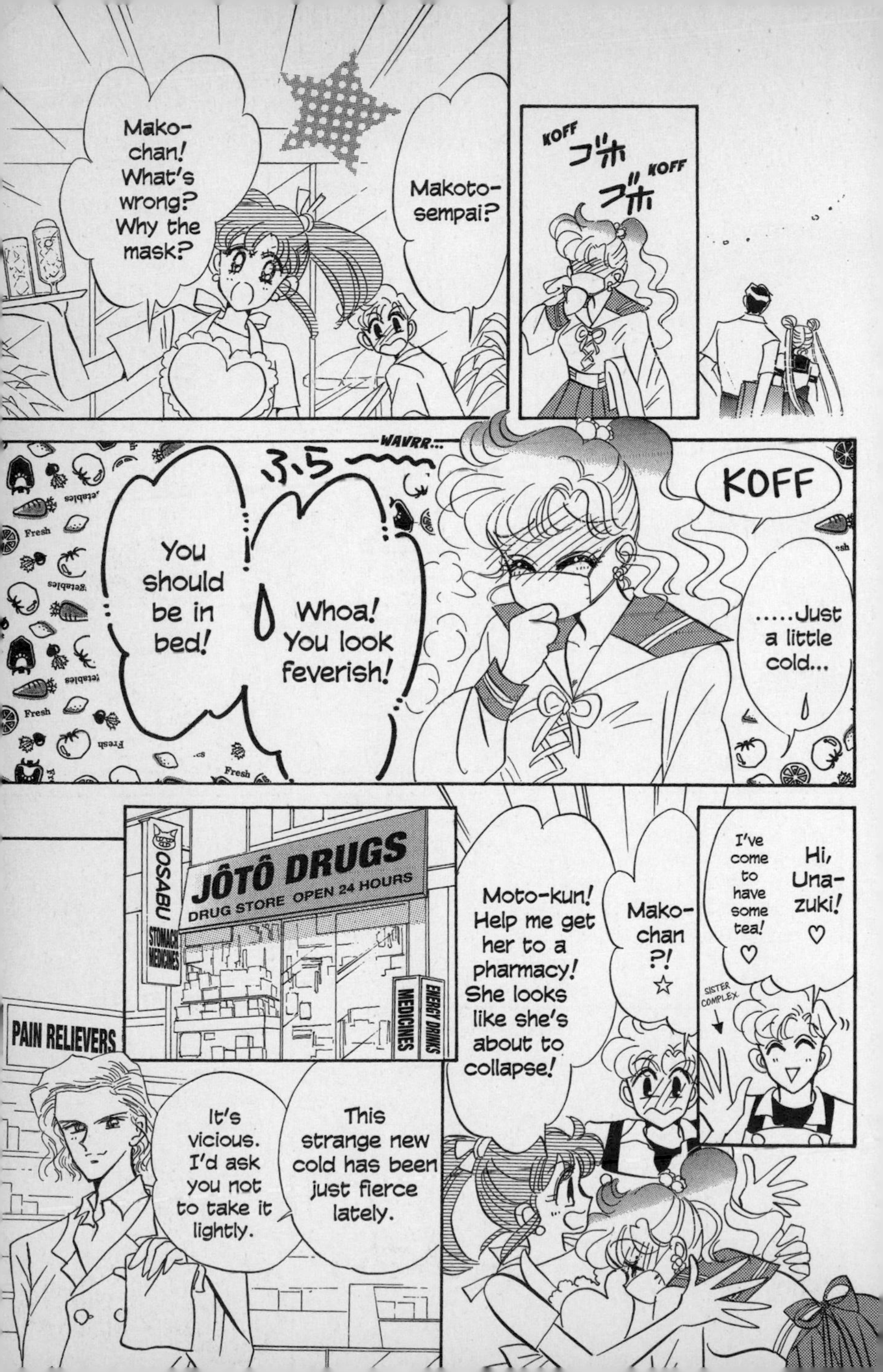
KOFF
ゴホ
KOFF
ゴホ
Makoto-sempai?
Mako-chan! What's wrong? Why the mask?
KOFF
.....Just a little cold...
WAVRR...
ふら〜〜
Whoa! You look feverish!
You should be in bed!
Hi, Una-zuki! ♡
I've come to have some tea! ♡
SISTER COMPLEX.
Mako-chan?! ☆
Moto-kun! Help me get her to a pharmacy! She looks like she's about to collapse!
JÔTÔ DRUGS
DRUG STORE OPEN 24 HOURS
OSABU
STOMACH MEDICINES
MEDICINES
ENERGY DRINKS
PAIN RELIEVERS
This strange new cold has been just fierce lately.
It's vicious. I'd ask you not to take it lightly.

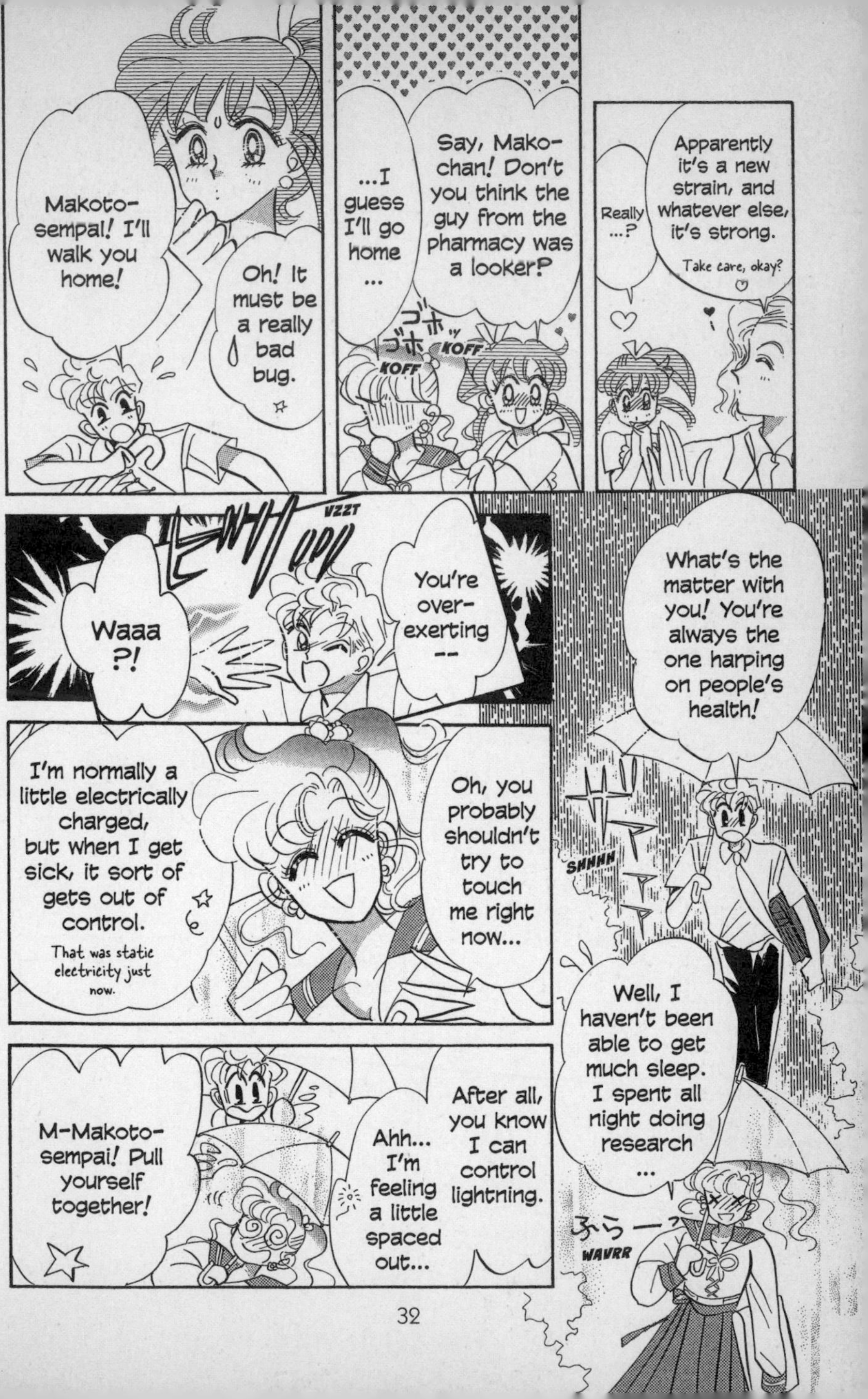
Apparently it's a new strain, and whatever else, it's strong.
Take care, okay?
Really ...?
Say, Mako-chan! Don't you think the guy from the pharmacy was a looker?
...I guess I'll go home ...
ゴホッ ゴホ
KOFF KOFF
Oh! It must be a really bad bug.
Makoto-sempai! I'll walk you home!
What's the matter with you! You're always the one harping on people's health!
SHHHH
Well, I haven't been able to get much sleep. I spent all night doing research ...
ふらーっ
WAVRR
You're over-exerting --
VZZT
Waaa ?!
Oh, you probably shouldn't try to touch me right now...
I'm normally a little electrically charged, but when I get sick, it sort of gets out of control.
That was static electricity just now.
After all, you know I can control lightning.
Ahh... I'm feeling a little spaced out...
M-Makoto-sempai! Pull yourself together!

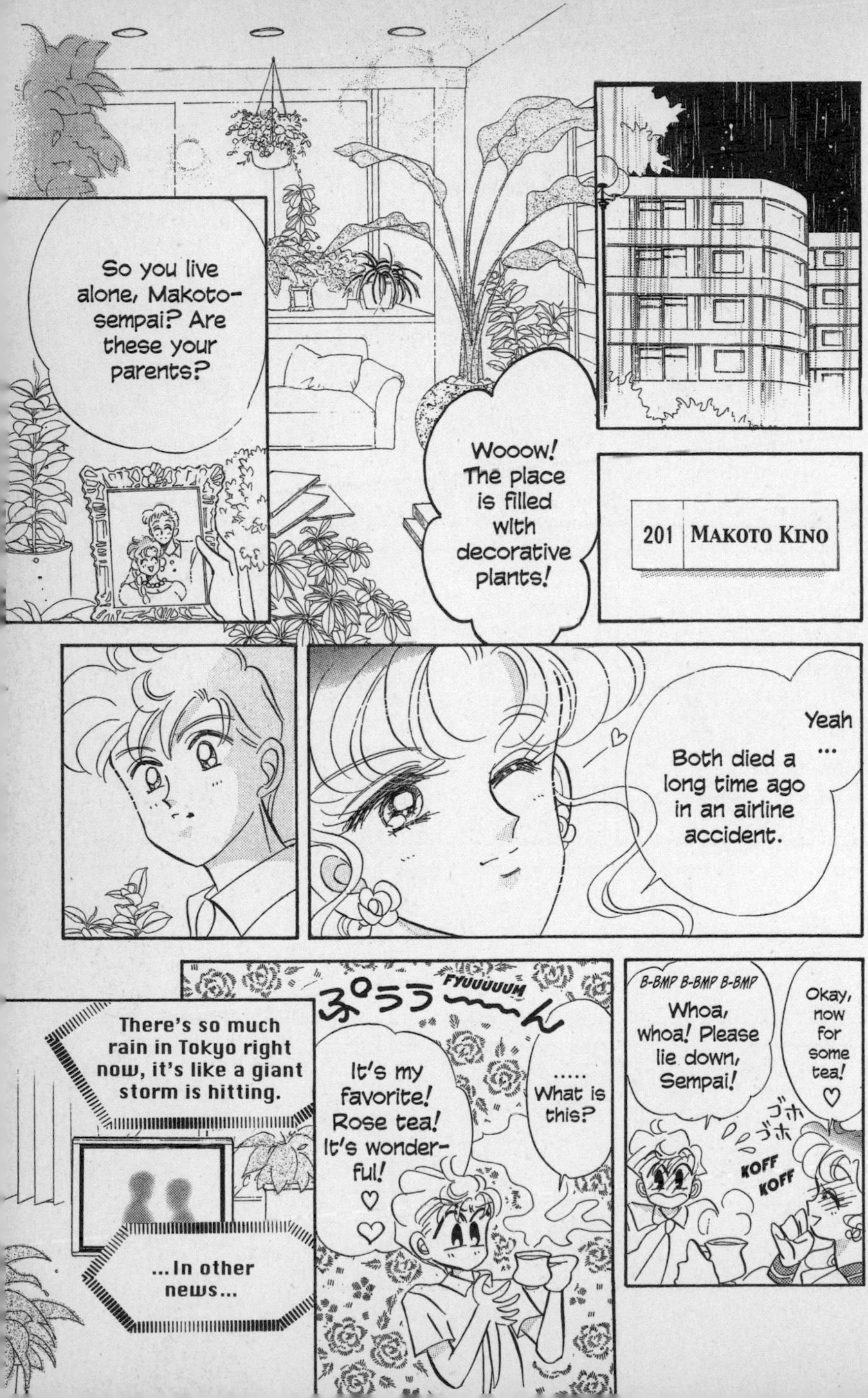
201 MAKOTO KINO
Wooow! The place is filled with decorative plants!
So you live alone, Makoto-sempai? Are these your parents?
Yeah ...
Both died a long time ago in an airline accident.
Okay, now for some tea! ♡
B-BMP B-BMP B-BMP
Whoa, whoa! Please lie down, Sempai!
ゴホゴホ
KOFF KOFF
ぷううーん
FYUUUUUM
..... What is this?
It's my favorite! Rose tea! It's wonderful! ♡ ♡
There's so much rain in Tokyo right now, it's like a giant storm is hitting.
...In other news...

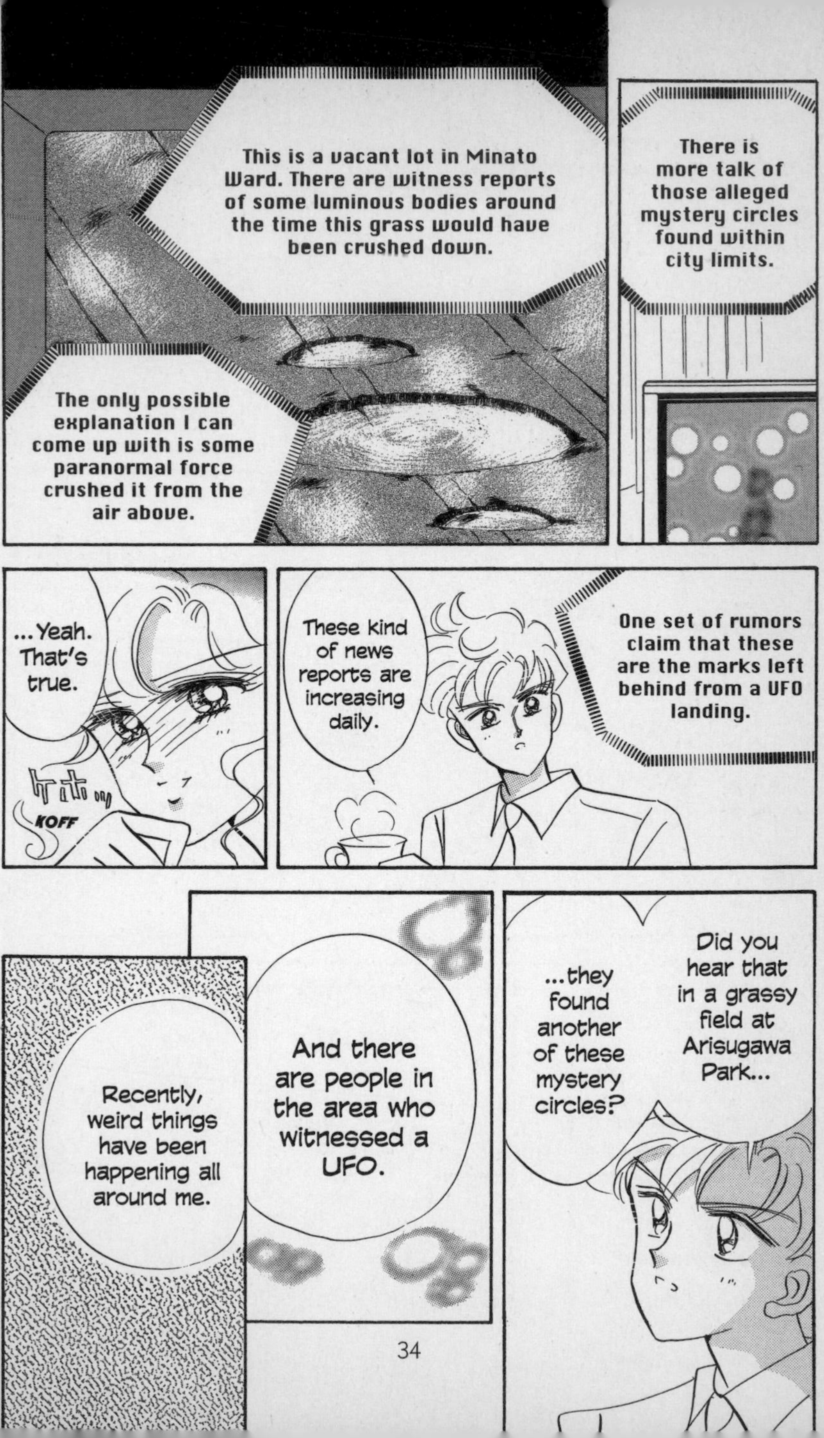
There is more talk of those alleged mystery circles found within city limits.
This is a vacant lot in Minato Ward. There are witness reports of some luminous bodies around the time this grass would have been crushed down.
The only possible explanation I can come up with is some paranormal force crushed it from the air above.
One set of rumors claim that these are the marks left behind from a UFO landing.
These kind of news reports are increasing daily.
...Yeah. That's true.
KOFF
Did you hear that in a grassy field at Arisugawa Park...
...they found another of these mystery circles?
And there are people in the area who witnessed a UFO.
Recently, weird things have been happening all around me.

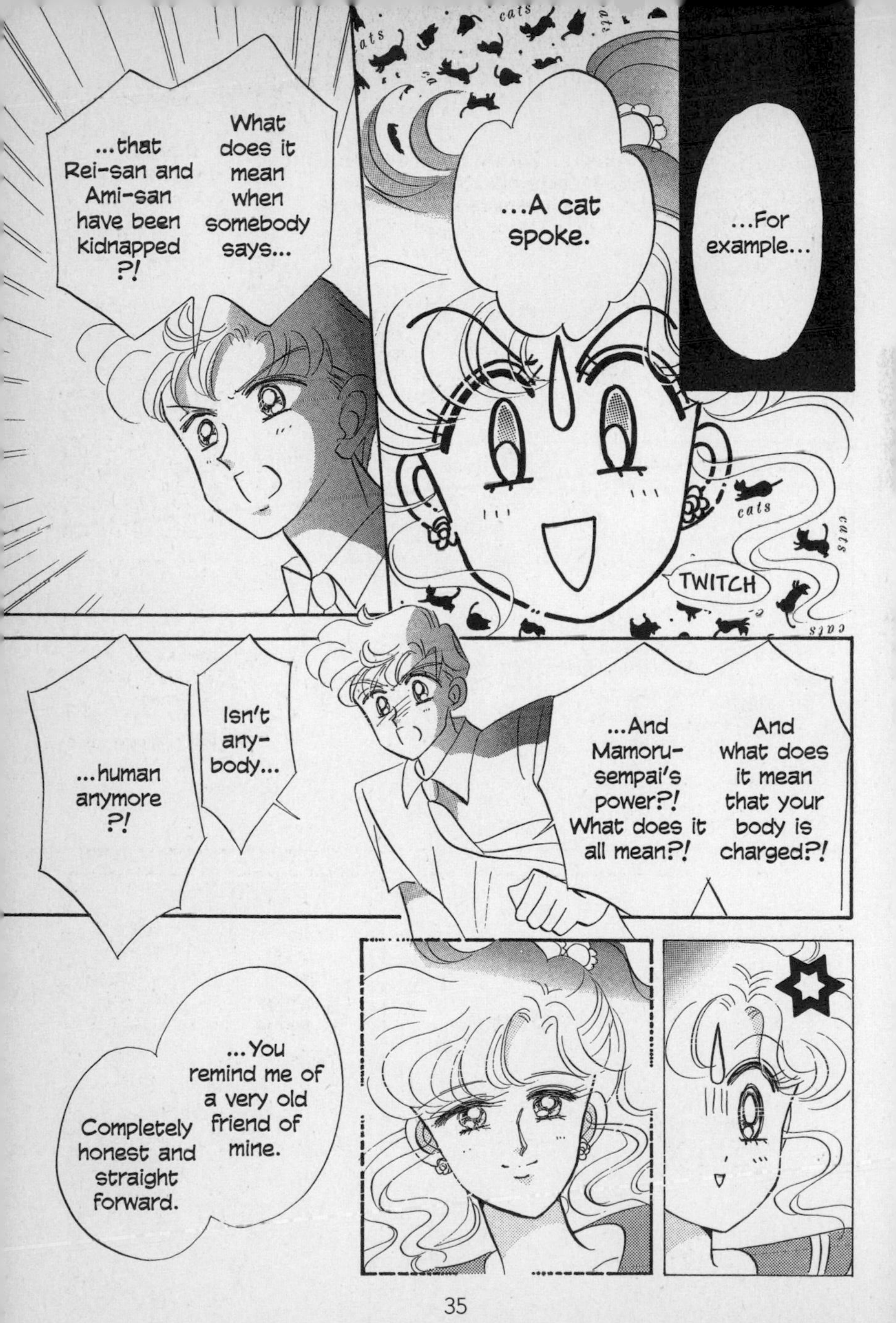
...For example...
...A cat spoke.
TWITCH
What does it mean when somebody says...
...that Rei-san and Ami-san have been kidnapped?!
And what does it mean that your body is charged?!
...And Mamoru-sempai's power?! What does it all mean?!
Isn't anybody...
...human anymore?!
...You remind me of a very old friend of mine.
Completely honest and straight forward.

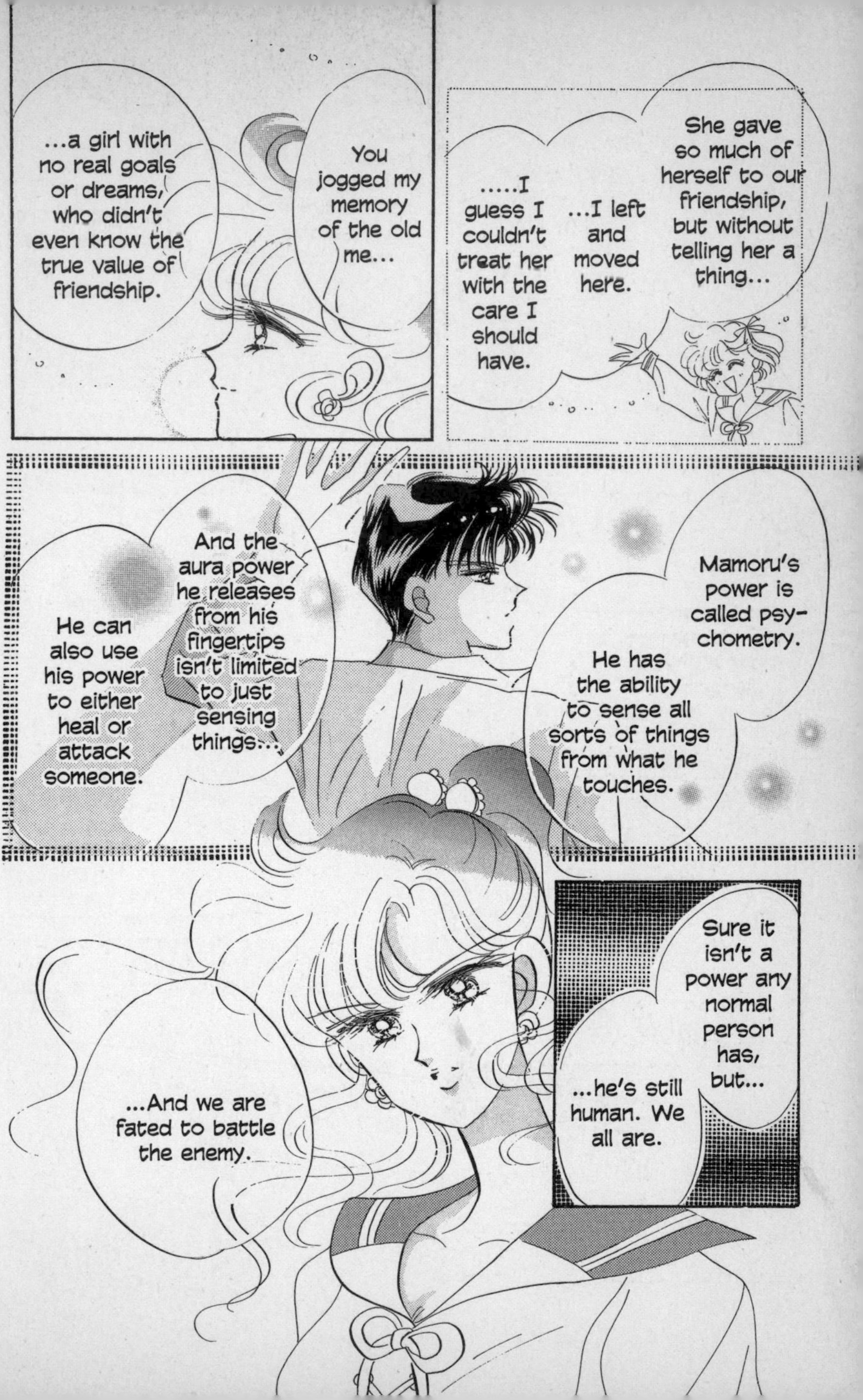
She gave so much of herself to our friendship, but without telling her a thing...
...I left and moved here.
.....I guess I couldn't treat her with the care I should have.
You jogged my memory of the old me...
...a girl with no real goals or dreams, who didn't even know the true value of friendship.
Mamoru's power is called psy-chometry.
He has the ability to sense all sorts of things from what he touches.
And the aura power he releases from his fingertips isn't limited to just sensing things...
He can also use his power to either heal or attack someone.
Sure it isn't a power any normal person has, but...
...he's still human. We all are.
...And we are fated to battle the enemy.

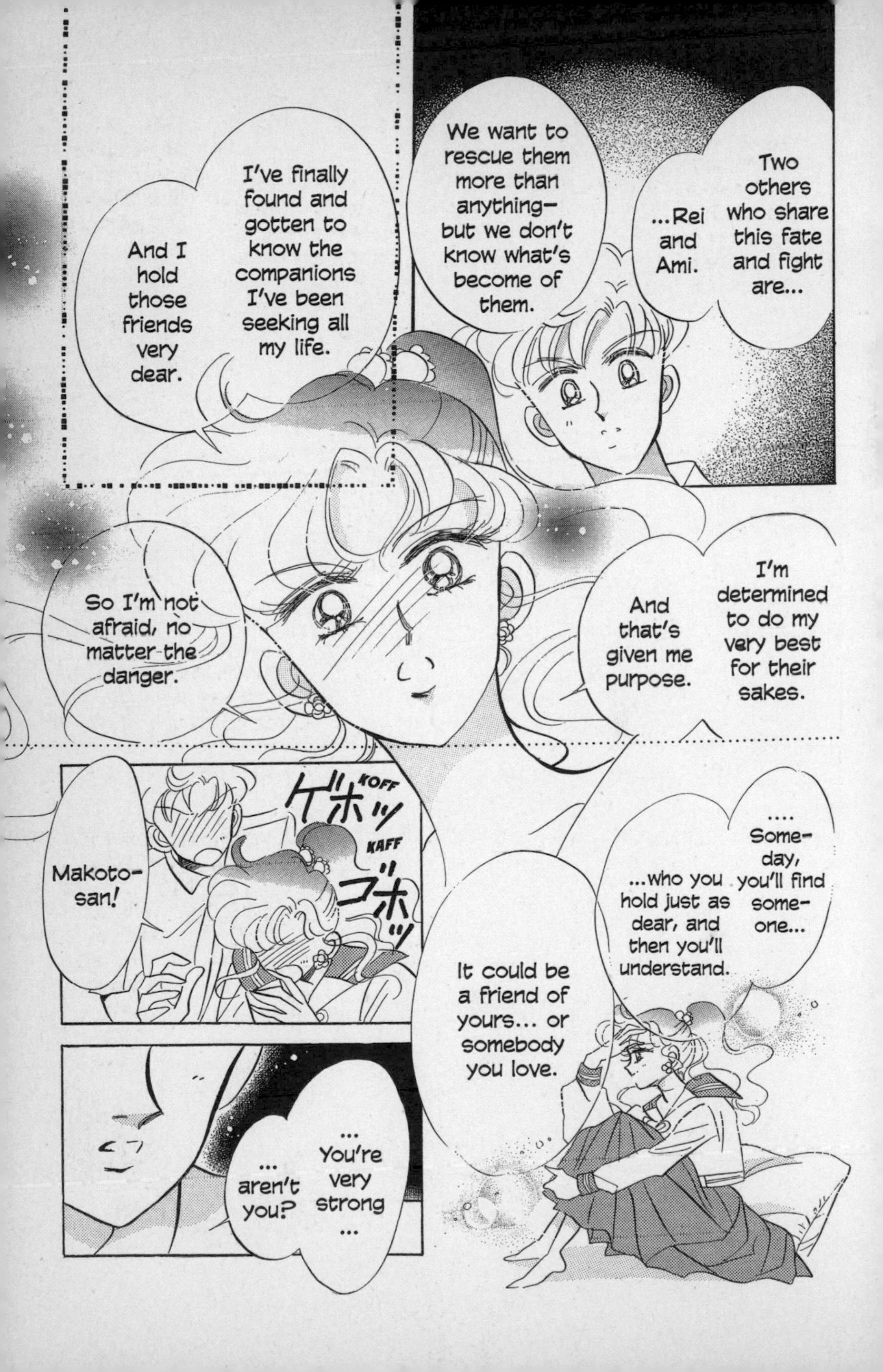
Two others who share this fate and fight are...
...Rei and Ami.
We want to rescue them more than anything— but we don't know what's become of them.
I've finally found and gotten to know the companions I've been seeking all my life.
And I hold those friends very dear.
I'm determined to do my very best for their sakes.
And that's given me purpose.
So I'm not afraid, no matter the danger.
.... Someday, you'll find someone...
...who you hold just as dear, and then you'll understand.
It could be a friend of yours... or somebody you love.
ゲボッ KOFF
ゴボッ KAFF
Makoto-san!
... You're very strong ...
... aren't you?

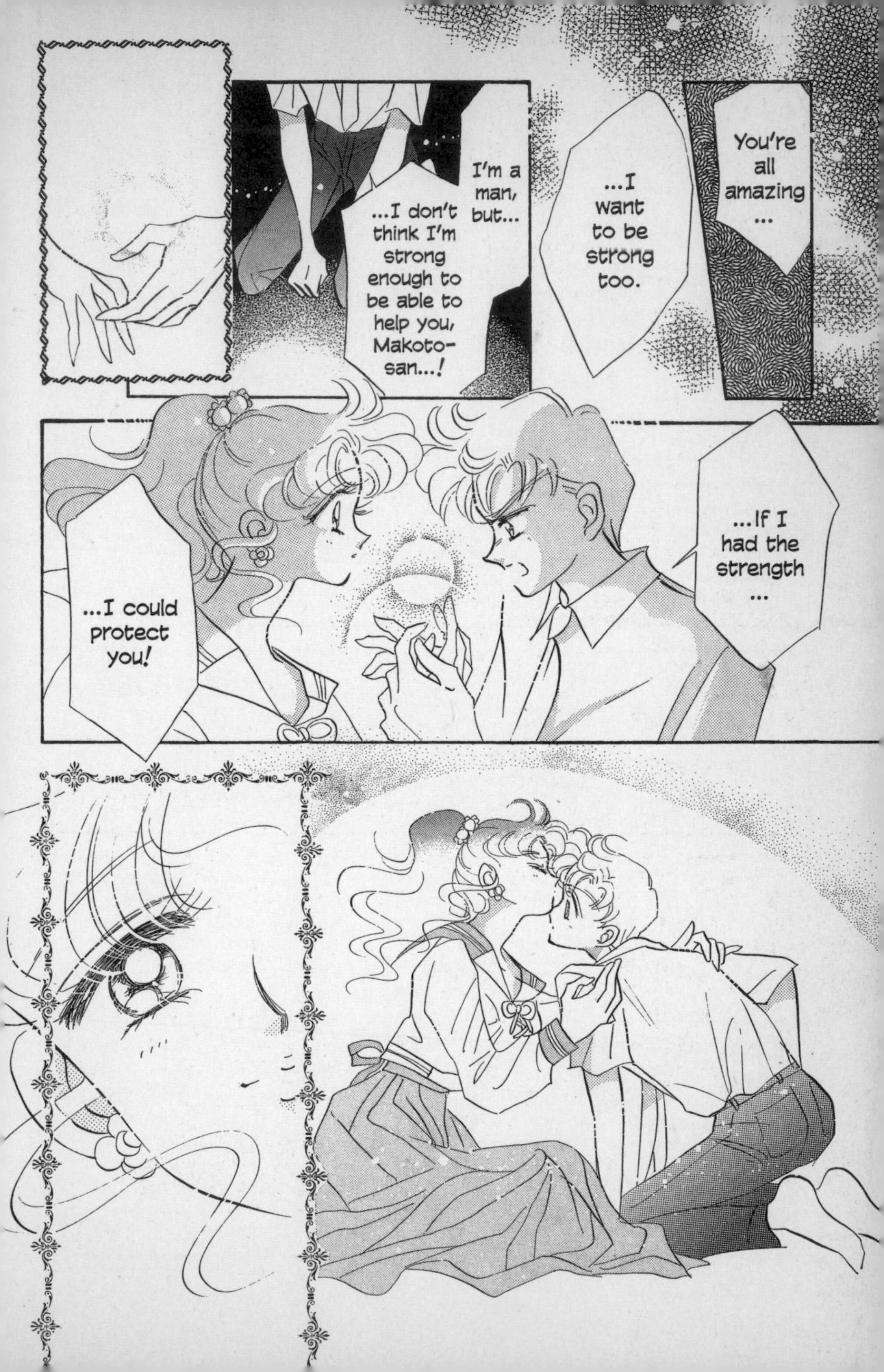
You're all amazing ...
...I want to be strong too.
I'm a man, but...
...I don't think I'm strong enough to be able to help you, Makoto-san...!
...If I had the strength ...
...I could protect you!

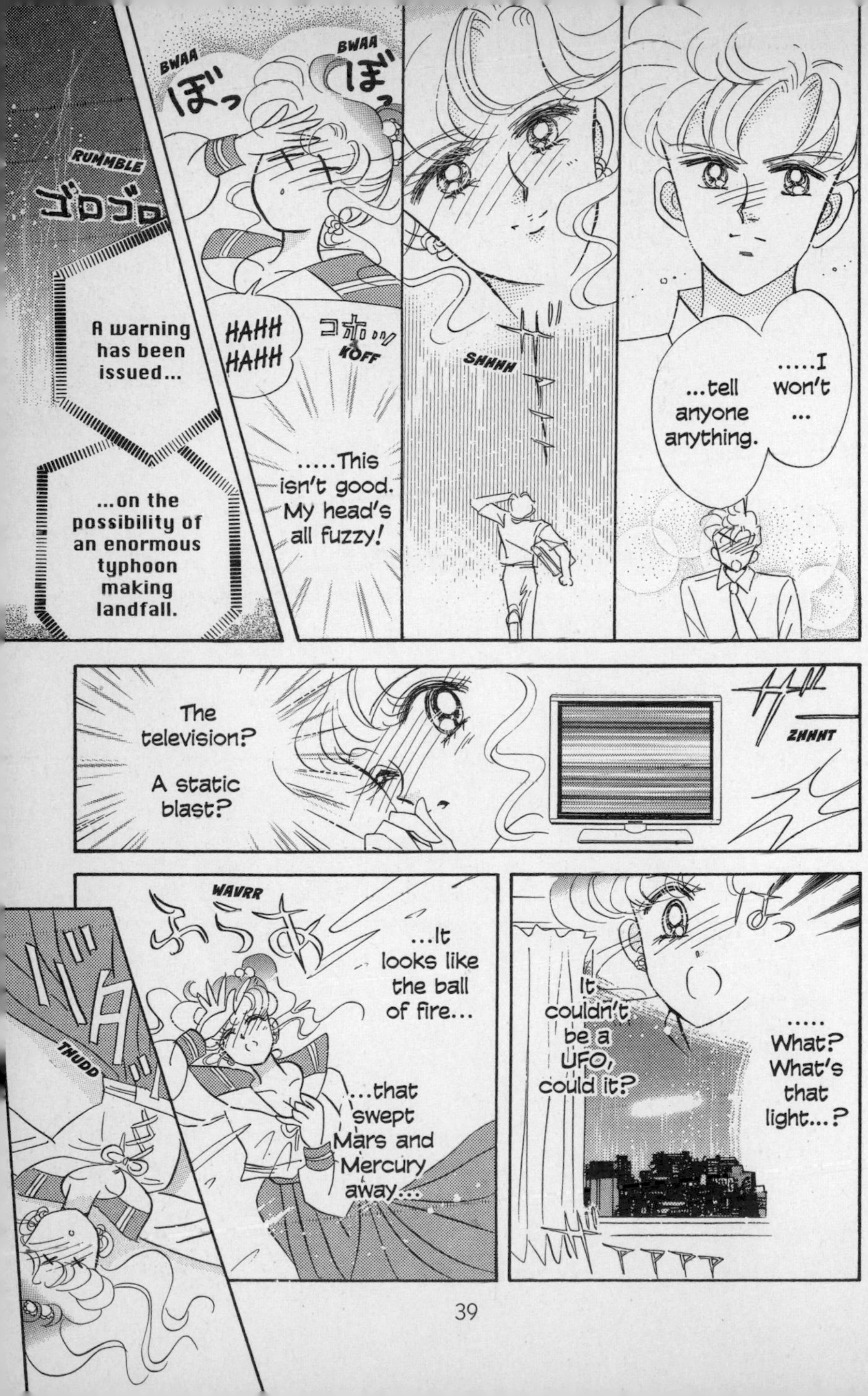
.....I won't ...
...tell anyone anything.
SHHHH
BWAA
BWAA
HAHH HAHH
KOFF
.....This isn't good. My head's all fuzzy!
RUMMBLE
A warning has been issued...
...on the possibility of an enormous typhoon making landfall.
ZHHHT
The television?
A static blast?
.....What? What's that light...?
It couldn't be a UFO, could it?
WAVRR
...It looks like the ball of fire...
...that swept Mars and Mercury away...
THUDD

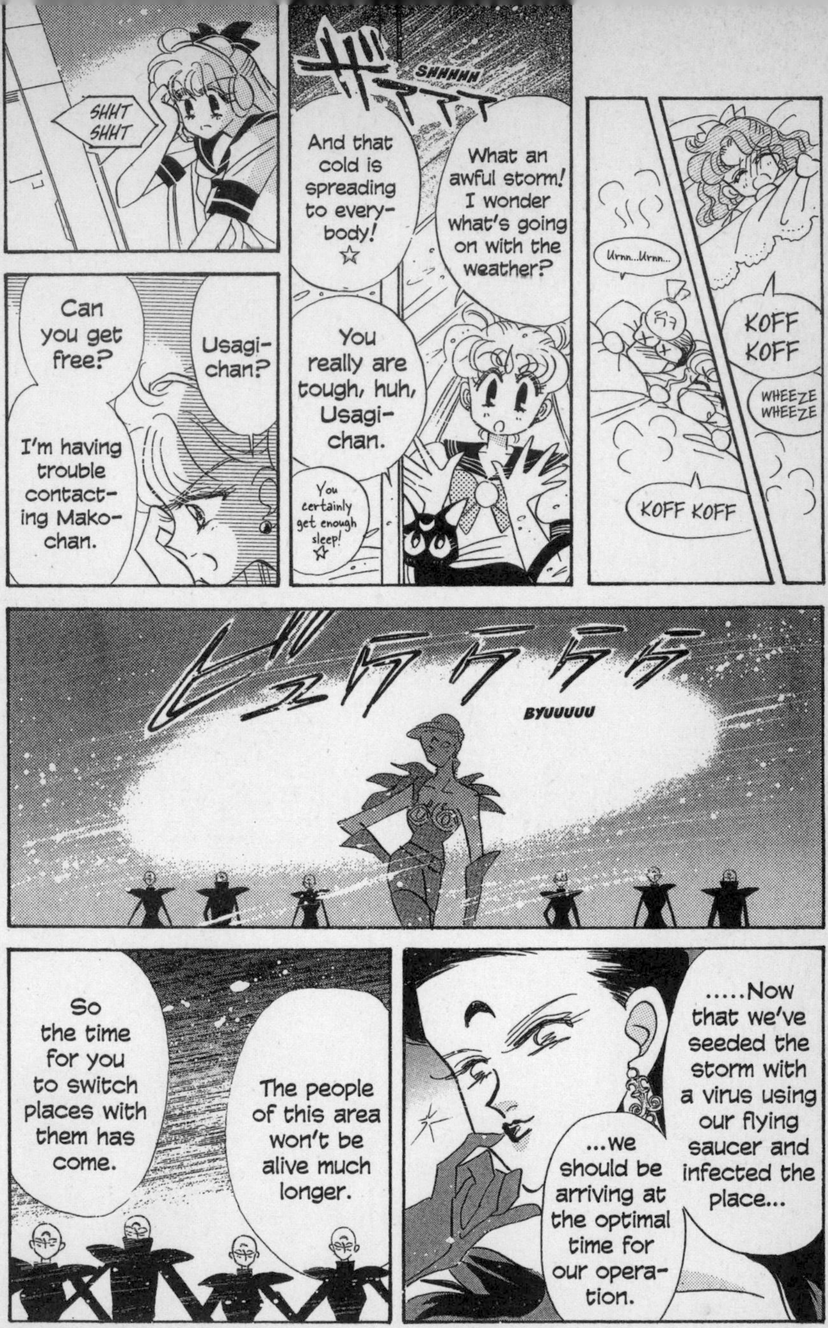
Urnn...Urnn...
KOFF KOFF
WHEEZE WHEEZE
KOFF KOFF
SHHHHH
What an awful storm! I wonder what's going on with the weather?
And that cold is spreading to every-body! ☆
You really are tough, huh, Usagi-chan.
You certainly get enough sleep! ☆
SHHT SHHT
Usagi-chan?
Can you get free?
I'm having trouble contact-ing Mako-chan.
BYUUUUU
.....Now that we've seeded the storm with a virus using our flying saucer and infected the place...
...we should be arriving at the optimal time for our opera-tion.
The people of this area won't be alive much longer.
So the time for you to switch places with them has come.

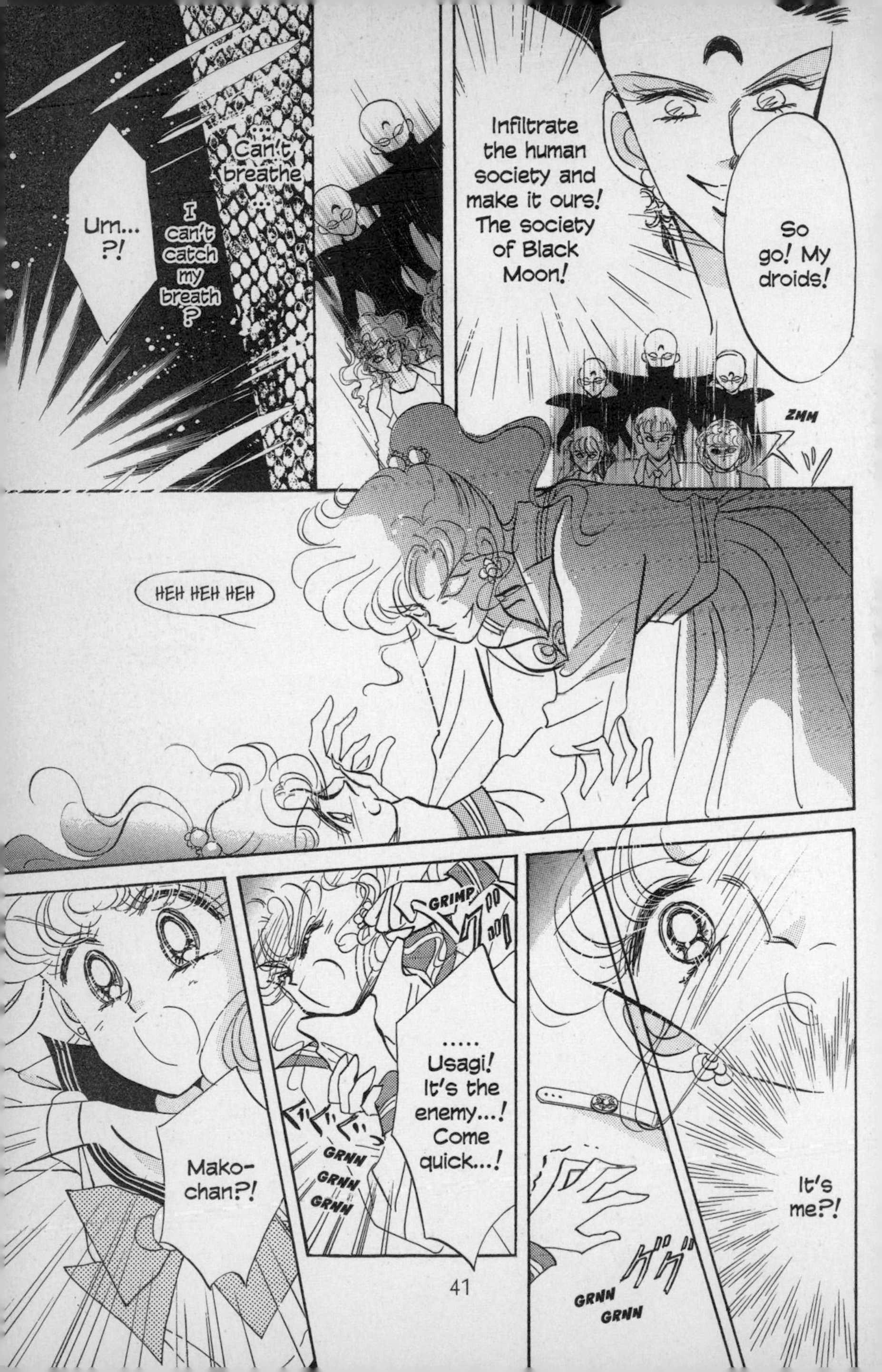
So go! My droids!
Infiltrate the human society and make it ours! The society of Black Moon!
ZMM
...Can't breathe...
I can't catch my breath?
Urn...?!
HEH HEH HEH
It's me?!
GRNN
GRNN
GRIMP
.....Usagi! It's the enemy...! Come quick...!
GRNN
GRNN
GRNN
Mako-chan?!

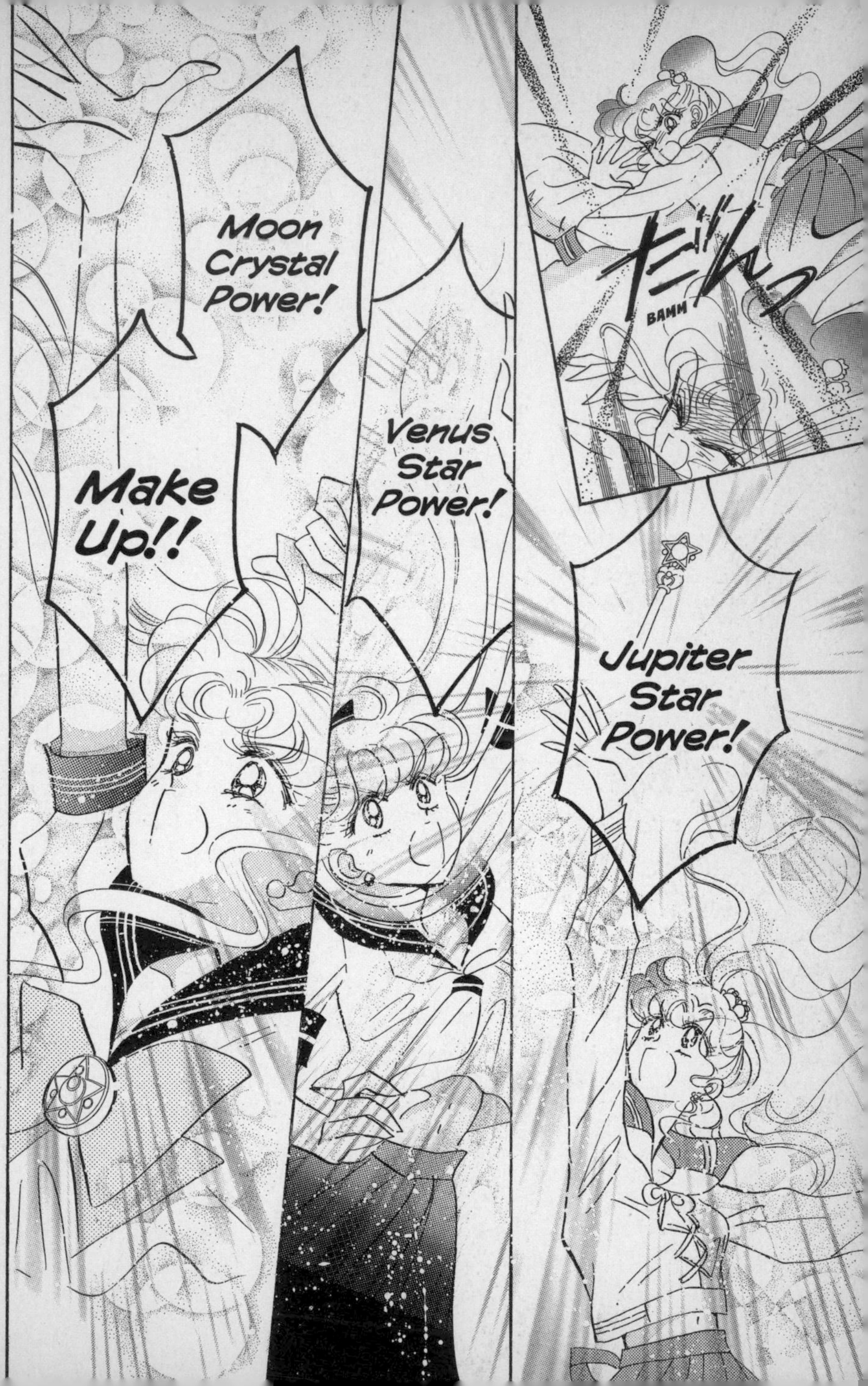
BAMM
Jupiter Star Power!
Venus Star Power!
Moon Crystal Power!
Make Up!!

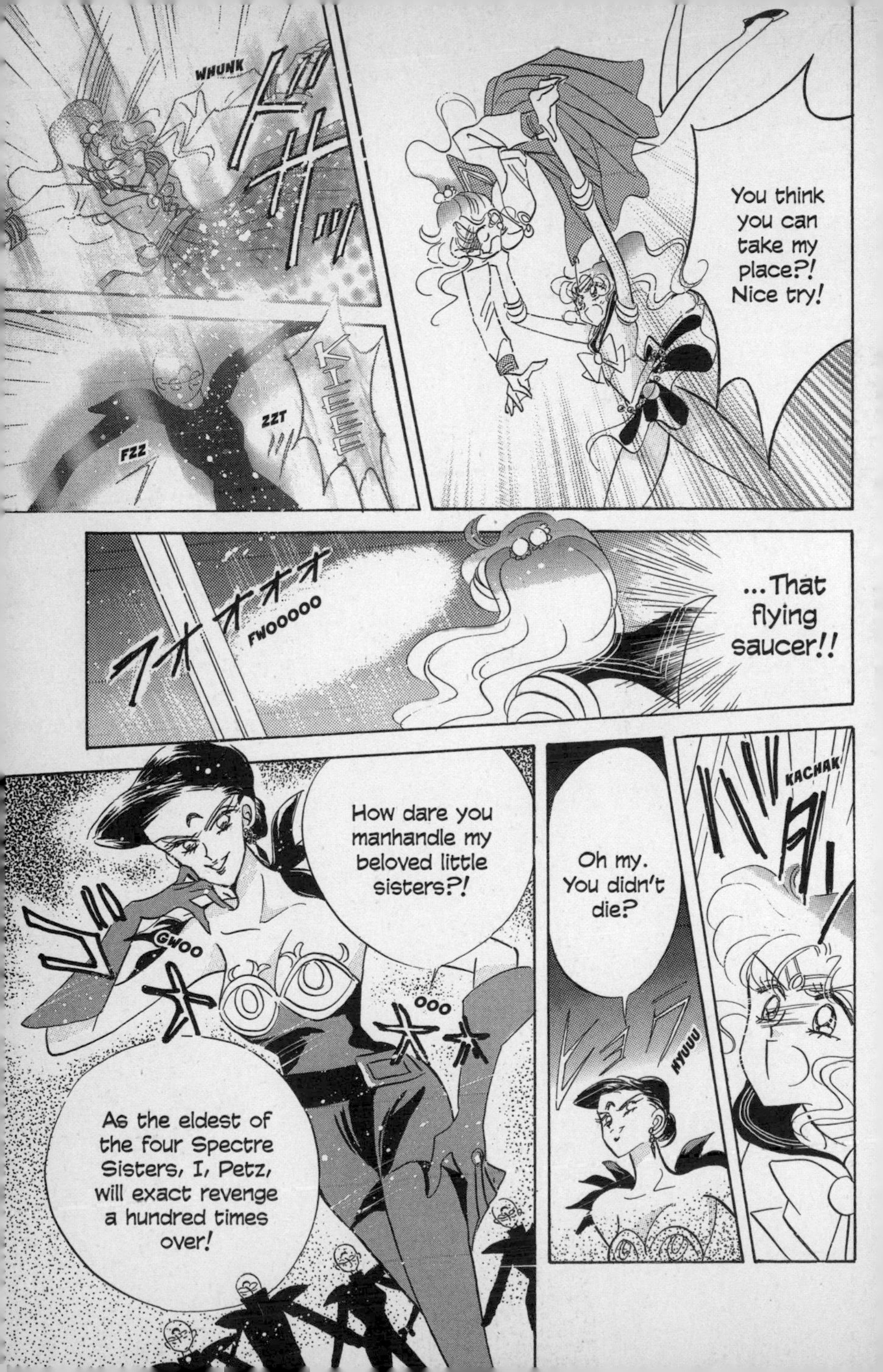
You think you can take my place?! Nice try!
WHUNK
KIEEE
ZZT
FZZ
...That flying saucer!!
FWOOOOO
KACHAK
Oh my. You didn't die?
HYUUU
How dare you manhandle my beloved little sisters?!
GWOO
OOO
As the eldest of the four Spectre Sisters, I, Petz, will exact revenge a hundred times over!

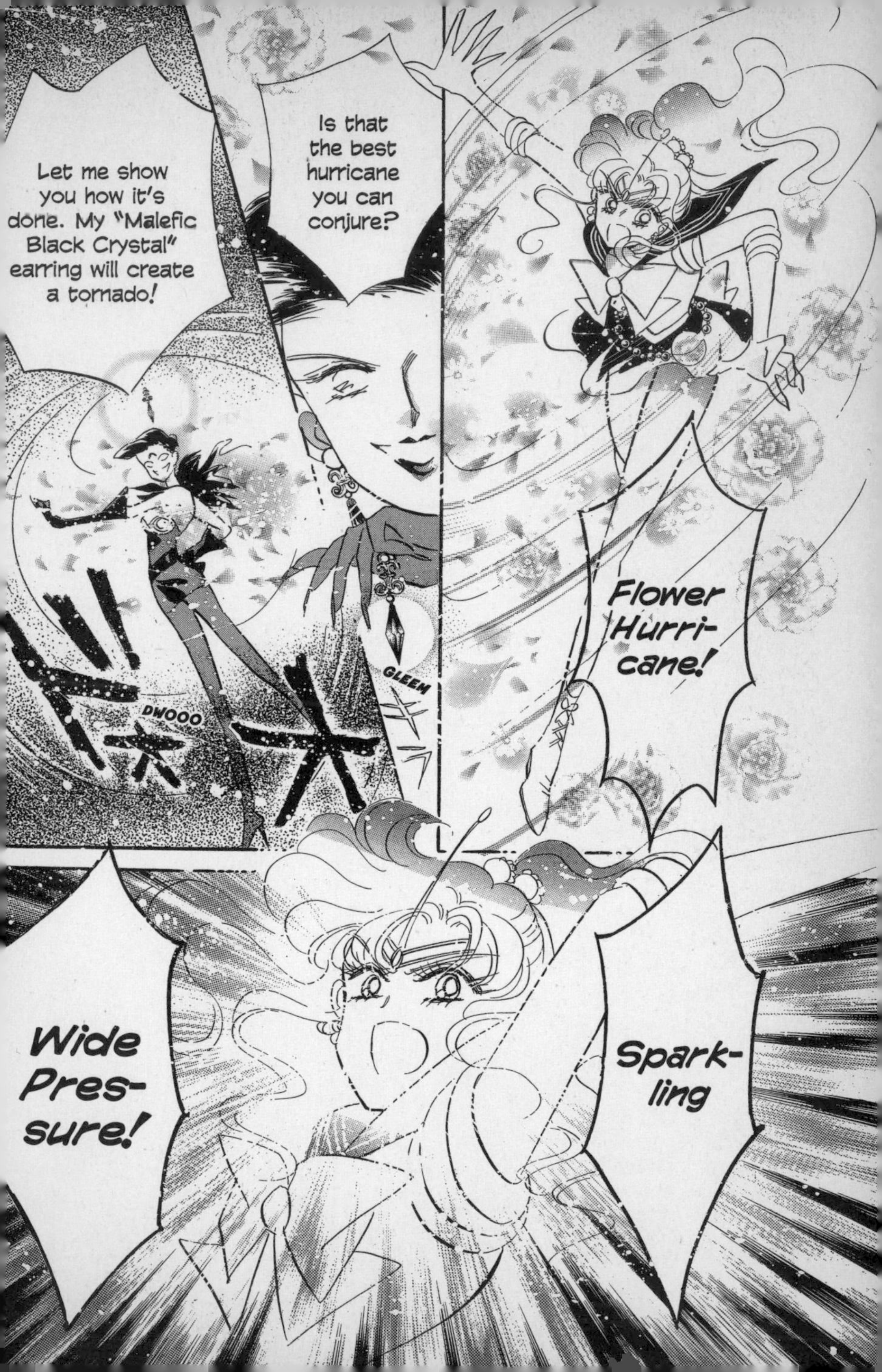
Flower Hurri-cane!
Is that the best hurricane you can conjure?
Let me show you how it's done. My "Malefic Black Crystal" earring will create a tornado!
GLEEM
DWOOO
Spark-ling
Wide Pres-sure!

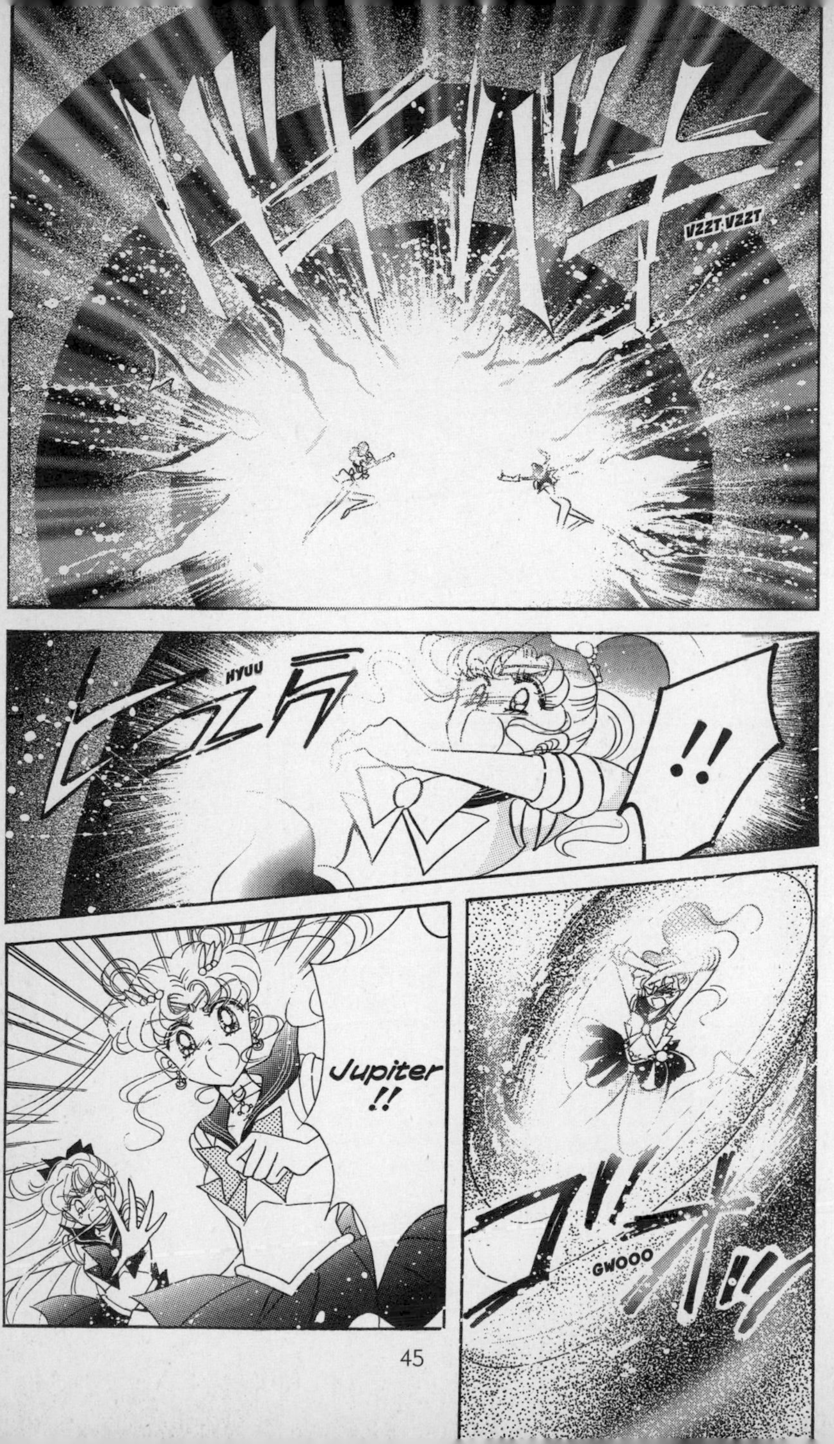
VZZT VZZT
HYUU
!!
GWOOO
Jupiter !!

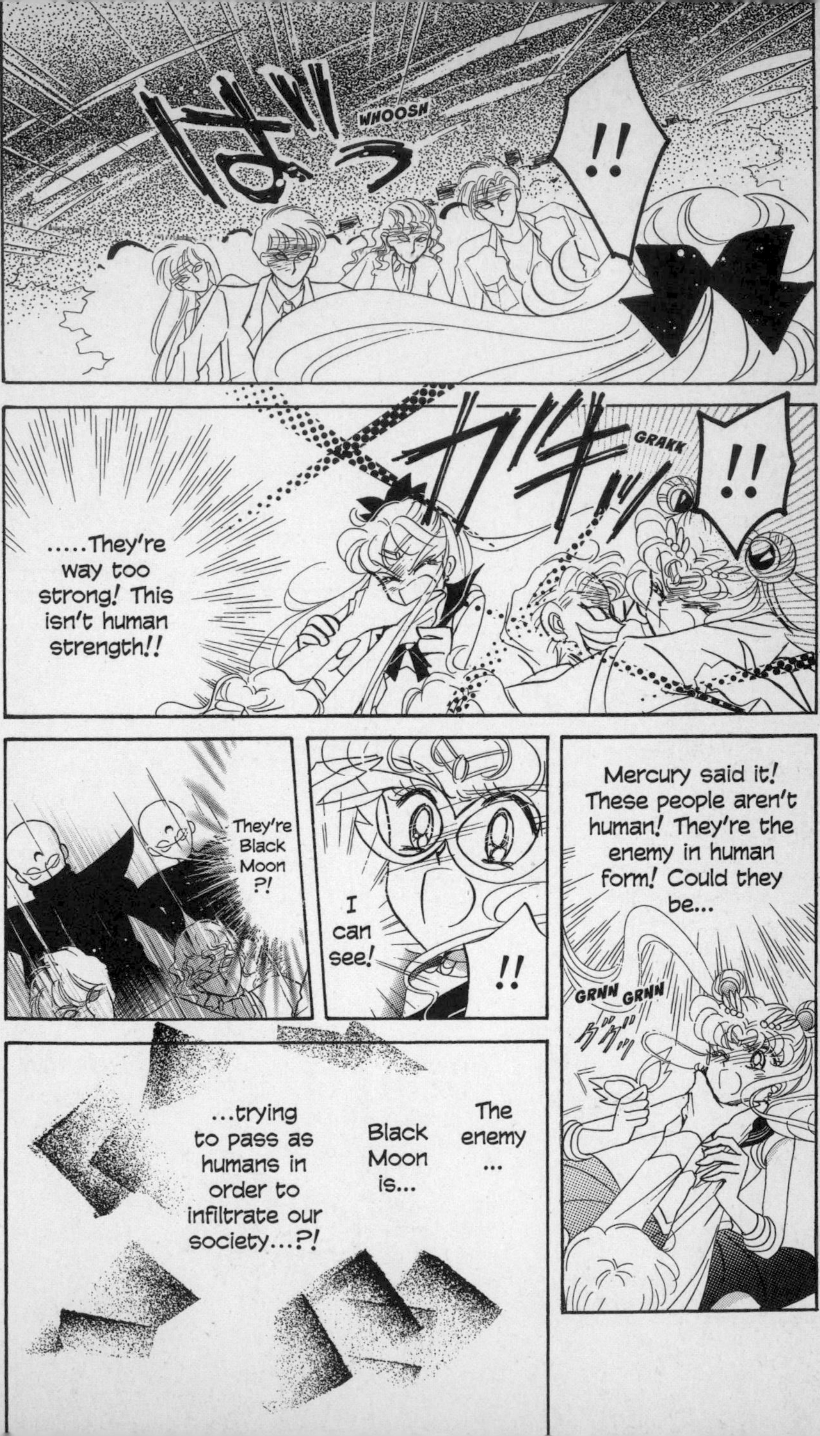
WHOOSH
!!
GRAKK
!!
.....They're way too strong! This isn't human strength!!
Mercury said it! These people aren't human! They're the enemy in human form! Could they be...
GRNN GRNN
!!
I can see!
They're Black Moon ?!
The enemy ...
Black Moon is...
...trying to pass as humans in order to infiltrate our society...?!

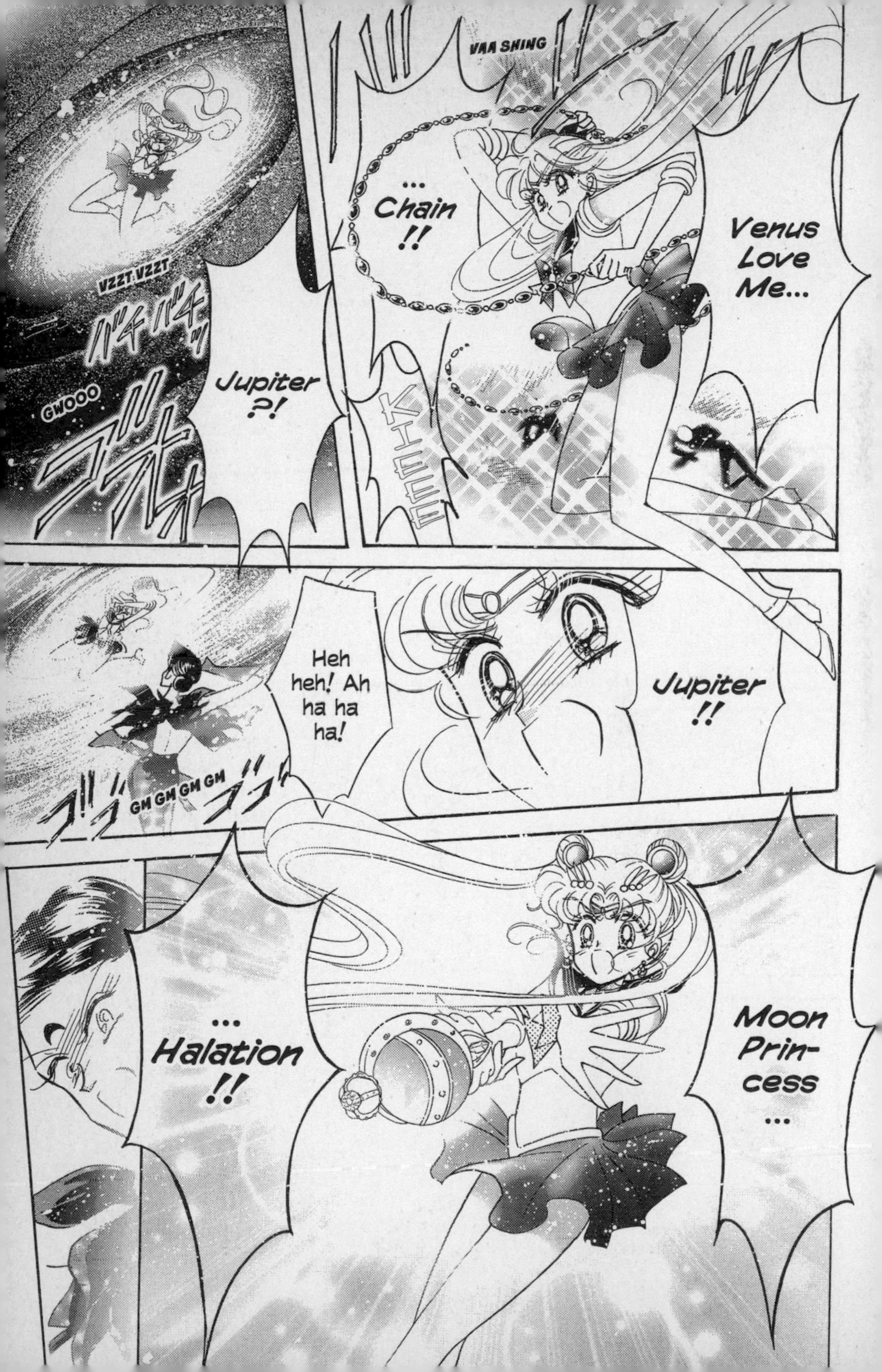
VAA SHING
Venus Love Me...
... Chain !!
KIEEE
VZZT VZZT
GWOOO
Jupiter ?!
Jupiter !!
Heh heh! Ah ha ha ha!
GM GM GM GM
Moon Prin-cess ...
... Halation !!

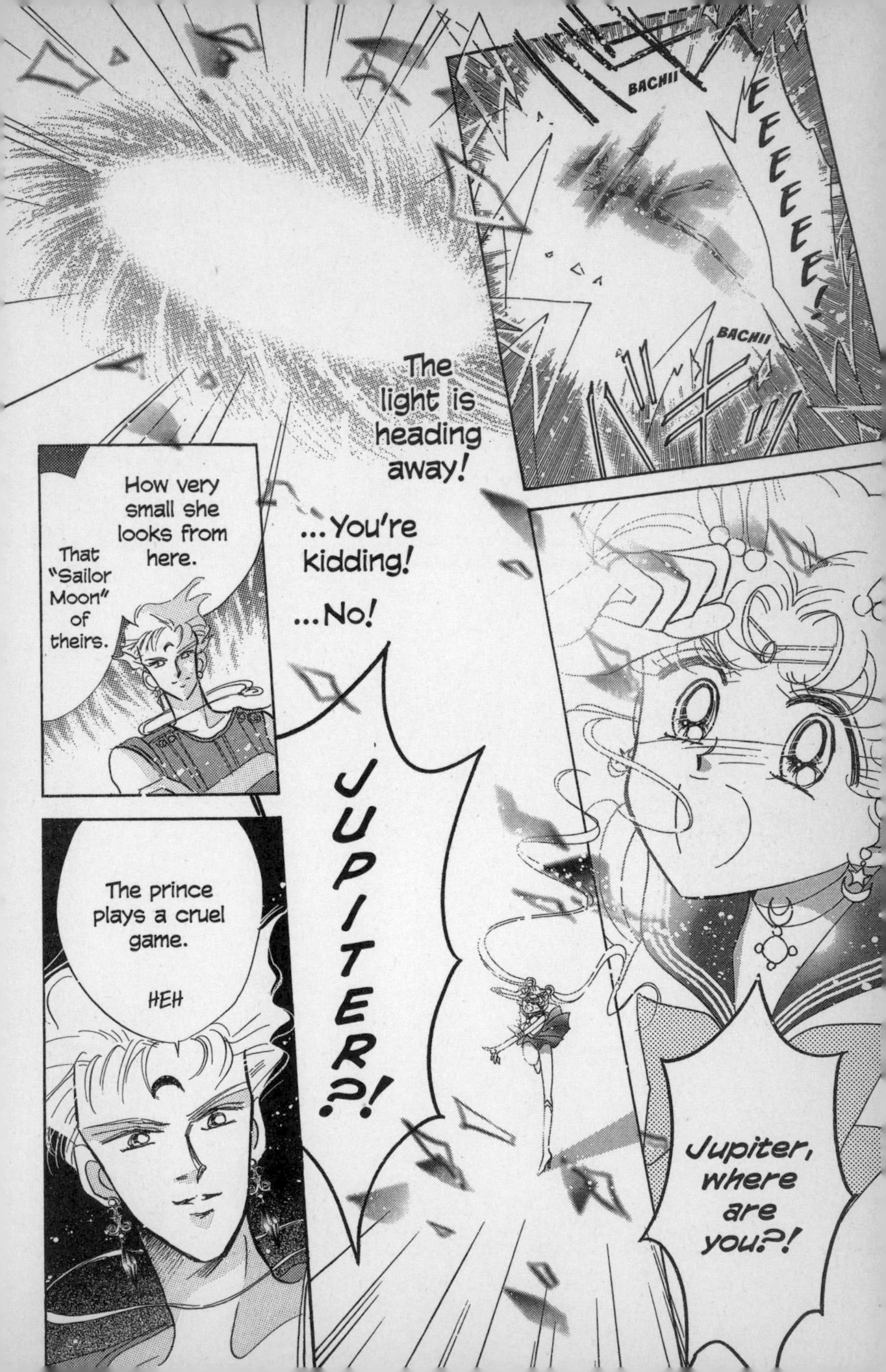
BACHII
EEEEEE!
BACHII
The light is heading away!
...You're kidding!
...No!
Jupiter, where are you?!
JUPITER?!
How very small she looks from here.
That "Sailor Moon" of theirs.
The prince plays a cruel game.
HEH

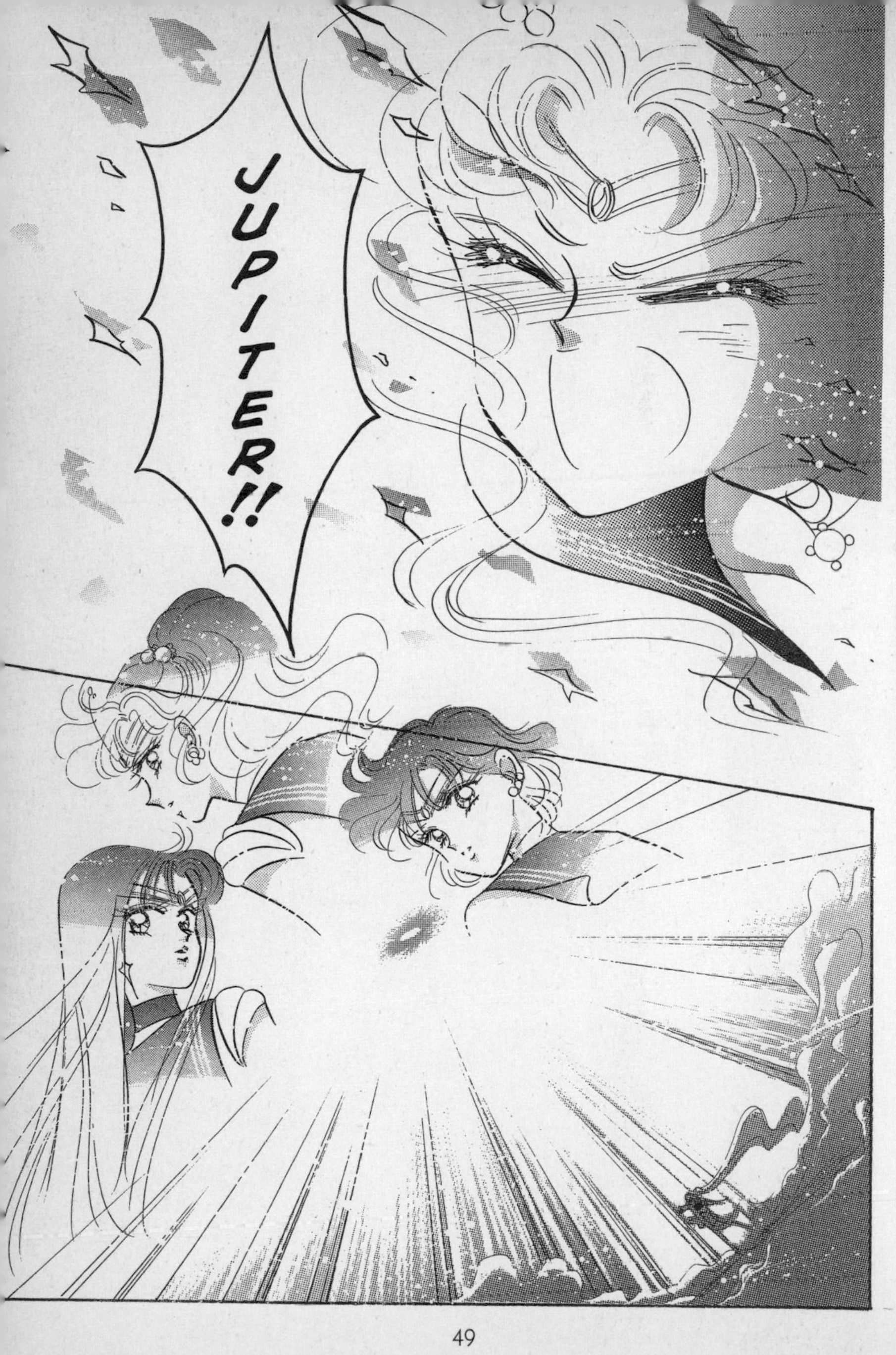
JUPITER!!

Pretty Guardian ✶ Sailor Moon

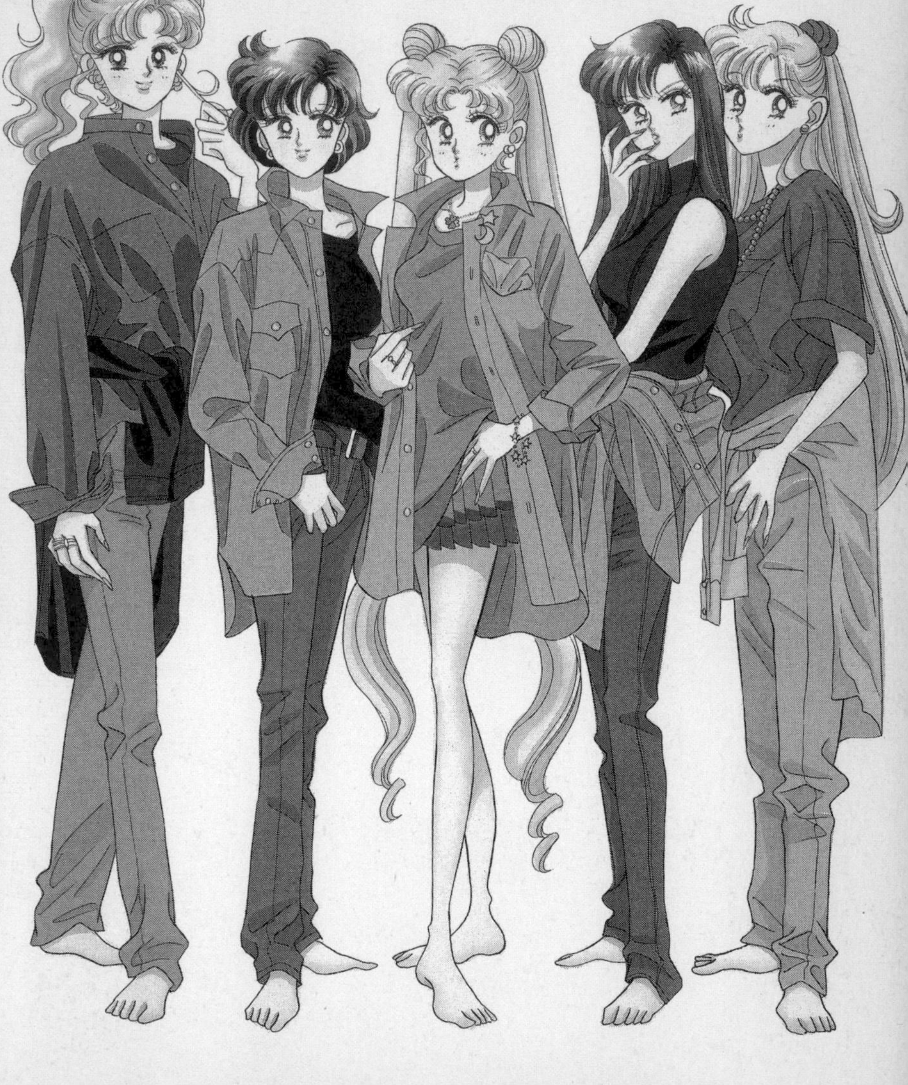

Act 18 Invasion, Sailor Venus

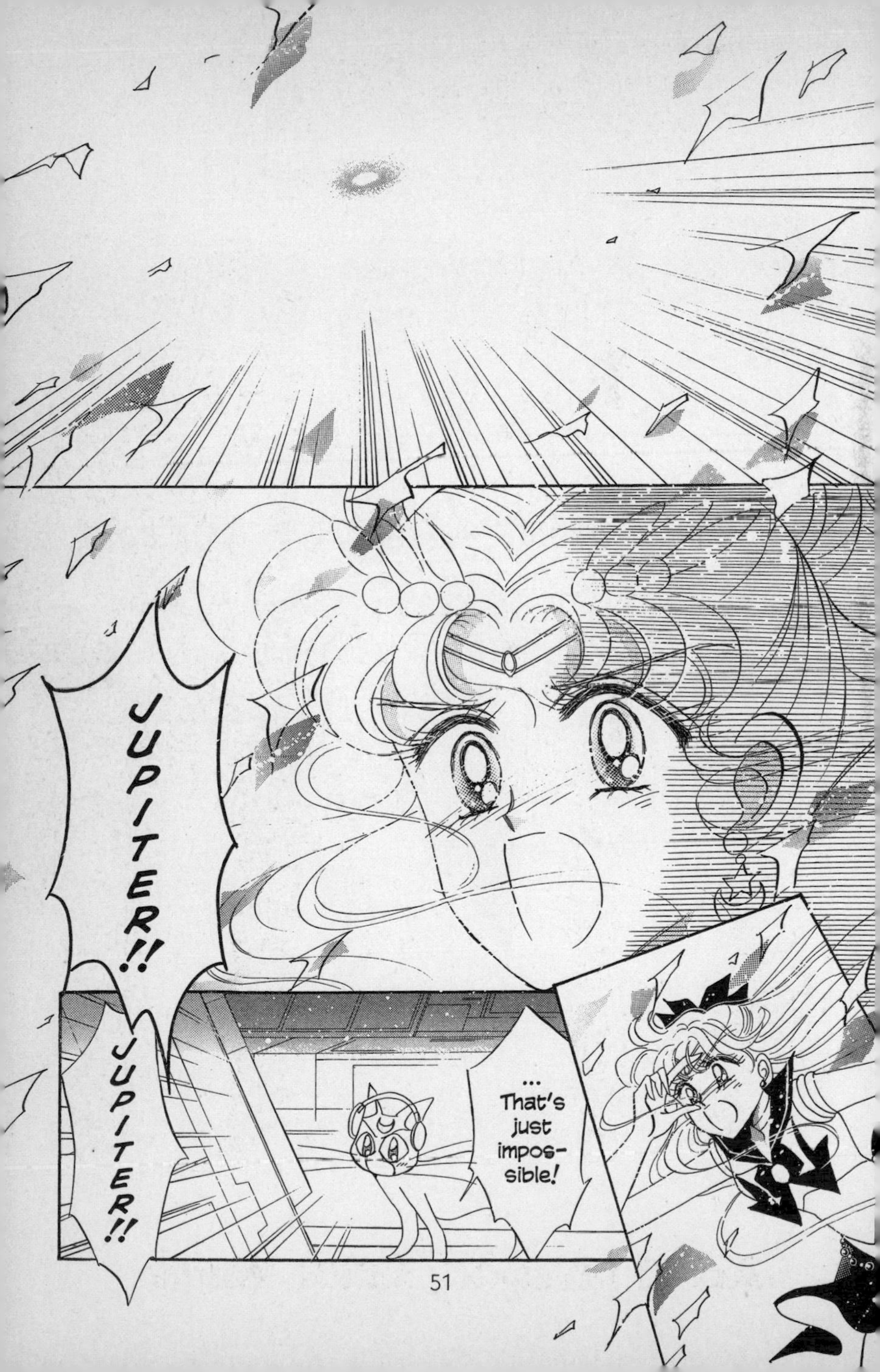
JUPITER!!
... That's just impossible!
JUPITER!!

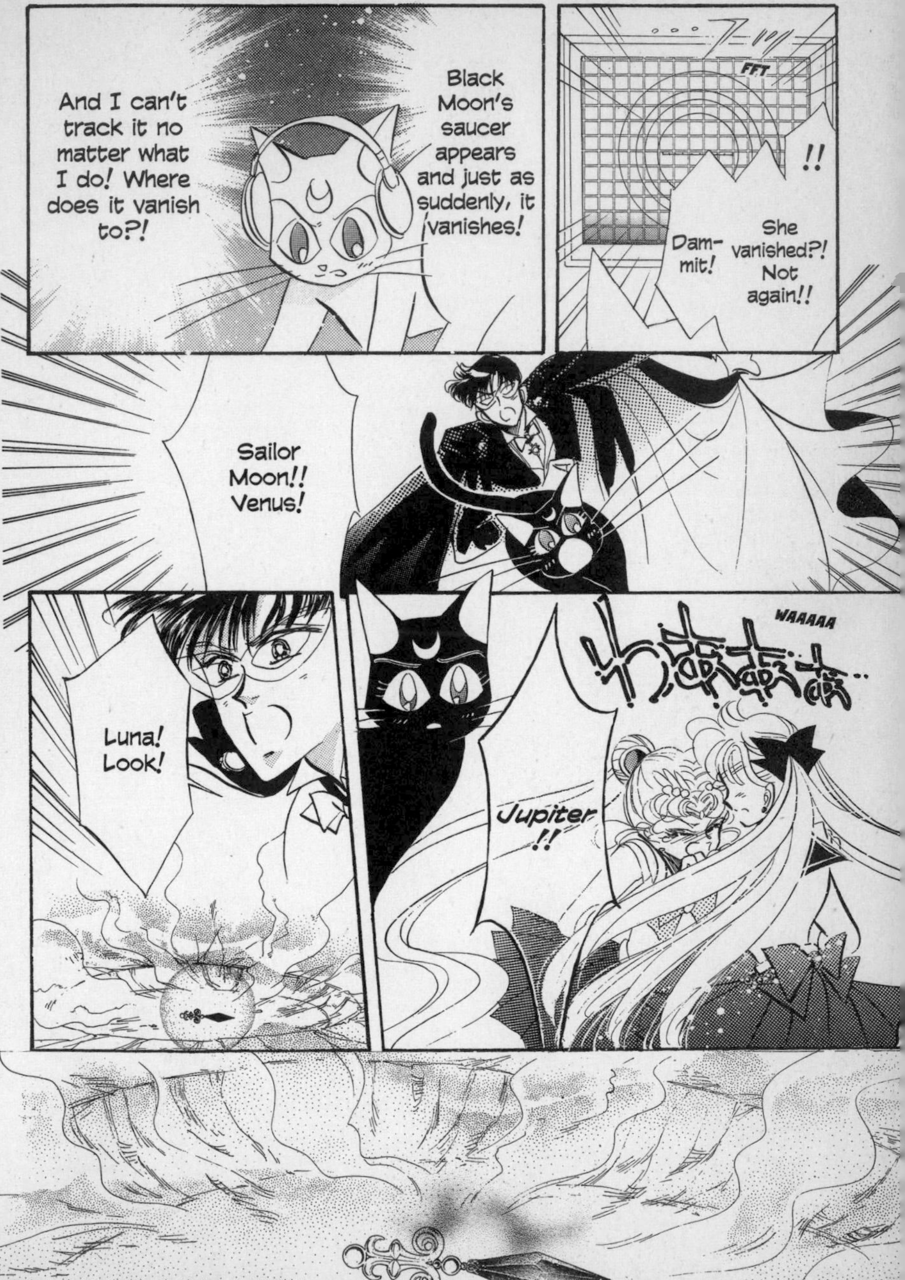
FFT
!!
She vanished?! Not again!!
Dam-mit!
Black Moon's saucer appears and just as suddenly, it vanishes!
And I can't track it no matter what I do! Where does it vanish to?!
Sailor Moon!! Venus!
WAAAAA
Jupiter !!
Luna! Look!

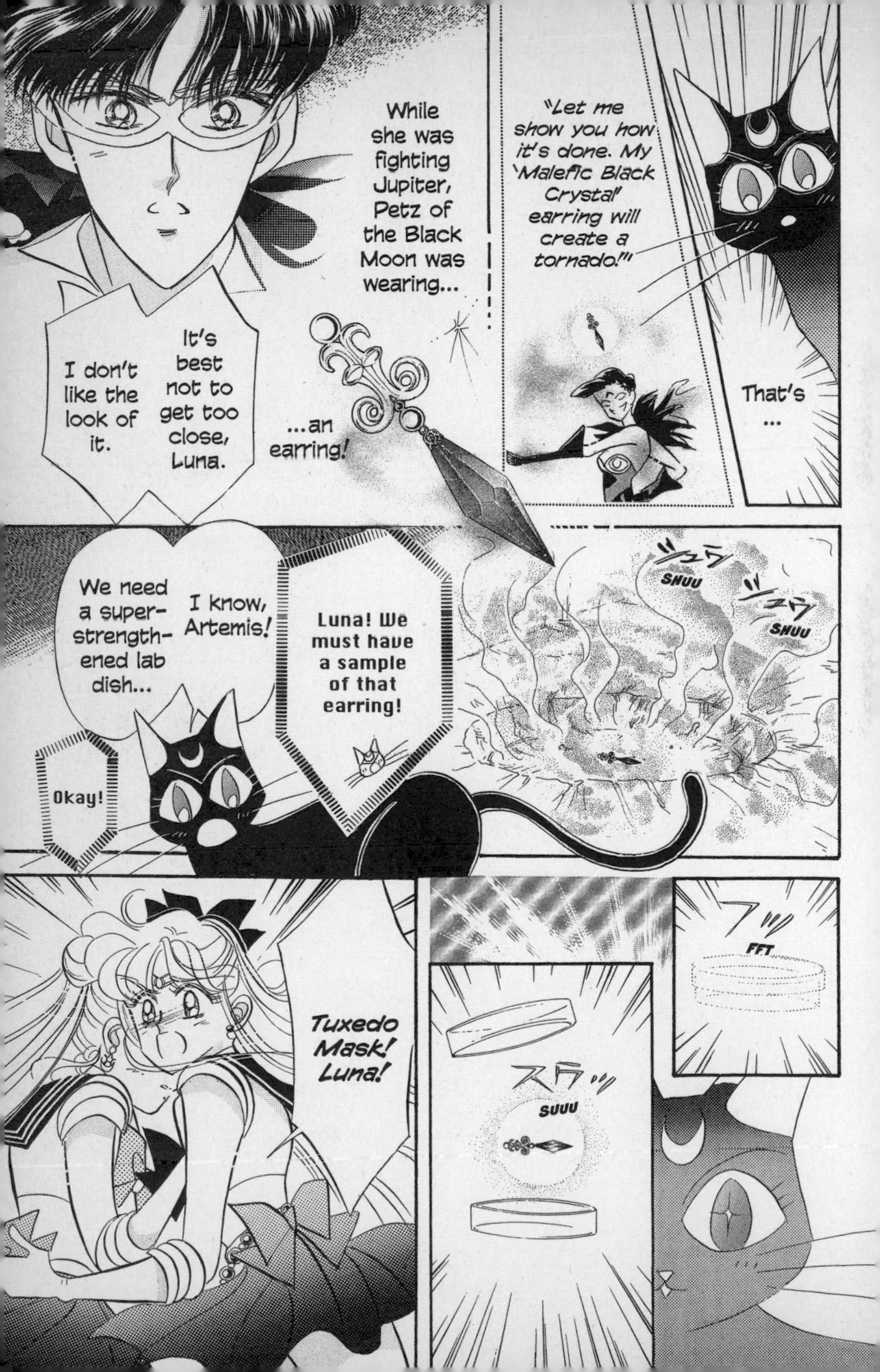
"Let me show you how it's done. My 'Malefic Black Crystal' earring will create a tornado!"
That's ...
While she was fighting Jupiter, Petz of the Black Moon was wearing...
...an earring!
It's best not to get too close, Luna.
I don't like the look of it.
SHUU
SHUU
Luna! We must have a sample of that earring!
I know, Artemis!
We need a super-strengthened lab dish...
Okay!
FFT
SUUU
Tuxedo Mask! Luna!

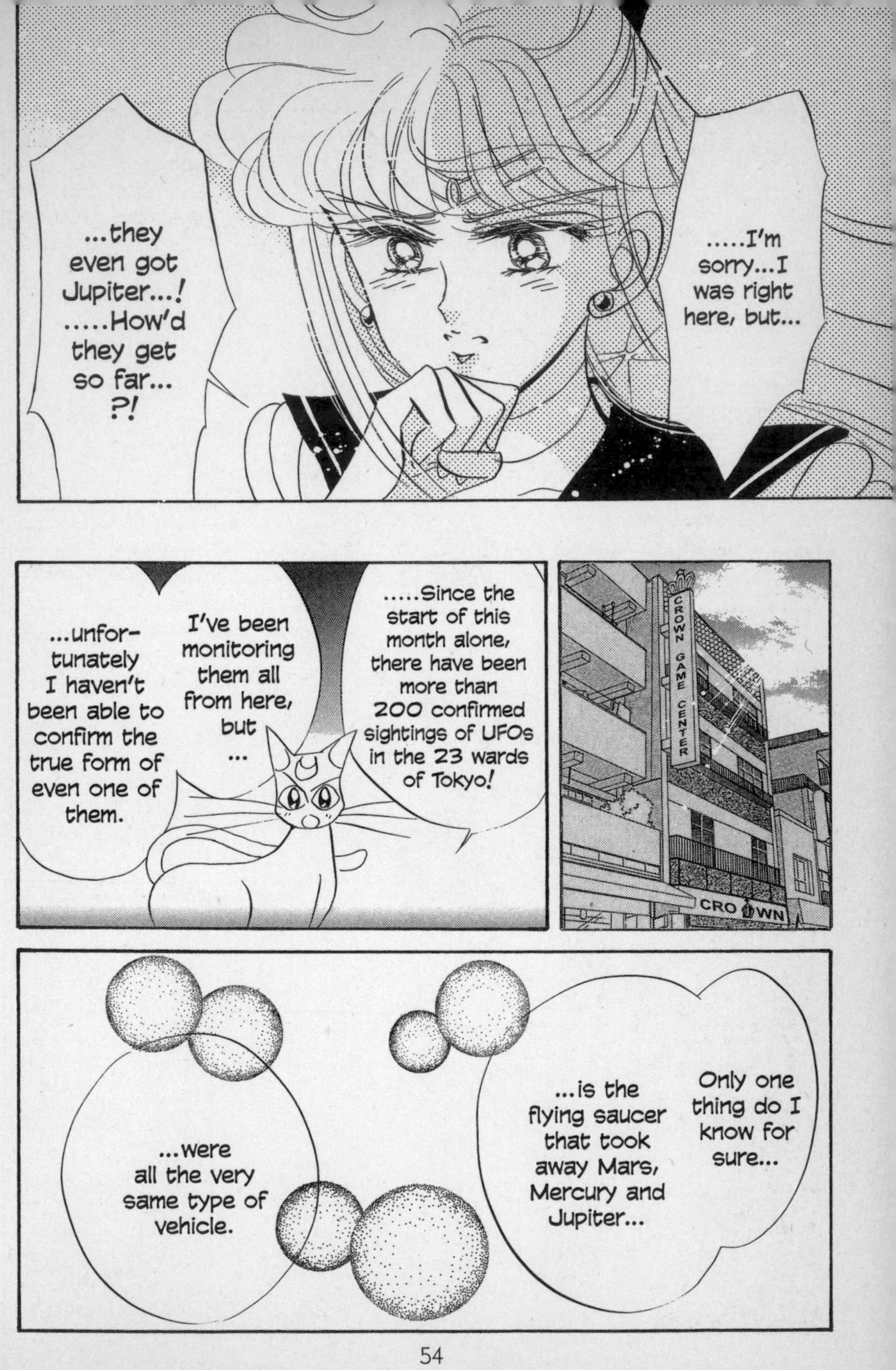
.....I'm sorry...I was right here, but...
...they even got Jupiter...! .....How'd they get so far...?!
CROWN GAME CENTER
.....Since the start of this month alone, there have been more than 200 confirmed sightings of UFOs in the 23 wards of Tokyo!
I've been monitoring them all from here, but ...
...unfor-tunately I haven't been able to confirm the true form of even one of them.
Only one thing do I know for sure...
...is the flying saucer that took away Mars, Mercury and Jupiter...
...were all the very same type of vehicle.

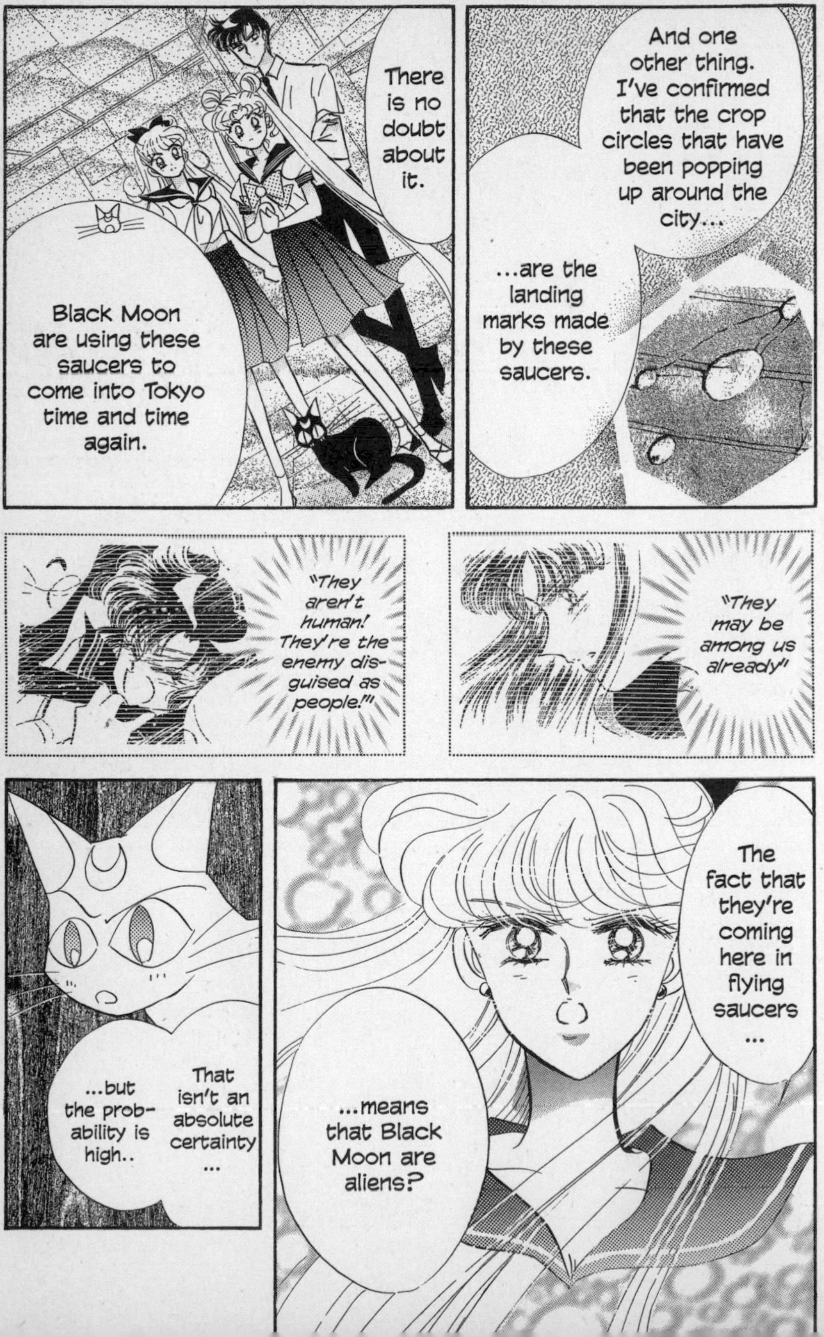
And one other thing. I've confirmed that the crop circles that have been popping up around the city...
...are the landing marks made by these saucers.
There is no doubt about it.
Black Moon are using these saucers to come into Tokyo time and time again.
"They may be among us already"
"They aren't human! They're the enemy disguised as people!"
The fact that they're coming here in flying saucers ...
...means that Black Moon are aliens?
That isn't an absolute certainty ...
...but the probability is high..

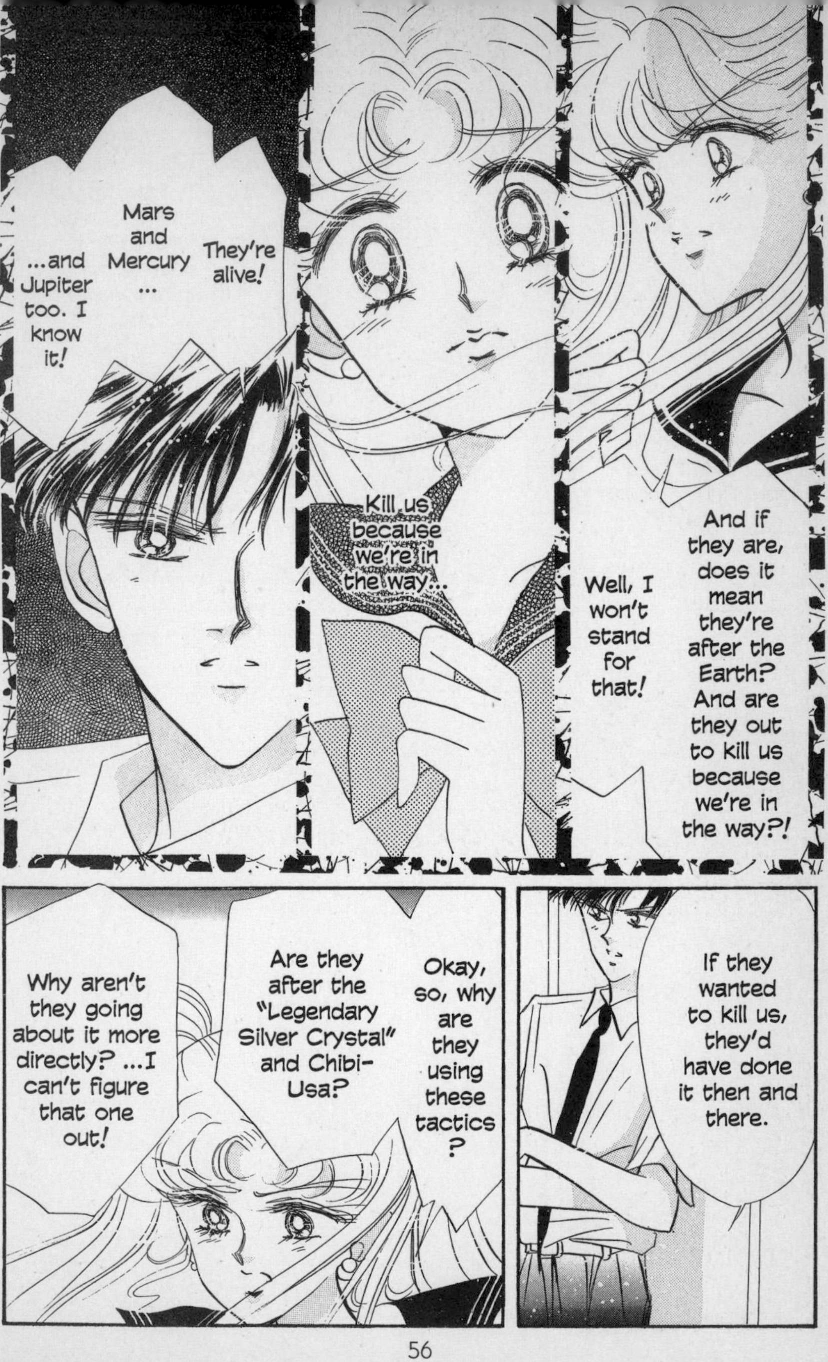
And if they are, does it mean they're after the Earth? And are they out to kill us because we're in the way?!
Well, I won't stand for that!
Kill us because we're in the way...
They're alive!
Mars and Mercury ...
...and Jupiter too. I know it!
If they wanted to kill us, they'd have done it then and there.
Okay, so, why are they using these tactics?
Are they after the "Legendary Silver Crystal" and Chibi-Usa?
Why aren't they going about it more directly? ...I can't figure that one out!

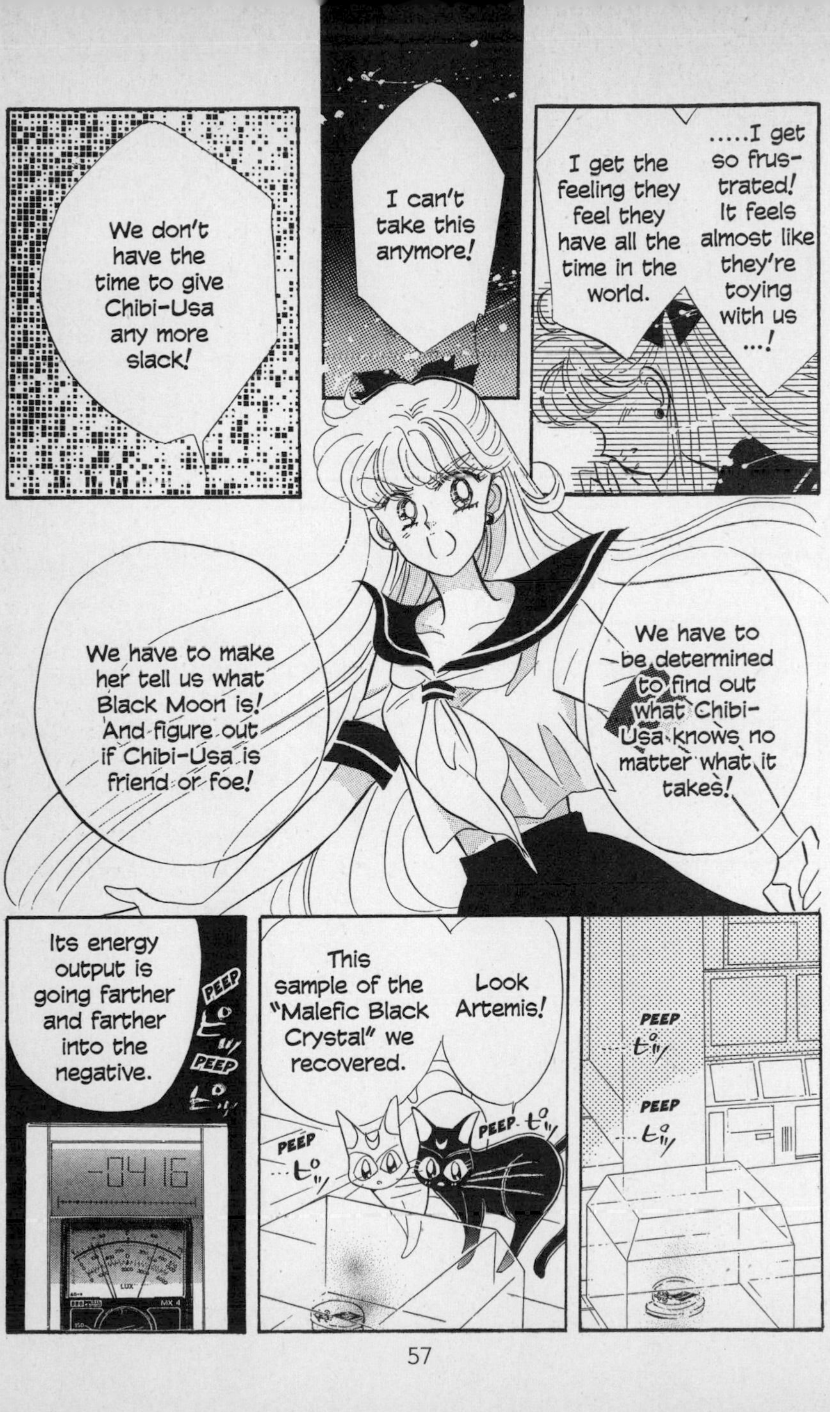
.....I get so frus-trated! It feels almost like they're toying with us ...!
I get the feeling they feel they have all the time in the world.
I can't take this anymore!
We don't have the time to give Chibi-Usa any more slack!
We have to be determined to find out what Chibi-Usa knows no matter what it takes!
We have to make her tell us what Black Moon is! And figure out if Chibi-Usa is friend or foe!
PEEP
PEEP
Look Artemis!
This sample of the "Malefic Black Crystal" we recovered.
PEEP
PEEP
Its energy output is going farther and farther into the negative.
PEEP
PEEP
-04 16
LUX
MX 4

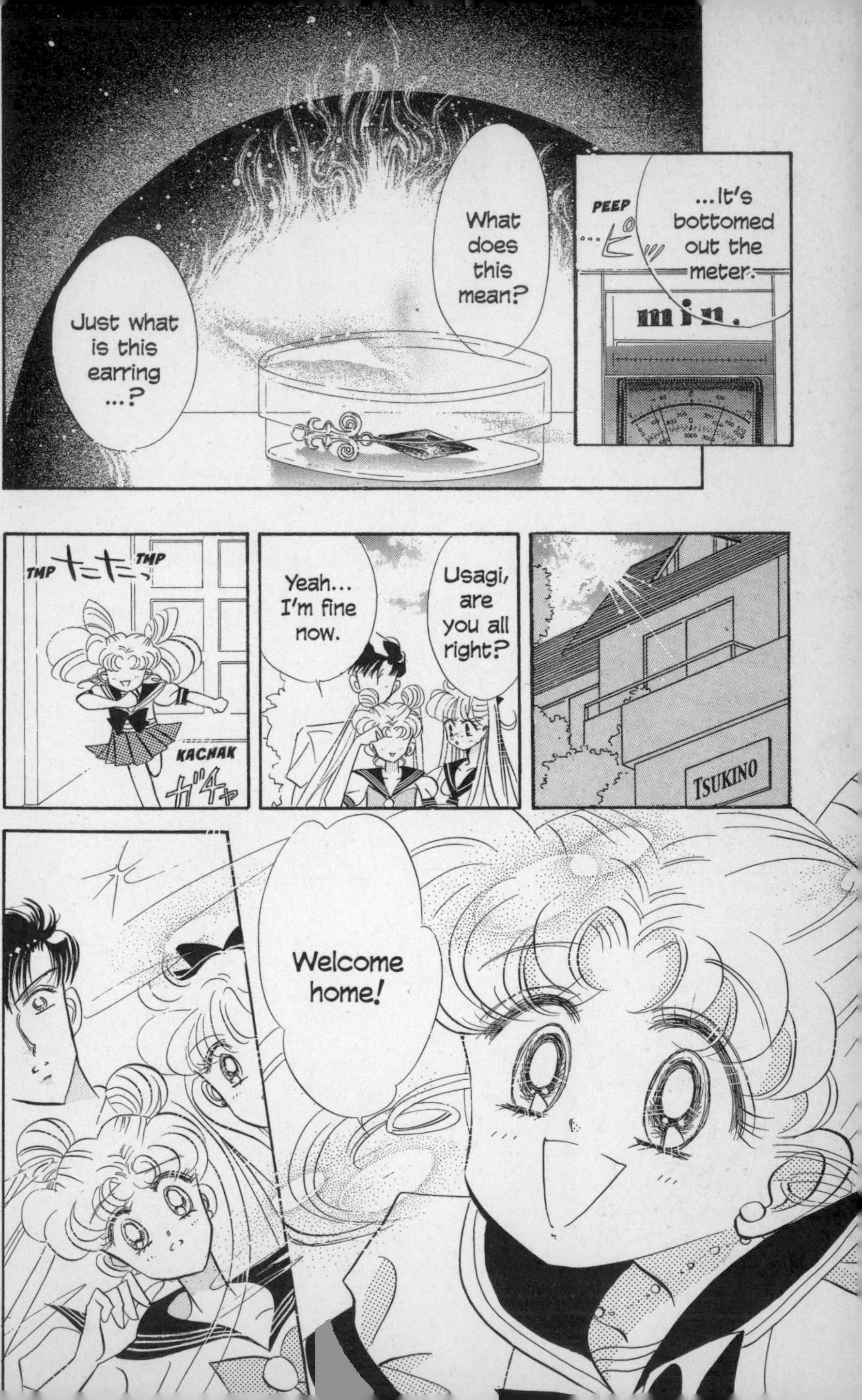
PEEP
...It's bottomed out the meter.
min.
What does this mean?
Just what is this earring ...?
TSUKINO
Usagi, are you all right?
Yeah... I'm fine now.
TMP
TMP
KACHAK
Welcome home!

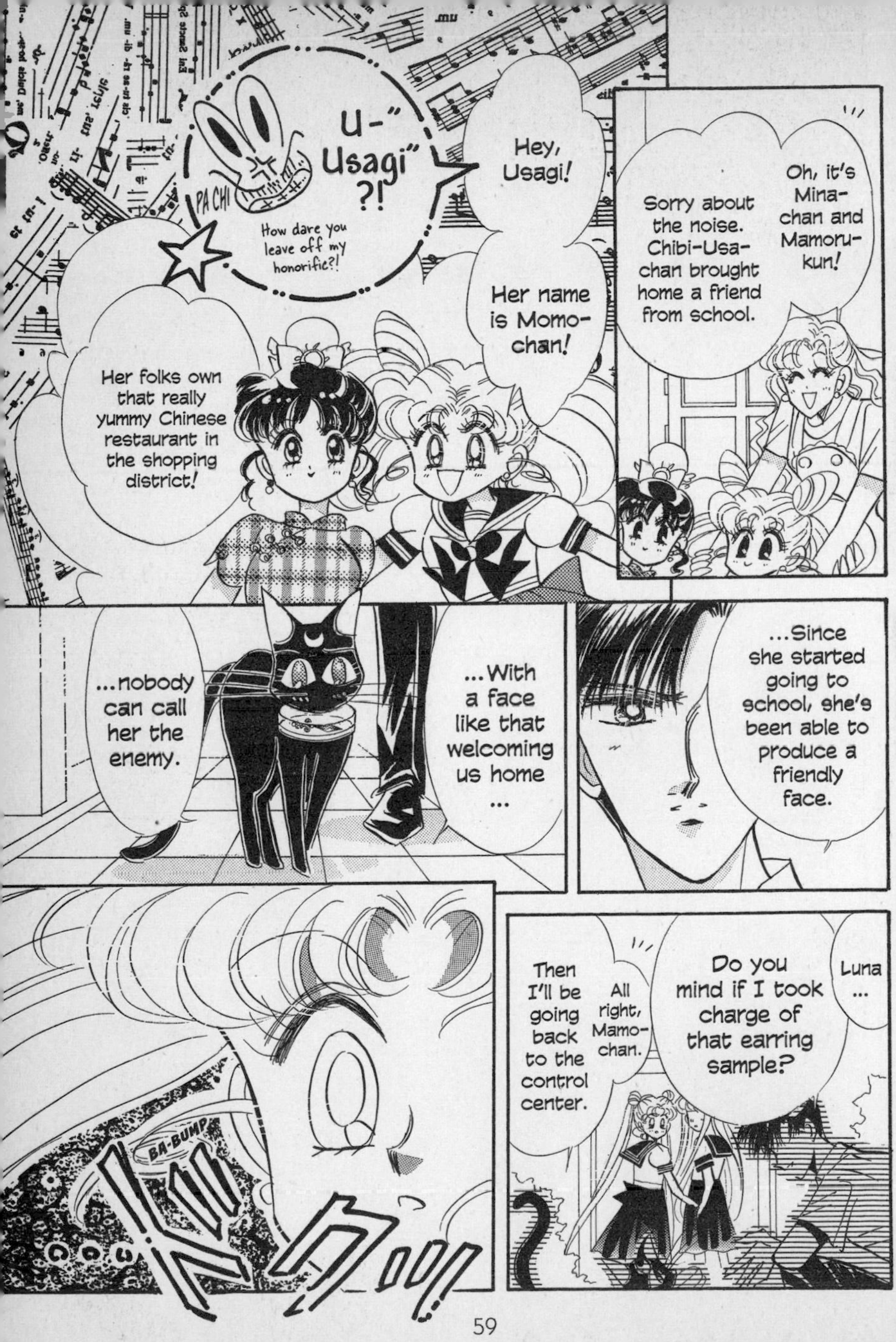
Oh, it's Mina-chan and Mamoru-kun!
Sorry about the noise. Chibi-Usa-chan brought home a friend from school.
Hey, Usagi!
U-"Usagi"?!
How dare you leave off my honorific?!
PA CHI
Her name is Momo-chan!
Her folks own that really yummy Chinese restaurant in the shopping district!
...Since she started going to school, she's been able to produce a friendly face.
...With a face like that welcoming us home ...
...nobody can call her the enemy.
Luna ...
Do you mind if I took charge of that earring sample?
All right, Mamo-chan.
Then I'll be going back to the control center.
BA-BUMP

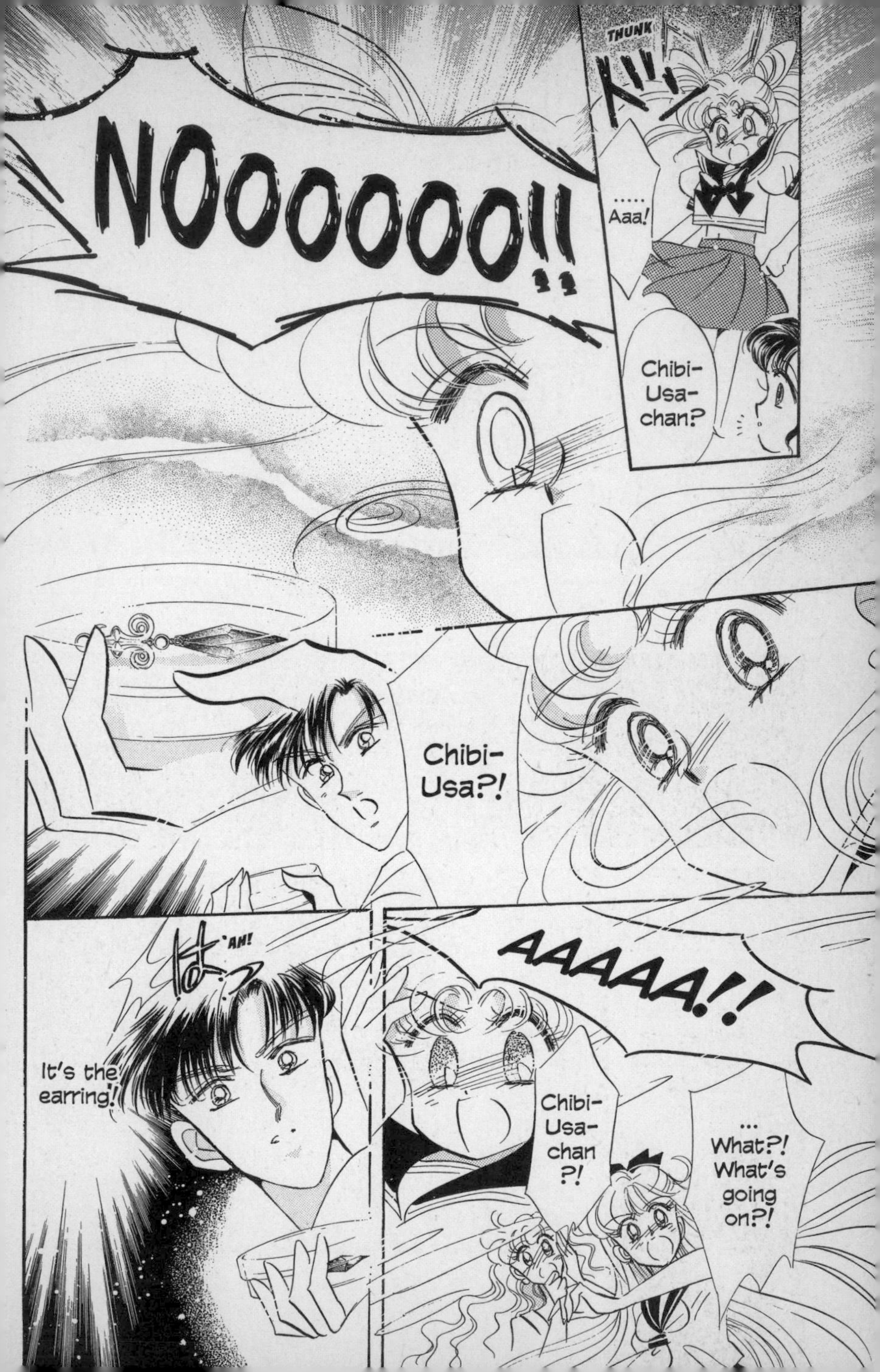

THUNK
.....
Aaa!
Chibi-Usa-chan?
NOOOOOOO!!
Chibi-Usa?!
AAAAA!!
... What?! What's going on?!
Chibi-Usa-chan?!
AH!
It's the earring!

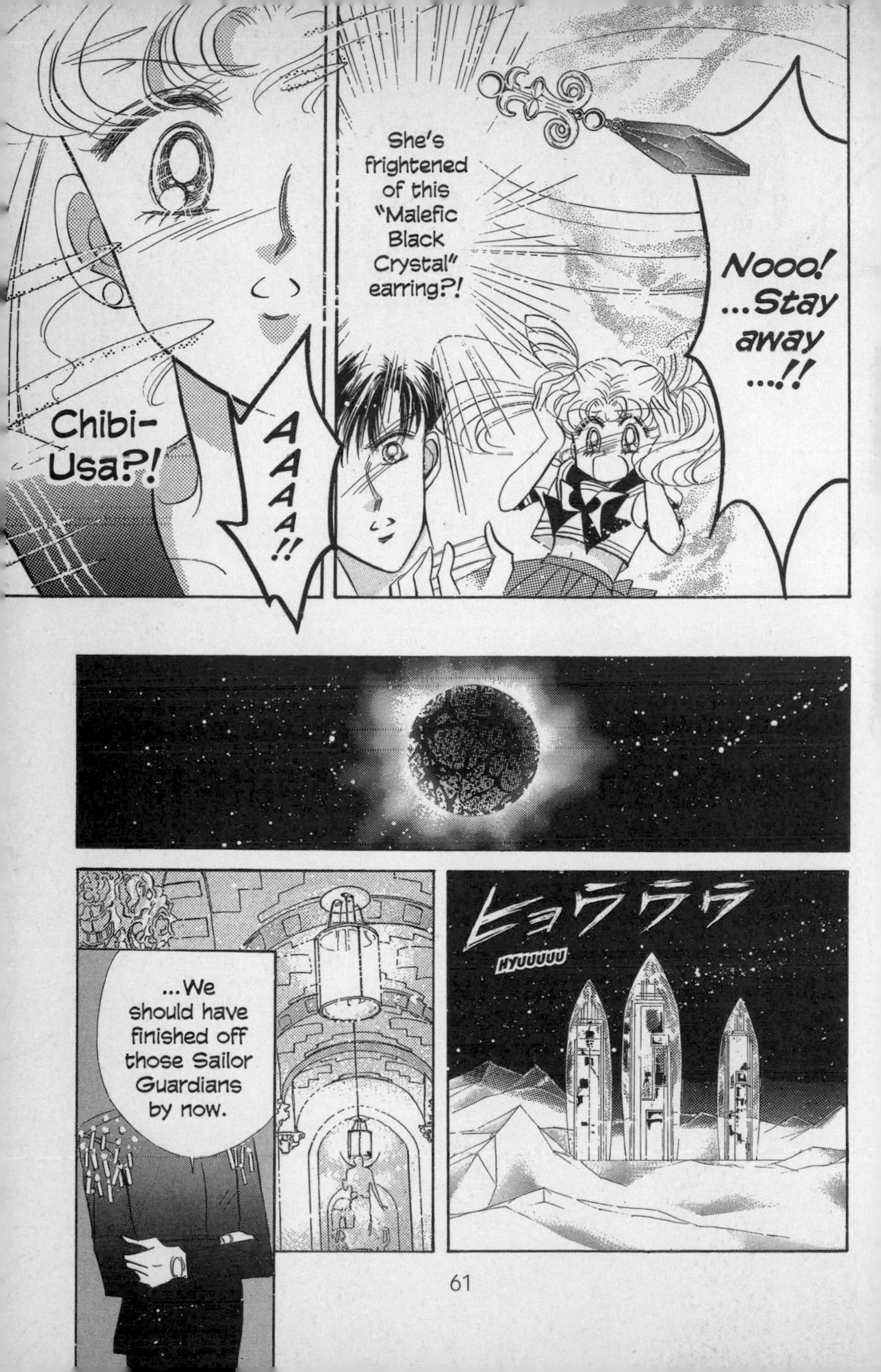
Nooo! ...Stay away ...!!
She's frightened of this "Malefic Black Crystal" earring?!
AAAA!!
Chibi-Usa?!
ヒョラララ
HYUUUUU
...We should have finished off those Sailor Guardians by now.

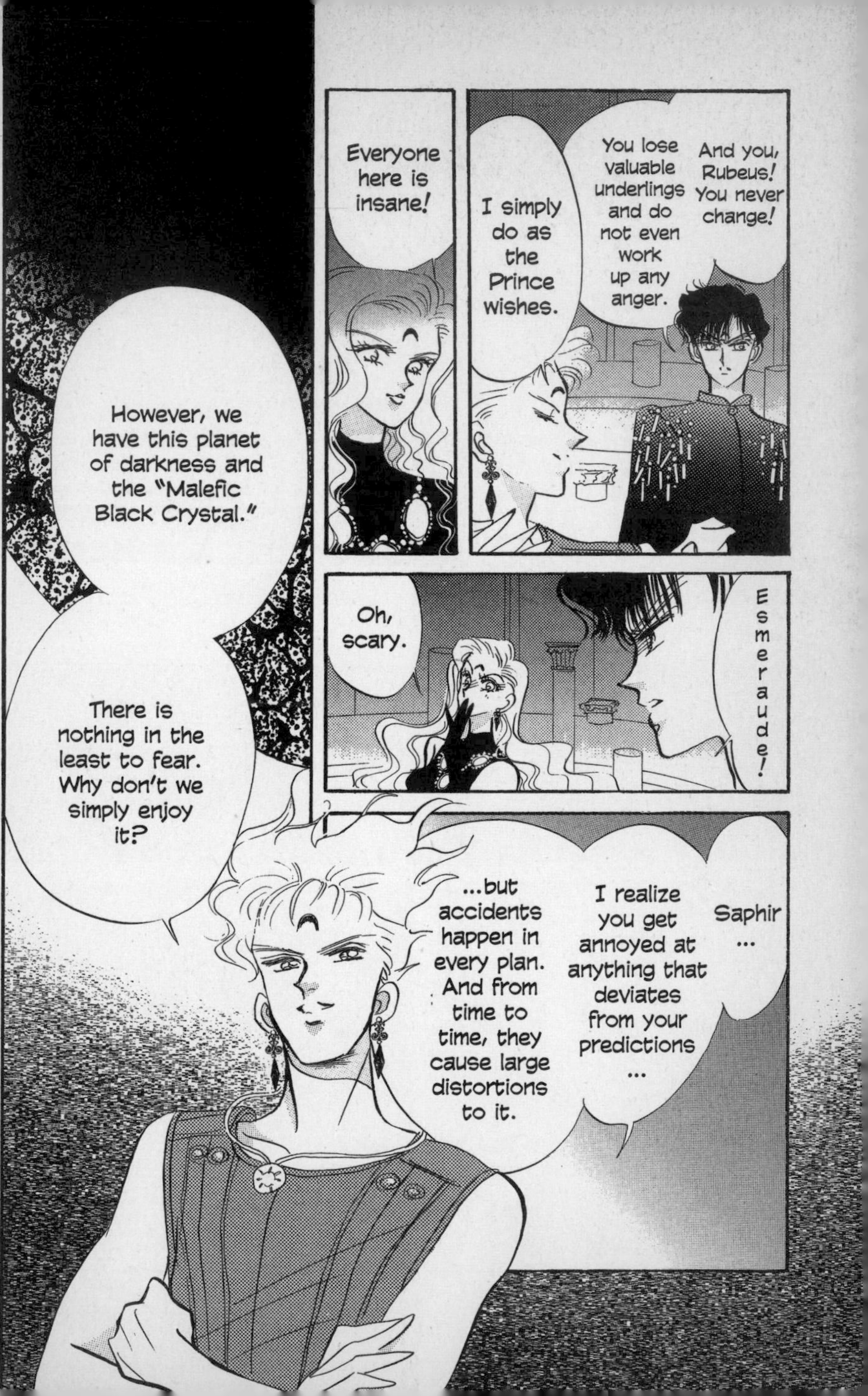
And you, Rubeus! You never change!
You lose valuable underlings and do not even work up any anger.
I simply do as the Prince wishes.
Everyone here is insane!
Esmeraude!
Oh, scary.
Saphir ...
I realize you get annoyed at anything that deviates from your predictions ...
...but accidents happen in every plan. And from time to time, they cause large distortions to it.
However, we have this planet of darkness and the "Malefic Black Crystal."
There is nothing in the least to fear. Why don't we simply enjoy it?

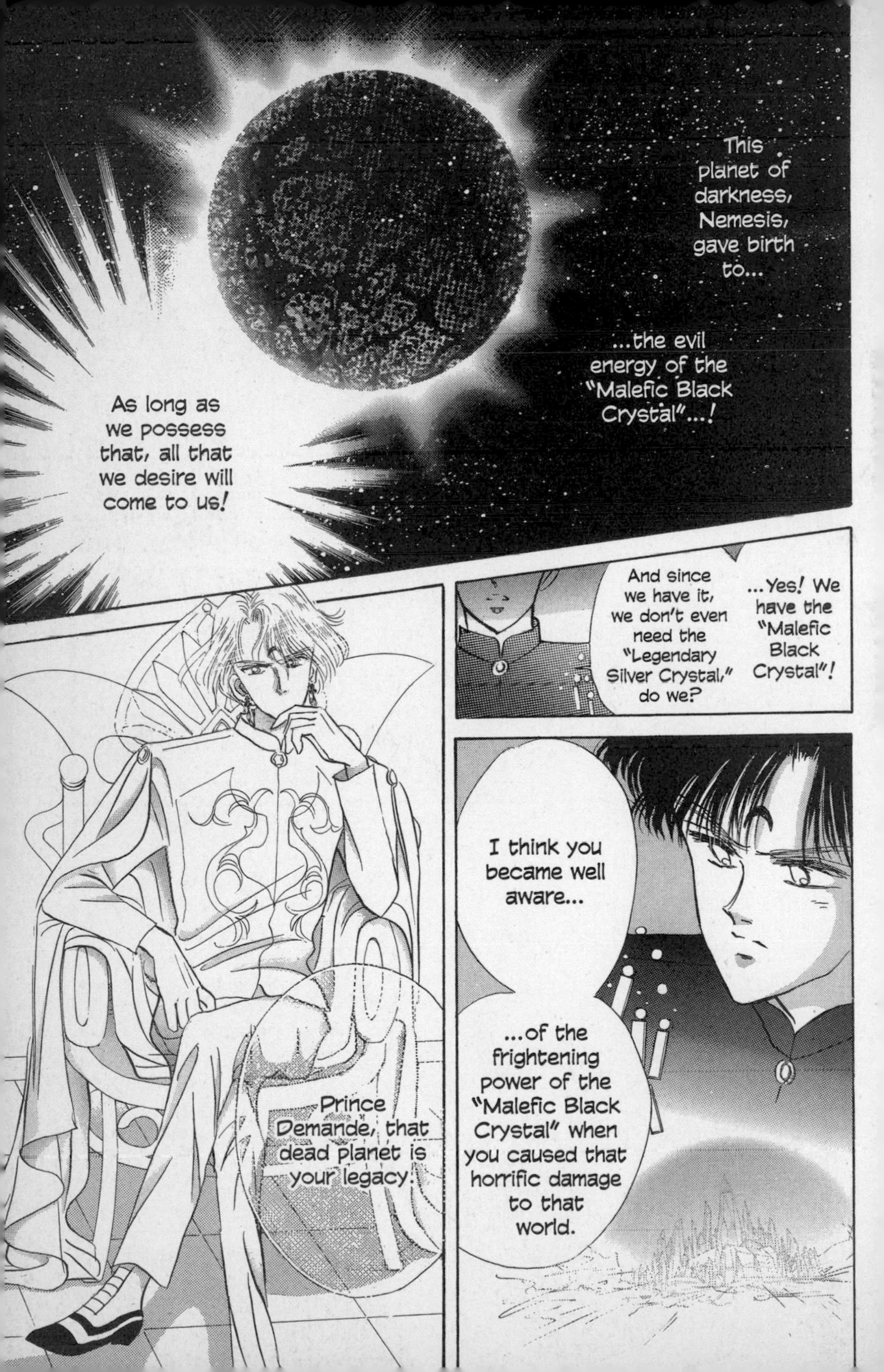
This planet of darkness, Nemesis, gave birth to...
...the evil energy of the "Malefic Black Crystal"...!
As long as we possess that, all that we desire will come to us!
...Yes! We have the "Malefic Black Crystal"!
And since we have it, we don't even need the "Legendary Silver Crystal," do we?
I think you became well aware...
...of the frightening power of the "Malefic Black Crystal" when you caused that horrific damage to that world.
Prince Demande, that dead planet is your legacy.

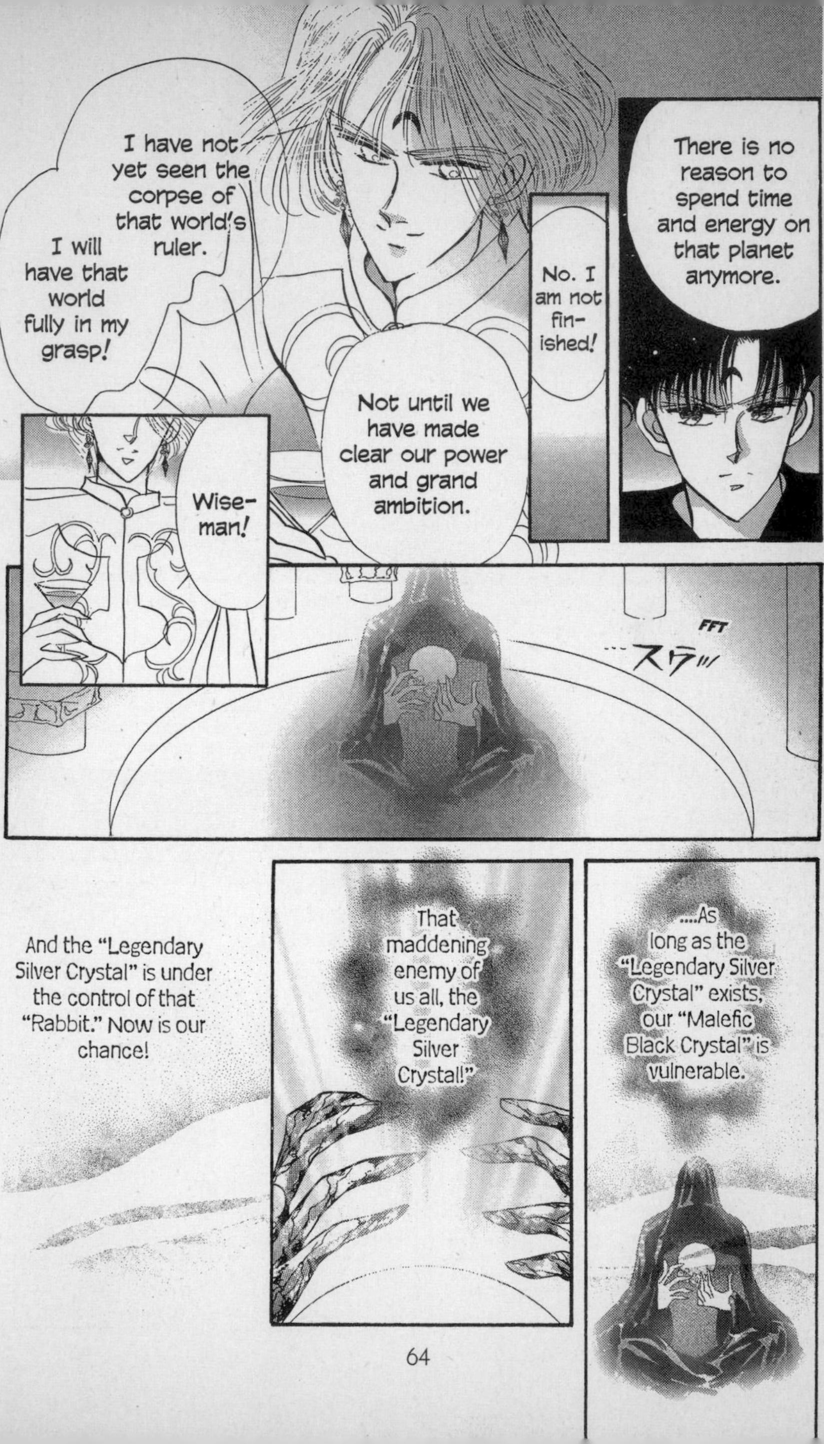

There is no reason to spend time and energy on that planet anymore.
No. I am not finished!
I have not yet seen the corpse of that world's ruler.
I will have that world fully in my grasp!
Not until we have made clear our power and grand ambition.
Wise-man!
FFT
...スラッ
....As long as the "Legendary Silver Crystal" exists, our "Malefic Black Crystal" is vulnerable.
That maddening enemy of us all, the "Legendary Silver Crystal!"
And the "Legendary Silver Crystal" is under the control of that "Rabbit." Now is our chance!

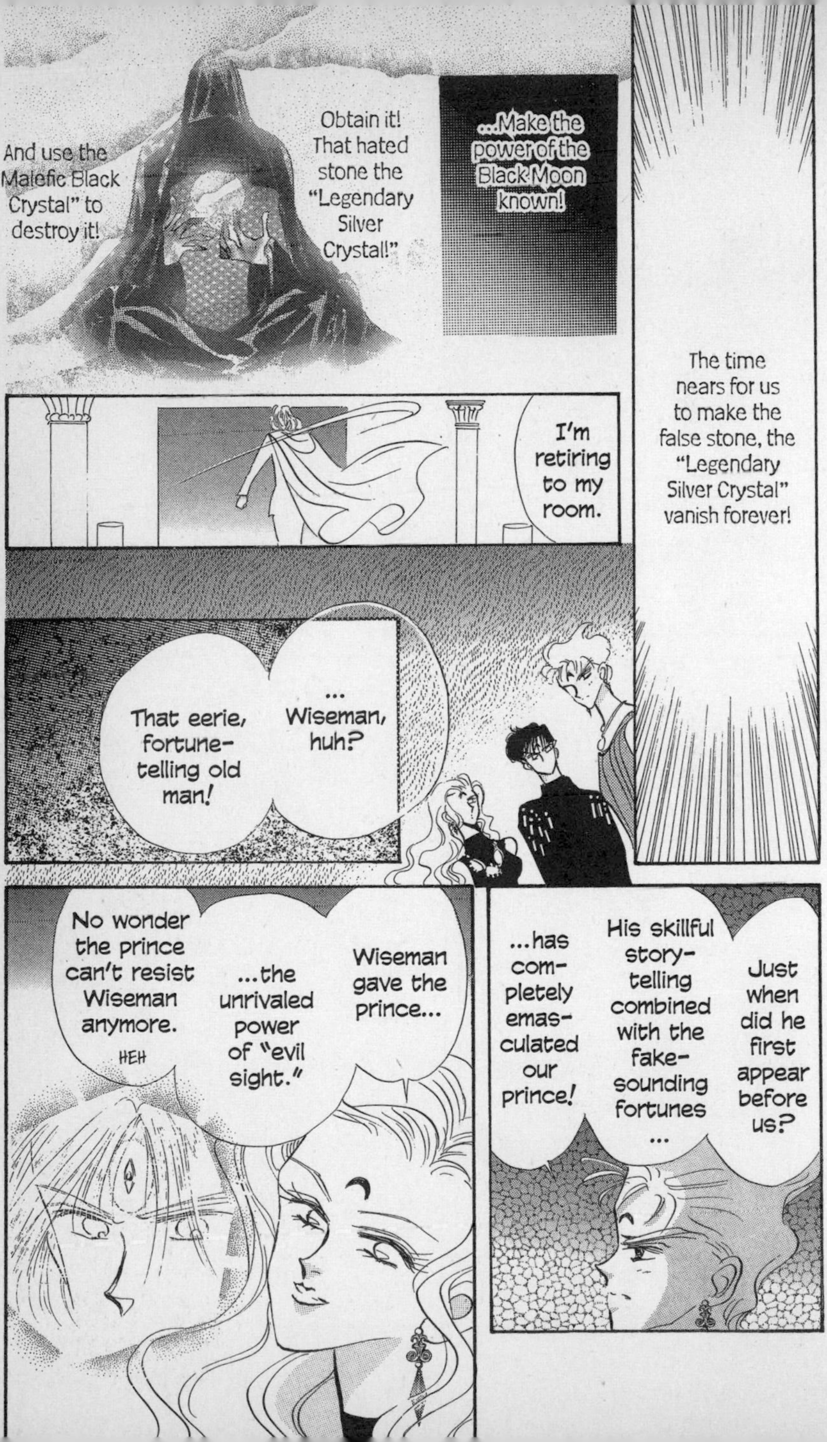
The time nears for us to make the false stone, the "Legendary Silver Crystal" vanish forever!
...Make the power of the Black Moon known!
Obtain it! That hated stone the "Legendary Silver Crystal!"
And use the "Malefic Black Crystal" to destroy it!
I'm retiring to my room.
... Wiseman, huh?
That eerie, fortune-telling old man!
Just when did he first appear before us?
His skillful story-telling combined with the fake-sounding fortunes ...
...has completely emasculated our prince!
Wiseman gave the prince...
...the unrivaled power of "evil sight."
No wonder the prince can't resist Wiseman anymore.
HEH

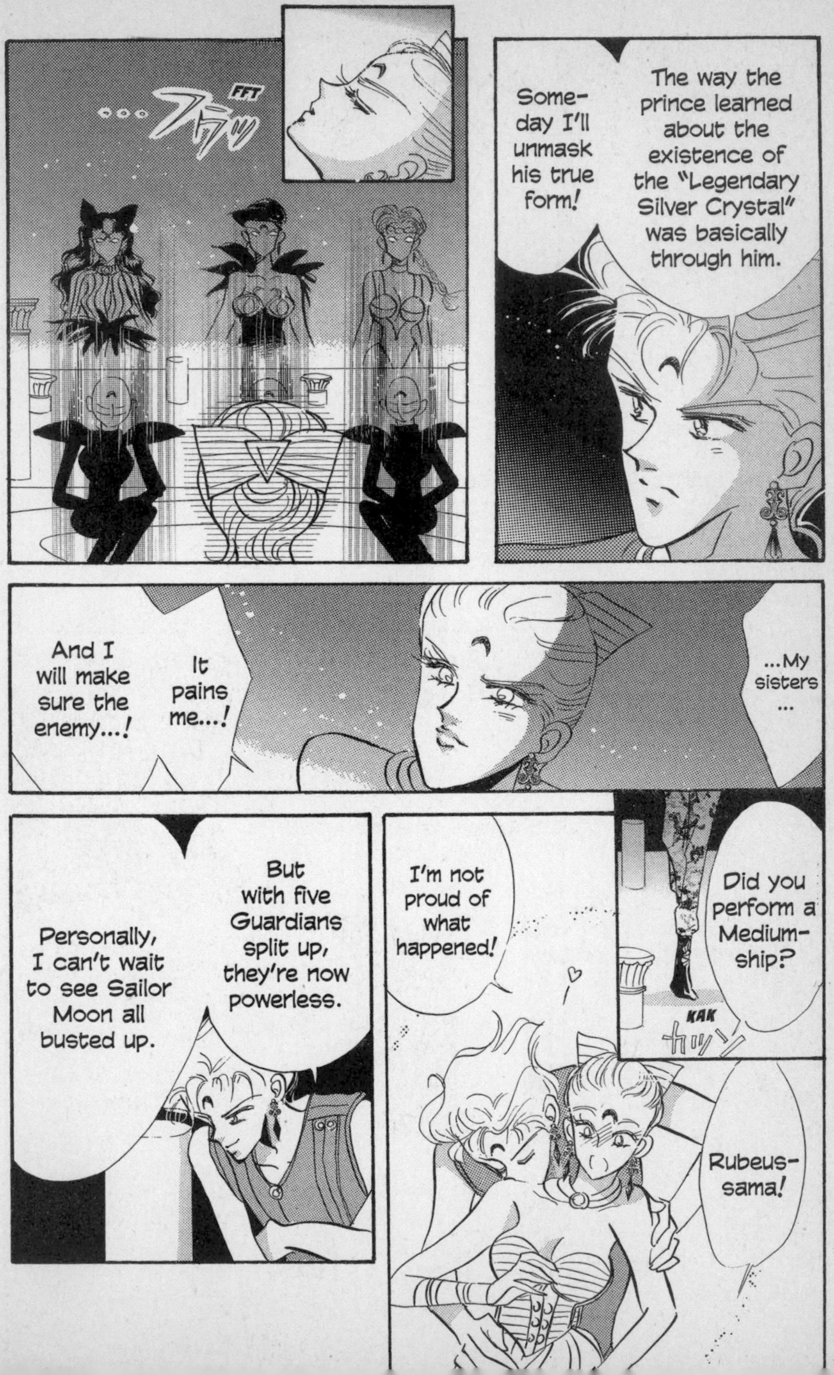

The way the prince learned about the existence of the "Legendary Silver Crystal" was basically through him.
Someday I'll unmask his true form!
FFT
...フラッ
...My sisters...
It pains me...!
And I will make sure the enemy...!
Did you perform a Medium-ship?
KAK
カツン
Rubeus-sama!
I'm not proud of what happened!
But with five Guardians split up, they're now powerless.
Personally, I can't wait to see Sailor Moon all busted up.

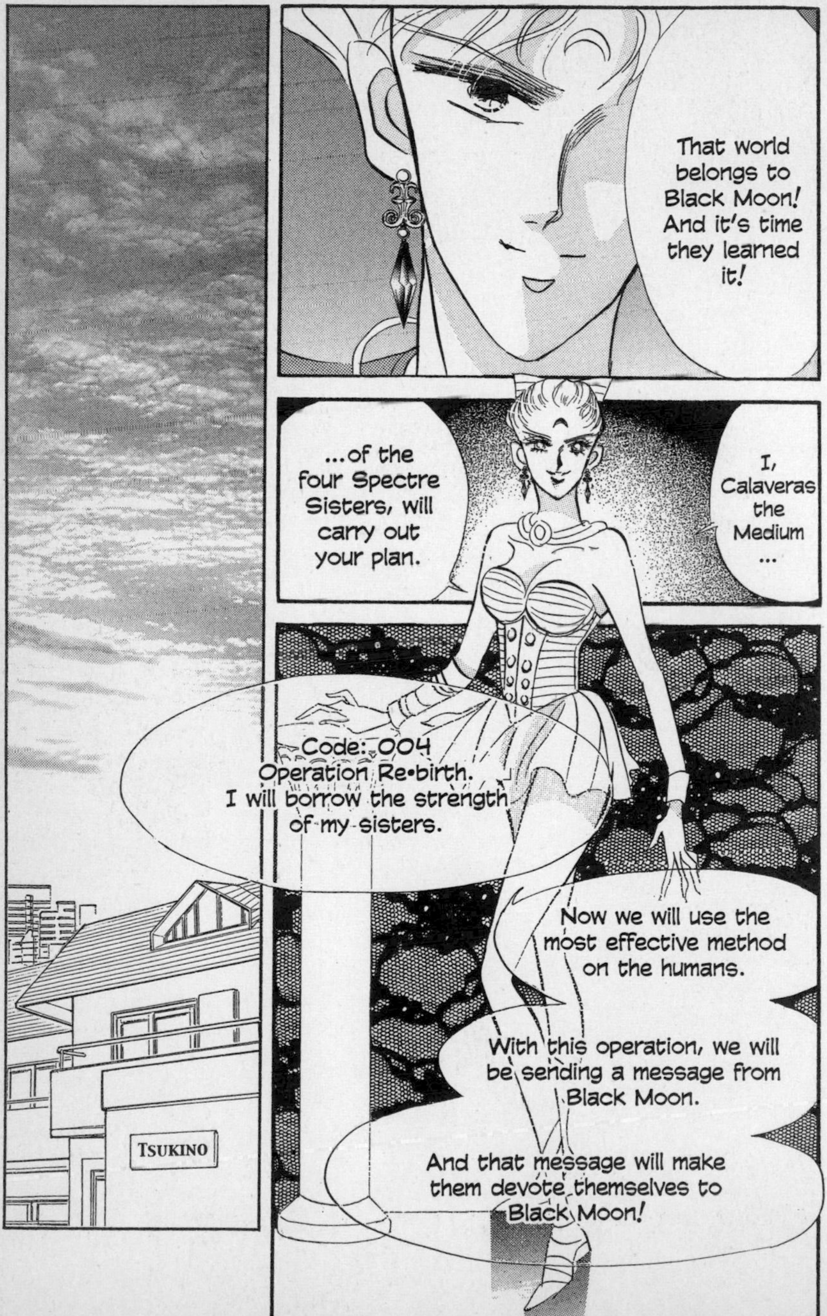
That world belongs to Black Moon! And it's time they learned it!
I, Calaveras the Medium ...
...of the four Spectre Sisters, will carry out your plan.
Code: 004 Operation Re•birth. I will borrow the strength of my sisters.
Now we will use the most effective method on the humans.
With this operation, we will be sending a message from Black Moon.
And that message will make them devote themselves to Black Moon!
TSUKINO

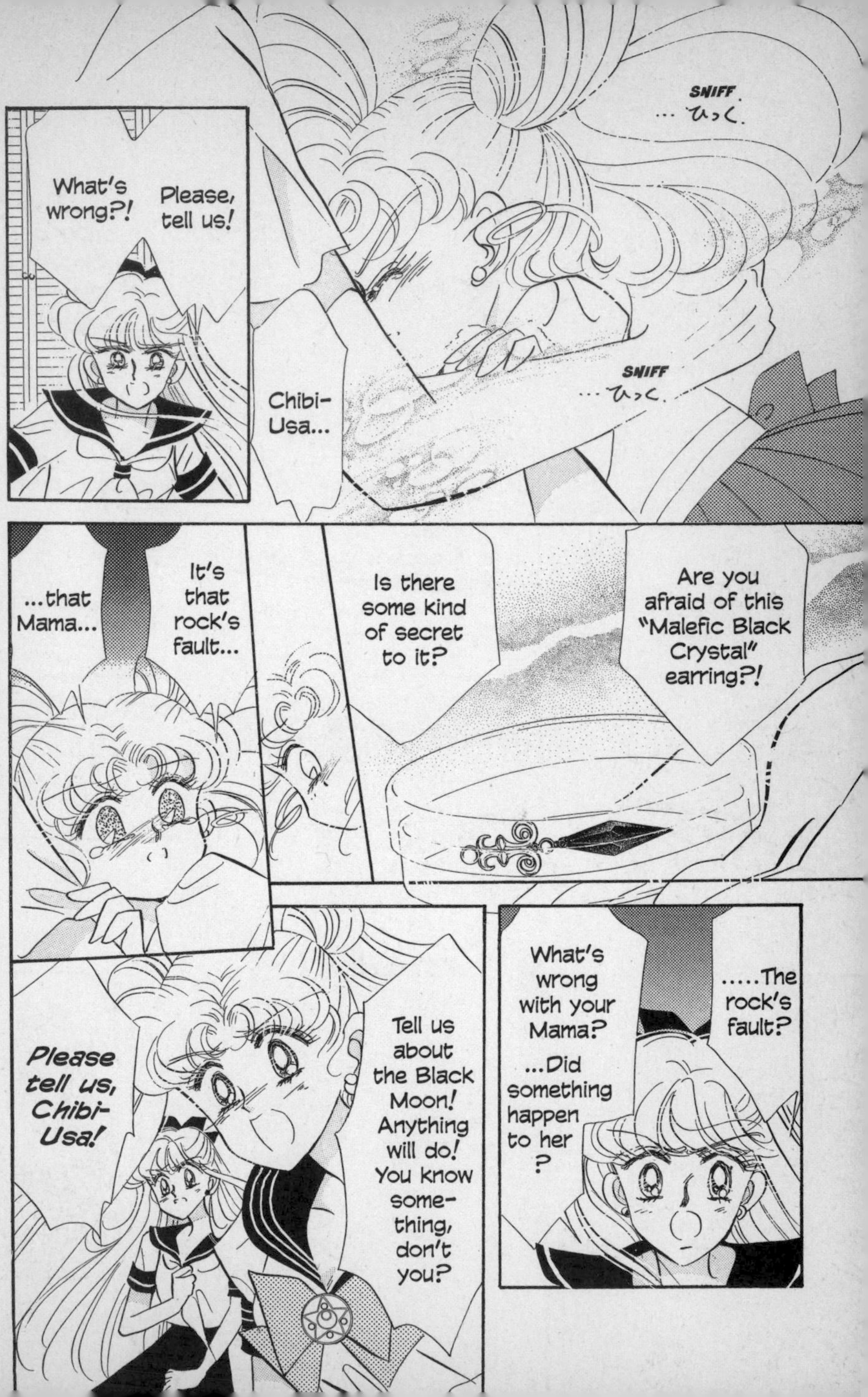
SNIFF
... ひっく.
SNIFF
... ひっく
Chibi-Usa...
Please, tell us!
What's wrong?!
Are you afraid of this "Malefic Black Crystal" earring?!
Is there some kind of secret to it?
It's that rock's fault...
...that Mama...
.....The rock's fault?
What's wrong with your Mama? ...Did something happen to her ?
Tell us about the Black Moon! Anything will do! You know something, don't you?
Please tell us, Chibi-Usa!

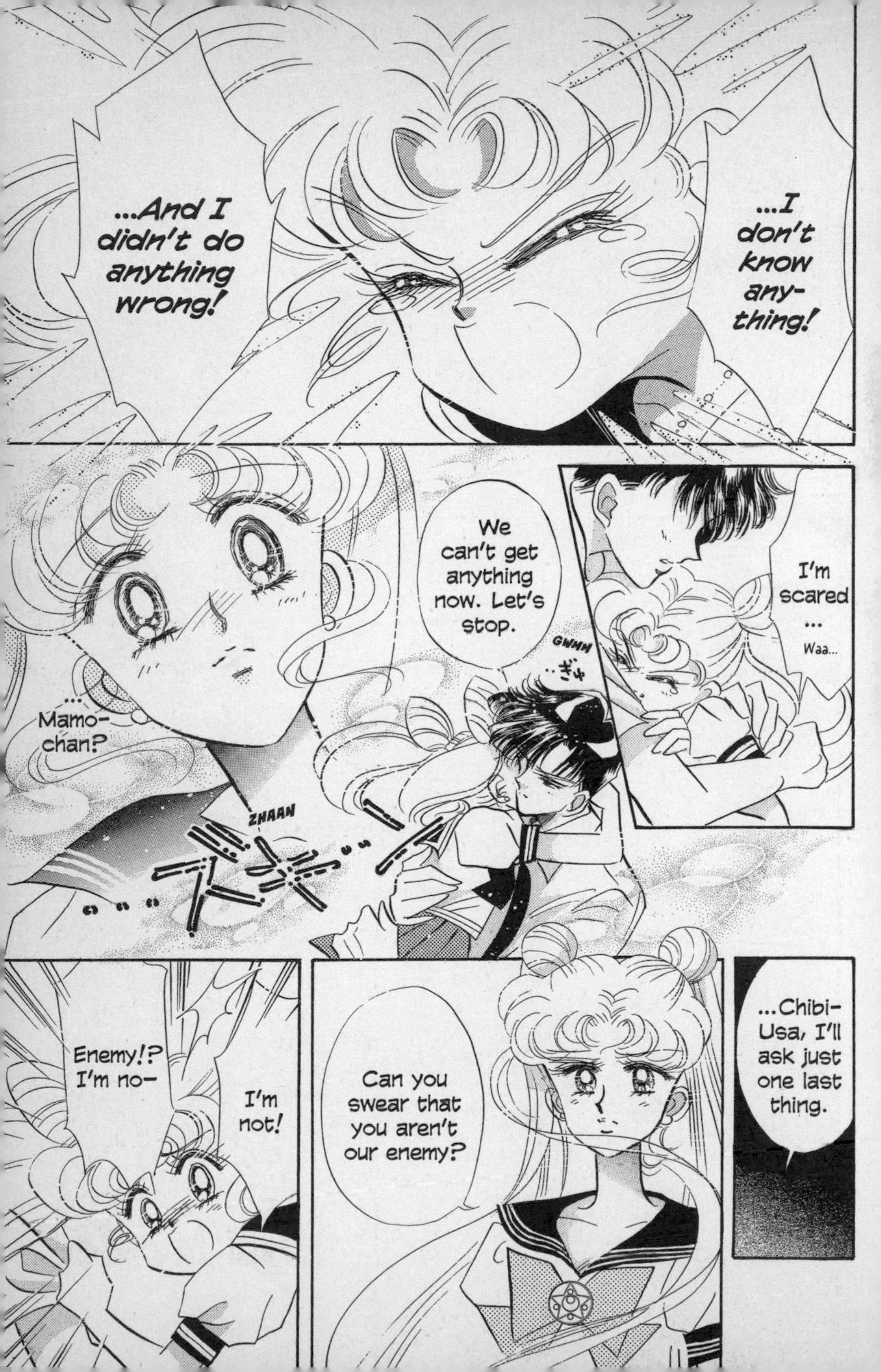
...I don't know any-thing!
...And I didn't do anything wrong!
I'm scared ...
Waa...
We can't get anything now. Let's stop.
GWMM
ぎゅ
...Mamo-chan?
ZHAAN
...Chibi-Usa, I'll ask just one last thing.
Can you swear that you aren't our enemy?
Enemy!? I'm no-
I'm not!

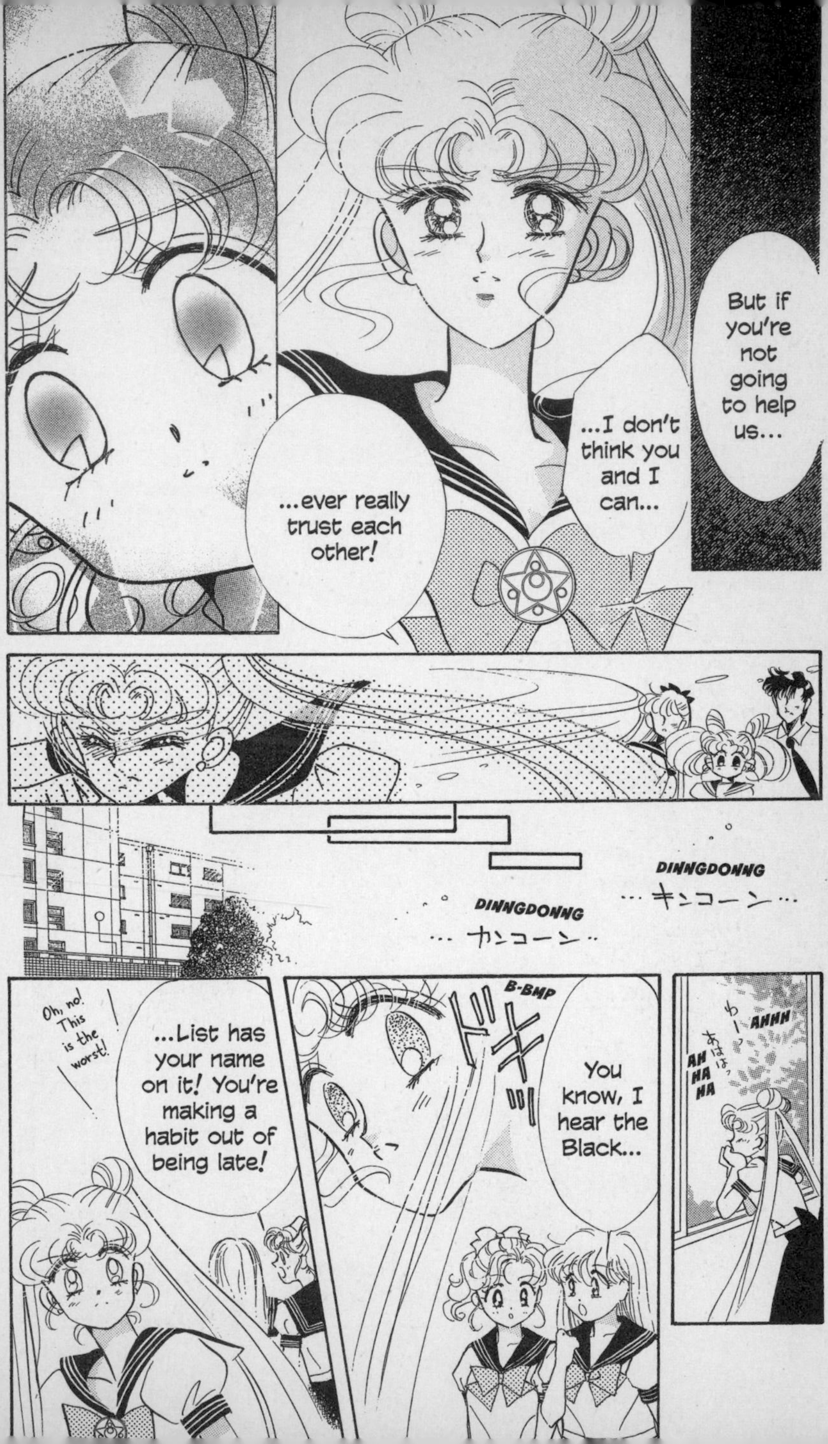
But if you're not going to help us...
...I don't think you and I can...
...ever really trust each other!
DINNGDONNG
・・・キンコーン・・・
DINNGDONNG
・・・カンコーン・・
AHHH
わー
AH HA HA
あははっ
B-BMP
ドキ
You know, I hear the Black...
...List has your name on it! You're making a habit out of being late!
Oh, no! This is the worst!

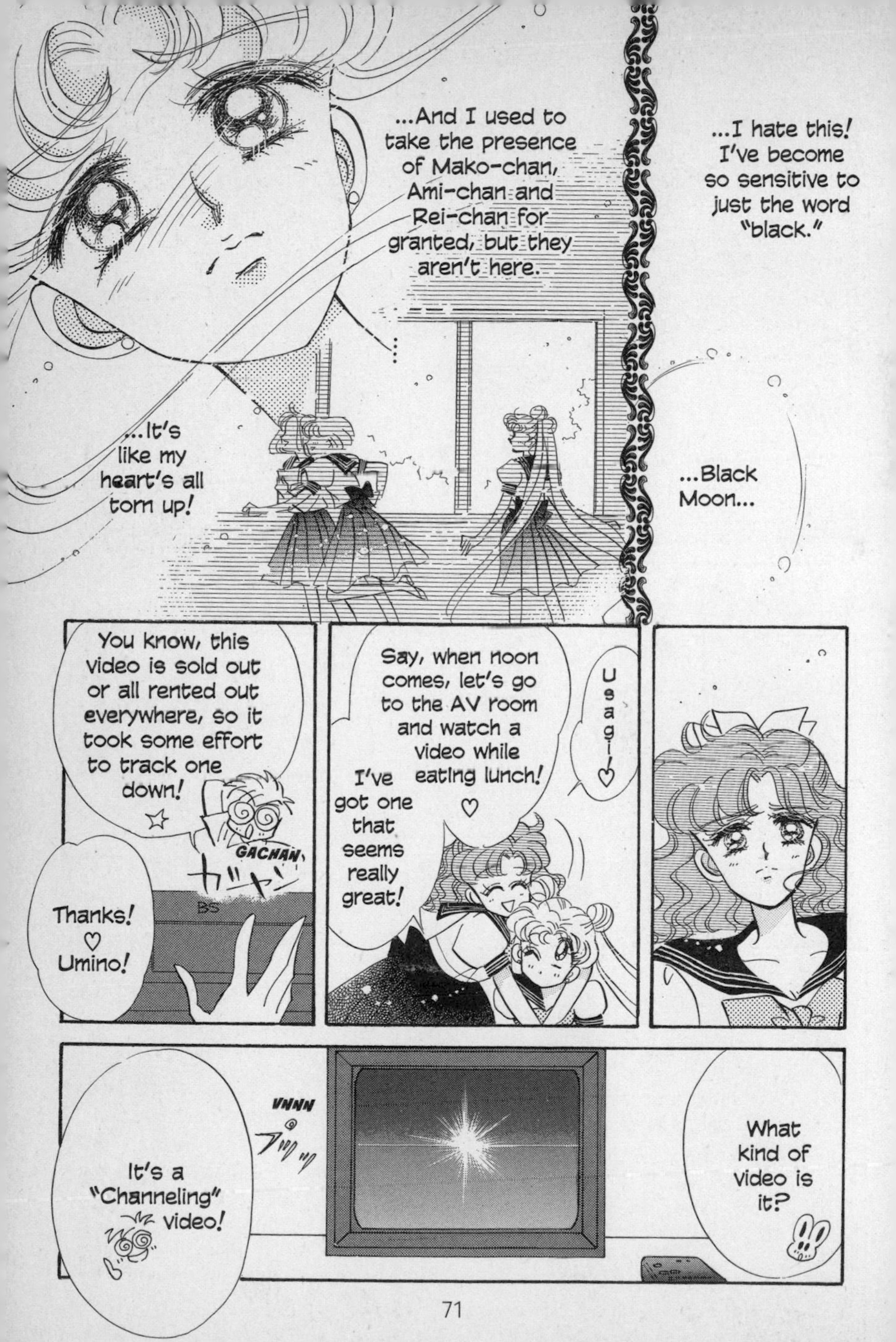
...I hate this! I've become so sensitive to just the word "black."
...Black Moon...
...And I used to take the presence of Mako-chan, Ami-chan and Rei-chan for granted, but they aren't here.
...It's like my heart's all torn up!
Usagi! ♡
Say, when noon comes, let's go to the AV room and watch a video while eating lunch! ♡
I've got one that seems really great!
You know, this video is sold out or all rented out everywhere, so it took some effort to track one down!
GACHAN
Thanks! ♡ Umino!
What kind of video is it?
VNNN
It's a "Channeling" video!

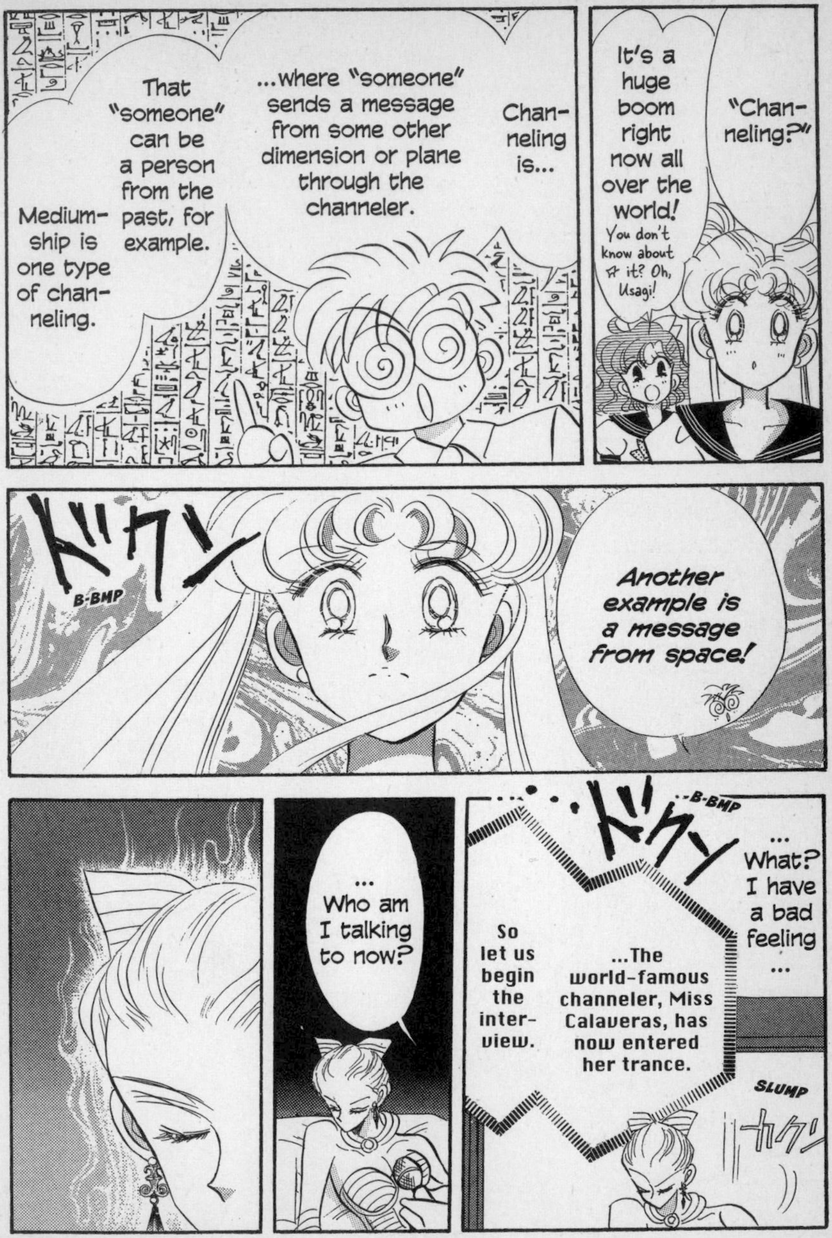
"Channeling?"
It's a huge boom right now all over the world!
You don't know about it? Oh, Usagi!
Channeling is...
...where "someone" sends a message from some other dimension or plane through the channeler.
That "someone" can be a person from the past, for example.
Mediumship is one type of channeling.
Another example is a message from space!
ドクン
B-BMP
...B-BMP
...ドクン
...What? I have a bad feeling...
...The world-famous channeler, Miss Calaveras, has now entered her trance.
So let us begin the interview.
SLUMP
カクン
...Who am I talking to now?

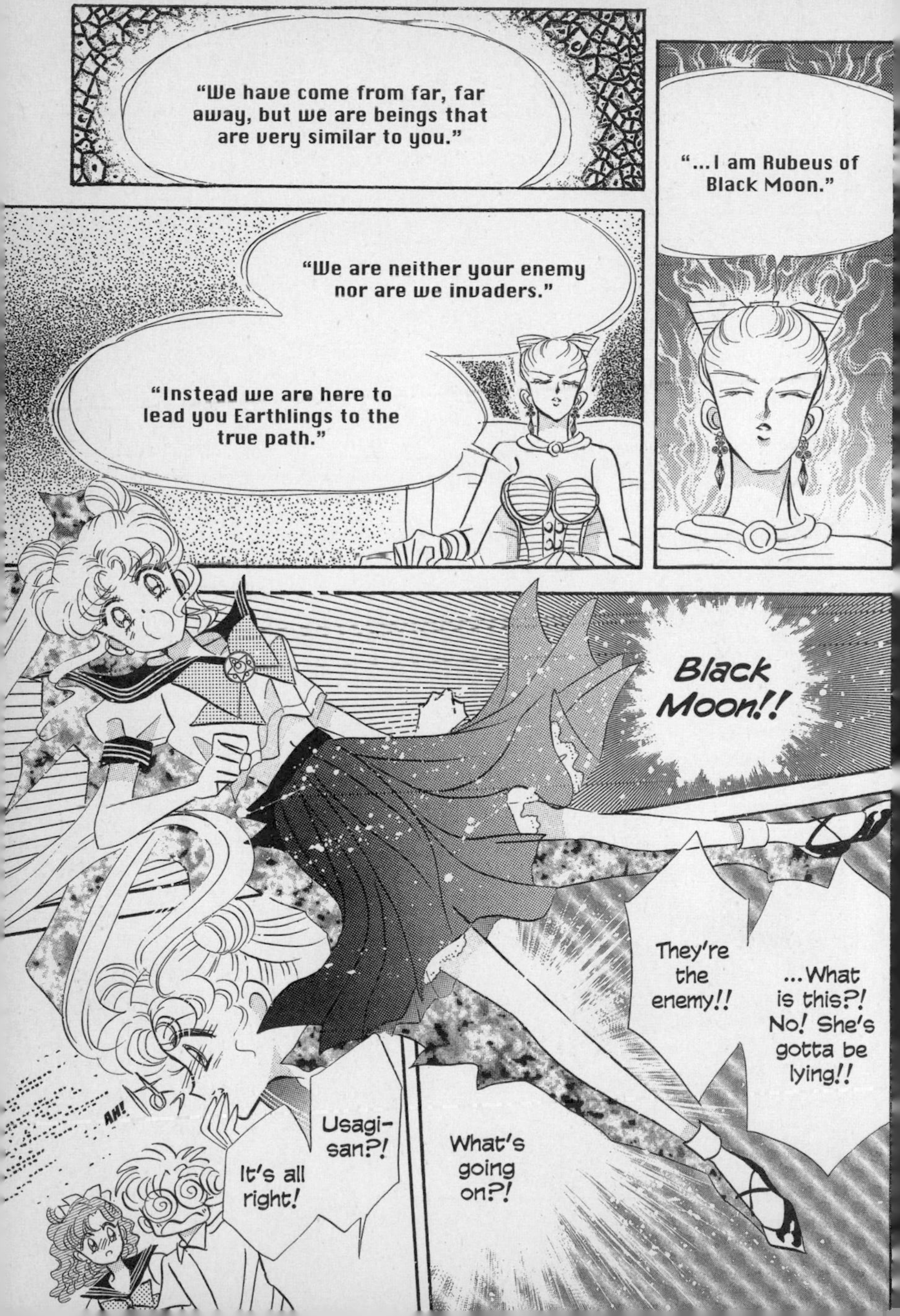
"...I am Rubeus of Black Moon."
"We have come from far, far away, but we are beings that are very similar to you."
"We are neither your enemy nor are we invaders."
"Instead we are here to lead you Earthlings to the true path."
Black Moon!!
...What is this?! No! She's gotta be lying!!
They're the enemy!!
What's going on?!
Usagi-san?!
It's all right!
AH!

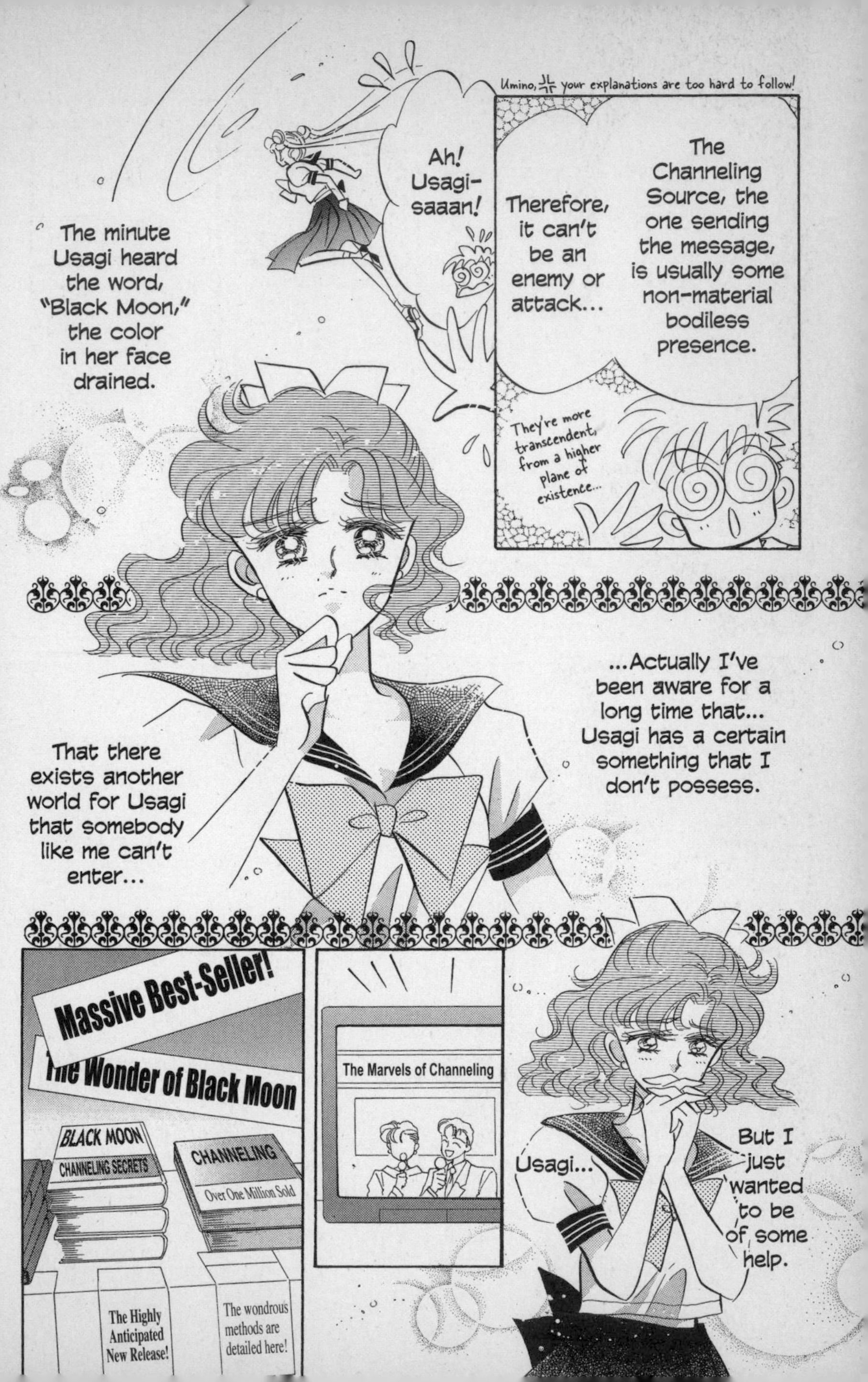
Umino, your explanations are too hard to follow!
The Channeling Source, the one sending the message, is usually some non-material bodiless presence.
Therefore, it can't be an enemy or attack...
They're more transcendent, from a higher plane of existence...
Ah! Usagi-saaan!
The minute Usagi heard the word, "Black Moon," the color in her face drained.
...Actually I've been aware for a long time that... Usagi has a certain something that I don't possess.
That there exists another world for Usagi that somebody like me can't enter...
But I just wanted to be of some help.
Usagi...
The Marvels of Channeling
Massive Best-Seller!
The Wonder of Black Moon
BLACK MOON
CHANNELING SECRETS
CHANNELING
Over One Million Sold
The Highly Anticipated New Release!
The wondrous methods are detailed here!

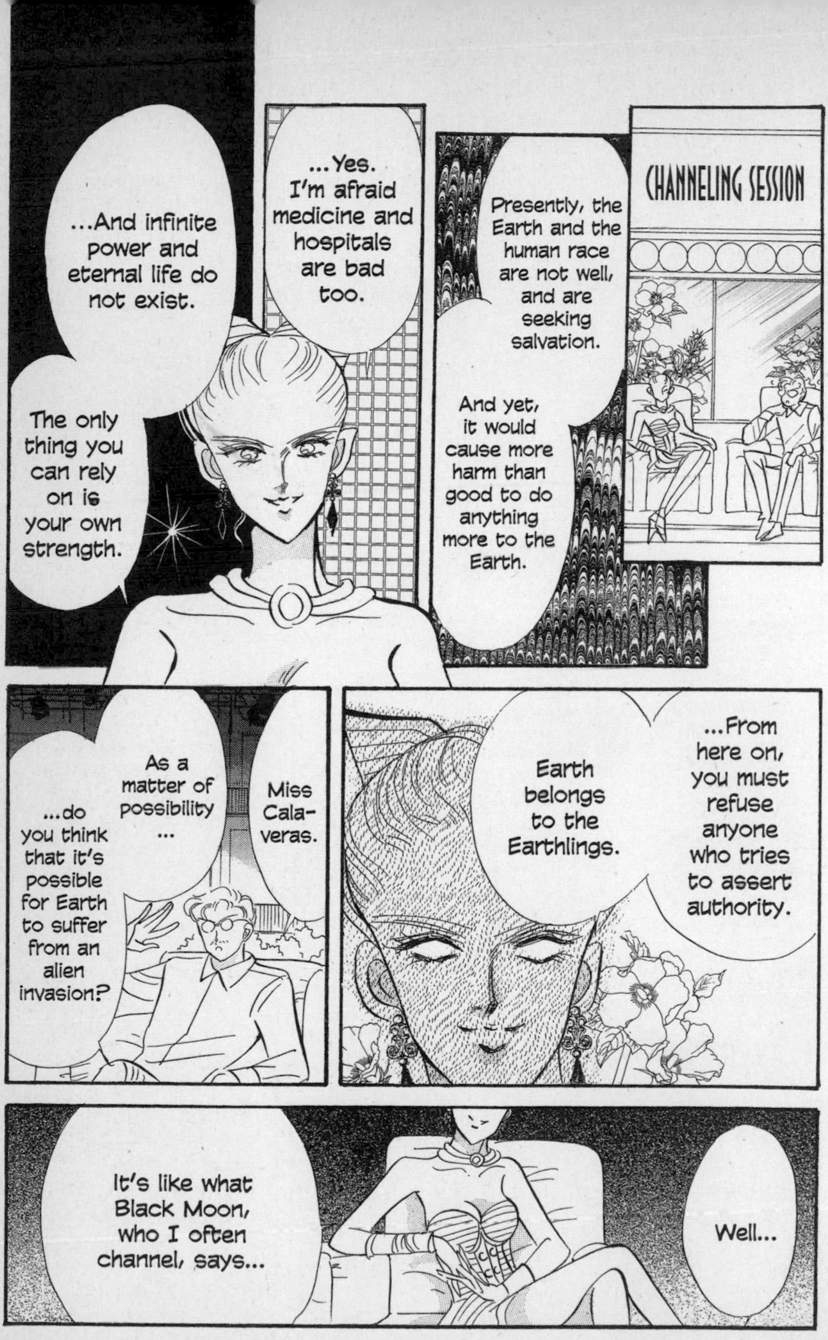
CHANNELING SESSION
Presently, the Earth and the human race are not well, and are seeking salvation.
And yet, it would cause more harm than good to do anything more to the Earth.
...Yes. I'm afraid medicine and hospitals are bad too.
...And infinite power and eternal life do not exist.
The only thing you can rely on is your own strength.
...From here on, you must refuse anyone who tries to assert authority.
Earth belongs to the Earthlings.
Miss Calaveras.
As a matter of possibility ...
...do you think that it's possible for Earth to suffer from an alien invasion?
Well...
It's like what Black Moon, who I often channel, says...

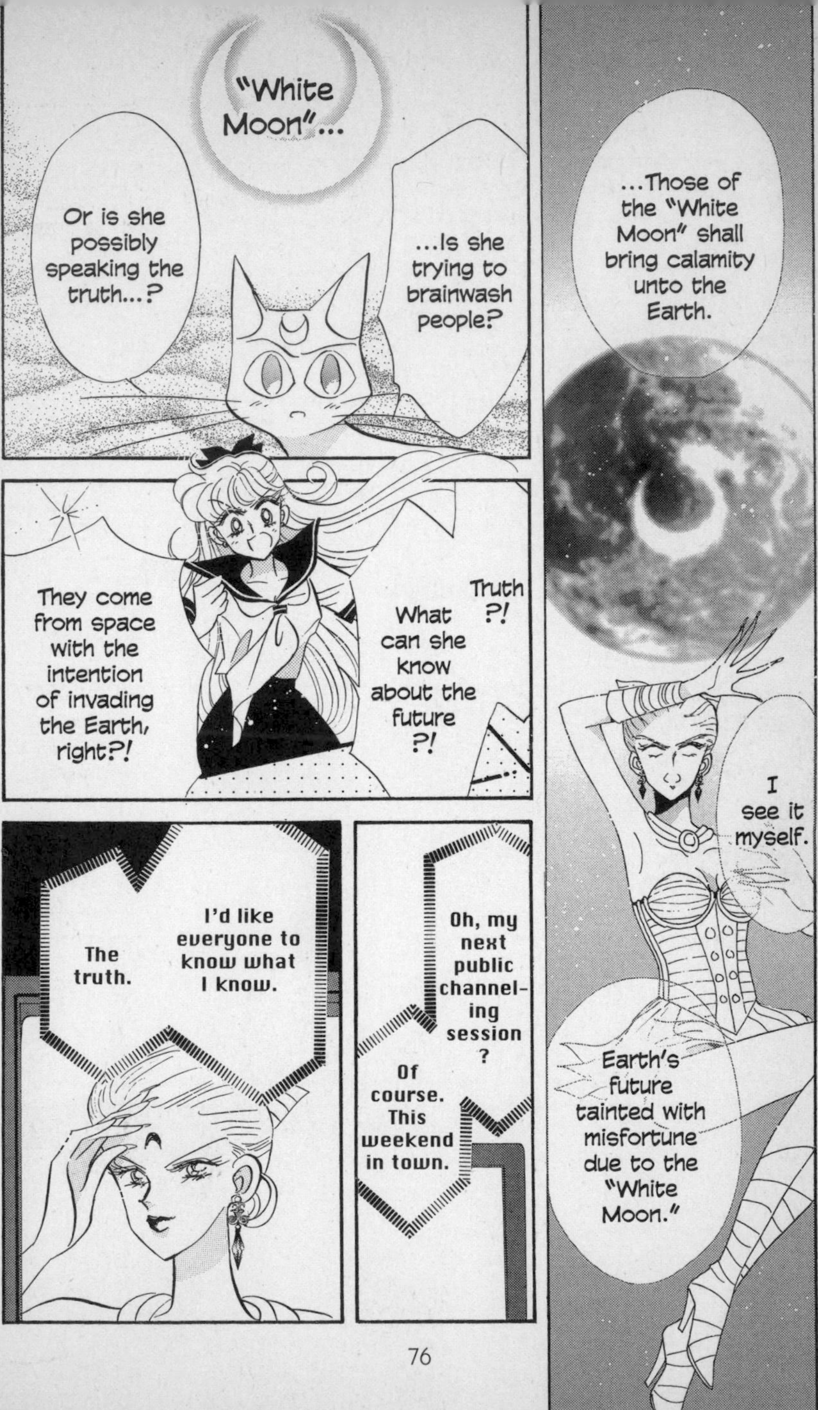
...Those of the "White Moon" shall bring calamity unto the Earth.
I see it myself.
Earth's future tainted with misfortune due to the "White Moon."
"White Moon"...
...Is she trying to brainwash people?
Or is she possibly speaking the truth...?
Truth ?!
What can she know about the future ?!
They come from space with the intention of invading the Earth, right?!
Oh, my next public channel-ing session ?
Of course. This weekend in town.
I'd like everyone to know what I know.
The truth.

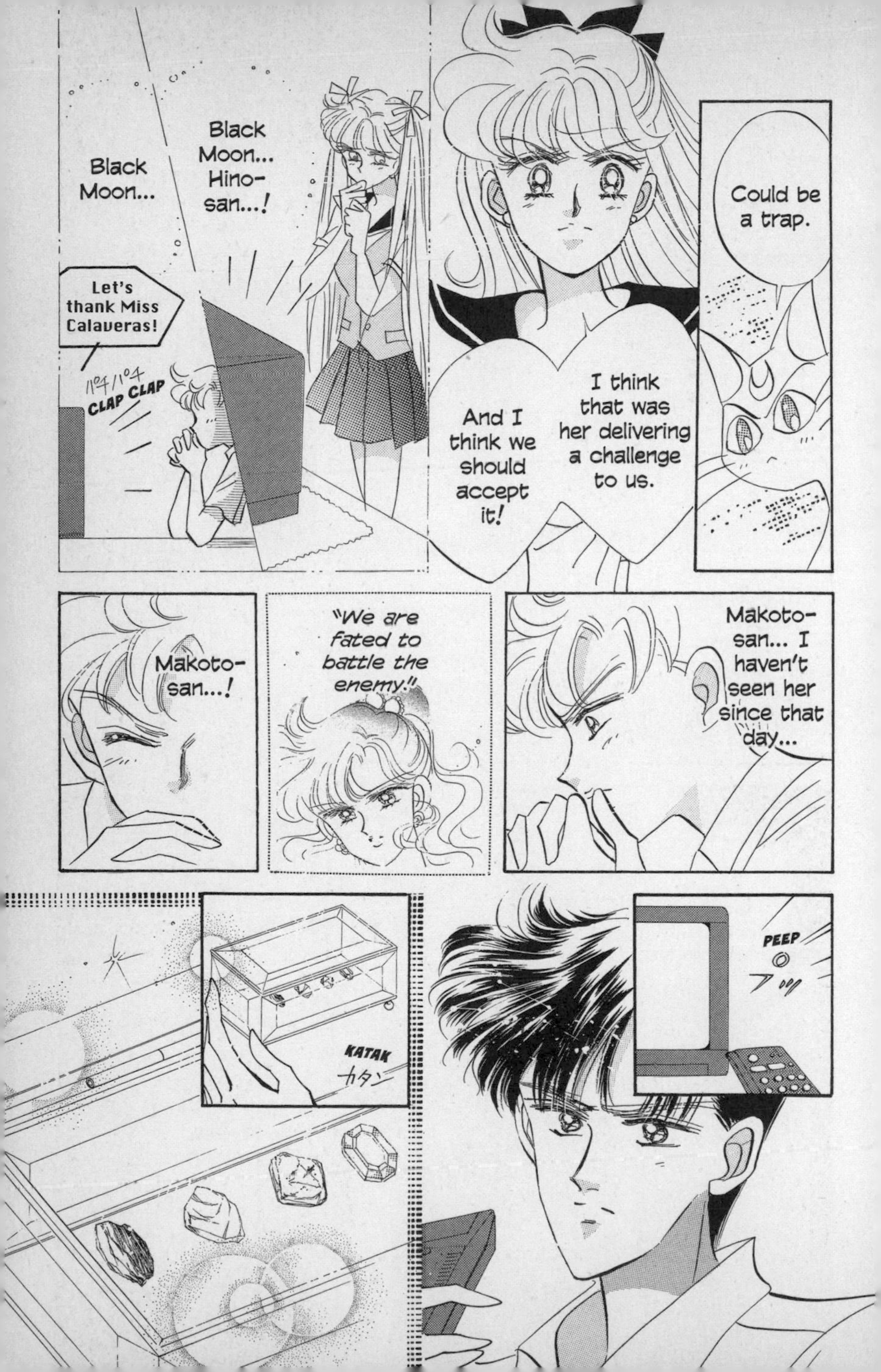

Could be a trap.
I think that was her delivering a challenge to us.
And I think we should accept it!
Black Moon... Hino-san...!
Black Moon...
Let's thank Miss Calaveras!
パチパチ CLAP CLAP
Makoto-san... I haven't seen her since that day...
"We are fated to battle the enemy."
Makoto-san...!
PEEP
KATAK カタン

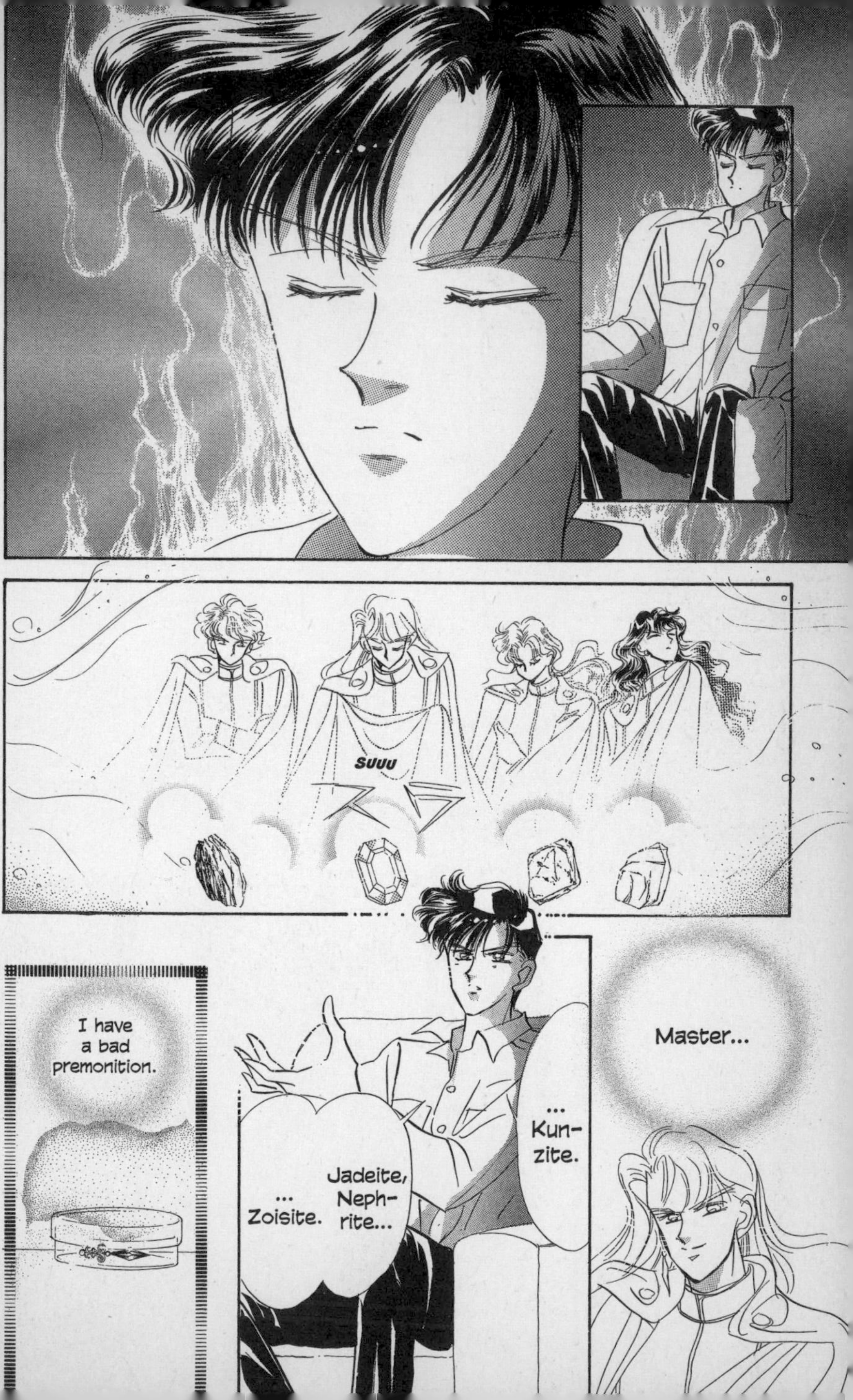
SUUU
Master...
... Kun-zite.
Jadeite, Neph-rite...
... Zoisite.
I have a bad premonition.

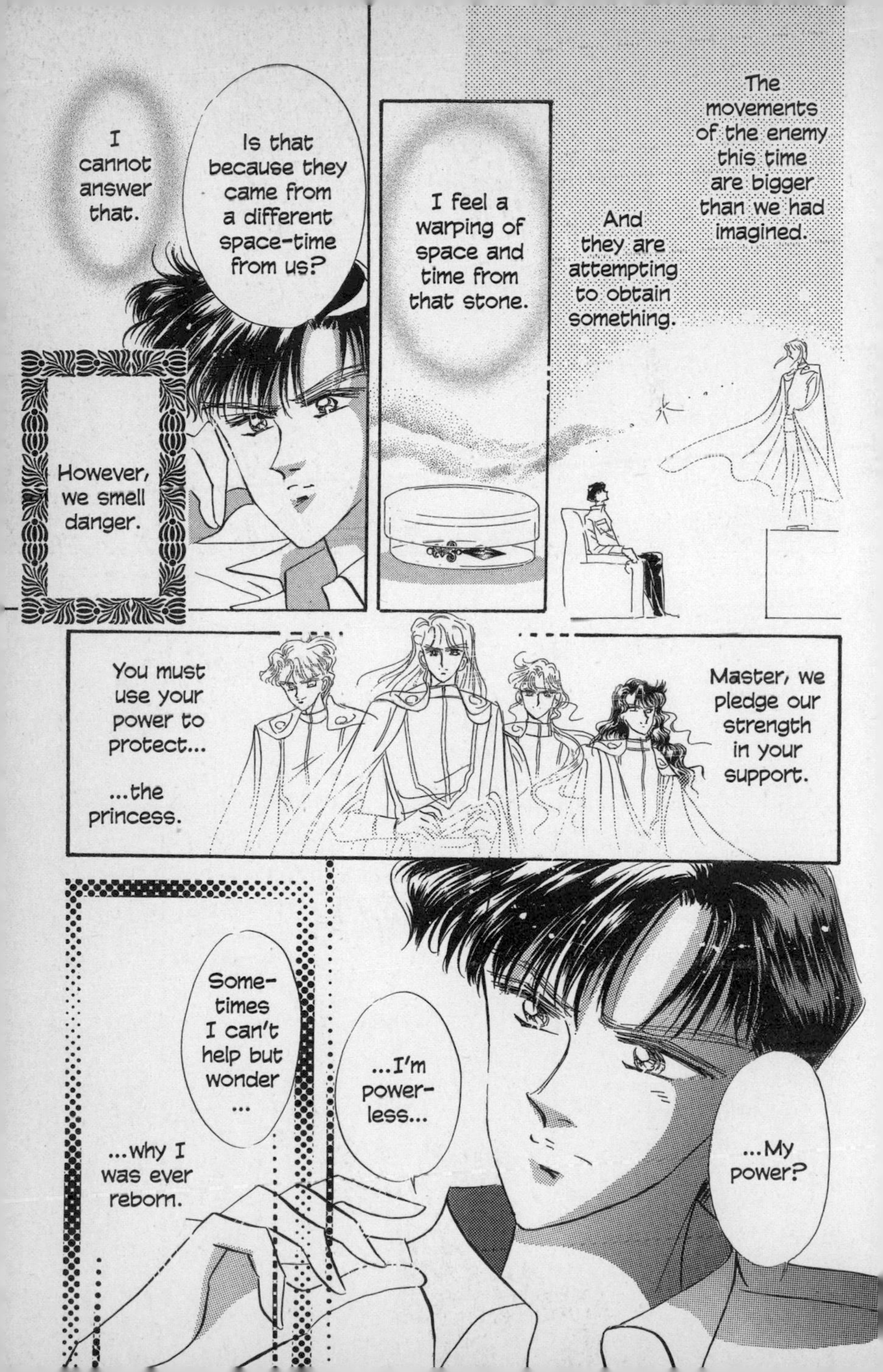
The movements of the enemy this time are bigger than we had imagined.
And they are attempting to obtain something.
I feel a warping of space and time from that stone.
Is that because they came from a different space-time from us?
I cannot answer that.
However, we smell danger.
Master, we pledge our strength in your support.
You must use your power to protect...
...the princess.
...My power?
...I'm powerless...
Sometimes I can't help but wonder...
...why I was ever reborn.

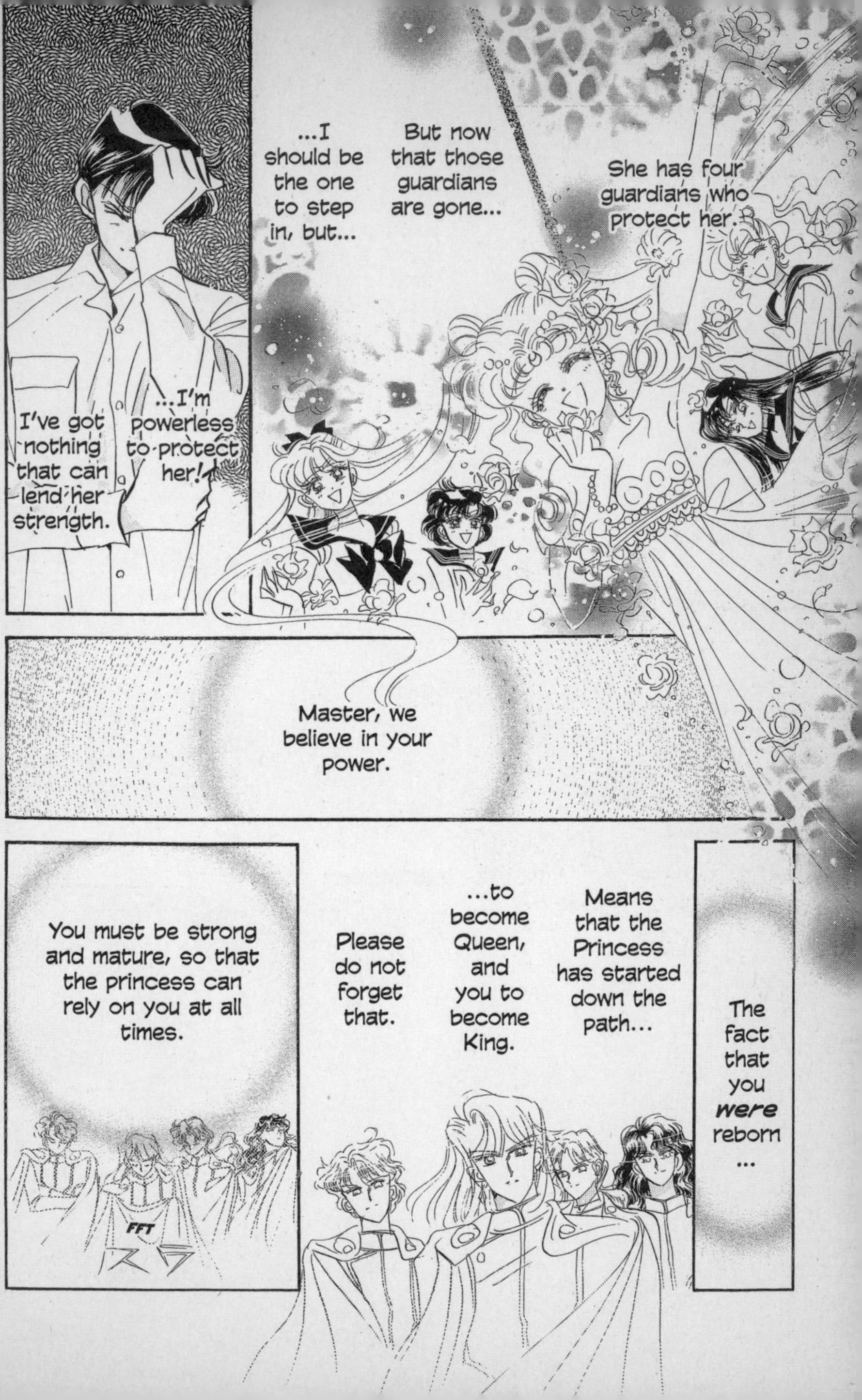

She has four guardians who protect her.
But now that those guardians are gone...
...I should be the one to step in, but...
...I'm powerless to protect her!
I've got nothing that can lend her strength.
Master, we believe in your power.
The fact that you *were* reborn...
Means that the Princess has started down the path...
...to become Queen, and you to become King.
Please do not forget that.
You must be strong and mature, so that the princess can rely on you at all times.
FFT

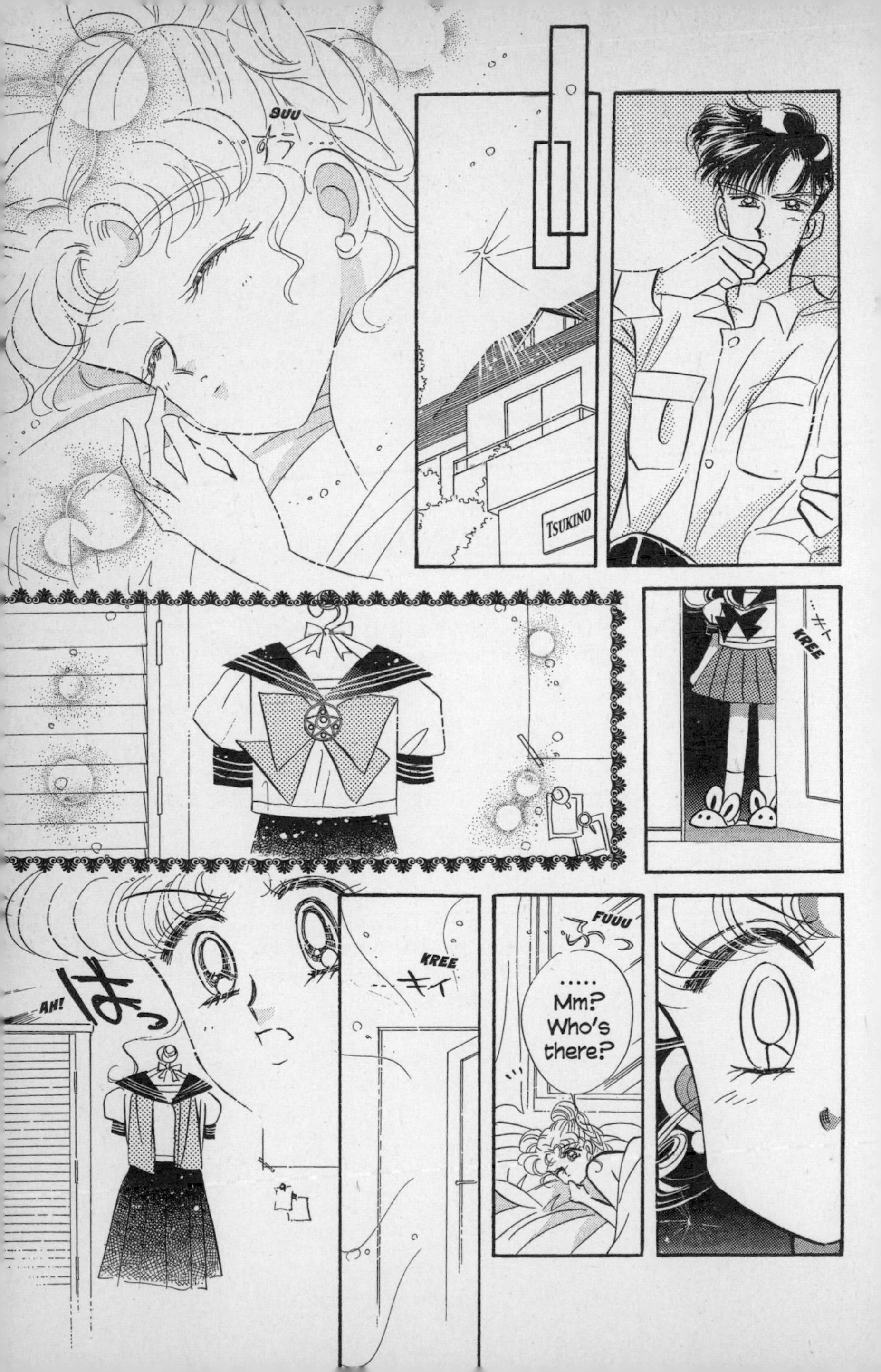
SUU
KREE
FUUU
..... Mm? Who's there?
KREE
AH!

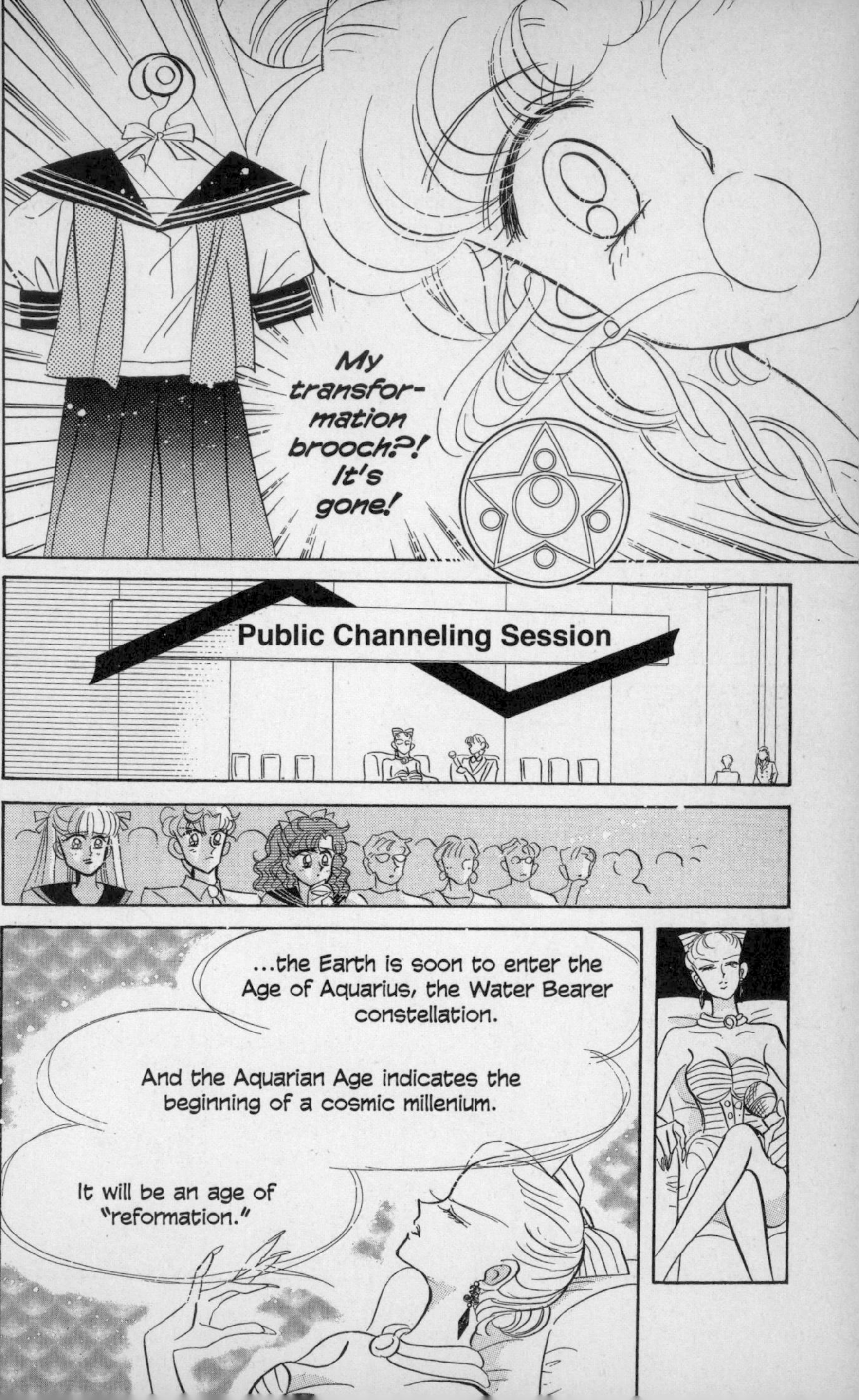
My transfor-mation brooch?! It's gone!
Public Channeling Session
...the Earth is soon to enter the Age of Aquarius, the Water Bearer constellation.
And the Aquarian Age indicates the beginning of a cosmic millenium.
It will be an age of "reformation."

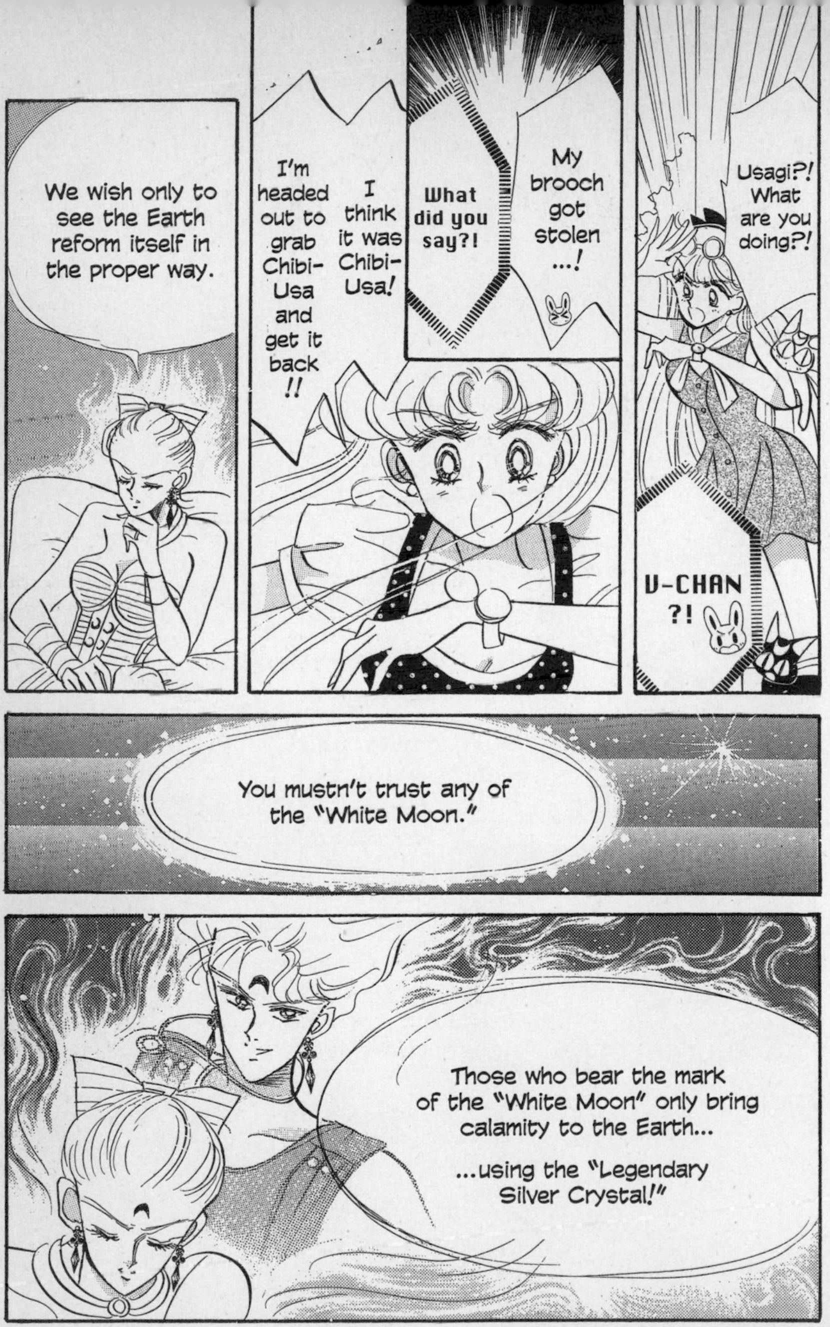
Usagi?! What are you doing?!
V-CHAN ?!
My brooch got stolen ...!
What did you say?!
I think it was Chibi-Usa!
I'm headed out to grab Chibi-Usa and get it back !!
We wish only to see the Earth reform itself in the proper way.
You mustn't trust any of the "White Moon."
Those who bear the mark of the "White Moon" only bring calamity to the Earth...
...using the "Legendary Silver Crystal!"

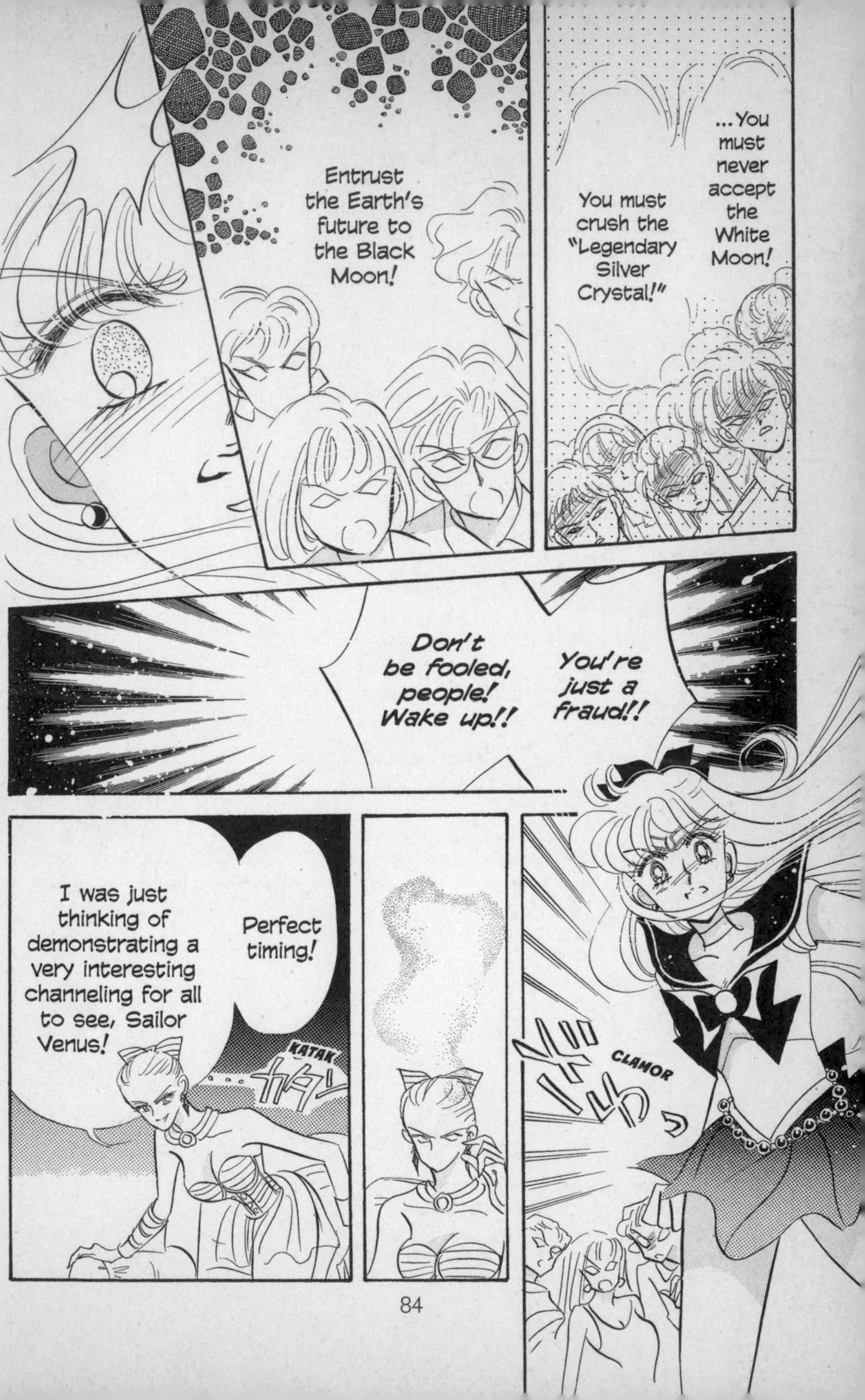
...You must never accept the White Moon!
You must crush the "Legendary Silver Crystal!"
Entrust the Earth's future to the Black Moon!
You're just a fraud!!
Don't be fooled, people! Wake up!!
CLAMOR
Perfect timing!
I was just thinking of demonstrating a very interesting channeling for all to see, Sailor Venus!
KATAK

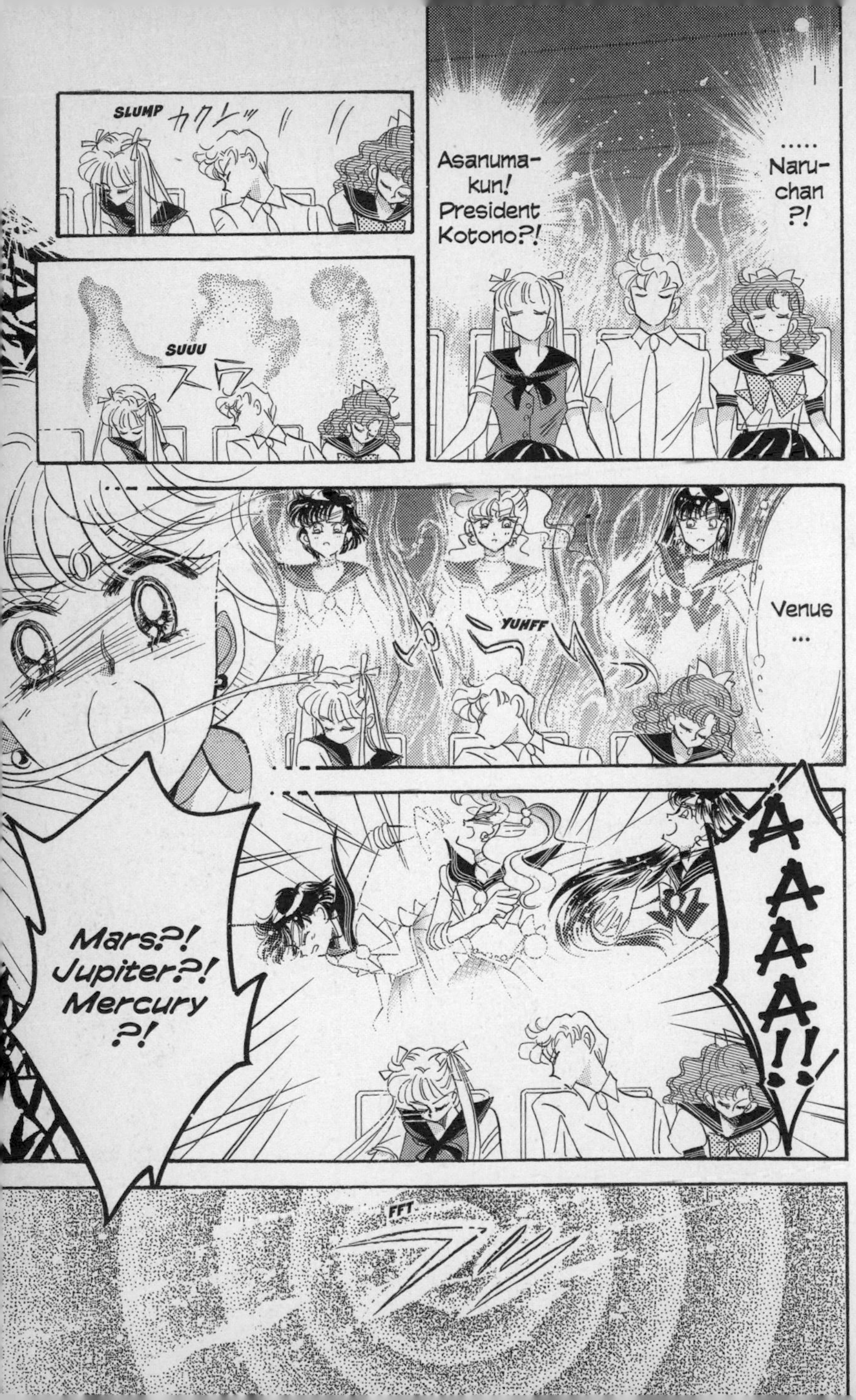

.....
Naru-chan?!
Asanuma-kun! President Kotono?!
SLUMP
カクンッ
SUUU
Venus ...
YUHFF
AAAA!!
Mars?! Jupiter?! Mercury?!
FFT

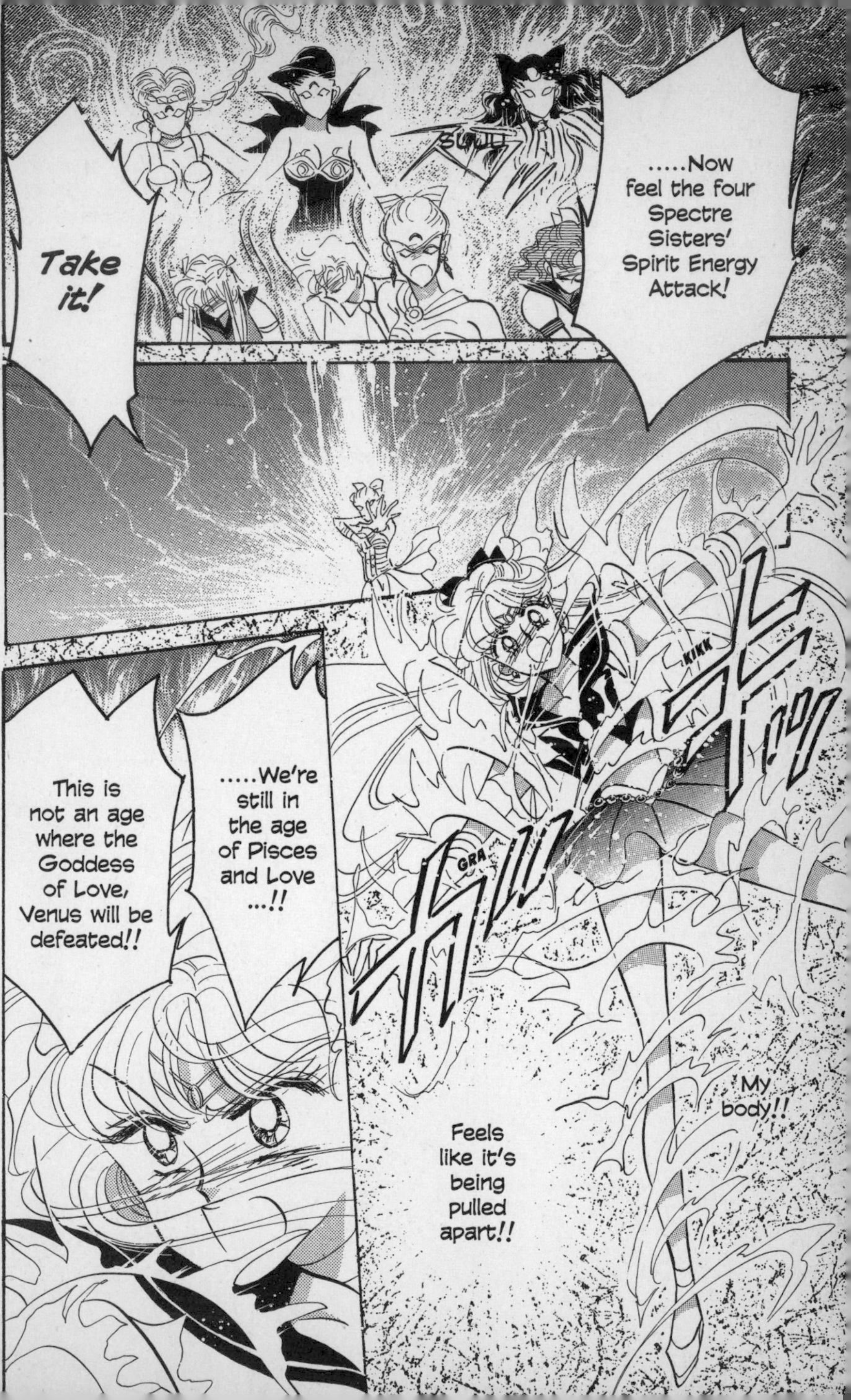
.....Now feel the four Spectre Sisters' Spirit Energy Attack!
SUUU
Take it!
KIKK
GRA
My body!!
Feels like it's being pulled apart!!
.....We're still in the age of Pisces and Love ...!!
This is not an age where the Goddess of Love, Venus will be defeated!!

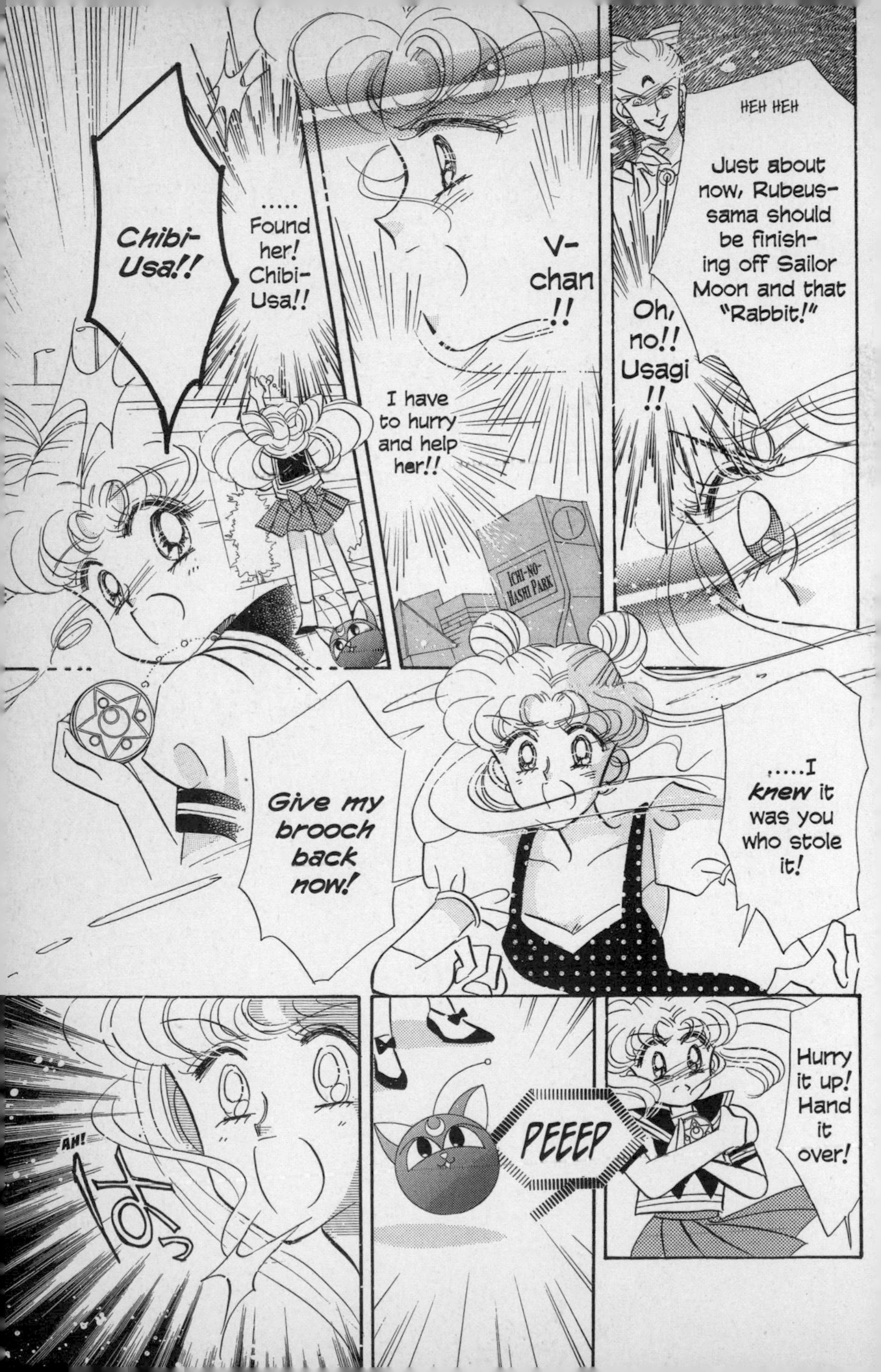
HEH HEH
Just about now, Rubeus-sama should be finishing off Sailor Moon and that "Rabbit!"
Oh, no!! Usagi!!
V-chan!!
I have to hurry and help her!!
..... Found her! Chibi-Usa!!
Chibi-Usa!!
ICHI-NO-HASHI PARK
.....I *knew* it was you who stole it!
Give my brooch back now!
Hurry it up! Hand it over!
PEEEP
AH!

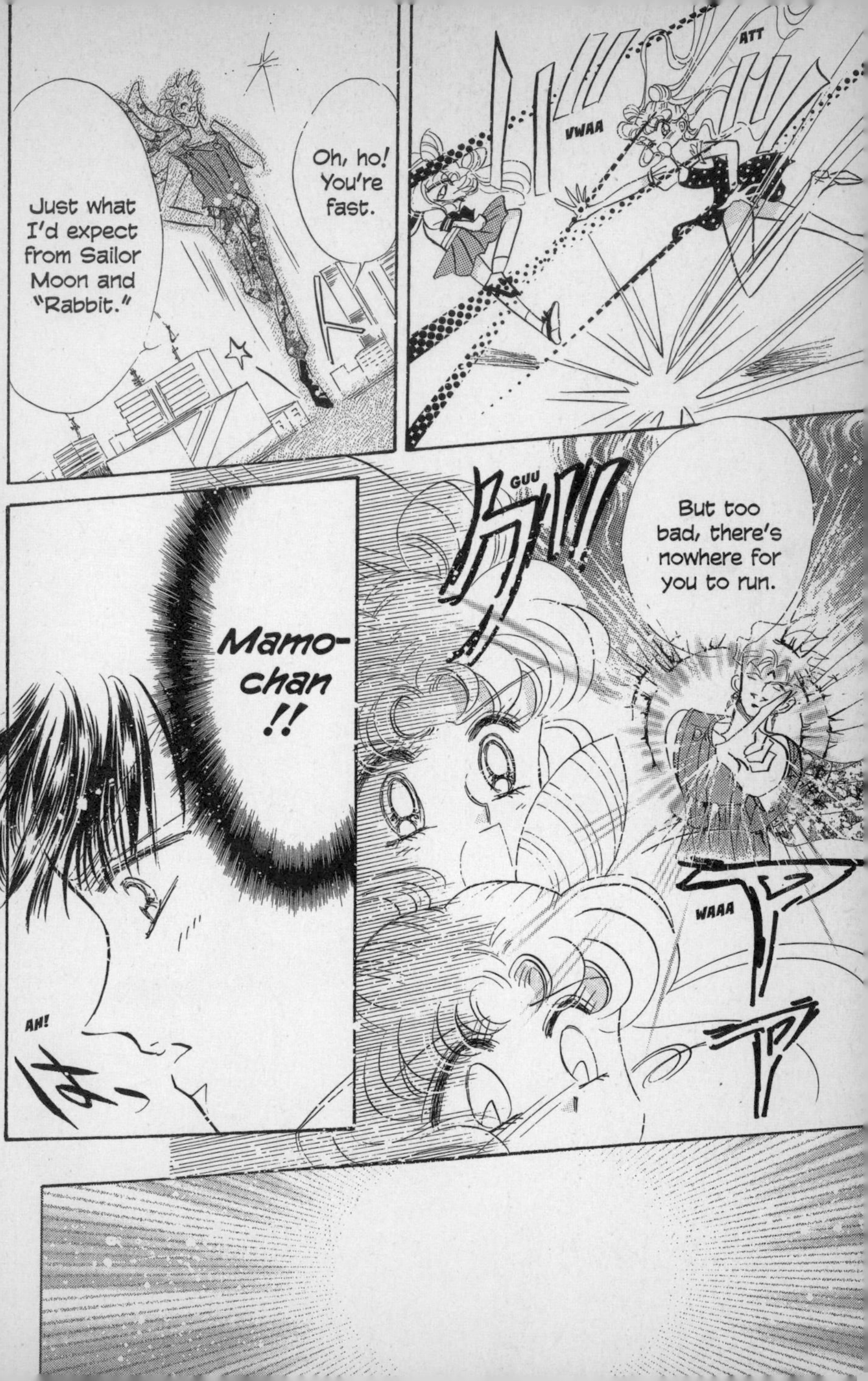
ATT
VWAA
Oh, ho! You're fast.
Just what I'd expect from Sailor Moon and "Rabbit."
GUU
But too bad, there's nowhere for you to run.
WAAA
Mamo-chan!!
AH!

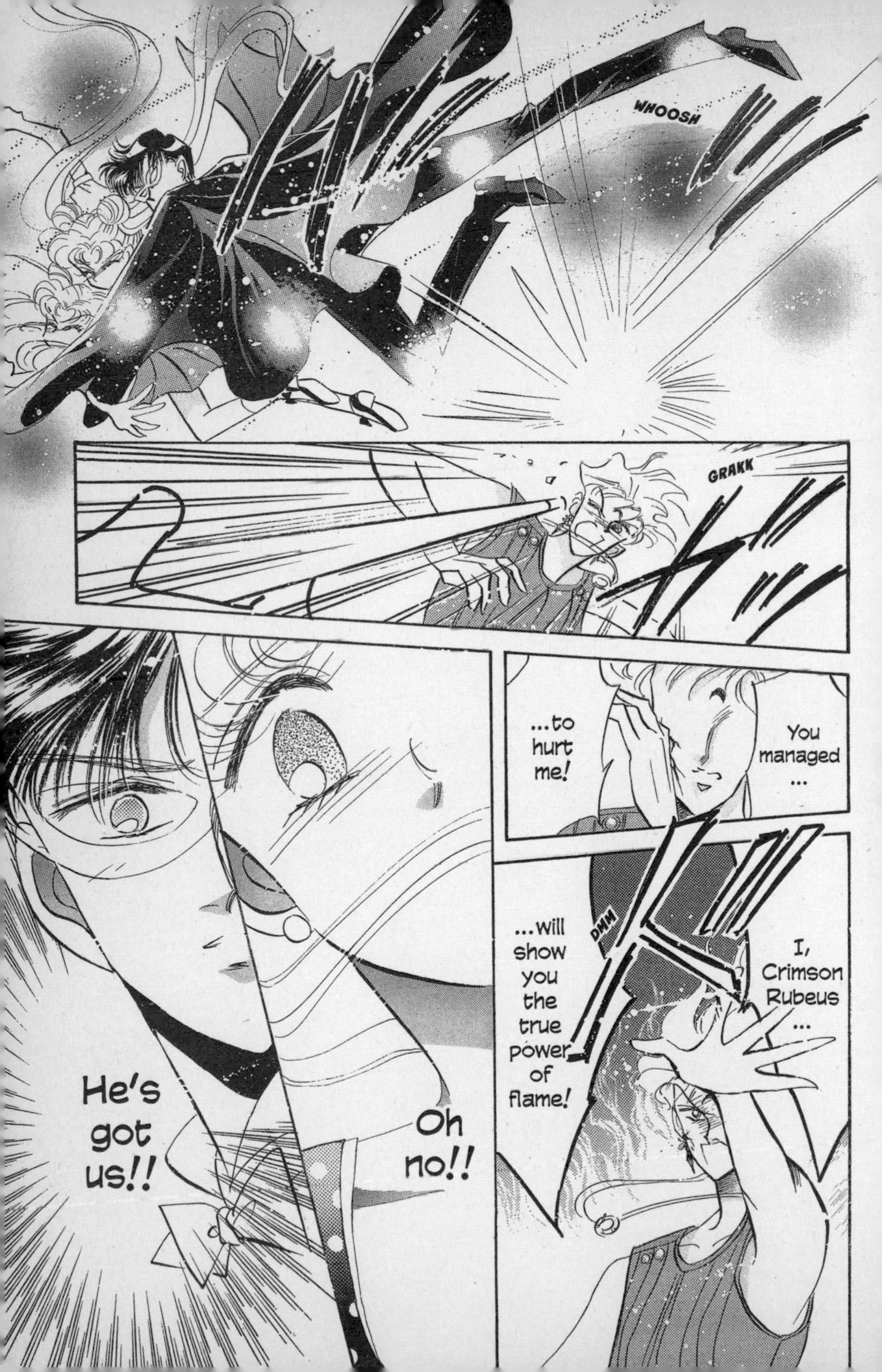
WHOOSH
GRAKK
You managed ...
...to hurt me!
I, Crimson Rubeus ...
...will show you the true power of flame!
DMM
Oh no!!
He's got us!!

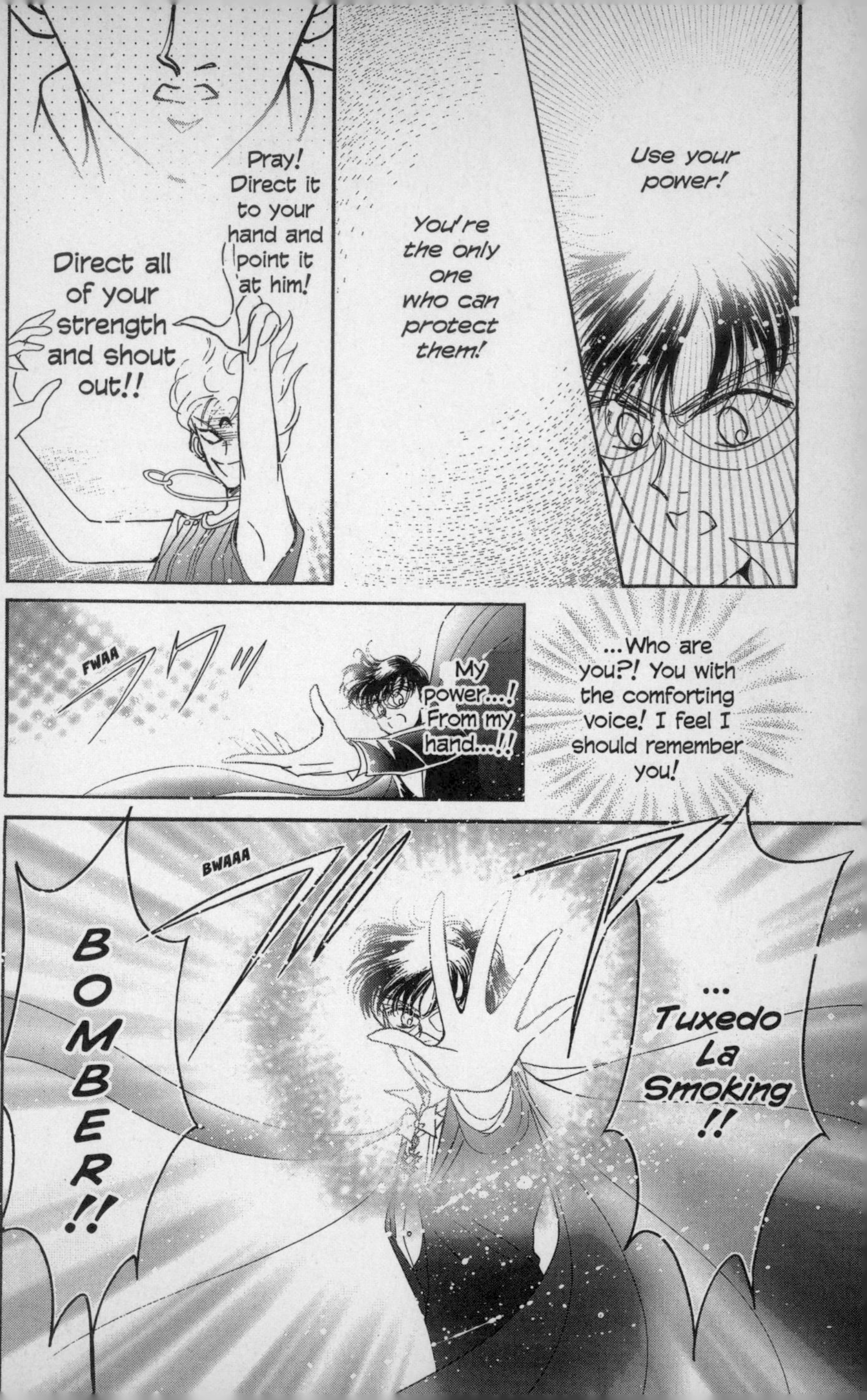

Use your power!
You're the only one who can protect them!
Pray! Direct it to your hand and point it at him!
Direct all of your strength and shout out!!
...Who are you?! You with the comforting voice! I feel I should remember you!
My power...! From my hand...!!
FWAA
BWAAA
... Tuxedo La Smoking !!
BOMBER!!

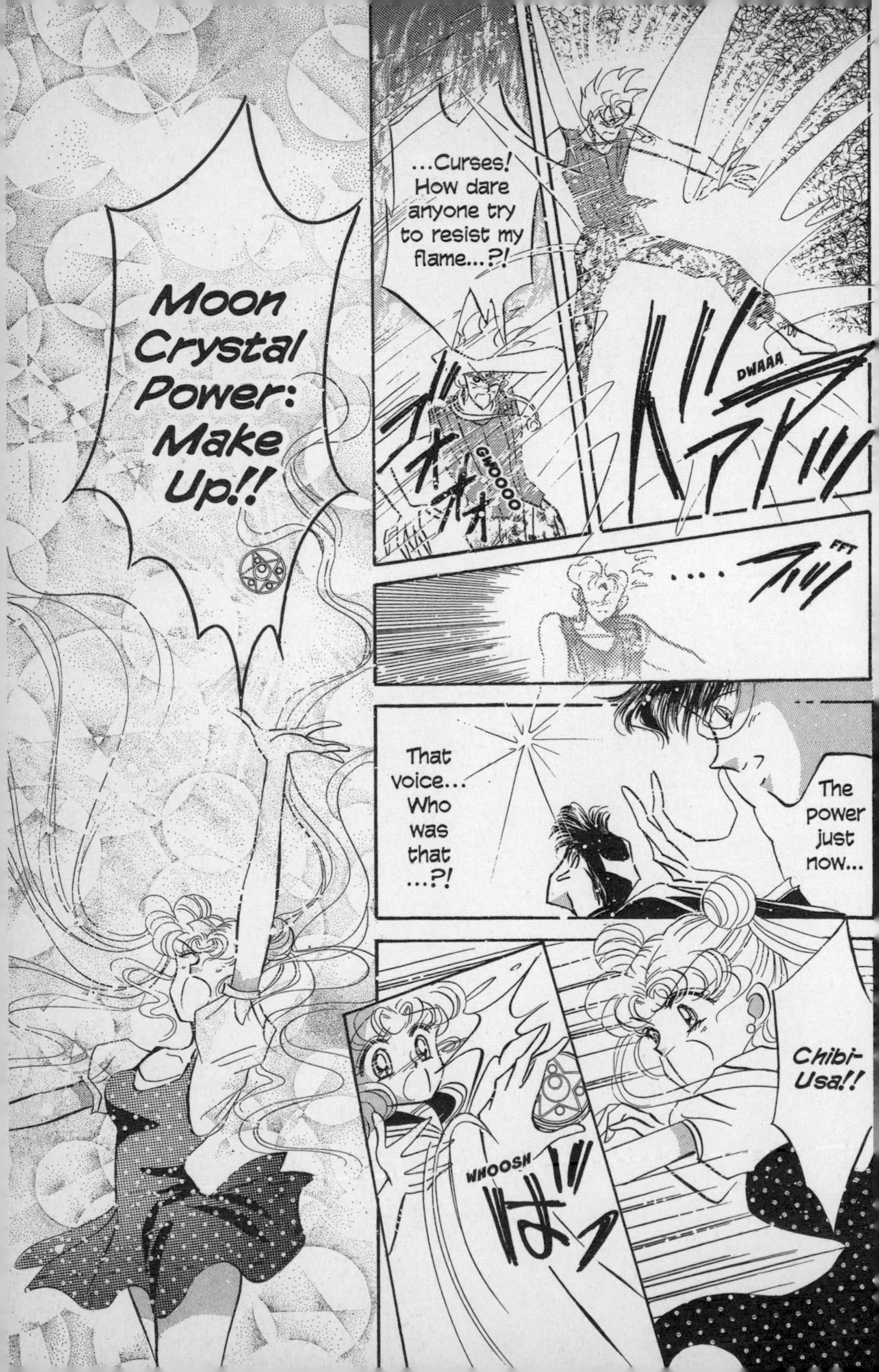
DWAAA
...Curses! How dare anyone try to resist my flame...?!
GWOOOOO
FFT
....
The power just now...
That voice... Who was that ...?!
Chibi-Usa!!
WHOOSH
Moon Crystal Power: Make Up!!

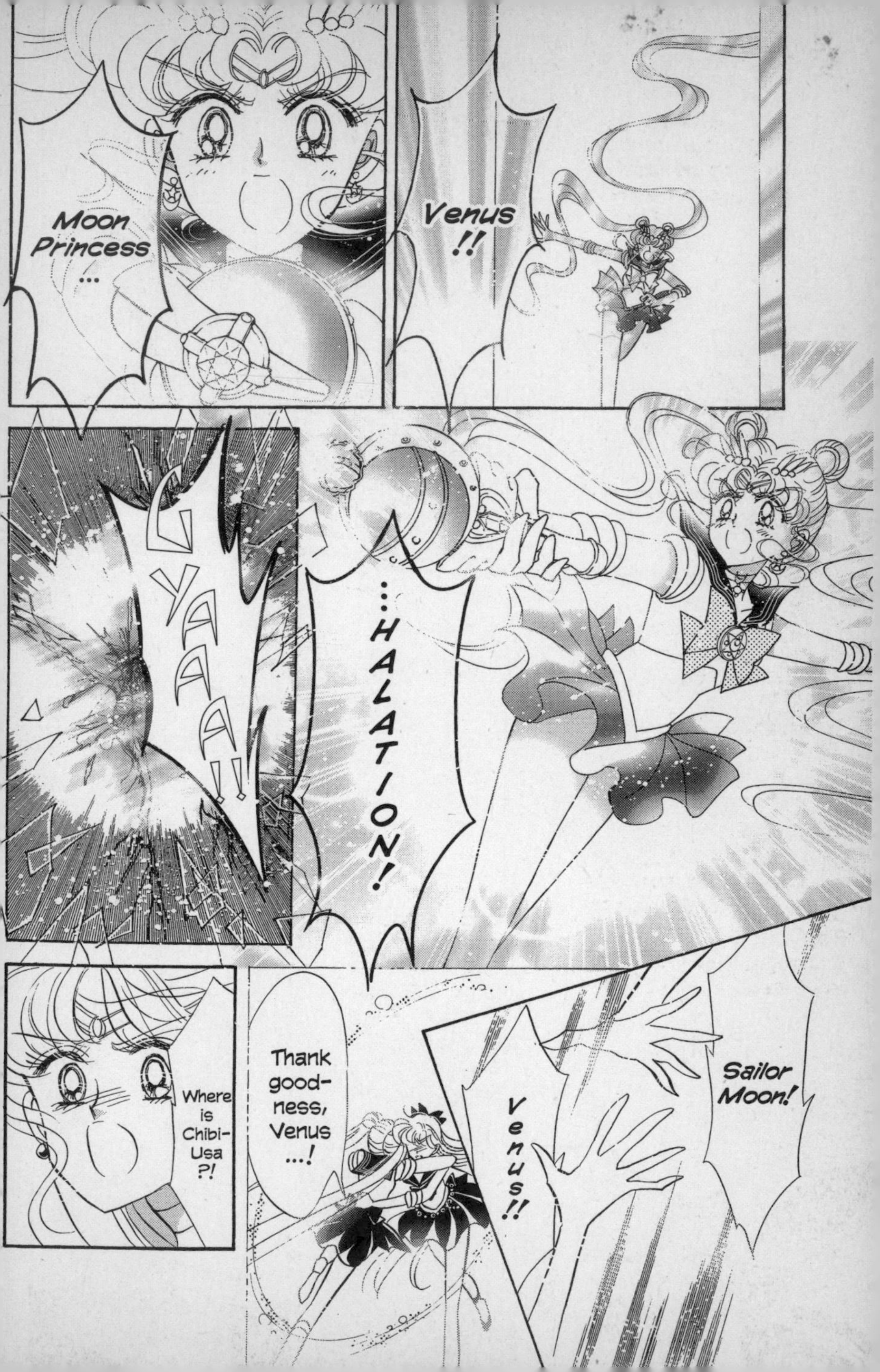
Venus !!
Moon Princess ...
...HALATION!
GYAAAA!!
Sailor Moon!
Venus!!
Thank goodness, Venus ...!
Where is Chibi-Usa ?!

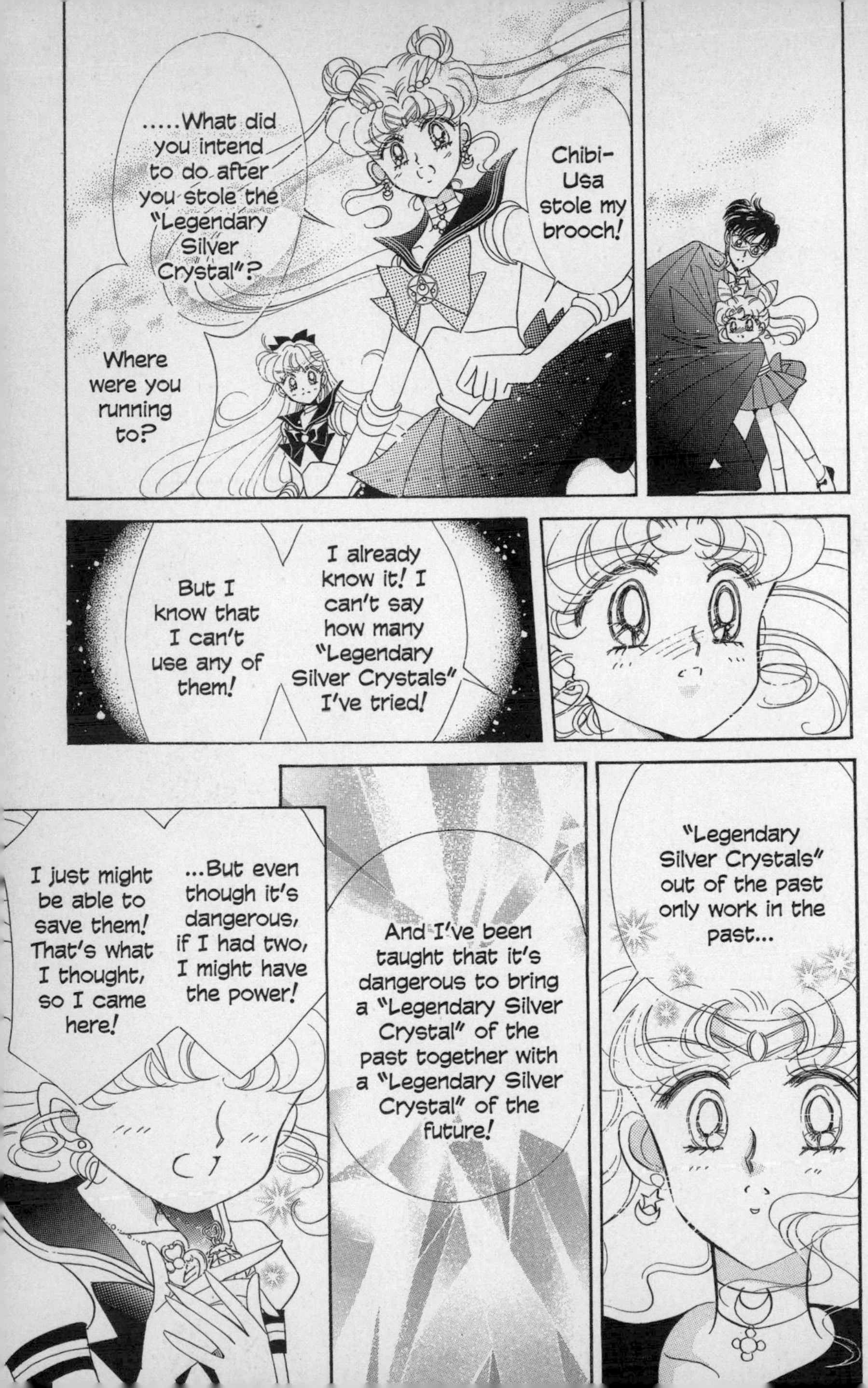
Chibi-Usa stole my brooch!
.....What did you intend to do after you stole the "Legendary Silver Crystal"?
Where were you running to?
I already know it! I can't say how many "Legendary Silver Crystals" I've tried!
But I know that I can't use any of them!
"Legendary Silver Crystals" out of the past only work in the past...
And I've been taught that it's dangerous to bring a "Legendary Silver Crystal" of the past together with a "Legendary Silver Crystal" of the future!
...But even though it's dangerous, if I had two, I might have the power!
I just might be able to save them! That's what I thought, so I came here!

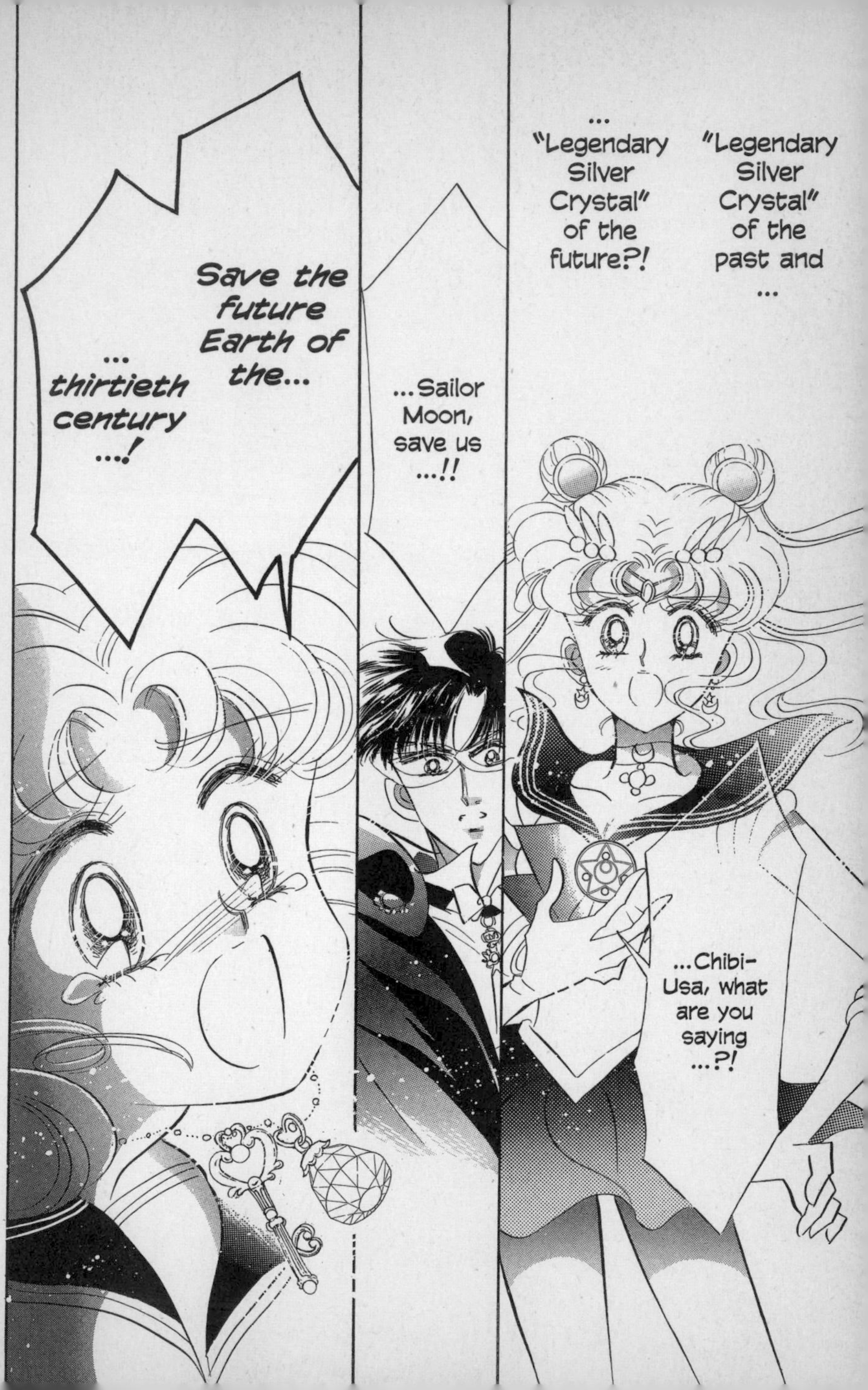
"Legendary Silver Crystal" of the past and ...
... "Legendary Silver Crystal" of the future?!
...Chibi-Usa, what are you saying ...?!
...Sailor Moon, save us ...!!
Save the future Earth of the...
... thirtieth century ...!

Act 19 Time Warp, Sailor Pluto

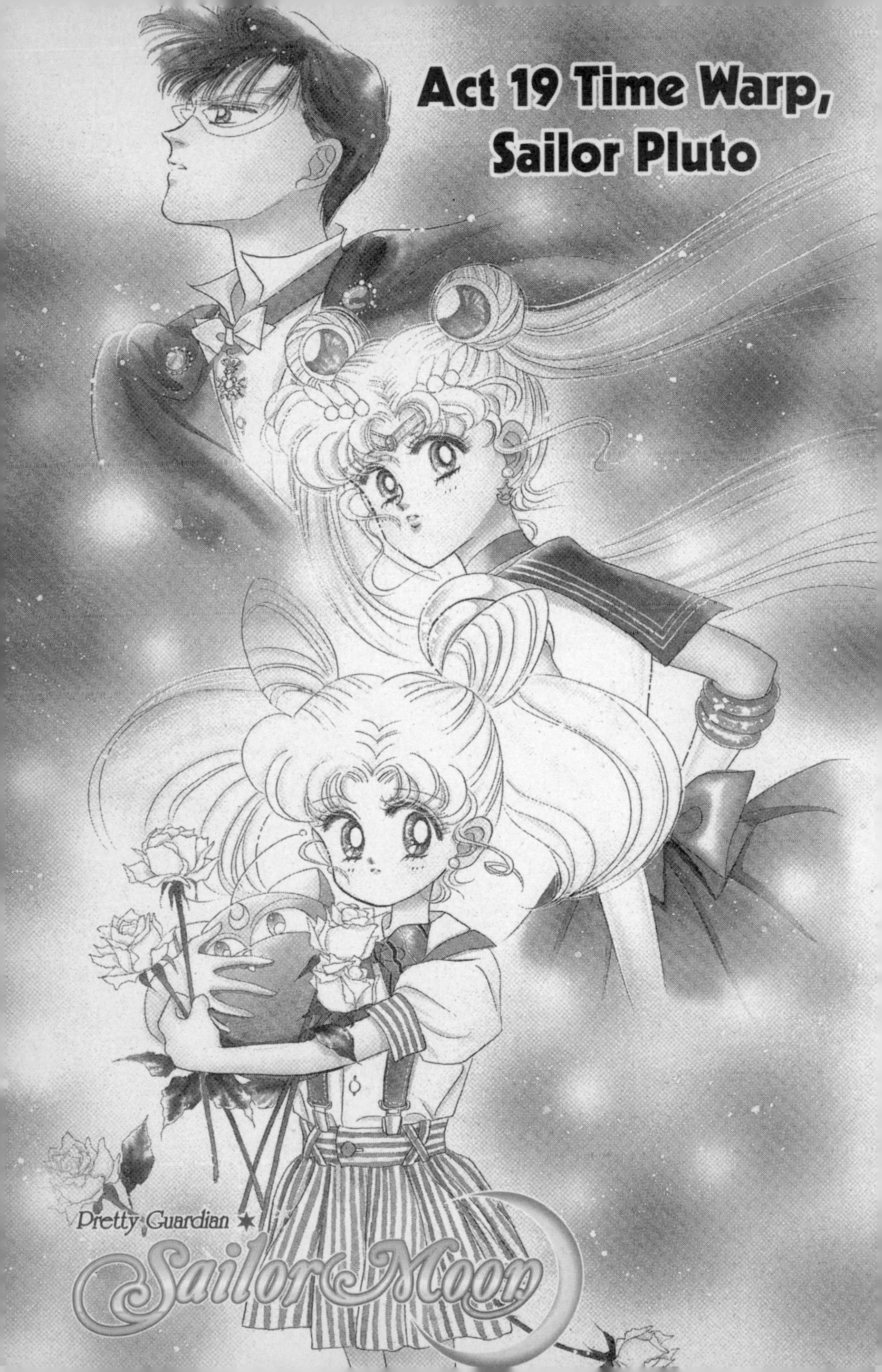
Pretty Guardian
Sailor Moon

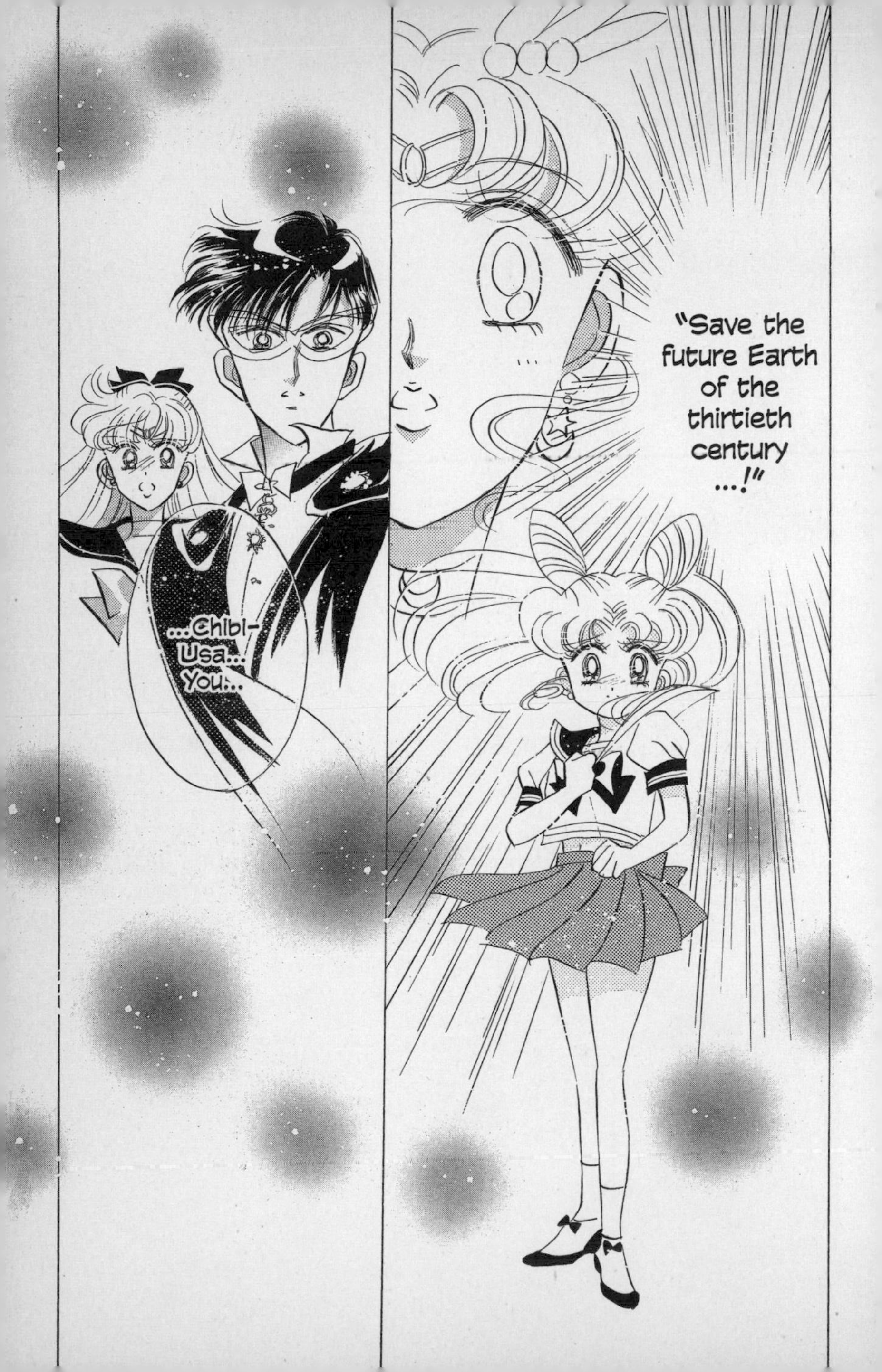
"Save the future Earth of the thirtieth century ...!"
...Chibi-Usa... You...

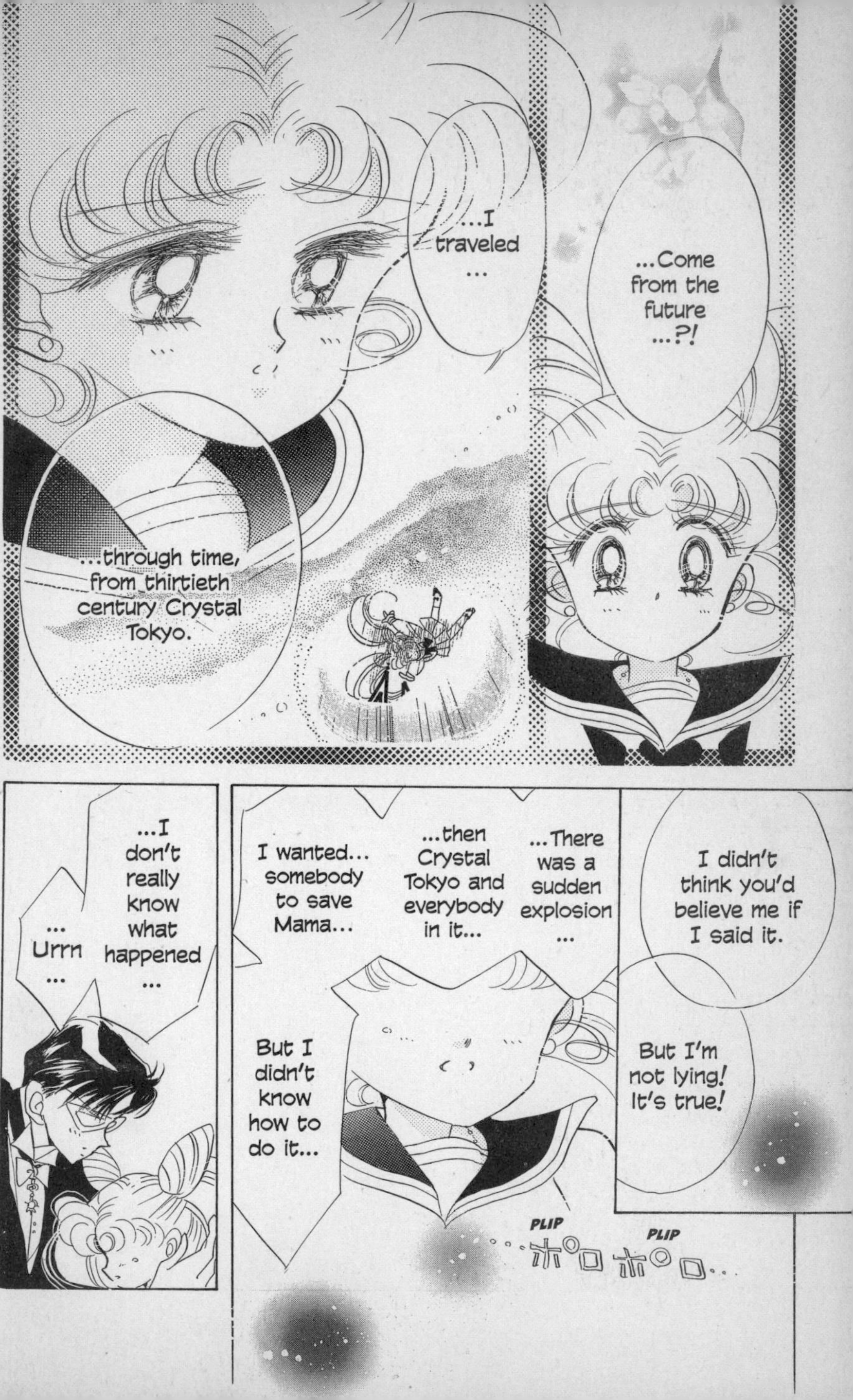
...Come from the future ...?!
...I traveled ...
...through time, from thirtieth century Crystal Tokyo.
I didn't think you'd believe me if I said it.
But I'm not lying! It's true!
...There was a sudden explosion ...
...then Crystal Tokyo and everybody in it...
I wanted... somebody to save Mama...
But I didn't know how to do it...
PLIP
PLIP
ポロポロ...
...I don't really know what happened ...
... Urrn ...

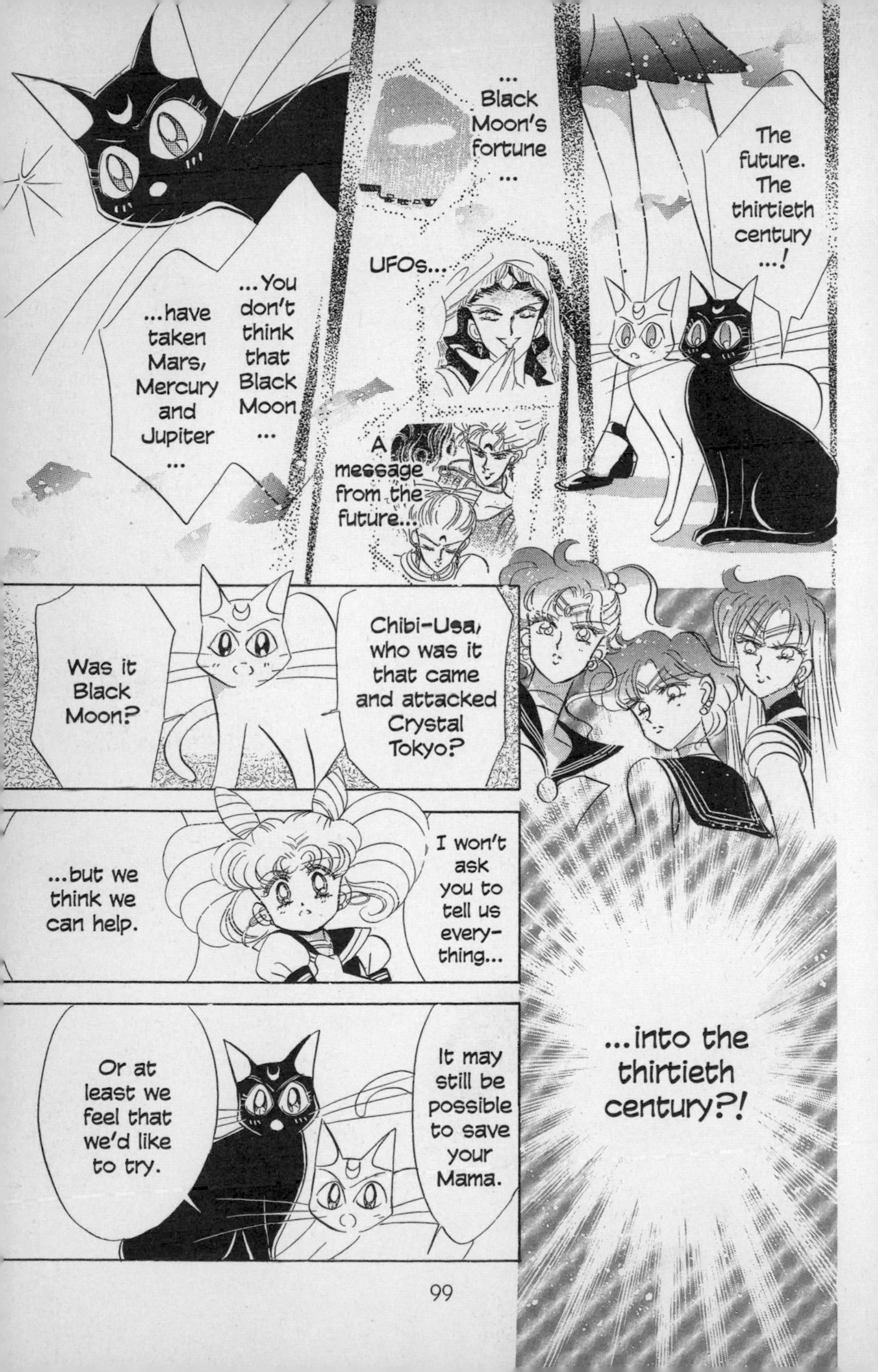

The future. The thirtieth century ...!
... Black Moon's fortune ...
UFOs...
A message from the future...
...You don't think that Black Moon ...
...have taken Mars, Mercury and Jupiter ...
...into the thirtieth century?!
Chibi-Usa, who was it that came and attacked Crystal Tokyo?
Was it Black Moon?
I won't ask you to tell us every-thing...
...but we think we can help.
It may still be possible to save your Mama.
Or at least we feel that we'd like to try.

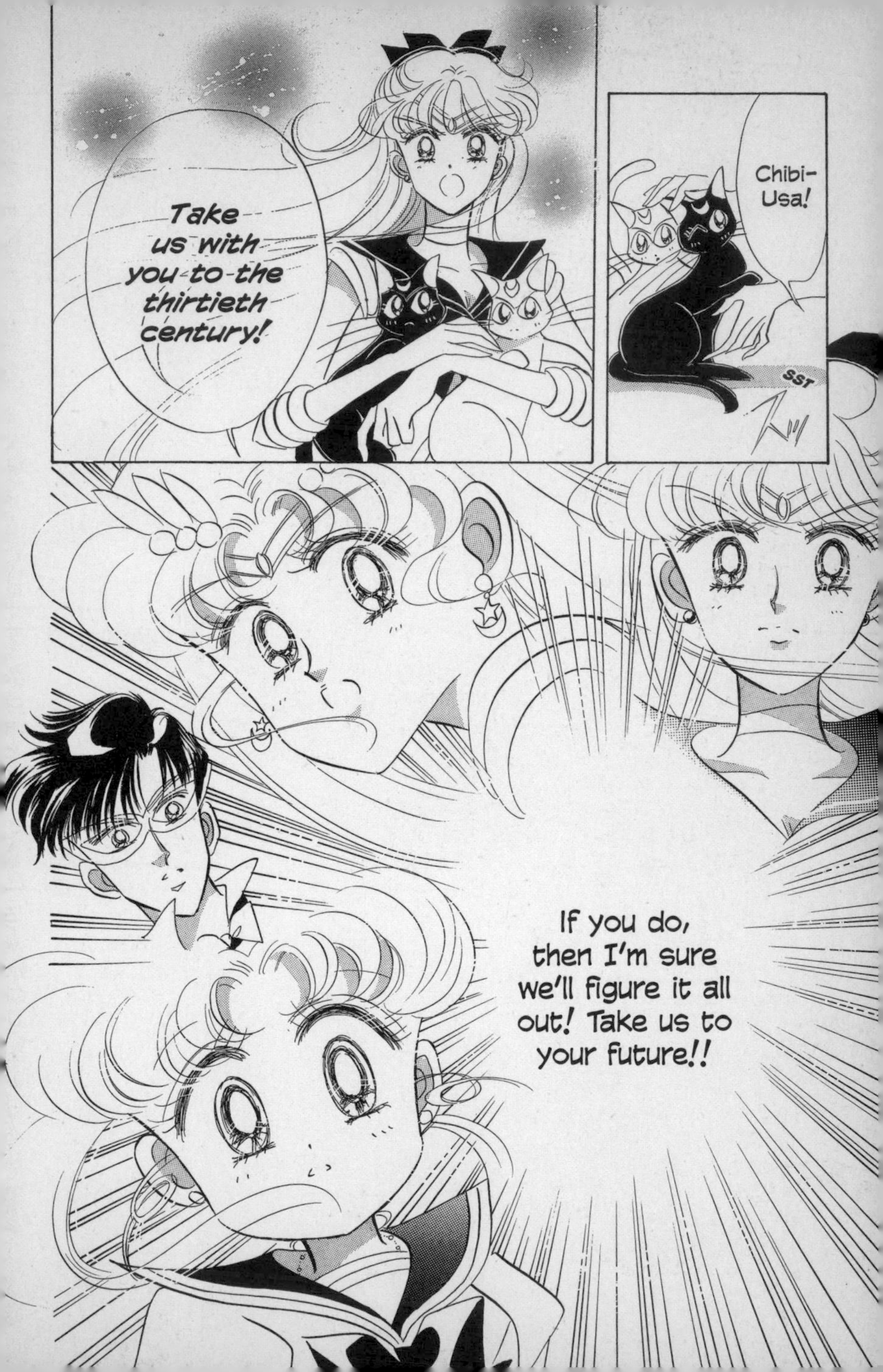

Chibi-Usa!
SST
Take us with you to the thirtieth century!
If you do, then I'm sure we'll figure it all out! Take us to your future!!

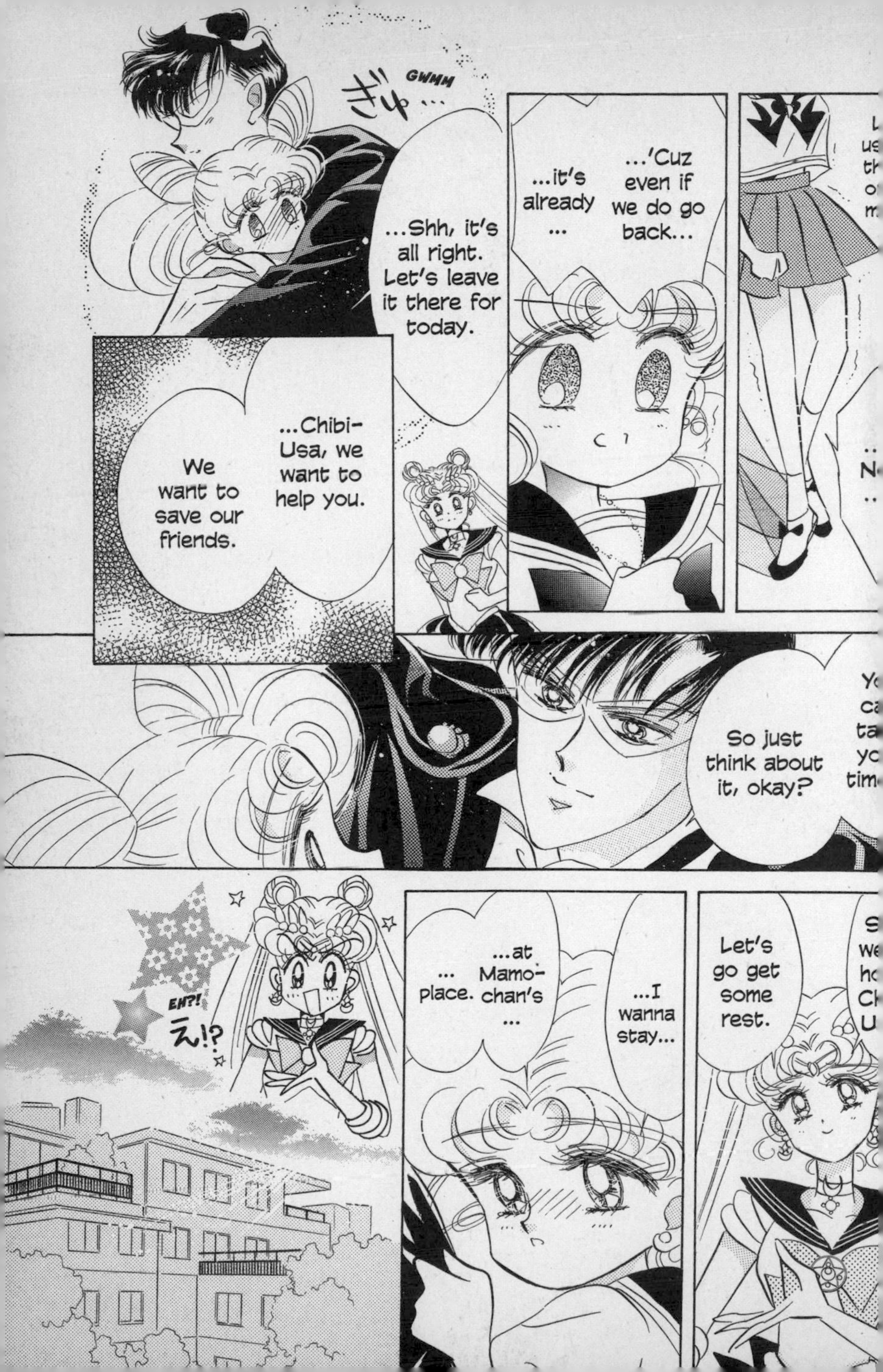
...'Cuz even if we do go back...
...it's already ...
GWMM
ぎゅ...
...Shh, it's all right. Let's leave it there for today.
...Chibi-Usa, we want to help you.
We want to save our friends.
So just think about it, okay?
Let's go get some rest.
...I wanna stay...
...at Mamo-chan's ...
... place.
EH?!
え!?

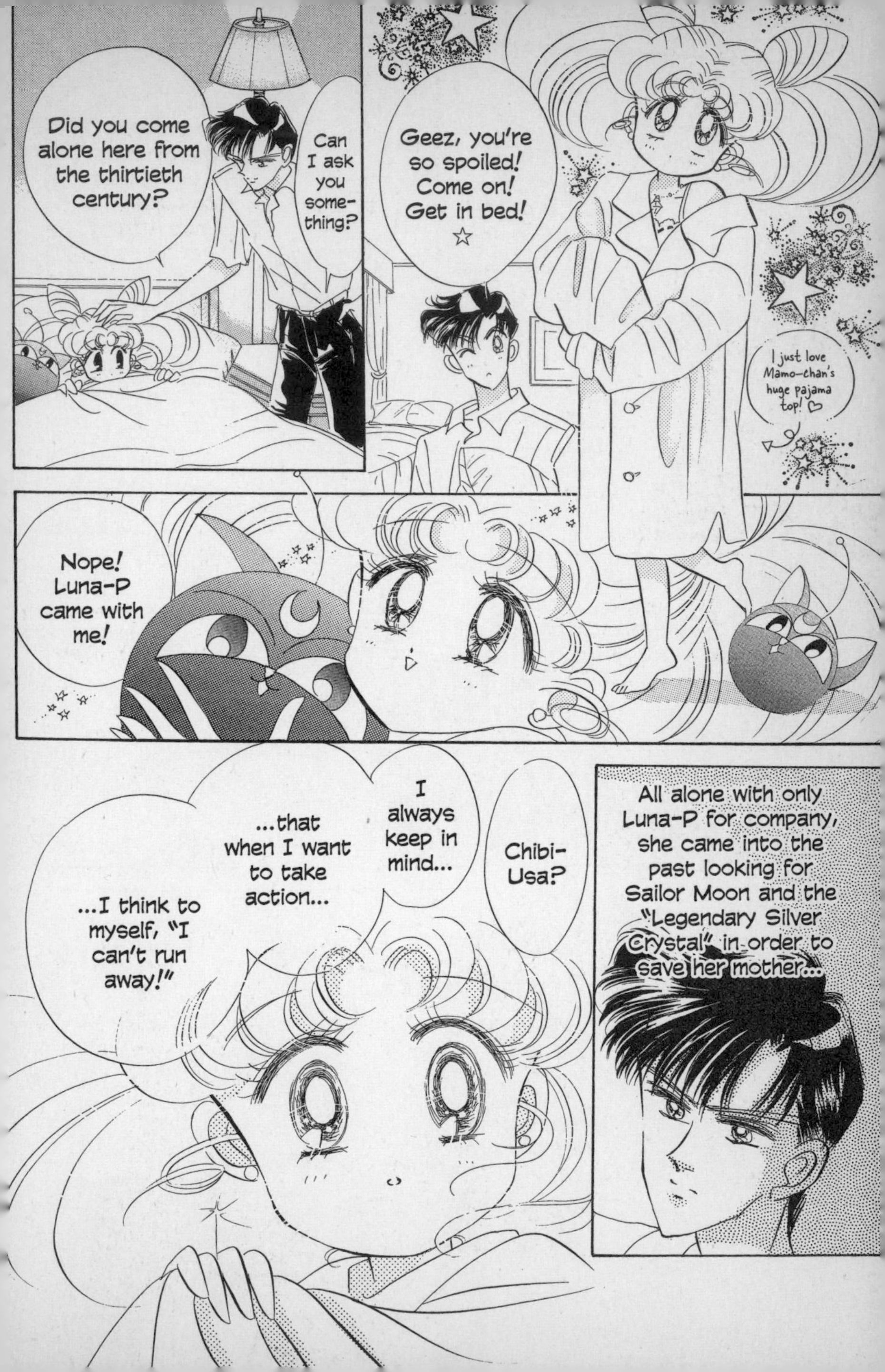
Geez, you're so spoiled! Come on! Get in bed! ☆
I just love Mamo-chan's huge pajama top! ♡
Can I ask you something?
Did you come alone here from the thirtieth century?
Nope! Luna-P came with me!
All alone with only Luna-P for company, she came into the past looking for Sailor Moon and the "Legendary Silver Crystal" in order to save her mother...
Chibi-Usa?
I always keep in mind...
...that when I want to take action...
...I think to myself, "I can't run away!"

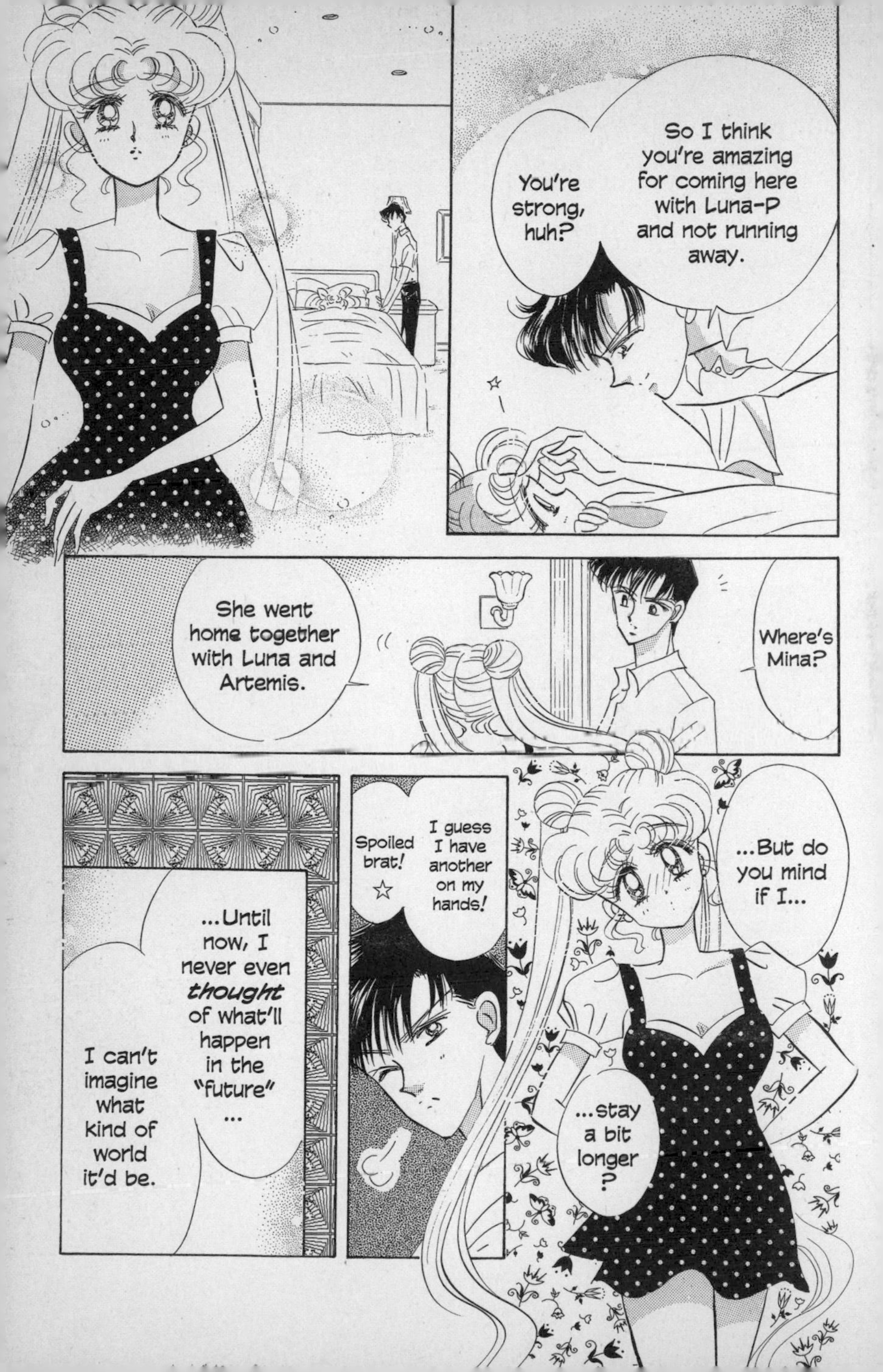
So I think you're amazing for coming here with Luna-P and not running away.
You're strong, huh?
Where's Mina?
She went home together with Luna and Artemis.
...But do you mind if I...
...stay a bit longer?
I guess I have another on my hands!
Spoiled brat! ☆
...Until now, I never even *thought* of what'll happen in the "future"...
I can't imagine what kind of world it'd be.

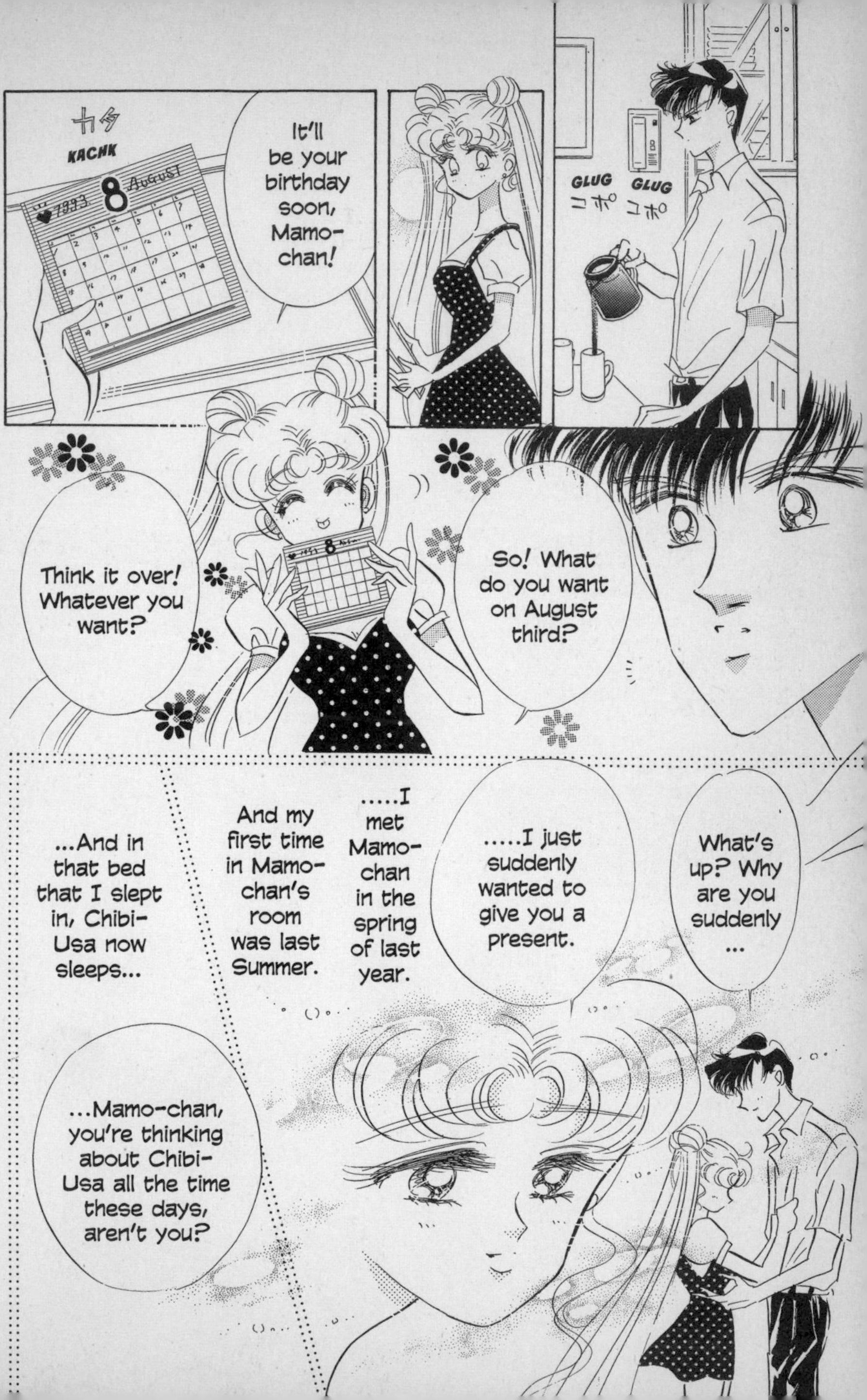
GLUG GLUG
コポ コポ
カタ
KACHK
1993 8 AUGUST
It'll be your birthday soon, Mamo-chan!
So! What do you want on August third?
Think it over! Whatever you want?
What's up? Why are you suddenly ...
.....I just suddenly wanted to give you a present.
.....I met Mamo-chan in the spring of last year.
And my first time in Mamo-chan's room was last Summer.
...And in that bed that I slept in, Chibi-Usa now sleeps...
...Mamo-chan, you're thinking about Chibi-Usa all the time these days, aren't you?

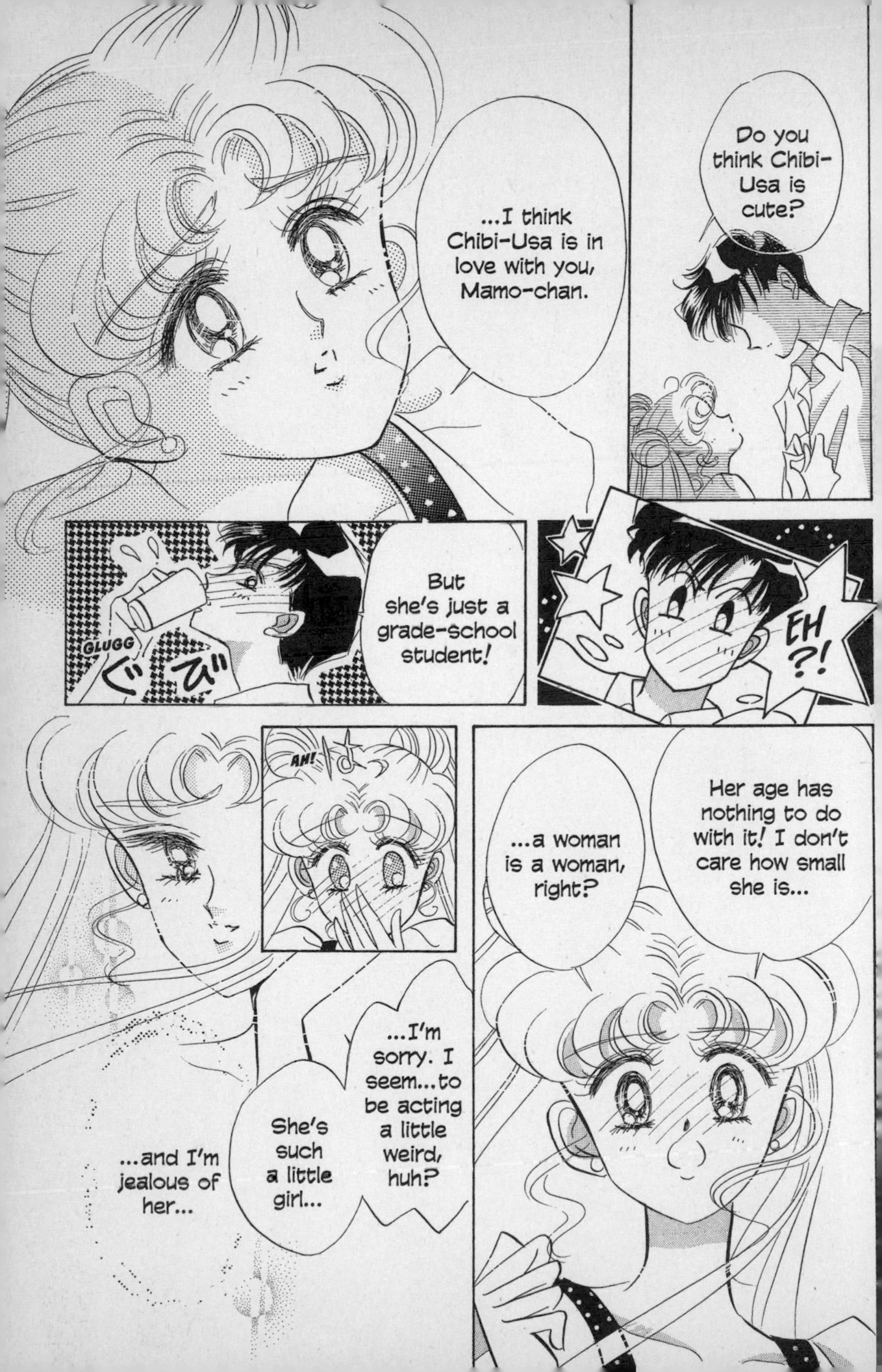
Do you think Chibi-Usa is cute?
...I think Chibi-Usa is in love with you, Mamo-chan.
EH?!
But she's just a grade-school student!
GLUGG
Her age has nothing to do with it! I don't care how small she is...
...a woman is a woman, right?
AH!
...I'm sorry. I seem...to be acting a little weird, huh?
She's such a little girl...
...and I'm jealous of her...

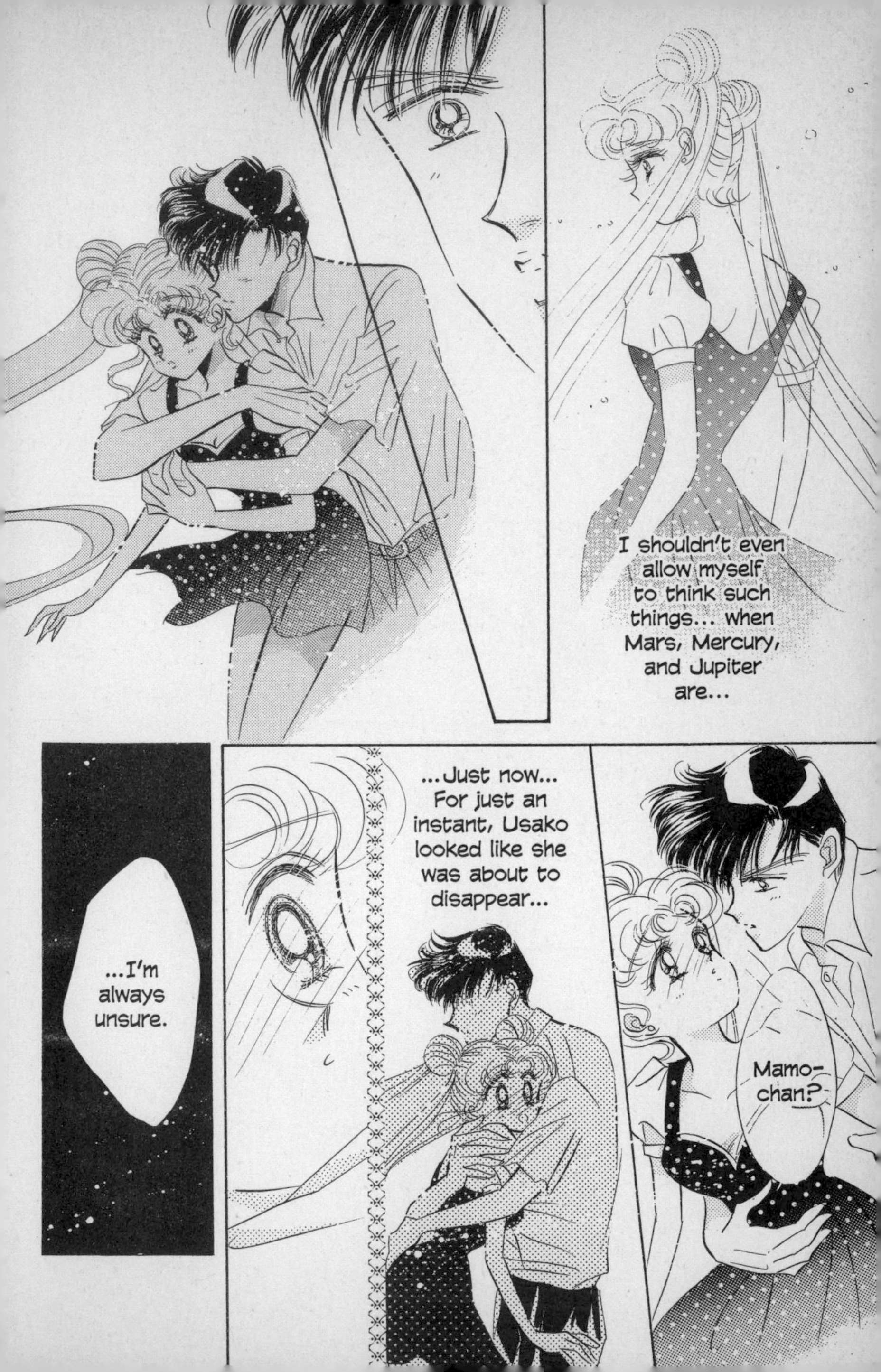
I shouldn't even allow myself to think such things... when Mars, Mercury, and Jupiter are...
Mamo-chan?
...Just now... For just an instant, Usako looked like she was about to disappear...
...I'm always unsure.

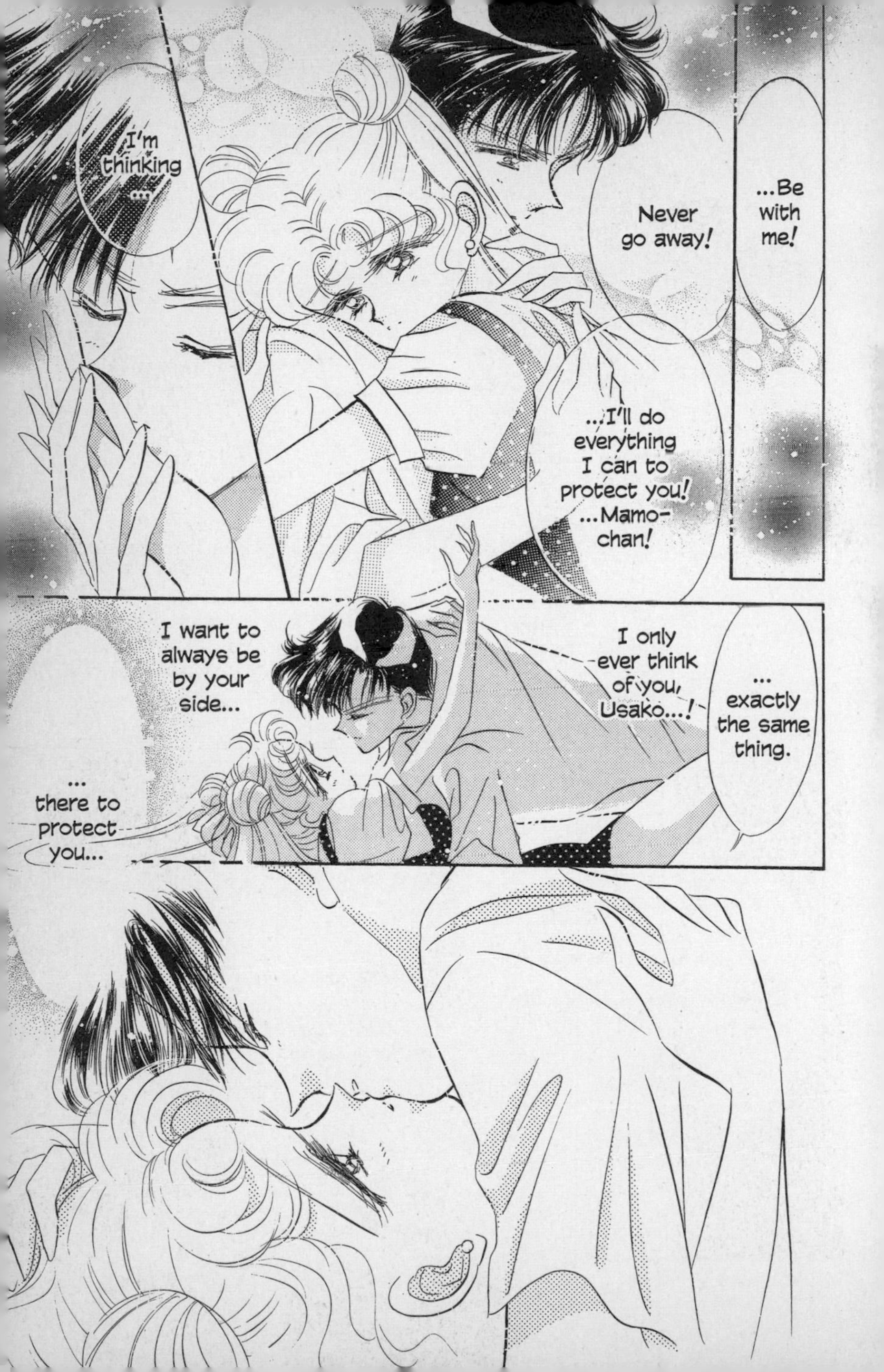
...Be with me!
Never go away!
...I'll do everything I can to protect you! ...Mamo-chan!
I'm thinking ...
... exactly the same thing.
I only ever think of you, Usako...!
I want to always be by your side...
... there to protect you...

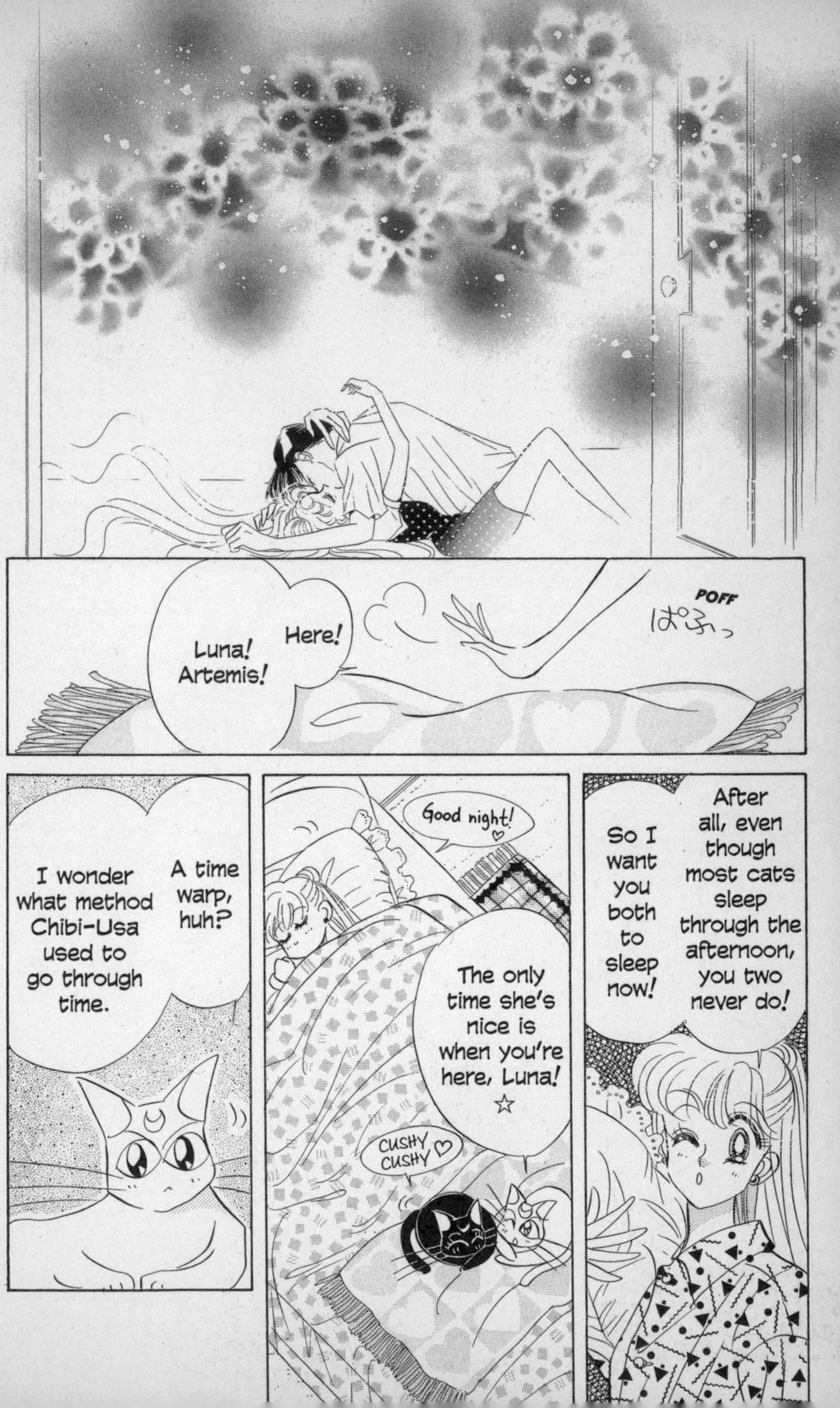
POFF
ぱふっ
Here!
Luna! Artemis!
After all, even though most cats sleep through the afternoon, you two never do!
So I want you both to sleep now!
Good night! ♡
The only time she's nice is when you're here, Luna! ☆
CUSHY CUSHY ♡
A time warp, huh?
I wonder what method Chibi-Usa used to go through time.

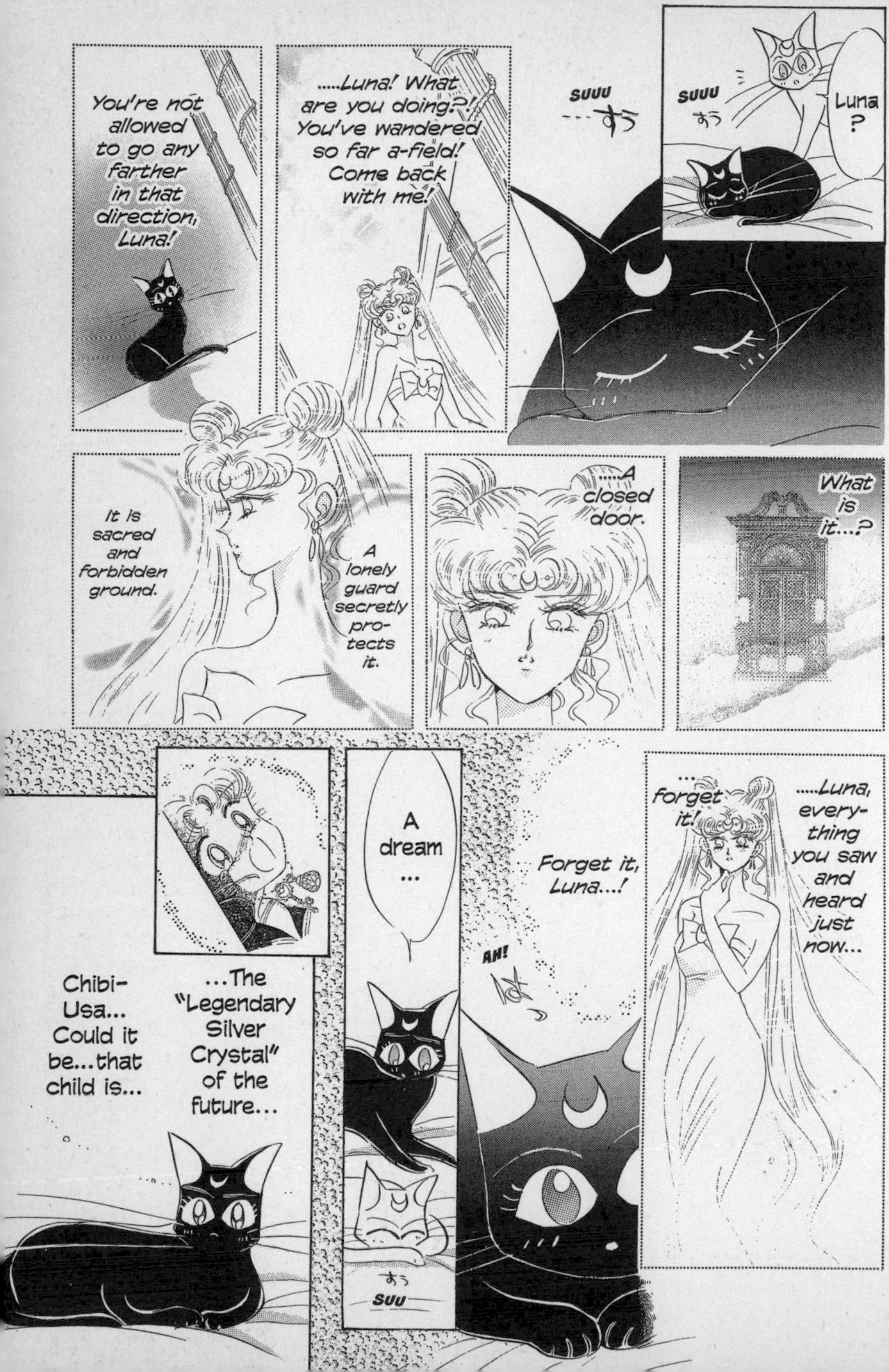
Luna ?
SUUU
すう
SUUU
すう
.....Luna! What are you doing?! You've wandered so far a-field! Come back with me!
You're not allowed to go any farther in that direction, Luna!
What is it...?
.....A closed door.
It is sacred and forbidden ground.
A lonely guard secretly protects it.
.....Luna, everything you saw and heard just now...
...forget it!
Forget it, Luna...!
AH!
はっ
A dream ...
すう
SUU
...The "Legendary Silver Crystal" of the future...
Chibi-Usa... Could it be...that child is...

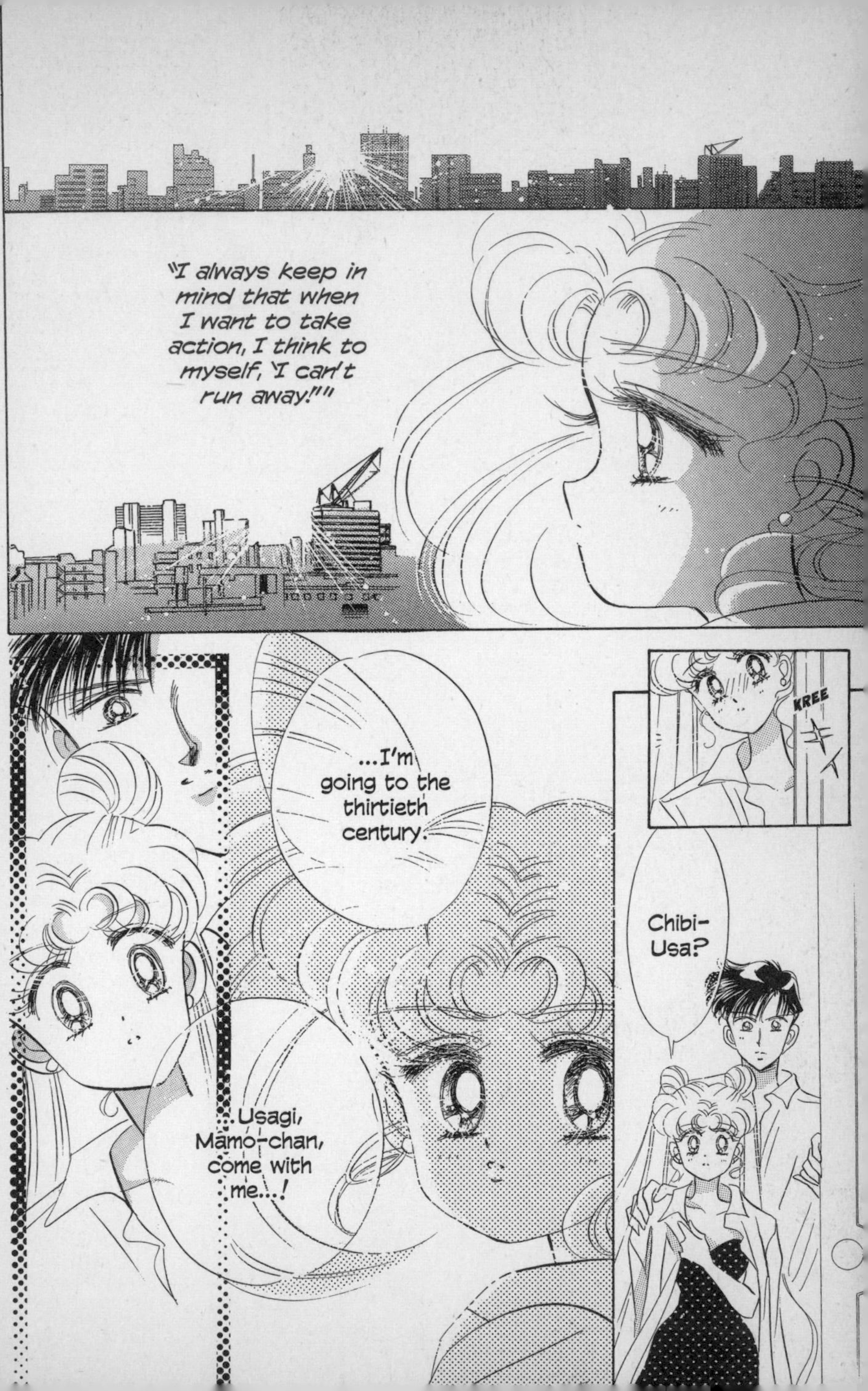
"I always keep in mind that when I want to take action, I think to myself, 'I can't run away!'"
KREE
Chibi-Usa?
...I'm going to the thirtieth century.
...Usagi, Mamo-chan, come with me...!

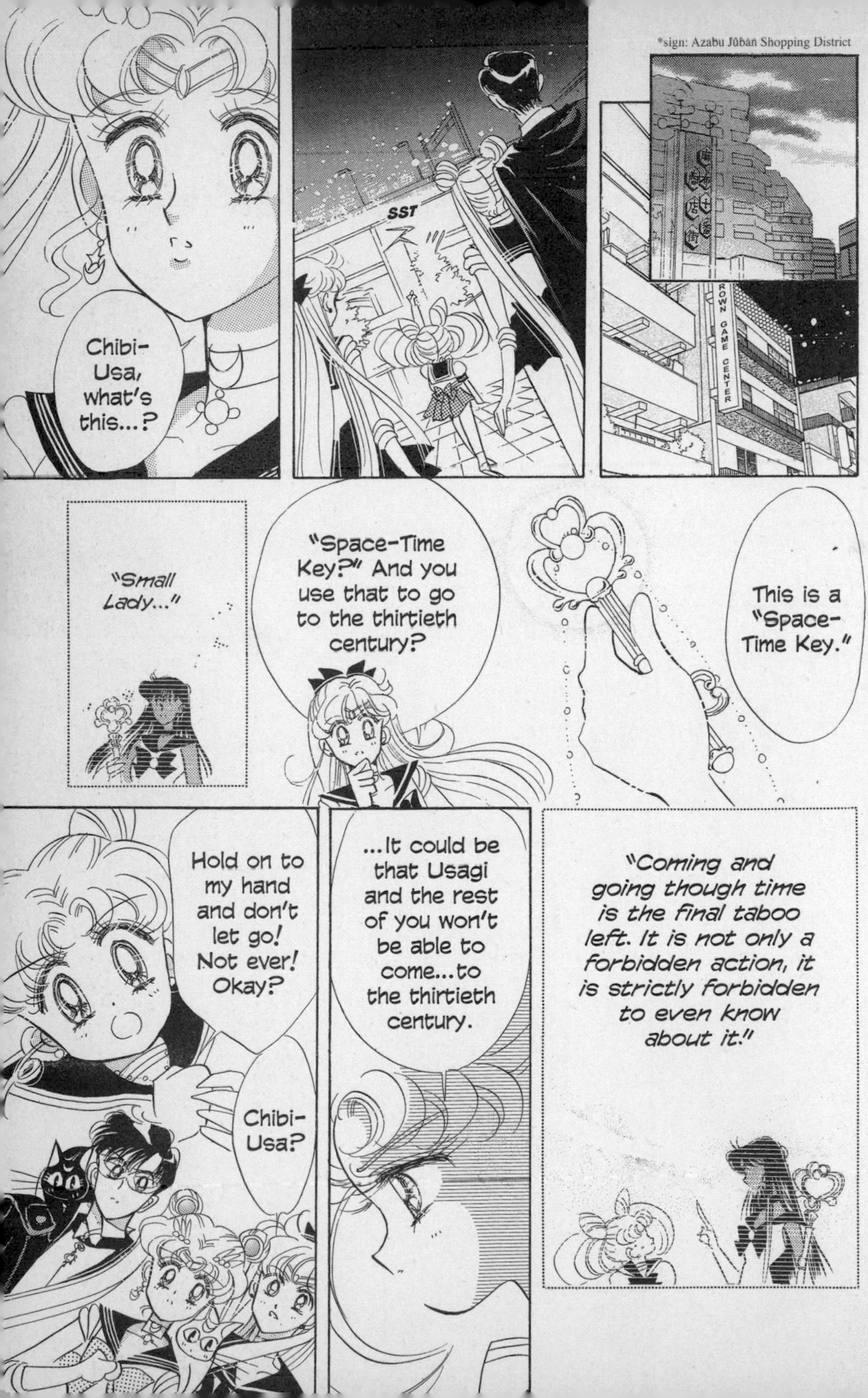
ROWN GAME CENTER
SST
Chibi-Usa, what's this...?
This is a "Space-Time Key."
"Space-Time Key?" And you use that to go to the thirtieth century?
"Small Lady..."
"Coming and going though time is the final taboo left. It is not only a forbidden action, it is strictly forbidden to even know about it."
...It could be that Usagi and the rest of you won't be able to come...to the thirtieth century.
Hold on to my hand and don't let go! Not ever! Okay?
Chibi-Usa?
*sign: Azabu Jûban Shopping District

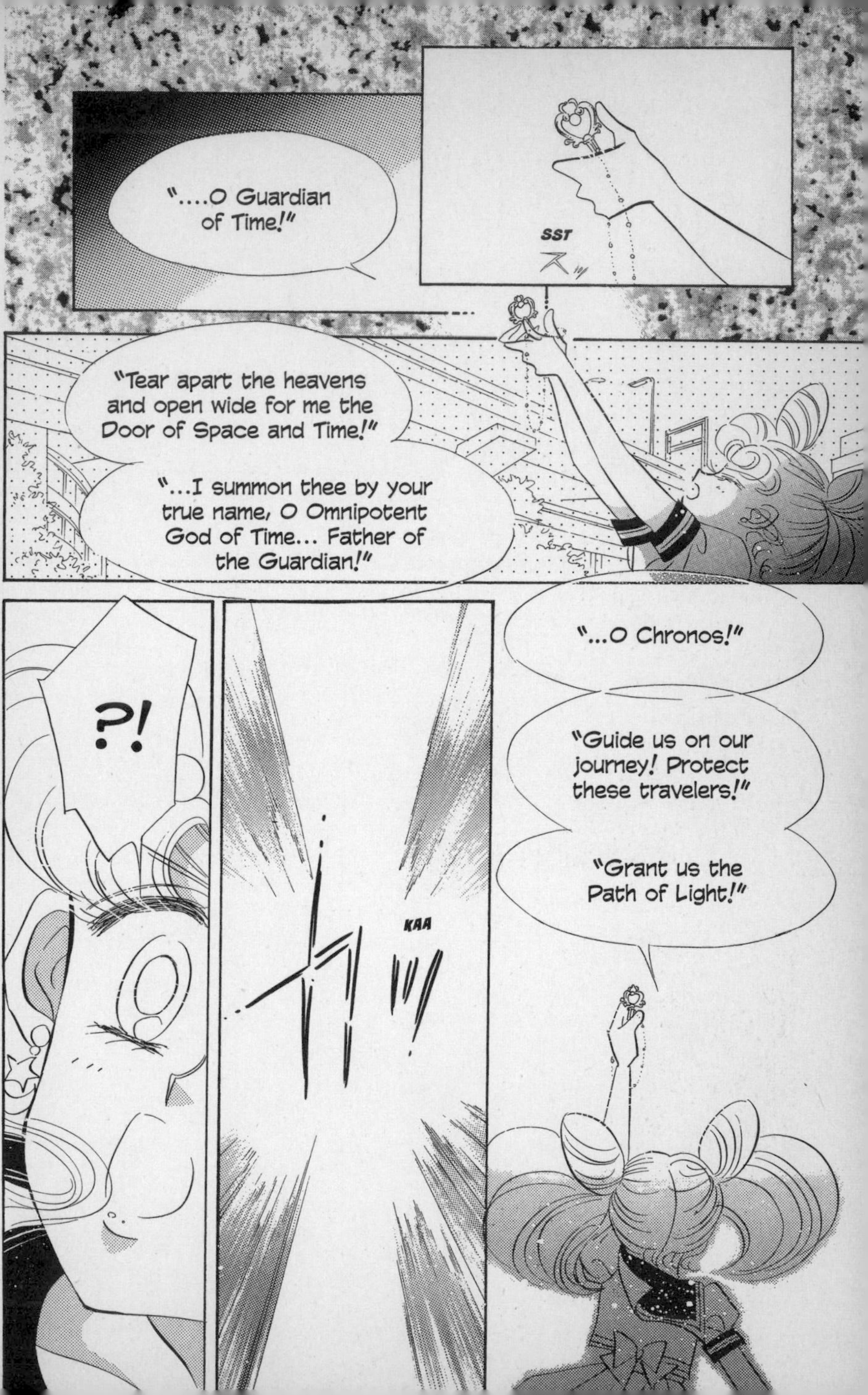
SST
スッ
"....O Guardian of Time!"
"Tear apart the heavens and open wide for me the Door of Space and Time!"
"...I summon thee by your true name, O Omnipotent God of Time... Father of the Guardian!"
"...O Chronos!"
"Guide us on our journey! Protect these travelers!"
"Grant us the Path of Light!"
KAA
?!

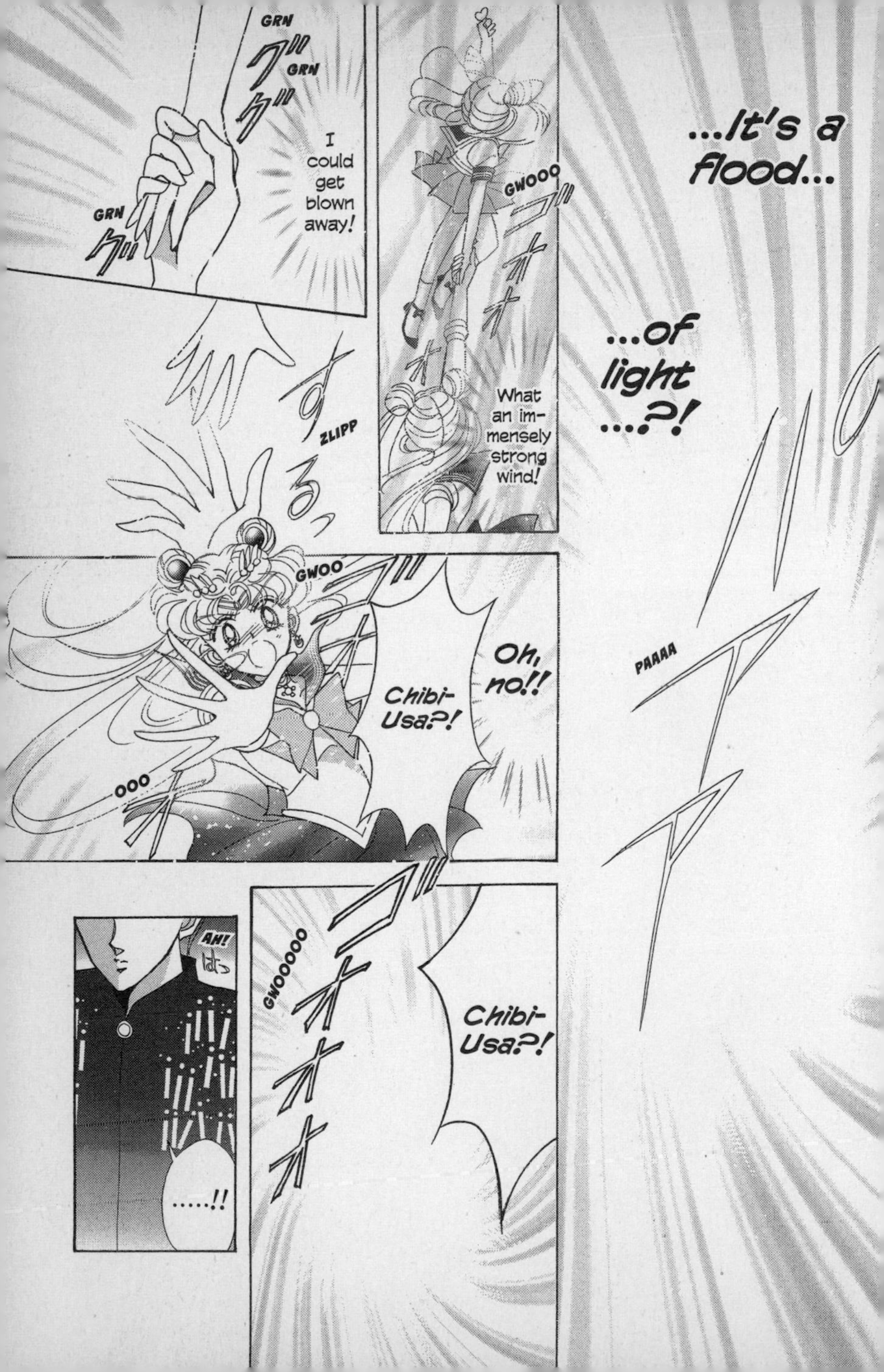
...It's a flood...
...of light ...?!
PAAAA
GWOOO
What an im-mensely strong wind!
GRN
GRN
I could get blown away!
GRN
ZLIPP
GWOO
Oh, no!!
Chibi-Usa?!
OOO
GWOOOOO
Chibi-Usa?!
AH!
.....!!

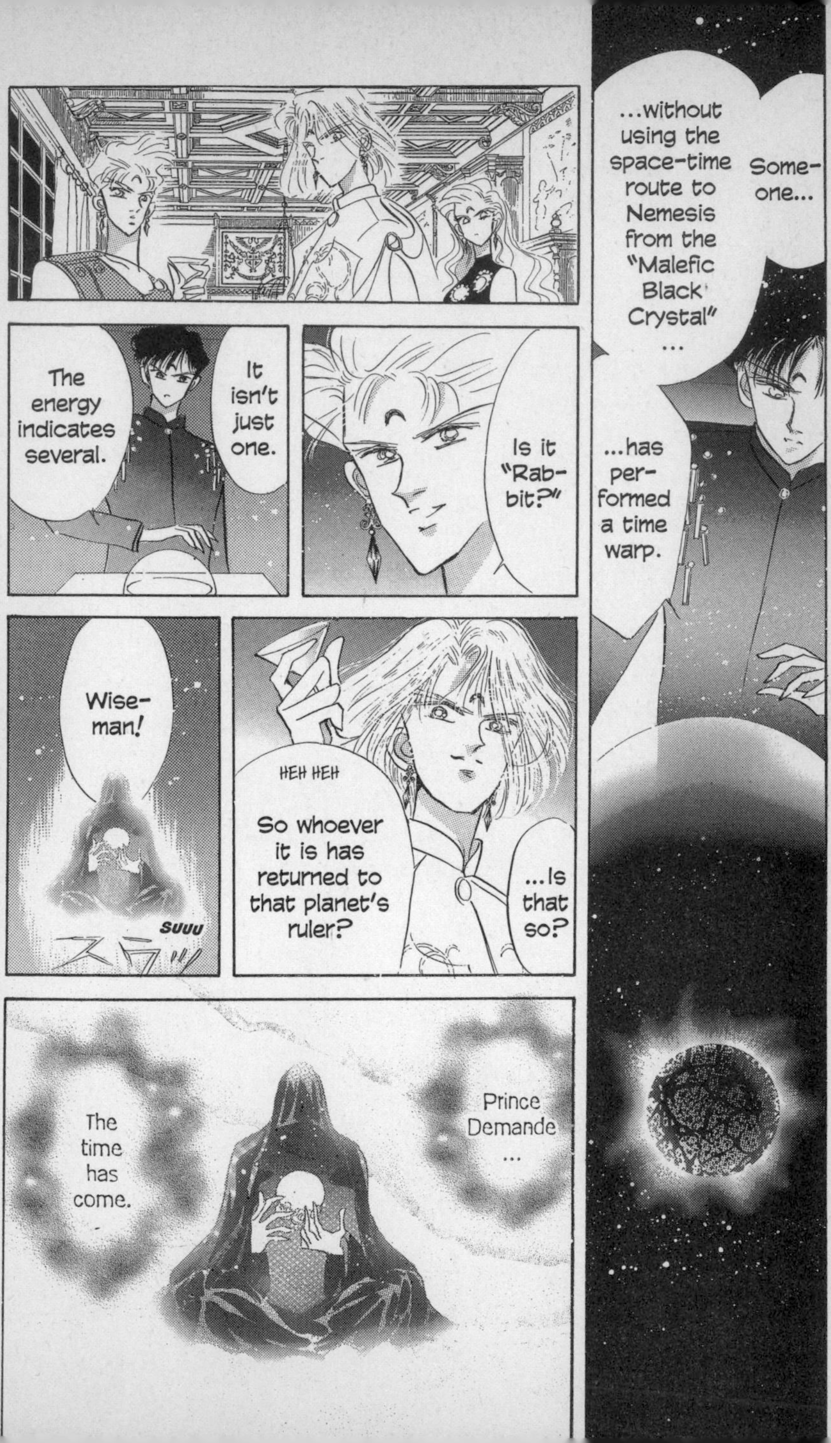
Some-one...
...without using the space-time route to Nemesis from the "Malefic Black Crystal"...
...has per-formed a time warp.
Is it "Rab-bit?"
It isn't just one.
The energy indicates several.
HEH HEH
So whoever it is has returned to that planet's ruler?
...Is that so?
Wise-man!
SUUU
Prince Demande...
The time has come.

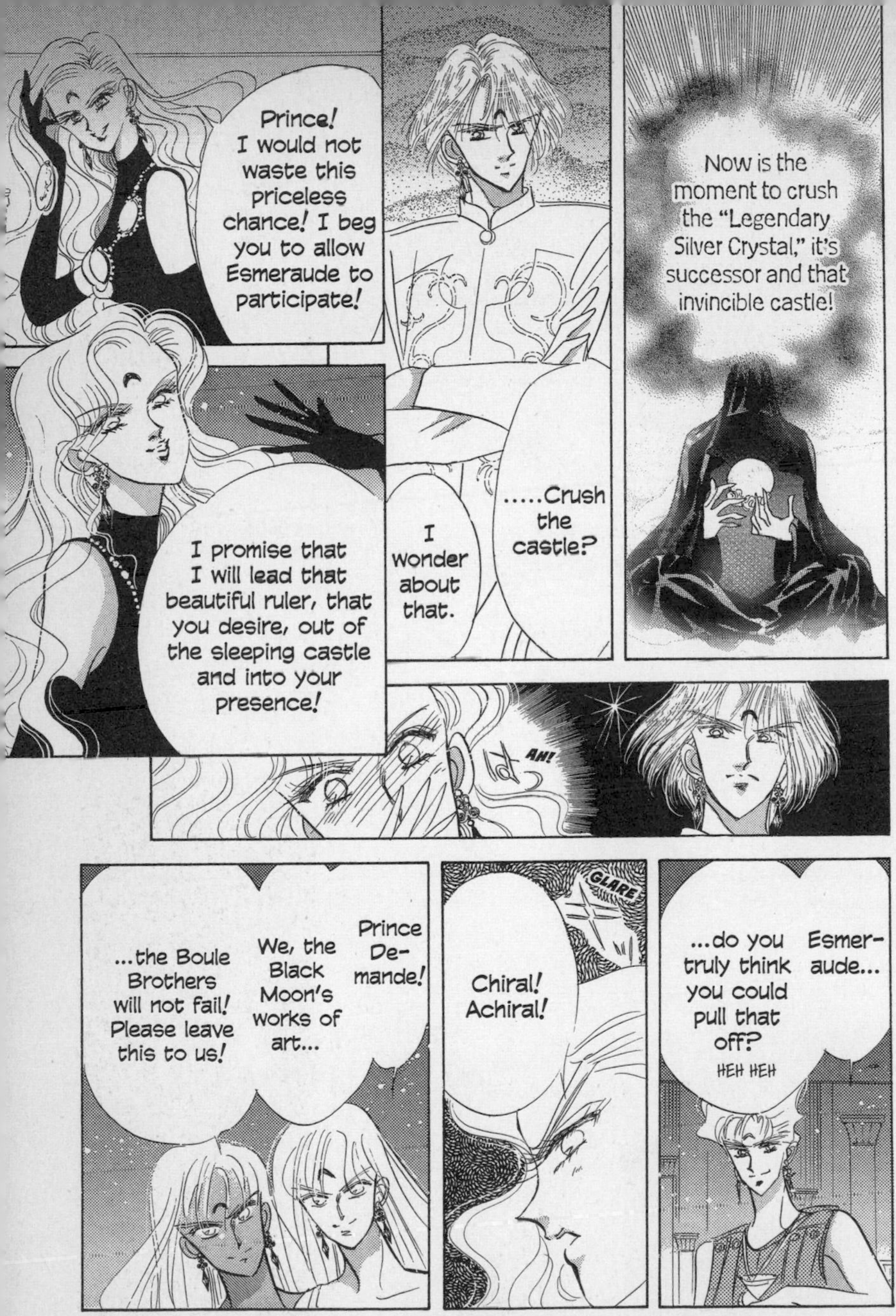
Now is the moment to crush the "Legendary Silver Crystal," it's successor and that invincible castle!
.....Crush the castle?
I wonder about that.
Prince! I would not waste this priceless chance! I beg you to allow Esmeraude to participate!
I promise that I will lead that beautiful ruler, that you desire, out of the sleeping castle and into your presence!
AH!
Esmer-aude...
...do you truly think you could pull that off?
HEH HEH
GLARE
Chiral! Achiral!
Prince De-mande!
We, the Black Moon's works of art...
...the Boule Brothers will not fail! Please leave this to us!

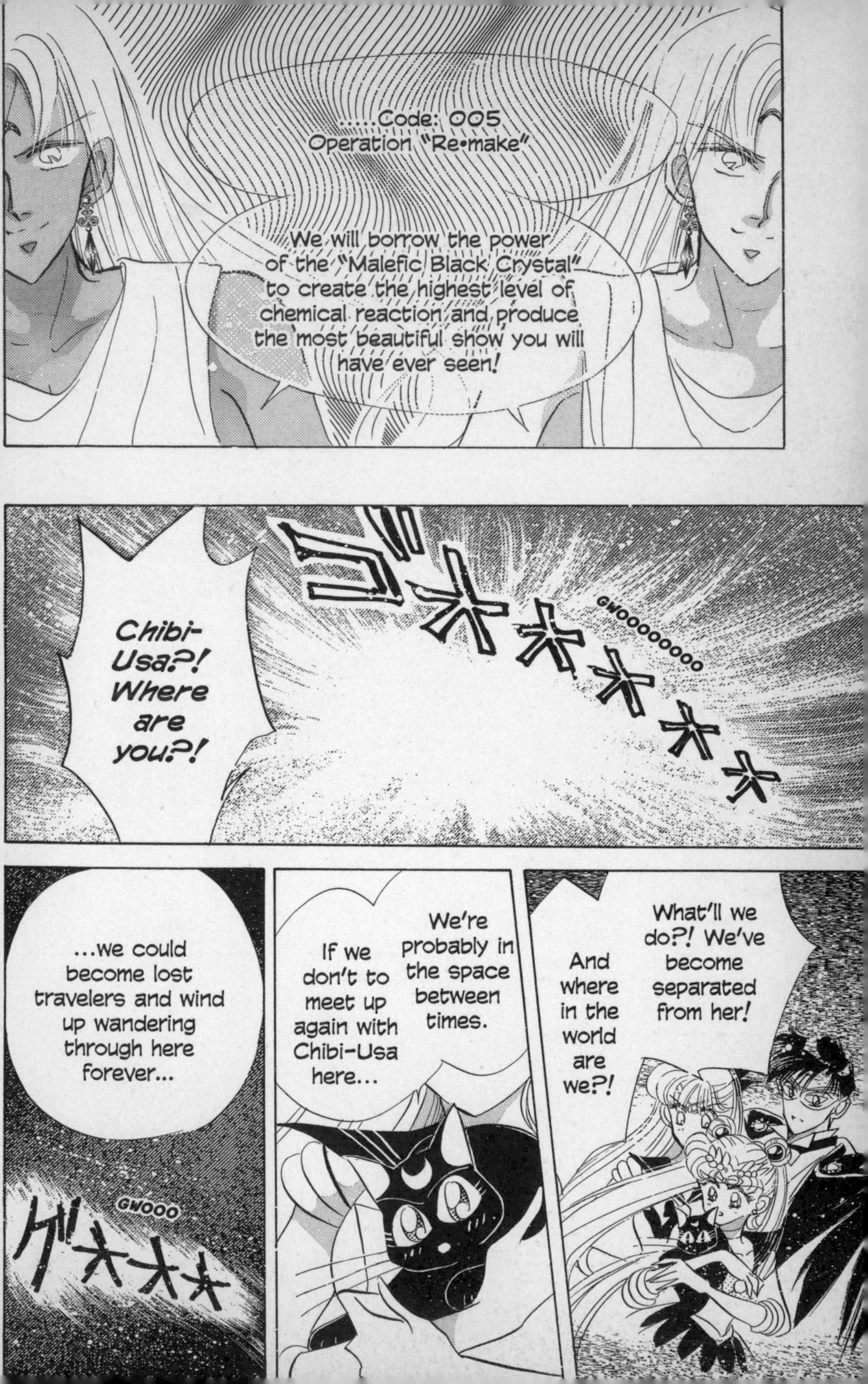
.....Code: 005
Operation "Re•make"
We will borrow the power of the "Malefic Black Crystal" to create the highest level of chemical reaction and produce the most beautiful show you will have ever seen!
GWOOOOOOOOO
Chibi-Usa?! Where are you?!
What'll we do?! We've become separated from her!
And where in the world are we?!
We're probably in the space between times.
If we don't to meet up again with Chibi-Usa here...
...we could become lost travelers and wind up wandering through here forever...
GWOOO

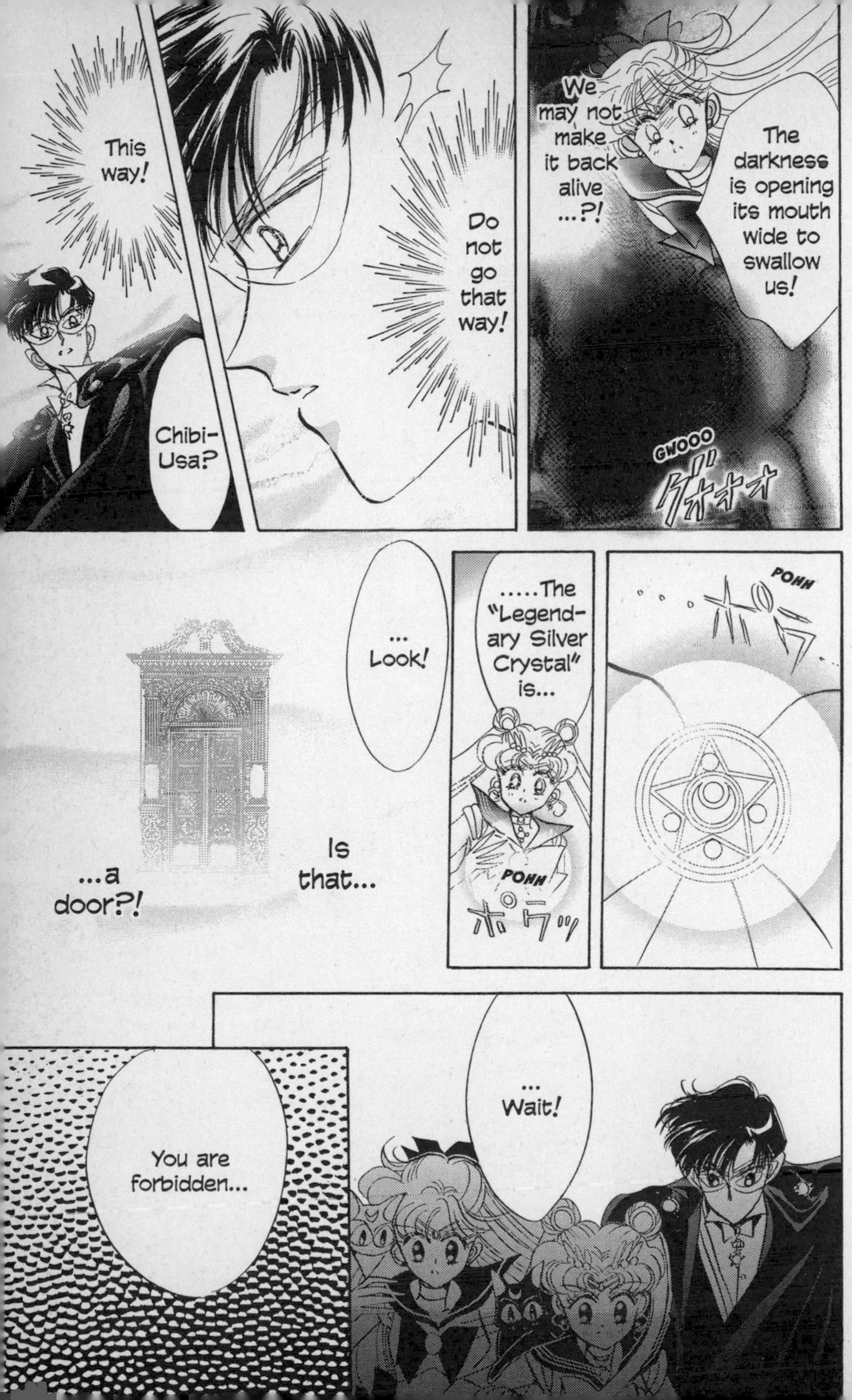
The darkness is opening its mouth wide to swallow us!
We may not make it back alive ...?!
GWOOO
Do not go that way!
This way!
Chibi-Usa?
POHN
.....The "Legendary Silver Crystal" is...
POHN
... Look!
Is that...
...a door?!
... Wait!
You are forbidden...

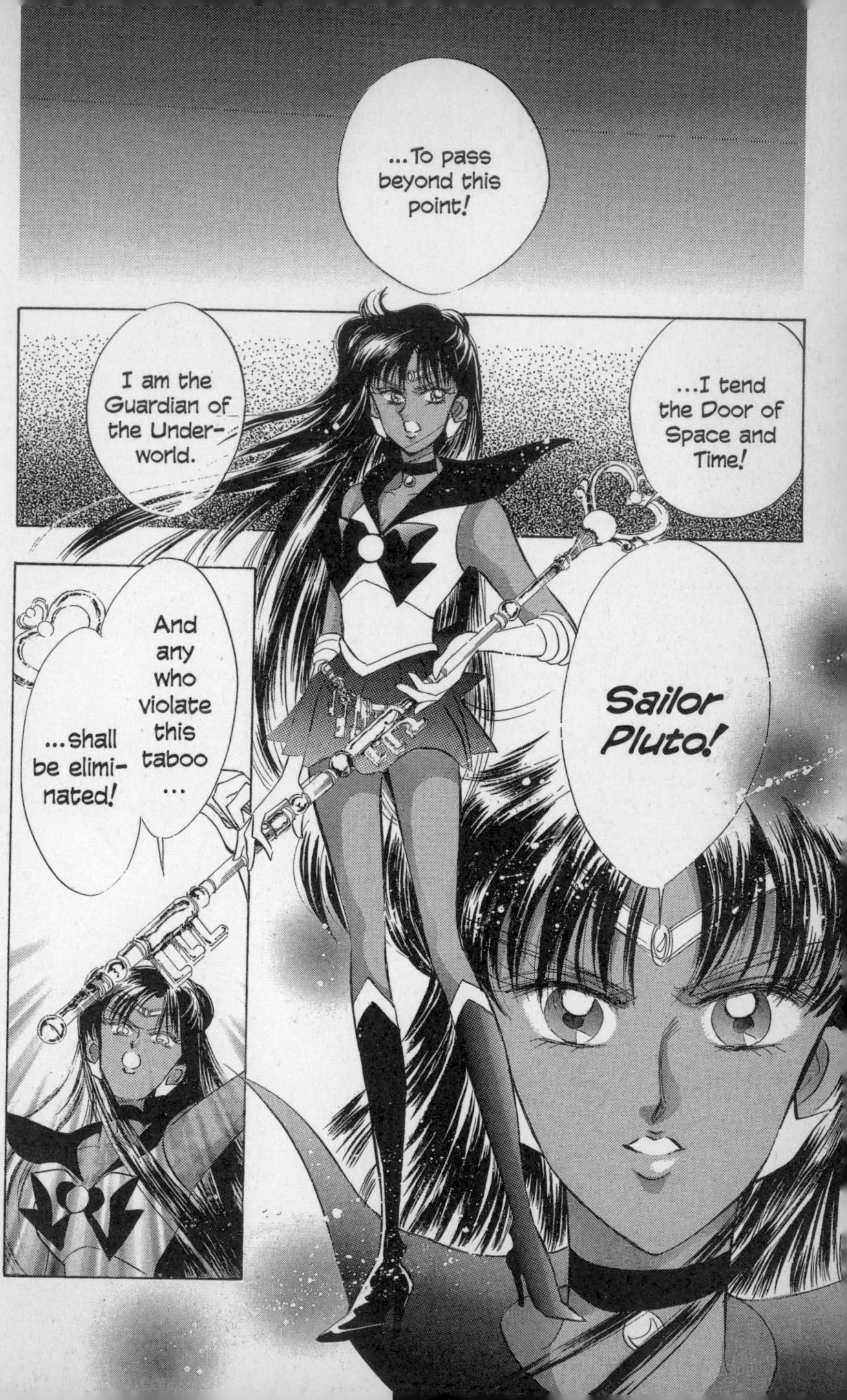
...To pass beyond this point!
I am the Guardian of the Under-world.
...I tend the Door of Space and Time!
Sailor Pluto!
And any who violate this taboo ...
...shall be elimi-nated!

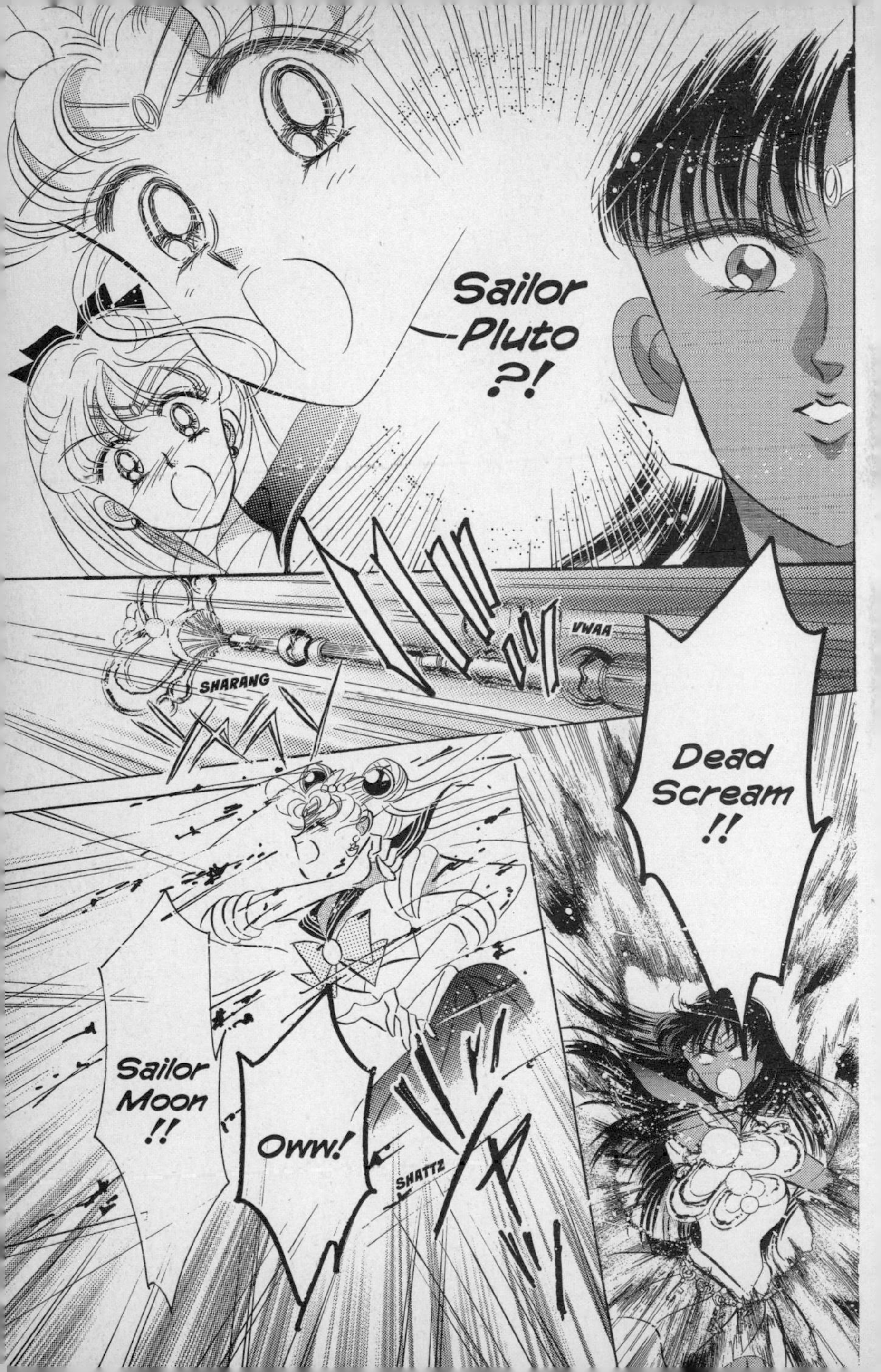
Sailor Pluto ?!
VWAA
SHARANG
Dead Scream !!
Oww!
SHATTZ
Sailor Moon !!

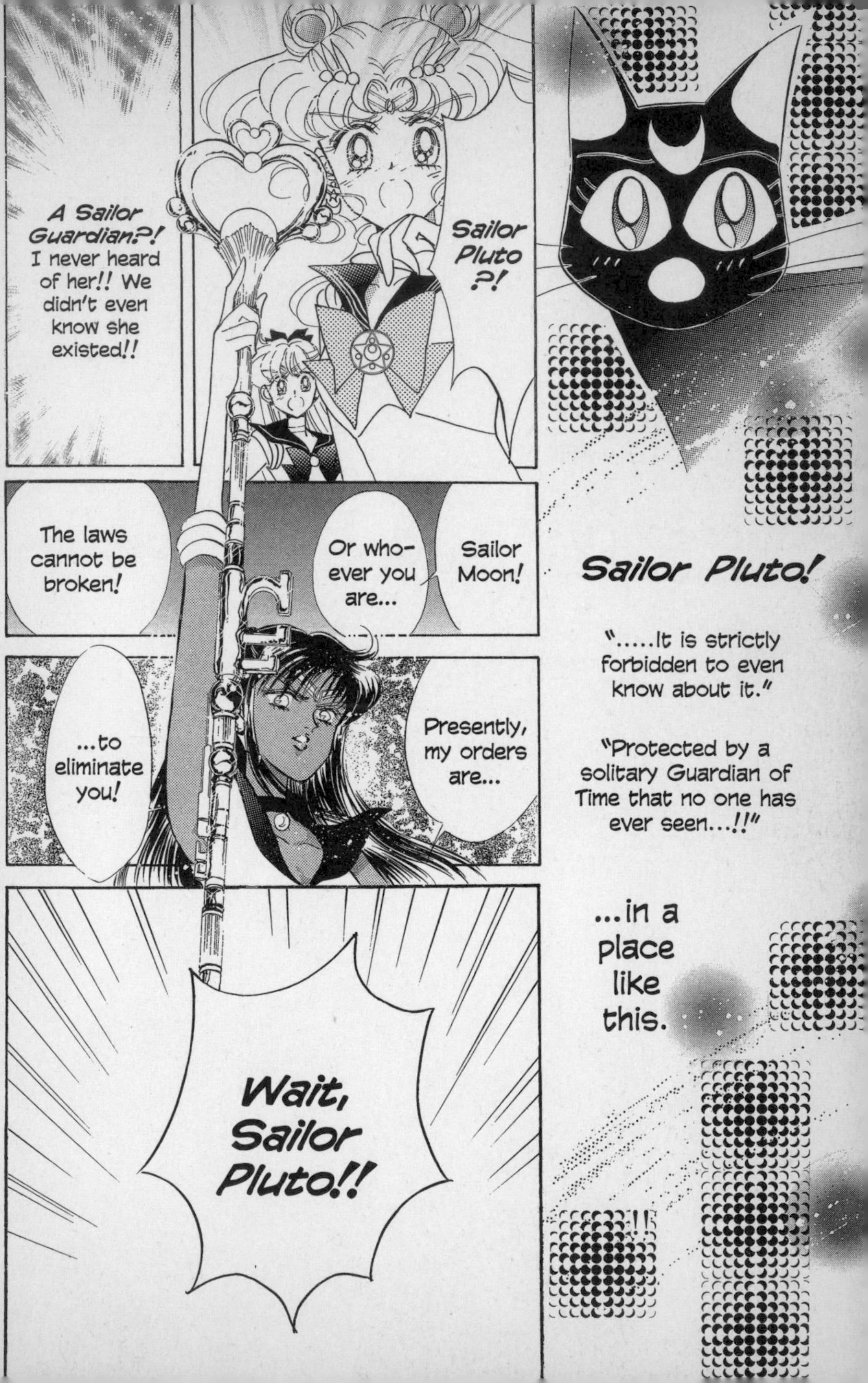
Sailor Pluto!
".....It is strictly forbidden to even know about it."
"Protected by a solitary Guardian of Time that no one has ever seen...!!"
...in a place like this.
!!
Sailor Pluto?!
A Sailor Guardian?! I never heard of her!! We didn't even know she existed!!
Sailor Moon!
Or who-ever you are...
The laws cannot be broken!
Presently, my orders are...
...to eliminate you!
Wait, Sailor Pluto!!

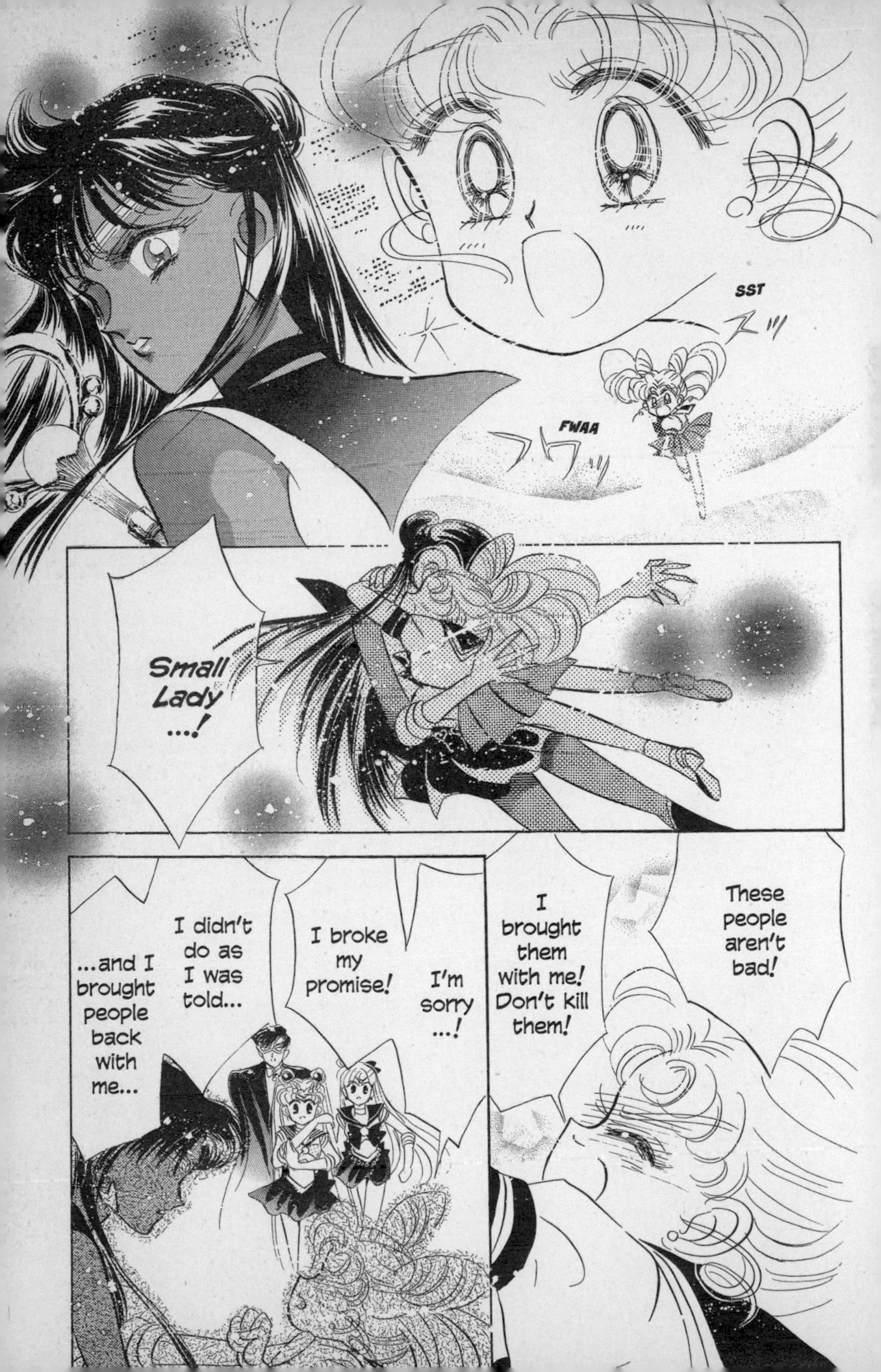
SST
スッ
FWAA
フワッ
Small Lady ...!
These people aren't bad!
I brought them with me! Don't kill them!
I'm sorry ...!
I broke my promise!
I didn't do as I was told...
...and I brought people back with me...

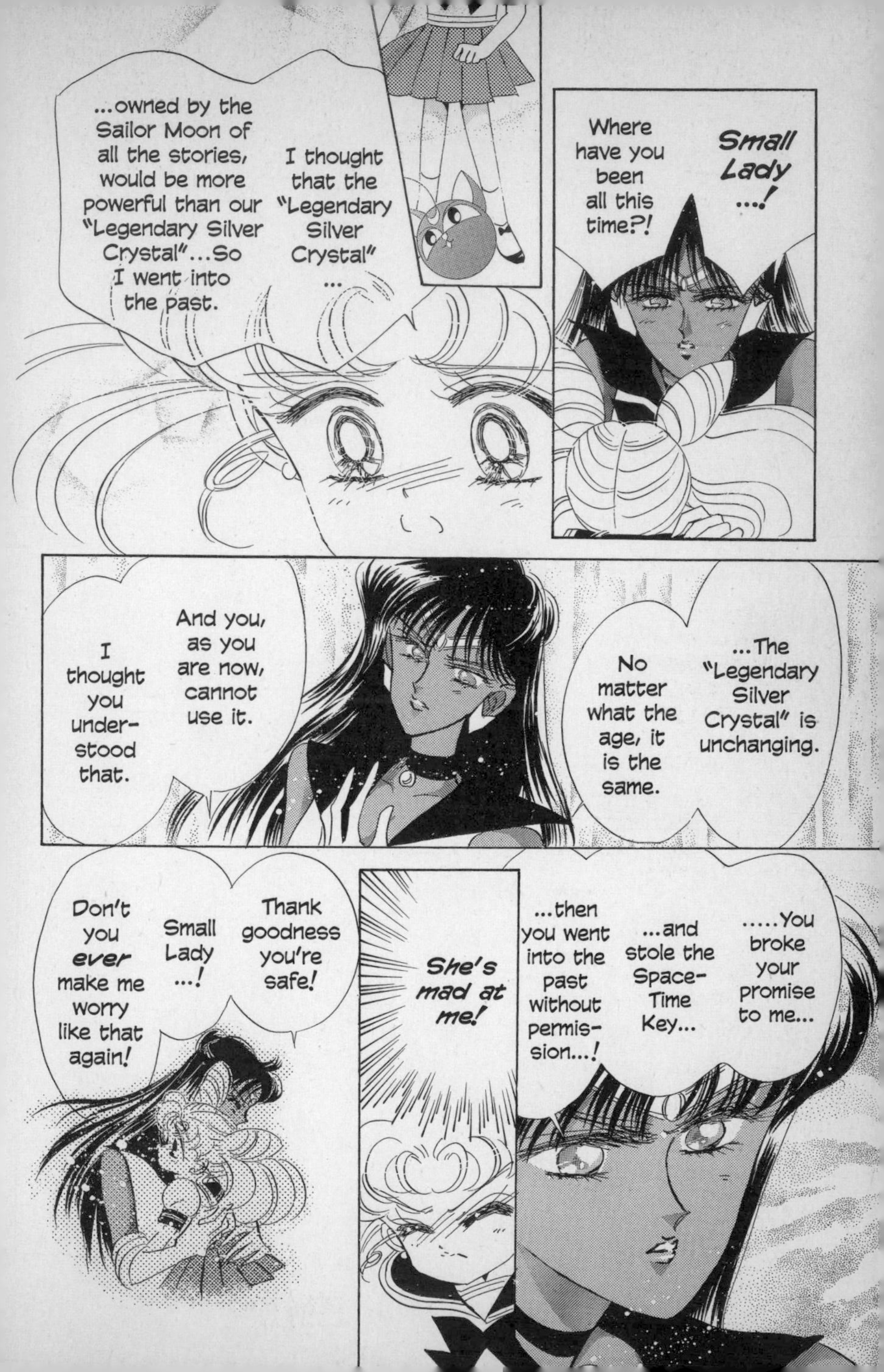
Small Lady...!
Where have you been all this time?!
I thought that the "Legendary Silver Crystal"...
...owned by the Sailor Moon of all the stories, would be more powerful than our "Legendary Silver Crystal"...So I went into the past.
...The "Legendary Silver Crystal" is unchanging.
No matter what the age, it is the same.
And you, as you are now, cannot use it.
I thought you understood that.
.....You broke your promise to me...
...and stole the Space-Time Key...
...then you went into the past without permission...!
She's mad at me!
Thank goodness you're safe!
Small Lady...!
Don't you ever make me worry like that again!

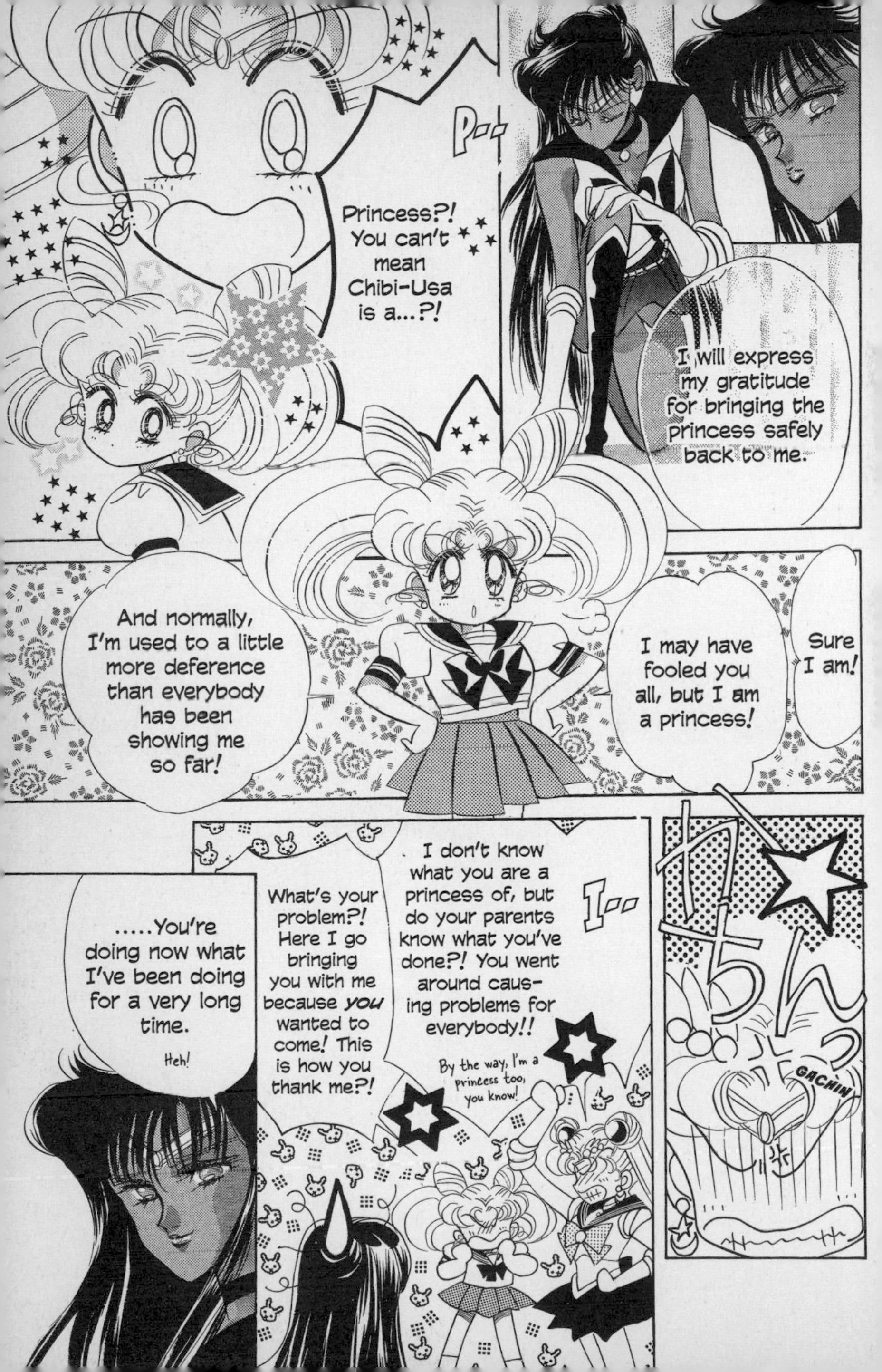
I will express my gratitude for bringing the princess safely back to me.
P--
Princess?! You can't mean Chibi-Usa is a...?!
Sure I am!
I may have fooled you all, but I am a princess!
And normally, I'm used to a little more deference than everybody has been showing me so far!
GACHIN
I--
I don't know what you are a princess of, but do your parents know what you've done?! You went around caus-ing problems for everybody!!
What's your problem?! Here I go bringing you with me because *you* wanted to come! This is how you thank me?!
By the way, I'm a princess too, you know!
.....You're doing now what I've been doing for a very long time.
Heh!

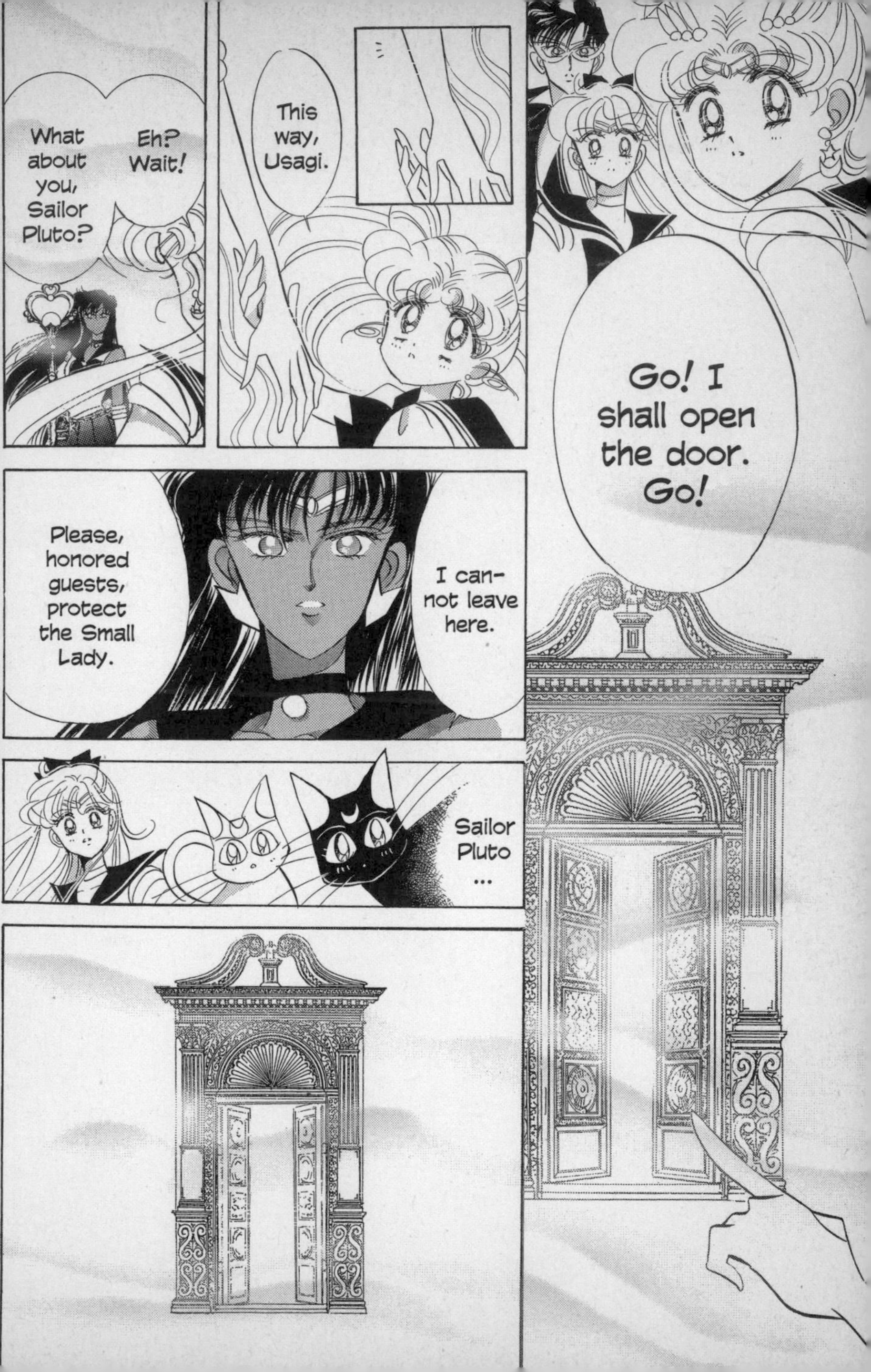
Go! I shall open the door. Go!
This way, Usagi.
Eh? Wait!
What about you, Sailor Pluto?
I can-not leave here.
Please, honored guests, protect the Small Lady.
Sailor Pluto ...

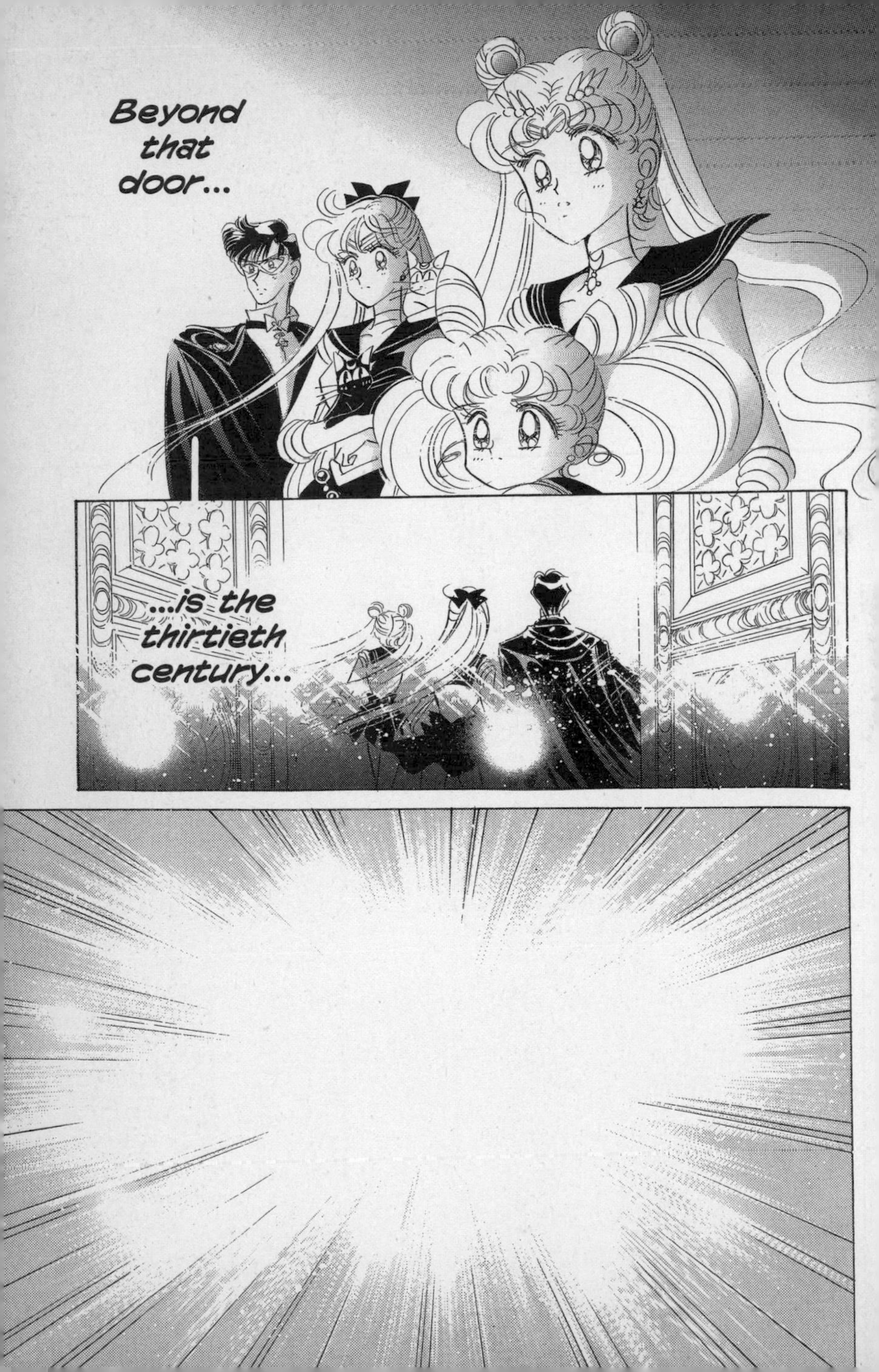
Beyond that door...
...is the thirtieth century...

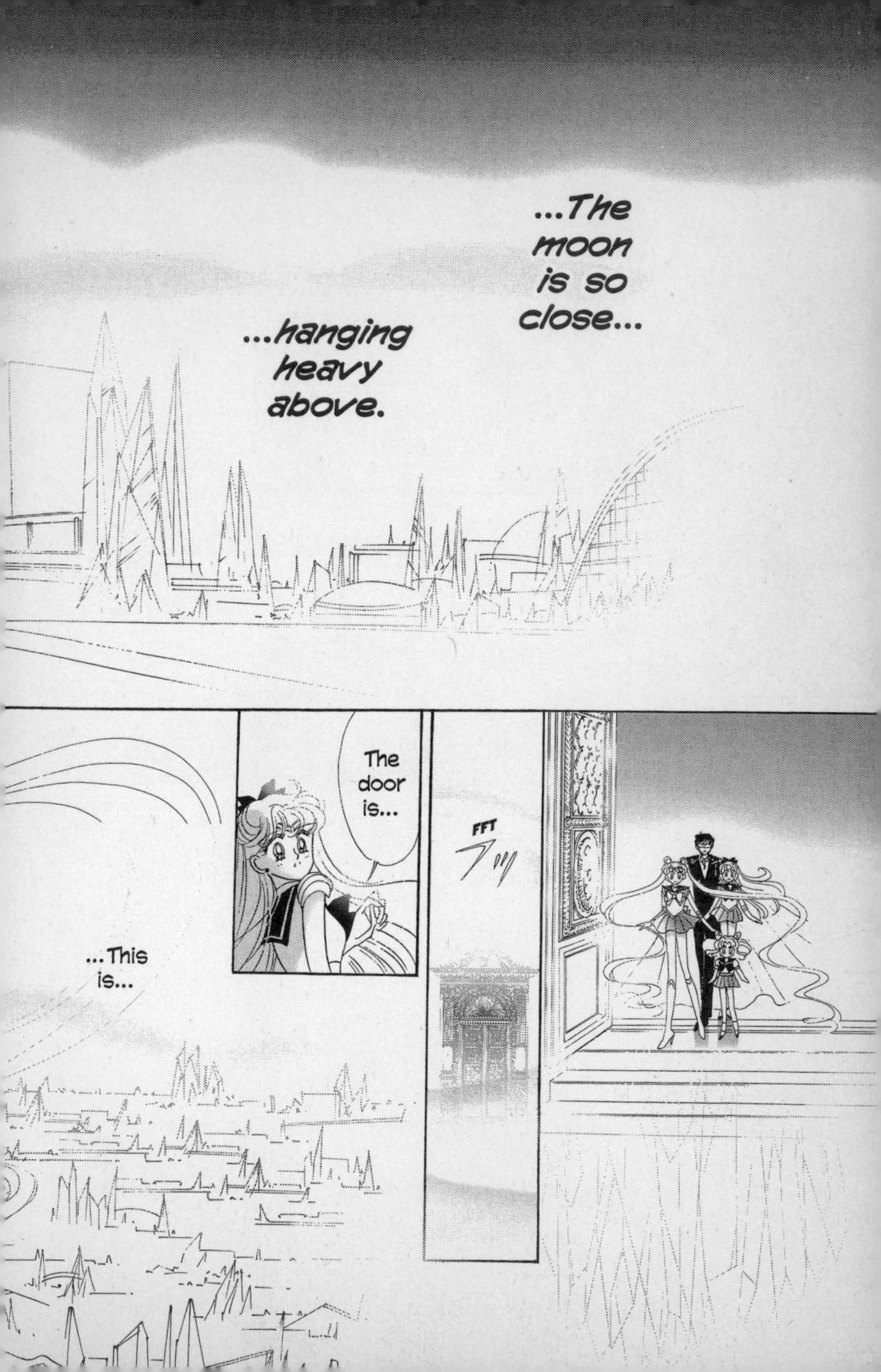
...The moon is so close...
...hanging heavy above.
FFT
The door is...
...This is...

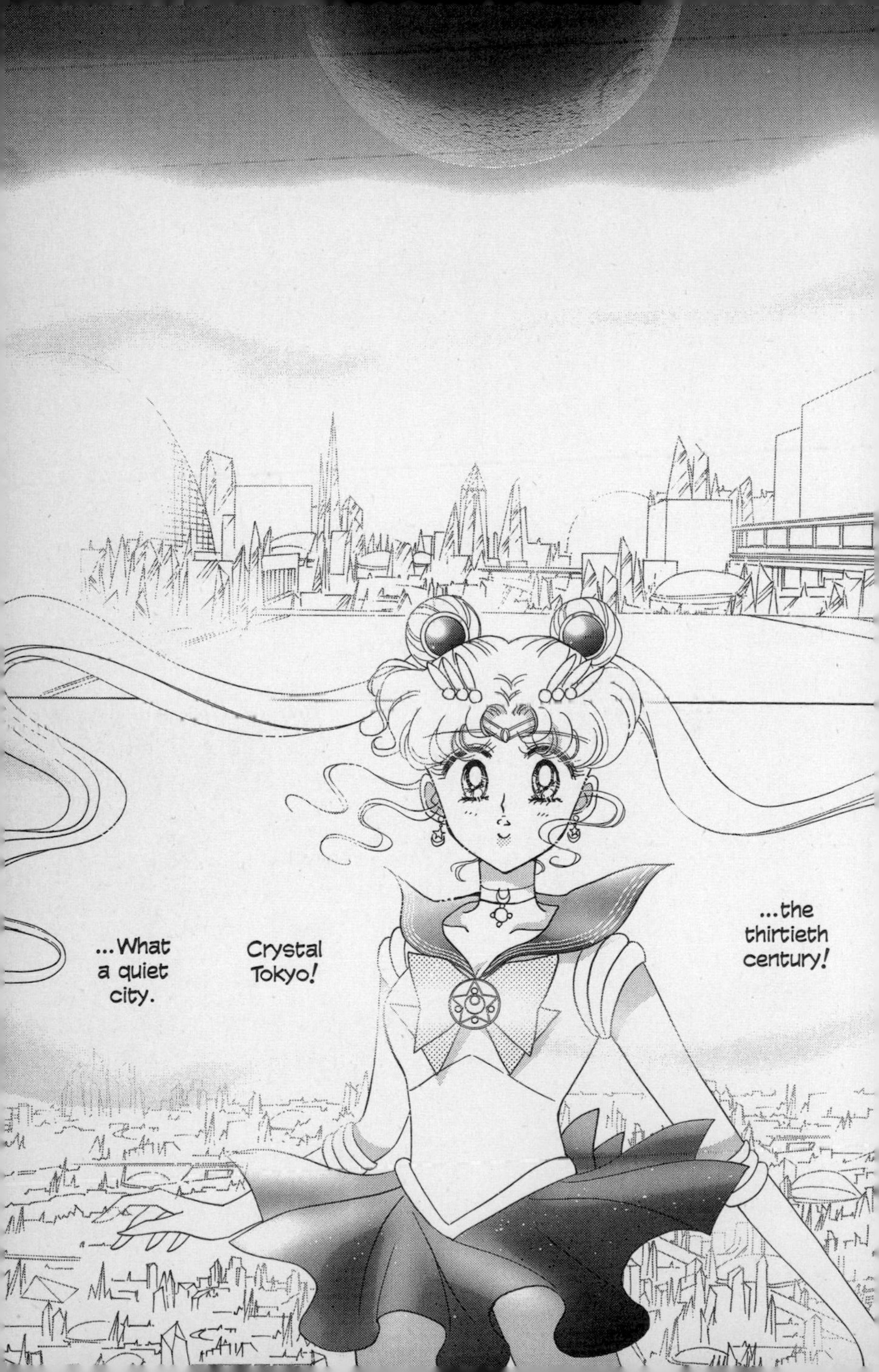
...the thirtieth century!
Crystal Tokyo!
...What a quiet city.

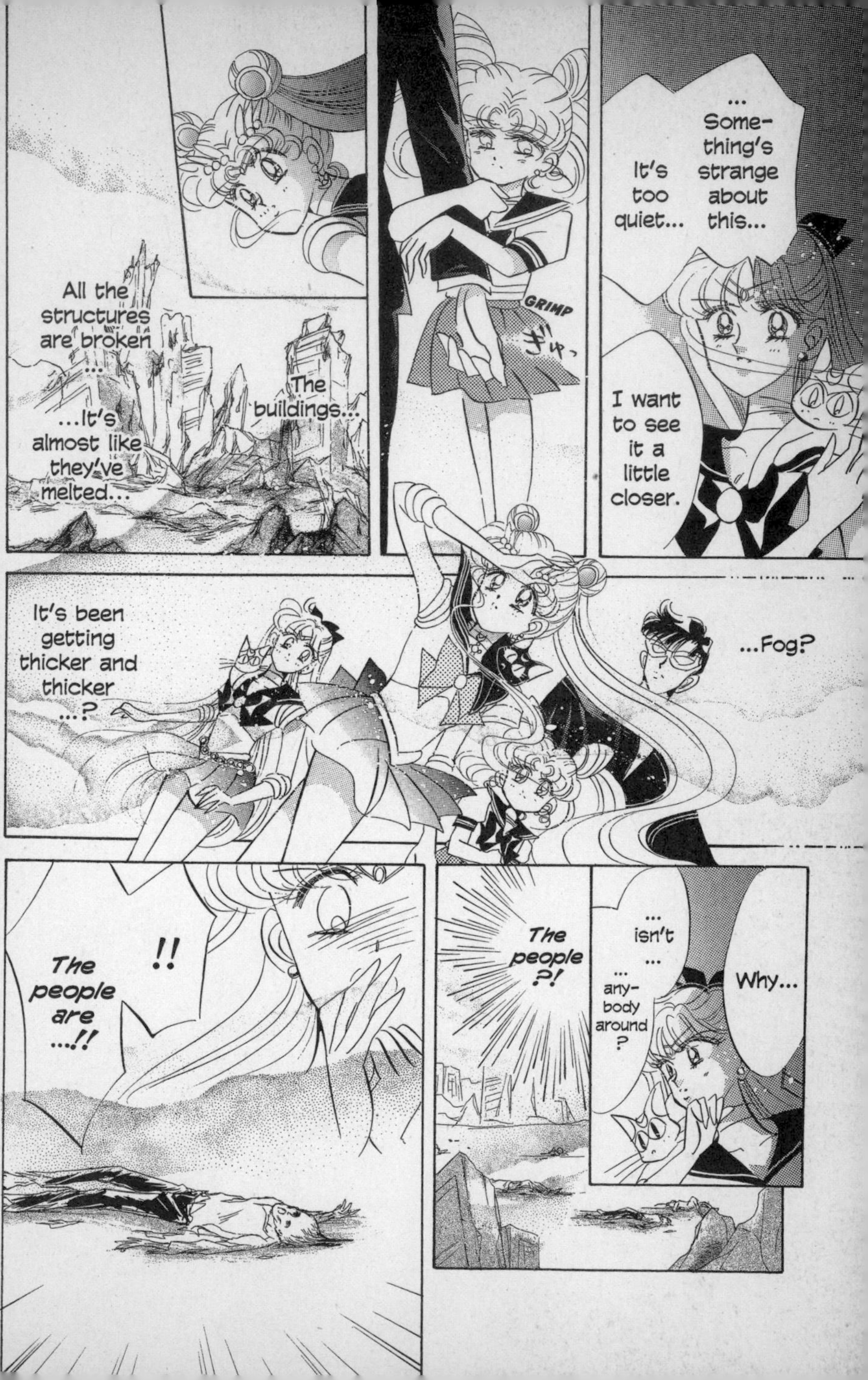
... Something's strange about this...
It's too quiet...
I want to see it a little closer.
GRIMP
ぎゅっ
The buildings...
All the structures are broken ...
...It's almost like they've melted...
...Fog?
It's been getting thicker and thicker ...?
Why...
... isn't ... ... anybody around ?
The people ?!
!!
The people are ...!!

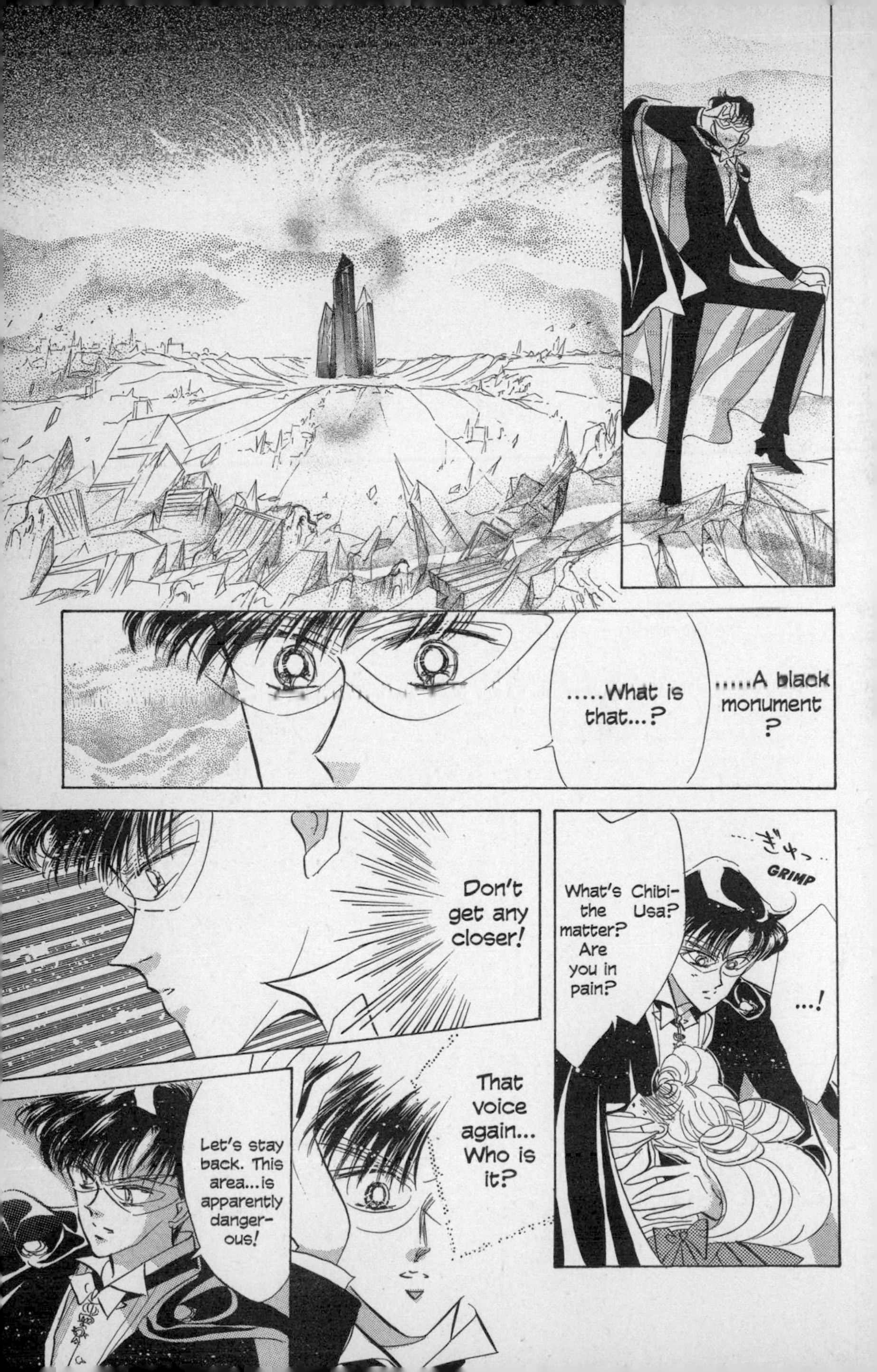

.....A black monument?
.....What is that...?
...ぎゅっ...
GRIMP
Chibi-Usa? What's the matter? Are you in pain?
...!
Don't get any closer!
That voice again... Who is it?
Let's stay back. This area...is apparently danger-ous!

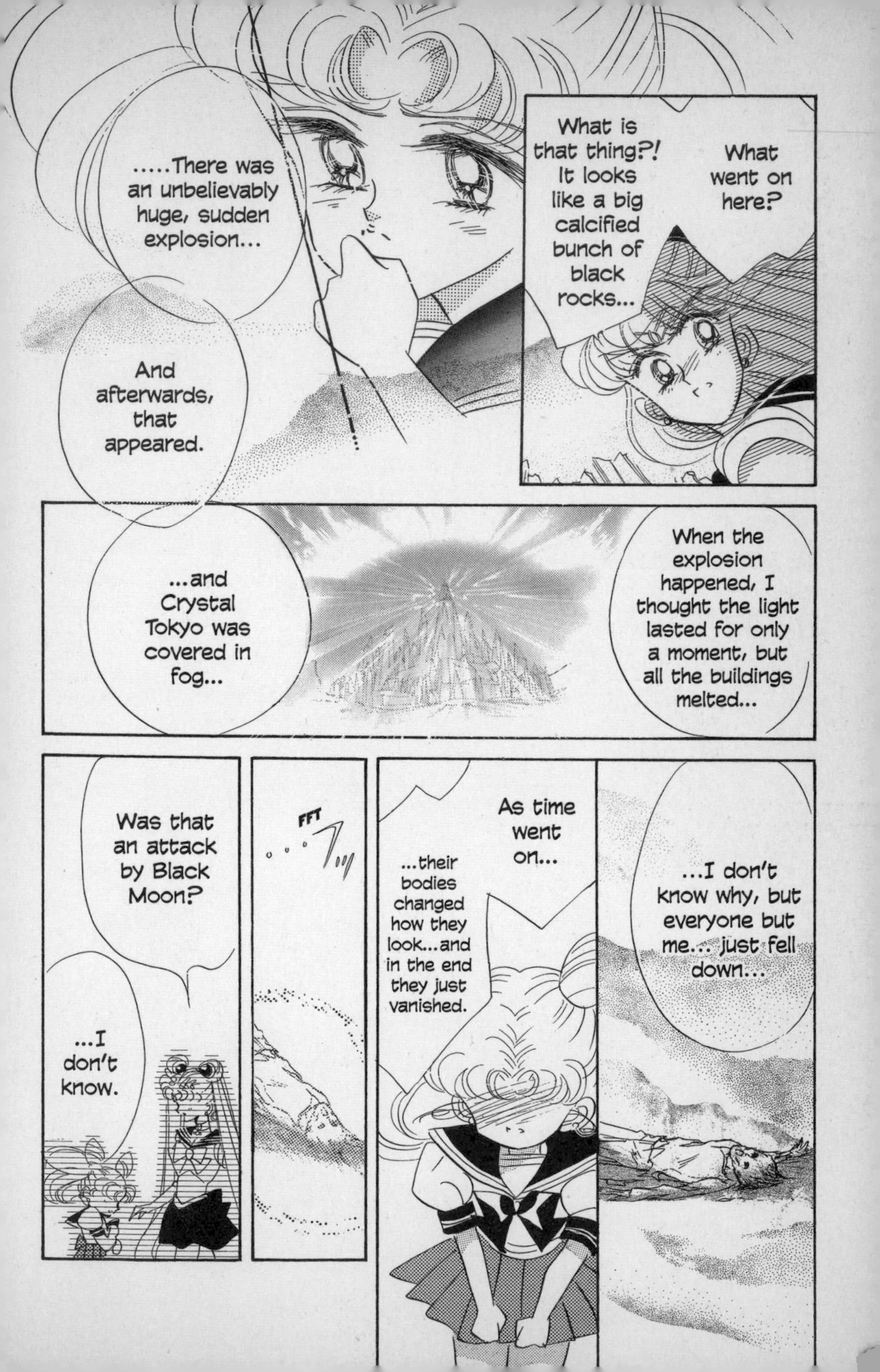
What went on here?
What is that thing?! It looks like a big calcified bunch of black rocks...
.....There was an unbelievably huge, sudden explosion...
And afterwards, that appeared.
When the explosion happened, I thought the light lasted for only a moment, but all the buildings melted...
...and Crystal Tokyo was covered in fog...
...I don't know why, but everyone but me... just fell down...
As time went on...
...their bodies changed how they look...and in the end they just vanished.
FFT
Was that an attack by Black Moon?
...I don't know.

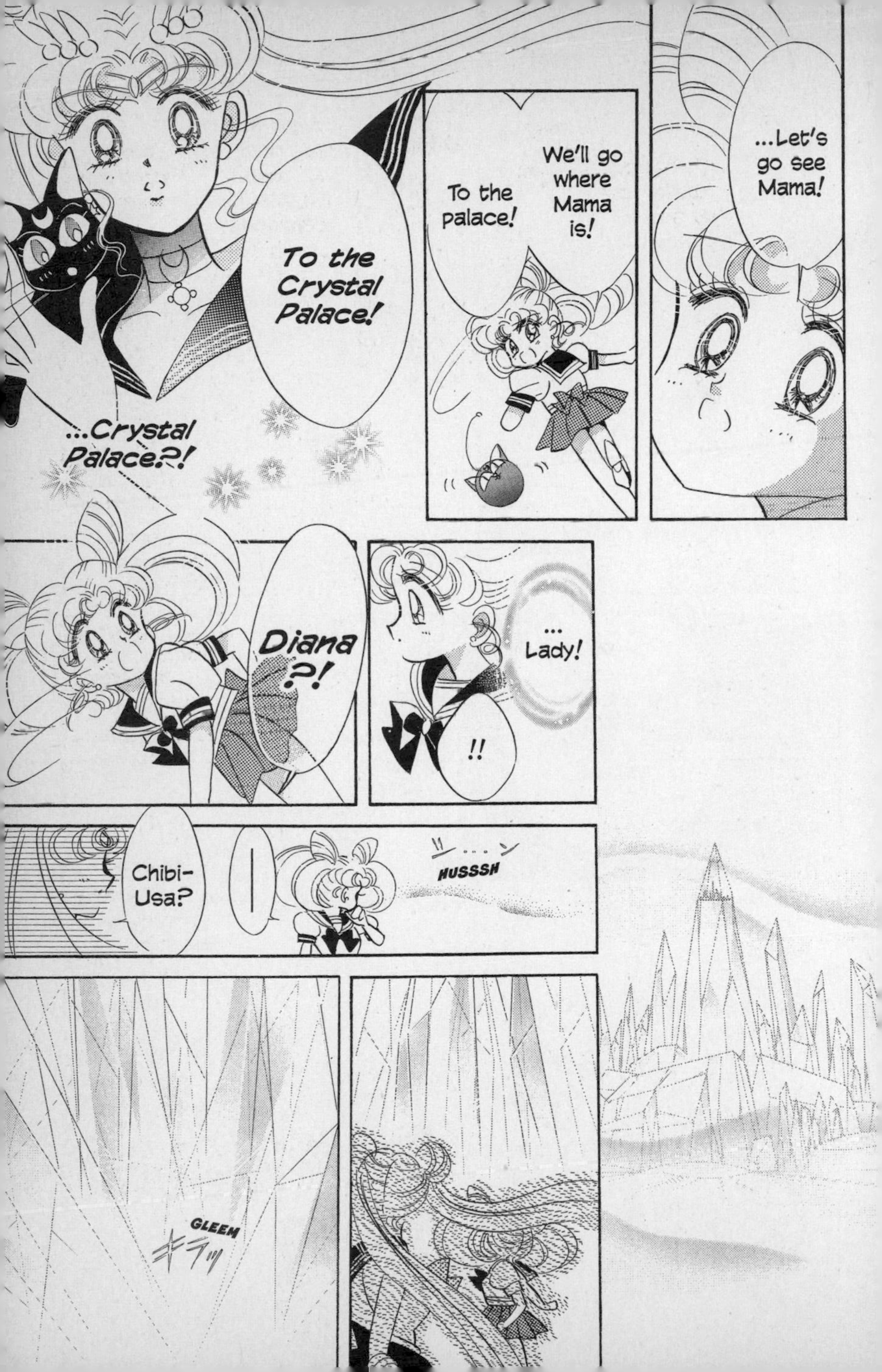
...Let's go see Mama!
We'll go where Mama is!
To the palace!
To the Crystal Palace!
...Crystal Palace?!
... Lady!
!!
Diana?!
HUSSSH
Chibi-Usa?
GLEEM
ギラッ

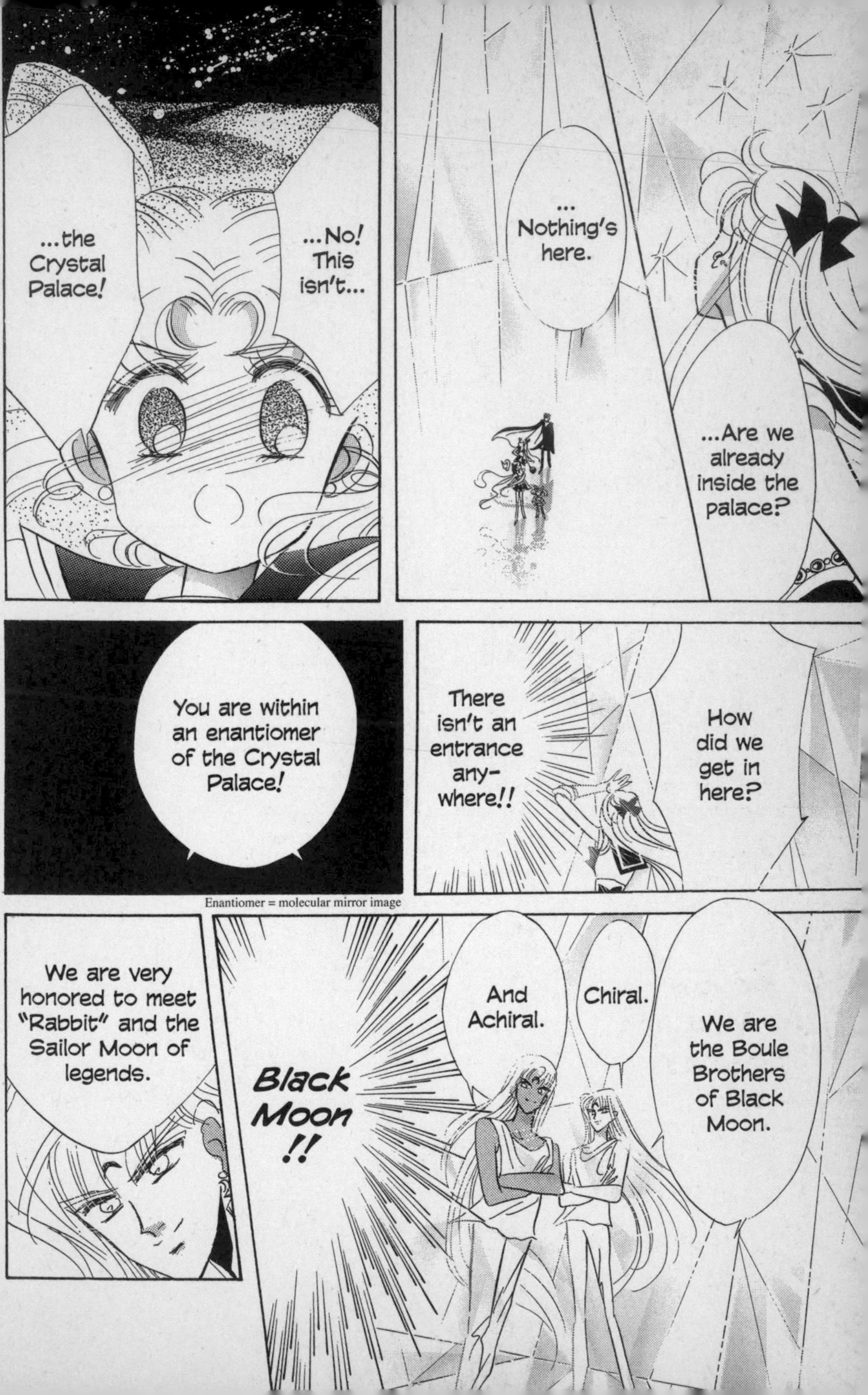
...Nothing's here.
...Are we already inside the palace?
...No! This isn't...
...the Crystal Palace!
How did we get in here?
There isn't an entrance any-where!!
You are within an enantiomer of the Crystal Palace!
We are the Boule Brothers of Black Moon.
Chiral.
And Achiral.
Black Moon!!
We are very honored to meet "Rabbit" and the Sailor Moon of legends.
Enantiomer = molecular mirror image

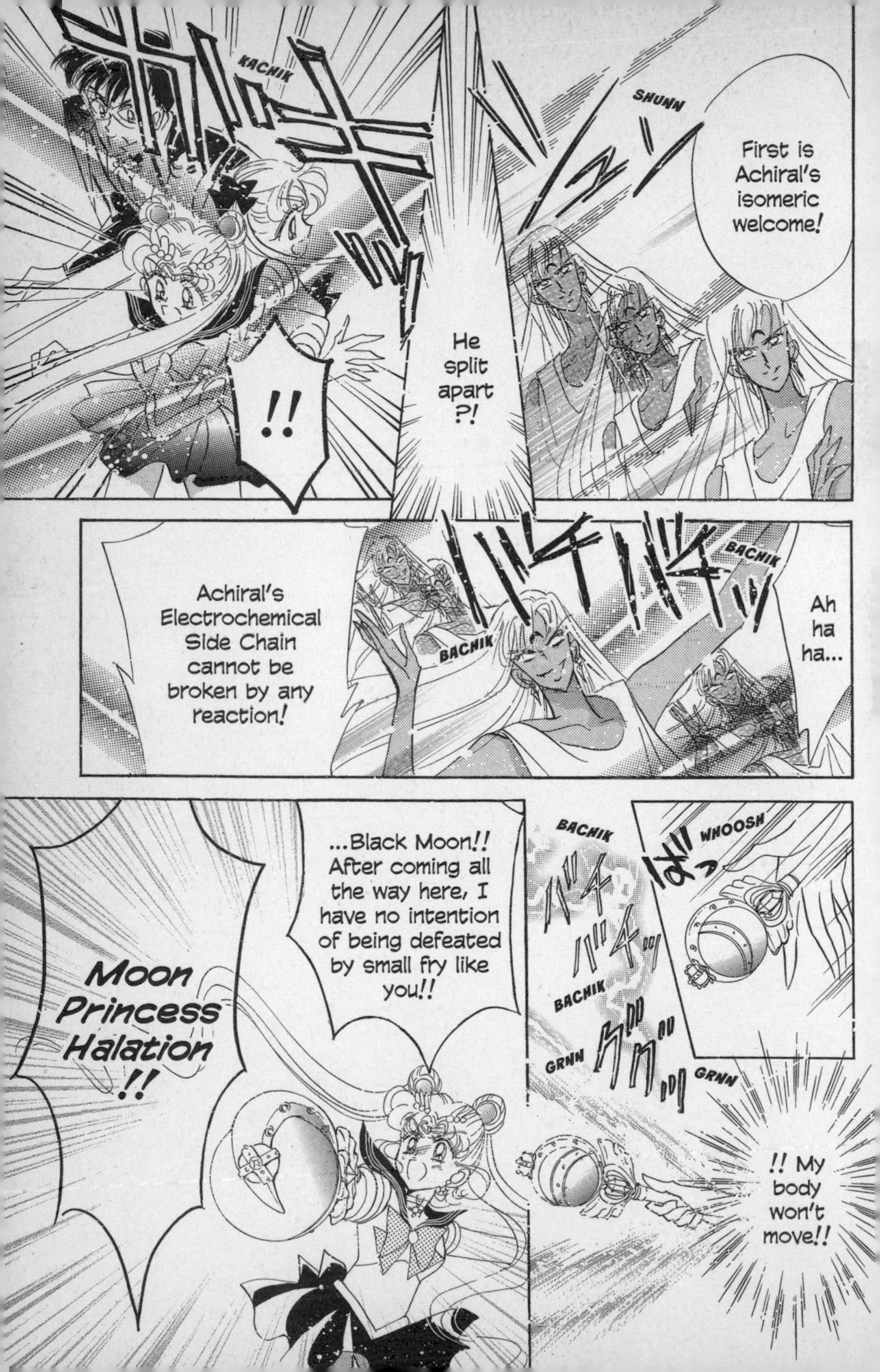
SHUNN
First is Achiral's isomeric welcome!
He split apart?!
KACHIK
!!
Ah ha ha...
BACHIK
BACHIK
Achiral's Electrochemical Side Chain cannot be broken by any reaction!
WHOOSH
BACHIK
BACHIK
GRNN
GRNN
!! My body won't move!!
...Black Moon!! After coming all the way here, I have no intention of being defeated by small fry like you!!
Moon Princess Halation!!

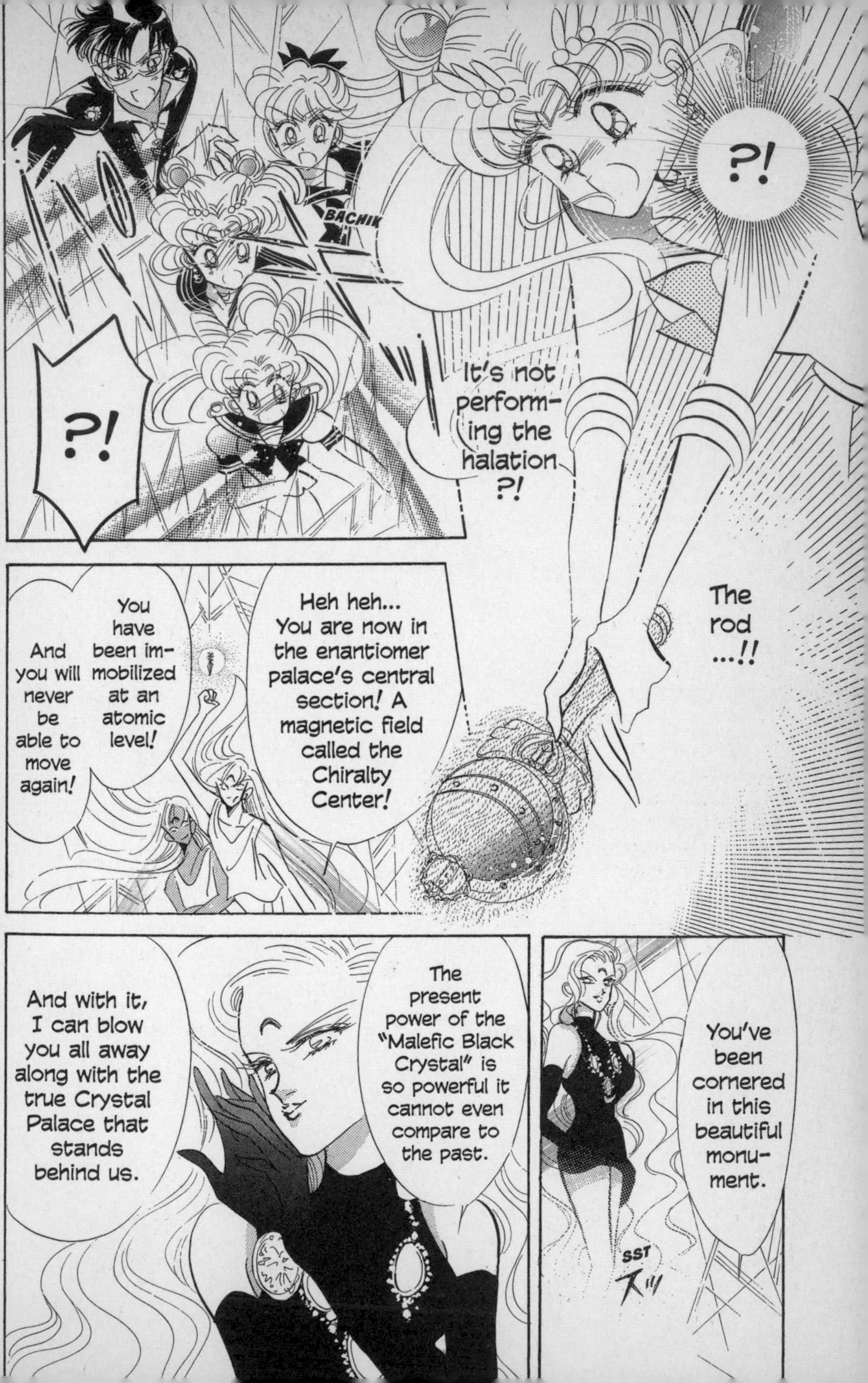
?!
BACHIK
It's not perform-ing the halation ?!
?!
The rod ...!!
Heh heh... You are now in the enantiomer palace's central section! A magnetic field called the Chiralty Center!
You have been im-mobilized at an atomic level!
And you will never be able to move again!
You've been cornered in this beautiful monu-ment.
SST
The present power of the "Malefic Black Crystal" is so powerful it cannot even compare to the past.
And with it, I can blow you all away along with the true Crystal Palace that stands behind us.

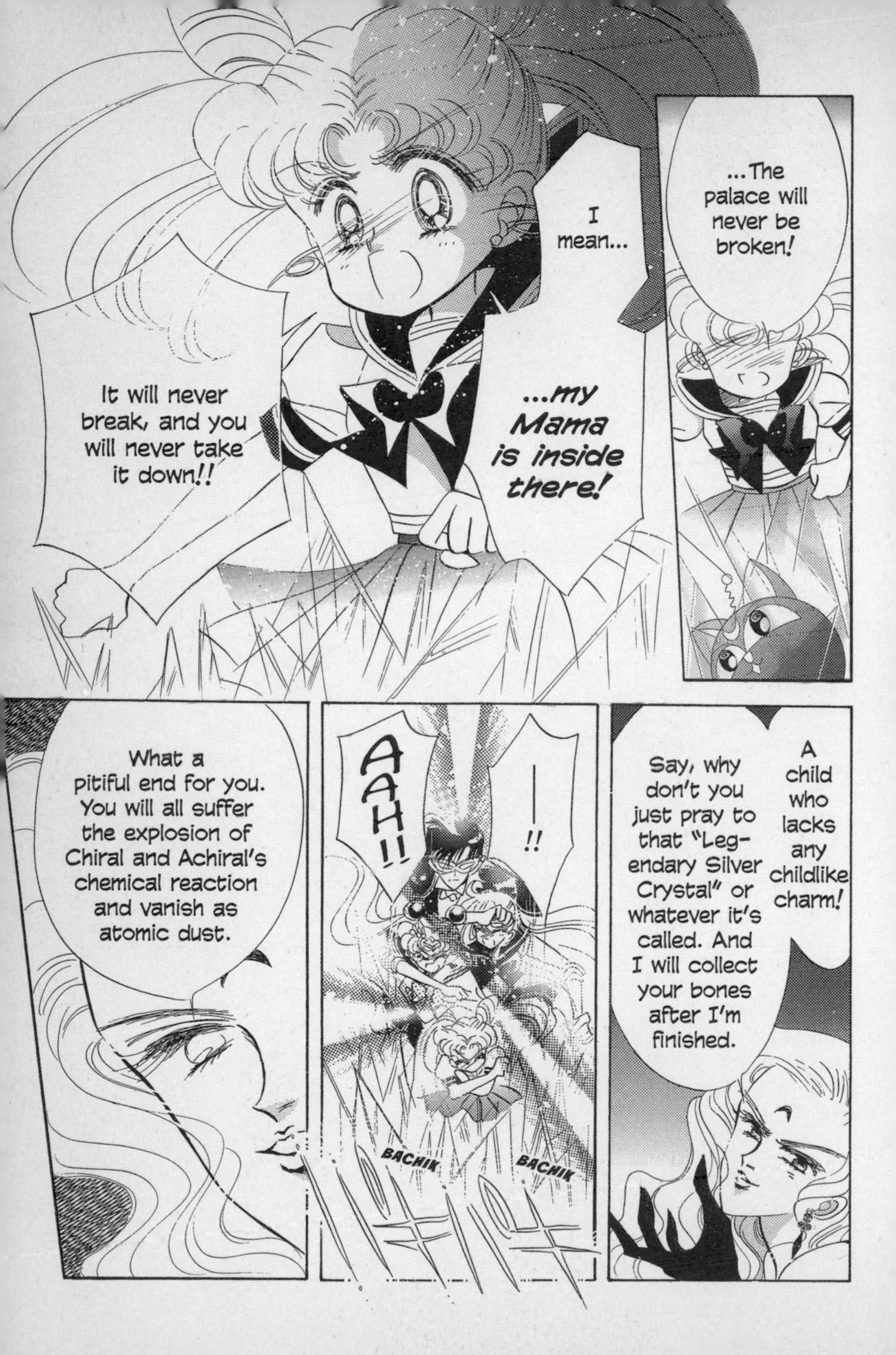
...The palace will never be broken!
I mean...
...my Mama is inside there!
It will never break, and you will never take it down!!
A child who lacks any childlike charm!
Say, why don't you just pray to that "Legendary Silver Crystal" or whatever it's called. And I will collect your bones after I'm finished.
—!!
AAH!!
BACHIK
BACHIK
What a pitiful end for you. You will all suffer the explosion of Chiral and Achiral's chemical reaction and vanish as atomic dust.

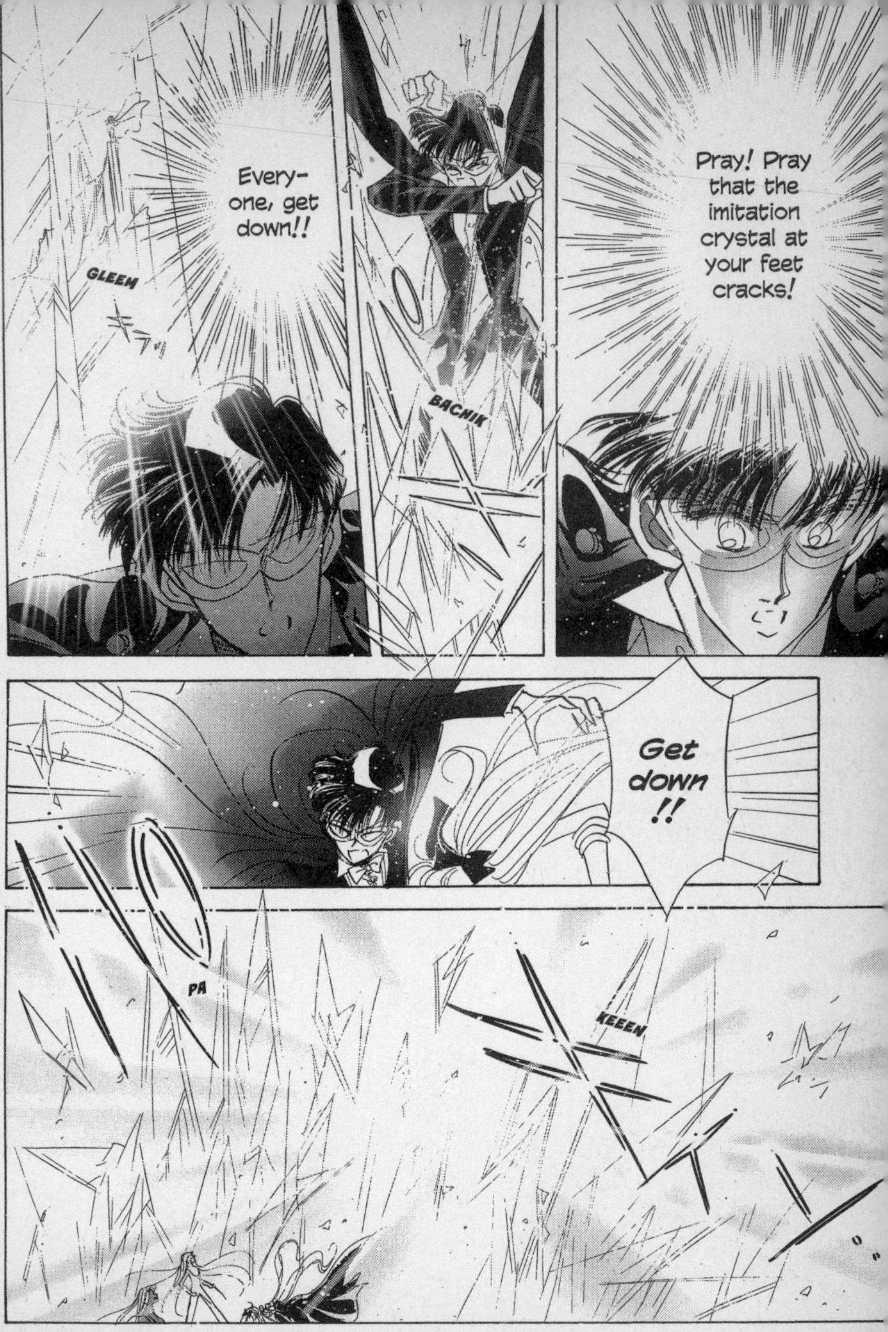
Pray! Pray that the imitation crystal at your feet cracks!
BACHIK
Every-one, get down!!
GLEEM
Get down!!
KEEEN
PA

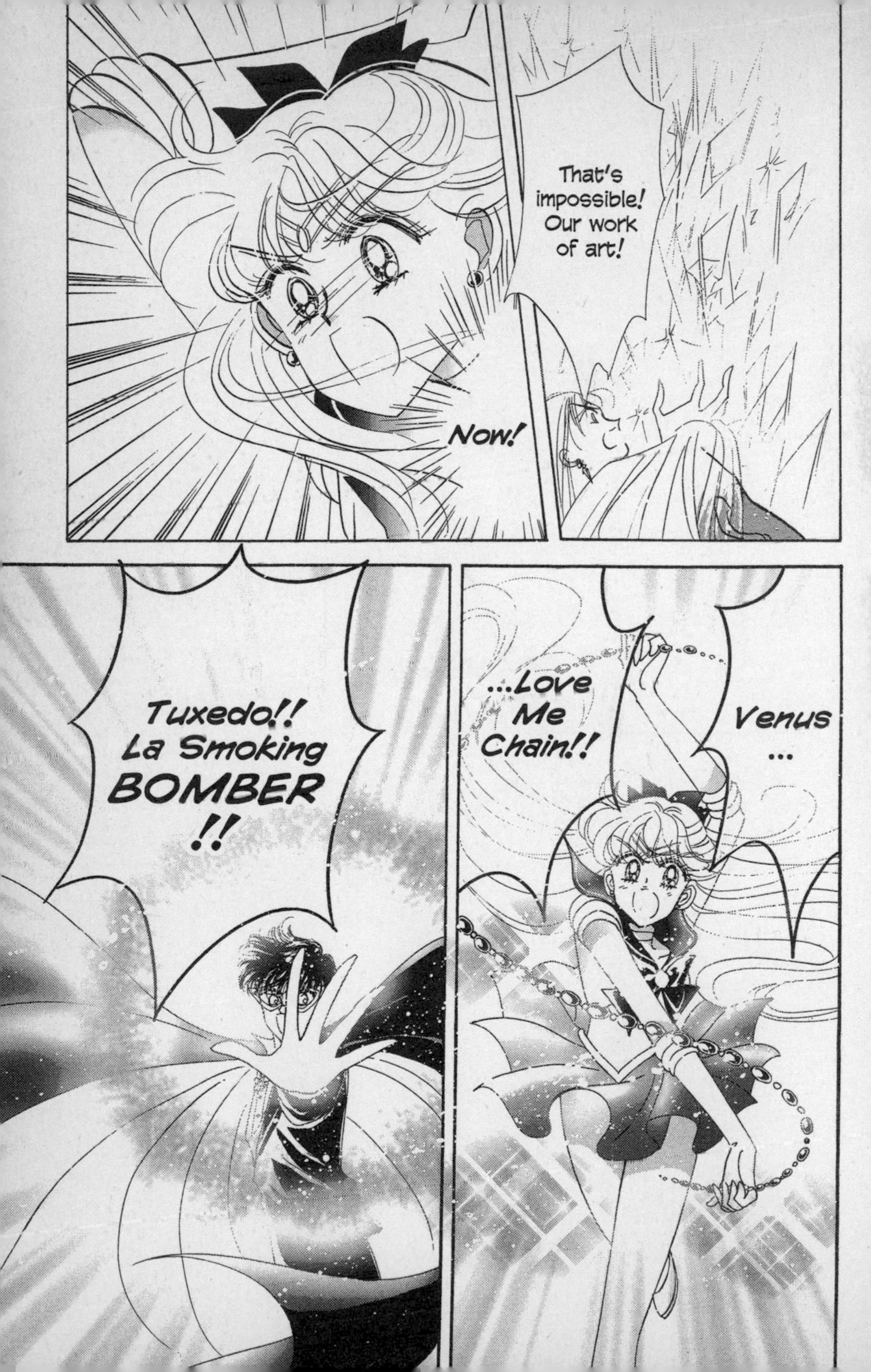
That's impossible! Our work of art!
Now!
Venus ...
...Love Me Chain!!
Tuxedo!! La Smoking BOMBER !!

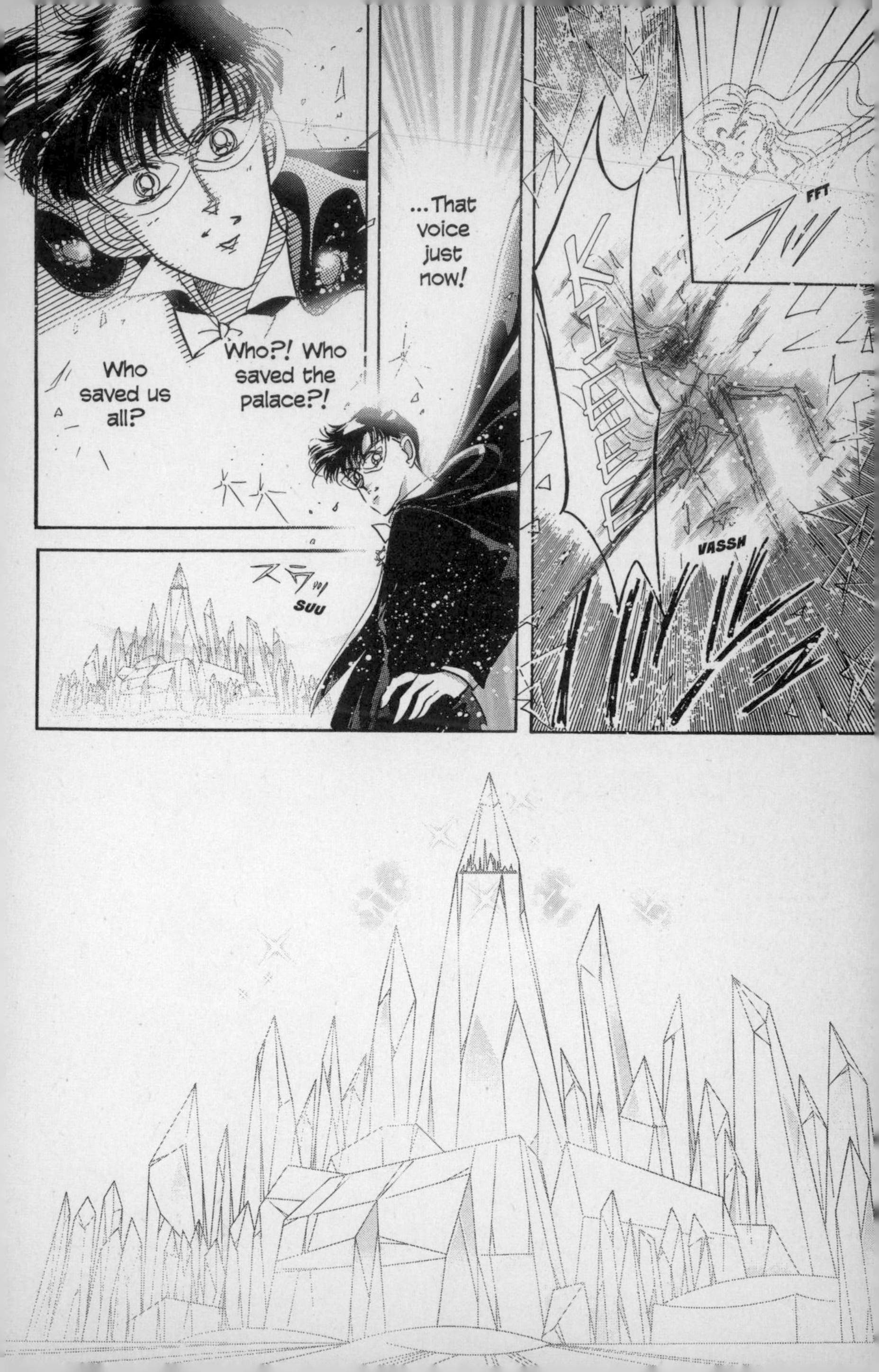
FFT
KIEEEE
VASSH
...That voice just now!
Who?! Who saved the palace?!
Who saved us all?
SUU

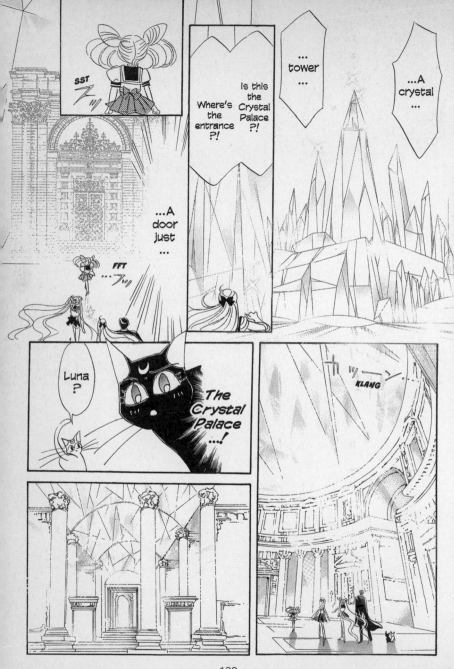

...A crystal...

...tower...

Is this the Crystal Palace ?!

Where's the entrance ?!

SST

...A door just...

FFT

Luna ?

The Crystal Palace ...!

KLANG

139

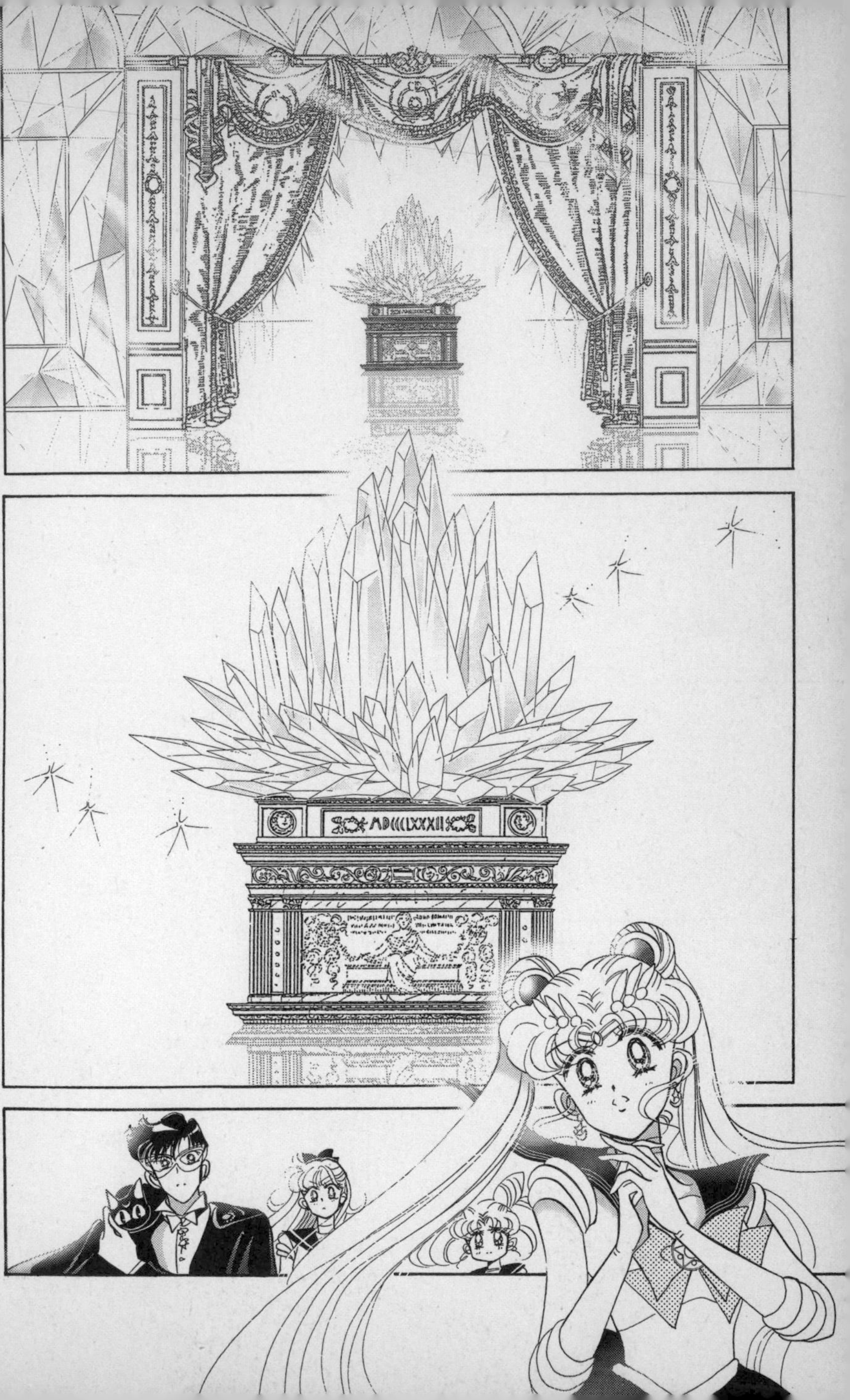
MDCCCCLXXXII

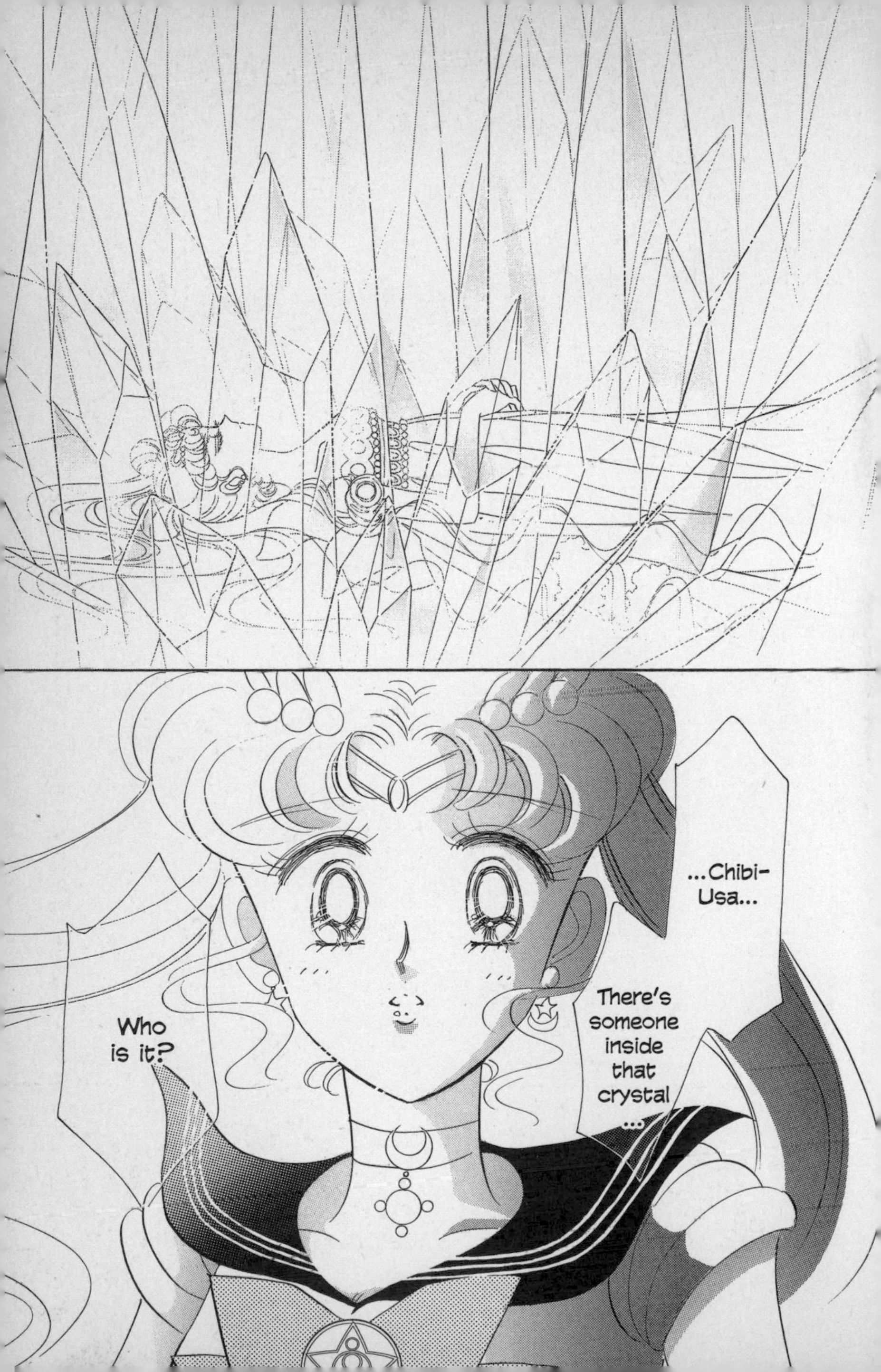
...Chibi-Usa...
There's someone inside that crystal ...
Who is it?

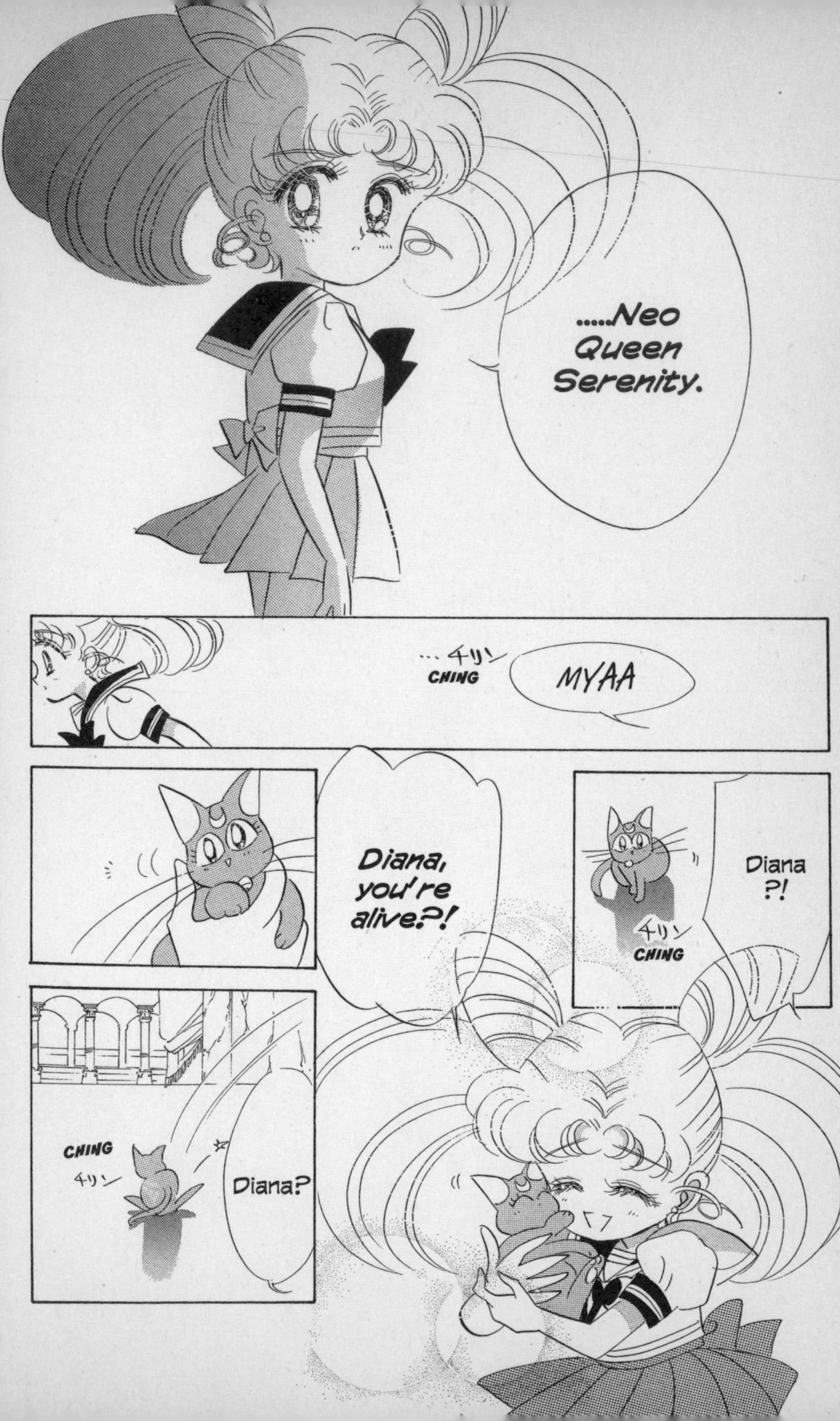

......Neo Queen Serenity.
MYAA
... チリン
CHING
Diana ?!
チリン
CHING
Diana, you're alive?!
Diana?
CHING
チリン

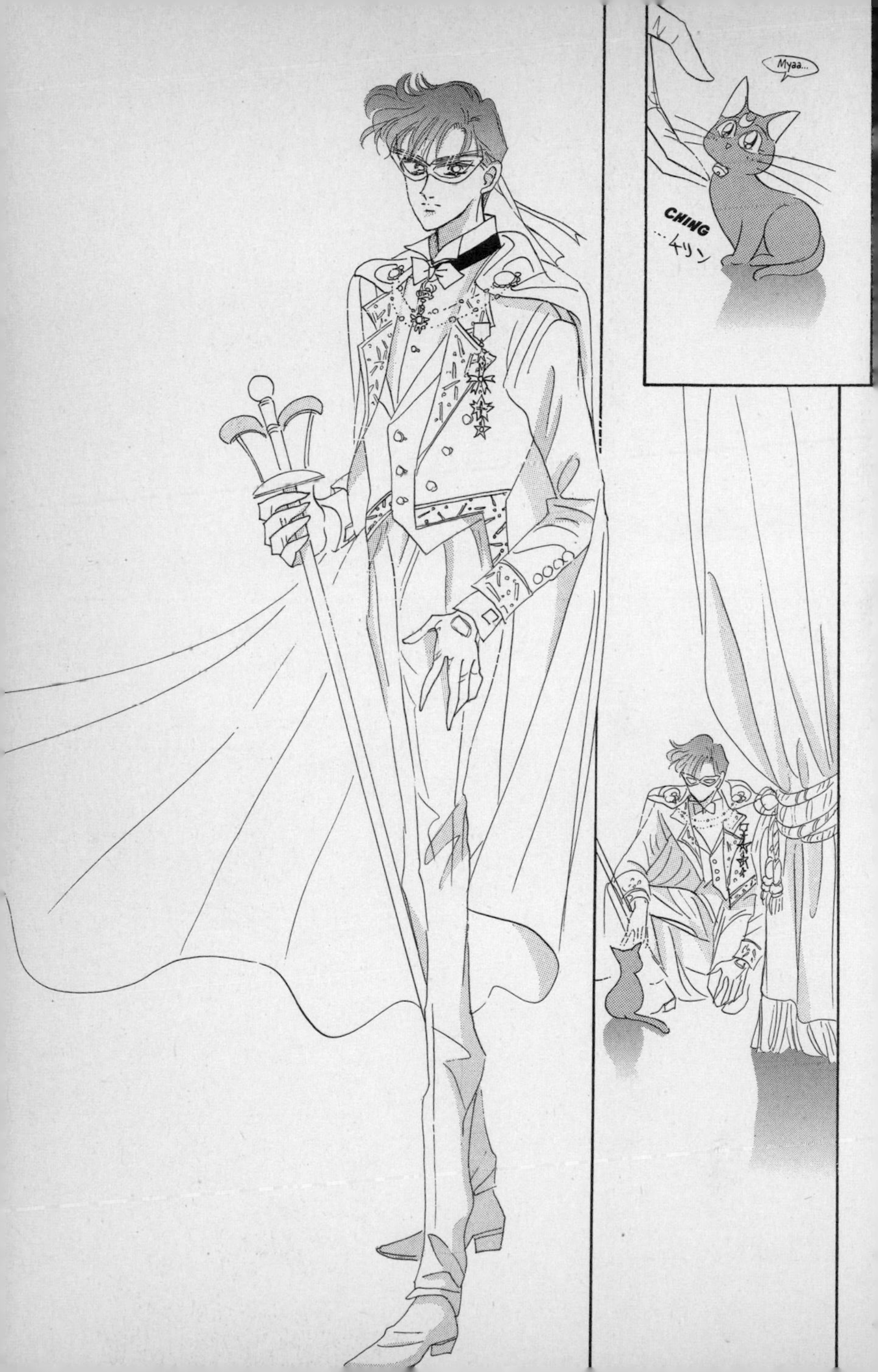
Myaa...
CHING
…チリン

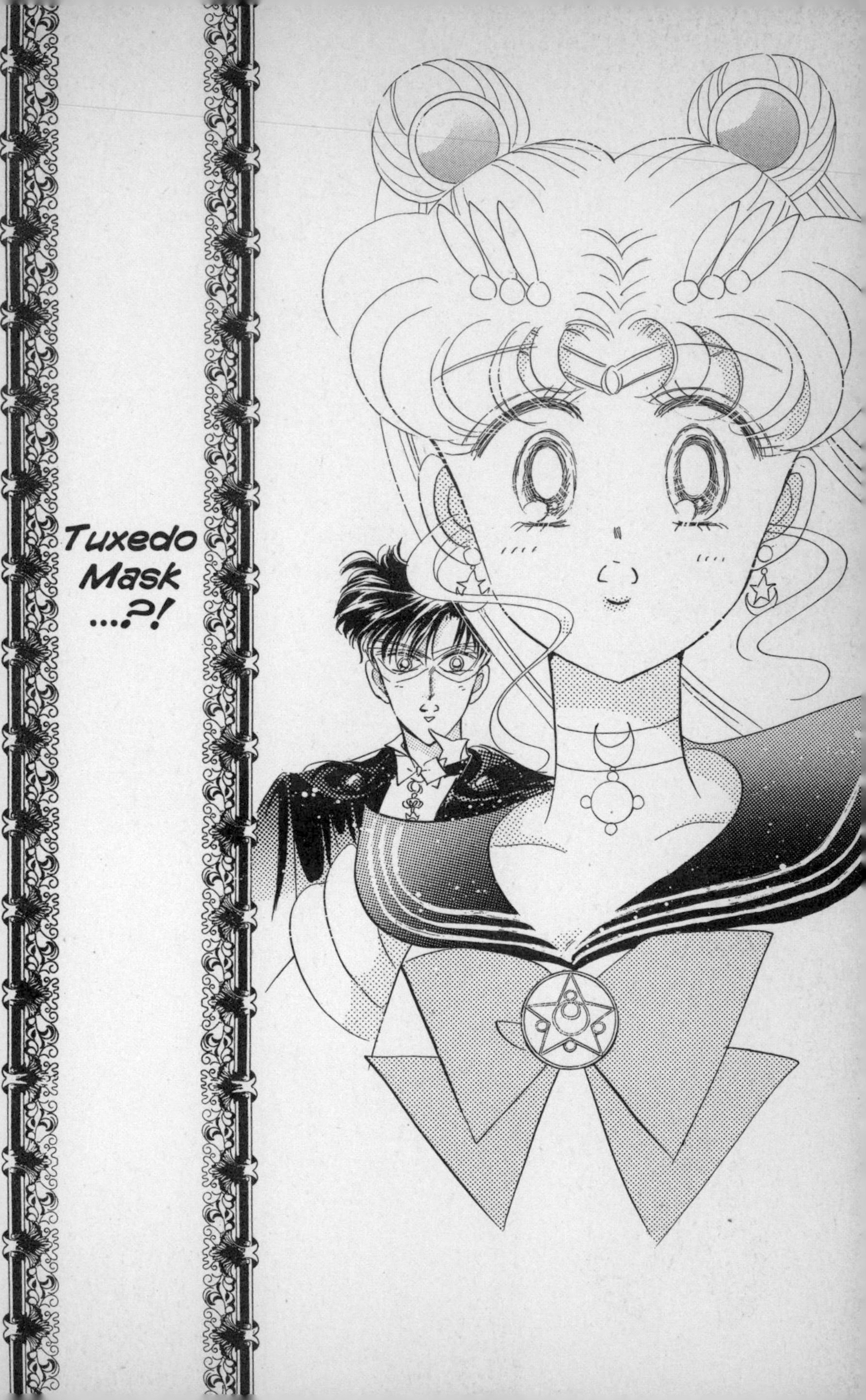
Tuxedo Mask ...?!

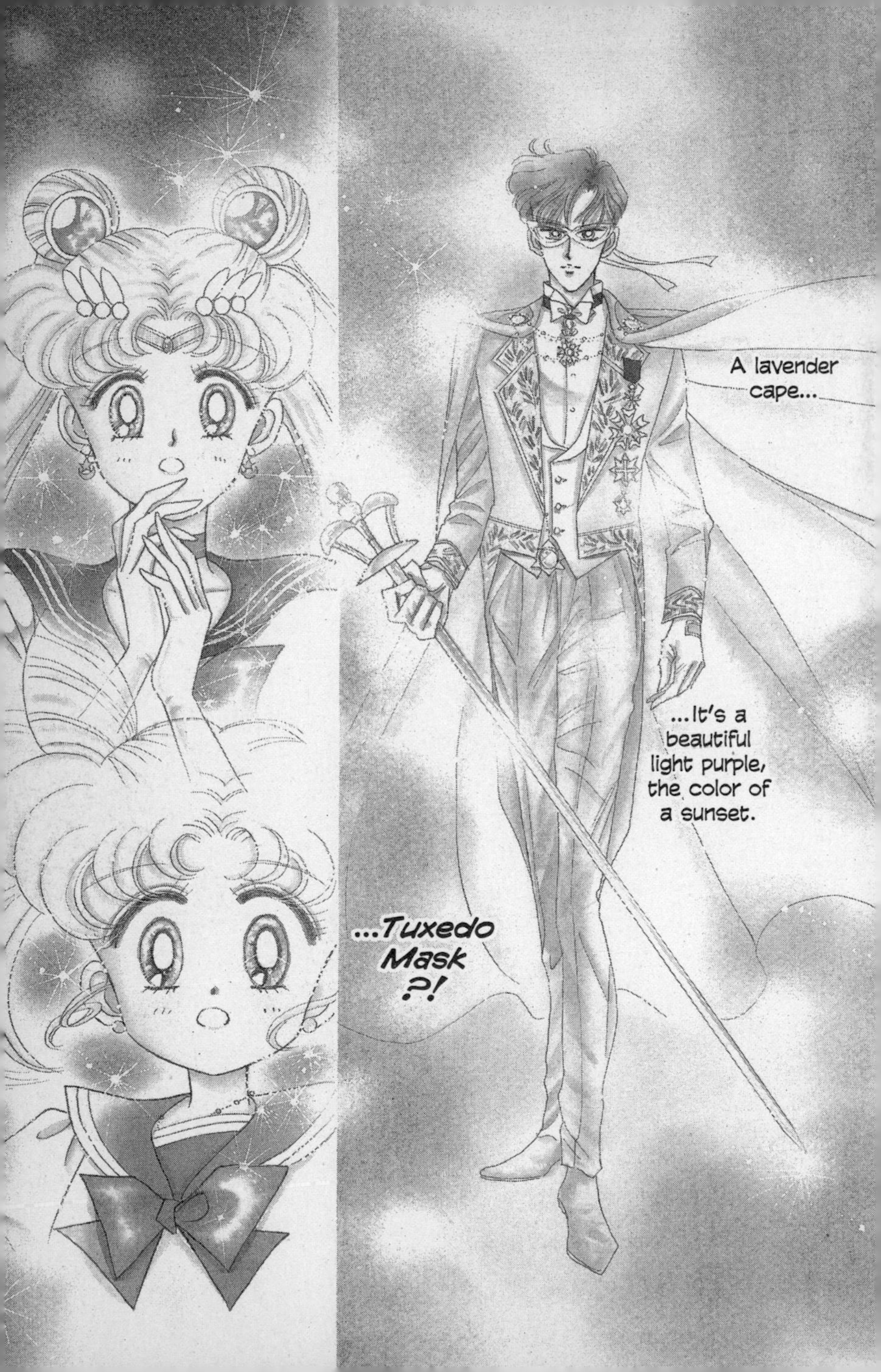
A lavender cape...
...It's a beautiful light purple, the color of a sunset.
...Tuxedo Mask ?!

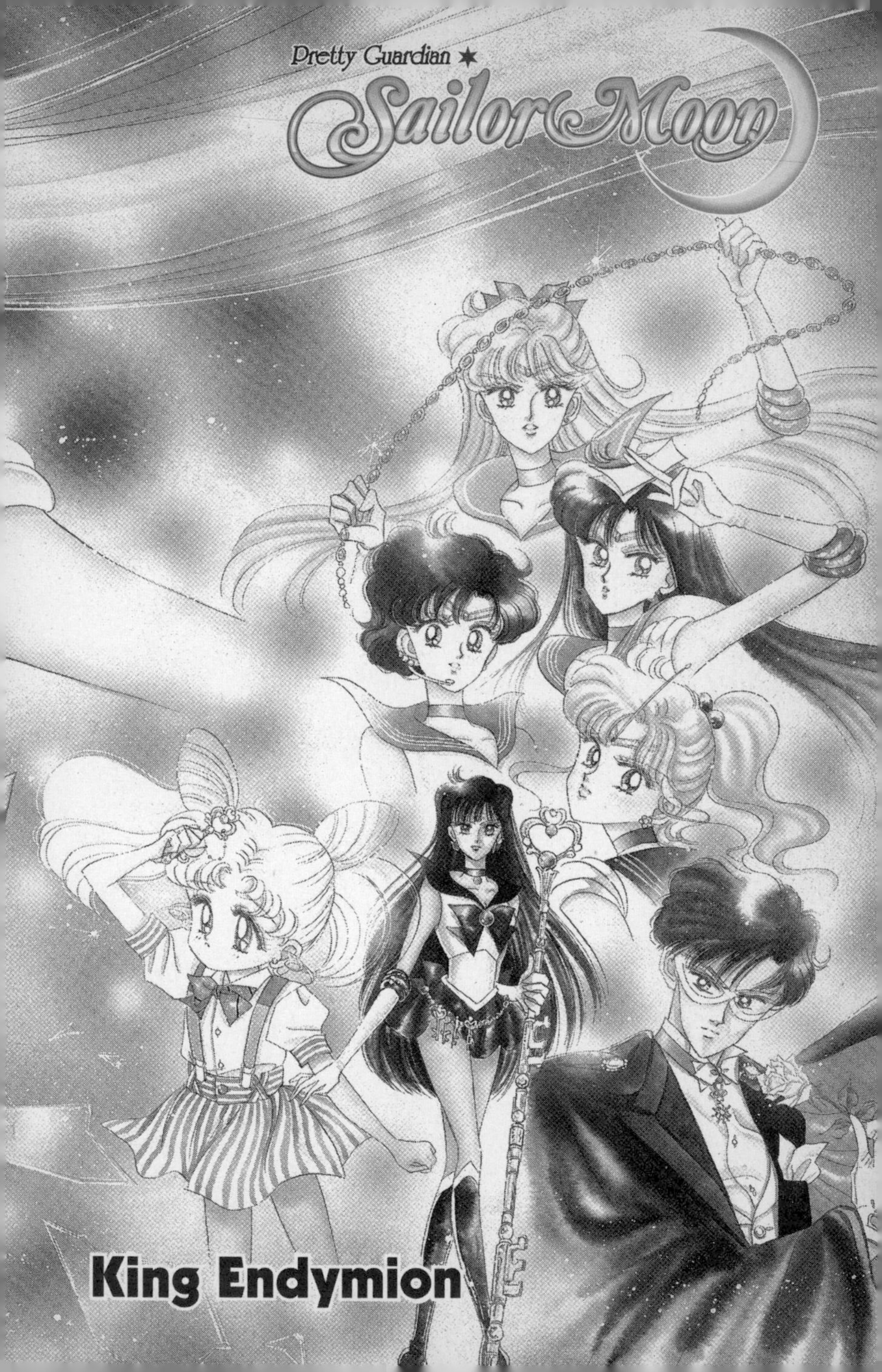
Pretty Guardian
Sailor Moon
King Endymion

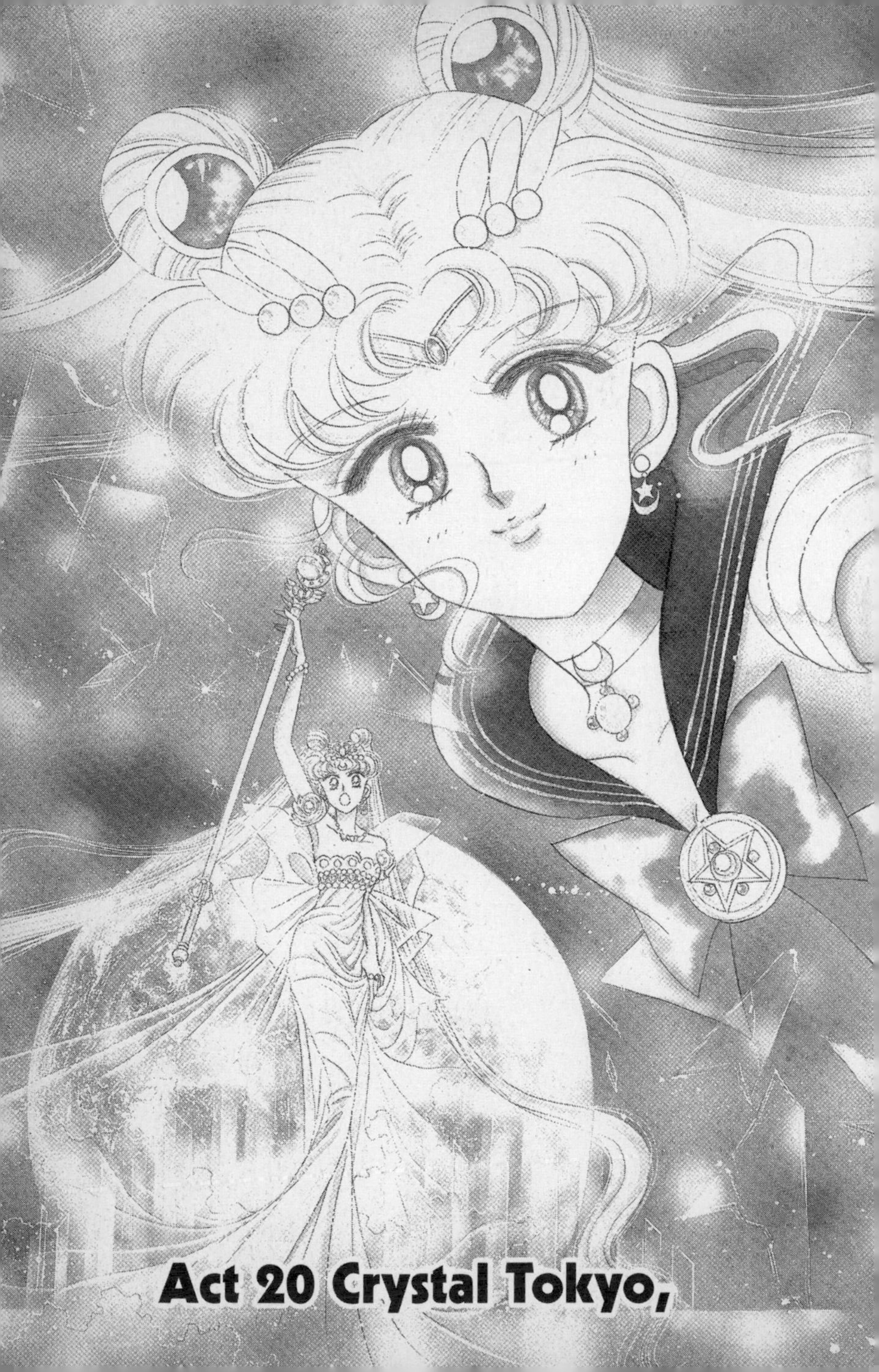
Act 20 Crystal Tokyo,

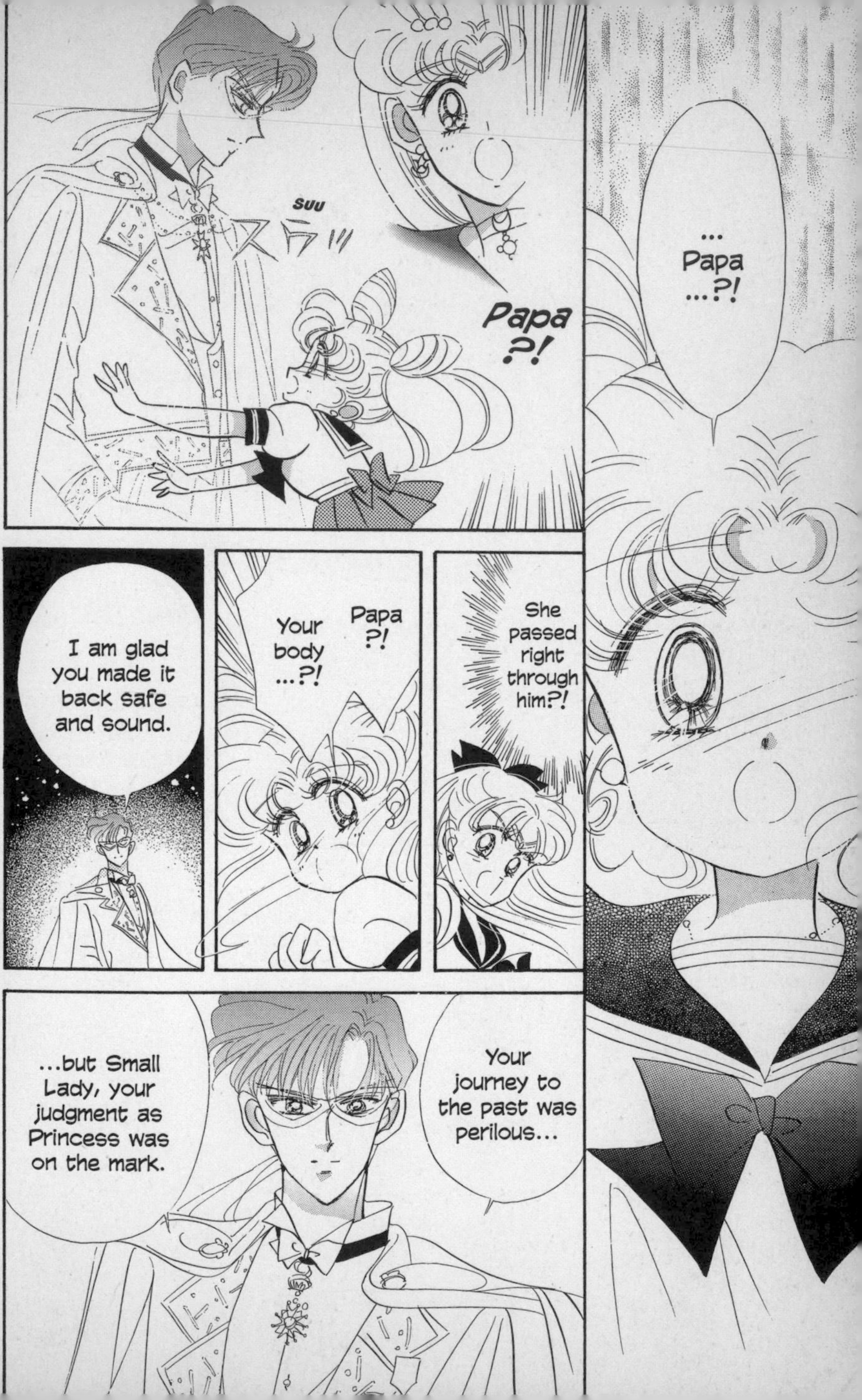

... Papa ...?!
SUU
スラッ
Papa ?!
She passed right through him?!
Papa ?!
Your body ...?!
I am glad you made it back safe and sound.
Your journey to the past was perilous...
...but Small Lady, your judgment as Princess was on the mark.

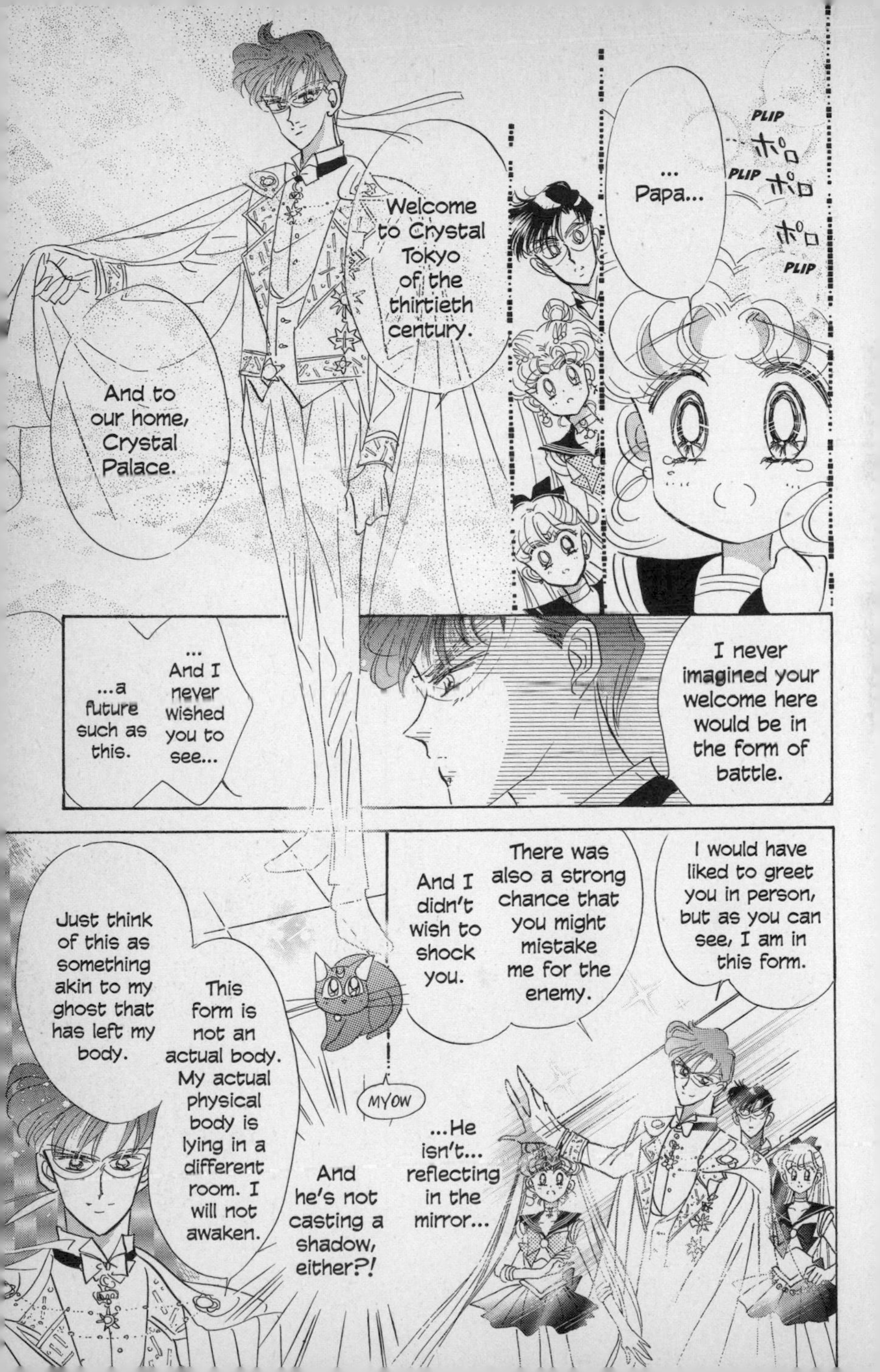
PLIP ポロ
PLIP ポロ
ポロ PLIP
... Papa...
Welcome to Crystal Tokyo of the thirtieth century.
And to our home, Crystal Palace.
I never imagined your welcome here would be in the form of battle.
... And I never wished you to see...
...a future such as this.
I would have liked to greet you in person, but as you can see, I am in this form.
There was also a strong chance that you might mistake me for the enemy.
And I didn't wish to shock you.
...He isn't... reflecting in the mirror...
And he's not casting a shadow, either?!
MYOW
This form is not an actual body. My actual physical body is lying in a different room. I will not awaken.
Just think of this as something akin to my ghost that has left my body.

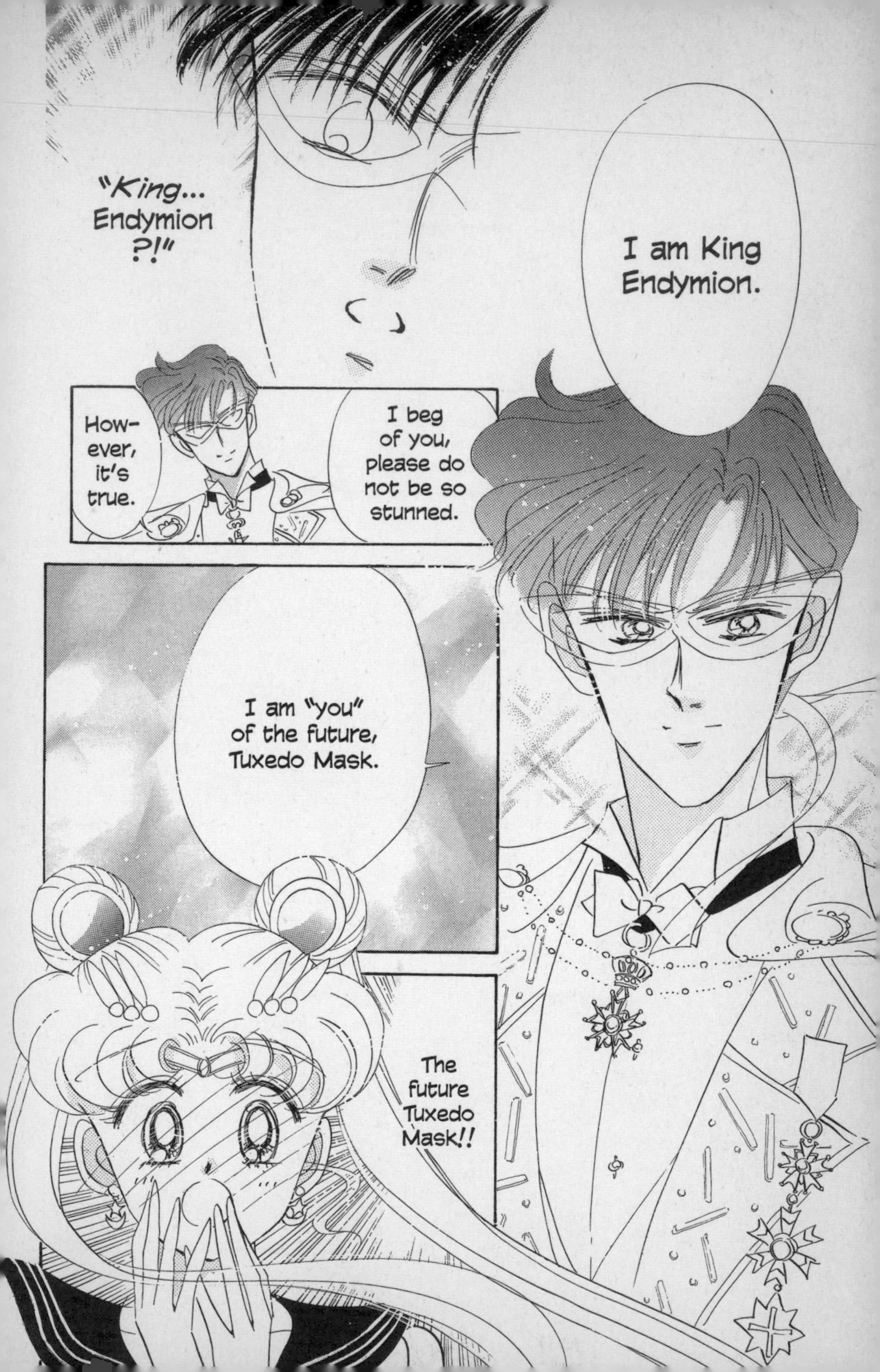
"King... Endymion ?!"
I am King Endymion.
I beg of you, please do not be so stunned.
How-ever, it's true.
I am "you" of the future, Tuxedo Mask.
The future Tuxedo Mask!!

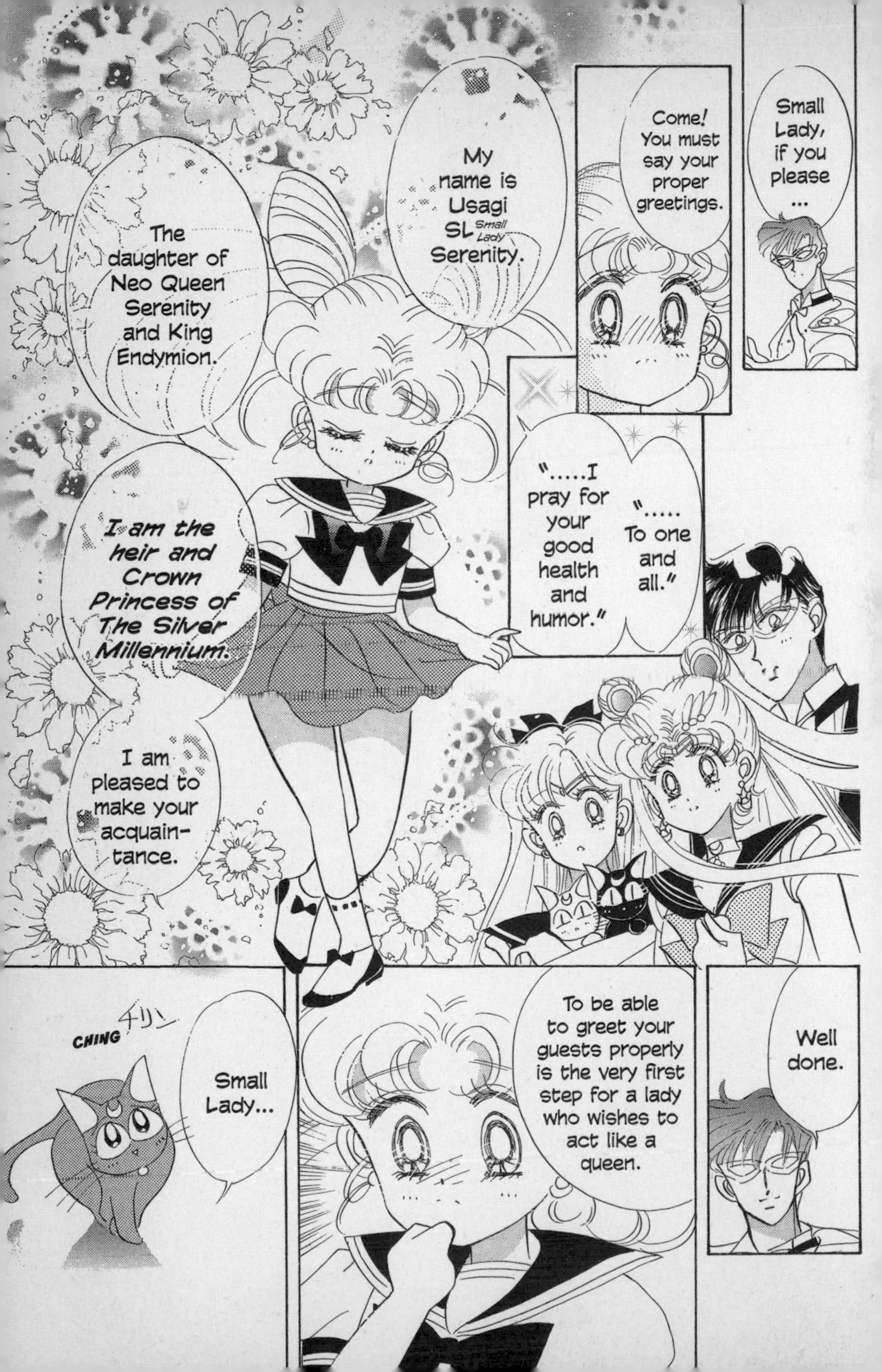
Small Lady, if you please ...
Come! You must say your proper greetings.
My name is Usagi SL Small Lady Serenity.
The daughter of Neo Queen Serenity and King Endymion.
I am the heir and Crown Princess of The Silver Millennium.
I am pleased to make your acquaintance.
".....I pray for your good health and humor."
"..... To one and all."
Well done.
To be able to greet your guests properly is the very first step for a lady who wishes to act like a queen.
Small Lady...
CHING

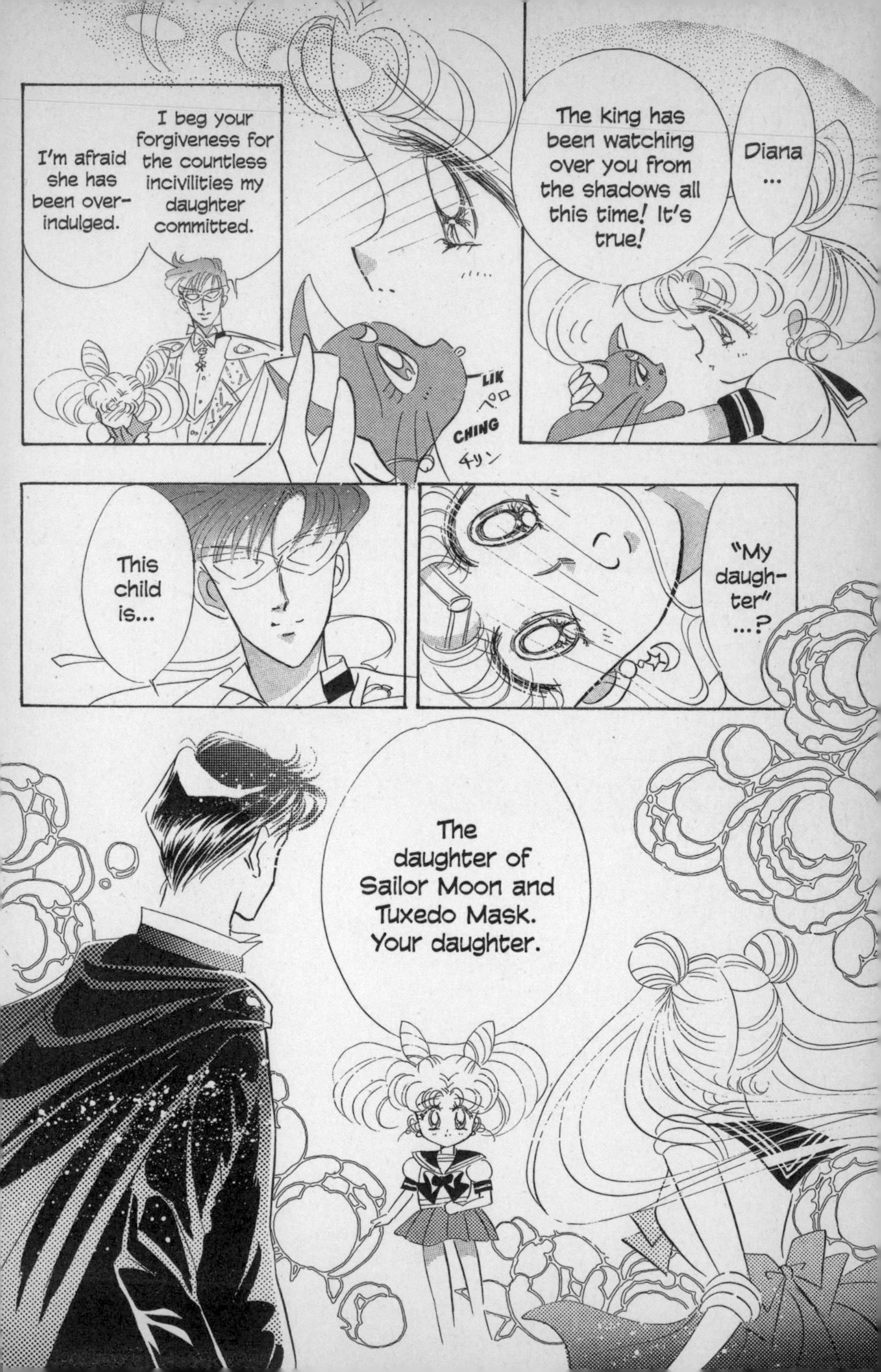
Diana ...
The king has been watching over you from the shadows all this time! It's true!
LIK
ペロ
CHING
チリン
I beg your forgiveness for the countless incivilities my daughter committed.
I'm afraid she has been over-indulged.
"My daughter" ...?
This child is...
The daughter of Sailor Moon and Tuxedo Mask. Your daughter.

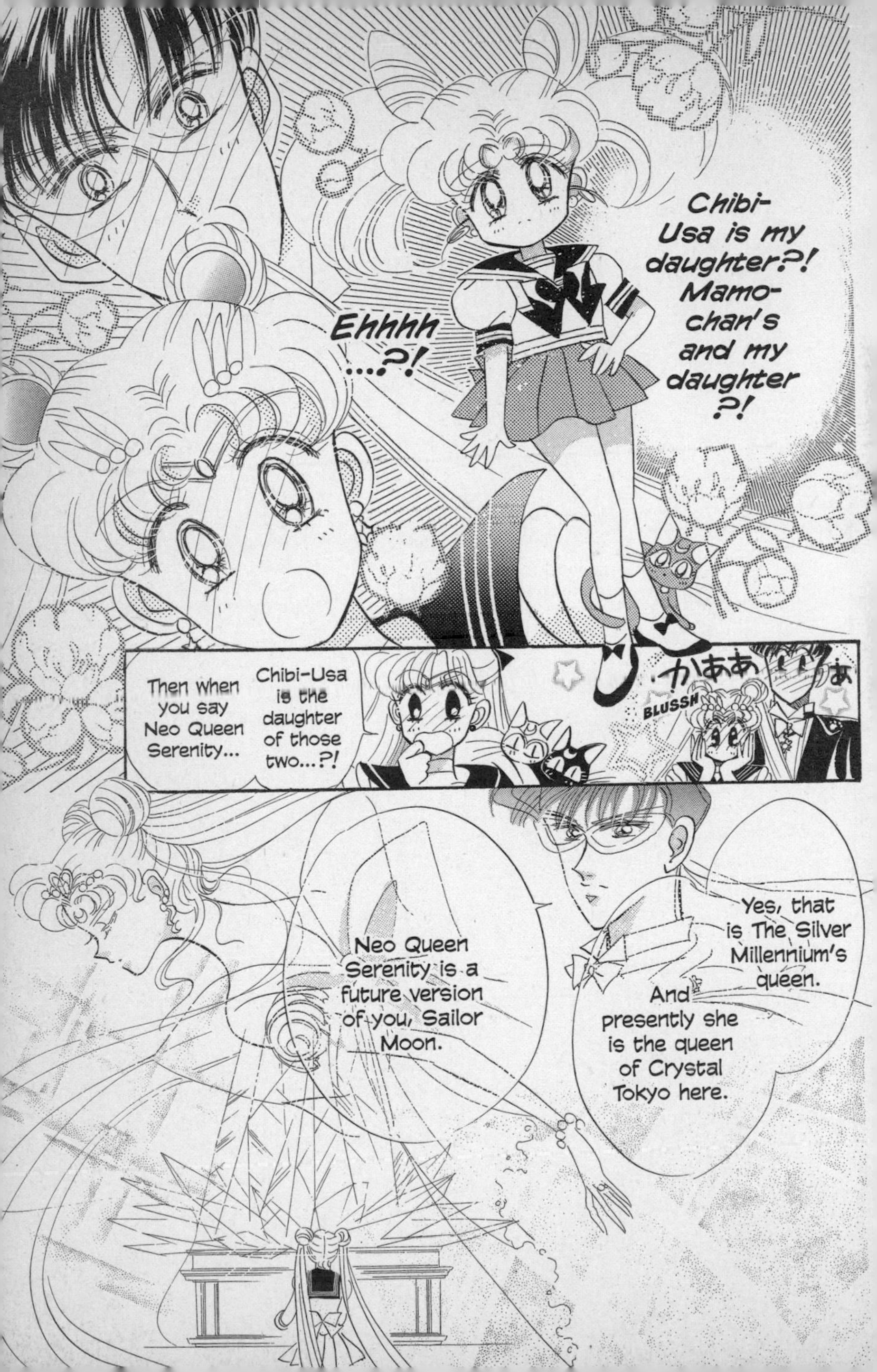
Chibi-Usa is my daughter?! Mamo-chan's and my daughter?!
Ehhhh ...?!
かああ あ
BLUSSH
Chibi-Usa is the daughter of those two...?!
Then when you say Neo Queen Serenity...
Yes, that is The Silver Millennium's queen.
And presently she is the queen of Crystal Tokyo here.
Neo Queen Serenity is a future version of you, Sailor Moon.

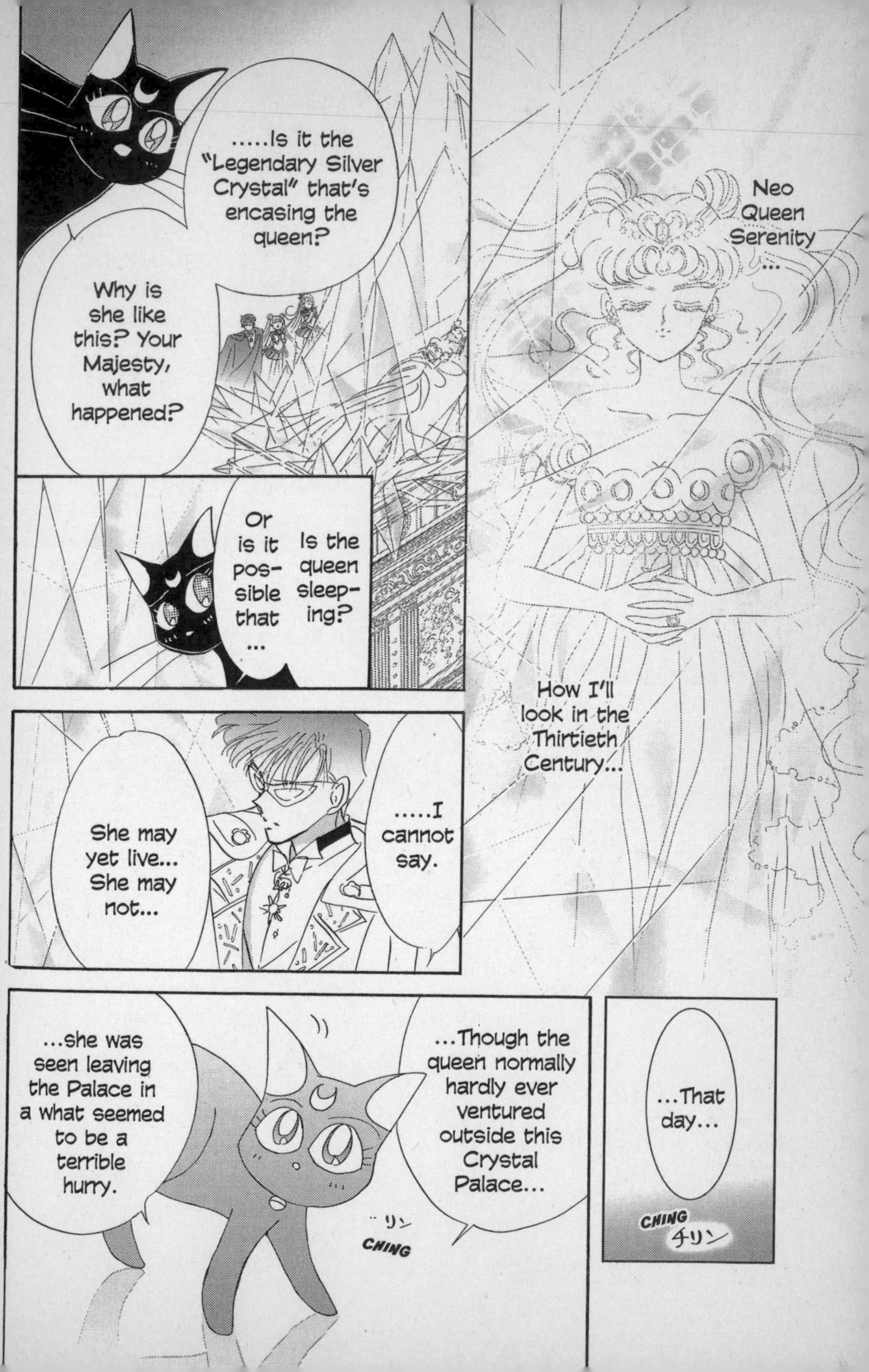
Neo Queen Serenity...
How I'll look in the Thirtieth Century...
.....Is it the "Legendary Silver Crystal" that's encasing the queen?
Why is she like this? Your Majesty, what happened?
Is the queen sleeping?
Or is it possible that...
.....I cannot say.
She may yet live... She may not...
...That day...
CHING
チリン
...Though the queen normally hardly ever ventured outside this Crystal Palace...
...she was seen leaving the Palace in a what seemed to be a terrible hurry.
‥リン
CHING

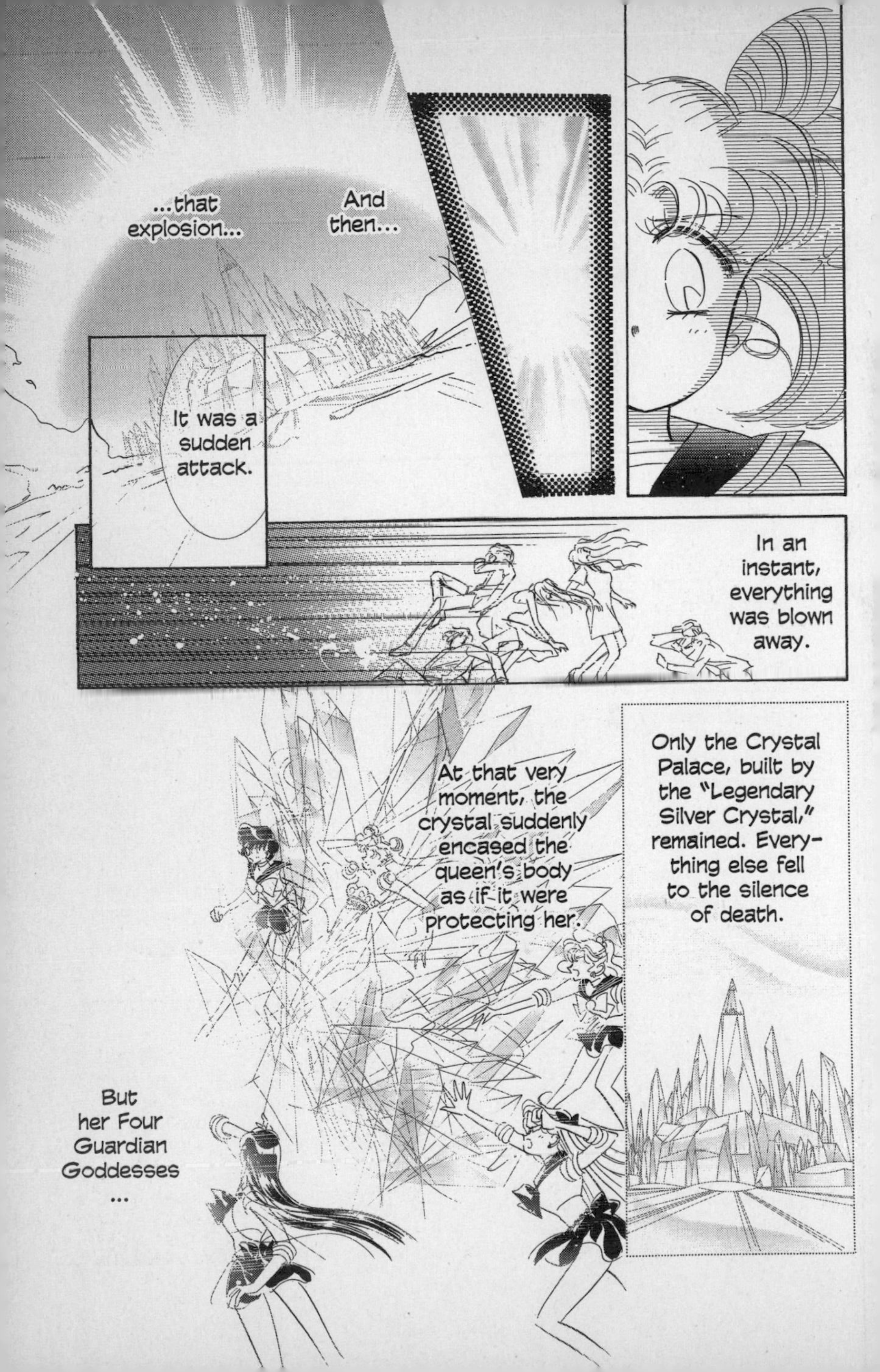
And then...
...that explosion...
It was a sudden attack.
In an instant, everything was blown away.
Only the Crystal Palace, built by the "Legendary Silver Crystal," remained. Every-thing else fell to the silence of death.
At that very moment, the crystal suddenly encased the queen's body as if it were protecting her.
But her Four Guardian Goddesses ...

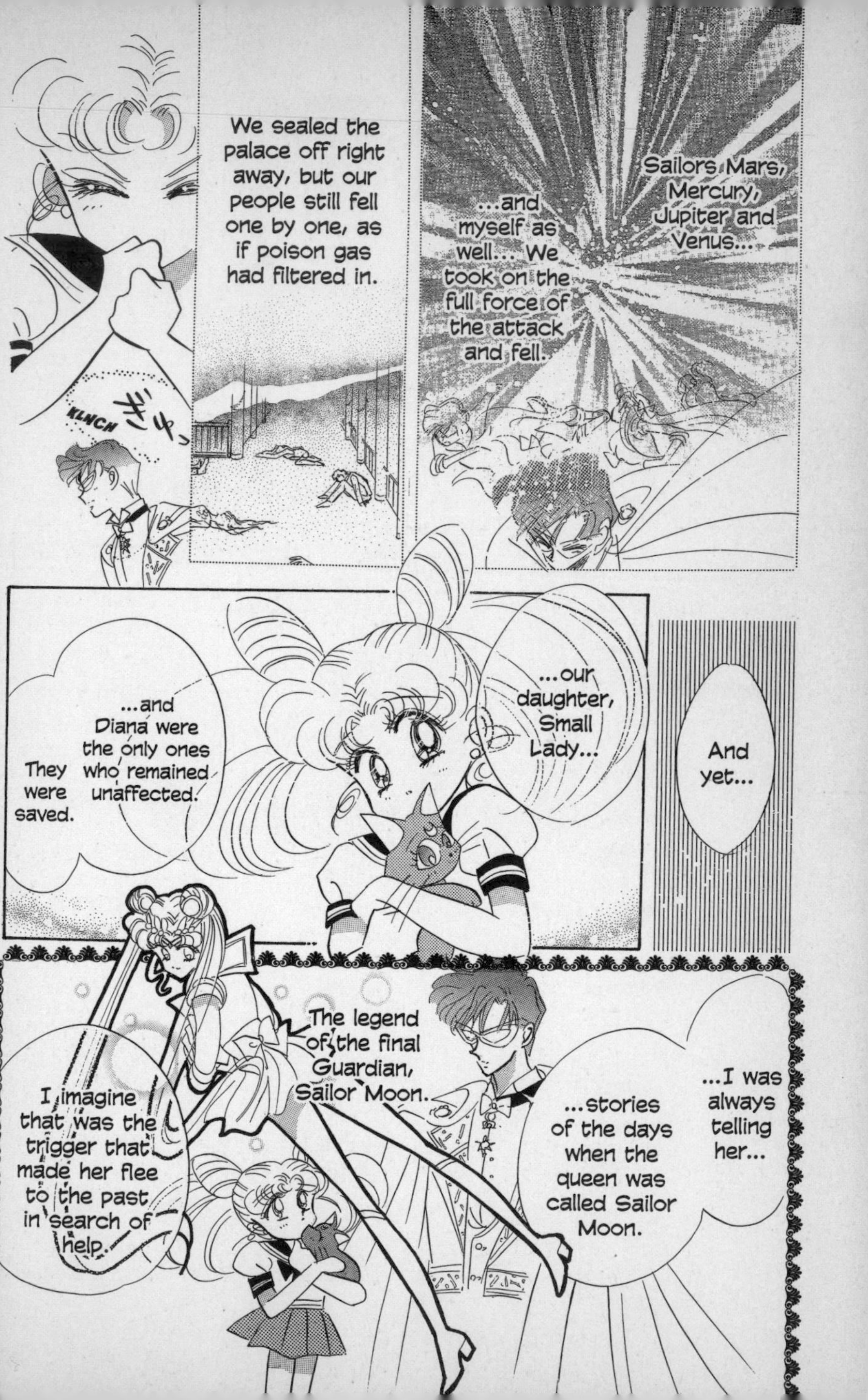
Sailors Mars, Mercury, Jupiter and Venus...
...and myself as well... We took on the full force of the attack and fell.
We sealed the palace off right away, but our people still fell one by one, as if poison gas had filtered in.
KLNCH
ギュッ
And yet...
...our daughter, Small Lady...
...and Diana were the only ones who remained unaffected.
They were saved.
...I was always telling her...
...stories of the days when the queen was called Sailor Moon.
The legend of the final Guardian, Sailor Moon.
I imagine that was the trigger that made her flee to the past in search of help.

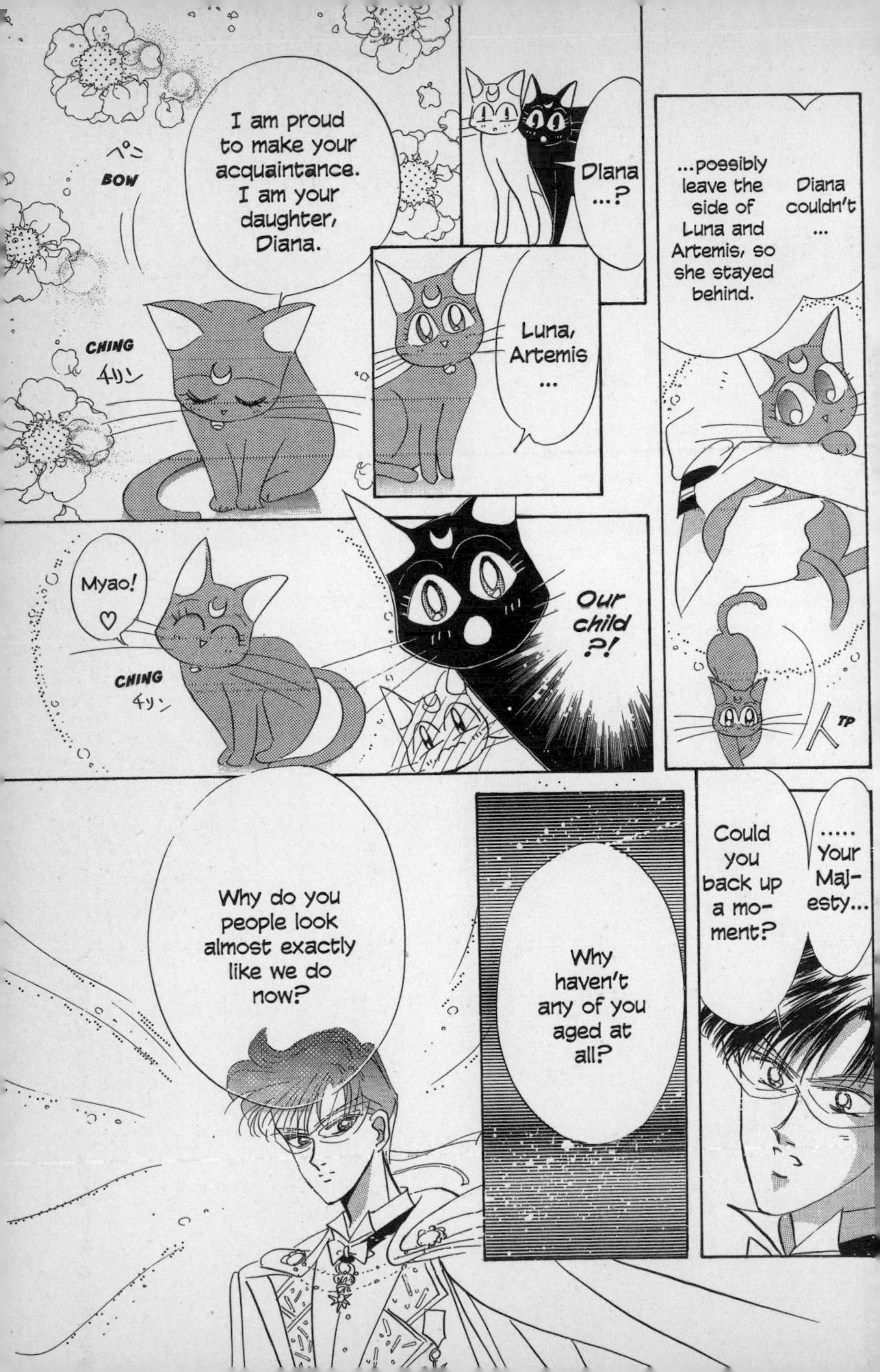
Diana couldn't ...
...possibly leave the side of Luna and Artemis, so she stayed behind.
TP
Diana ...?
I am proud to make your acquaintance. I am your daughter, Diana.
ペこ
BOW
CHING
チリン
Luna, Artemis ...
Our child ?!
Myao! ♡
CHING
チリン
..... Your Maj-esty...
Could you back up a mo-ment?
Why haven't any of you aged at all?
Why do you people look almost exactly like we do now?

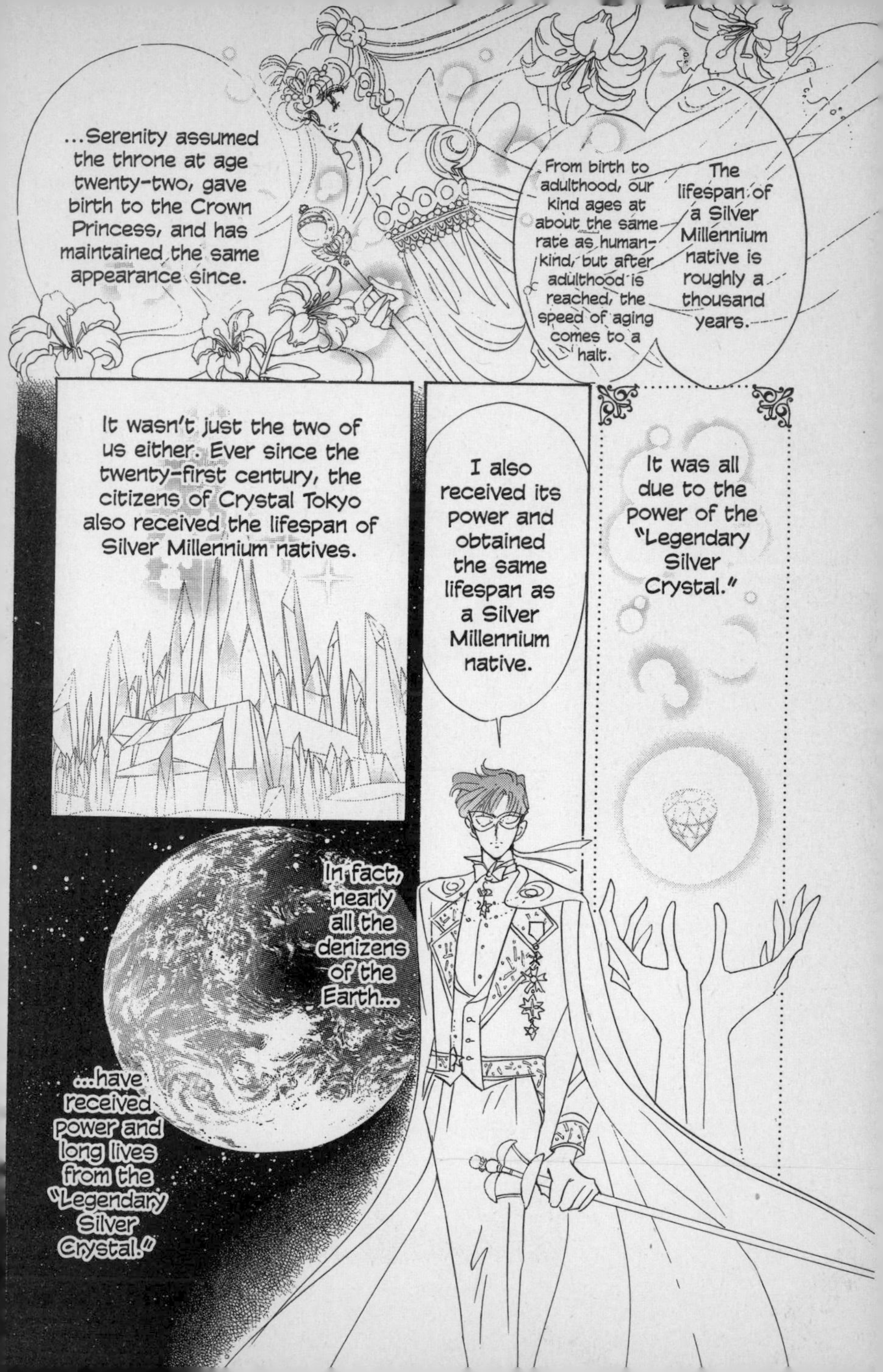
The lifespan of a Silver Millennium native is roughly a thousand years.
From birth to adulthood, our kind ages at about the same rate as humankind, but after adulthood is reached, the speed of aging comes to a halt.
...Serenity assumed the throne at age twenty-two, gave birth to the Crown Princess, and has maintained the same appearance since.
It was all due to the power of the "Legendary Silver Crystal."
I also received its power and obtained the same lifespan as a Silver Millennium native.
It wasn't just the two of us either. Ever since the twenty-first century, the citizens of Crystal Tokyo also received the lifespan of Silver Millennium natives.
In fact, nearly all the denizens of the Earth...
...have received power and long lives from the "Legendary Silver Crystal."

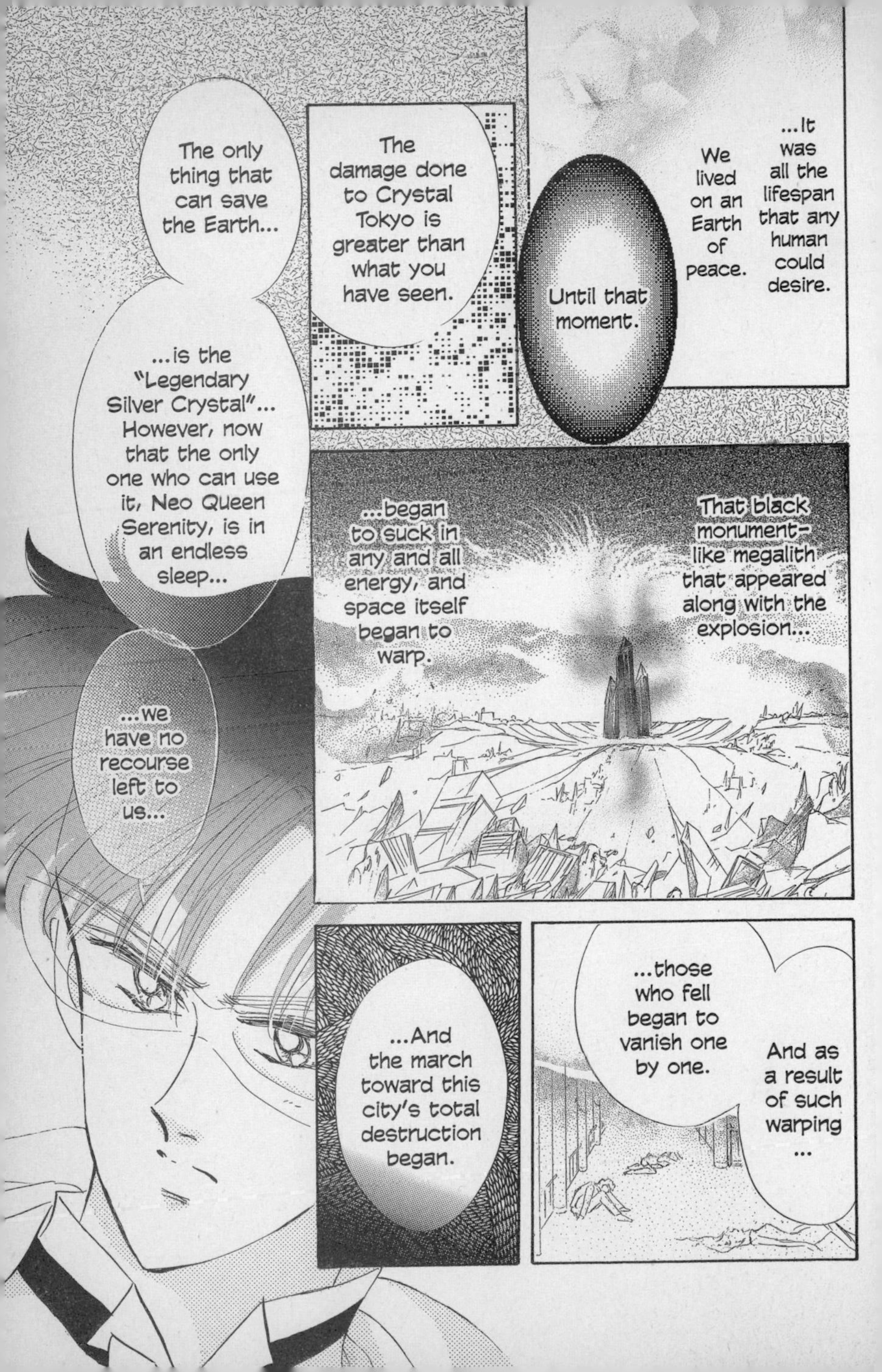
...It was all the lifespan that any human could desire.
We lived on an Earth of peace.
Until that moment.
That black monument-like megalith that appeared along with the explosion...
...began to suck in any and all energy, and space itself began to warp.
And as a result of such warping ...
...those who fell began to vanish one by one.
...And the march toward this city's total destruction began.
The damage done to Crystal Tokyo is greater than what you have seen.
The only thing that can save the Earth...
...is the "Legendary Silver Crystal"... However, now that the only one who can use it, Neo Queen Serenity, is in an endless sleep...
...we have no recourse left to us...

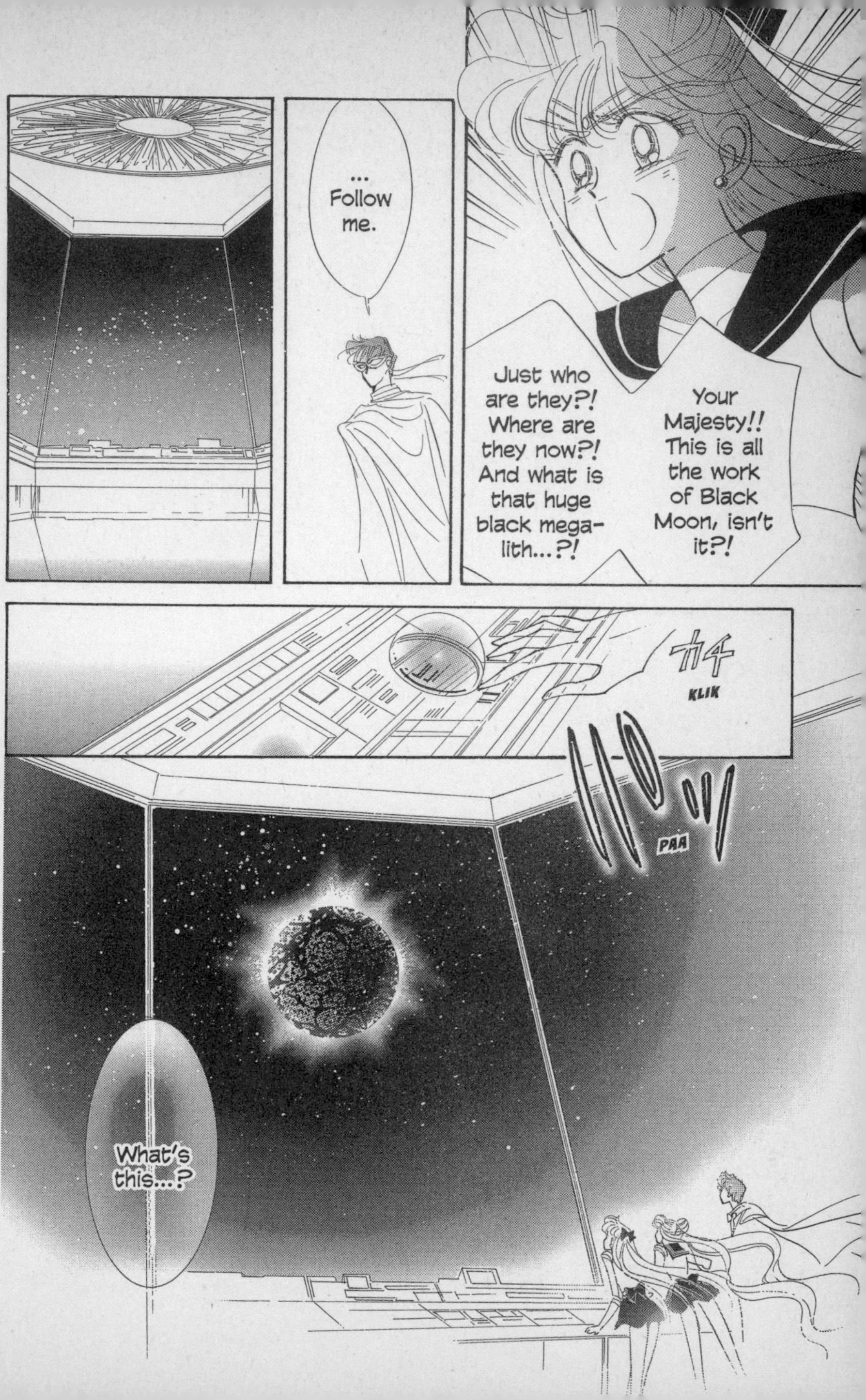
Your Majesty!! This is all the work of Black Moon, isn't it?!
Just who are they?! Where are they now?! And what is that huge black megalith...?!
... Follow me.
カチ
KLIK
PAA
What's this...?

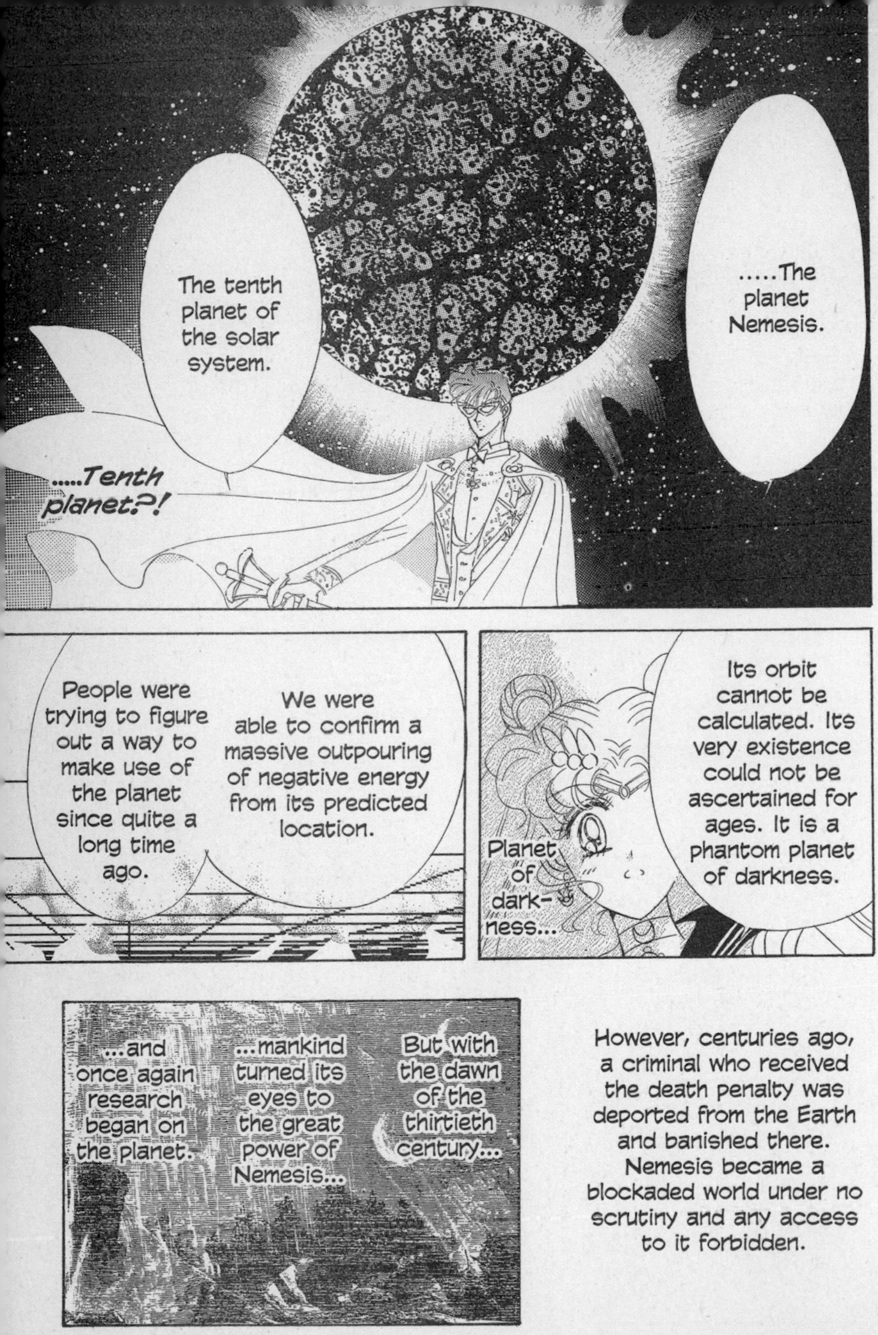
.....The planet Nemesis.
The tenth planet of the solar system.
.....Tenth planet?!
Its orbit cannot be calculated. Its very existence could not be ascertained for ages. It is a phantom planet of darkness.
Planet of dark-ness...
We were able to confirm a massive outpouring of negative energy from its predicted location.
People were trying to figure out a way to make use of the planet since quite a long time ago.
However, centuries ago, a criminal who received the death penalty was deported from the Earth and banished there. Nemesis became a blockaded world under no scrutiny and any access to it forbidden.
But with the dawn of the thirtieth century...
...mankind turned its eyes to the great power of Nemesis...
...and once again research began on the planet.

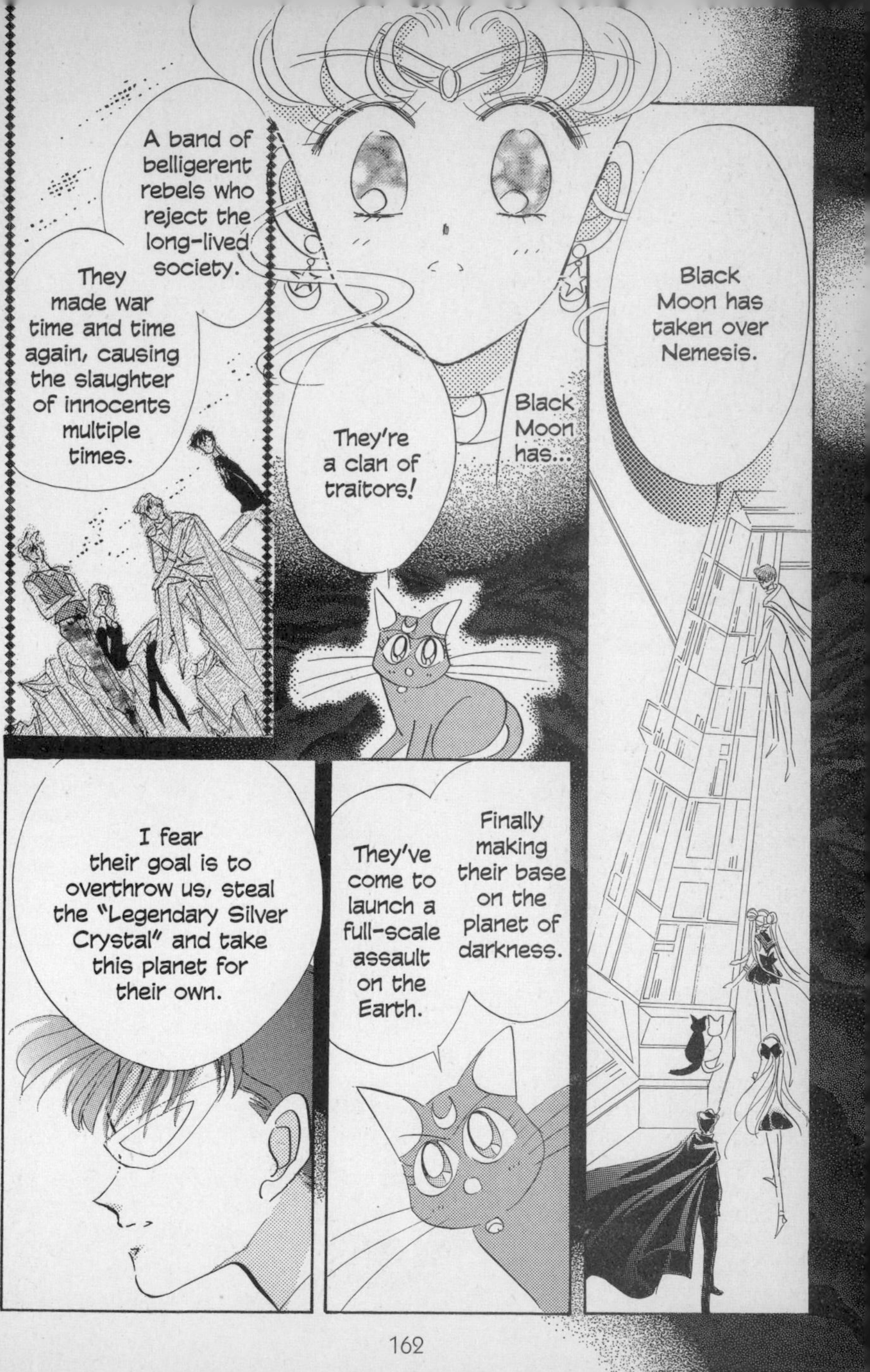
Black Moon has taken over Nemesis.
Black Moon has...
They're a clan of traitors!
A band of belligerent rebels who reject the long-lived society.
They made war time and time again, causing the slaughter of innocents multiple times.
Finally making their base on the planet of darkness.
They've come to launch a full-scale assault on the Earth.
I fear their goal is to overthrow us, steal the "Legendary Silver Crystal" and take this planet for their own.

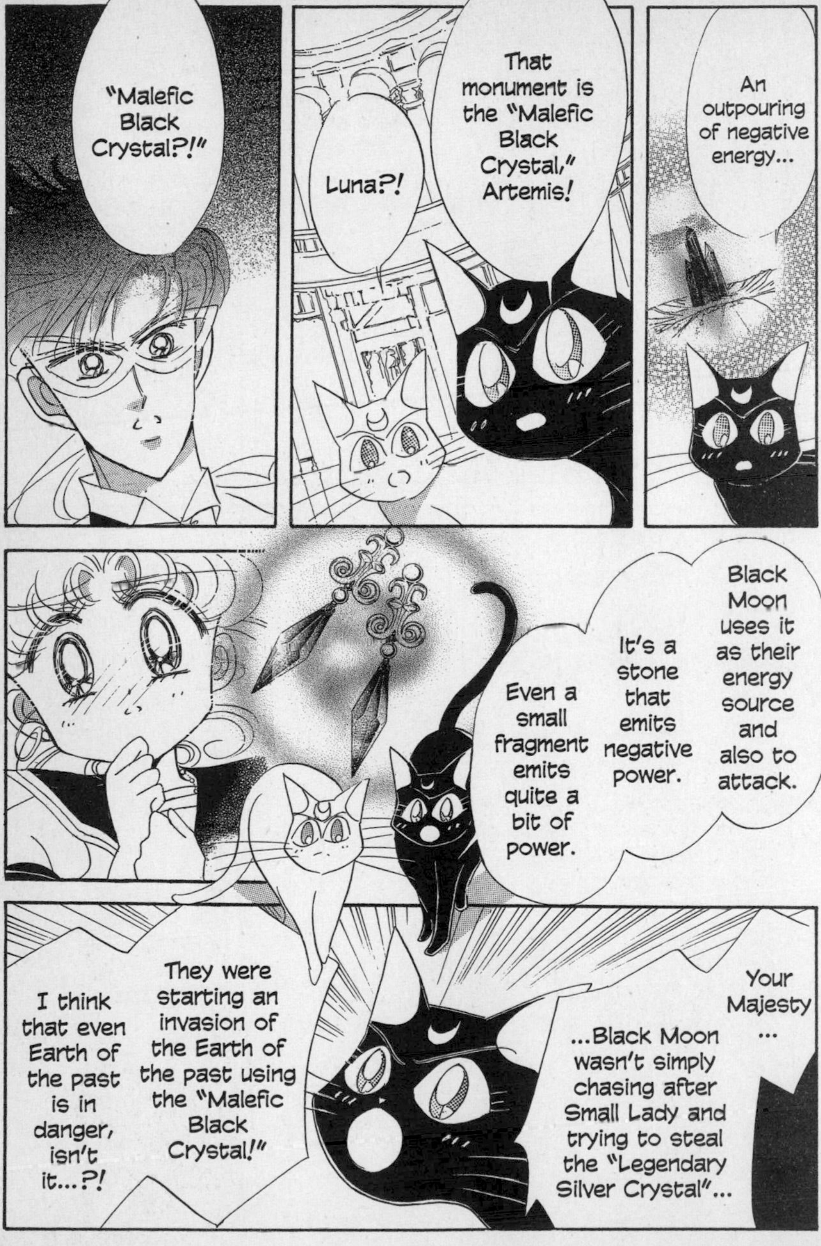
An outpouring of negative energy...
That monument is the "Malefic Black Crystal," Artemis!
Luna?!
"Malefic Black Crystal?!"
Black Moon uses it as their energy source and also to attack.
It's a stone that emits negative power.
Even a small fragment emits quite a bit of power.
Your Majesty ...
...Black Moon wasn't simply chasing after Small Lady and trying to steal the "Legendary Silver Crystal"...
They were starting an invasion of the Earth of the past using the "Malefic Black Crystal!"
I think that even Earth of the past is in danger, isn't it...?!

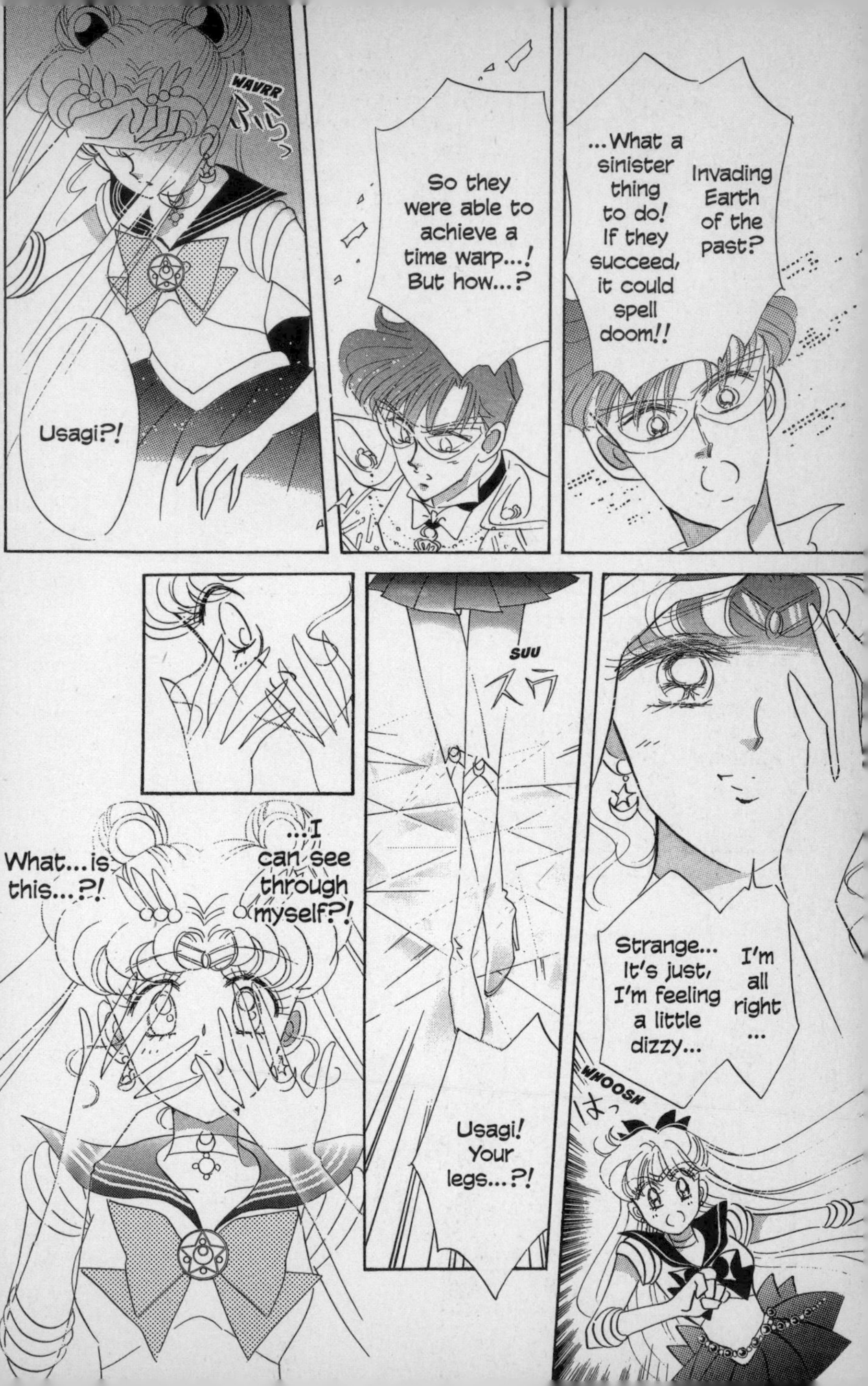
Invading Earth of the past?
...What a sinister thing to do! If they succeed, it could spell doom!!
So they were able to achieve a time warp...! But how...?
WAVRR
ふらっ
Usagi?!
I'm all right ...
Strange... It's just, I'm feeling a little dizzy...
WHOOSH
はっ
SUU
スウ
Usagi! Your legs...?!
...I can see through myself?!
What...is this...?!

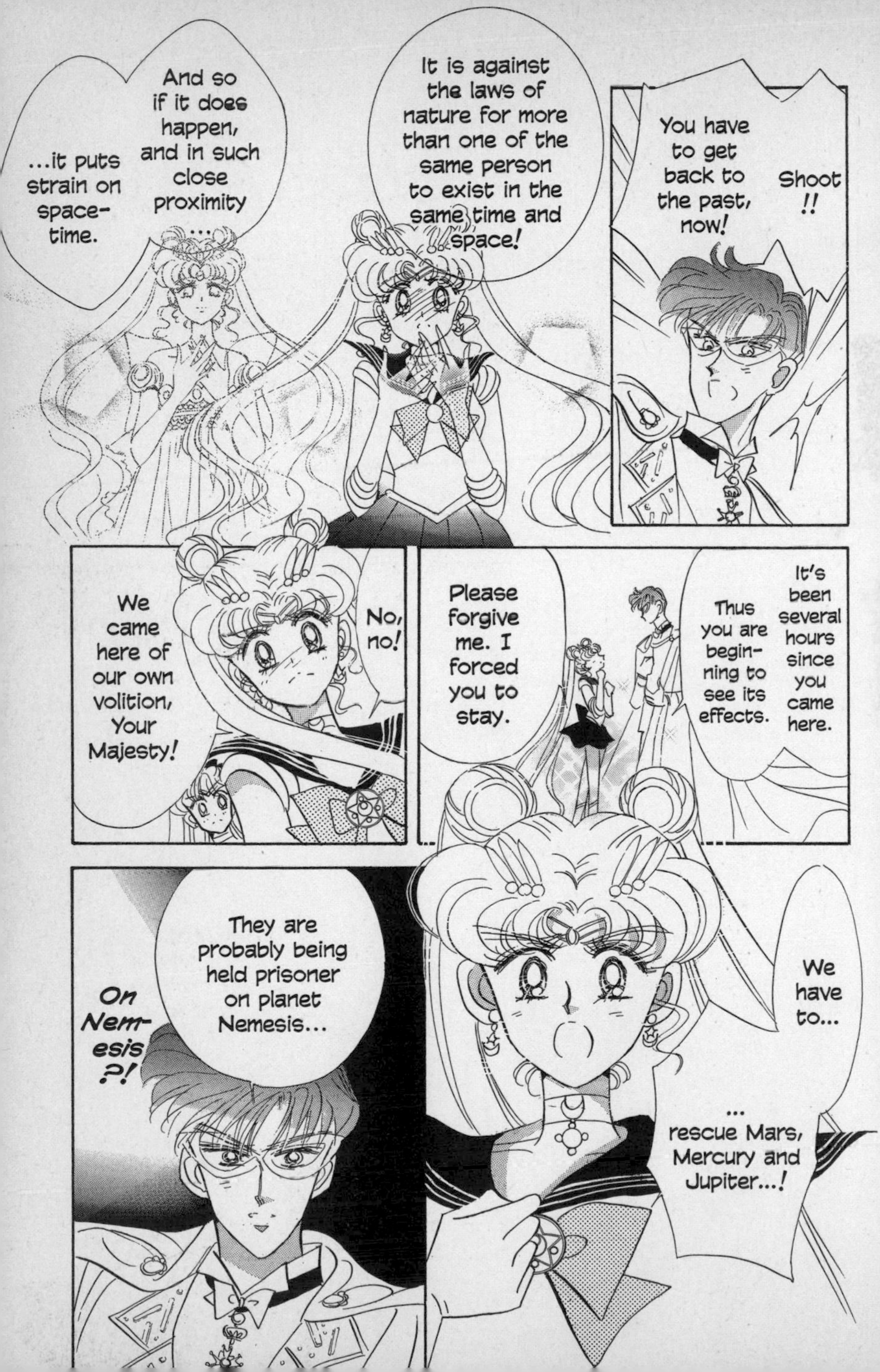
Shoot!!
You have to get back to the past, now!
It is against the laws of nature for more than one of the same person to exist in the same time and space!
And so if it does happen, and in such close proximity...
...it puts strain on space-time.
It's been several hours since you came here.
Thus you are beginning to see its effects.
Please forgive me. I forced you to stay.
No, no!
We came here of our own volition, Your Majesty!
We have to...
...rescue Mars, Mercury and Jupiter...!
They are probably being held prisoner on planet Nemesis...
On Nemesis?!

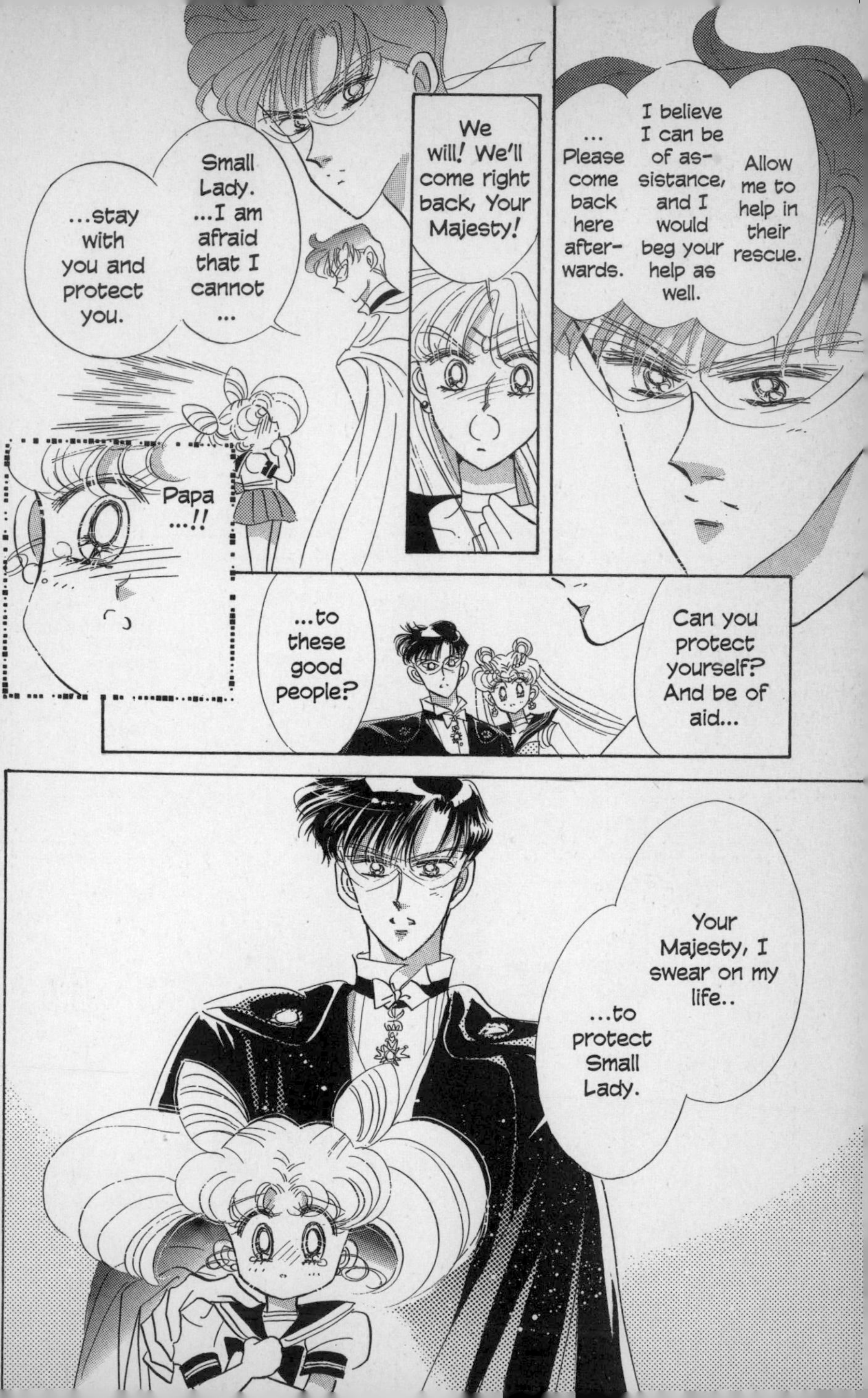
Allow me to help in their rescue.
I believe I can be of as-sistance, and I would beg your help as well.
... Please come back here after-wards.
We will! We'll come right back, Your Majesty!
Small Lady. ...I am afraid that I cannot ...
...stay with you and protect you.
Papa ...!!
Can you protect yourself? And be of aid...
...to these good people?
Your Majesty, I swear on my life..
...to protect Small Lady.

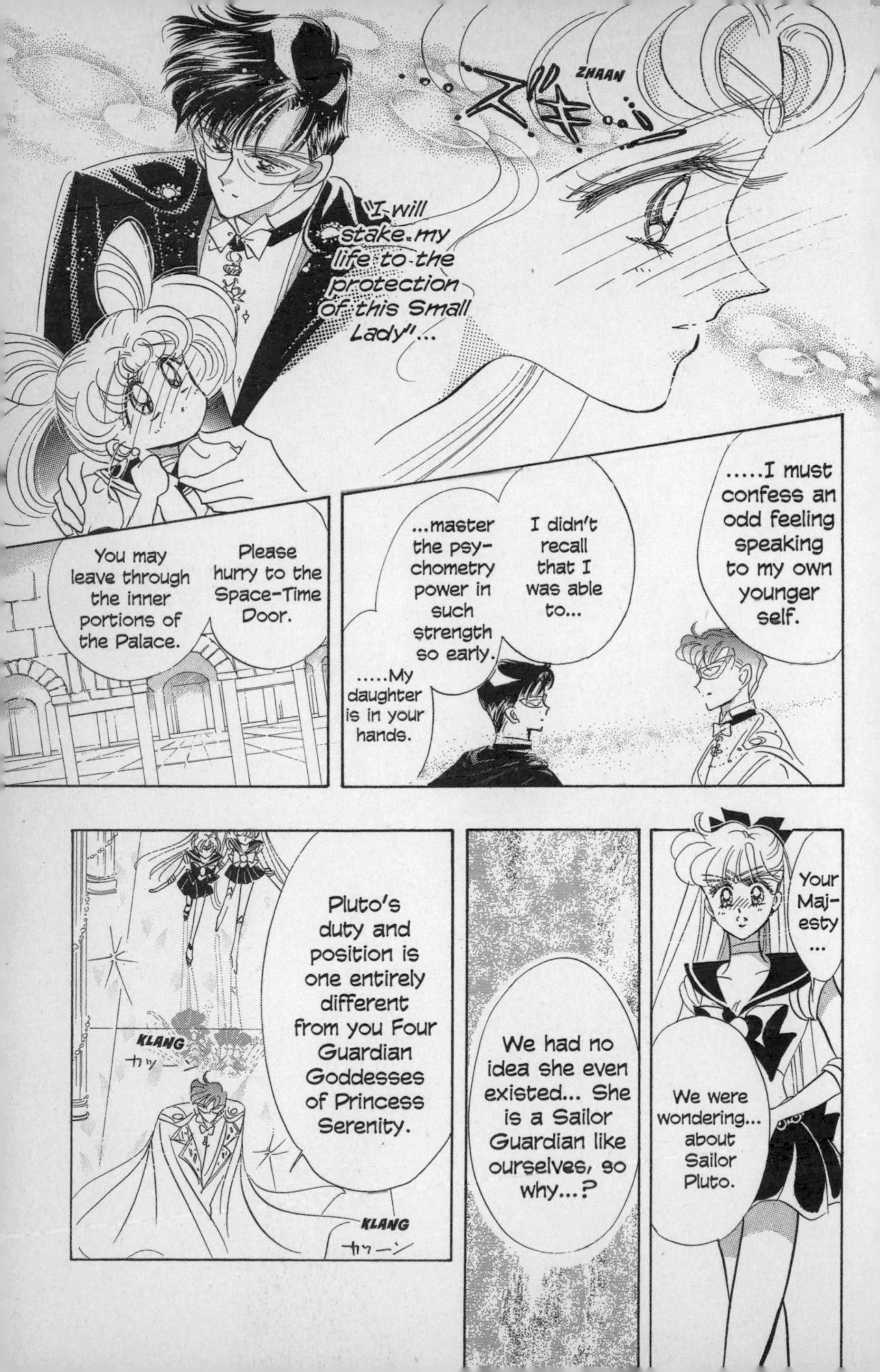
ZHAAN
"I will stake my life to the protection of this Small Lady"...
.....I must confess an odd feeling speaking to my own younger self.
I didn't recall that I was able to...
...master the psychometry power in such strength so early.
.....My daughter is in your hands.
Please hurry to the Space-Time Door.
You may leave through the inner portions of the Palace.
Your Majesty...
We were wondering... about Sailor Pluto.
We had no idea she even existed... She is a Sailor Guardian like ourselves, so why...?
Pluto's duty and position is one entirely different from you Four Guardian Goddesses of Princess Serenity.
KLANG
KLANG

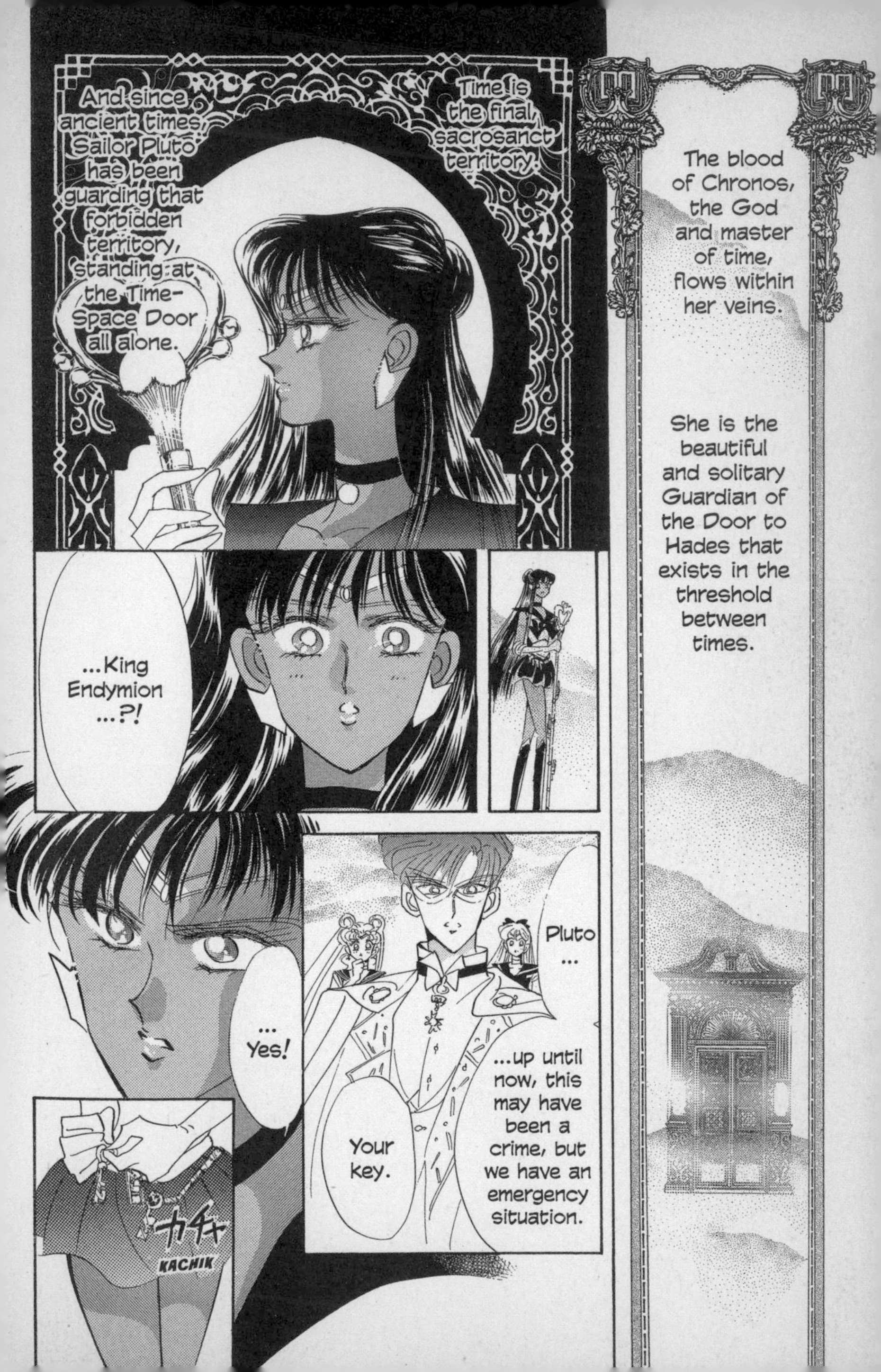
The blood of Chronos, the God and master of time, flows within her veins.
She is the beautiful and solitary Guardian of the Door to Hades that exists in the threshold between times.
Time is the final, sacrosanct territory.
And since ancient times, Sailor Pluto has been guarding that forbidden territory, standing at the Time-Space Door all alone.
...King Endymion ...?!
Pluto ...
...up until now, this may have been a crime, but we have an emergency situation.
Your key.
... Yes!
カチャ
KACHIK

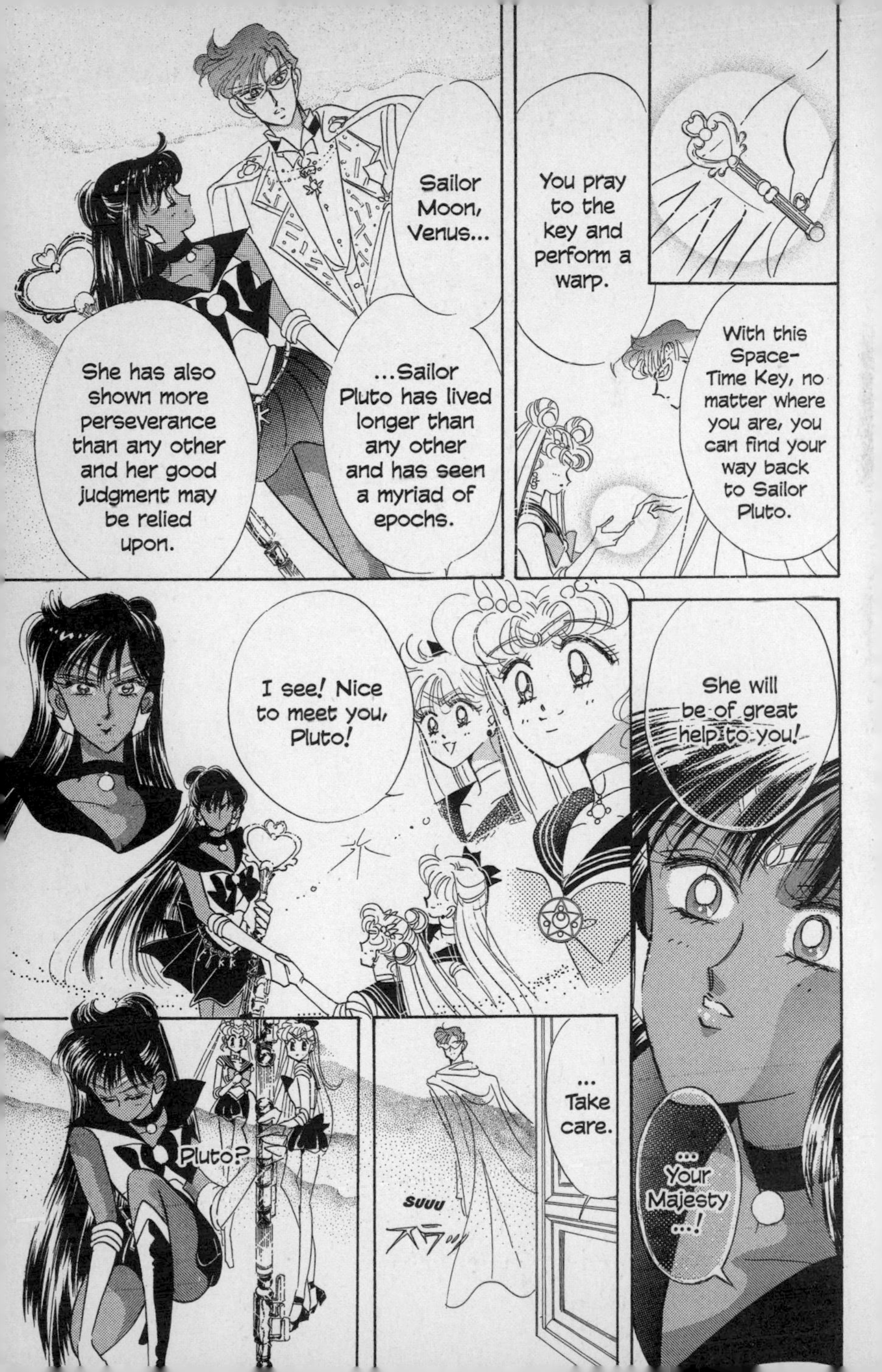
With this Space-Time Key, no matter where you are, you can find your way back to Sailor Pluto.
You pray to the key and perform a warp.
Sailor Moon, Venus...
...Sailor Pluto has lived longer than any other and has seen a myriad of epochs.
She has also shown more perseverance than any other and her good judgment may be relied upon.
She will be of great help to you!
I see! Nice to meet you, Pluto!
... Take care.
SUUU
スラッ
... Your Majesty ...!
Pluto?

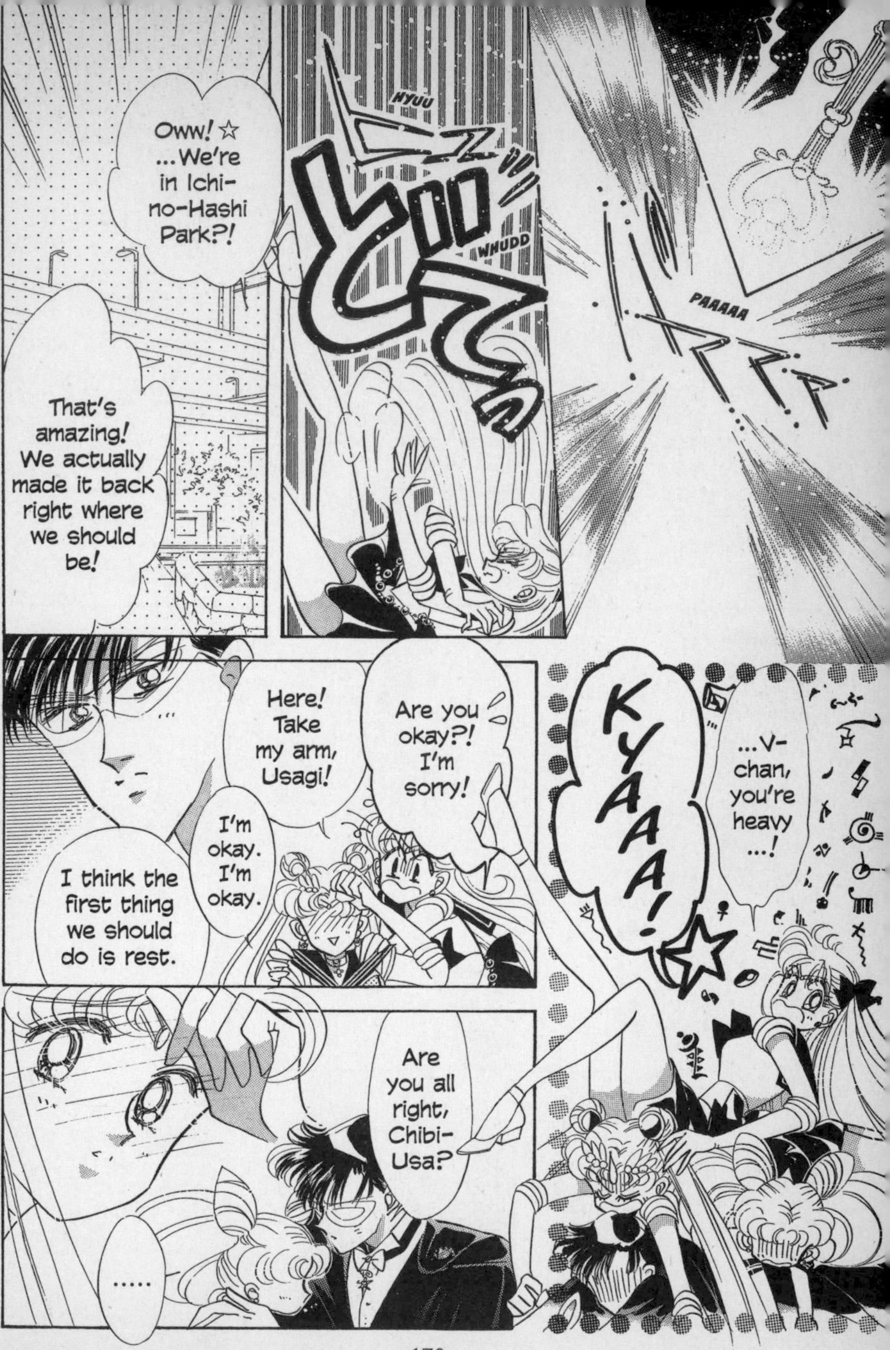
PAAAAA
HYUU
WHUDD
Oww! ☆ ...We're in Ichi-no-Hashi Park?!
That's amazing! We actually made it back right where we should be!
KYAAA!
...V-chan, you're heavy...!
Are you okay?! I'm sorry!
Here! Take my arm, Usagi!
...
I'm okay. I'm okay.
I think the first thing we should do is rest.
Are you all right, Chibi-Usa?
.....

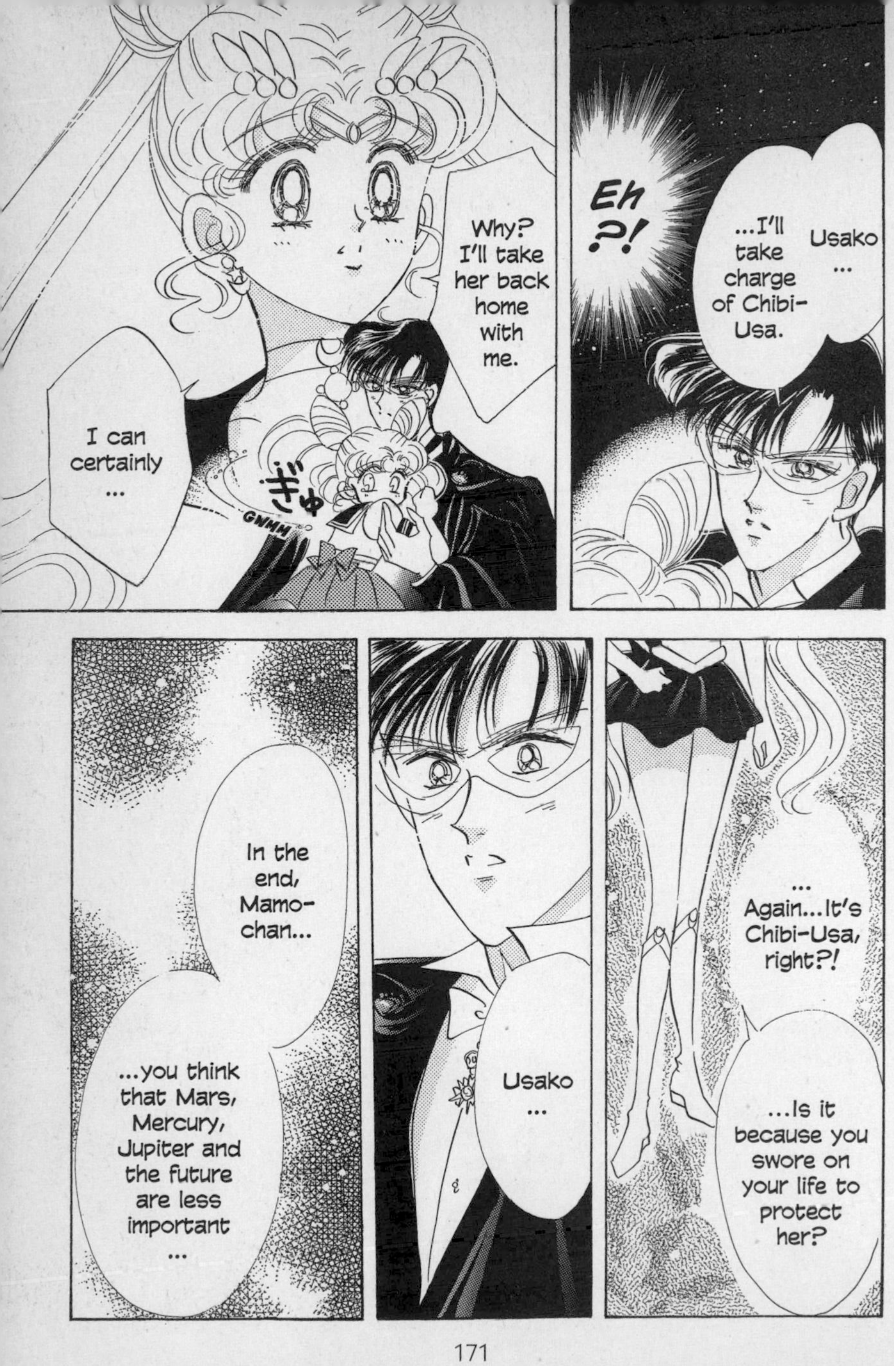
Usako ...
...I'll take charge of Chibi-Usa.
Eh ?!
Why? I'll take her back home with me.
I can certainly ...
ぎゅ
GNMM
... Again...It's Chibi-Usa, right?!
...Is it because you swore on your life to protect her?
Usako ...
In the end, Mamo-chan...
...you think that Mars, Mercury, Jupiter and the future are less important ...

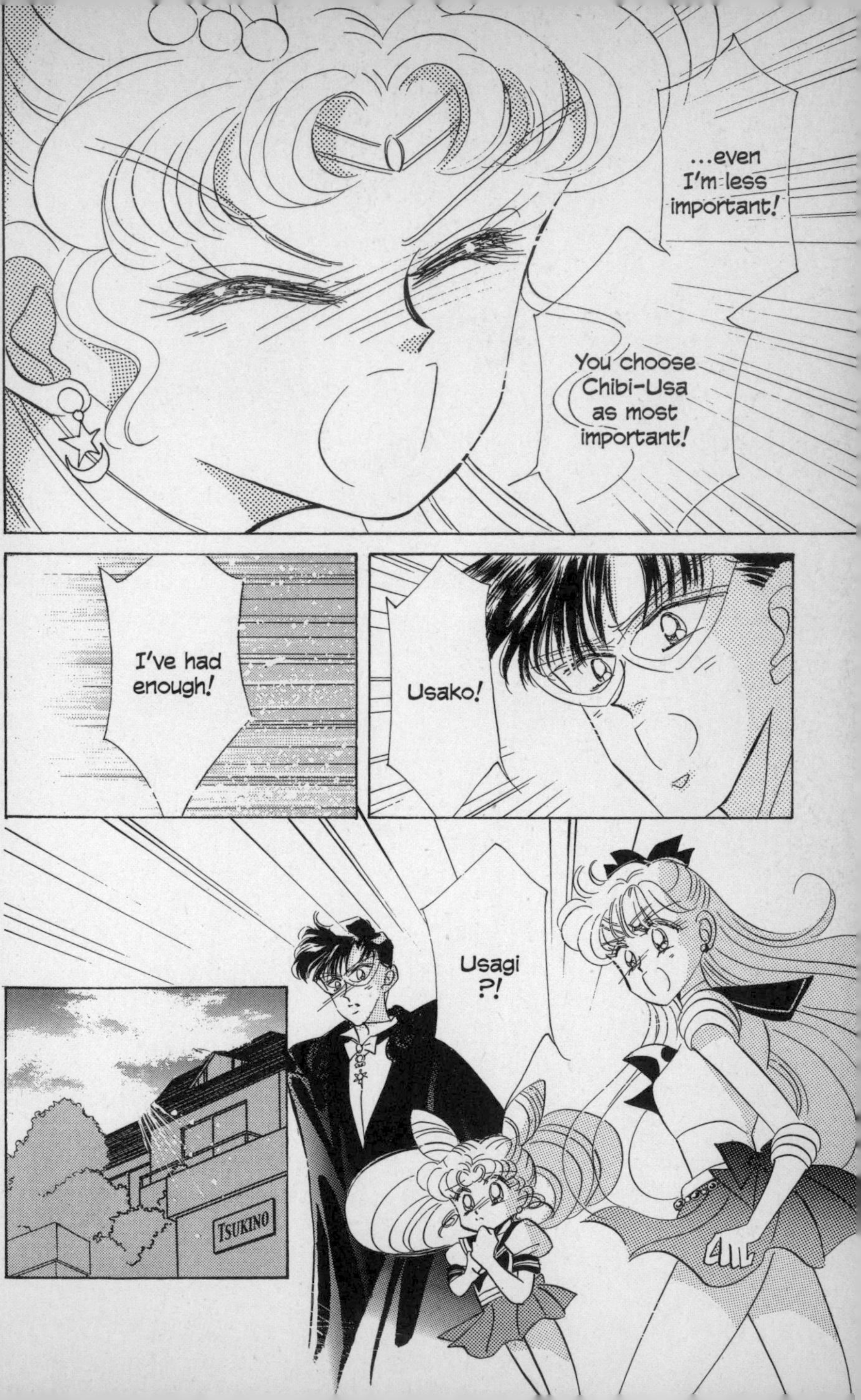
...even I'm less important!
You choose Chibi-Usa as most important!
Usako!
I've had enough!
Usagi ?!
TSUKINO

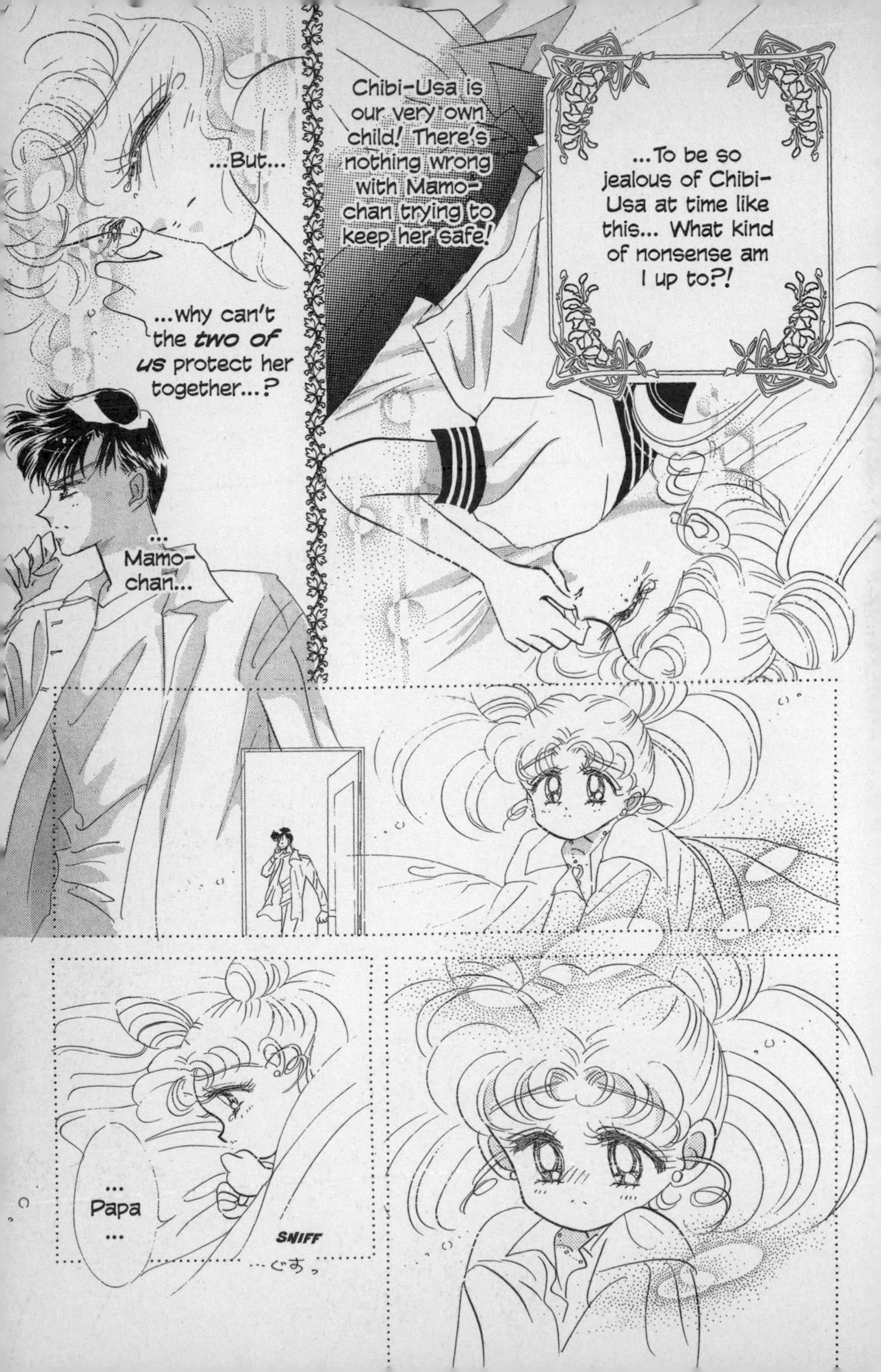
...To be so jealous of Chibi-Usa at time like this... What kind of nonsense am I up to?!
Chibi-Usa is our very own child! There's nothing wrong with Mamo-chan trying to keep her safe!
...But...
...why can't the *two of us* protect her together...?
... Mamo-chan...
... Papa ...
SNIFF
ぐすっ

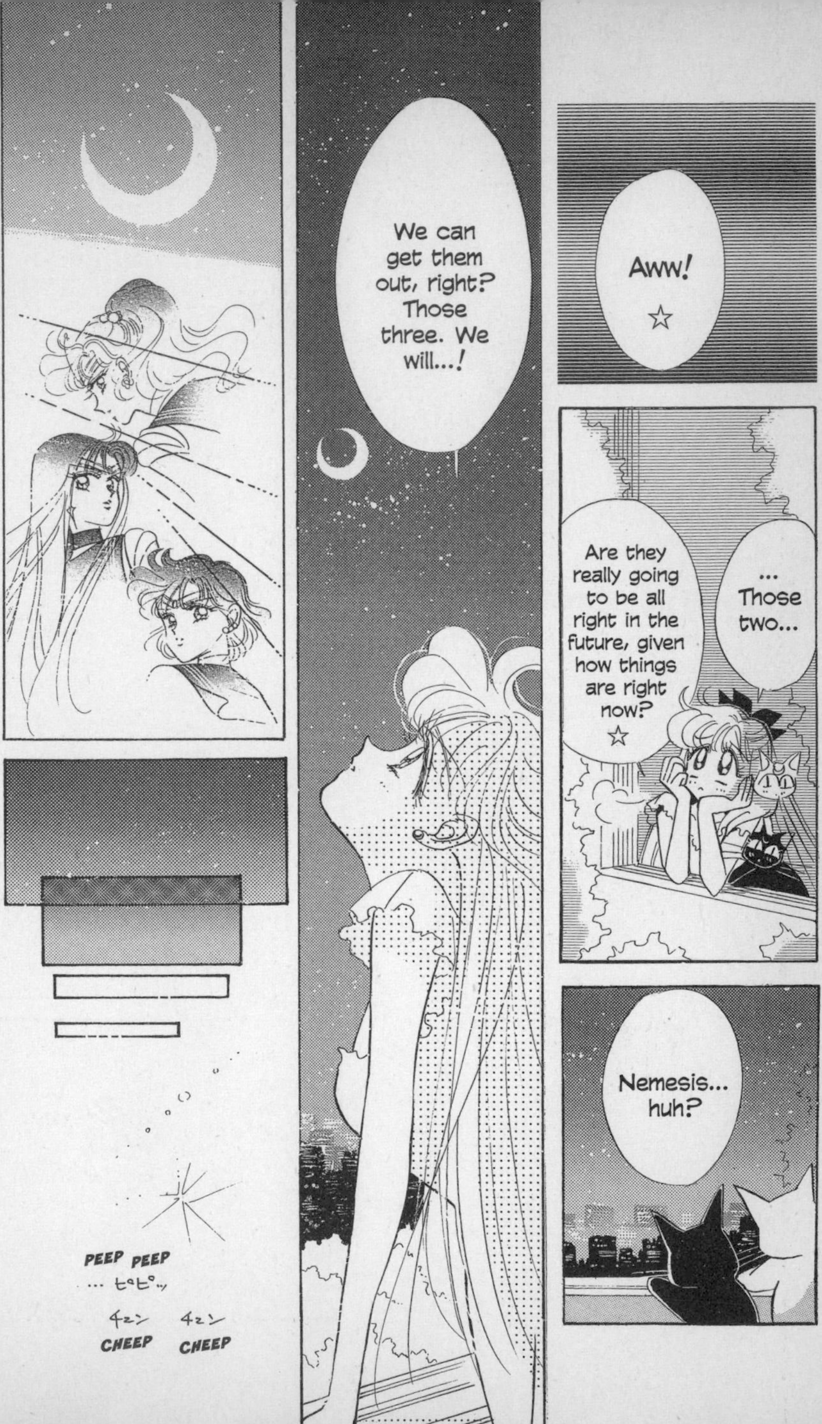
Aww! ☆
... Those two...
Are they really going to be all right in the future, given how things are right now? ☆
Nemesis... huh?
We can get them out, right? Those three. We will...!
PEEP PEEP
... ピピッ
チュン
CHEEP
チュン
CHEEP

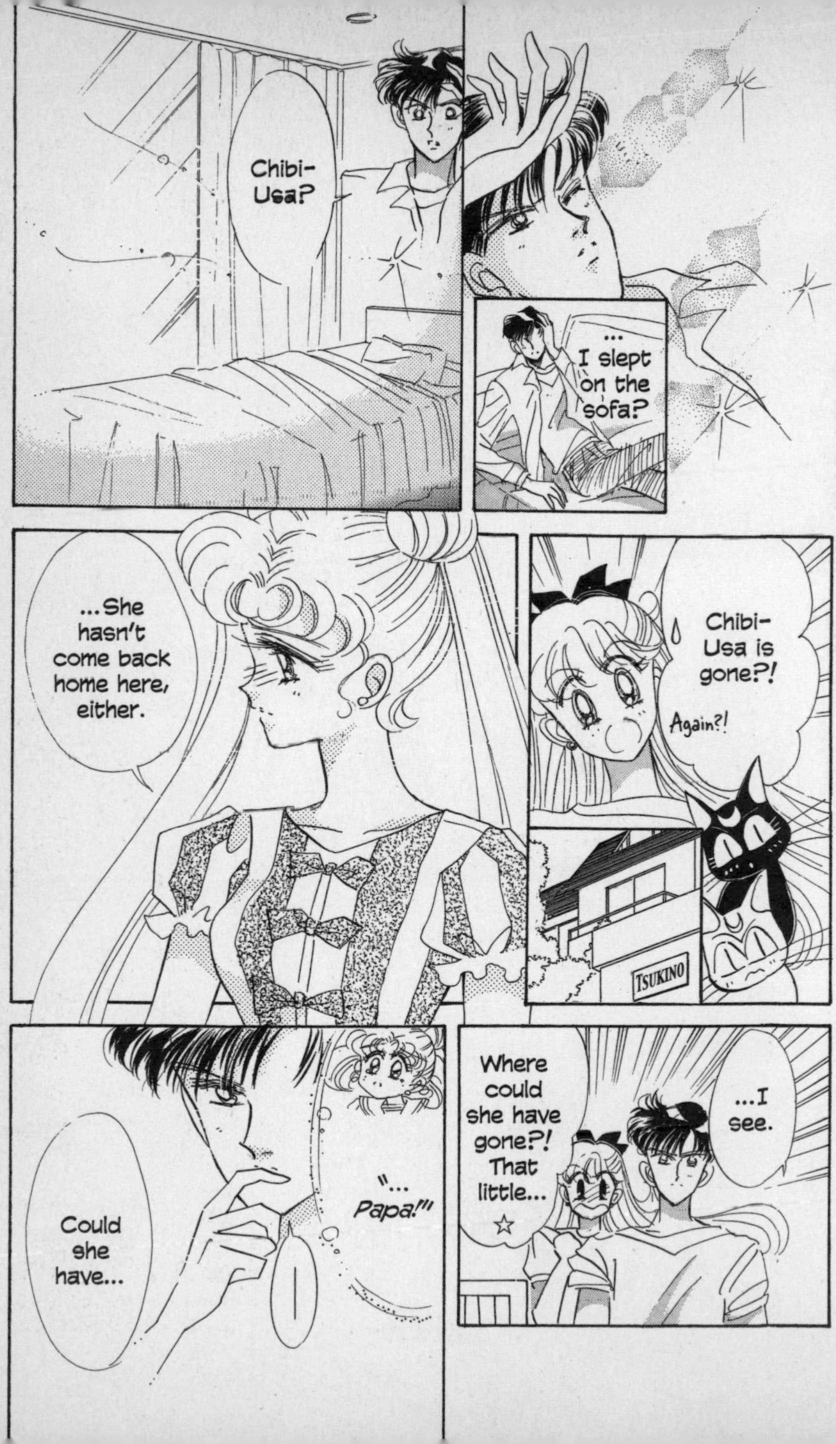
... I slept on the sofa?
Chibi-Usa?
Chibi-Usa is gone?!
Again?!
TSUKINO
...She hasn't come back home here, either.
...I see.
Where could she have gone?! That little... ☆
"... Papa!"
Could she have...

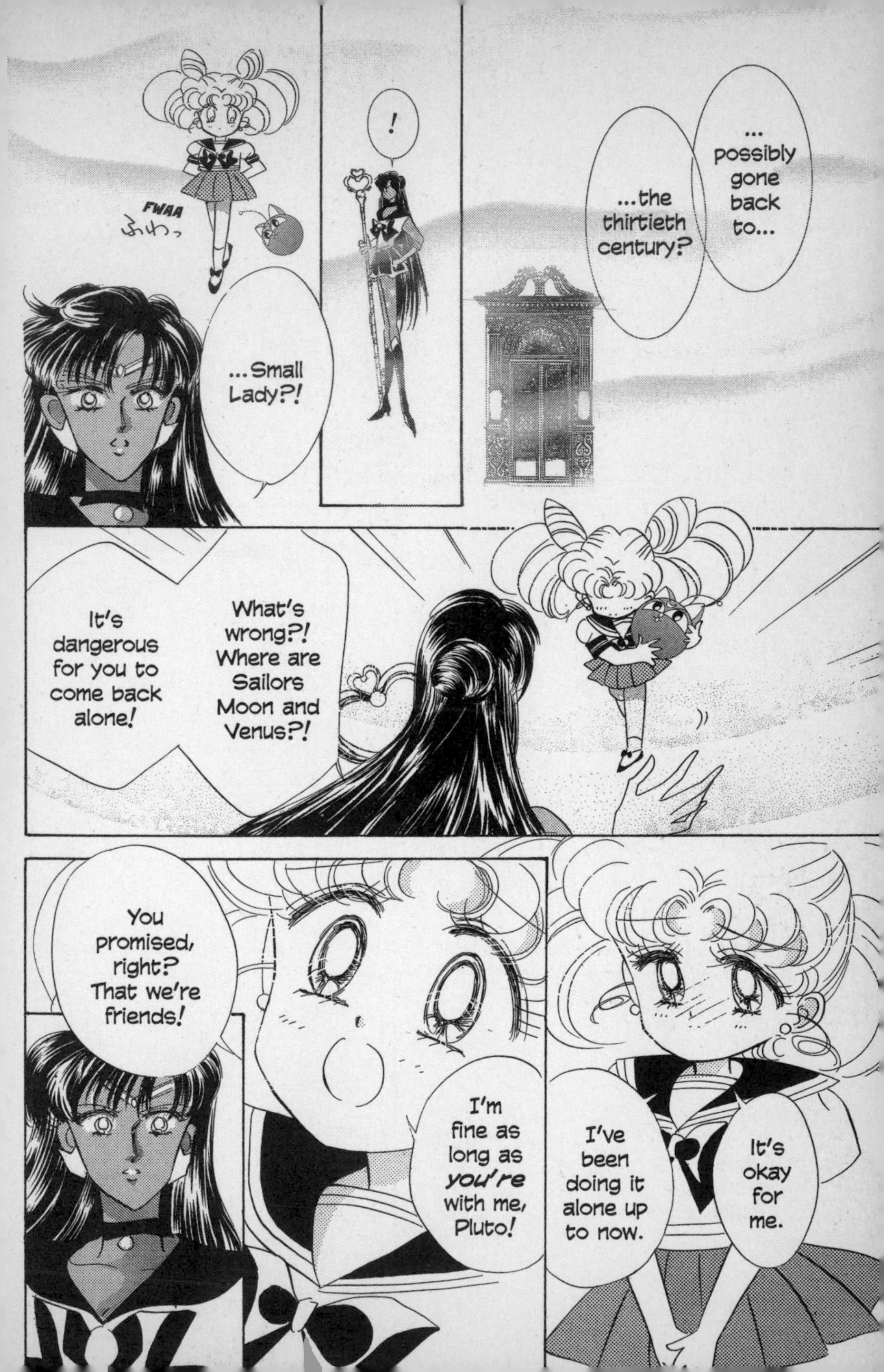
...possibly gone back to...
...the thirtieth century?
!
FWAA
ふわっ
...Small Lady?!
What's wrong?! Where are Sailors Moon and Venus?!
It's dangerous for you to come back alone!
It's okay for me.
I've been doing it alone up to now.
I'm fine as long as *you're* with me, Pluto!
You promised, right? That we're friends!

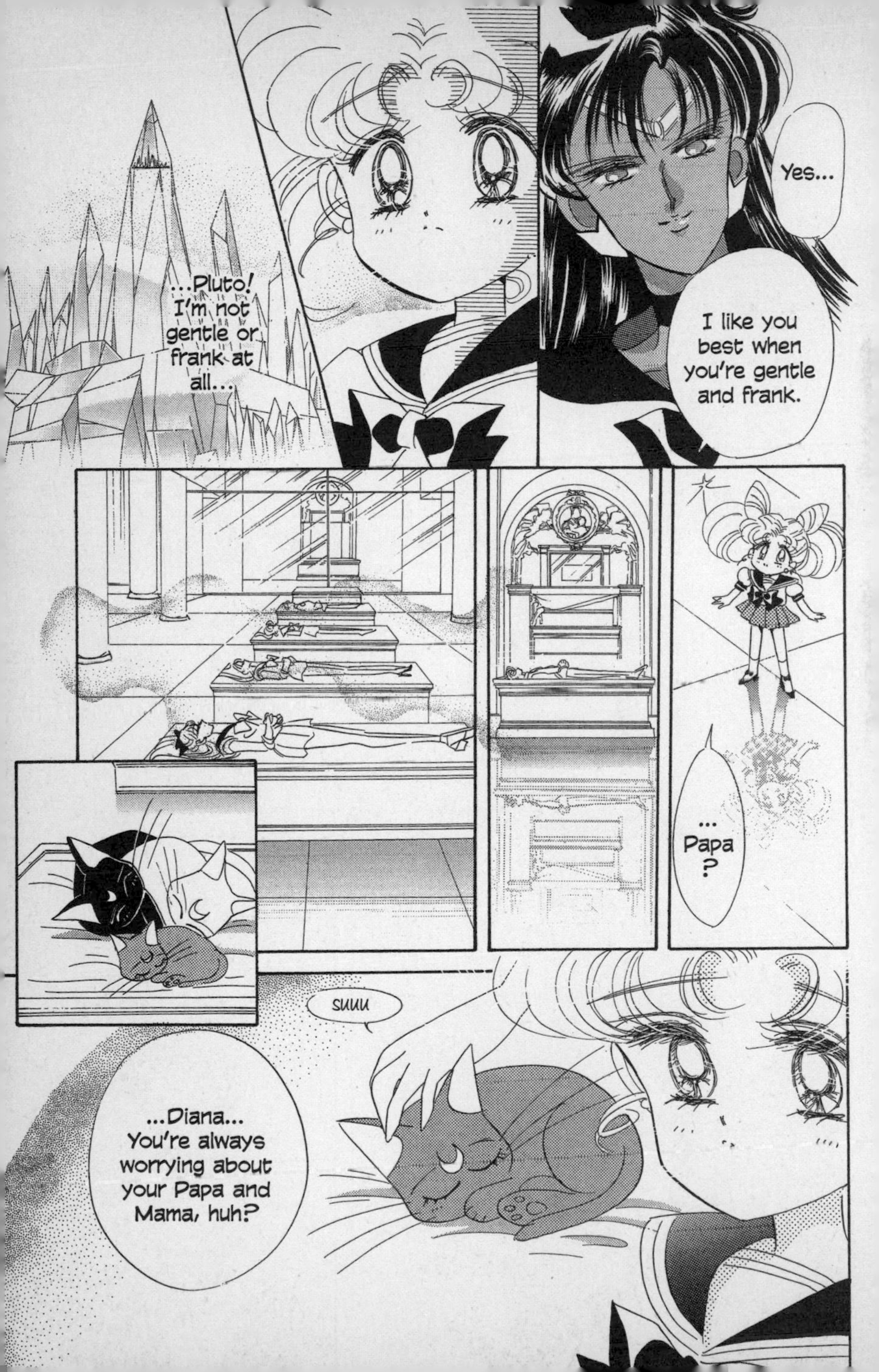
Yes...
I like you best when you're gentle and frank.
...Pluto! I'm not gentle or frank at all...
...Papa?
SUUU
...Diana... You're always worrying about your Papa and Mama, huh?

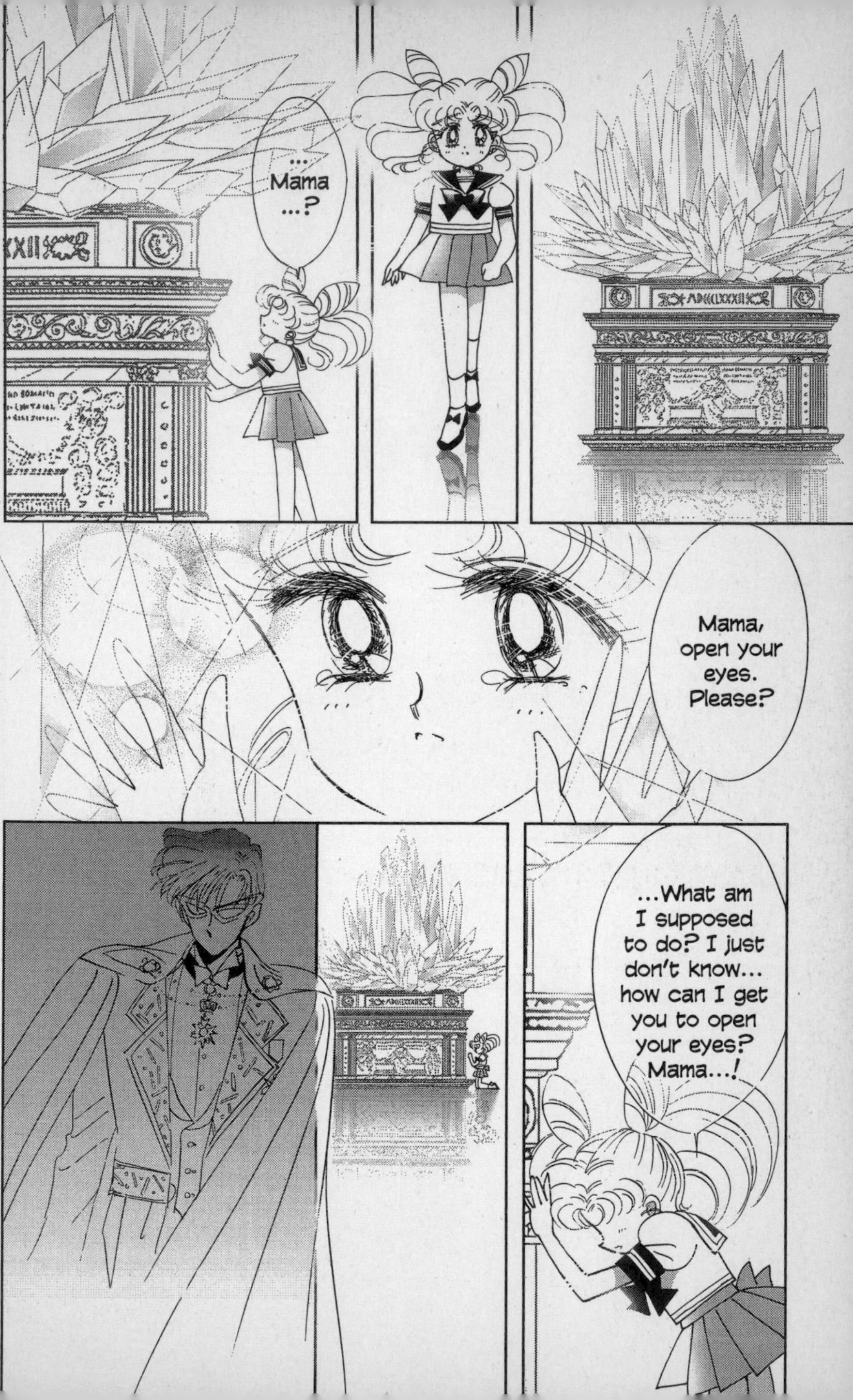
... Mama ...?
Mama, open your eyes. Please?
...What am I supposed to do? I just don't know... how can I get you to open your eyes? Mama...!

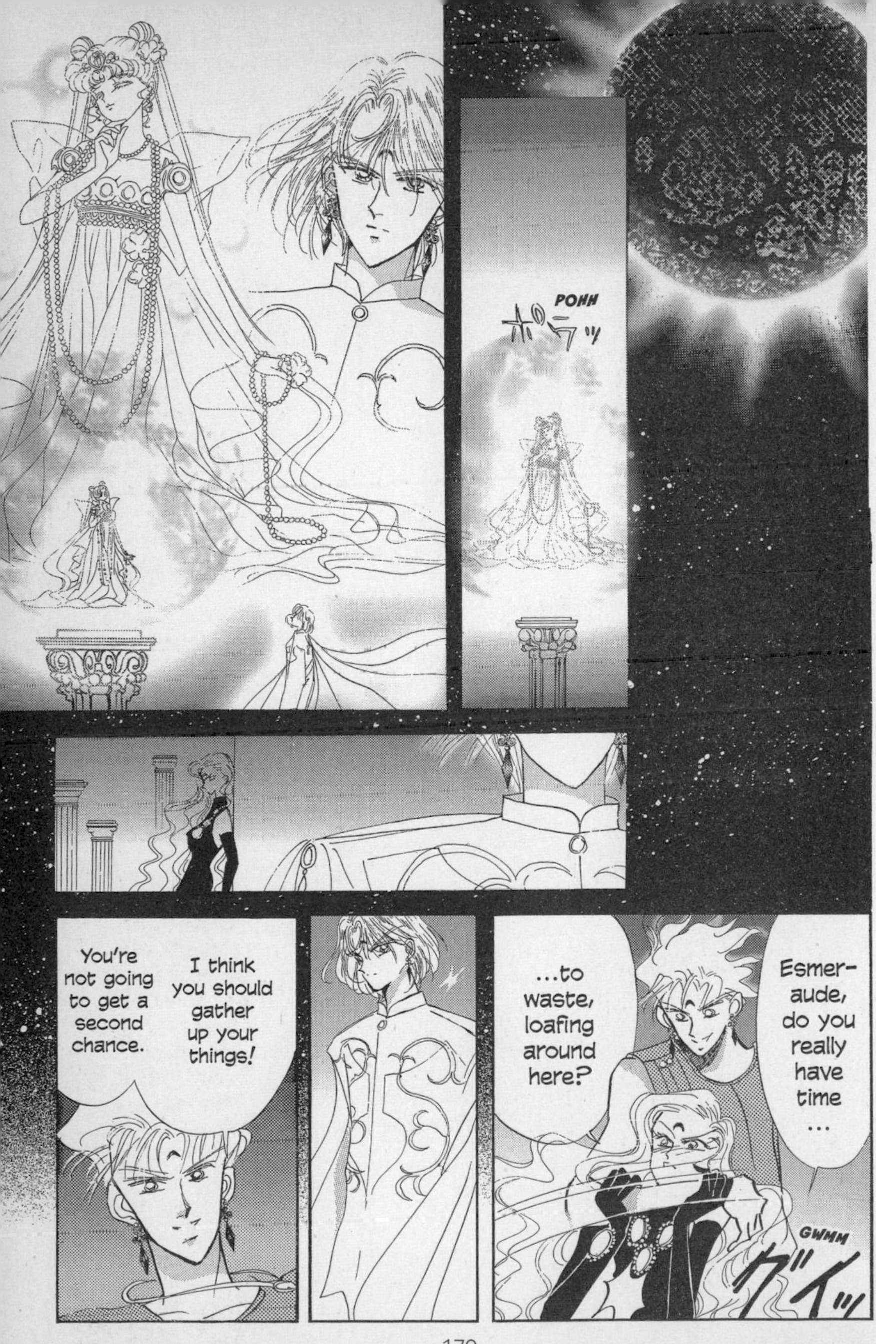
POHH
Esmer-aude, do you really have time ...
...to waste, loafing around here?
GWMM
I think you should gather up your things!
You're not going to get a second chance.

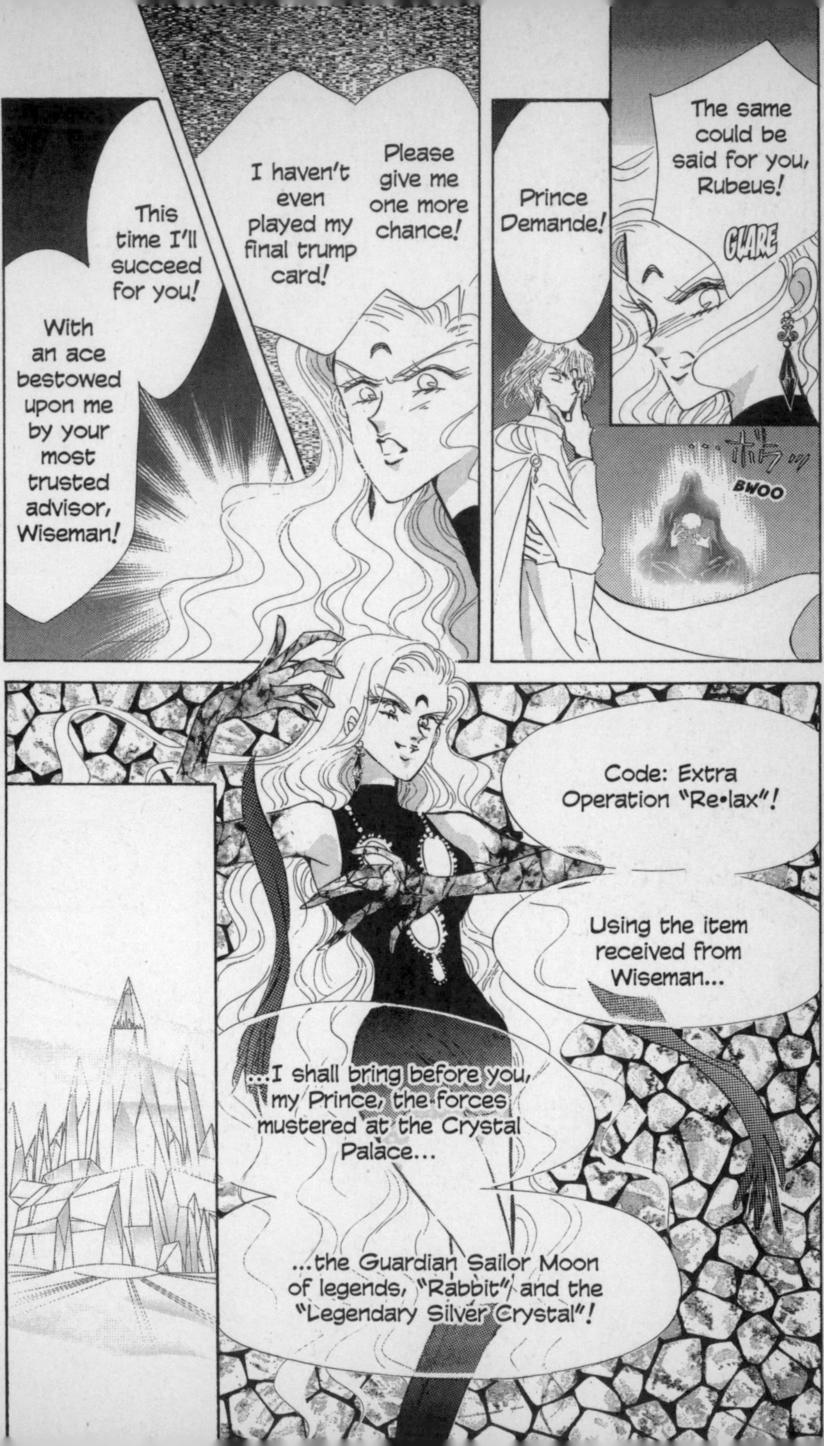

The same could be said for you, Rubeus!
GLARE
BWOO
Prince Demande!
Please give me one more chance!
I haven't even played my final trump card!
This time I'll succeed for you!
With an ace bestowed upon me by your most trusted advisor, Wiseman!
Code: Extra Operation "Re•lax"!
Using the item received from Wiseman...
...I shall bring before you, my Prince, the forces mustered at the Crystal Palace...
...the Guardian Sailor Moon of legends, "Rabbit" and the "Legendary Silver Crystal"!

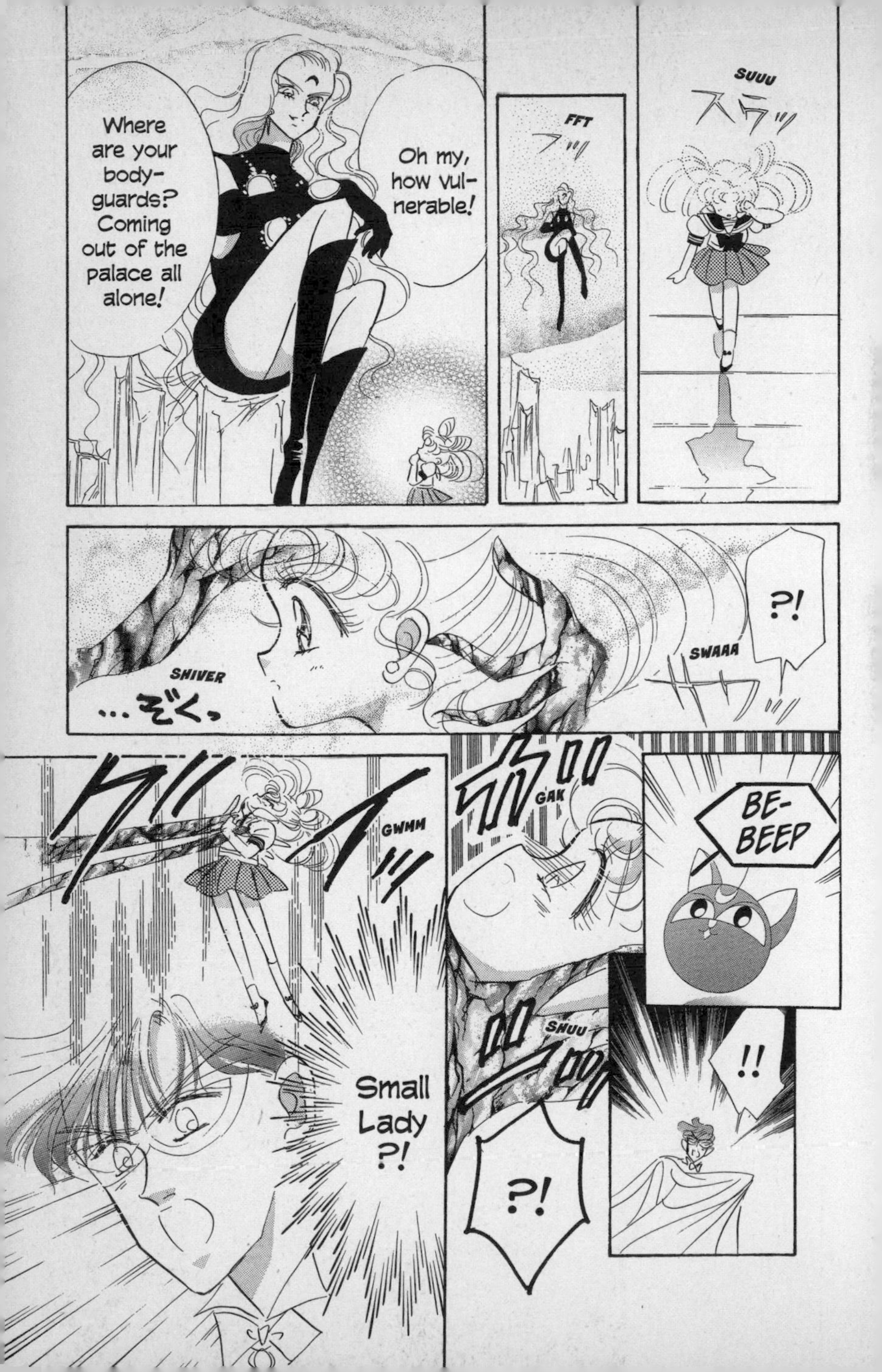
SUUU
スラッ
FFT
Oh my, how vul-nerable!
Where are your body-guards? Coming out of the palace all alone!
?!
SWAAA
SHIVER
...ぞくっ
BE-BEEP
!!
GAK
SHUU
?!
GWMM
Small Lady?!

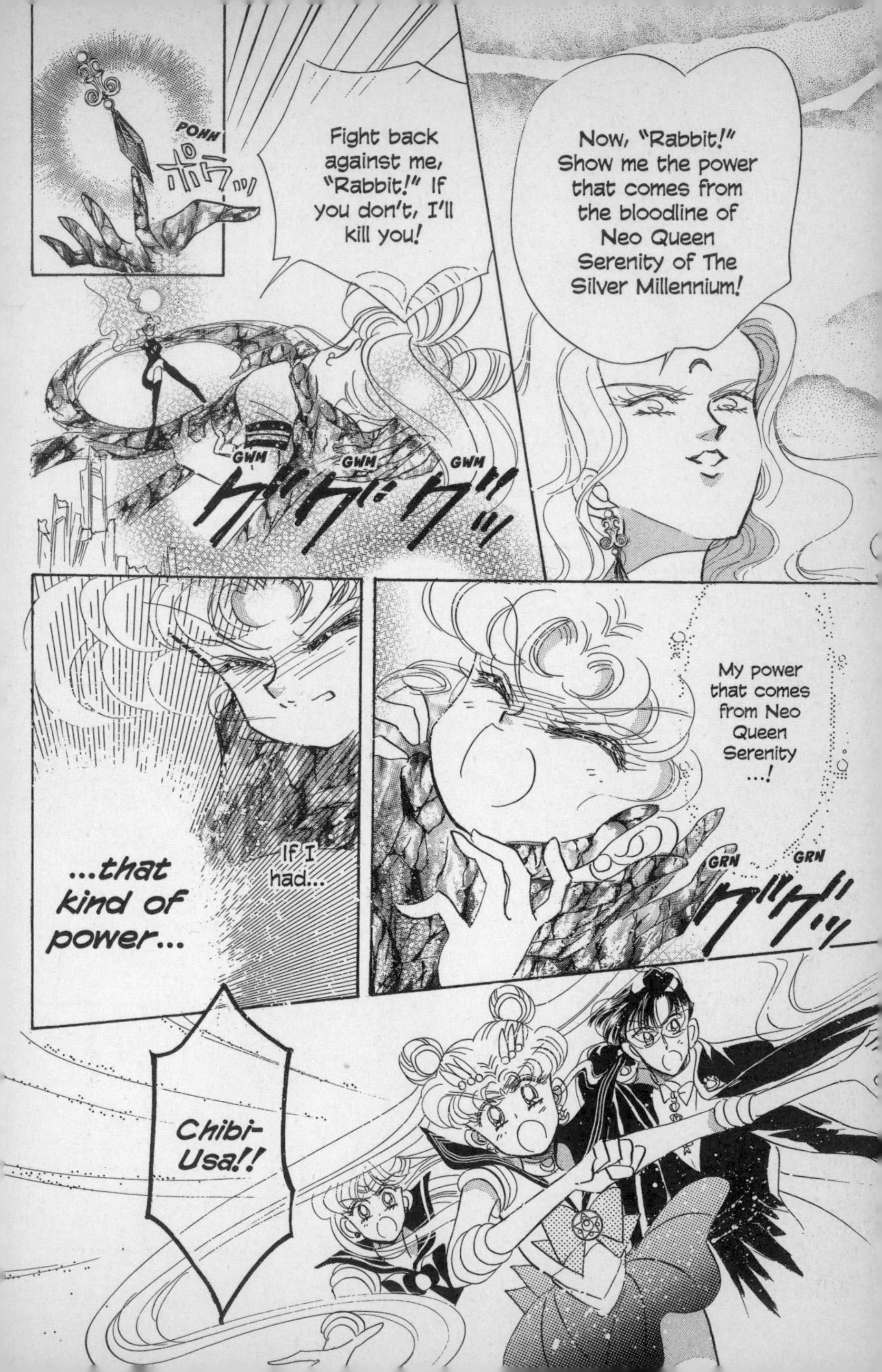
Now, "Rabbit!" Show me the power that comes from the bloodline of Neo Queen Serenity of The Silver Millennium!
Fight back against me, "Rabbit!" If you don't, I'll kill you!
POHN
GWM GWM GWM
My power that comes from Neo Queen Serenity ...!
GRN GRN
If I had...
...that kind of power...
Chibi-Usa!!

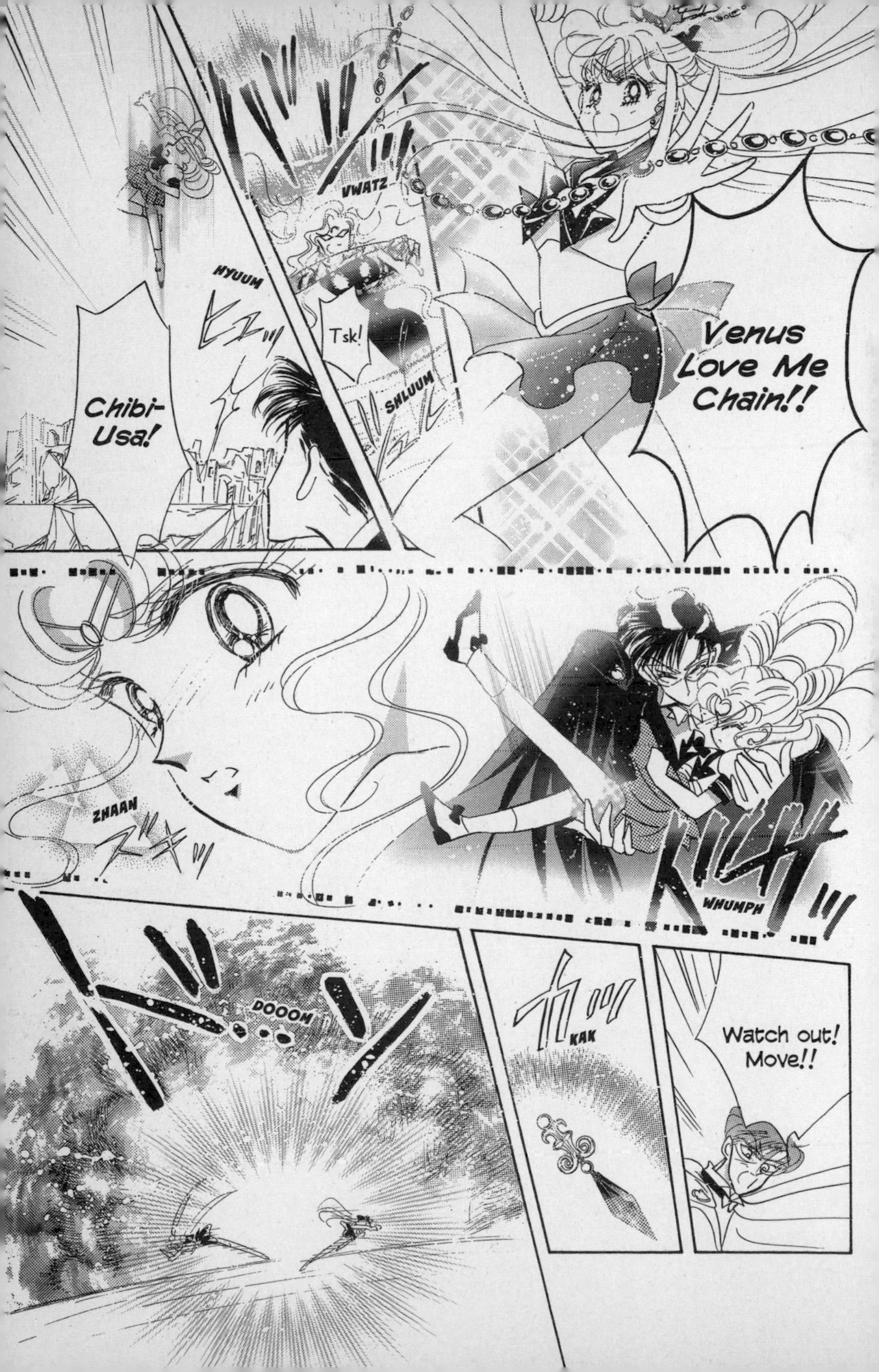

Venus Love Me Chain!!
VWATZ
Tsk!
SHLUUM
HYUUM
Chibi-Usa!
WHUMPH
ZHAAN
Watch out! Move!!
KAK
DOOOM

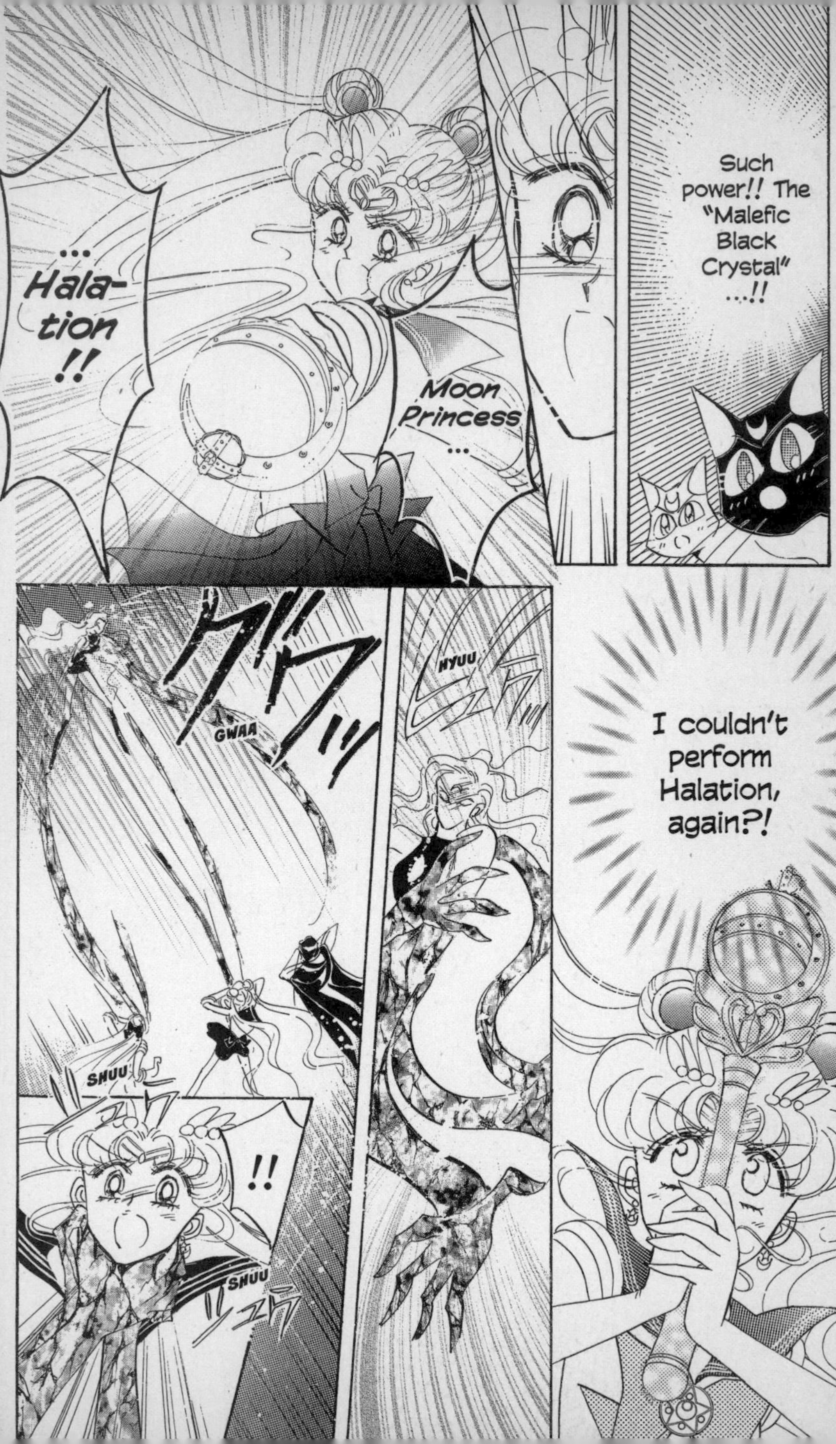

Such power!! The "Malefic Black Crystal" ...!!
Moon Princess ...
... Halation!!
I couldn't perform Halation, again?!
HYUU
GWAA
SHUU
!!
SHUU

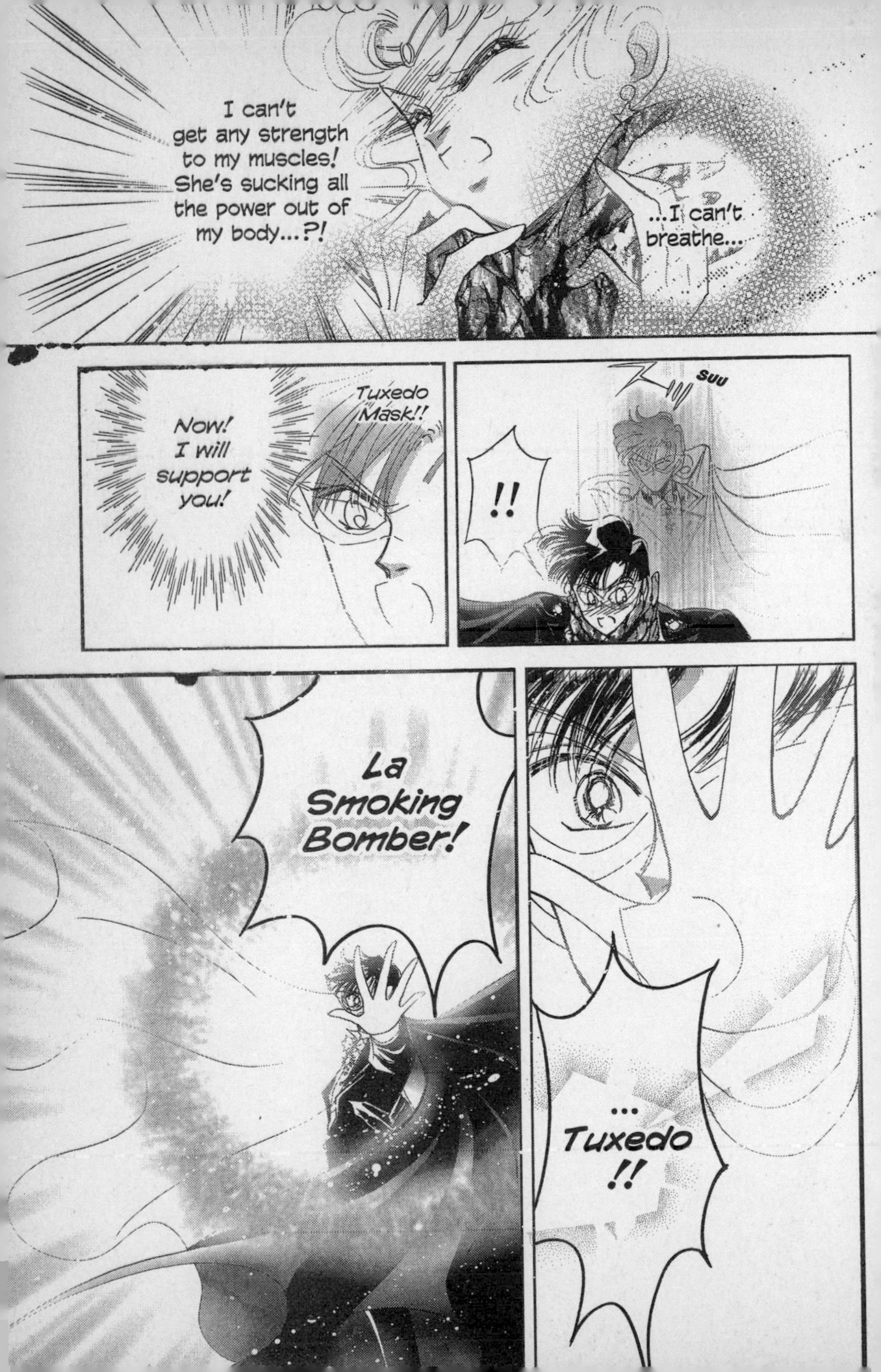
...I can't breathe...
I can't get any strength to my muscles! She's sucking all the power out of my body...?!
SUU
!!
Tuxedo Mask!!
Now! I will support you!
...Tuxedo!!
La Smoking Bomber!

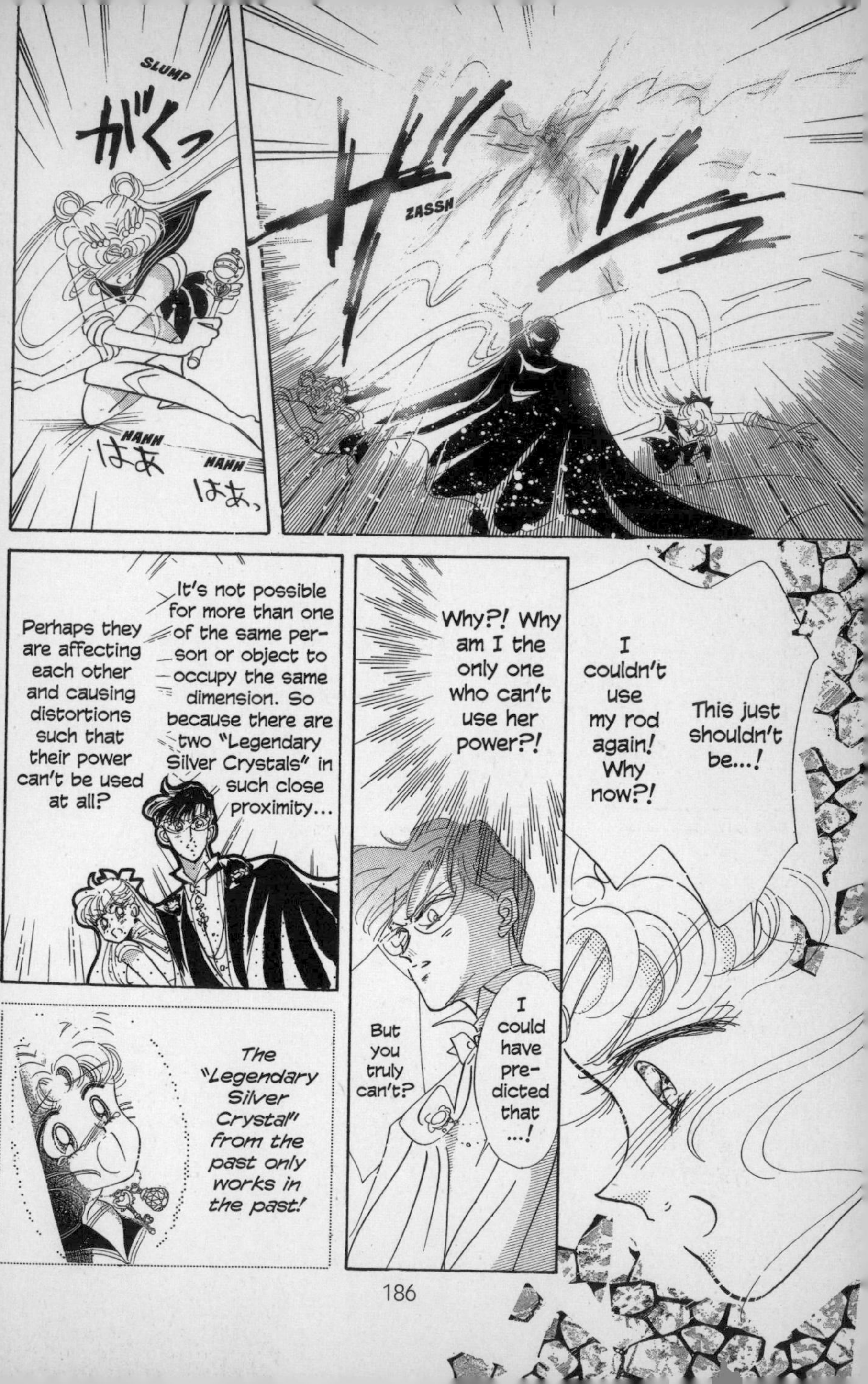
ザザッ
ZASSH
がくっ
SLUMP
はあ
HANN
はあっ
HANN
This just shouldn't be...!
I couldn't use my rod again! Why now?!
Why?! Why am I the only one who can't use her power?!
I could have predicted that...!
But you truly can't?
It's not possible for more than one of the same person or object to occupy the same dimension. So because there are two "Legendary Silver Crystals" in such close proximity...
Perhaps they are affecting each other and causing distortions such that their power can't be used at all?
The "Legendary Silver Crystal" from the past only works in the past!

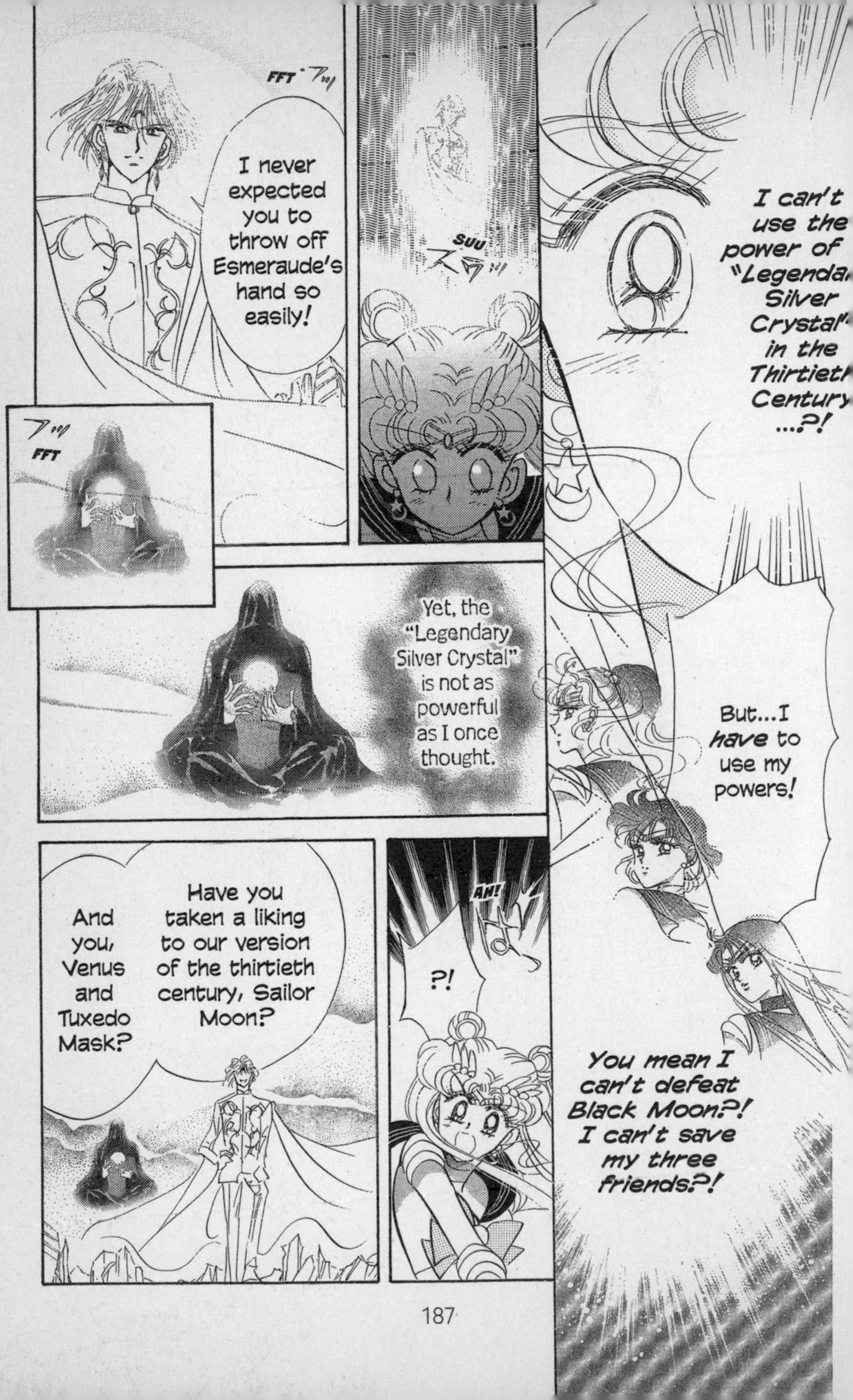

I can't use the power of "Legenda Silver Crystal" in the Thirtiet Century ...?!
But...I have to use my powers!
You mean I can't defeat Black Moon?! I can't save my three friends?!
SUU
FFT
I never expected you to throw off Esmeraude's hand so easily!
FFT
Yet, the "Legendary Silver Crystal" is not as powerful as I once thought.
AH!
?!
Have you taken a liking to our version of the thirtieth century, Sailor Moon?
And you, Venus and Tuxedo Mask?

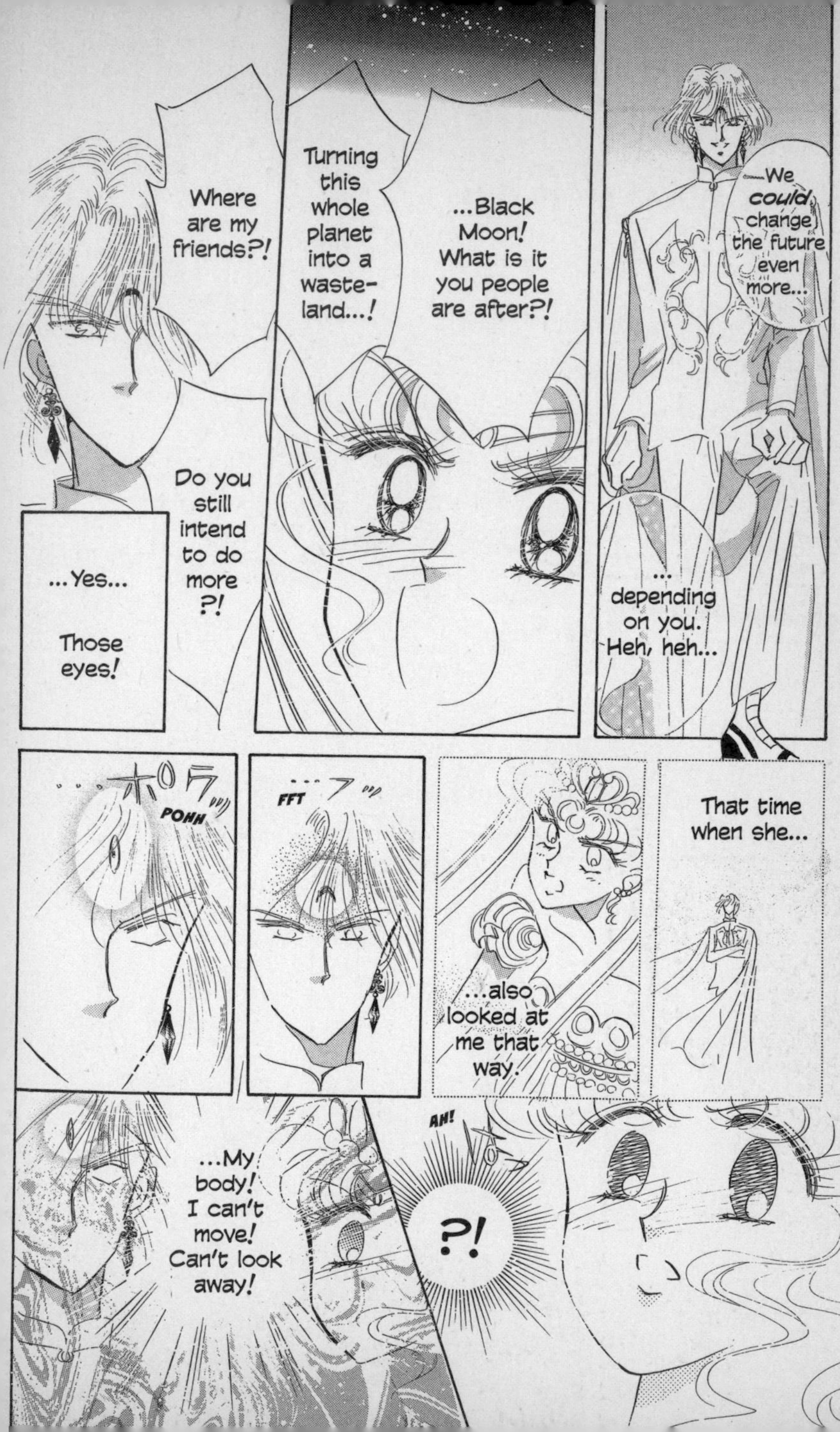
—We could change the future even more...
...depending on you. Heh, heh...
...Black Moon! What is it you people are after?!
Turning this whole planet into a waste-land...!
Where are my friends?!
Do you still intend to do more?!
...Yes...
Those eyes!
That time when she...
...also looked at me that way.
FFT
POHN
AH!
?!
...My body! I can't move! Can't look away!

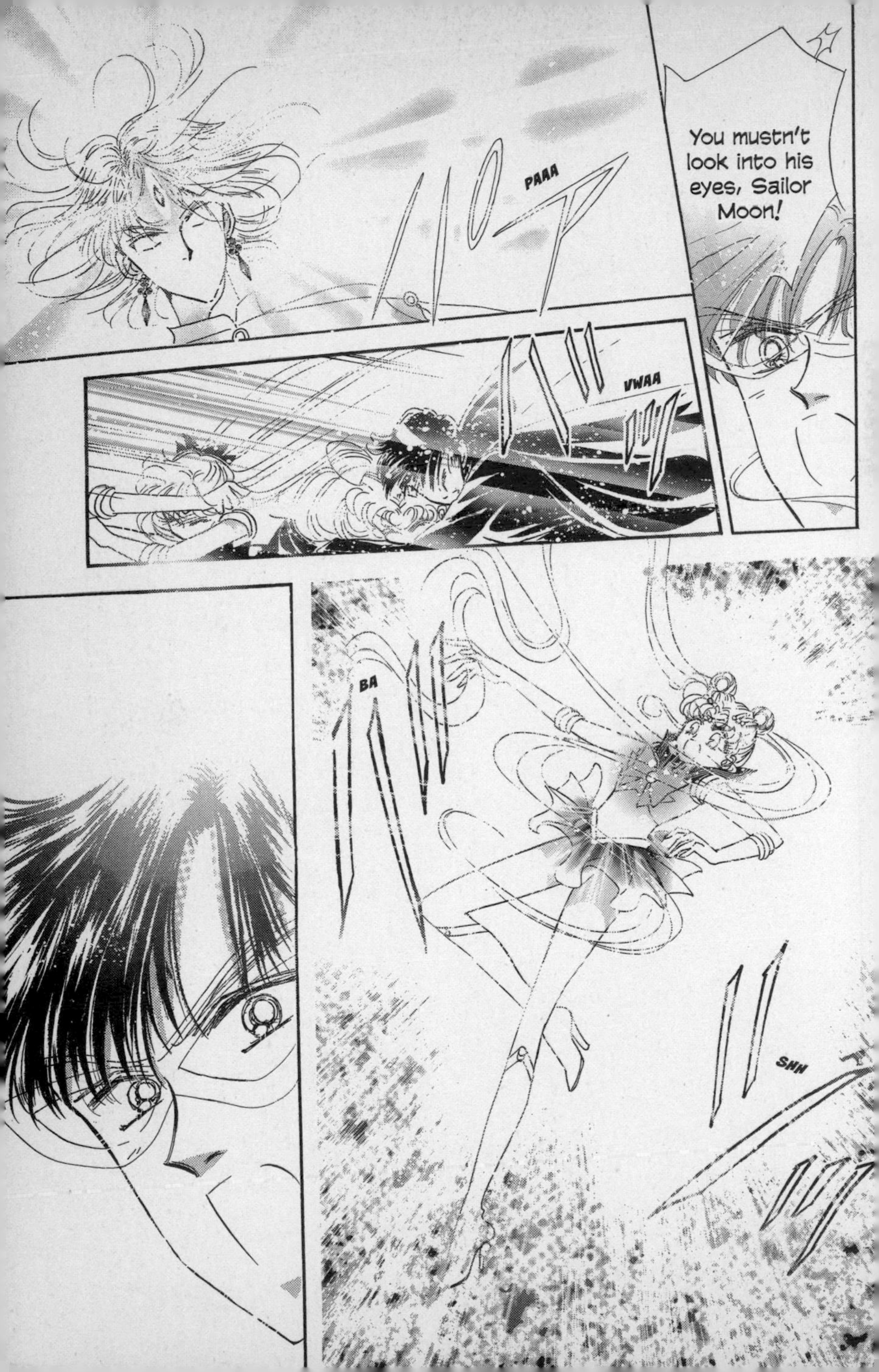
You mustn't look into his eyes, Sailor Moon!
PAAA
VWAA
BA
SHN

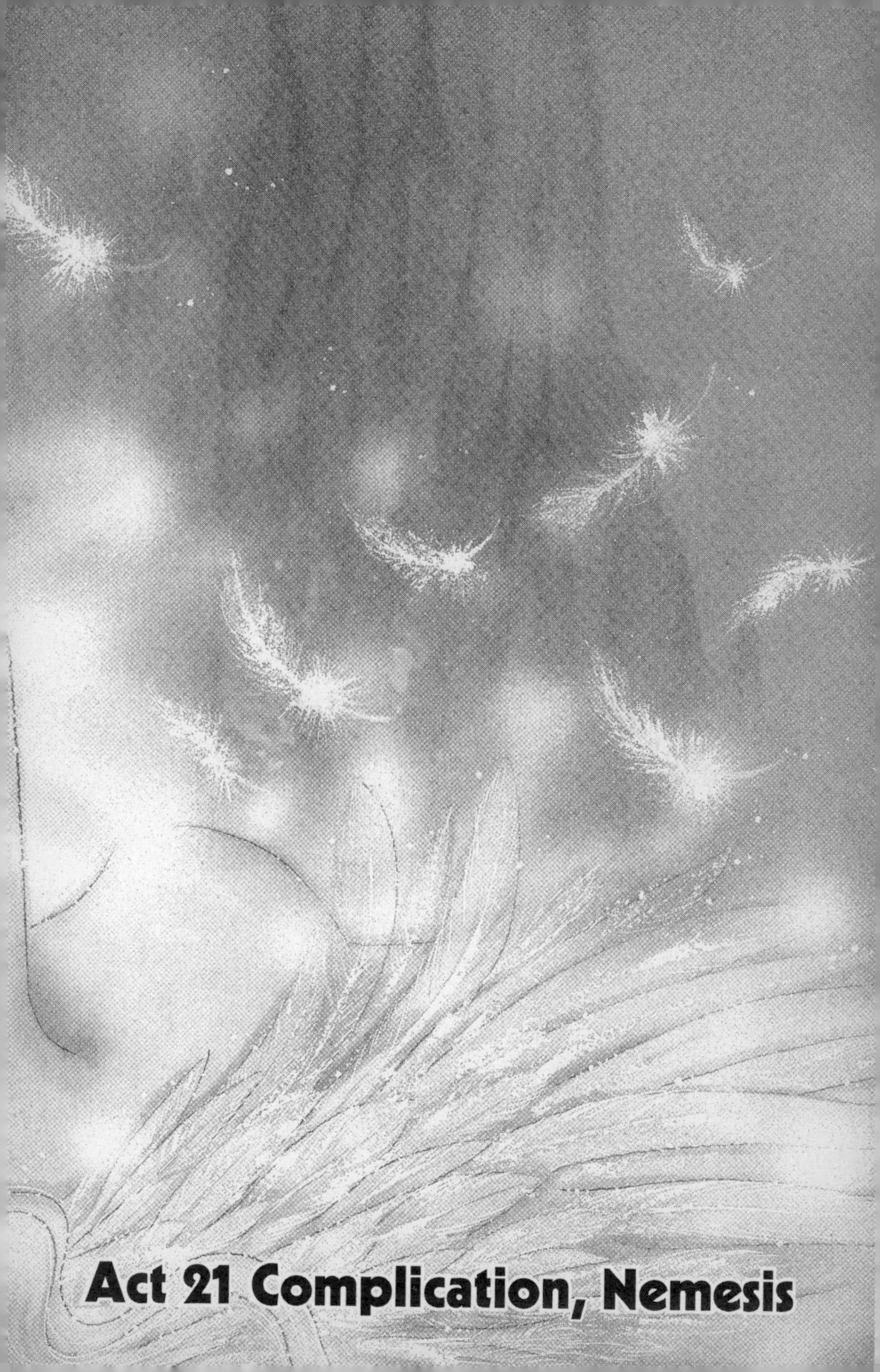

Act 21 Complication, Nemesis

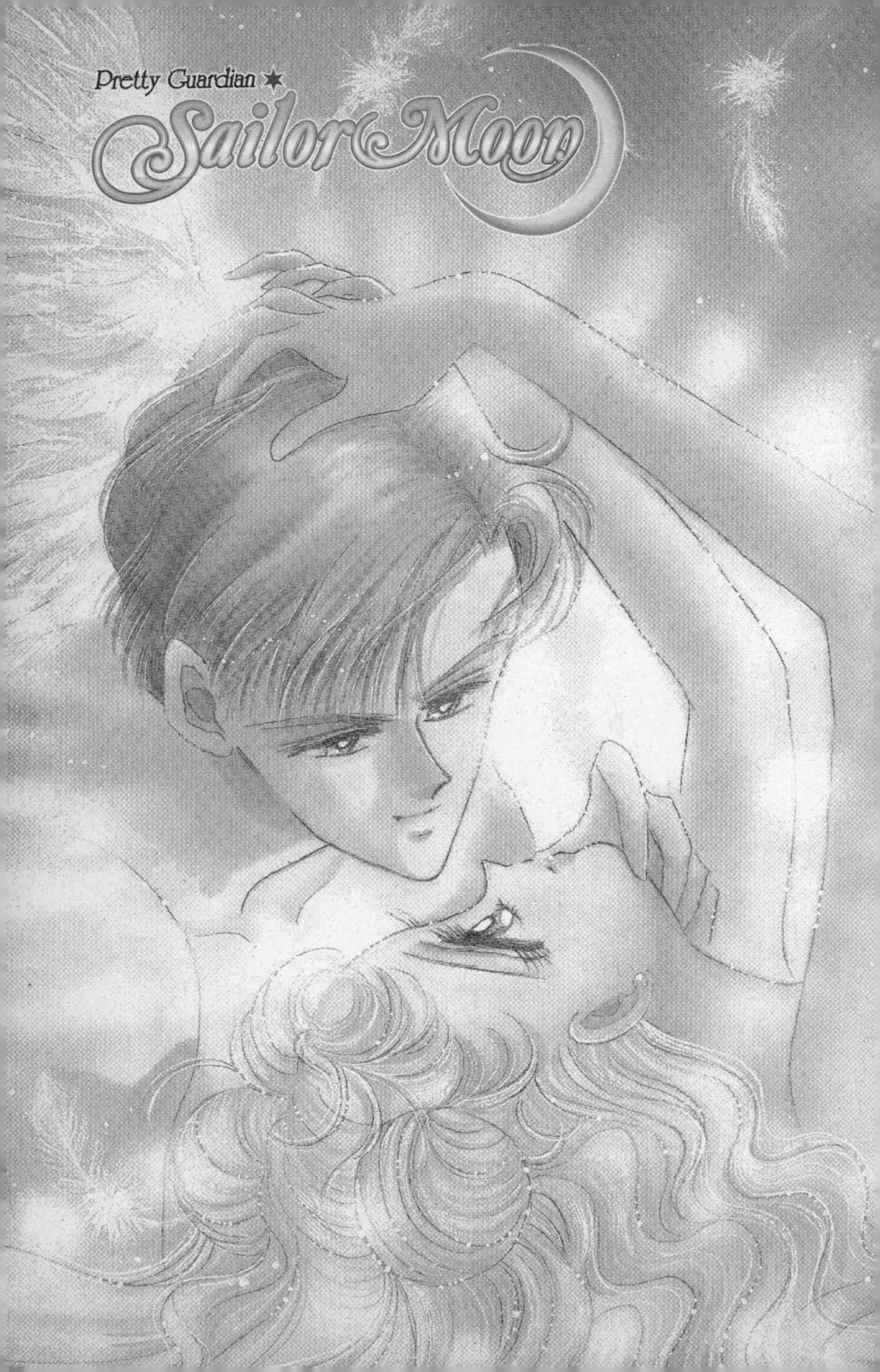
Pretty Guardian
Sailor Moon

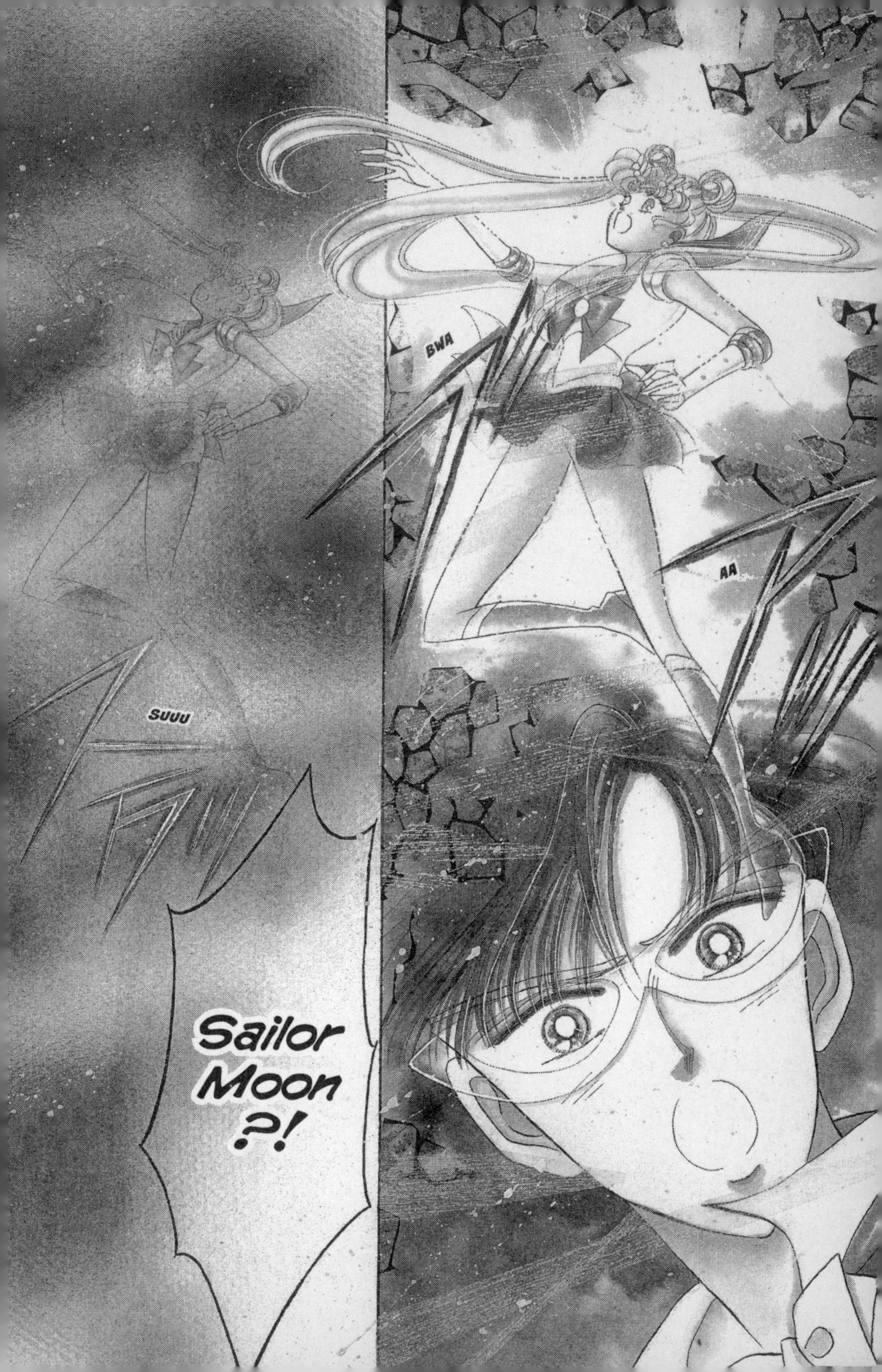
BWA
AA
SUUU
Sailor Moon ?!

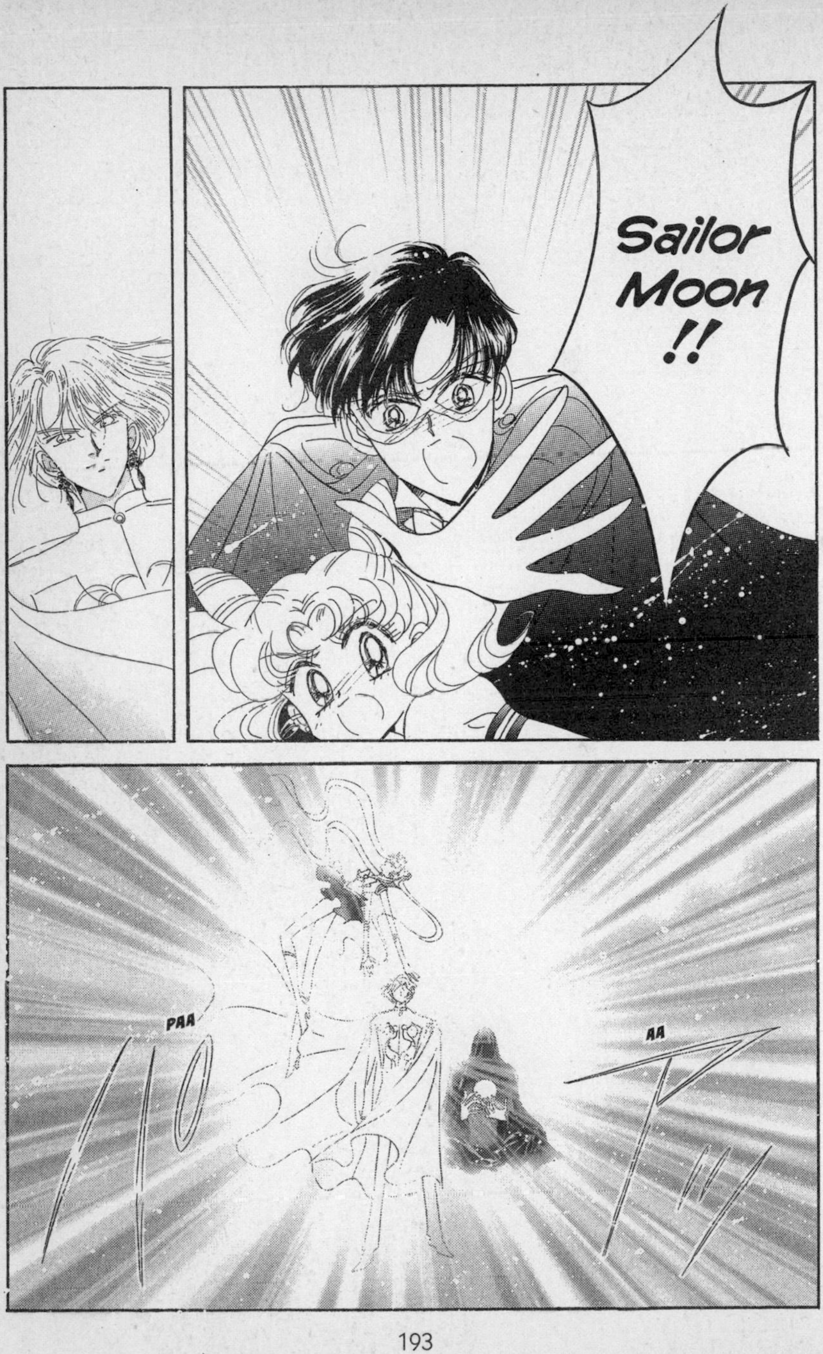
Sailor Moon !!
PAA
AA

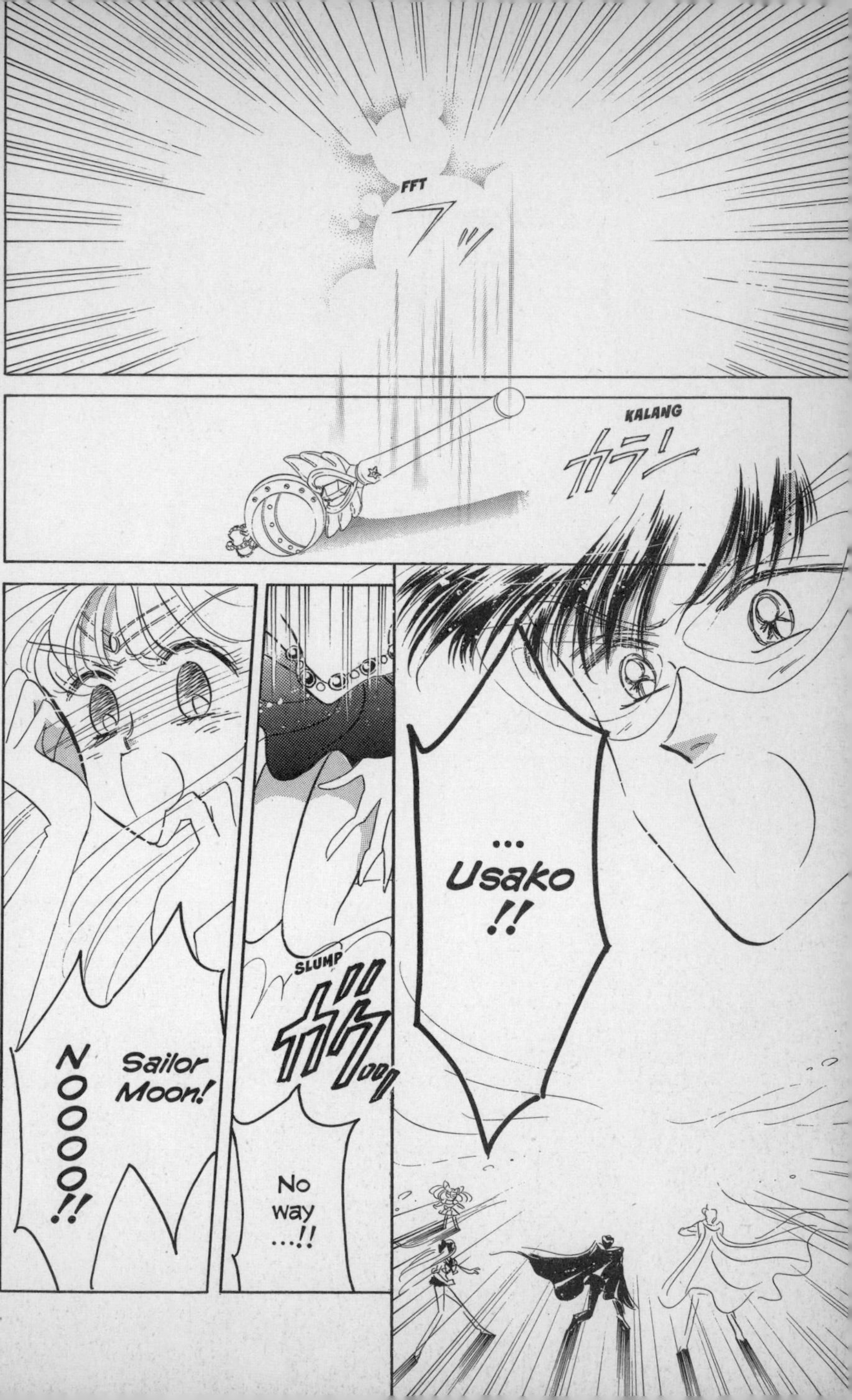
FFT
フッ
KALANG
カラン
... Usako !!
SLUMP
ガクッ
No way ...!!
Sailor Moon!
NOOOOO!!

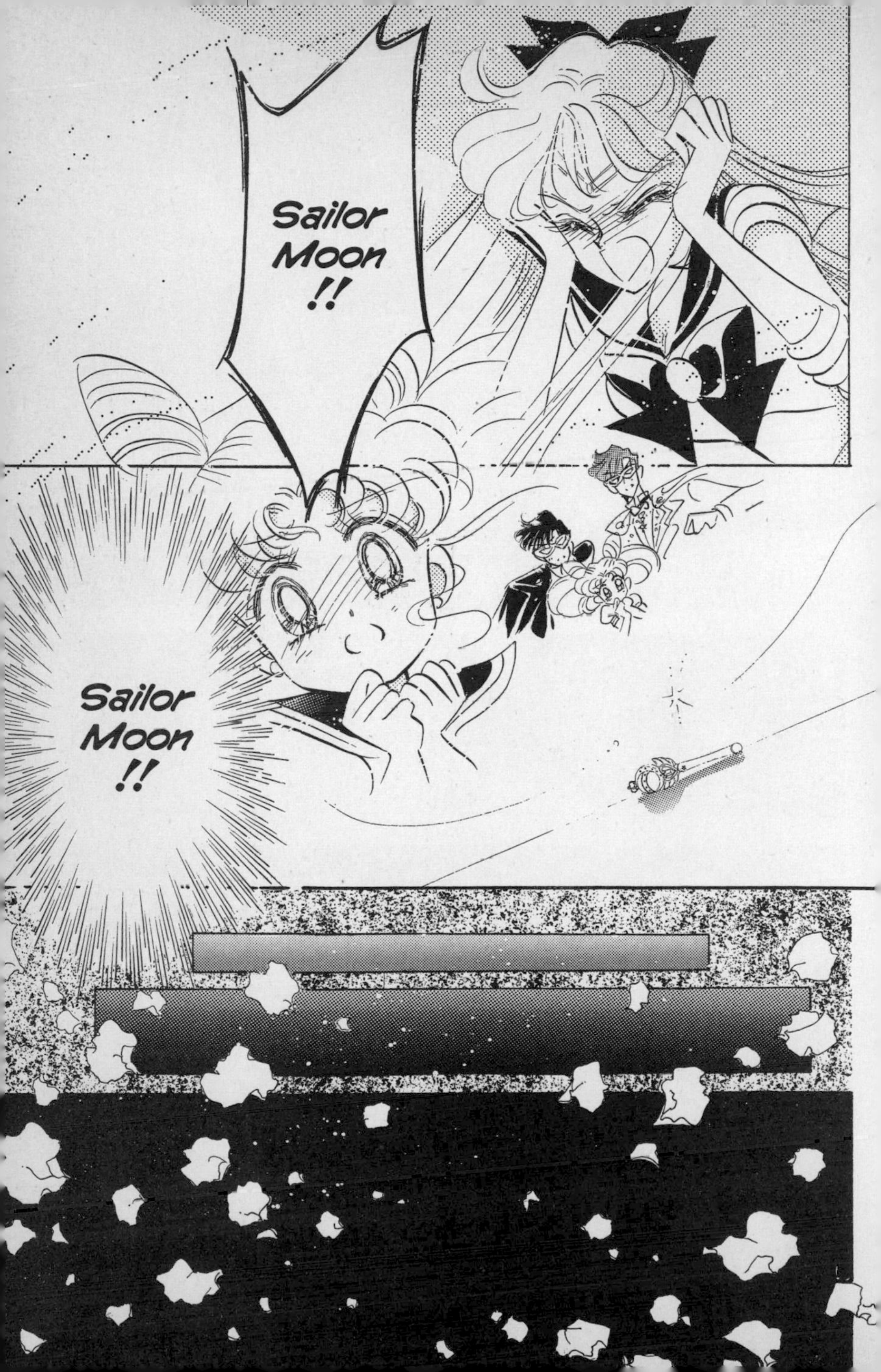
Sailor Moon !!
Sailor Moon !!

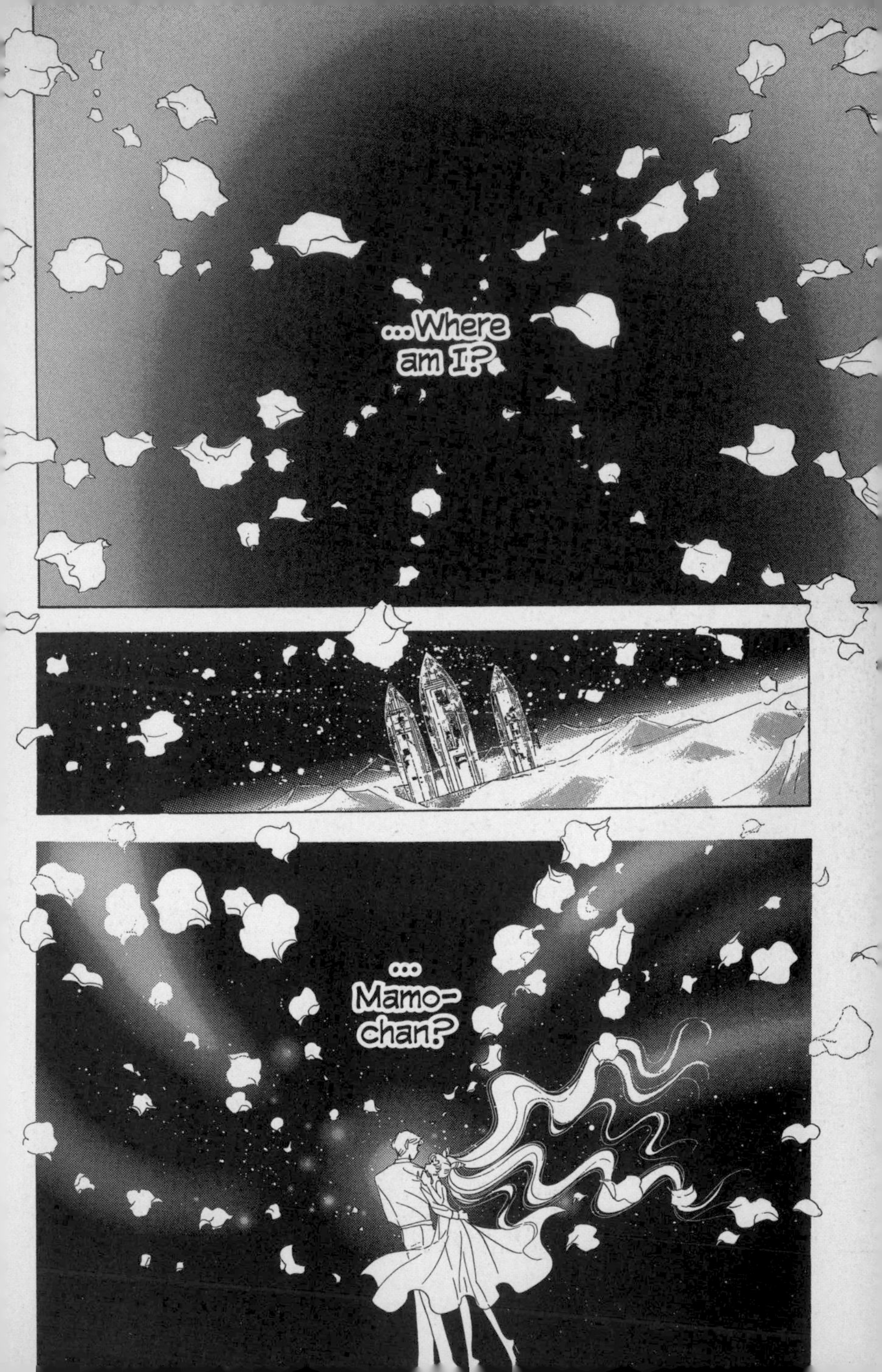
...Where am I?
...Mamo-chan?

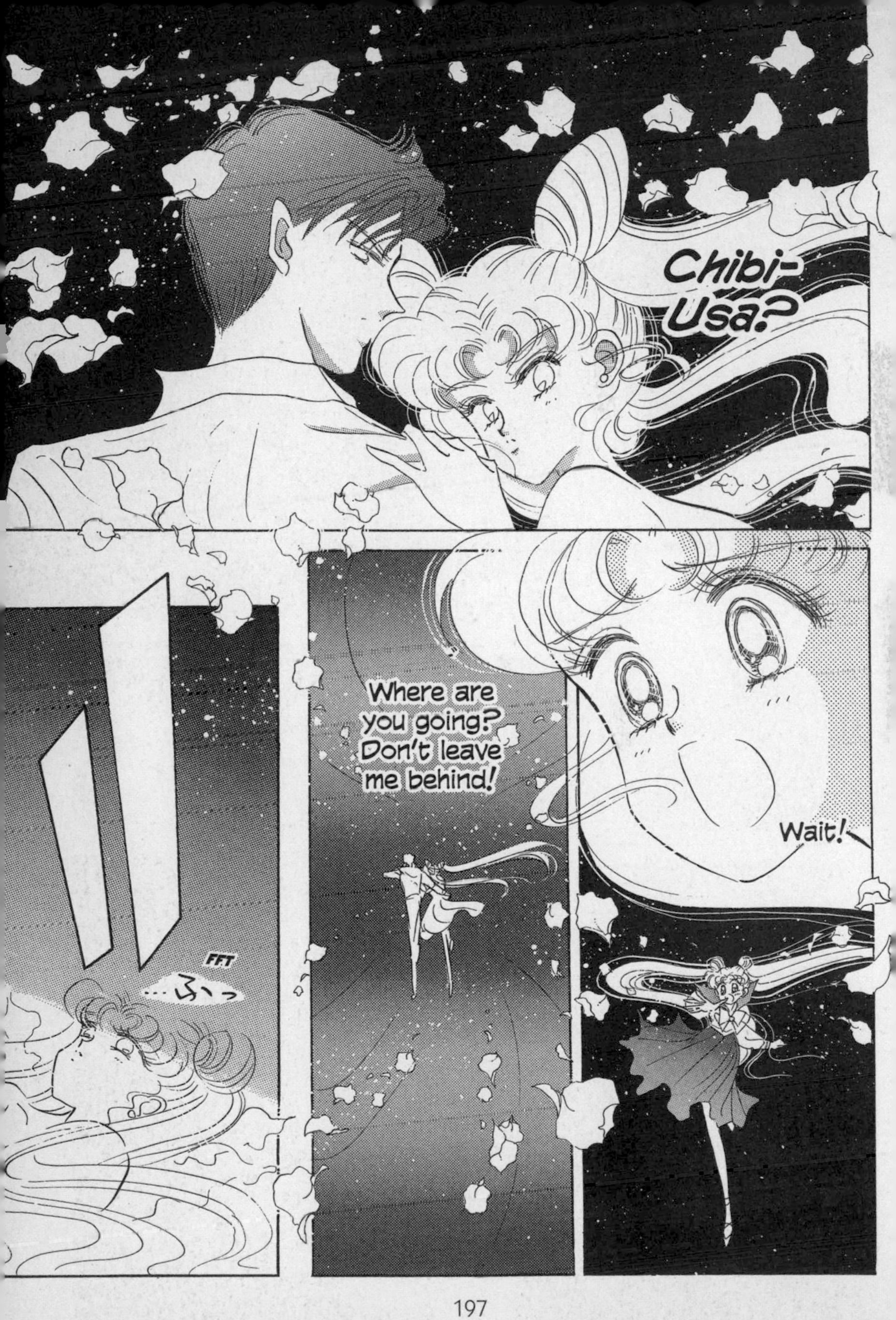
Chibi-Usa?
Wait!
Where are you going? Don't leave me behind!
FFT
…ふっ

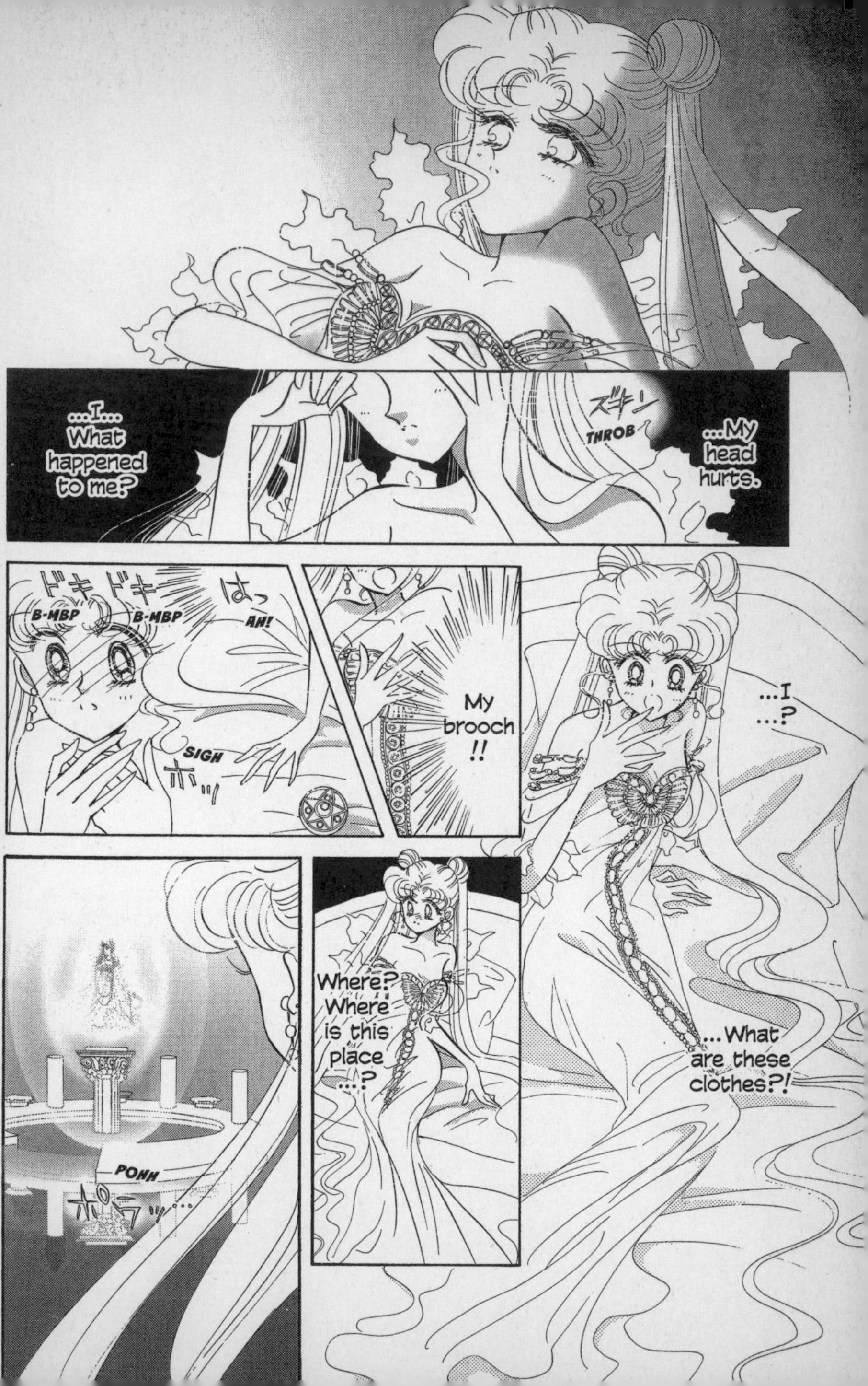
...My head hurts.
ズキン
THROB
...I... What happened to me?
...I ...?
...What are these clothes?!
My brooch!!
ドキドキ
B-MBP B-MBP
はっ
AH!
SIGH
ホッ
Where? Where is this place ...?
PONH
ポワッ...

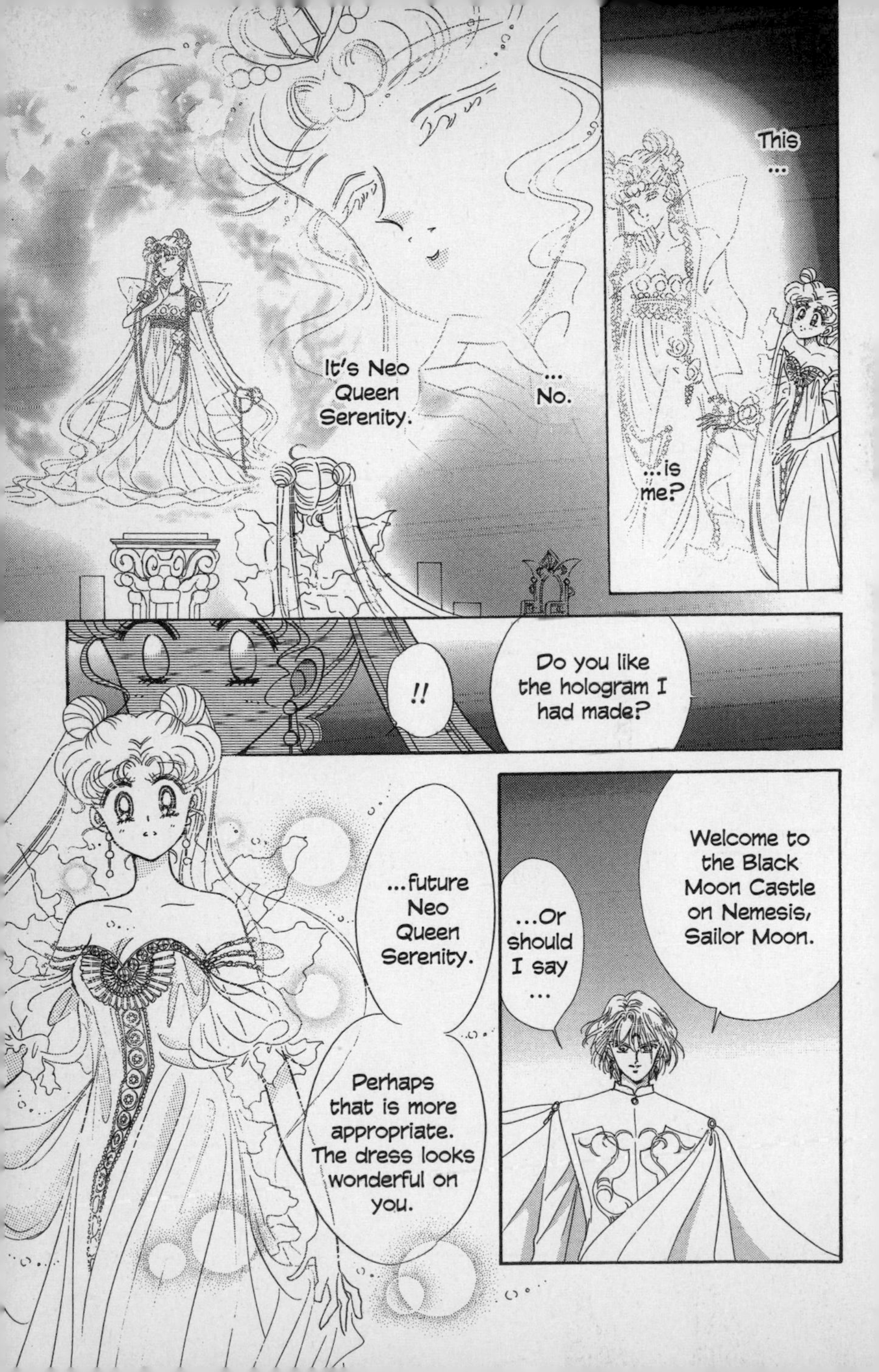
This ...
...is me?
... No.
It's Neo Queen Serenity.
Do you like the hologram I had made?
!!
Welcome to the Black Moon Castle on Nemesis, Sailor Moon.
...Or should I say ...
...future Neo Queen Serenity.
Perhaps that is more appropriate. The dress looks wonderful on you.

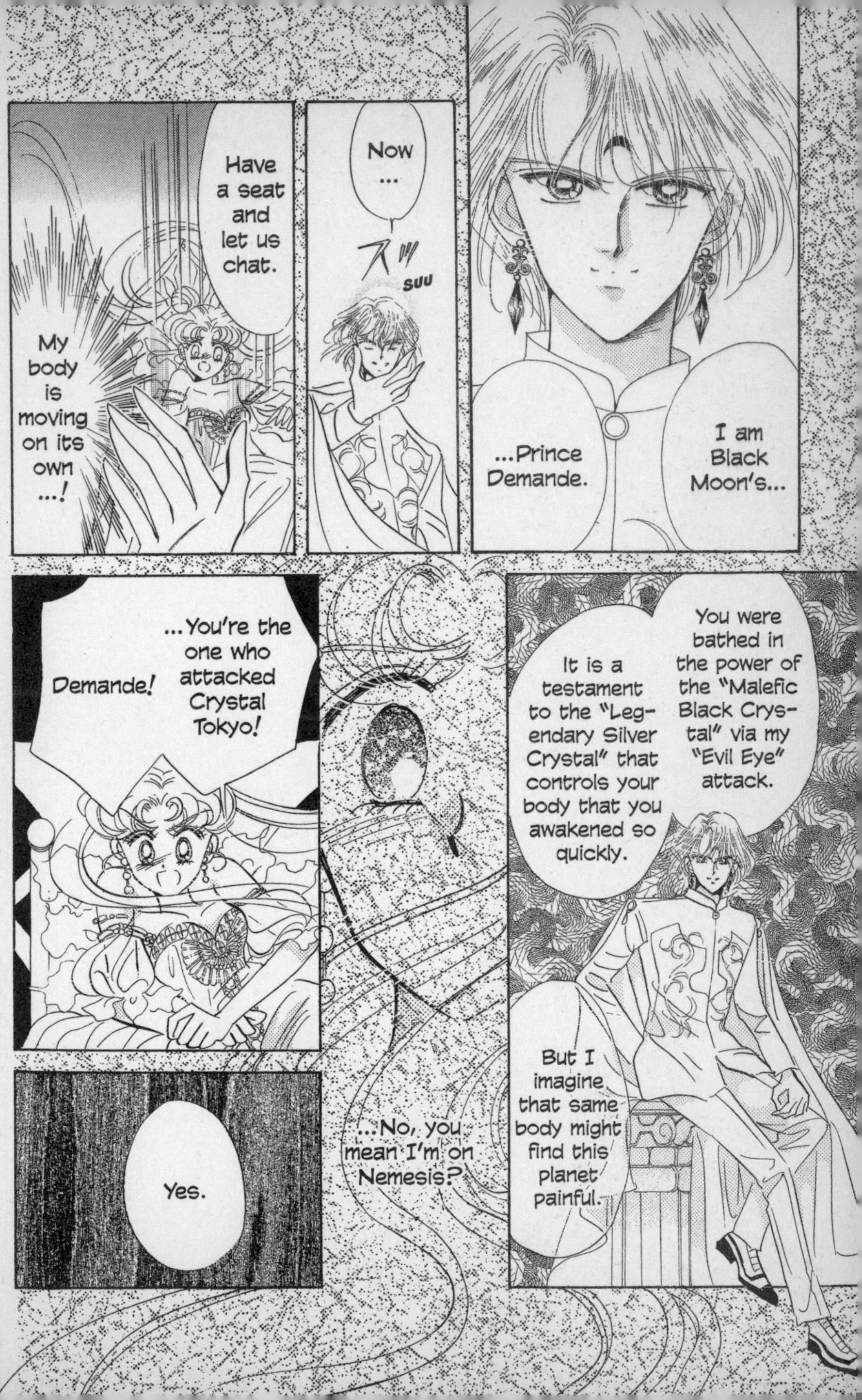

I am Black Moon's...
...Prince Demande.
Now ...
スッ
SUU
Have a seat and let us chat.
My body is moving on its own ...!
You were bathed in the power of the "Malefic Black Crys-tal" via my "Evil Eye" attack.
It is a testament to the "Leg-endary Silver Crystal" that controls your body that you awakened so quickly.
But I imagine that same body might find this planet painful.
...No, you mean I'm on Nemesis?
Demande!
...You're the one who attacked Crystal Tokyo!
Yes.

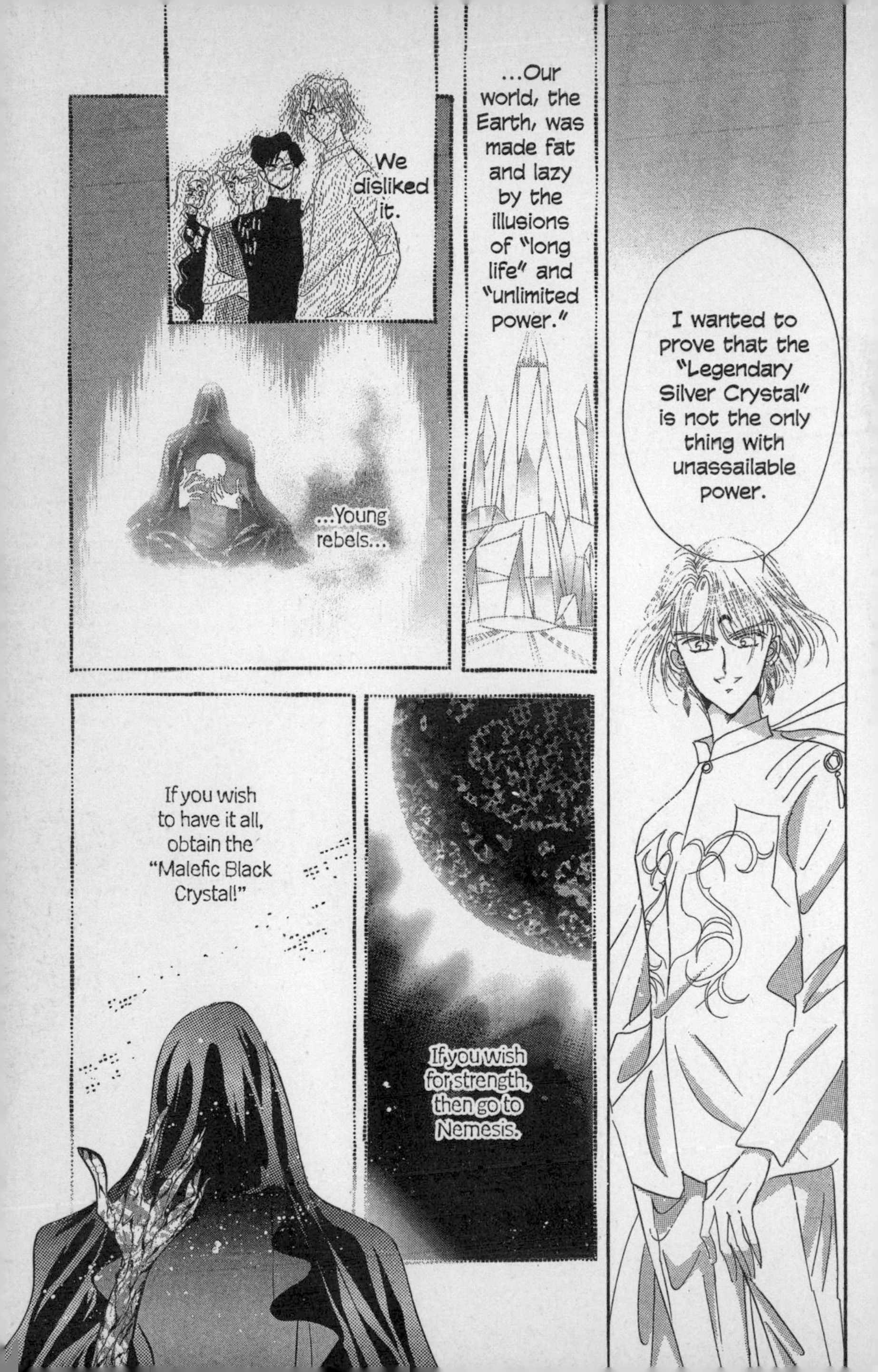
I wanted to prove that the "Legendary Silver Crystal" is not the only thing with unassailable power.
...Our world, the Earth, was made fat and lazy by the illusions of "long life" and "unlimited power."
We disliked it.
...Young rebels...
If you wish for strength, then go to Nemesis.
If you wish to have it all, obtain the "Malefic Black Crystal!"

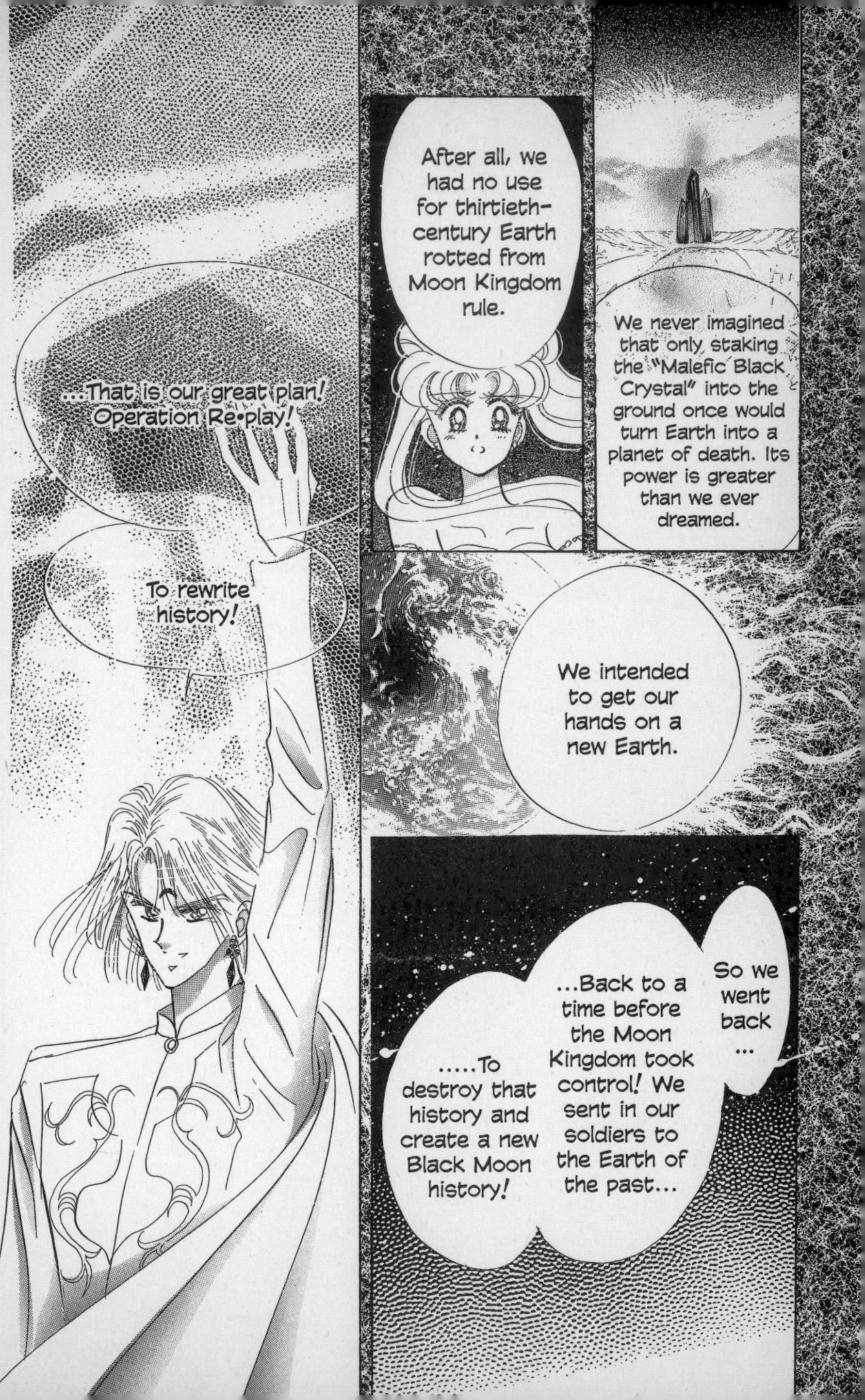
We never imagined that only staking the "Malefic Black Crystal" into the ground once would turn Earth into a planet of death. Its power is greater than we ever dreamed.
After all, we had no use for thirtieth-century Earth rotted from Moon Kingdom rule.
We intended to get our hands on a new Earth.
So we went back ...
...Back to a time before the Moon Kingdom took control! We sent in our soldiers to the Earth of the past...
.....To destroy that history and create a new Black Moon history!
...That is our great plan! Operation Re•play!
To rewrite history!

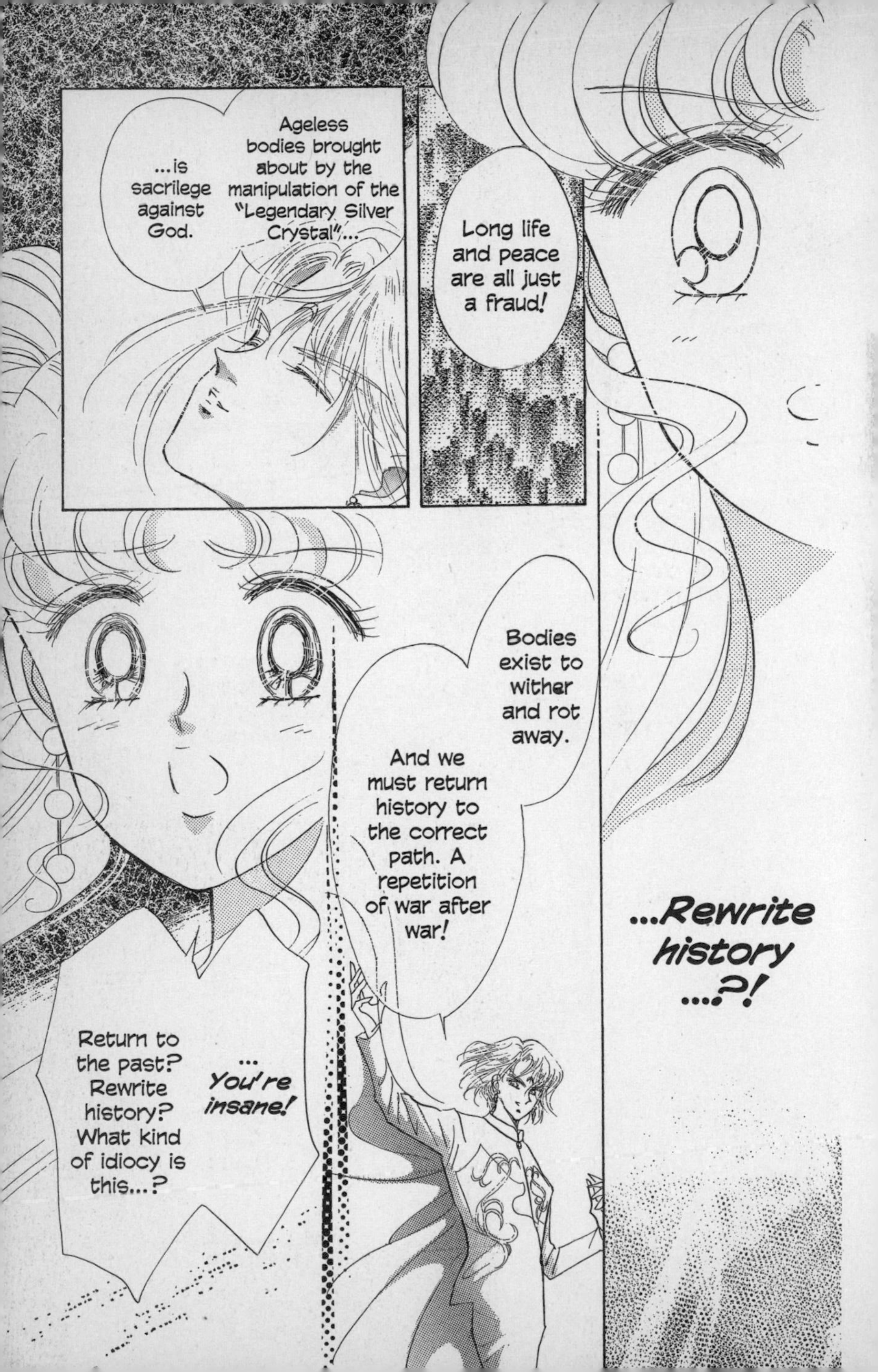
...Rewrite history ...?!
Long life and peace are all just a fraud!
Ageless bodies brought about by the manipulation of the "Legendary Silver Crystal"...
...is sacrilege against God.
Bodies exist to wither and rot away.
And we must return history to the correct path. A repetition of war after war!
Return to the past? Rewrite history? What kind of idiocy is this...?
... You're insane!

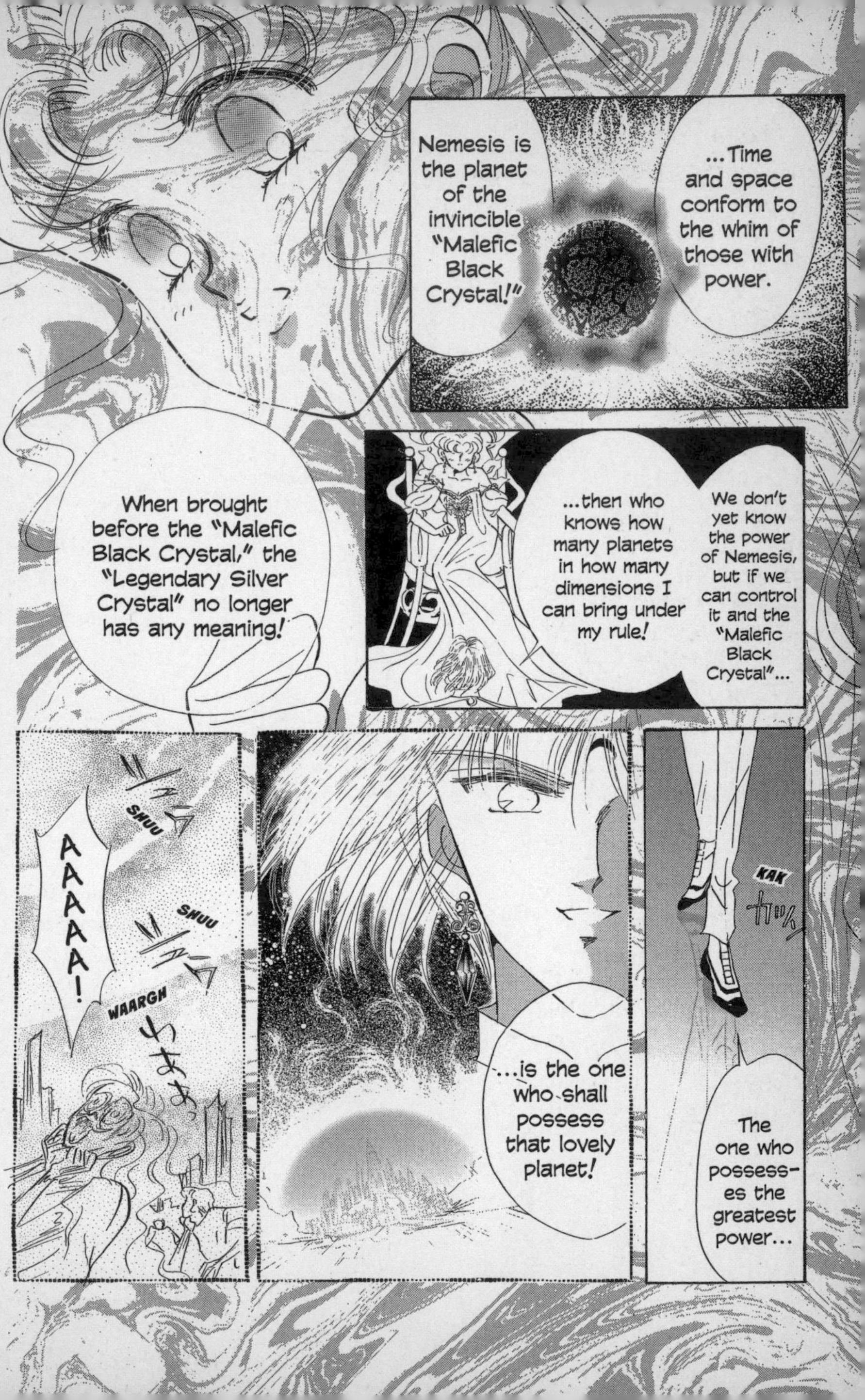
...Time and space conform to the whim of those with power.
Nemesis is the planet of the invincible "Malefic Black Crystal!"
We don't yet know the power of Nemesis, but if we can control it and the "Malefic Black Crystal"...
...then who knows how many planets in how many dimensions I can bring under my rule!
When brought before the "Malefic Black Crystal," the "Legendary Silver Crystal" no longer has any meaning!
KAK
The one who possess-es the greatest power...
...is the one who shall possess that lovely planet!
SHUU
SHUU
AAAAA!
WAARGH

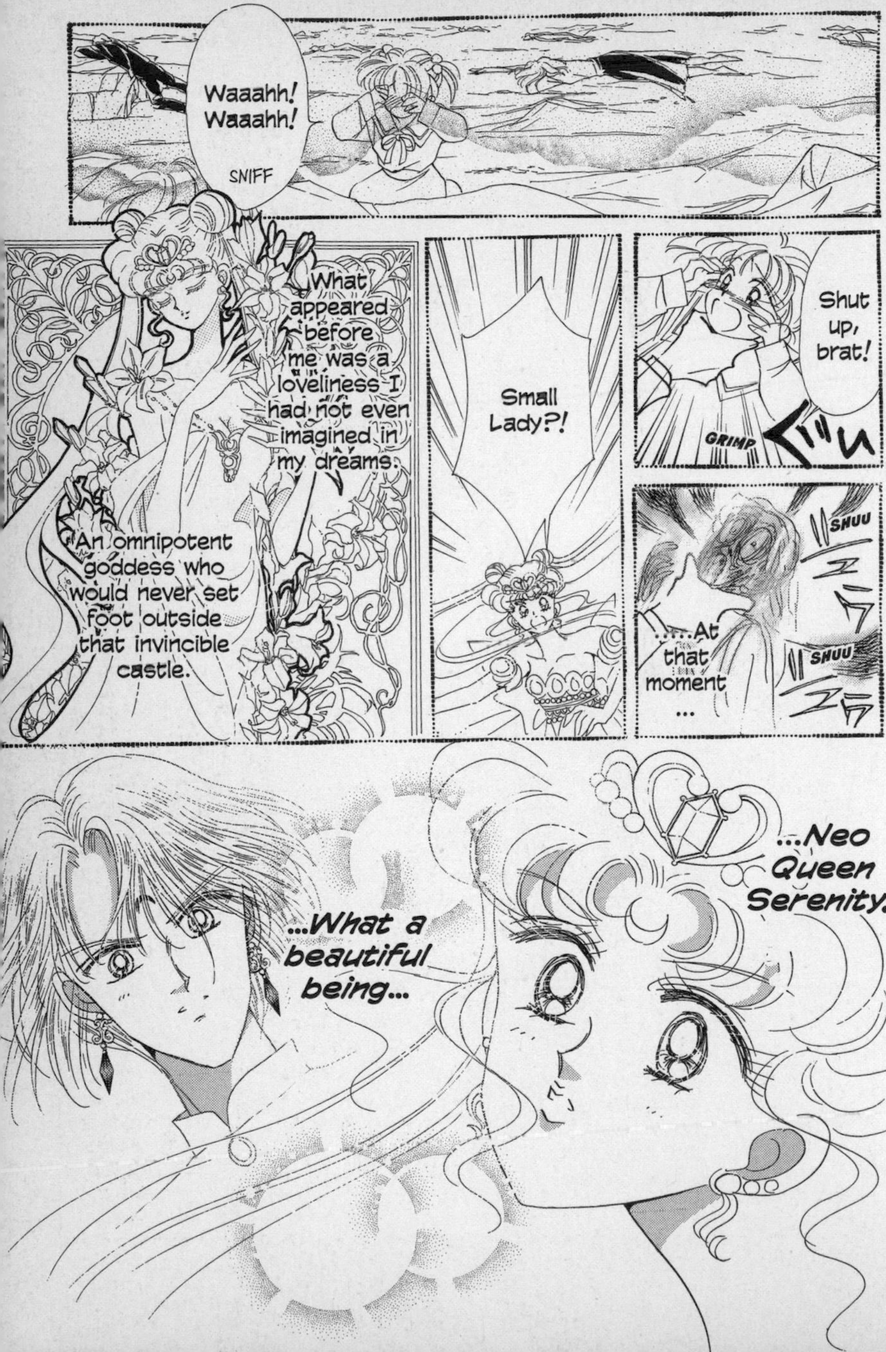
Waaahh! Waaahh!
SNIFF
Shut up, brat!
GRIMP
SHUU
.....At that moment ...
SHUU
Small Lady?!
What appeared before me was a loveliness I had not even imagined in my dreams.
An omnipotent goddess who would never set foot outside that invincible castle.
...Neo Queen Serenity!
...What a beautiful being...

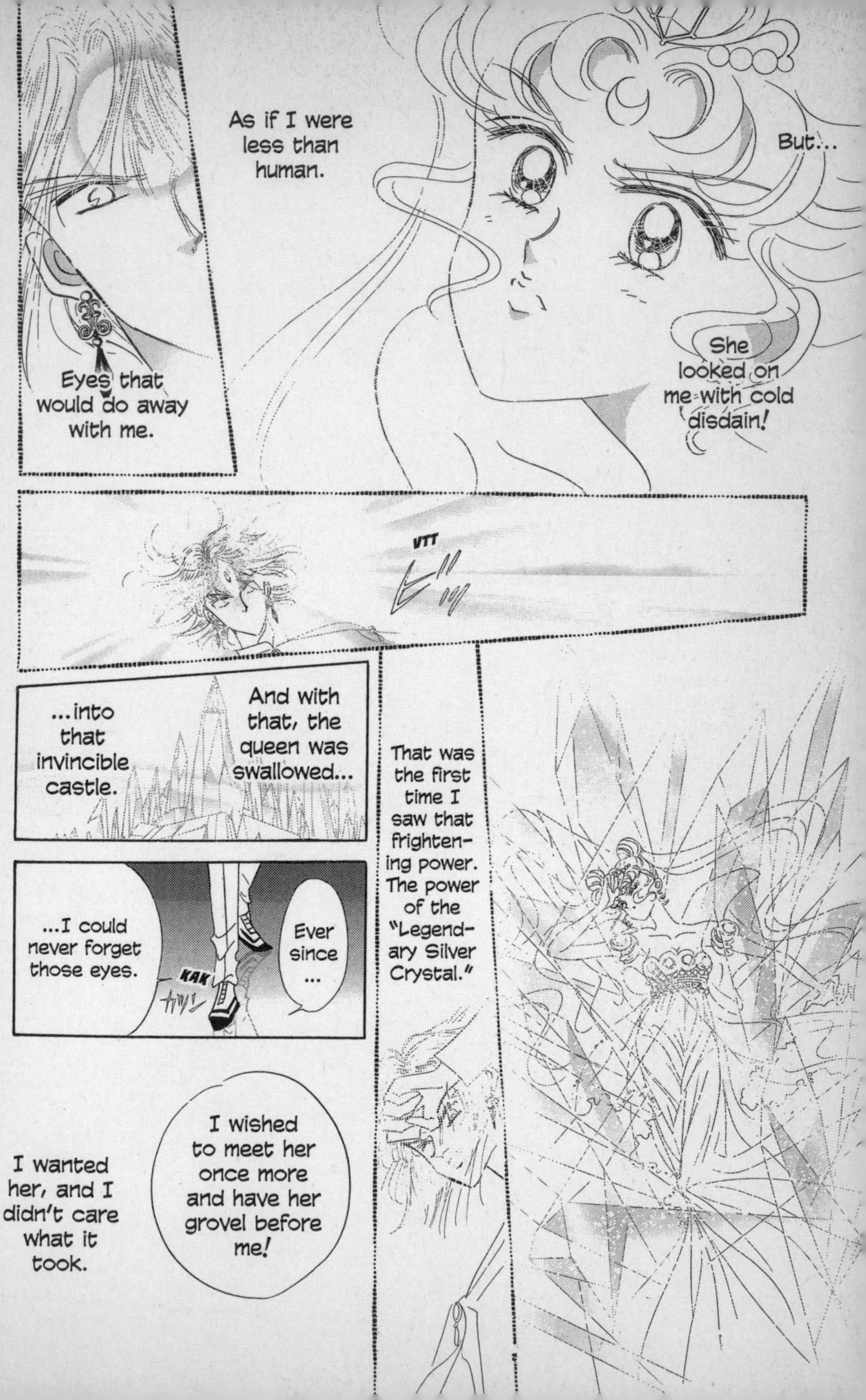
But...
She looked on me with cold disdain!
As if I were less than human.
Eyes that would do away with me.
VTT
That was the first time I saw that frightening power. The power of the "Legendary Silver Crystal."
And with that, the queen was swallowed...
...into that invincible castle.
Ever since...
...I could never forget those eyes.
KAK
I wished to meet her once more and have her grovel before me!
I wanted her, and I didn't care what it took.

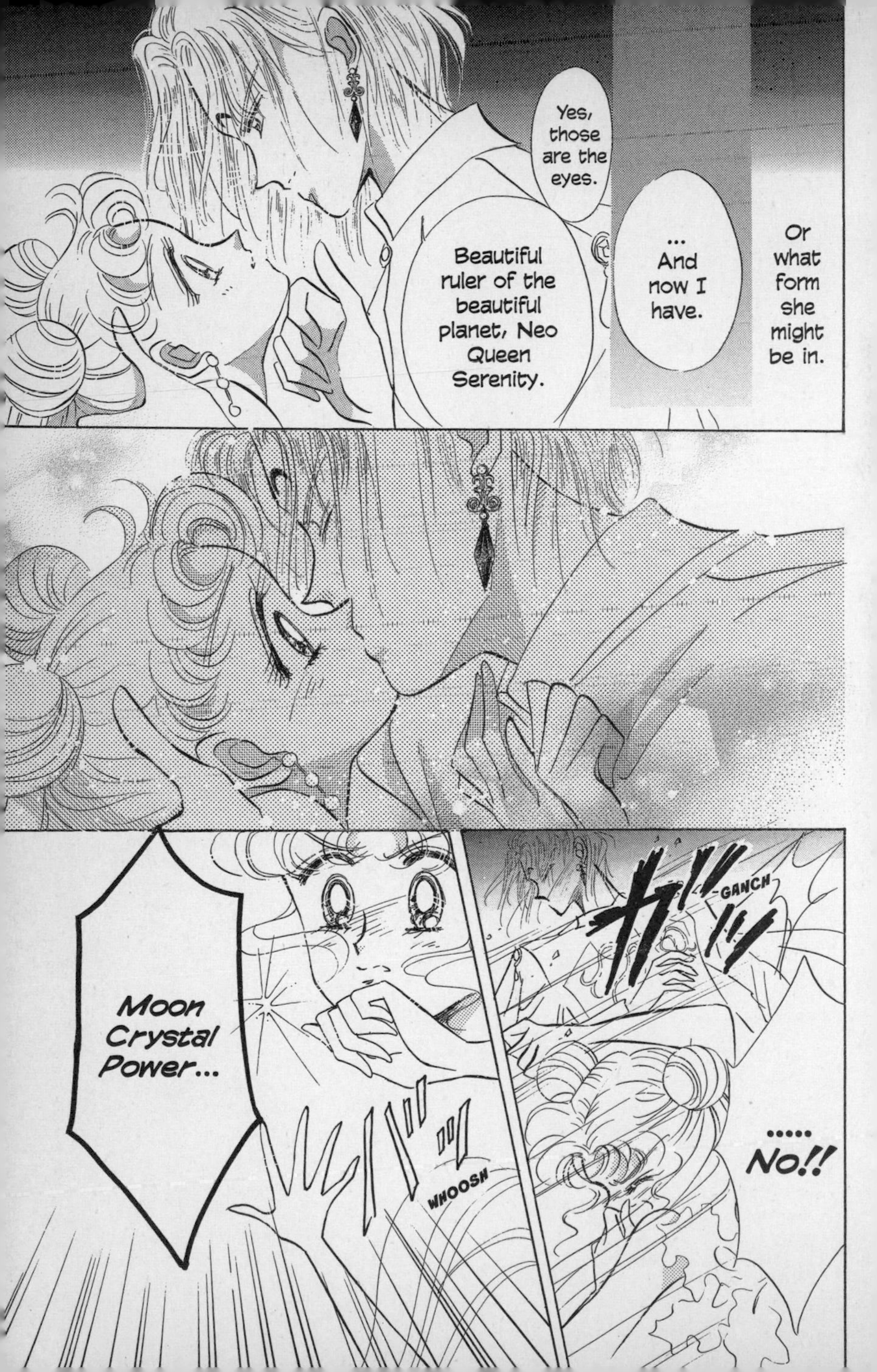
Yes, those are the eyes.
Or what form she might be in.
... And now I have.
Beautiful ruler of the beautiful planet, Neo Queen Serenity.
GANCH
..... No!!
Moon Crystal Power...
WHOOSH

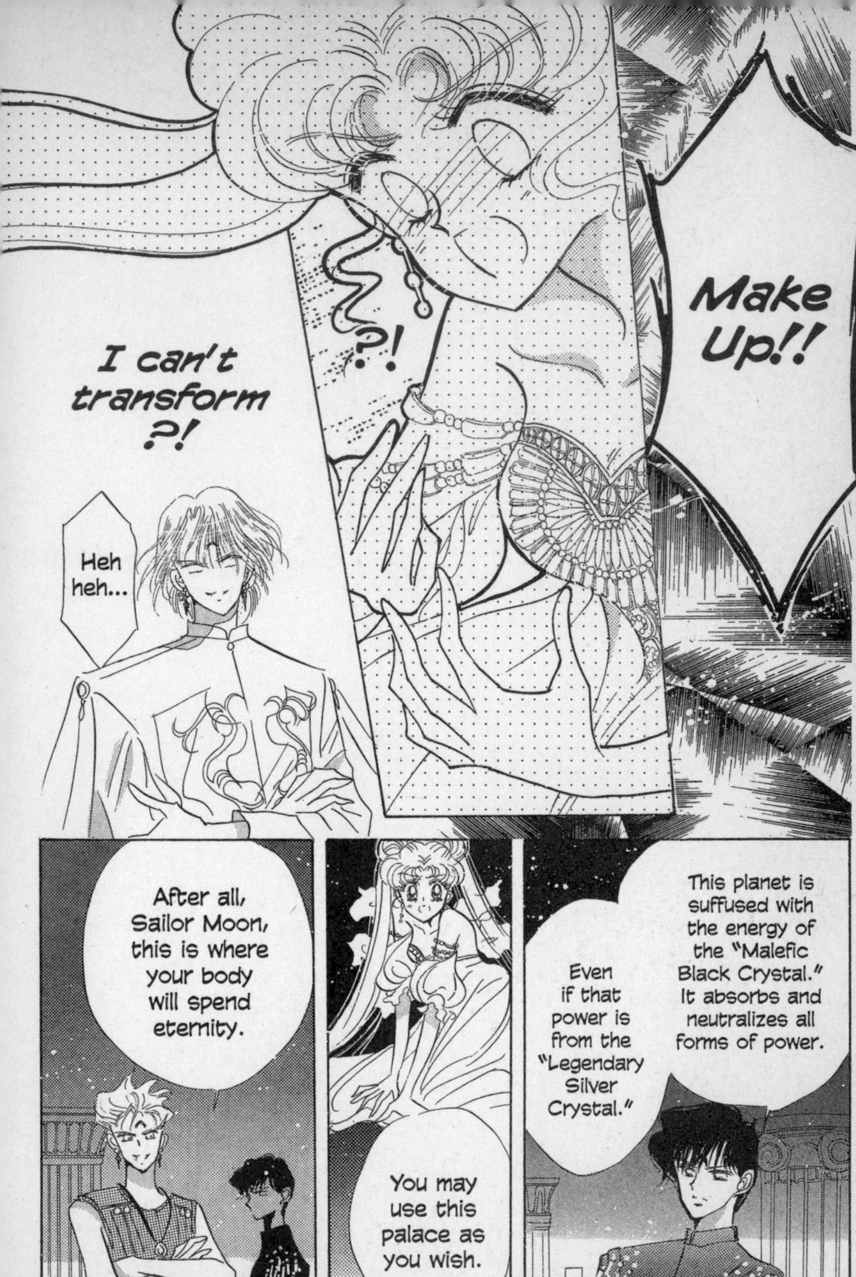
Make Up!!
?!
I can't transform ?!
Heh heh...
This planet is suffused with the energy of the "Malefic Black Crystal." It absorbs and neutralizes all forms of power.
Even if that power is from the "Legendary Silver Crystal."
You may use this palace as you wish.
After all, Sailor Moon, this is where your body will spend eternity.

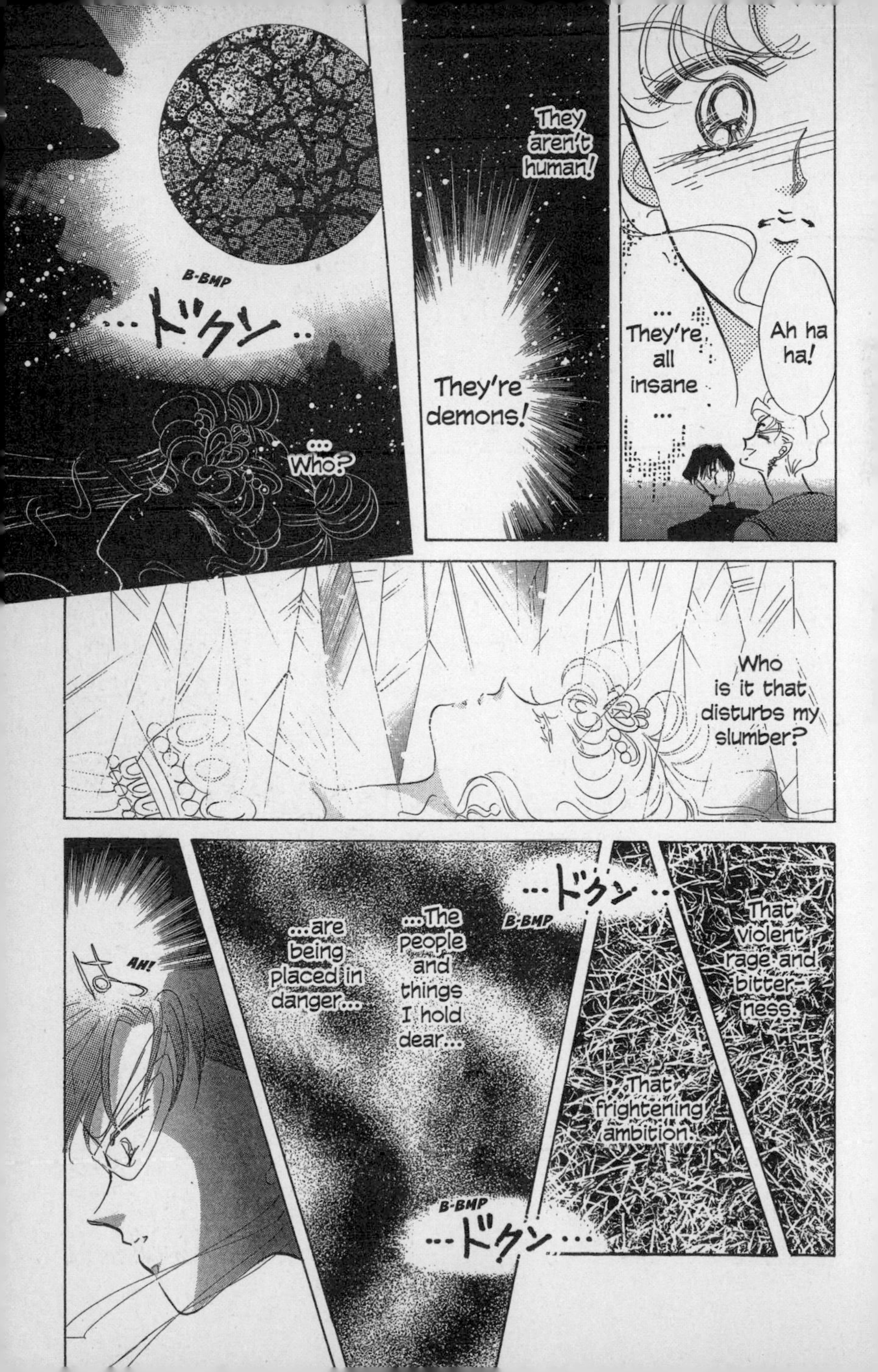

Ah ha ha!
... They're all insane ...
They aren't human!
They're demons!
B-BMP
...ドクン...
...Who?
Who is it that disturbs my slumber?
That violent rage and bitterness.
That frightening ambition.
...ドクン...
B-BMP
...The people and things I hold dear...
...are being placed in danger...
B-BMP
...ドクン...
AH!

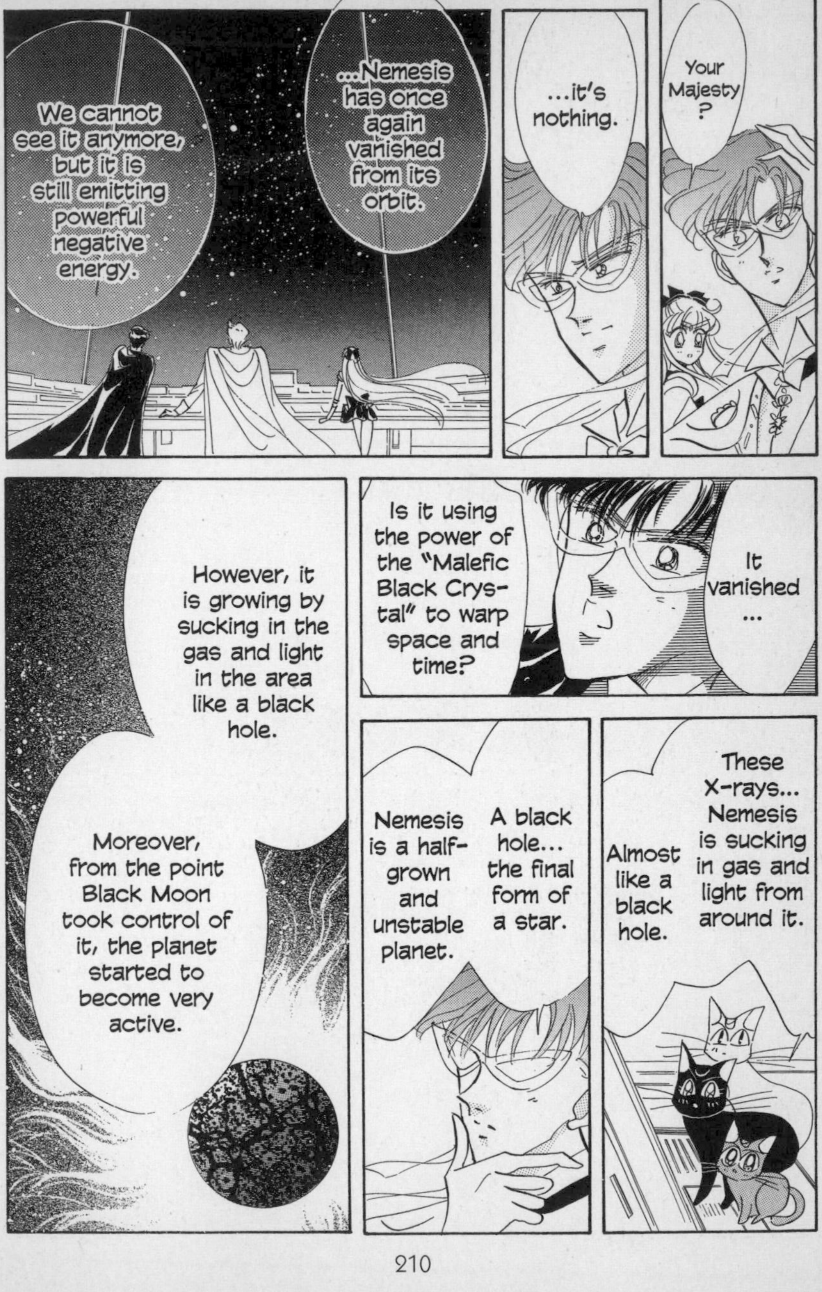
Your Majesty ?
...it's nothing.
...Nemesis has once again vanished from its orbit.
We cannot see it anymore, but it is still emitting powerful negative energy.
It vanished ...
Is it using the power of the "Malefic Black Crys-tal" to warp space and time?
These X-rays... Nemesis is sucking in gas and light from around it.
Almost like a black hole.
A black hole... the final form of a star.
Nemesis is a half-grown and unstable planet.
However, it is growing by sucking in the gas and light in the area like a black hole.
Moreover, from the point Black Moon took control of it, the planet started to become very active.

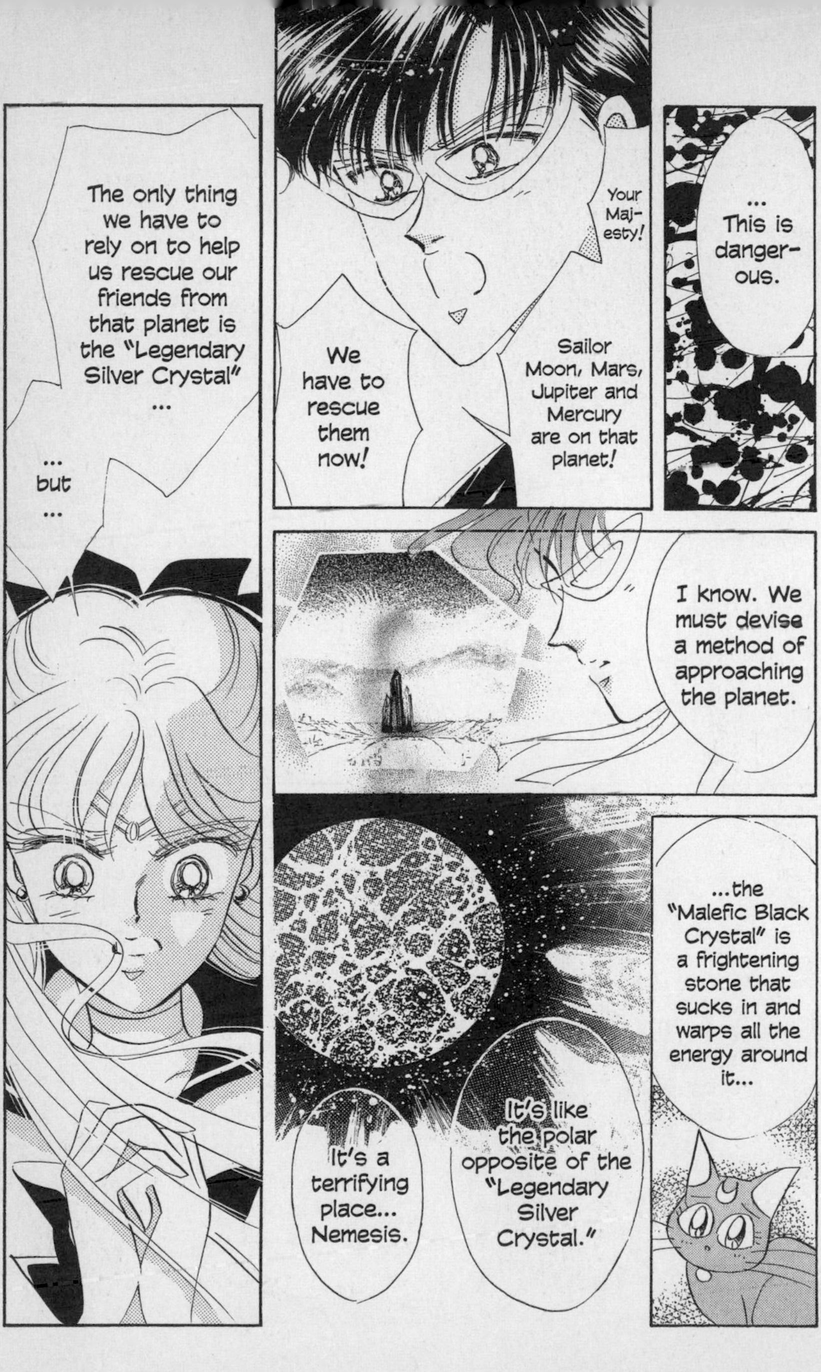
... This is danger- ous.
Your Maj- esty!
Sailor Moon, Mars, Jupiter and Mercury are on that planet!
We have to rescue them now!
I know. We must devise a method of approaching the planet.
...the "Malefic Black Crystal" is a frightening stone that sucks in and warps all the energy around it...
It's like the polar opposite of the "Legendary Silver Crystal."
It's a terrifying place... Nemesis.
The only thing we have to rely on to help us rescue our friends from that planet is the "Legendary Silver Crystal" ...
... but ...

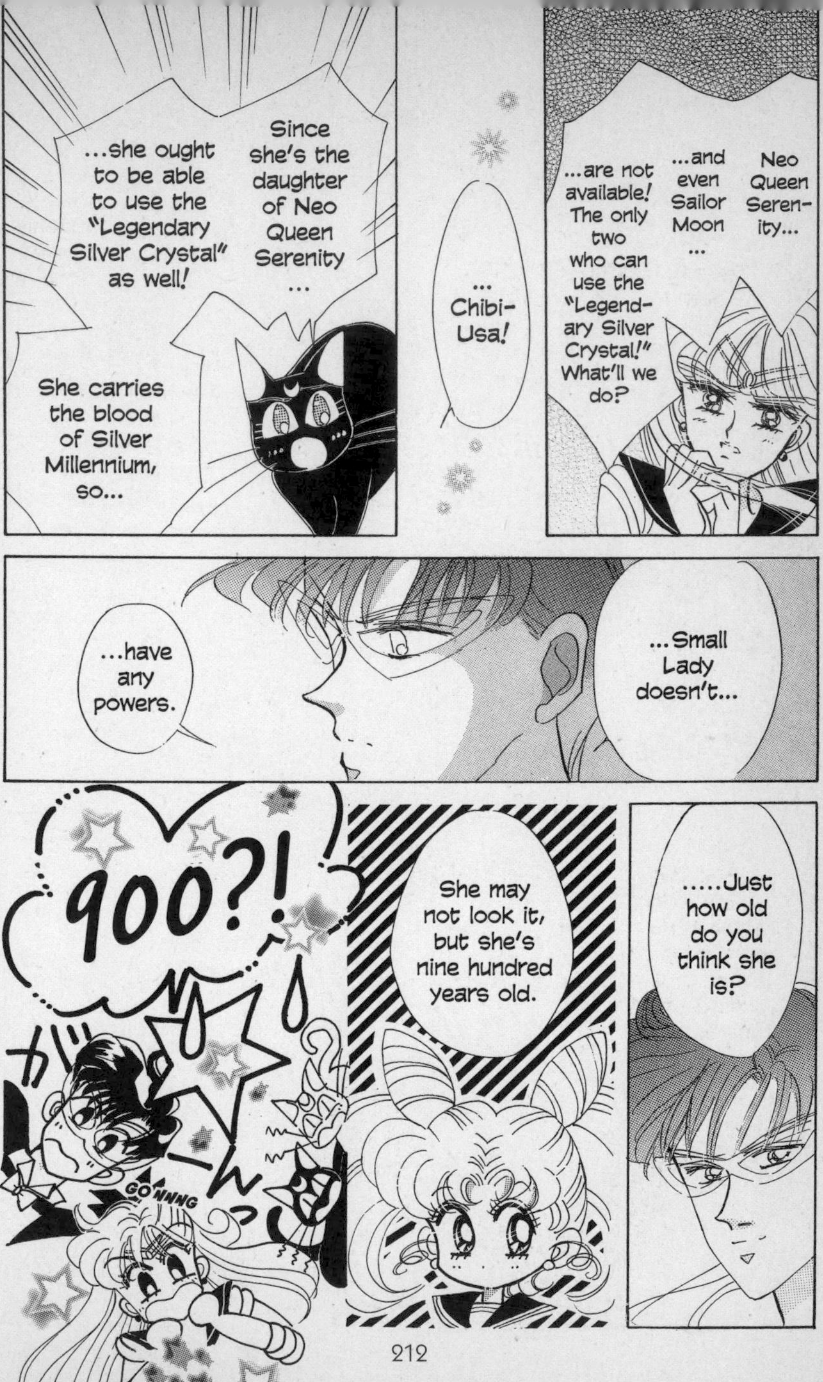
Neo Queen Seren-ity...
...and even Sailor Moon...
...are not available! The only two who can use the "Legend-ary Silver Crystal!" What'll we do?
...Chibi-Usa!
Since she's the daughter of Neo Queen Serenity...
...she ought to be able to use the "Legendary Silver Crystal" as well!
She carries the blood of Silver Millennium, so...
...Small Lady doesn't...
...have any powers.
.....Just how old do you think she is?
She may not look it, but she's nine hundred years old.
900?!
GONNNG

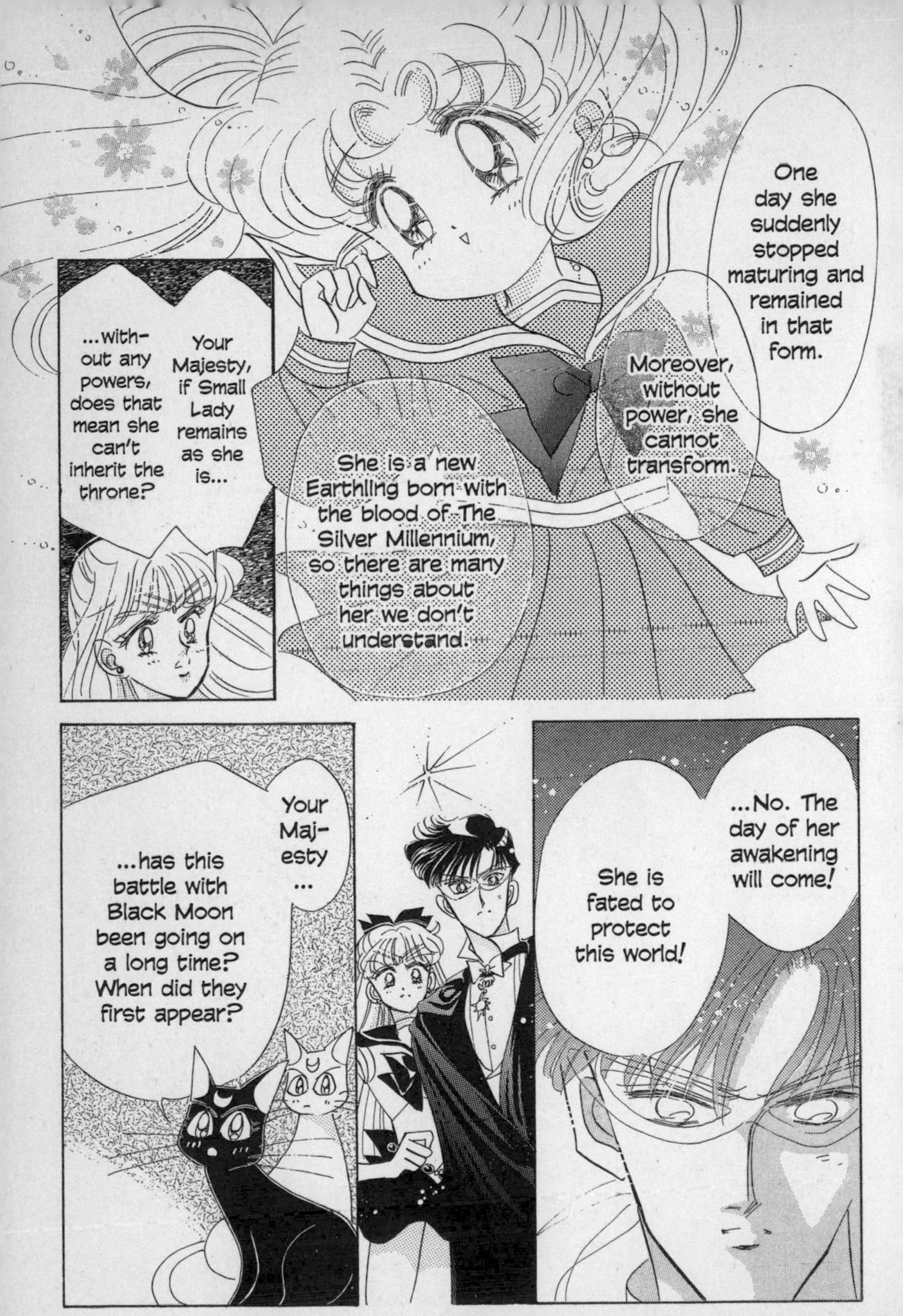
One day she suddenly stopped maturing and remained in that form.
Moreover, without power, she cannot transform.
She is a new Earthling born with the blood of The Silver Millennium, so there are many things about her we don't understand.
Your Majesty, if Small Lady remains as she is...
...without any powers, does that mean she can't inherit the throne?
...No. The day of her awakening will come!
She is fated to protect this world!
Your Majesty...
...has this battle with Black Moon been going on a long time? When did they first appear?

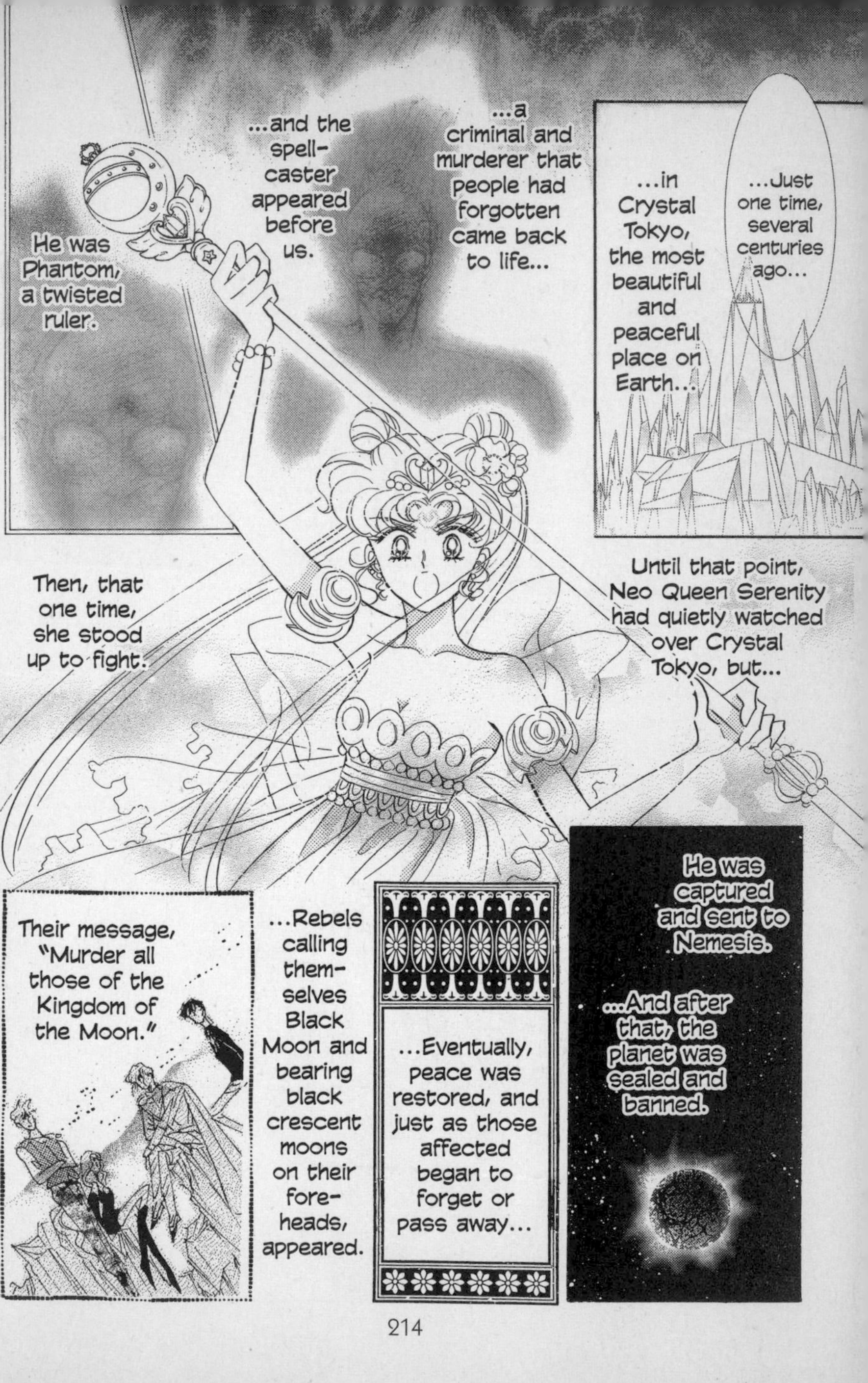
...Just one time, several centuries ago...
...in Crystal Tokyo, the most beautiful and peaceful place on Earth...
...a criminal and murderer that people had forgotten came back to life...
...and the spell-caster appeared before us.
He was Phantom, a twisted ruler.
Until that point, Neo Queen Serenity had quietly watched over Crystal Tokyo, but...
Then, that one time, she stood up to fight.
He was captured and sent to Nemesis.
...And after that, the planet was sealed and banned.
...Eventually, peace was restored, and just as those affected began to forget or pass away...
...Rebels calling themselves Black Moon and bearing black crescent moons on their foreheads, appeared.
Their message, "Murder all those of the Kingdom of the Moon."

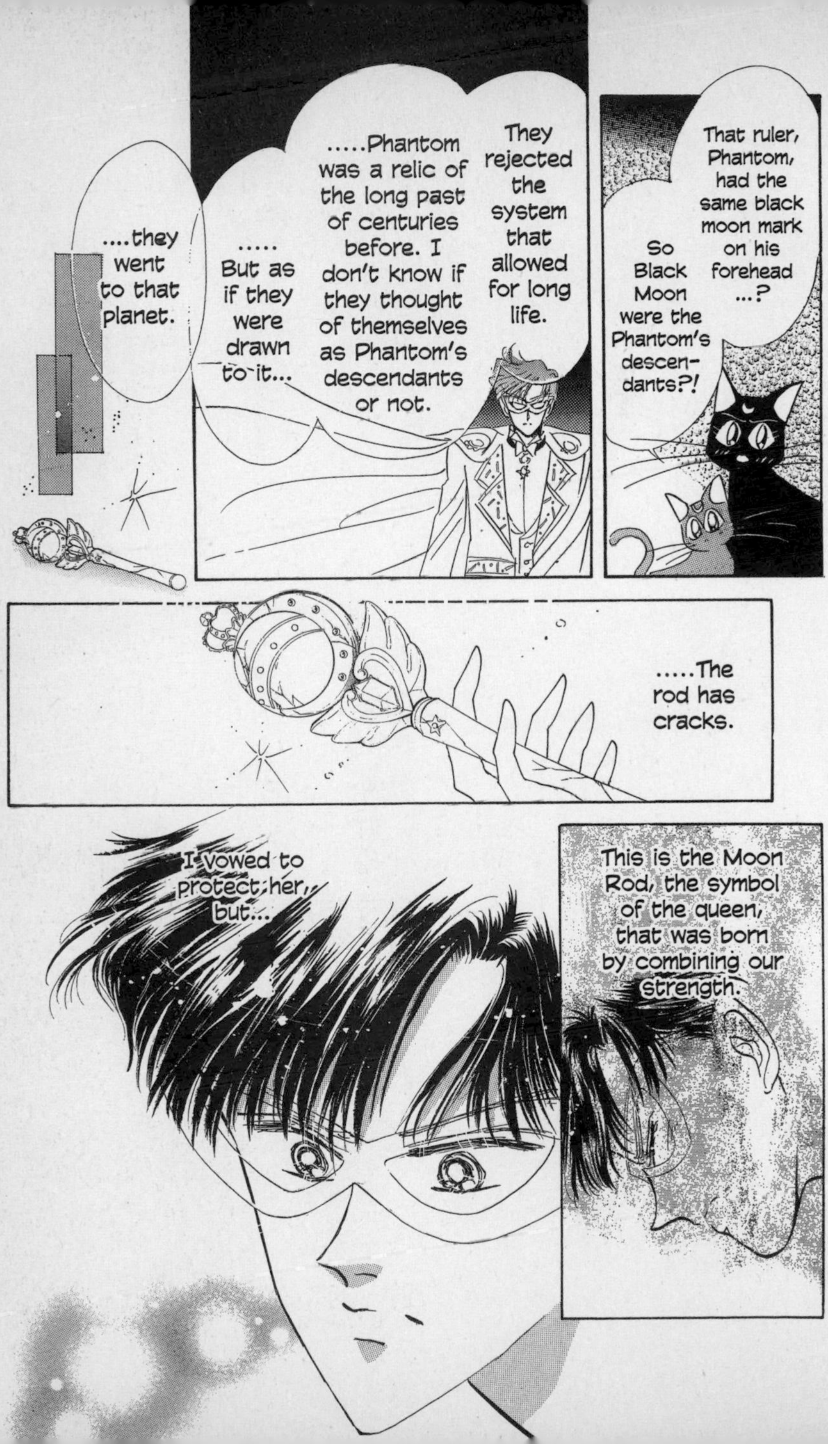
That ruler, Phantom, had the same black moon mark on his forehead ...?
So Black Moon were the Phantom's descendants?!
They rejected the system that allowed for long life.
.....Phantom was a relic of the long past of centuries before. I don't know if they thought of themselves as Phantom's descendants or not.
..... But as if they were drawn to it...
....they went to that planet.
.....The rod has cracks.
This is the Moon Rod, the symbol of the queen, that was born by combining our strength.
I vowed to protect her, but...

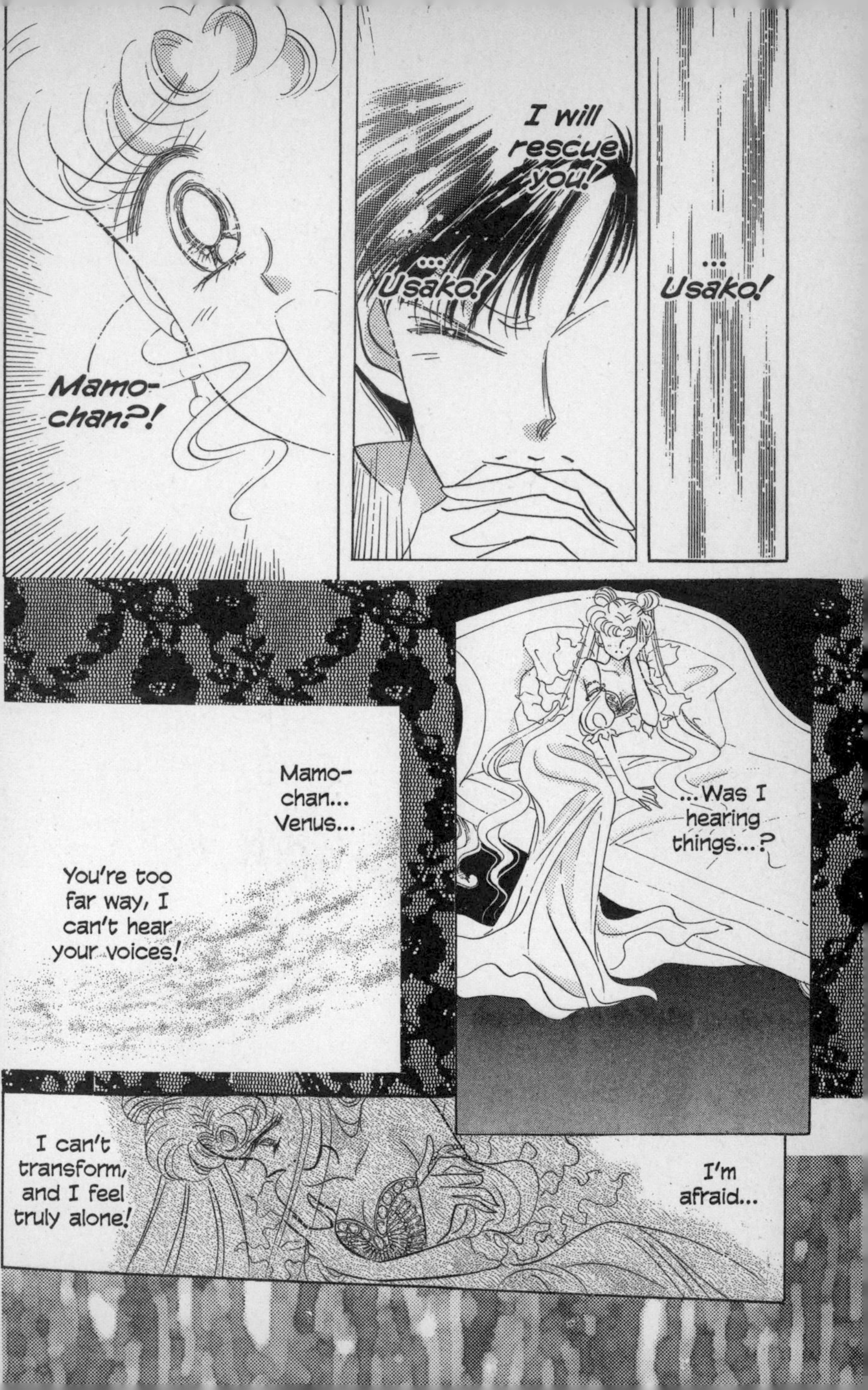
...Usako!
I will rescue you!
...Usako!
Mamo-chan?!
...Was I hearing things...?
Mamo-chan... Venus...
You're too far way, I can't hear your voices!
I'm afraid...
I can't transform, and I feel truly alone!

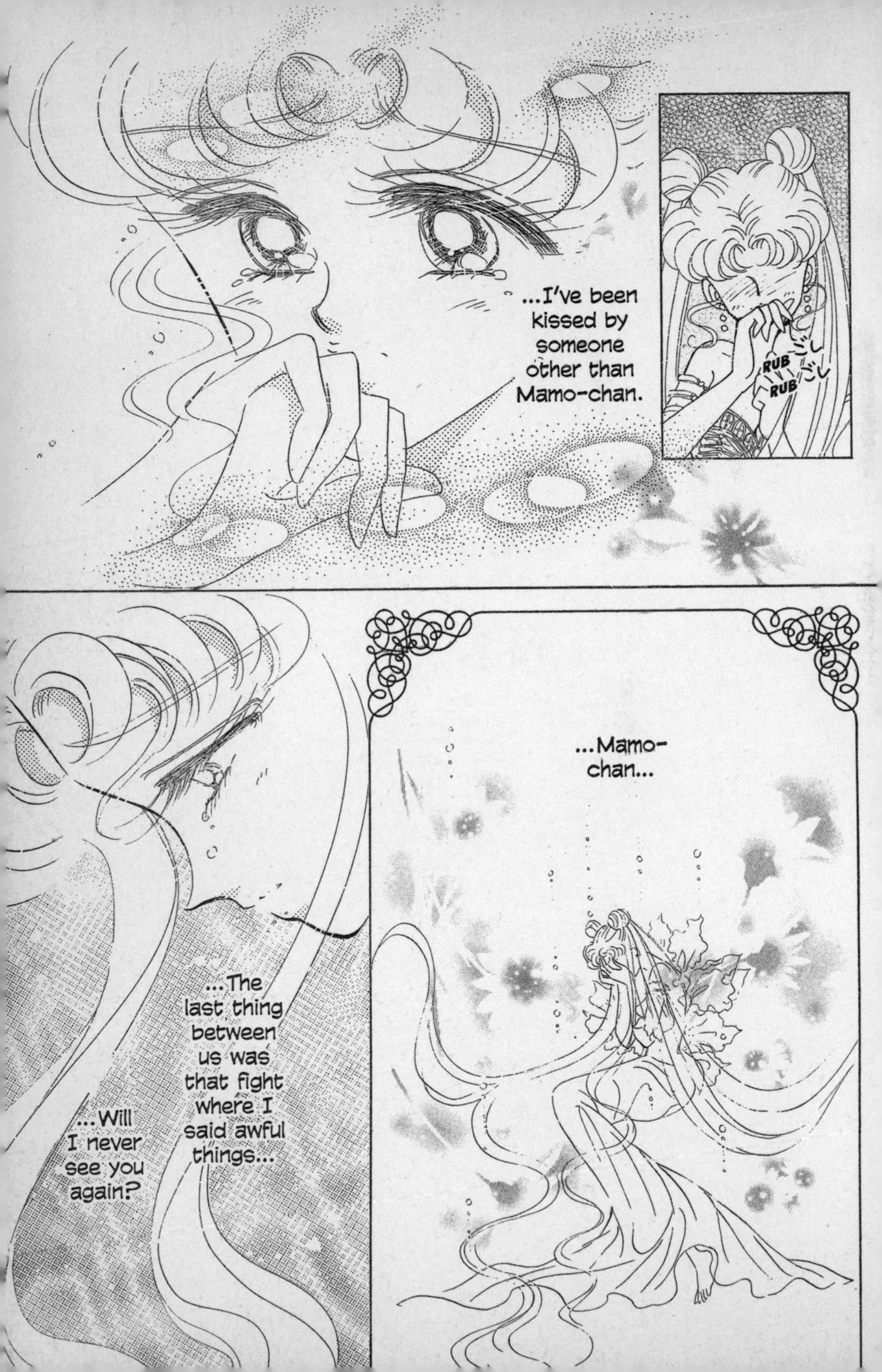
RUB ごし
RUB ごし
...I've been kissed by someone other than Mamo-chan.
...Mamo-chan...
...The last thing between us was that fight where I said awful things...
...Will I never see you again?

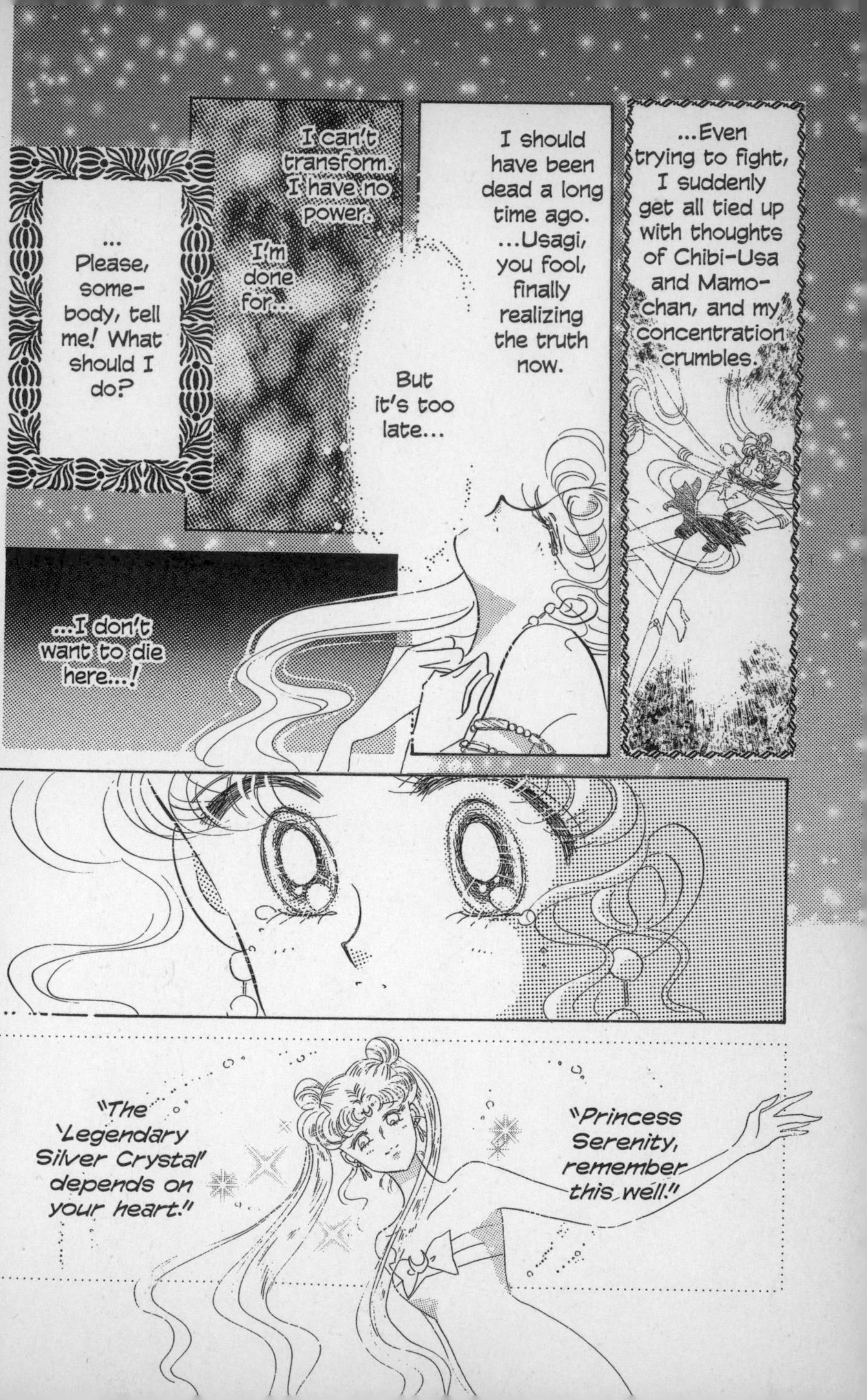
...Even trying to fight, I suddenly get all tied up with thoughts of Chibi-Usa and Mamo-chan, and my concentration crumbles.
I should have been dead a long time ago. ...Usagi, you fool, finally realizing the truth now.
But it's too late...
I can't transform. I have no power.
I'm done for...
...Please, somebody, tell me! What should I do?
...I don't want to die here...!
"Princess Serenity, remember this well."
"The 'Legendary Silver Crystal' depends on your heart."

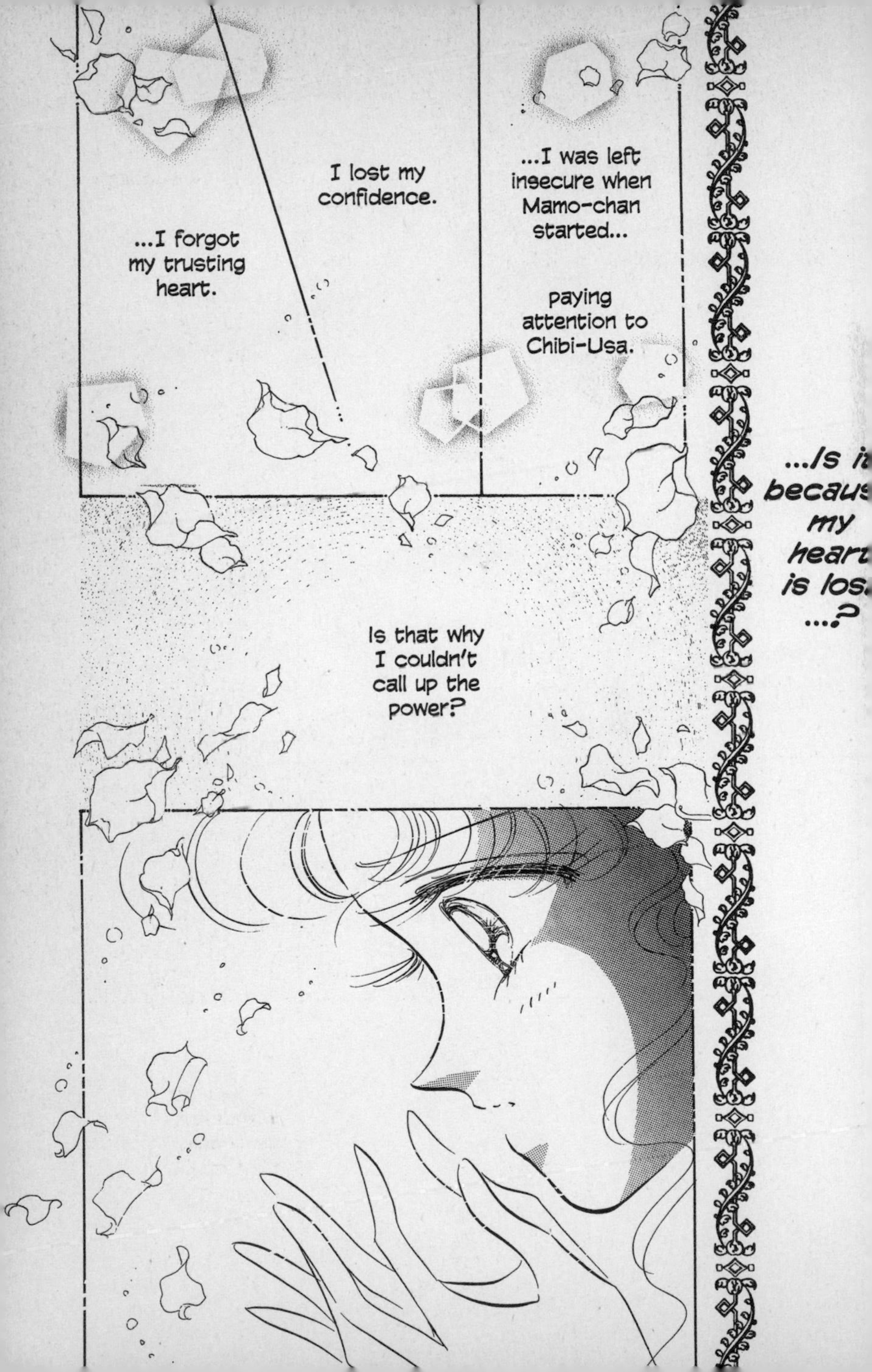
...I was left insecure when Mamo-chan started...
paying attention to Chibi-Usa.
I lost my confidence.
...I forgot my trusting heart.
Is that why I couldn't call up the power?
...Is i becaus my heart is los ...?

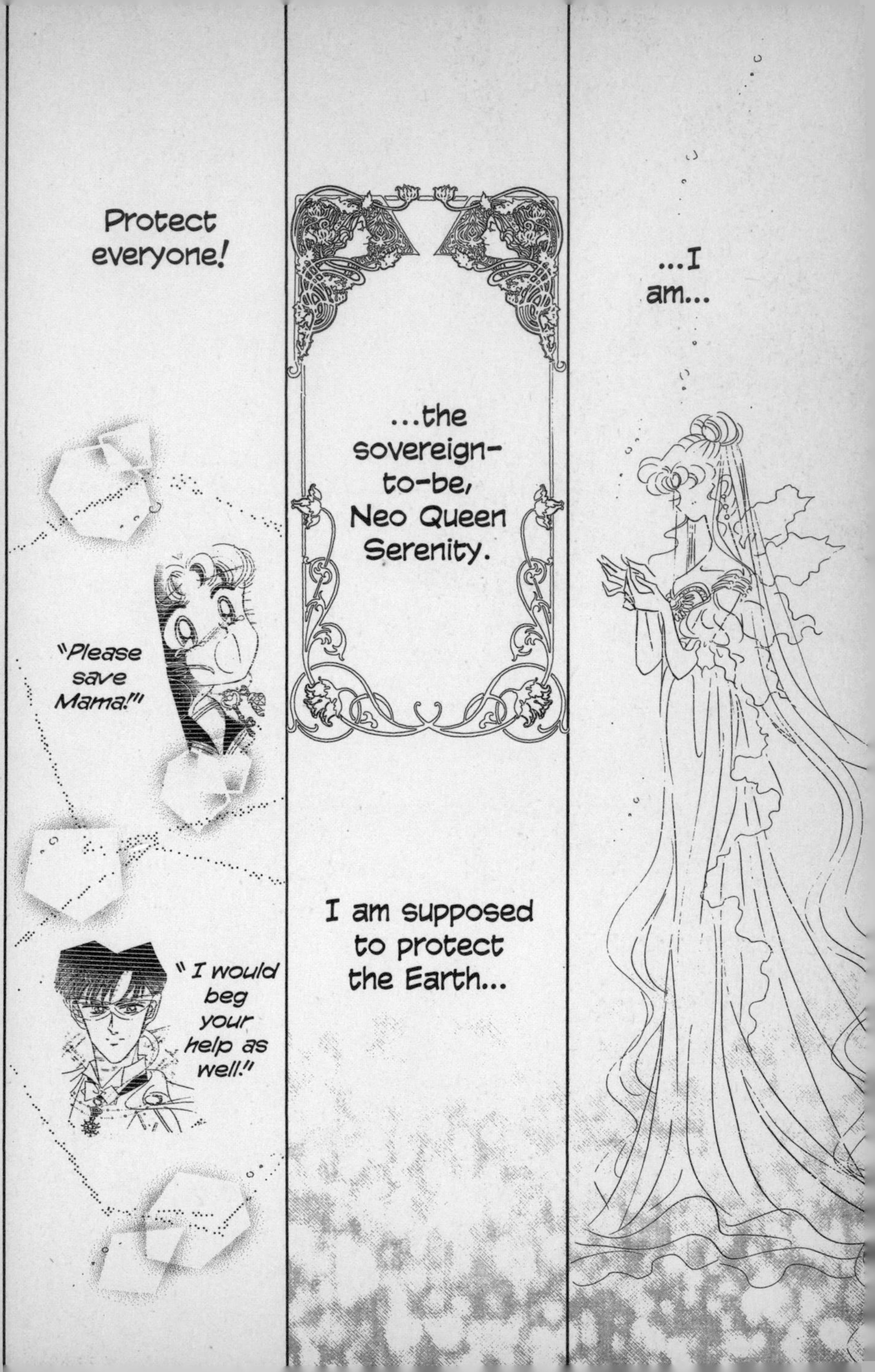
...I am...
...the sovereign-to-be, Neo Queen Serenity.
I am supposed to protect the Earth...
Protect everyone!
"Please save Mama!"
"I would beg your help as well."

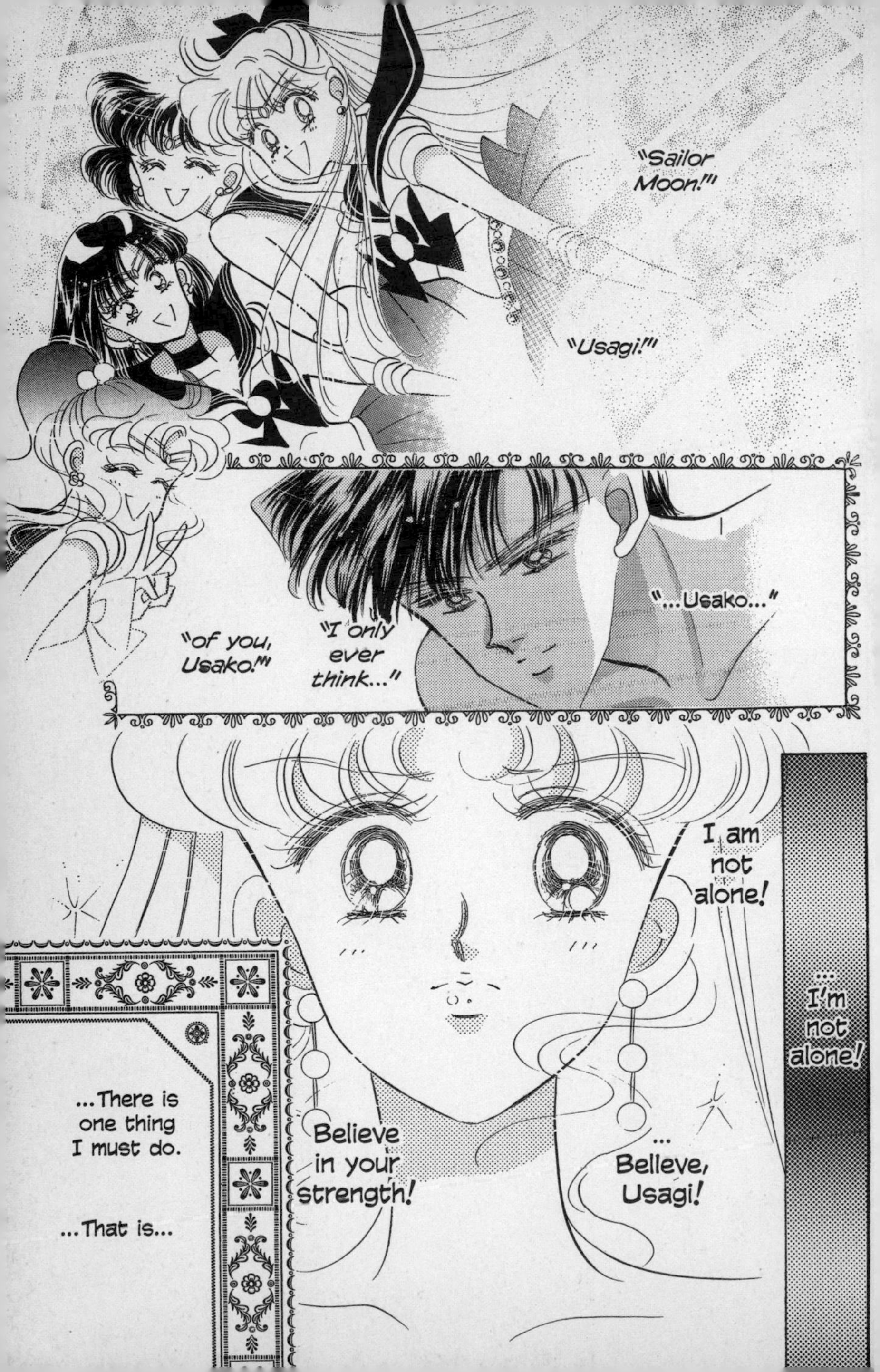
"Sailor Moon!"
"Usagi!"
"...Usako..."
"I only ever think..."
"of you, Usako!"
I am not alone!
...I'm not alone!
...Believe, Usagi!
Believe in your strength!
...There is one thing I must do.
...That is...

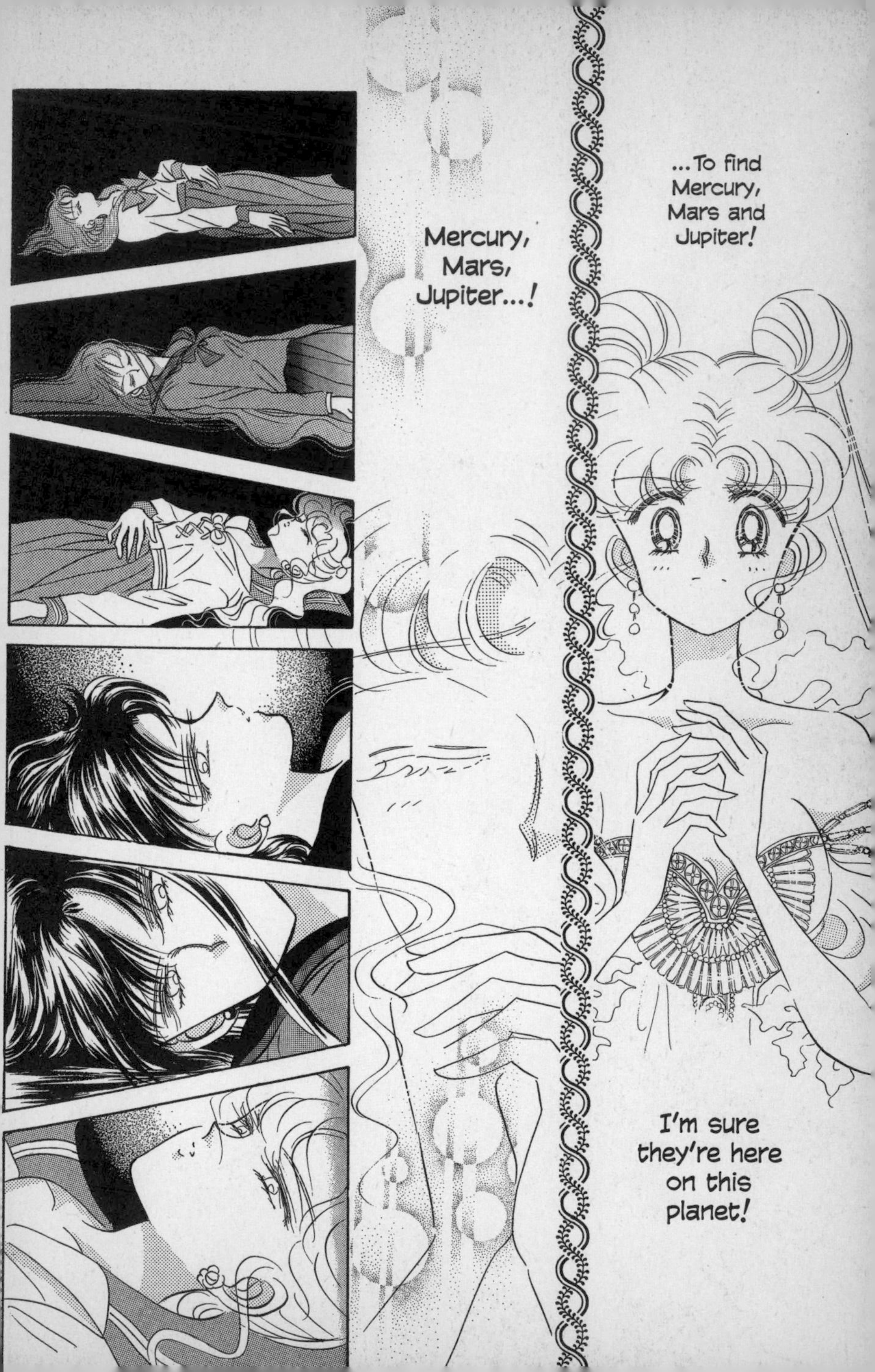
...To find Mercury, Mars and Jupiter!
I'm sure they're here on this planet!
Mercury, Mars, Jupiter...!

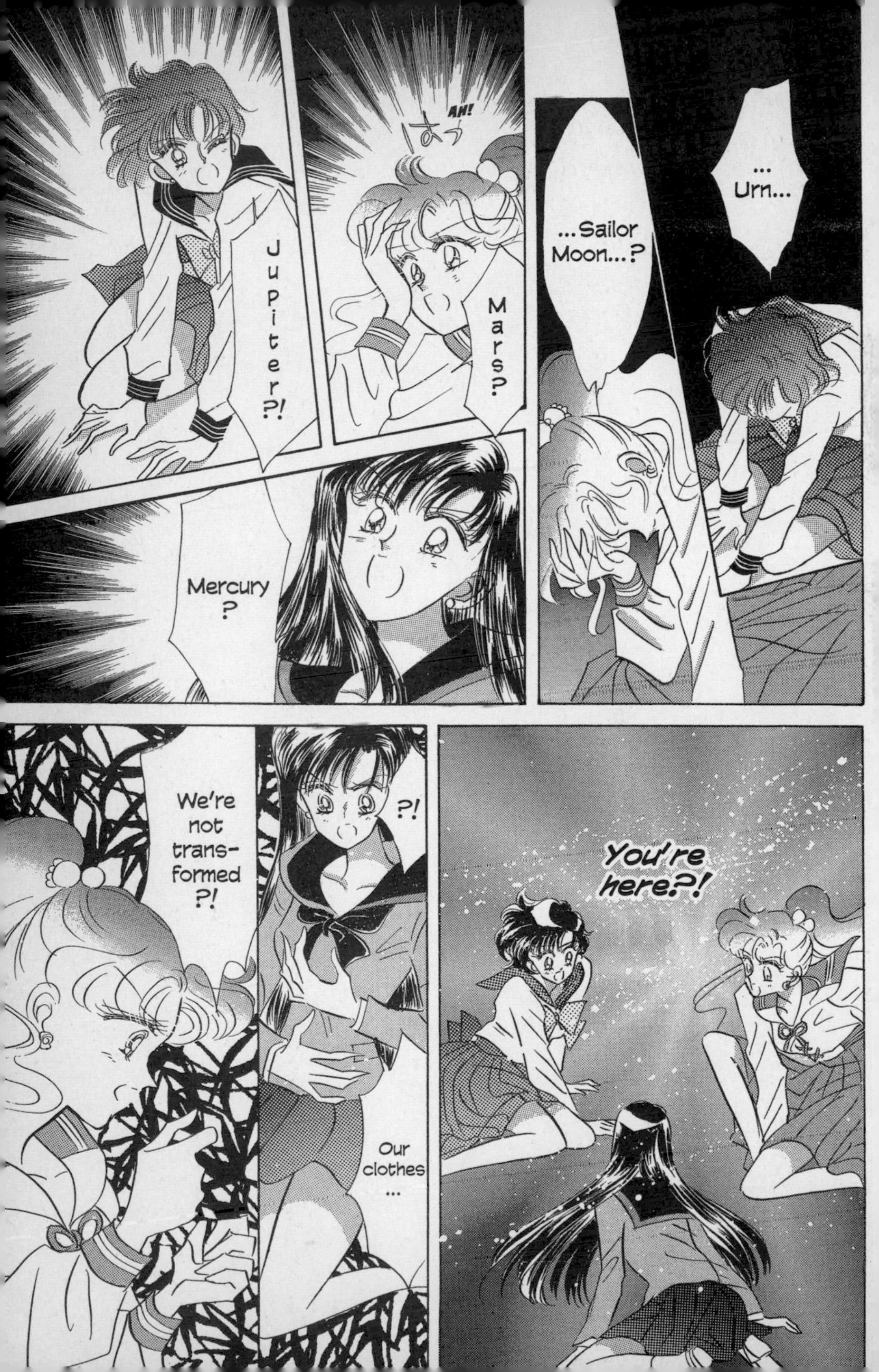
... Urn...
...Sailor Moon...?
AH!
あっ
Mars?
Jupiter?!
Mercury ?
You're here?!
?!
Our clothes ...
We're not trans- formed ?!

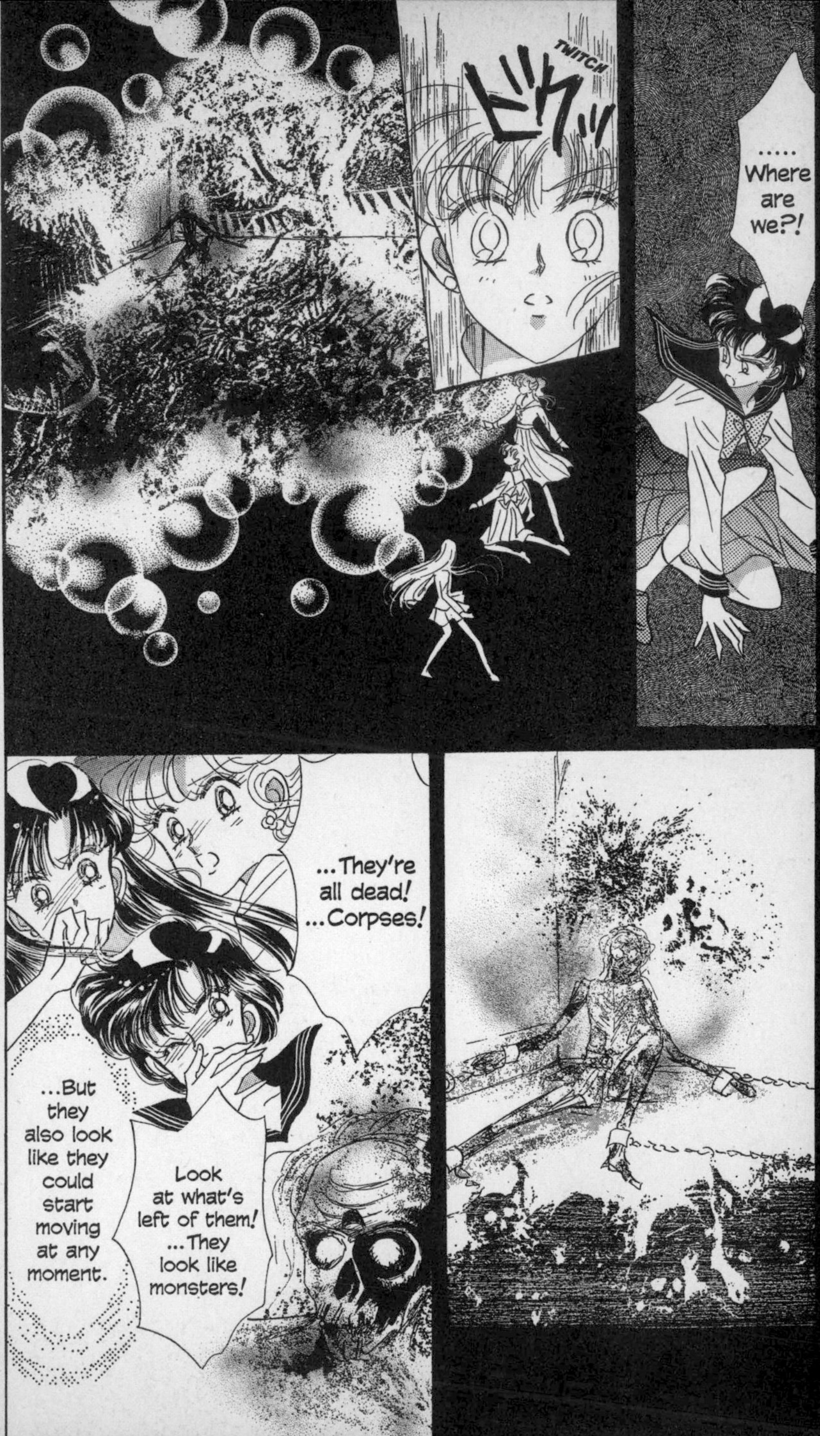
.....
Where are we?!
TWITCH
ドクッ
...They're all dead! ...Corpses!
Look at what's left of them! ...They look like monsters!
...But they also look like they could start moving at any moment.

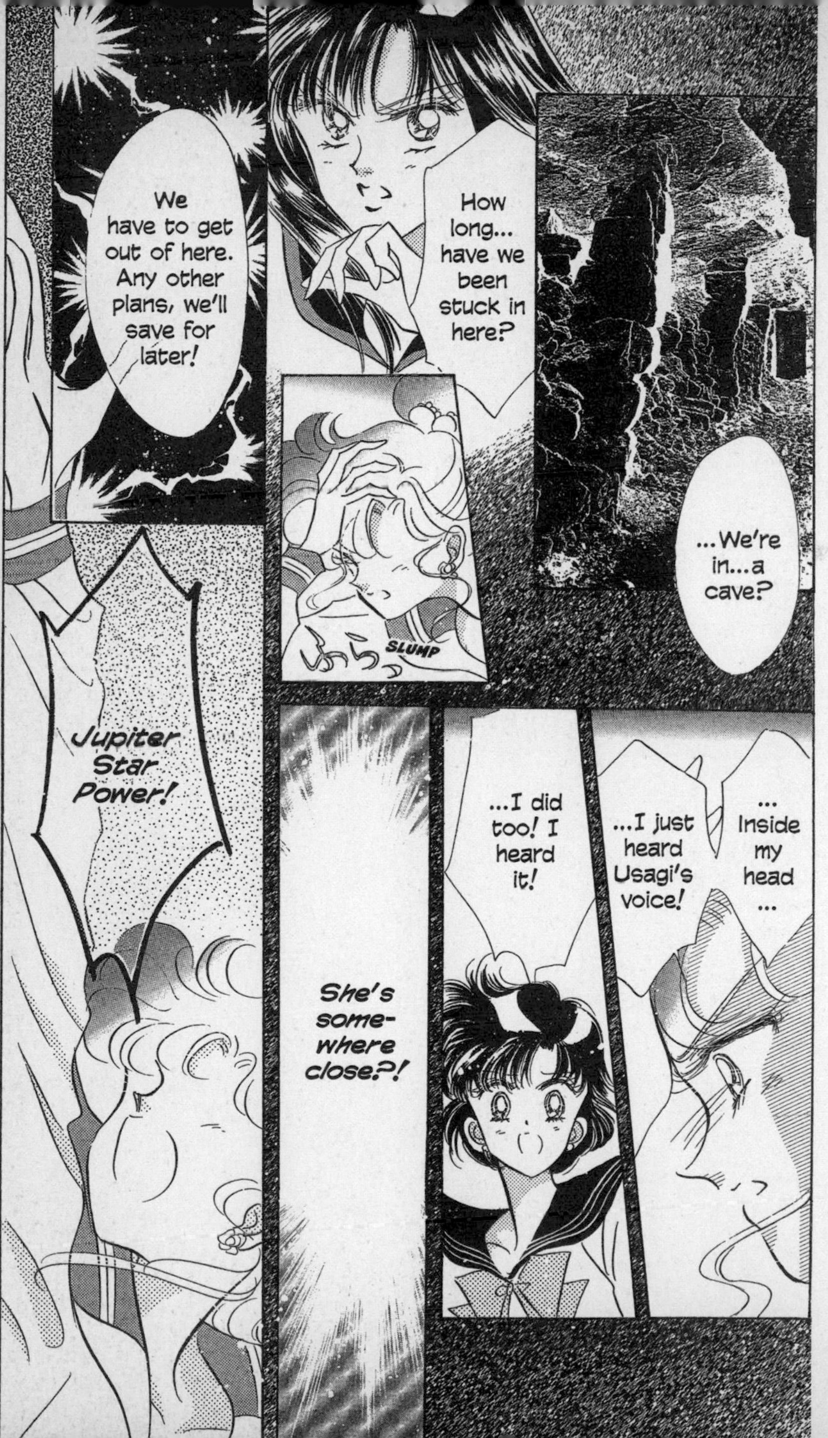
...We're in...a cave?
How long... have we been stuck in here?
ふらっ
SLUMP
We have to get out of here. Any other plans, we'll save for later!
... Inside my head ...
...I just heard Usagi's voice!
...I did too! I heard it!
She's some-where close?!
Jupiter Star Power!

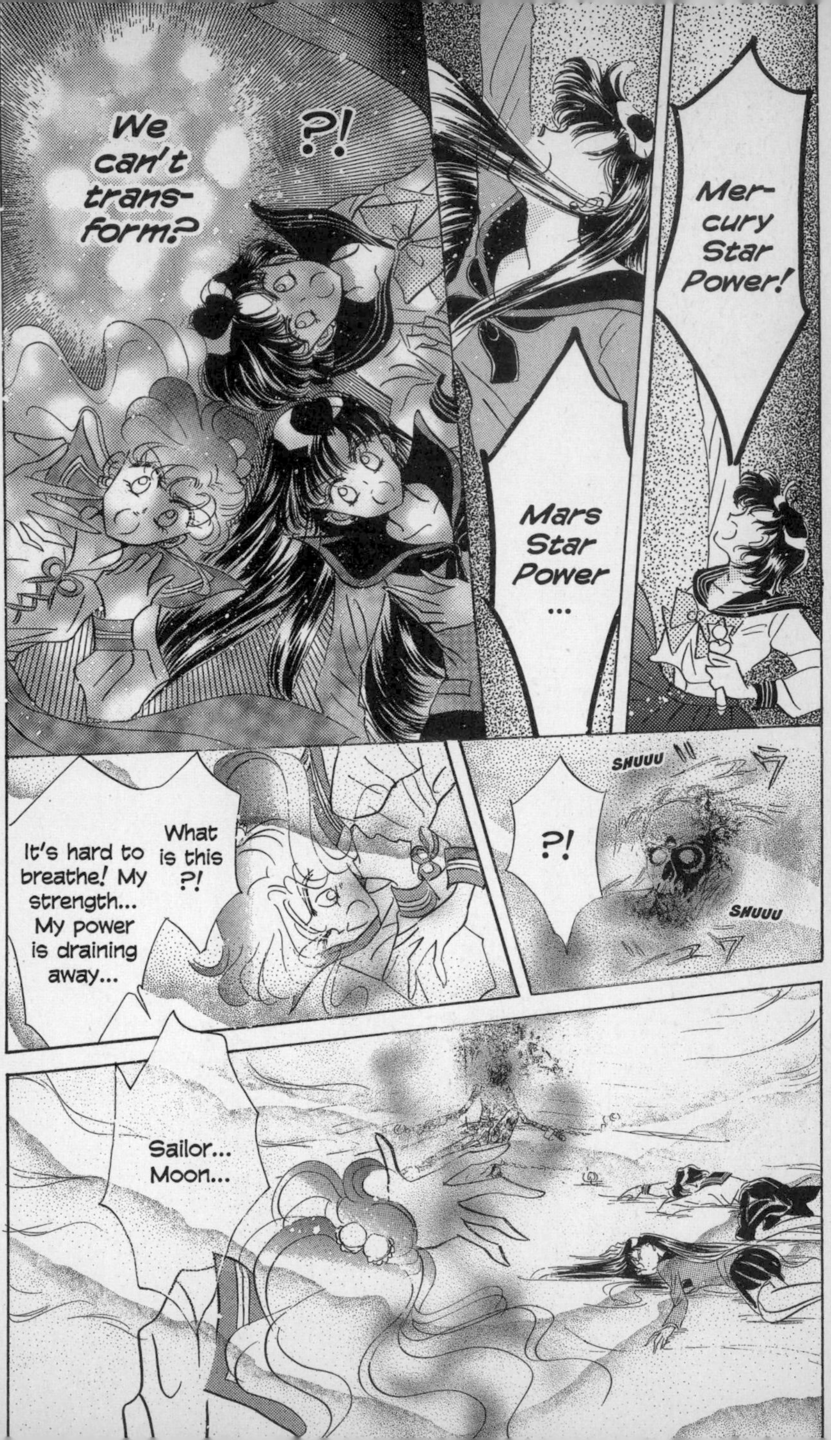
Mercury Star Power!
Mars Star Power ...
?!
We can't transform?
SHUUU
?!
SHUUU
What is this ?!
It's hard to breathe! My strength... My power is draining away...
Sailor... Moon...

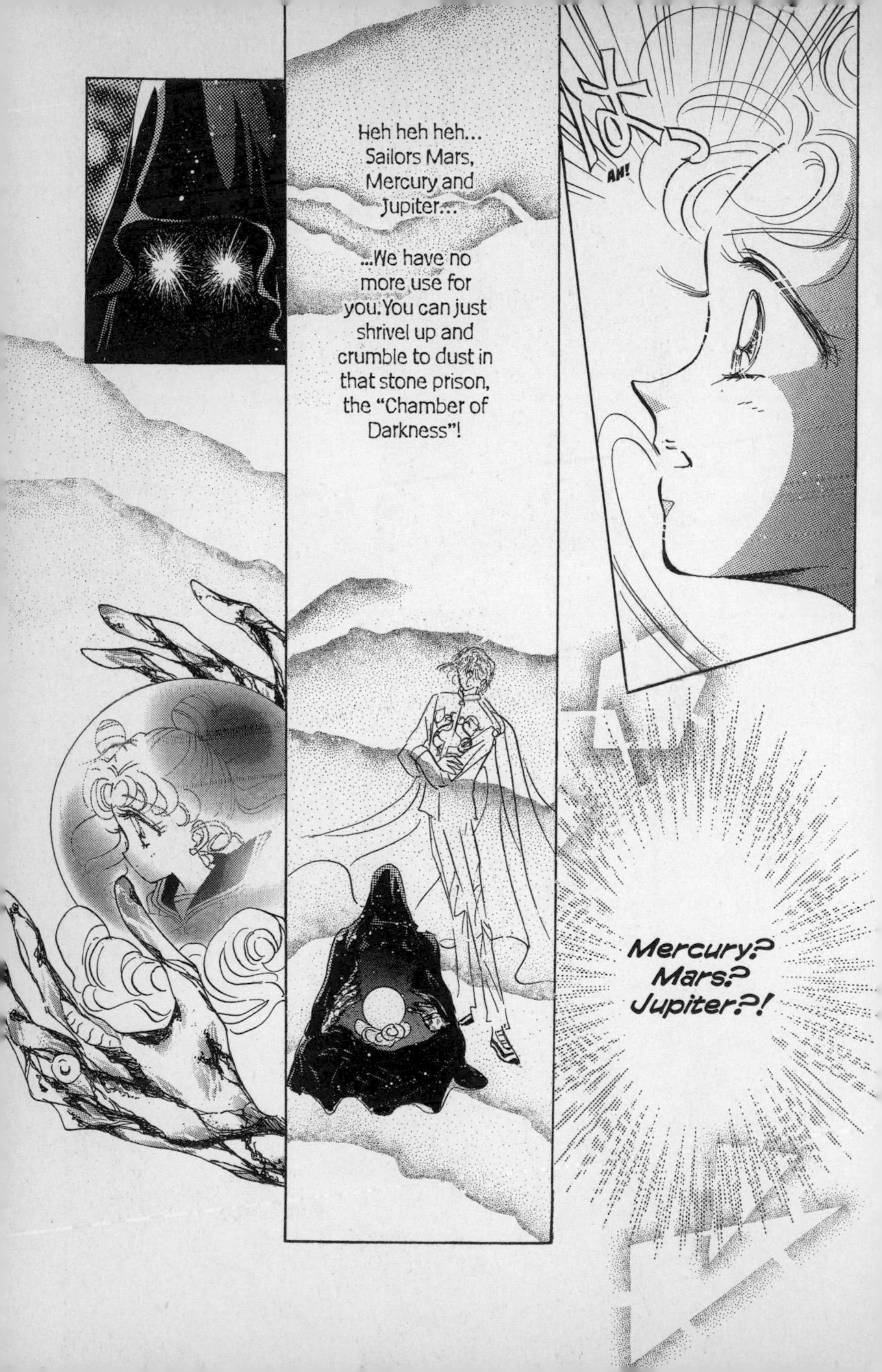
AH!
Mercury? Mars? Jupiter?!
Heh heh heh... Sailors Mars, Mercury and Jupiter...
...We have no more use for you. You can just shrivel up and crumble to dust in that stone prison, the "Chamber of Darkness"!

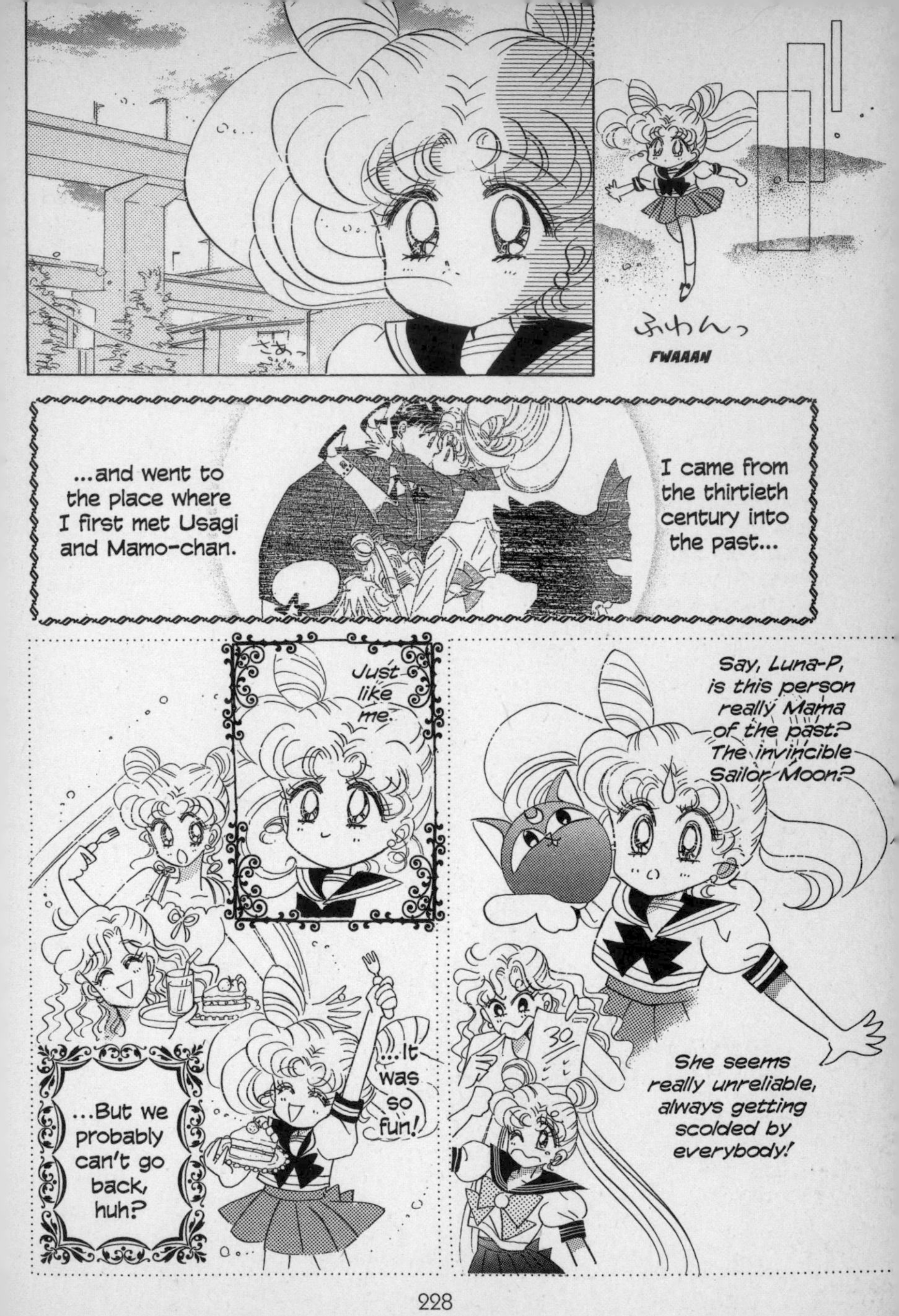
ふわんっ
FWAAAN
さあっ
I came from the thirtieth century into the past...
...and went to the place where I first met Usagi and Mamo-chan.
Say, Luna-P, is this person really Mama of the past? The invincible Sailor Moon?
She seems really unreliable, always getting scolded by everybody!
Just like me.
...It was so fun!
...But we probably can't go back, huh?

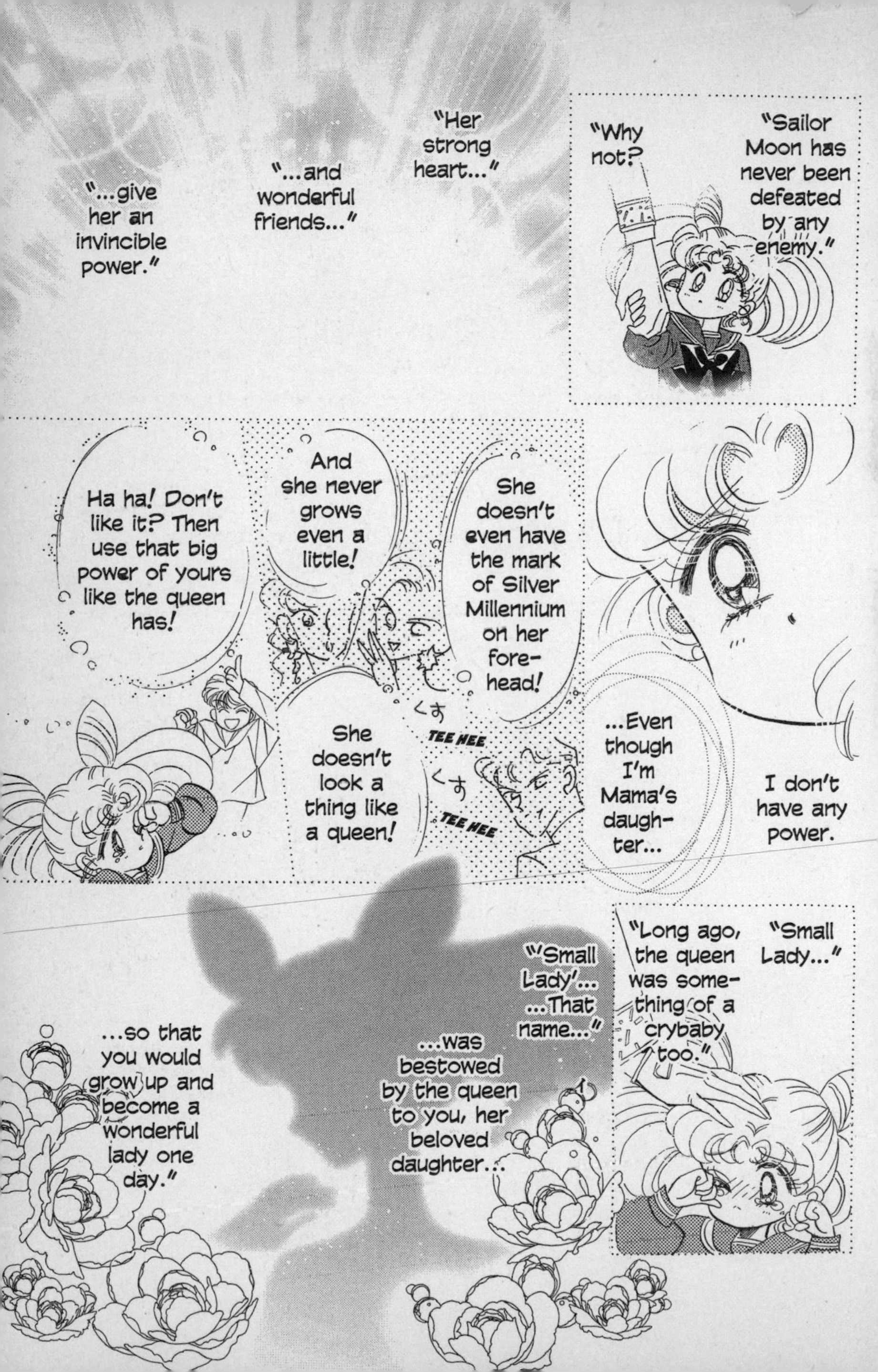
"Sailor Moon has never been defeated by any enemy."
"Why not?
"Her strong heart..."
"...and wonderful friends..."
"...give her an invincible power."
I don't have any power.
...Even though I'm Mama's daughter...
She doesn't even have the mark of Silver Millennium on her forehead!
And she never grows even a little!
くす
TEE HEE
くす
TEE HEE
She doesn't look a thing like a queen!
Ha ha! Don't like it? Then use that big power of yours like the queen has!
"Small Lady..."
"Long ago, the queen was something of a crybaby too."
"'Small Lady'... ...That name..."
...was bestowed by the queen to you, her beloved daughter...
...so that you would grow up and become a wonderful lady one day."

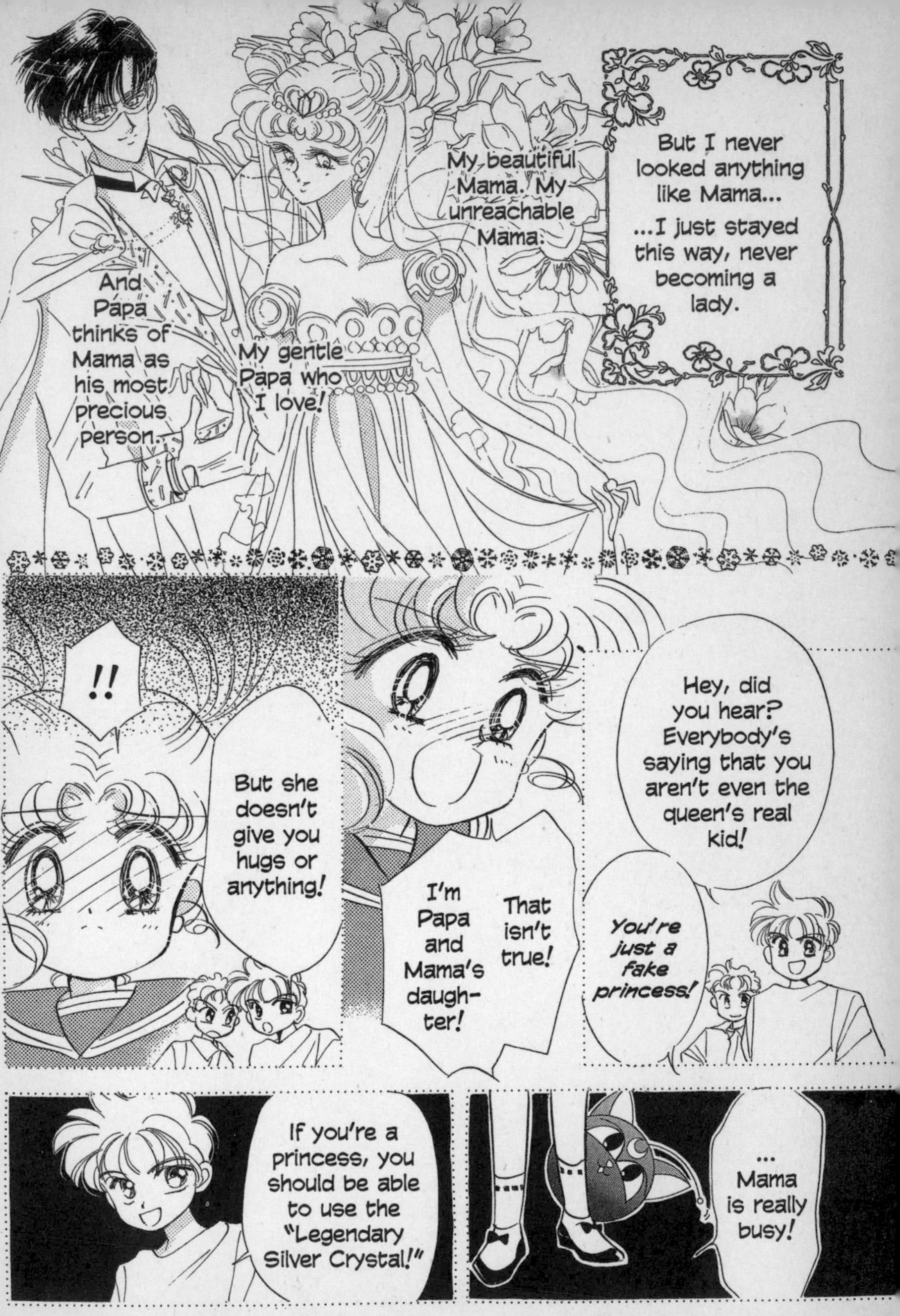
But I never looked anything like Mama...
...I just stayed this way, never becoming a lady.
My beautiful Mama. My unreachable Mama.
My gentle Papa who I love!
And Papa thinks of Mama as his most precious person.
Hey, did you hear? Everybody's saying that you aren't even the queen's real kid!
You're just a fake princess!
That isn't true!
I'm Papa and Mama's daughter!
But she doesn't give you hugs or anything!
!!
... Mama is really busy!
If you're a princess, you should be able to use the "Legendary Silver Crystal!"

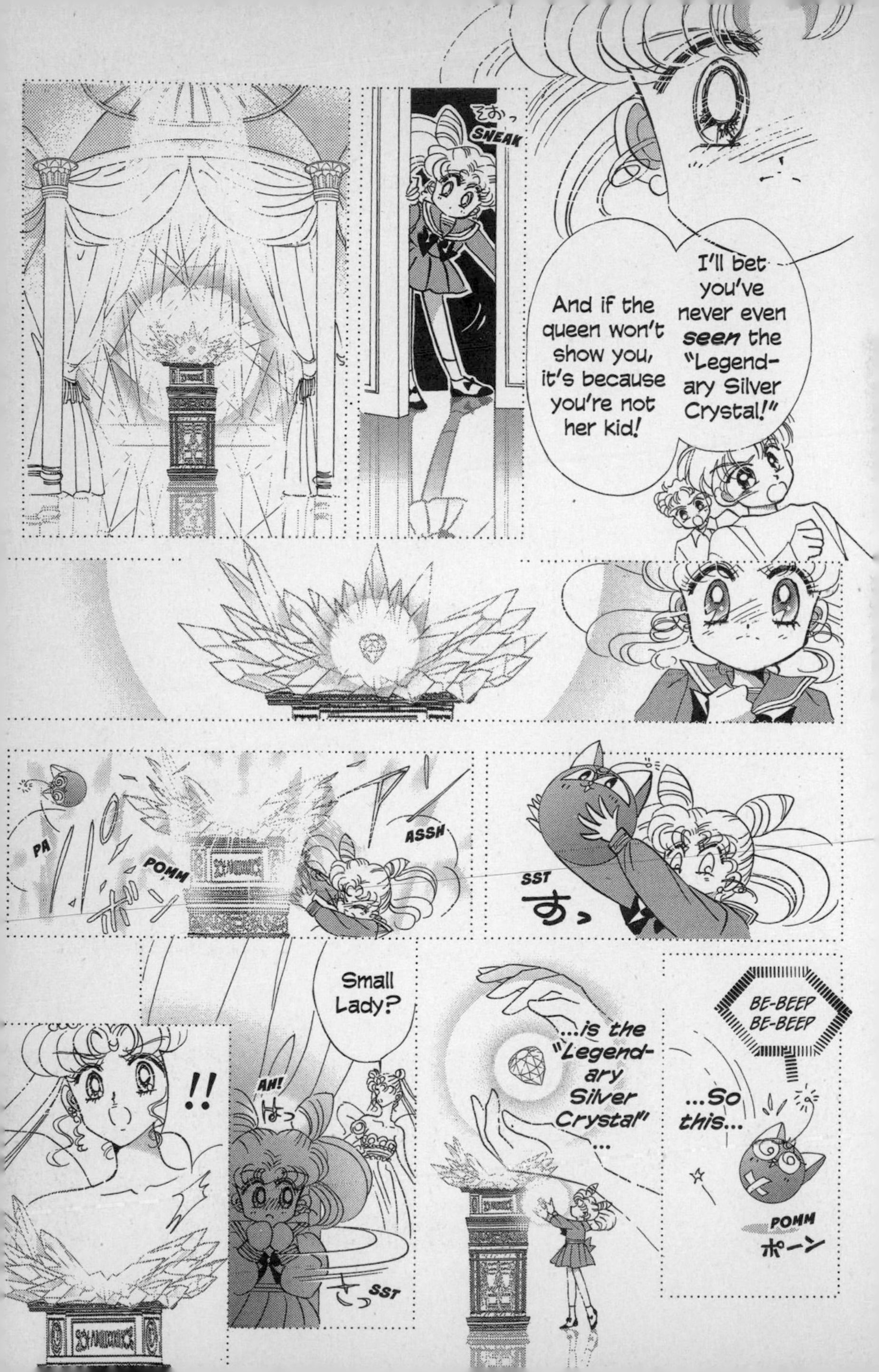
I'll bet you've never even seen the "Legendary Silver Crystal!"
And if the queen won't show you, it's because you're not her kid!
そおっ SNEAK
SST すっ
ASSH
POMM ボン
PA
BE-BEEP BE-BEEP
...So this...
POMM ポーン
...is the "Legendary Silver Crystal"...
Small Lady?
AH! はっ
SST さっ
!!

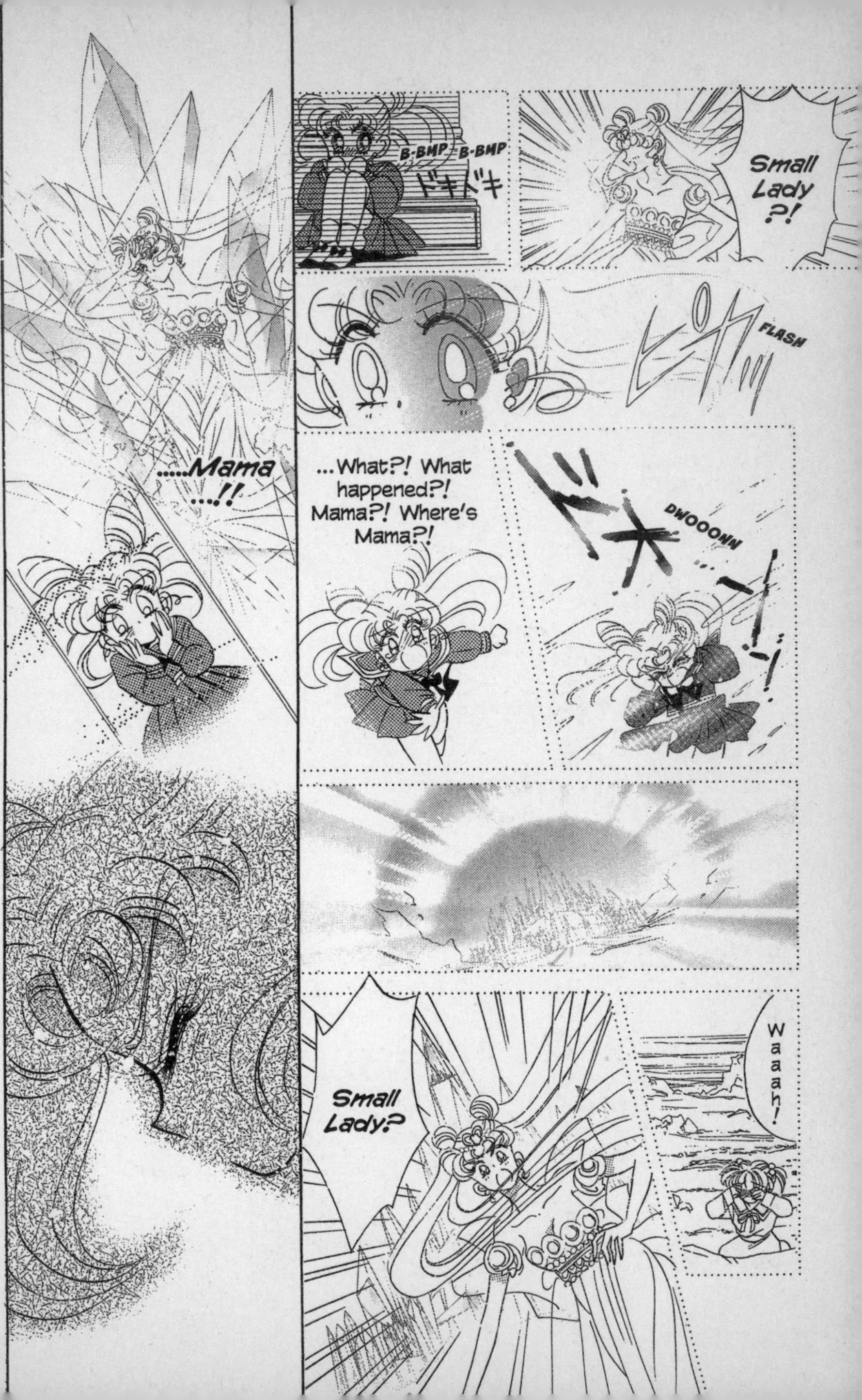
Small Lady ?!
B-BMP B-BMP
ドキドキ
FLASH
ピカッ
DWOOONN
ドォーン
...What?! What happened?! Mama?! Where's Mama?!
Waaah!
Small Lady?
.....Mama ....!!

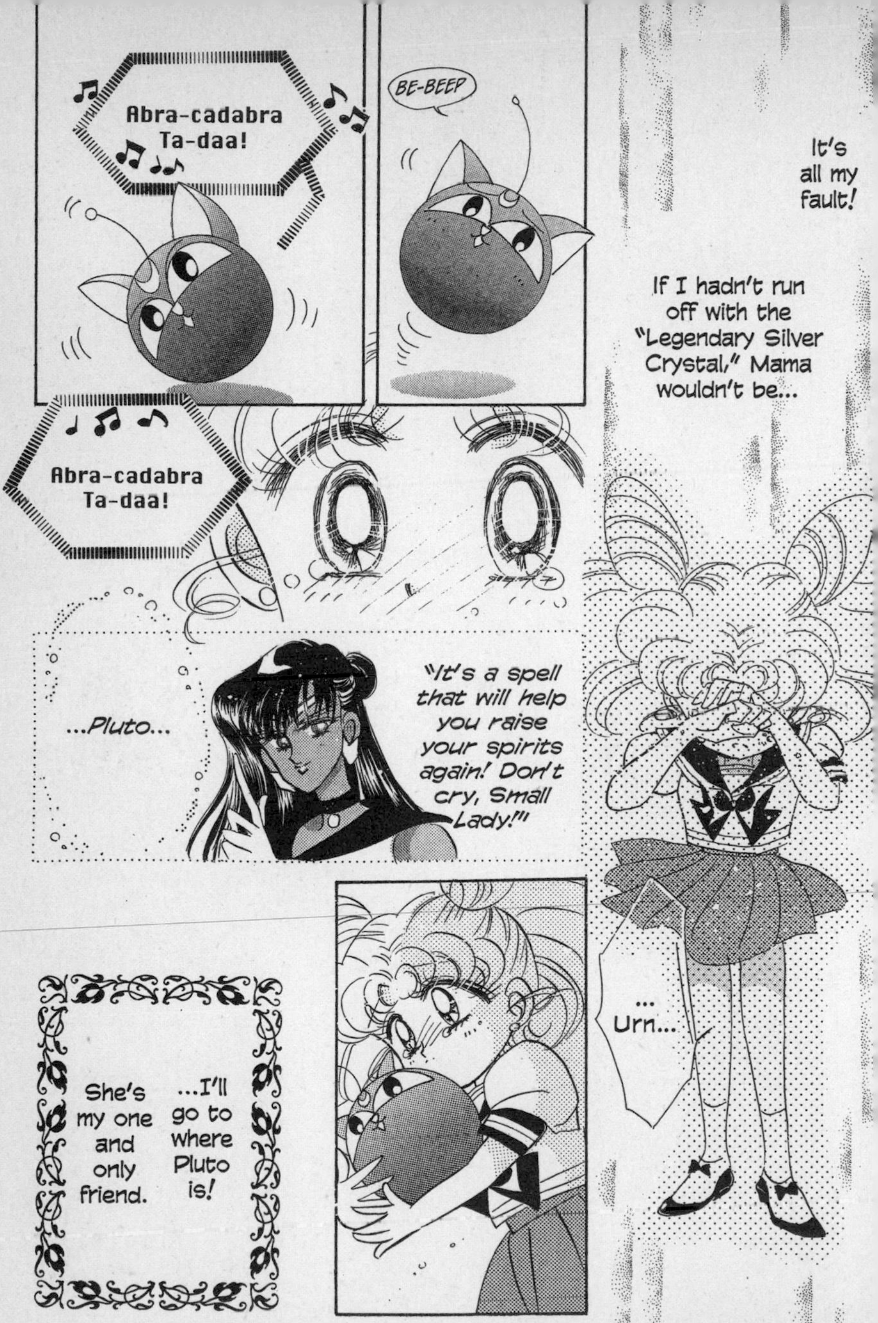
It's all my fault!
If I hadn't run off with the "Legendary Silver Crystal," Mama wouldn't be...
... Urn...
BE-BEEP
Abra-cadabra Ta-daa!
Abra-cadabra Ta-daa!
"It's a spell that will help you raise your spirits again! Don't cry, Small Lady!"
...Pluto...
...I'll go to where Pluto is!
She's my one and only friend.

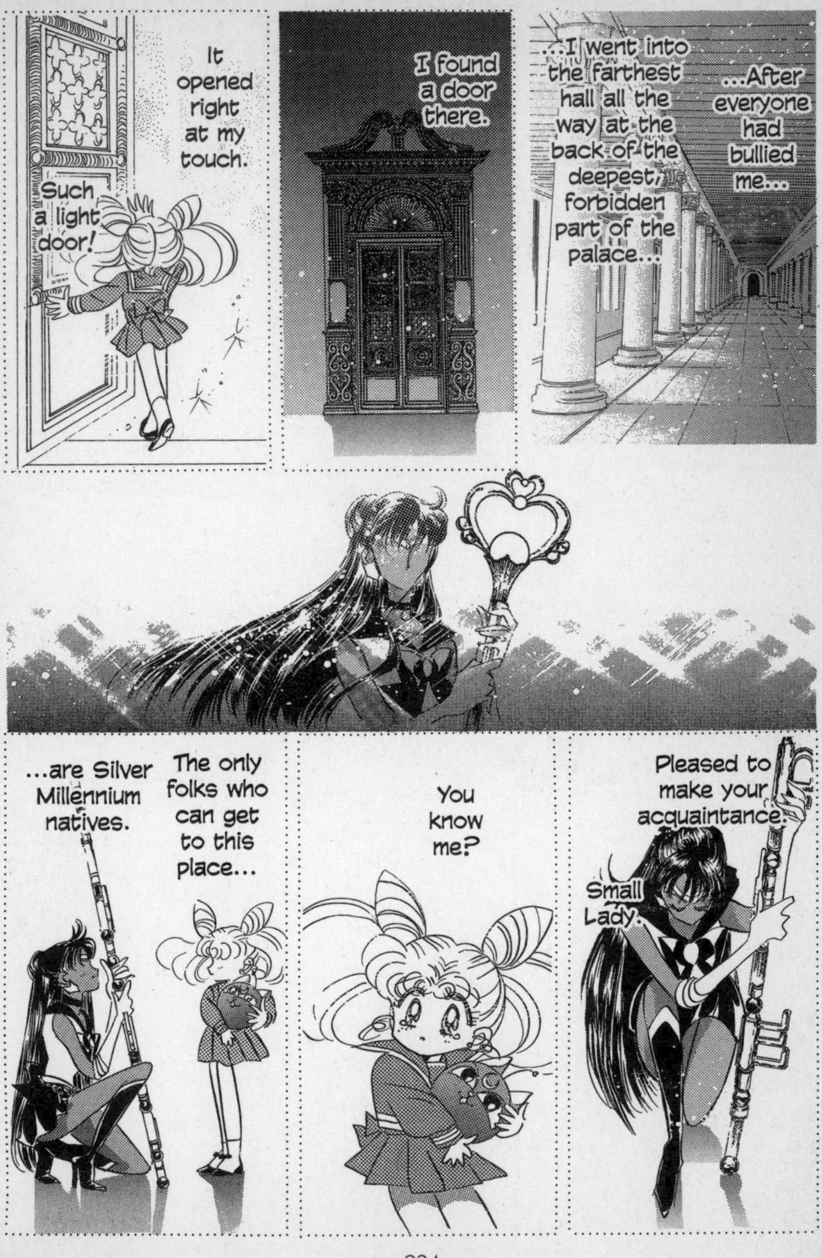
...After everyone had bullied me...
...I went into the farthest hall all the way at the back of the deepest, forbidden part of the palace...
I found a door there.
It opened right at my touch.
Such a light door!
Pleased to make your acquaintance.
Small Lady.
You know me?
The only folks who can get to this place...
...are Silver Millennium natives.

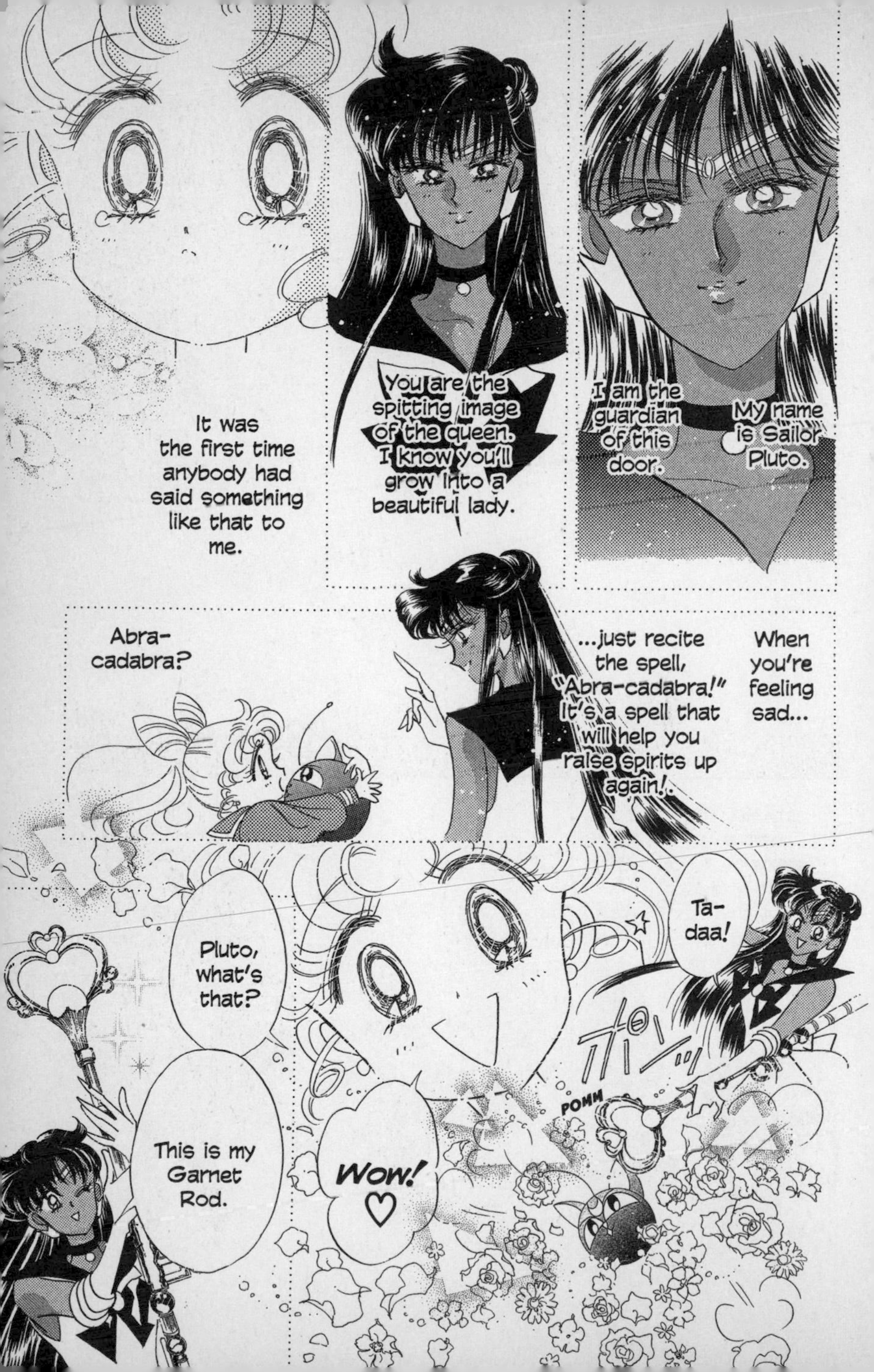
My name is Sailor Pluto.
I am the guardian of this door.
You are the spitting image of the queen. I know you'll grow into a beautiful lady.
It was the first time anybody had said something like that to me.
When you're feeling sad...
...just recite the spell, "Abra-cadabra!" It's a spell that will help you raise spirits up again!.
Abra-cadabra?
Ta-daa!
POMM
Wow! ♡
Pluto, what's that?
This is my Garnet Rod.

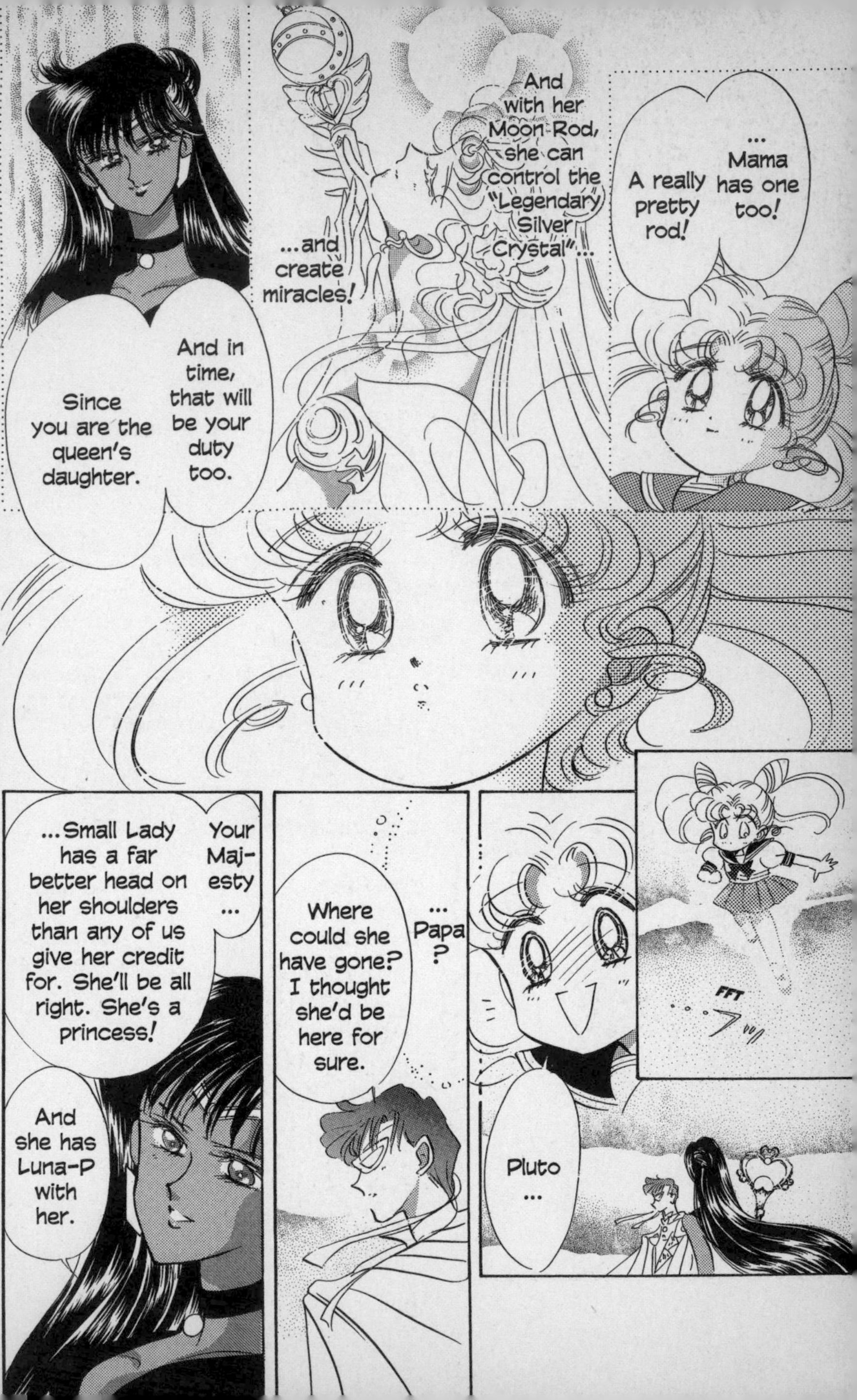

A really pretty rod! ... Mama has one too!
And with her Moon Rod, she can control the "Legendary Silver Crystal"...
...and create miracles!
Since you are the queen's daughter. And in time, that will be your duty too.
FFT
Pluto ...
... Papa ?
Where could she have gone? I thought she'd be here for sure.
Your Maj-esty ...
...Small Lady has a far better head on her shoulders than any of us give her credit for. She'll be all right. She's a princess!
And she has Luna-P with her.

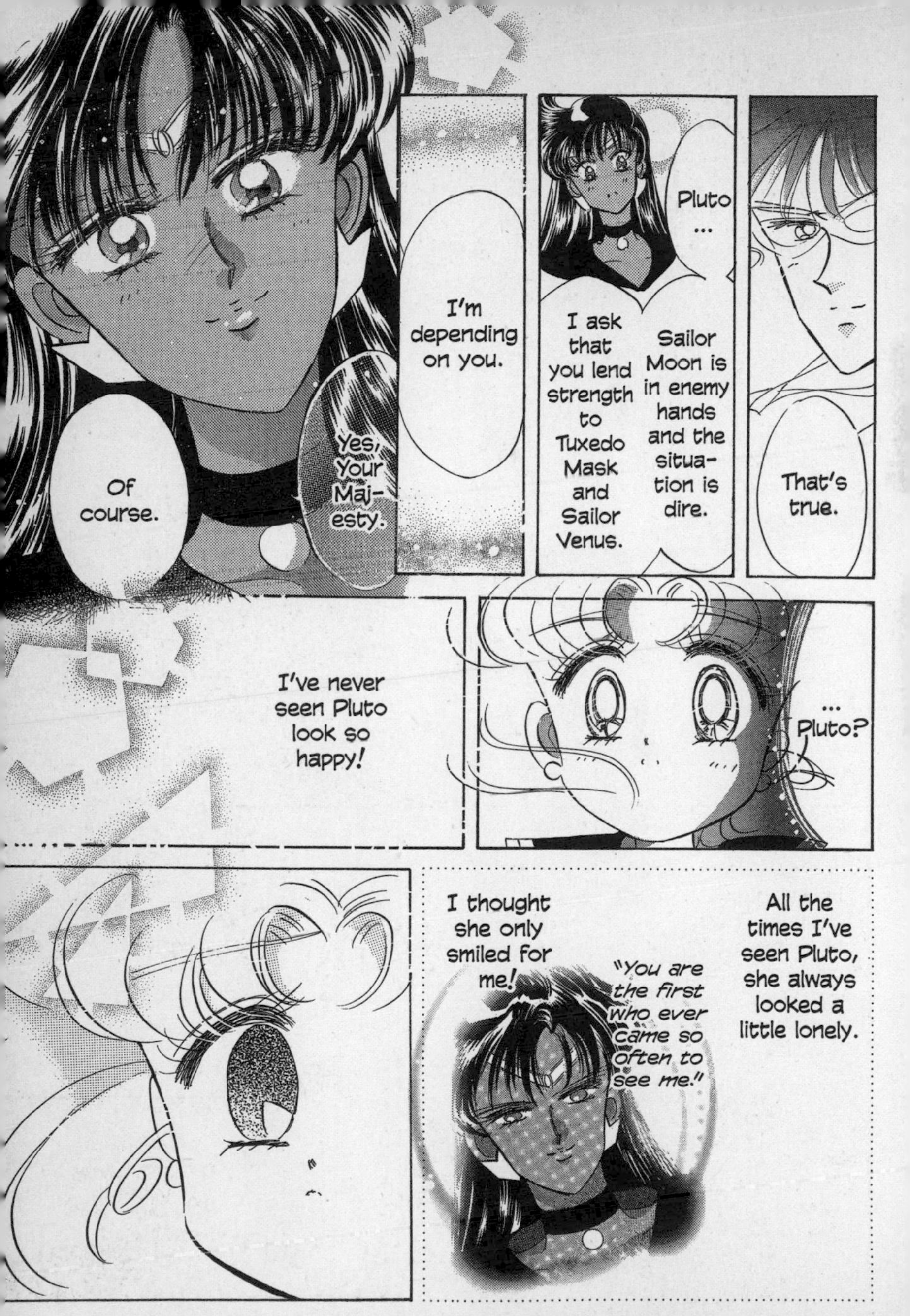
That's true.
Pluto ...
Sailor Moon is in enemy hands and the situation is dire.
I ask that you lend strength to Tuxedo Mask and Sailor Venus.
I'm depending on you.
Yes, Your Majesty.
Of course.
... Pluto?
I've never seen Pluto look so happy!
All the times I've seen Pluto, she always looked a little lonely.
"You are the first who ever came so often to see me."
I thought she only smiled for me!

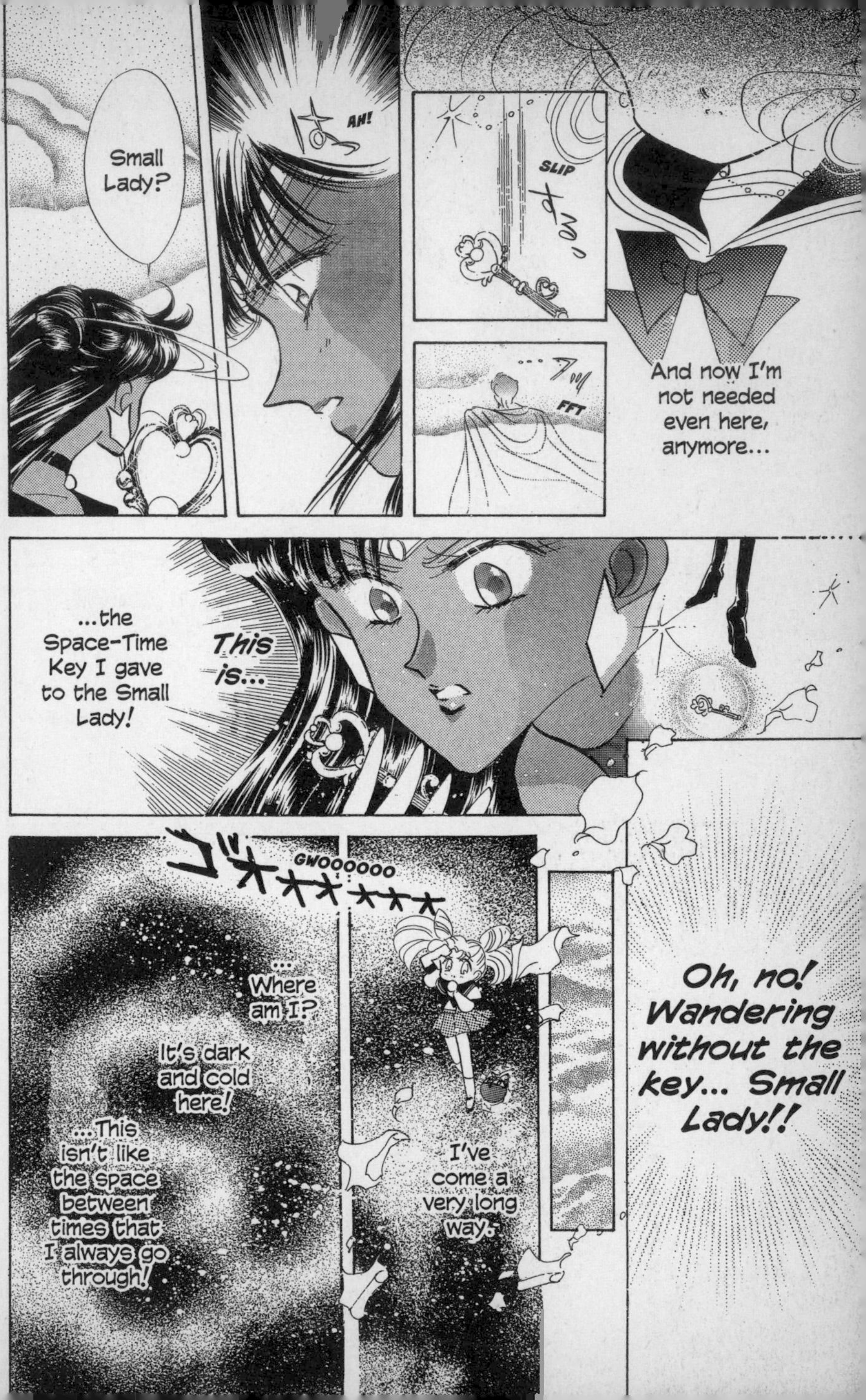
And now I'm not needed even here, anymore...
SLIP
FFT
AH!
Small Lady?
This is...
...the Space-Time Key I gave to the Small Lady!
Oh, no! Wandering without the key... Small Lady!!
GWOOOOOO
I've come a very long way.
... Where am I?
It's dark and cold here!
...This isn't like the space between times that I always go through!

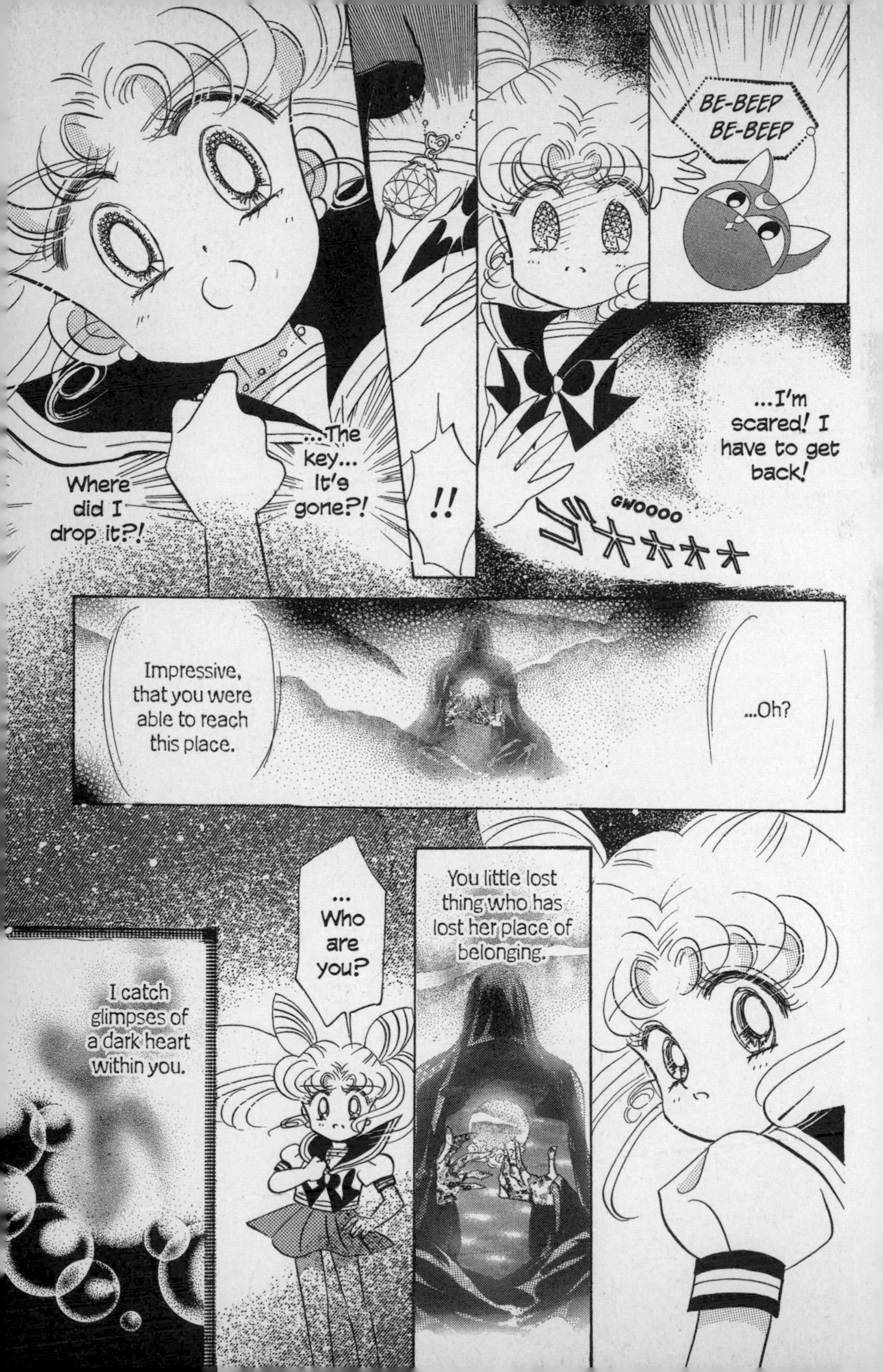
BE-BEEP BE-BEEP
...I'm scared! I have to get back!
GWOOOO
!!
...The key... It's gone?!
Where did I drop it?!
...Oh?
Impressive, that you were able to reach this place.
You little lost thing who has lost her place of belonging.
... Who are you?
I catch glimpses of a dark heart within you.

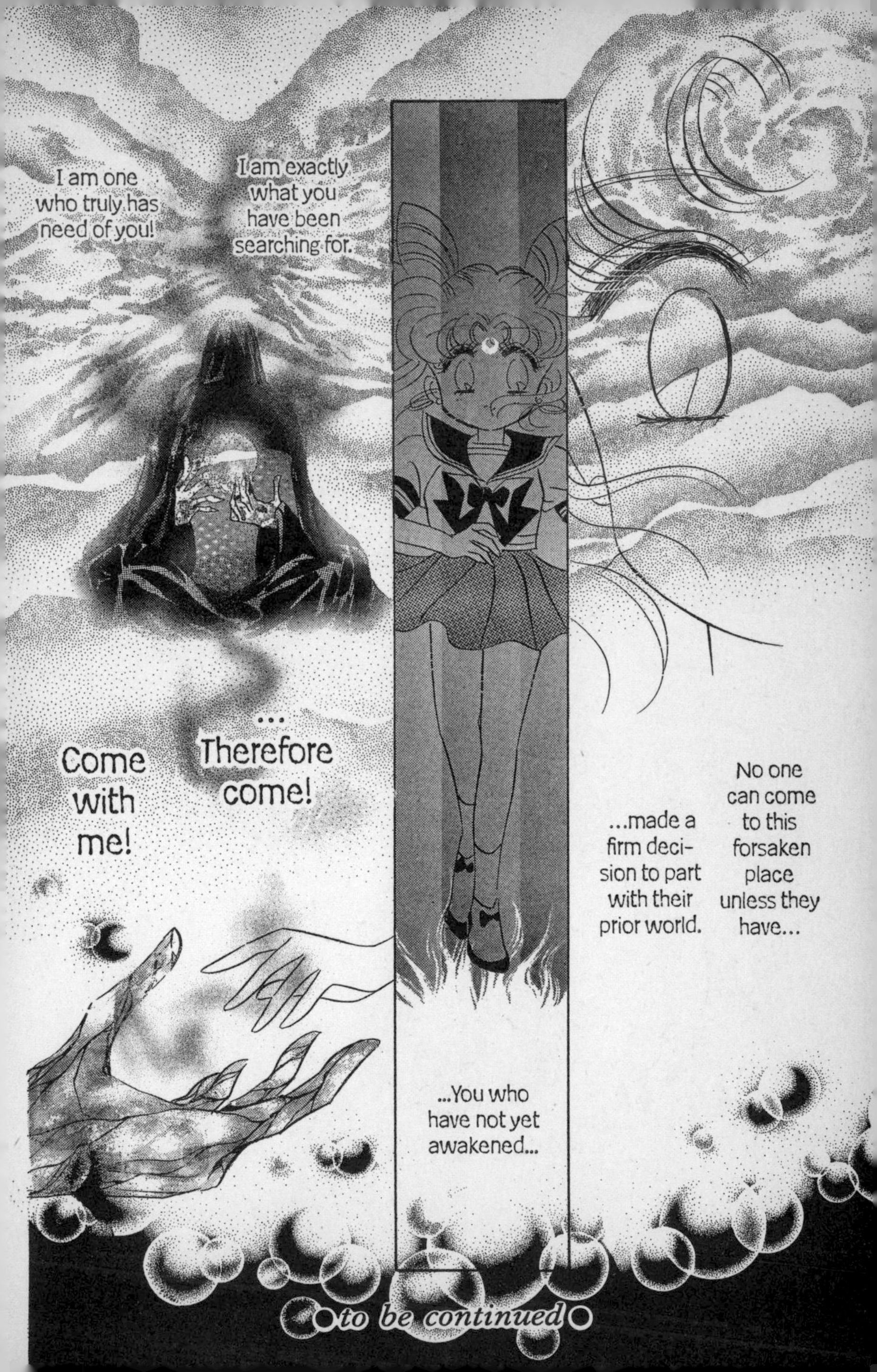
No one can come to this forsaken place unless they have...
...made a firm decision to part with their prior world.
...You who have not yet awakened...
I am exactly what you have been searching for.
I am one who truly has need of you!
...Therefore come!
Come with me!
to be continued

Translation Notes

Japanese is a tricky language for most Westerners, and translation is often more art than science. For your edification and reading pleasure, here are notes on some of the places where we could have gone in a different direction with our translation of the work, or where a Japanese cultural reference is used.

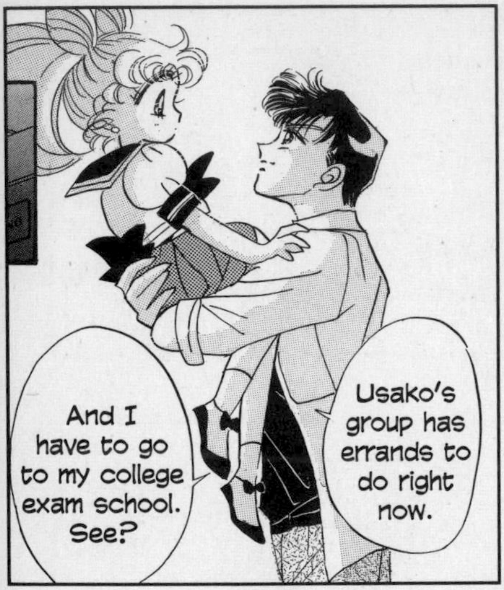
Usako's group has errands to do right now.
And I have to go to my college exam school. See?

Page 17, College Exam School
There are special schools where students go after normal school hours are over to help bone up for their college entrance exams. Since a student's college entrance exams determine the quality of college they goes to, and that college determines the quality of job they have after graduation (as well as a good portion of their social status), the tests they take to get into college are the most important tests of a Japanese student's life. So it's no wonder that an entire industry of schools has developed around the college entrance exams.

Page 17, Shabu-shabu
Shabu-shabu is a hot-pot dish where one takes thinly sliced meat (usually beef) and swishes it back and forth in boiling water or broth until it is cooked enough to eat. Then it is dipped in a thin sauce then eaten. In a normal Shabu-shabu meal, other meats and veggies are cooked the same way, but there are usually side dishes as well.

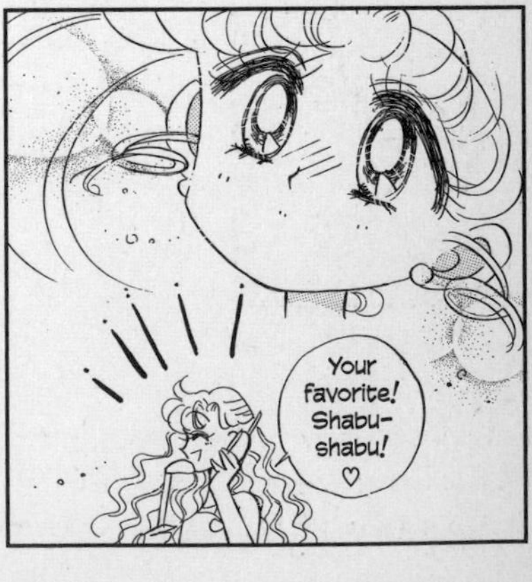
Your favorite! Shabu-shabu! ♡

Page 21, Rainy Season
June is the rainy season in Japan where it rains nearly every day and is pretty much cloudy all month. Forgetting your umbrella during the season usually means a good drenching on your way home.

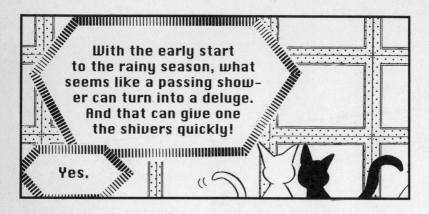

With the early start to the rainy season, what seems like a passing show-er can turn into a deluge. And that can give one the shivers quickly!
Yes.

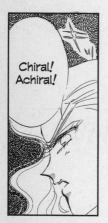

Chiral! Achiral!

Page 117, Chiral, Achiral
A chiral molecule is a molecule that is not identical to its mirror image, and thus cannot be superimposed onto it. An achiral molecule is identical to and can be superimposed upon its mirror image.

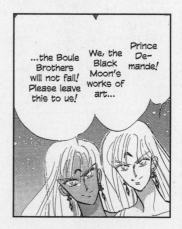

Prince De-mande!
We, the Black Moon's works of art...
...the Boule Brothers will not fail! Please leave this to us!

Page 117, Boule
A Boule is a term used in chemistry to describe a crystal ingot that is made by artificial means. In the Japanese version, the kanji for their name is the Japanese word for "artificial," but it has furigana pronunciation guide that says, "Boule."

Page 135, Chemical Terms

This sequence uses a lot of chemical terms such as enantiomer, electrochemical side chain, isomer and chiralty center. Unfortunately, while Takeuchi-sensei is trained as a chemist, this translator is not. You are welcome to look up the meanings yourself. If you can make sense of them, I would congratulate you on being a more chemistry-inclined person than myself. Although the chemical terms bear a relationship to the events in the manga, like most manga, it is not necessary to know exactly what the terms mean to make sense of the story.

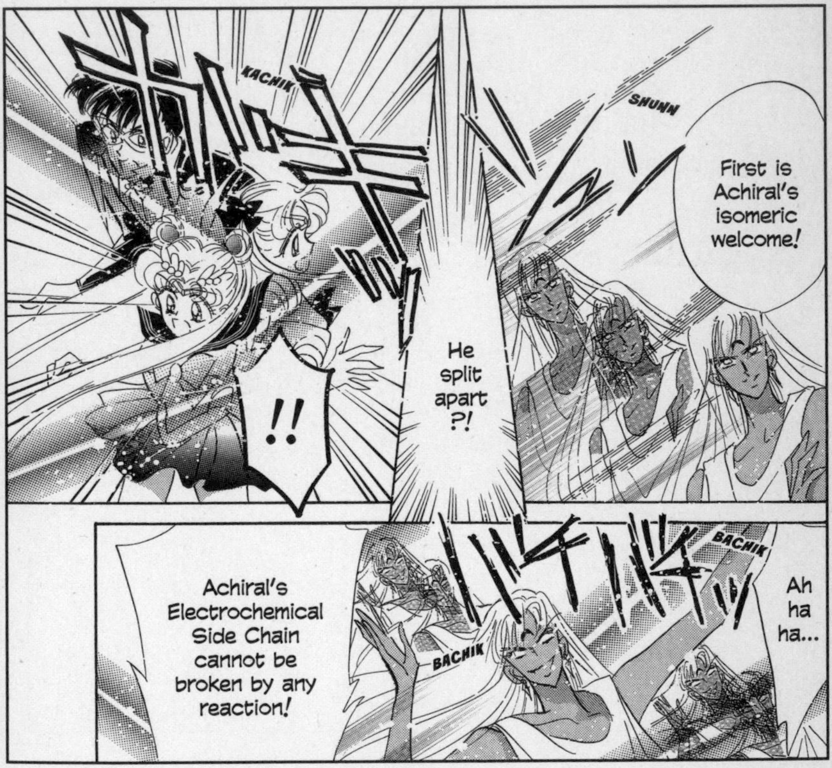
SHUNN
First is Achiral's isomeric welcome!
He split apart?!
KACHIK
!!
Ah ha ha...
BACHIK
BACHIK
Achiral's Electrochemical Side Chain cannot be broken by any reaction!